"Philosophers rarely write big books that could change the world, but ***Blood Oil*** is such a book. Wenar does not shy away from the horrific consequences of current trade practices, nor from the philosophical arguments needed to show that this trade rests on ethically indefensible assumptions. Yet instead of leaving us to despair, he offers realistic ways of bringing about change that would make the world a better and fairer place."—**Peter Singer**, Princeton University, author of *One World* and *The Most Good You Can Do*

"Have you ever worried that your spending might be supporting the 'rulers and sadistic militias' that blight so many countries in Africa and around the world? Or that your purchases of oil are supporting injustice and oppression, just as British purchases of sugar once supported the enslavement of Africans? Leif Wenar has written the indispensable guide, combining politics, economics, and ethics to tell us just how and why we are all involved, and what we ought to do to make the world a better place." —**Angus Deaton**, Princeton University, Nobel Prize Winner in Economics, 2015

"This book is one of those rare manifestos that awaken people to a pressing ethical issue by changing the way they see the world. Whether or not its recommendations are practicable today, *Blood Oil* is a fantastically stimulating read: analytic, informative, rationally optimistic, and written with erudition and panache."—**Steven Pinker**, Harvard University, author of *The Better Angels of Our Nature* and *How the Mind Works*

"Leif Wenar's objective is to devise ways in which the vicious circle at heart of many development failures can be broken, so that odious regimes can be prevented from appropriating natural resources to their own advantage and saddling future generation with much diminished national wealth. Most importantly the book derives practical proposals on how such objectives are to be achieved. The book's conclusions will be of great interest to all those working in international development, and particularly to national governments and international organizations."—**Branko Milanovic**, CUNY Graduate School, former World Bank Lead Economist, Author of *Worlds Apart* and *The Haves and the Have-Nots*

"It is time that we woke up to the fact that the level of our dependence on certain resources means that we let ourselves be blackmailed by tyrants.

Our comfort is purchased by collusion with regimes that are responsible for high levels of human misery, injustice and bigotry. This courageous and forceful book challenges us to make the hard decision that might change this worsening situation. It is a serious and urgent appeal to the conscience of the West."—**Rowan Williams**, former Archbishop of Canterbury and Leader of the Anglican Communion

"***Blood Oil*** is an inspiring book. It will make you think differently about everything you buy—from cell phones to children's toys—and make you realize just how complicit we have become in the rights-crushing autocracies that produce the raw materials from which these everyday products are made. But ***Blood Oil*** also lays out, in careful detail, a clean trade strategy that will bring our complicity to an end and help poor people recover sovereignty over their resources. It is also a delight to read: free of jargon and ideology, an engaging, ironic and eloquent tour de force of moral passion."—**Michael Ignatieff**, Harvard University, author of *The Lesser Evil: Political Ethics in an Age of Terror*

"This is a long-awaited study of power in the contemporary world, in oil markets and the often corrupted power-plays that they engender. Leif Wenar is a philosopher with profound understanding of the daily, practical world. His big book should become required reading."—**Lord Carlile of Berriew**, Independent Reviewer of UK Terrorism Legislation 2001–11

"As consumers we depend every day on global supply chains tainted by exploitation and injustice. Leif Wenar's detailed and incisive study of the trade in oil and other "blood" resources, and of its moral and legal background, is the most sustained analysis yet of the responsibilities we bear as beneficiaries of the plunder of authoritarians and kleptocrats. Not everyone will agree with Wenar's moral arguments and policy recommendations but anyone who reads this book will see the urgency of the problem." —**Charles Beitz**, Princeton University, author of *Political Theory and International Relations* and *The Idea of Human Rights*

"Leif Wenar puts the oldest principles of ownership and justice to new use in his attack on the human disaster that is the notorious 'resource curse.' His proposal is original, exact, and morally admirable. It should stir us away from the coldly comforting idea that some peoples will always be poor and tyrannically governed. This is a fine marriage of moral seriousness and institutional imagination."—**Jedediah Purdy**, Duke University, author of *For Common Things* and *After Nature: A Politics for the Anthropocene*

"'Telling the person in the seat next to you that you are interested in philosophy' observes Leif Wenar, 'will often result in an uninterrupted flight.' This lively book gives strong evidence that interruption is sometimes a wise course of action. Writing in an engaging, conversational style, Wenar trenchantly and provocatively explores one of the great moral challenges of our time. Although the benefits from development and global connectedness—in which we are all inescapably complicit—have been huge, some of those benefits have flowed to people who have systematically made the lives of others desperate and miserable."—**John Mueller**, Ohio State University and the Cato Institute, co-author of *Chasing Ghosts: The Policing of Terrorism*

"Blood Oil is a brilliant inquiry into ethical implications of our dependence on the petroleum trade—and the uncomfortable fact that it fuels many violent conflicts and funds a large fraction of the world's autocrats. Wenar shows that much of this oil has been stolen from the citizens who rightfully own it, nests this issue in the historic struggle for the right of self-determination, and suggests a way to rectify this injustice that is surprisingly practical. This book is not merely a major scholarly achievement; it is both politically urgent and compulsively readable."—**Michael Ross**, UCLA, author of *The Oil Curse: How Petroleum Wealth Shapes the Development of Nations*

Blood Oil

Blood Oil

Tyrants, Violence, and the Rules That Run the World

LEIF WENAR

OXFORD
UNIVERSITY PRESS

OXFORD
UNIVERSITY PRESS

Oxford University Press is a department of the
University of Oxford. It furthers the University's objective
of excellence in research, scholarship, and education
by publishing worldwide.

Oxford New York
Auckland Cape Town Dar es Salaam Hong Kong Karachi
Kuala Lumpur Madrid Melbourne Mexico City Nairobi
New Delhi Shanghai Taipei Toronto

With offices in
Argentina Austria Brazil Chile Czech Republic France Greece
Guatemala Hungary Italy Japan Poland Portugal Singapore
South Korea Switzerland Thailand Turkey Ukraine Vietnam

Published in the United States of America by
Oxford University Press
198 Madison Avenue, New York, NY 10016

Library of Congress Cataloging-in-Publication Data
Wenar, Leif.
Blood oil : tyrants, violence, and the rules that run the world / Leif Wenar.
pages cm
Includes bibliographical references and index.
ISBN 978-0-19-026292-1 (hardback)
1. Petroleum industry and trade—Political aspects. 2. Natural resources—Political aspects.
3. Economic policy. 4. Geopolitics. I. Title.
HD9560.5.W46 2015
338.2'7285—dc23 2015023440

9 8 7 6 5 4 3 2 1

Printed in the United States of America
on acid-free paper

Divide and rule, the politician cries;
Unite and lead, is watchword of the wise.

—Goethe

Contents

Introduction

THE MOTHER OF INVENTIONS

Grab your smart phone, that small piece of matter with which you call, text, email, search, read, film, and game. What you're holding is a symphony of elements: of aluminum and silicon, lithium in the battery, tin in the solder, tungsten in the vibrating alert, and exotic metals like yttrium and lanthanum in the screen and the camera. Think of those unique molecules that make up the microarchitecture of your device. Every atom was extracted from the ground, from some exact point on the planet's surface. All of your phone is natural resources. The feast of reason that it offers you is set on the periodic table; its flow of soul rushes through the earth, the mother of all our inventions.

Our desires can be so absorbing, we forget the marvelous swirls of molecules that secure their satisfaction. You are impatient to get home, your foot presses slightly down on the pedal. You need to talk to a colleague in Sydney, you tap your finger on the mouse twice. Your flight to Paris will take you to a meeting, or to a lover. You may not think that as the airplane takes off—with the carbon-titanium in the fuselage, the steel in the landing gear, the kerosene in the fuel tanks, its precision guidance systems, and all the passengers with their tech—it becomes a miniature Earth in partial orbit. The miraculous multinational constructions that connect us with each other approach our own bodies in their intricacy, and we take their operation as much for granted as we press them into action.

What we read, drive, wear, and eat are mixtures of matter drawn from all over our globalized world; we continually consume united nations' goods.

It would be fascinating to trace the origins of what we own, and let's imagine that there's an app for that. Imagine your phone has an app called Supply Chains that tracks all the parts of any good back to their sources. You point the phone's camera at your shirt or ring or watch, and the screen shows a branching tree of components and subcomponents, each labeled with its origin. You bought your shirt at Macy's, and the app shows it was sewn in Italy from fabric made in China of polymer threads spun in India made from petroleum refined in South Korea that was extracted in Brunei. Your ring, you discover, holds a diamond that was polished in Israel after transiting through Dubai from a mine in Zimbabwe. Switching to the map function and pointing the camera at your watch, you see the supply chains behind the watch components snaking all around the world, rivulets of raw materials flowing into creeks of manufacturing combining into streams of assembly merging into a river of transport flowing toward you. Pointing your phone at your sunglasses shows them progressively disassembling like a multistage firework, the pieces spreading out across the world until the raw materials separate into liquids and melt into rocks that fly back under the ground.

The supply chains that bring us the earth's bounty are one of our species' great achievements. To make your shoes, a troupe of humans performed an elaborate dance across several continents, the complexity of their choreography surpassing any Balanchine ballet. And your shoes are only one global product. Could we see all the supply chains for all goods at once, glowing on the earth's surface, we would see a system of billions of nodes making trillions of connections, resembling nothing more than a florescent cross-section of the human brain spread across the map. And this brain-like web is growing. Over the past generation, global trade in goods has quadrupled in volume, connecting people ever more physically while the Internet has connected them socially.[1] And in fact, these two systems have grown in symbiosis: the web of supply chains building and powering the Internet, while the Internet controls the dynamic, frenetic world wide web of supply chains that brings our molecules to us.

THE LIFE MACHINE

Think of sitting in the stands of a stadium that has an unusual clock: once every second, a 3,500-pound block of metal drops from the sky and crashes onto the field. That is how much aluminum the world uses.[2] And aluminum is not humanity's big metal. In the stadium with the steel clock, each falling block is an earth-shaking fifty tons, landing each and every second, 24/7. That is global iron production.[3] Those massive amounts of matter going into production fit the size of the consumer who is demanding the molecules: seven billion humans (can we even comprehend it), each one with the daily desires of an individual life. It is, in the end, the combined desires of humanity that draw raw materials out of the ground and into the global network of supply chains. A billion cubic meters of wood every year? We need that much to make our houses and pianos, tissues and valentines.[4]

The global manufacturing that turns the raw into the wanted is enormously extensive. Twenty-two million tons of copper goes through the world's factories each year, mostly cast into pipes and drawn into wires for our rapidly urbanizing human population.[5] Production along the global assembly lines is also minutely intensive. To make a single capacitor, a Japanese firm makes holes one micron deep in a film of aluminum one hundred microns thick.[6] (Think of drilling three hundred thousand holes into a grain of rice, then turning it over and drilling another three hundred thousand on the other side.) And that capacitor is just one step along a global assembly line that produces one phone—a phone that goes, perhaps, to a megaslum in Kenya, to a mother who can now use it to discover where she can find fresh water today.[7]

Is this global economy, so impressive at both the macro and micro levels, the greatest of all human creations? Whether we think so will depend on what we value, including the value we put on human lives. The worldwide web of supply chains is a life machine, a single device helping to sustain *Homo sapiens* at its prodigious modern size. Here again we see two systems in symbiosis—humans and their supply chains—each growing the other and making the other more robust.

This is a centuries-long symbiotic relation, flourishing on both sides and especially since 1945. Many more people now earn a living producing goods for foreigners than before, while many more foreign-made electronics and medicines and seeds flow to them. Partly because of this global symbiosis, the average lifespan of humans is today longer than it has ever been. A smaller proportion of women die in childbirth than ever before. Child malnutrition is at its lowest level ever, while literacy rates worldwide have never been higher.[8] Most impressive has been the recent reduction in severe poverty—the reduction in the percentage of humans living each day on what

$1.25 can buy in America. The mainstream estimate is that during a recent twenty-year stretch of increasing global integration, the percentage of the developing world living in such extreme poverty shrank by more than half, from 43 to 21 percent.[9]

Global rates of maternal mortality, child malnutrition, literacy, and poverty are still nowhere close to acceptable, and this book will explain one reason why. Humanity's recent successes also come with serious challenges—climate change, resource depletion, financial crises, food insecurity, and more—which we will also explore. Still, the good-news statistics on human development may hearten us. These large numbers mark enrichments in the human experience of life. Our worldwide web of supply chains dazzles as it transforms rocks, mud, and wood into what billions need and want. Our recent successes give us hope that we can improve this life machine so that it enriches human experience even more. As the economist Angus Deaton writes:

> In the years since World War II... rapid economic growth in many countries has delivered hundreds of millions of people from destitution. Material wellbeing has risen as death rates have fallen, and people are living longer and richer lives... Not only has the world added four billion people over the past half-century, but the seven billion who are alive today have also, on average, much better lives than their parents and grandparents...
>
> This is a story of progress... where life expectancy sometimes increased at (the apparently impossible rate of) several years each year... The world is a healthier place now than at almost any time in the past. People live longer, they are taller and stronger, and their children are less likely to be sick or to die. Better health makes life better in and of itself, and it allows us to do more with our lives, to work more effectively, to earn more, to spend more time learning, and to enjoy more and better time with our families and friends.[10]

THE CURSE OF NATURAL RESOURCES

In the very big picture, the recent history of our species, we see much good news: longer lives, more literacy, less poverty, better health. Yet we also hear sirens off in the distance: war in the Middle East, tyranny in the Persian

Gulf, sexual violence in Africa. We sense that we might be connected to this suffering and injustice through global supply chains. Isn't that Saudi oil we fill our cars with? Maybe conflict minerals are inside our computers? Those sirens sound faint to us because they are so far away. But we suspect that up close, they must be blasting.

We can approach one of those distant sirens gingerly, with slow steps that will bring us closer without suddenly bursting our ears. Let us walk slowly toward Africa and the Congo, starting with a speech by a US senator:

> Without knowing it, tens of millions of people in the United States may be putting money in the pockets of some of the worst human rights violators in the world, simply by using a cell phone or laptop computer.[11]

And now a step closer, with an American activist deeply involved in Congolese affairs:

> For decades, all of the benefits of eastern Congo's vast mineral resource wealth have gone to those with the biggest guns... These minerals include gold, tin, tantalum and tungsten used in cell phones, computers and jewelry.[12]

And another step closer, with a newspaper story on a Congolese hospital in what a UN expert described as "the rape capital of the world":

> The number of women and children raped in the Democratic Republic of the Congo has risen dramatically because of a surge in rebel militia activity... The leader of Heal Africa's project dealing with sexual violence said: "The numbers are rising because several armed groups... have increased their activities over several months. In times of fighting you usually see also rape, refugees, stealing, killing and the burning of houses going up."[13]

And even closer, with a local report on the FDLR, a militia whose leadership includes former *génocidaires* from Rwanda:

> Wherever it is in control, the FDLR organizes the illegal exploitation of mines and forests... The relationship between the FDLR

> and the local Congolese population is reminiscent of that between master and slaves.[14]

With one more step, we are on the ground, with a doctor in his clinic:

> Denis Mukwege, a Congolese gynecologist, cannot bear to listen to the stories his patients tell him anymore. Every day, 10 new women and girls who have been raped show up at his hospital. Many have been so sadistically attacked from the inside out, butchered by bayonets and assaulted with chunks of wood, that their reproductive and digestive systems are beyond repair…In almost all the reported cases, the culprits are described as young men with guns, and in the deceptively beautiful hills here, there is no shortage of them: poorly paid and often mutinous government soldiers; homegrown militias called the Mai-Mai who slick themselves with oil before marching into battle; members of paramilitary groups originally from Uganda and Rwanda who have destabilized this area over the past 10 years in a quest for gold and all the other riches that can be extracted from Congo's exploited soil…
>
> Few seem to be spared. Dr. Mukwege said his oldest patient was 75, his youngest 3. "Some of these girls whose insides have been destroyed are so young that they don't understand what happened to them," Dr. Mukwege said. "They ask me if they will ever be able to have children, and it's hard to look into their eyes."[15]

Sirens have been blasting in the Congo for years. This long-running conflict is "The World's Worst War," with hundreds of thousands of conflict-related deaths at the least, and perhaps deaths approaching Holocaust levels.[16] And alarms have been sounding in the Congo as far back as we can hear. Joseph Conrad called the exploitation of the Congo's resources "the vilest scramble for loot that ever disfigured the history of human conscience," and he wrote *Heart of Darkness* to convey its horror.[17]

All is not well amidst the wonders we have made. One link in global supply chains is distorted, defective, unclean. At this link, trade works less like a life machine than its opposite. This defective link is the first link, where raw materials like petroleum, metals, and gems are extracted from the ground. There is something about extracting such resources that risks disaster. Consider, for example, the countries that extract a lot of oil.[18]

For forty years, oil states have been noisy distractions to the quiet successes of the developing world. While non-oil states have generally been getting richer, freer, and more peaceful, the oil states are no richer, no more free, and no more peaceful than they were in 1980. Many oil states have even gotten worse—Gabon's average income fell by almost half over the quarter century from 1980; Iraq's fell by a full 85 percent. Long internal conflicts have ravaged countries like Algeria, Angola, Colombia, and Nigeria. Two headline figures are that these oil states are *50 percent more likely* to be ruled by an authoritarian government, and poorer ones are *twice as likely* to experience civil war, as non-oil states. The oil states are also more financially opaque and volatile on average than non-oil states, and for reasons we will see, they allow women fewer opportunities to enter politics or to work outside the home.

These figures show what political scientists call the "resource curse."[19] The NGO Freedom House rates countries by the degree to which they secure civil liberties and political rights—today, only one-sixth of the world's oil is in countries rated as "free."[20] Extracting resources tends to fuel corruption and to damage institutions, while burning out social trust.[21] Reliance on extractive resources also correlates with more frequent and longer civil wars, some as brutal as those in Chechnya, Sudan, and Syria.[22] Many countries rich with natural resources are also full of very poor people. About 40 percent of the resource-rich world lives on less than $2 a day, and—unlike in the rest of the world—poverty has been rising while governance has been deteriorating.[23] And again these alarms have been sounding for ages. Adam Smith said that no projects are more ruinous to a nation than digging for silver and gold, and Karl Marx wrote of the "extirpation, enslavement and entombment in mines" of indigenous peoples in his day.[24]

This book is about why sirens sound where natural resources are extracted—and about why they sometimes scream right beside us. It is about upgrading the global economy without damaging the supply chains on which so much depends. Much of the book is about oil, by far the world's most valuable commodity as well as its most divisive one. As we will see, the bad-news stories radiating from oil states have a source that poisons countries rich with gems and metals too. We will see why so many have spoken of resource wealth as a curse—and how those resources end up cursing us too.

By Part IV of the book, the path to a better world will open ahead of us. The West can lead the world through the next global revolution—a revolution as important as the ending of the slave trade and the liberation of the colonies from empires. Leading this revolution will make us more secure at home, more trusted abroad, and better able to solve pressing global problems like climate change as well. By the end of the book, we will be able to see our place in the history of human progress, with a clearer view of how we can help create a more united humanity, prepared to meet the challenges of its future.

Like Dante's journey, however, what we pass through will get much worse before it gets much better. Like Dante, first we must survey the infernal world we are in.

THE OIL AROUND US, ON US, IN US

Let's look more deeply into our connections as consumers to the resource curse overseas, starting with the biggest natural resource of all: oil. In 2012, the average American household spent $2,912 a year buying gasoline.[25] That's a fair amount of money, and we can track where the dollars went. The oil companies got $465 for transporting, refining, and selling the oil; the federal government took just over $165 in tax. Most of the rest went to buy the crude oil itself. Tracing those dollars back to oil-producing countries, we find that $275 went to authoritarian regimes. The average American household paid $275 to some of the world's most repressive and dangerous rulers, just by filling up.

If this interests us enough to look into it, we will find that our situation is even worse than we thought. Consumers send money to dictators when buying gasoline—and when they shop too. Petrochemicals from oil are used to make everything from clothes to furniture to perfumes to vitamins. Consumers may buy authoritarian oil when they buy bottled water and magazines, jackets and cosmetics, televisions and tablets, crayons and toothpaste, luggage and corn flakes. And not just corn flakes: oil-derived nitrogen is used to grow most major crops, and so is inside most of the food in every grocery store. Oil also powers over 90 percent of the world's transportation. So the cost of authoritarian oil may be part of the price of any product that has been carried by a ship, plane, or truck—which is nearly everything on the shelves. Unless you walk to buy your food at an organic Amish farm, your shopping will be saturated with oil at every stage. Every time we go to the checkout—in a shop or online—we may be sending some of our cash to foreign strongmen.

The complexities of global markets hide all of this from us—what we see around us are just the cornucopias of retail. And it's not clear what we could do about it anyway. After all, the Saudi royals who are selling us oil are major American allies, and the oil companies between us and them are gigantic global firms (the *Forbes* top-twenty includes five oil companies).[26] The whole system of authoritarian oil is deeply entrenched not only in our own economy but in the world economy too. If we happen to think of the victims of the authoritarians who are getting our cash, it's likely not with indifference but more with a feeling of helplessness—what, after all, could we possibly do for them?

We're not the first to feel helpless about being connected to suffering and injustice by global markets. In eighteenth-century England, the issue was not "authoritarian oil" but "slave sugar." Sugar harvested by slaves in the Caribbean was a mainstay of British overseas trade, and the British elites were heavily involved. The richest members of the British parliament owned slave plantations, and the Church of England had such extensive holdings that the Church's brand (burnt into the slaves' chests) was recognized on every Caribbean island. The leaders of the first modern consumer boycott—the boycott against slave sugar—tried to punch through their day's "business as usual" by connecting consumers mentally to the slaves. In an extraordinary pamphlet of 1791, the campaigner William Fox wrote:

> If we purchase the commodity we participate in the crime. The slave dealer, the slave holder, and the slave driver, are virtually agents of the consumer, and may be considered as employed and hired by him to procure the commodity... In every pound of sugar used... we may be considered as consuming two ounces of human flesh.[27]

Are we like the British in 1791? Should we apply Fox's words to us: "The oil company and the authoritarian ruler are virtually agents of the consumer, and may be considered as employed and hired by him to procure the commodity..."? Could we even conceive of an oil boycott?

DO WE REALLY HAVE TO CARE ABOUT THIS?

I am reading an interesting book, I feel engaged with it, but there is no real chance that I will act differently after reading it or that it will make a difference in my life. There are, after all, so very many people in the world; we must be hardened to most of their fates. Picture in your mind a ten-year-old boy, and entertain the fantasy that today he will start a busy life of shaking hands with one new person every second. After seventy-five years, he still would not have met the number of people who live right now in absolute poverty.[28] Being frank with ourselves, we know that our fellow human beings, who exist in such huge numbers, are suffering and dying all the time. If all the screams and pleas of those being tortured right now sounded in your room, you would go deaf—and the same for the sobs of those bereaved by injustice. We have to be a bit hard of hearing day-to-day, insensible enough to get on with life in a world of relentless misery and death.

The philosopher (who is a professional imaginer) will try to enliven our senses to the disasters at the far ends of global supply chains. Imagine, the philosopher says, that from now you will have to barter for goods instead of paying cash. To get a smoke alarm for your house, you will need to hand over a torch that will set fire to three huts with the families inside. A handheld game console for your child will cost you a rifle that will be used in an assault on a refugee camp. As you fill your fuel tank, you watch a screen above the pump showing live CCTV from inside a wretched, sweaty prison. You pay the cashier with six dozen plastic handcuffs that will be used on the next wave of pro-democracy protesters as they are taken to that prison (you will see the imprisoned protestors on the screen the next time you fill up).

"People need to think," says a Nigerian activist, "that when they turn their heat on in Europe they're spilling pollution into the Niger Delta." "We need a new law," says an American standup, "that owners of SUVs are automatically in the military reserve. Then they can go get their own goddamn oil."[29] Philosophers, campaigners, comedians: all try to tighten the mental links between consumers here and calamities there. These imaginings are based on a thought about our connection to suffering and injustice abroad, which captures our attention because the thought is our own, lingering at the edges of our awareness and sometimes at the center. The idea is that we are connected to others' misery, that our spending powers those sirens sounding so far away. How real is this theory? How close is that hypothesis to fact?

Consumers could be connected to misery if their spending funds it. For example: cruel rulers and bloody rebels could sell natural resources that flow down supply chains to consumers, while money that consumers pay for finished goods flows back up the supply chains to those rulers and rebels. Another connection would be through incentives. Consumers who today buy goods made from the resources of troubled lands could be creating incentives for those troubles to continue tomorrow.[30]

Both of these theories are correct. We do fund human suffering when we make our everyday purchases, and our shopping today does incentivize injustice tomorrow. More, we have been connected to oppression and conflict, corruption and poverty, throughout our lives. As we will see, consumer spending for natural resources prolonged the life of the Soviet regime as well as apartheid in South Africa; it sustained both Pol Pot and Saddam Hussein in power; it helped pay for the genocide in Darfur; and it fired vicious conflicts in Angola and Sierra Leone. Without change, we—and then our children—will be cinched to such afflictions forever.

THE FOG OF WARES

But surely our money also goes to good places too? When we pull our gaze up from the disasters in some resource-exporting countries, we see that not all such countries look so bad. Some, in fact, seem to be doing quite well. Norway has oil, Botswana has diamonds, Chile has copper—and these countries have flourished. Our linkage through supply chains to the people in those lands looks win-win. We enjoy the goods made from their raw materials; they use the money from selling those raw materials to become better off. These are the connections that we want with everyone in our supply chains—this is how we want the global market to work. So when does our everyday spending go to "good" countries, and when does it go to "bad" countries? When are we wedded to weal and when to woe?

It is in the nature of the global market that this is so hard to know. Revisualize the huge network of supply chains for all commodities glowing on the earth's surface, billions of nodes making trillions of connections like neurons in a human brain. There are now crowd-sourced websites that can help shoppers to understand the supply chains behind at least a few products, and so the sources of a few of the natural resources in the products they buy.[31] Yet for major commodities like petroleum, supply chains are not public (in fact, as we will see, they are kept secret). And today's supply chains, like neurons in a brain, continually shift their linkages. The rubber in a condom bought from a shop one day might come from Indonesian trees, the next day it might be from India; we cannot track at that level of detail. Even if you could somehow label all the shelves in the stores nearest you with the origins of the raw materials in the goods on sale, the labels would be unreliable after the first restocking.

The way that global supply chains merge together further deepens the fog of wares. Call this the problem of intermediate goods. Only one in five diamonds, for instance, ends up in jewelry—most go onto drill bits used in mining. Diamonds harvested from the bloody fields in Zimbabwe may have been fixed onto a drill used to extract oil from Mexico, which was then refined into gasoline that filled the truck that brought oranges to your supermarket.[32] The next orange you pick up may be, in this remote sense, a "blood orange"—you simply cannot know.

We simply cannot know exactly which products are tainted by moral toxicity in their supply chains. Yet we can be sure the taint is there. "Taint" is a third kind of connection between consumers and producers, beyond contribution and incentivization. If you thought that there was a 10 percent chance the cocoa in your favorite chocolate had been picked by young children forced to work long hours in harsh conditions, would you still buy it? What if it were a 1 percent chance? And yet there is a much higher chance that we are bringing home products made with resources forcibly taken from some of the most violated people in the world. Our moral taint is a certainty: as we will see, we all own stolen goods.

CURSES ON US

The resource curse not only taints us, it threatens us as well. The resource curse is always in the news—it was visible, for example in the big international stories of 2014–15. In Africa, Ebola overwhelmed three countries whose health systems were still feeble after years of mineral-fueled authoritarianism and war—and the fear of the epidemic spread to America. Putin of Russia—his treasury full from years of high oil prices—projected force into Ukraine and Syria while cranking up threats to the West. Western countries sent air power to combat an oil-funded army calling itself Islamic State, which attracted young recruits to fight in the fractured oil states of Iraq and Syria. The chaos in Syria spattered into neighboring states and sent refugees fleeing toward Europe. The resource curse is in the headlines you see today. By the end of Part I, you will see it everywhere.

Recall that among developing states, oil states, are 50 percent more likely to have authoritarian rulers, rulers who are sustained in power with our money. The next time your country sends its military to dislodge a petrocrat like Saddam Hussein or Muammar Gaddafi, it may be that money you paid at the pump helped to buy the missiles that will be launched at your pilots and the bullets that will be shot at your young soldiers. Recall also that poorer oil states are twice as likely to suffer civil conflict. The next time you are stuck in an airport security line, waiting to take off your coat or shoes, you might reflect that the (failed) Nigerian underwear bomber and the (failed) Yemeni cargo plane bomber and the (deadly) Boston Marathon bombers came from oil-producing regions long destabilized by violence. Or you might reflect on whose nationals flew the planes into the World Trade Center on 9/11.

As we will see in Part II, when we feed misery overseas, we should not be shocked when resentment bites us back. And the damage we take from the resource curse is not just directly from hostile authoritarians and aggressive extremists. We also damage ourselves by fighting over how to handle the lose-lose choices they give us. Iran, Iraq, Libya, Syria, Russia, other oil states: think of how poisonous our arguments have been for four decades over whether we should take military action or not, impose sanctions or not, or tighten our security against their terrorism at the expense of our personal freedoms. So much bad blood from our arguments—even between people of good will. Isn't there a way to go back to the source and dissolve these no-win choices before they once again divide us with such fire from each other?

Here we could spin off in any number of directions: to American imperialism, Islamic extremism, the rise of China, climate change, or fracking. We will get to all of these topics and more in this book. First, let's pause to see where we have found ourselves and then move forward.

EVERYWHERE IN CHAINS

The global market is a spectacular network of transformation and transportation, daily turning giant chunks of natural resources into macrocosms of products. The world's supply chains bring us the tech and fashion and airplanes that are the platforms of our plans, and that we would only with the greatest reluctance give up. More, these supply chains also bring the food, the energy, and the medicines that we as a human community could not do without. Seven billion is a lot to keep alive each day—not to speak of the many who are now living better than ever and the best-off who are living quite well indeed. Humanity needs the global market, the life machine it has created.

Within this market, many of the relations between suppliers and demanders are the win-win connections described by classical economics: suppliers send the goods, and demanders repay them for their efforts. Yet in some places, where natural resources like petroleum, metals, gems, and timber are extracted, the life machine malfunctions. Here supply chains hitch to resources and rip them out of the ground with disastrous results for those nearby. In these places, global demand is like a tornado touching down, or like a huge syringe penetrating the earth's skin, sucking raw materials into the sky. We saw the damage up close with a small scene from a Congolese village and in the large statistics correlating resource production with authoritarianism, civil conflict, corruption, gender inequality, and more. The widespread blessings of global trade contain within them the resource curse.

Were consumers aware of these cursed market connections—sending their spending to dictators and militias and corrupt officials today, and incentivizing more suffering and injustice tomorrow—most would not want them. The contribution of any one consumer to the resource curse is unknown, and it is well-nigh impossible for any consumer to find out which purchases involve him or her in it. Still, alert consumers will suspect that many of the goods they buy bear a moral taint from their resource-cursed origins. She may have blood on her hands—in the gold in her ring. He may have screams in his mouth, as he eats ice-cream made with oil-derived nitrogen. She may resent needing to shop every day in a globalized market that is structured by such pervasive injustice. He may have a queasy feeling that the resource curse that goes around abroad will come around to hurt those he loves. And she may dread the next impossible foreign policy crisis that will fill the airwaves with invective.

This problem is very deep. It is deep not only because global flows of tainted natural resources are so massive but also because the world depends on those flows of resources continuing. If the millions of barrels of authoritarian oil were to stop flowing tomorrow, the global economy would seize. Luxuries would become unaffordable for us, hundreds of thousands would lose their jobs, and millions overseas who have recently escaped severe poverty would fall back into destitution, if they survived the crash at all. The world runs on tainted resources, so we seem to be caught in a terrible bind. Our desire to live morally decent lives pulls against the practical necessity of sustaining our lifestyles, and lives around the world.

With one eye, we see the world's pulsating web of supply chains, growing in symbiotic relation with humanity. With the other eye, we see the global market grinding on, using blood to grease its gears. Both views are valid; we can see both at the same time. What we see with both eyes looks like a predicament distinctive of now.

Many challenges faced by our ancestors now seem morally simple, if practically daunting. See slaves in chains: break the chains. The Nazis are bombing your city: stop the Nazis. Many of our new challenges seem both morally and practically hard. With new problems like the resource curse and climate change, consumers face hypercomplex, opaque systems in which billions contribute small amounts to large, bad outcomes. Worse, it is the same systems that bring us the bounties of modern life that also bring us the threats. Breaking the world's slave chains: a moral triumph. Breaking the world's supply chains? Not an option.

Indeed, compared to the resource curse, even climate change looks easy. At least with climate change, the cause and cure are easily understood. Excessive emissions at millions of locations add up to excessive emissions overall: the simple solution would be to reduce the sum by reducing the summands. The hard part is reducing emissions fairly—and collective action to do that is hard because the relevant actor, humanity, has trouble getting its act together.[33] Yet the basic problem and solution of climate change are mentally simple—no more taxing than addition and subtraction.

The resource curse is tougher because at the micro level, nothing appears to be wrong. Think again of the raw materials used to make your daily purchases: distant deposits of ores and oil, foreign forests, antipodean gems. What draws those raw materials toward you are the market forces of supply and demand. The rules governing each stage of their journey to you are just the familiar rules of property and contract. Those who extract the resources sell to manufacturers, who sell to retailers, who sell to you. The money you spend goes to retailers, who buy from manufacturers, who buy from extractors. At each link, all we see is what Adam Smith called the human "propensity to truck, barter, and exchange one thing for another."[34] There is no "excess" at any link in the chain. Unlike climate change, the problem is not one of addition, so subtraction will not help.

The resource curse presents a collective action problem, but we cannot see, even in the abstract, what that action is. The supply chains that link us to the resource curse look to be made of very basic transactions: property flowing through contracts all the way from source to sale. The huge tapestry of the world's supply chains seems woven with a simple stitch. There appears to be no error we could rip back to and reweave. The resource curse seems just a gigantically bad byproduct of the global market.

We hear faint cries from the distant ends of supply chains, where the huge weight of global consumer demand crushes down on the bodies of those tortured by authoritarians or raped by militiamen. We read stories of people in resource-rich countries wilting from hunger, or rising against their dictator, or fighting in gruesome civil wars, or even plotting to murder people like us. We also see the profusion of luxuries and necessities that emerge from supply chains close to us—and there seems to be nothing but simple market exchanges between the cursed sources and the shelves of our stores. Tracing most raw materials through the world's opaque, ever-shifting supply chains is too hard, especially since many raw materials are used as intermediate goods in the chains. It's difficult to imagine being a Fair Trade consumer of oil.

As consumers, we seem stuck. Let's look again from a different angle.

YOU OWN SAUDI ARABIA

Take a quick inventory of the objects you have touched today (sheets, clothes, cosmetics, etc.). Those objects are made of molecules from many countries. Perhaps you woke today in Egypt. You may be wearing a bit of Spain around your waist, some Venezuela on your feet. There might be a bit of the Congo in your pocket, and quite possibly some Oman on your nose. It's like you've circumnavigated the globe in somersaults, with the soil of many countries sticking to you—or like a god rolled you into a ball and bowled you around the world, with money spilling out of your pockets all the way. You may soon bite into a nice slice of Italy topped with Sri Lanka: if you are what you eat, then we are the world. Looking at the molecules that go into and then make up your body—the food, drink, vitamins, drugs—you are a global citizen, a multilateral creation yourself. The heart of the most xenophobic American border patroller has Mexico within it. The Japanese racist cannot cleanse Korea from his blood.

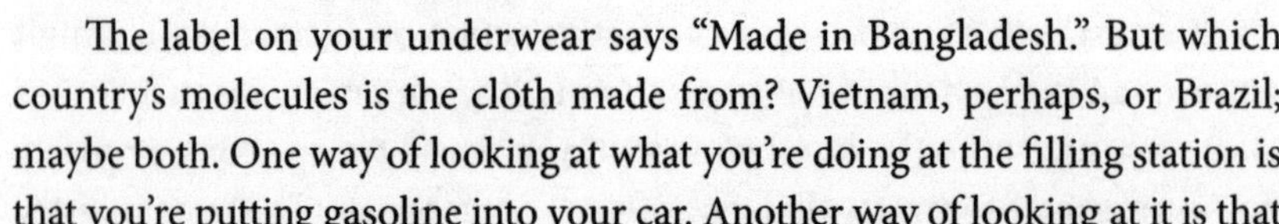

The label on your underwear says "Made in Bangladesh." But which country's molecules is the cloth made from? Vietnam, perhaps, or Brazil; maybe both. One way of looking at what you're doing at the filling station is that you're putting gasoline into your car. Another way of looking at it is that you're filling your car with the sovereign state of Angola. Or you could be filling your car with a mixture of Russia, Iraq, and Texas (as Marx said, money "brings together impossibilities, and forces contradictions to embrace"[35]). All of these atoms come from some exact point on the planet's surface: all were owned, at their origins, according to the laws of those countries. Supply chains are not only physical paths of molecules—they are chains of legal transactions, of property exchanged though contracts. What is now your property was once the property of others; the world's supply chains have put you into a legal relationship with many foreigners. This opens up a new perspective.

Let's choose something that is your property—say, your laptop—and trace the ownership of its components back through the links of its supply chains. You bought your laptop from a store, and the store bought that laptop from the manufacturer. The manufacturer bought all of the components of the laptop from its suppliers. If we trace back the property rights over one part of the computer—say, the plastic of the case—we will find the plastic feedstocks that were owned by a refinery, and then the oil that was owned by a trader that shipped the oil to the refinery. At the origin of this chain of legal titles, we find the oil owned, say, by the state of Saudi Arabia. You are in a legal relationship with the Saudi regime. Your legal ownership of your laptop depends upon the Saudi regime's legal ownership of a puddle of crude oil.

Or perhaps—a more profound question—should we say the Saudi regime's "alleged" ownership? The Saudi regime has declared that it owns all of the country's oil and that it has a right to sell off that oil. Yet why think that the Saudi regime has the authority to declare such a thing? Who put those men in charge of that country's petroleum? The Saudi regime's Basic Law says this:

> Government in the Kingdom of Saudi Arabia derives its authority from the Holy Qur'an and the sayings and customs of the Prophet.[36]

Do you have to believe *that* in order to own your laptop?

Perhaps you endorse the Saudi regime's authority for other reasons, which the regime itself would reject? Or perhaps you do not endorse the Saudi regime's authority at all? As you know, the Saudi regime has been repressive for decades, spending its huge oil revenues to crush all challenges to its rule. Certainly, we don't even want to think about invading the place—let's forget about *doing* anything whatsoever to Saudi Arabia. Yet when you shut your laptop and slip it into your bag, you do seem to be assuming some sort of justification, some implicit theory of property rights. So here is the precise question, for a moment of intense reflection: (how) did the Saudi regime legally sell the oil that made the plastic in the laptop that you now legally own?

Having no idea what the answer to this question could be is better than thinking the answer is obvious. And the answer will turn out to be surprising, gripping—one could even say wonderful were it not also part of the explanation of the suffering and injustice that comes with the resource curse. The answer is not obvious but will be worth the search, because finding the answer will point the way to lifting that curse.

TO SEE THE WORLD IN A DROP OF OIL

Thinking about the resource curse at the level of the consumer, we got stuck. Meditating on ownership frees us to go deeper. If we picture the world's law as a layer over its politics, and its politics as a layer over its economics, this book's analysis will take a core sample through all three strata to discover the ground truths of international trade in natural resources.

In this exploration, we will find the mechanisms in the life machine that maintain our species at its size, and the hidden political foundries in which the warped links in the world's supply chains are forged. We will search for why countries that export natural resources run greater risks of authoritarianism, civil war, corruption, gender oppression, and other disorders—and why some countries succeed with their resources while others suffer. We will find a chasm between old and new international law, and a cavern where all our charts say that good laws should be. We will detect hidden currents under the daily news flows about hostile petrocrats, bloody revolutions, failed states, terrorists, economic crises, and environmental damage. Digging into the political economy of natural resources will unearth the raw materials of the history that we are living through.

We can see much of the world in a drop of oil. Still, nothing explains everything; global events have more dimensions than any one vantage can survey. Law, politics, and economics are the resultants of many vectors, of various forces that reinforce and cancel; no system is monocausal or closed. There was of course more to 9/11 than oil. Those rapacious Congolese militiamen are not just greedy sadists searching for mineral loot—they are moving within the labyrinthine politics of their location. So even when we make progress in fighting the resource curse, this will not magically cure today's cursed countries, much less the Earth, of all troubles. There will still be bad governance, conflict, poverty, and terrorism. The curse's causes and cures are components of a larger whole; the chapters here light pixels in the global picture. Natural resources are not everything, but they certainly are something.

Finding solutions as deep as these problems will mean limning the foundations of the international system, asking how authoritarians, warlords, and corrupt elites continue to gain power through natural resources. Books written on these issues tend to highlight the West's foreign policy mistakes or its "addiction to oil"—and while there is truth in these theses, they are on the surface. Our search takes us deeper, delving through history, law, and the social sciences to find the global rules that channel power to these unaccountable men all day, every day—no matter what. We are looking for the practices that constantly, almost inevitably, empower today's violent, repressive, and corrupt actors, and in this search we will take nothing for granted about the wisdom or justice of the ways that the world has always worked.

The payoffs from taking a deeper view of resources will come in interpreting the world, and also in changing it. After Part I, the causes of the resource curse will be visible, and after Part II, our own contributions to it will be clear. Through these chapters, the challenge of the resource curse will begin to look less like the new challenge of climate change and more like the familiar challenges faced by our ancestors. Fighting the resource curse will turn out to be more like fighting slavery now seems to have been: morally simple, if practically daunting. The resource curse will look morally simple once we find the forces that drive it, now hiding in the light. When isolated, there will be no question that these forces are noxious and also dangerous. In Part III, we will find the principles that can counter the power that causes so much oppression and chaos worldwide.

The challenge of change will be daunting because the drivers of the resource curse are entrenched. We need to upgrade the global economy while not damaging its operation. Fortunately, the world is set for success. The principles we need are already widely believed, major treaties declaring these principles are already signed, powerful interests and ideals are already aligned. There is tremendous momentum in the right direction.

To lead in lifting the resource curse, Western countries only need to enforce their own principles, within their own borders, on their own soil.

This is crucial: the "we" in this book is we in the West; our leadership will come from putting our own houses in order. It is not for us to tell the Saudis or the Nigerians how to run their countries—those are matters for the Saudis, and for the Nigerians, to decide.

Our countries have to decide their own foreign policies, and we especially have to decide who we will trade with and how. Whatever decisions we make—to trade or not to trade, to trade under one set of rules or another—our decisions will have major implications for foreigners. This book hopes to present a persuasive case that we should decide to trade in accordance with our own deepest principles—instead of trading in violation of those principles, as we now do. Western countries should change their own rules of trade so as to respect the right of all peoples to take control over their own resources, and so to chart their own fates. Putting our own houses in order will help peoples everywhere to make their own lives better, and in time, this will make our lives better as well.

The West's leadership on resources will be the next stage of the global moral revolution that has already ended the Atlantic slave trade, liberated the colonies, overcome apartheid, and advanced human rights. Part IV sets out a plan of action that is ready to go today: a plan for statesmen, consumers, investors, leaders in civil society, and most of all, for citizens to act on now. Part V reflects on how remaking today's trade in natural resources will mesh with the larger history of human progress—how we can replace the rules that divide foreigners against each other, that divide foreigners against us, and that also divide us against ourselves.

We can find the flaws in global supply chains and fix them. We can quiet some of the sirens that blast far from us, and some set to blast close to us too. We can make a freer and more unified common life than we have yet achieved.

Need to Know Basis

The Facts About Resources, the Oil Companies, and the Oil Countries

This is a short chapter with some background information on natural resources that will be useful for reading the book.

First, a caveat. This book covers a lot, but it also leaves out a lot. There may be times when you read something here and think, "There's more to it than that." You will certainly be right, and you are warmly invited to enrich what you find on these pages with your own knowledge and views.

Second, a heads-up. Two topics will get less attention than some might expect in a book on natural resources: the early history of oil, and the environment. This is not because these topics are unimportant, but because they are covered well elsewhere.

So, for example, we will take for granted that oil was a major factor in great power politics before the last forty years, which is our period. Oil was both the goal and the fuel of many of the past century's wars, and control over oil was a steady priority for the big industrialized countries.

The basic facts of this history are not controversial, even among observers with quite different politics. So, for example, speaking of World War I, Britain's Lord Curzon declared, "The Allied cause had floated to victory upon a wave of oil."[1] Already in 1924, Calvin Coolidge remarked, "The supremacy of nations may be determined by the possession of available petroleum and its products."[2] About the industrial countries after World War II, Noam Chomsky wrote, "The 'golden age' of postwar development relied on cheap and abundant oil, kept that way largely by threat or use of force."[3] Those looking for a more detailed history of the role of oil in the struggles among nations will enjoy Daniel Yergin's book and documentary series *The Prize*.[4]

For similar reasons, there will also be relatively little here on the environment. Much of this story is well known. Mining and logging are usually intrusive industrial processes destructive of the preexisting natural order. Even if they are handled well (which they often are not), they risk polluting or poisoning the air and water, destroying fragile ecosystems, and disrupting the livelihoods and cultural practices of surrounding communities. Oil spills, gas flares, strip mines, and clear-cut forests are just a few of the phrases that evoke the damage these extractive industries can cause. (There is more on environmental damage on the website.[5])

Climate change is a major issue that will be taken up in the policy chapters toward the end of the book. There is no doubt that humanity's most dangerous and difficult climate challenges are bound up with our exploitation of natural resources, and especially with our energy and food systems. The book's position on climate change is that of the consensus report of the main international organization of climate scientists:

> Human influence on the climate system is clear... Continued emission of greenhouse gases will cause further warming and long-lasting changes in all components of the climate system, increasing the likelihood of severe, pervasive and irreversible impacts for people and ecosystems... Adaptation and mitigation are complementary strategies for reducing and managing the risks of climate change. Substantial emissions reductions over the next few decades can reduce climate risks in the 21st century and beyond... Mitigation can be more cost-effective using an integrated approach that combines measures to reduce energy use and the [greenhouse gas] intensity of end-use sectors, decarbonize energy supply, reduce net emissions and enhance carbon sinks in land-based sectors.[6]

A reasonable discussion of what to do about climate change would take another book. This book's policy recommendations will be compatible with any responsible plan. So again you are invited to add your own views on climate to what you read throughout the book. When we do take up the issue in Chapter 16, the good news will be that policies for fighting the resource curse will also make progress on climate change. One good way to start decarbonizing the energy supply is to stop buying blood oil.

Instead of retelling the stories about history and the environment, this chapter summarizes some of the less-known technological and economic dimensions of today's natural resource trade. From these angles, the familiar themes of conflict and destruction fade, and the stories are much more about successes. If one surveys how cleverly humanity supplies itself with fuels and raw materials, one may come away impressed. And even those who cannot bring themselves to admire anything related to oil may gain a new appreciation for how enmeshed our lives are with it. Having a sense of the technology and economics of the global resource systems gives one an advantage in understanding why the political and environmental problems surrounding resources have been so devilishly hard to solve.

THE CATHEDRALS OF MODERNITY

Travellers returning from a trip to Egypt or India or Italy may scan their home country with a critical eye. Where, after all, are our great wonders? Where are our pyramids? And what have we built that approaches the glorious Taj Mahal? Today, we are so much richer than the Italians of the Renaissance—and our architects can computer-design any fantasy. Yet what have we done with all of our wealth and technology, really? Have we created anything that can hold a candle to St. Peter's in Rome?

These travellers are looking in the wrong places. Unlike the ancient civilizations, our modern civilization does not invest its genius in glorifying its rulers or gods. Our best designers and biggest enterprises mostly strive to satisfy the daily desires of ordinary people. And that means that our architectural wonders are ugly monstrosities, hidden far from public view. Instead of the grandeur of pharaohs or popes, much of our engineering ingenuity is aimed at the shared need of all production and consumption, which is energy. Travellers looking to see the cathedrals of modernity should helicopter out to an oil platform.

The world's tallest skyscraper is the Burj Khalifa in Dubai—but an oil platform in the Gulf of Mexico stands more than two-thirds taller.[7] The One World Trade Center complex in New York has been called "the world's most expensive building"—it cost around $4 billion.[8] Australia's Gorgon gas project, which links subsea wells to a land-based plant, is estimated at $54 billion.[9]

Russia's Berkut platform is built to survive a sixty-foot tsunami—and to endure a 9.0 earthquake without interrupting its operations.[10] The Sevan Driller, floating off the coast of Brazil, can stretch its equipment through 12,000 feet of ocean and still drill a well to 40,000 feet—farther below the earth's surface than most commercial jets fly above it.[11] There are two man-made objects that can be seen with the naked eye from the surface of the moon—the Great Wall of China, and the Troll platform off the coast of Norway, which has in some years by itself supplied 12 percent of Europe's natural gas.[12] (From here on, natural gas will just be called *gas.*)

The oil industry is first and most about geology and engineering: about finding elusive pockets of molecules in the earth's crust, extracting them, transporting them, and refining them into useful products. Doing this today requires very sophisticated technology—for decades, the petroleum industry has been a major force for innovation. Imagine what it would take to drill to a closet-sized area half a mile down and seven miles away; that's been done off the coast of Russia. Subsurface imaging techniques like reverse time migration and full waveform inversion require huge amounts of artificial brainpower—and 4D seismic surveying captures gigantic caches of data. There already exist today what *Star Trek* fans would recognize as holodecks: immersive rooms where petroleum geologists walk through dynamically simulated oil reservoirs.

The outcome of innovation has been oceans of oil—transported through tubes that are as long as the Mississippi River and carried by ships five times heavier than the biggest aircraft carrier.[13] The world uses 1,000 barrels of oil—that is, 42,000 gallons of oil—each and every . . . second. Imagine four Olympic-sized swimming pools full of dark liquid disappearing into showers of tiny sparks, once a minute. This liquid is being used everywhere around the world, helping humans to live in unprecedented numbers and in the remotest locations. The geniuses of the ancient world would not know how to take the first step of the engineering feats that we hardly notice. The Romans were so proud of their aqueducts; few of us give a thought to the oleoducts that sustain modern civilization worldwide.[14]

The reason that oil is so much with us is that—ignoring the politics and the environment for the moment—it is such a brilliant energy source for transportation. Oil fuels are easy to move, relatively light and stable, and pack lots of punch: a gallon of oil contains about the same energy as ten pounds of coal, seventeen pounds of wood, and (comparing again to ancient civilizations) fifty days of slave labor.[15] If you tried to fly a 737 using today's best batteries instead of jet fuel, you would need to load batteries that weighed twenty-two times more than the plane itself.[16]

The fact to remember here is that today, over 90 percent of the world's transportation runs on oil—that's almost every car, truck, ship, and plane on Earth. The world's fleet is oil-powered today because (again holding politics and the environment aside) oil has for years been the best engineering solution to the challenge of moving people and goods. Right now, any machine that travels on land, air, or sea is very likely powered by oil. It may well be that every human being and every man-made thing you can see right now has been moved to where it is by tiny oil sparks.

THE ROAR OF FOSSILS

You will hear fossils today—perhaps you hear them right now, in the rumble of explosions of droplets of fossil fuel that power a car or truck or jet. Or perhaps now you hear an electric motor, or a stereo speaker, or the hum of the lights: the energy making that noise still likely comes from breaking chemical bonds formed in ages past, inside coal or natural gas. Oil is humanity's main energy source for transportation—coal and gas are its main energy sources for electricity. These three fossil fuels together produce around 85 percent of humanity's energy: right now, humans burn fossils for most of their power.

Almost all energy on Earth comes, ultimately, from the sun. It was the sun that radiated the energy that grew the organisms whose fossils we now burn. In a sense, the fossil fuels are congealed sunlight—or one can think of them as extremely efficient solar batteries. The energy that speeds you toward your holiday, or that carries your voice across continents, is energy that comes from a particle of sunlight, buried for eons beneath the earth.[17]

Coal, oil, and gas are solid, liquid, and gaseous forms of carbon and hydrogen (thus "hydrocarbons"). They differ in how many carbon atoms are stuck together in their molecules—a lot in coal, some in oil, a few in gas. Their carbon was bonded inside organisms, mostly plankton (not dinosaurs) that floated in ancient seas. The energy inside these organisms was preserved as they sank, were buried, and were compacted during sedimentation. As Jean-Paul Sartre said of coal, a fossil fuel is "a source of accumulated energy derived from vanished vegetable matter; one might describe it as capital bequeathed to mankind by other living beings."[18] About 200,000 pounds of plants went into making each gallon of our gasoline.[19]

Energy transitions change the human condition—as Marx said, "The windmill gives you society with the feudal lord; the steam-mill, society with the industrial capitalist."[20] The transition from biomass (wood and dung) to fossil fuels during the Industrial Revolution was humankind's most momentous energy transition since the domestication of fire. With coal as power, the graph of the world's population, which had climbed very slowly for millennia, suddenly rocketed upward. As Ralph Waldo Emerson said, "Coal is a portable climate. It carries the heat of the tropics to Labrador and the Polar circle; and it is the means of transporting itself whithersoever it is wanted… [A] half-ounce of coal will draw two tons a mile, and coal carries coal, by rail and by boat, to make Canada as warm as Calcutta, and with its comfort brings its industrial power."[21] The intrafossil transition from coal to oil as humanity's main energy source (which happened around 1970) was not as momentous. Still, this was the transition from the world of the steam train and steamship to the automobile and airplane.[22] Recently, the global energy mix has been shifting away from oil toward gas, with renewables still small but coming more online.[23]

It's no accident that the Book of Genesis identifies light with creation, and that the Book of John links it to life. The forms of energy available to a civilization shape its fundamentals, like its demographics and its modes of production. Fuels influence what desires humans can satisfy, and so also what further desires they can afford to have. If you look at humanity's per-capita energy use today, it's as though each human being has twenty-three servants working for him or her, every hour of every day.[24]

Life as we know it, certainly we ourselves, would not exist were it not for humanity's transition to fossil fuels. Still, there is no reason to fetishize or revile any particular energy source. Coal has done much for us, but it is now likely time to switch away from it. If safe, transportable cold fusion were invented tomorrow (the nightmare of the sheikhs), we could leapfrog renewables and transition away from fossils in a generation. Energy sources are means for humans to satisfy and extend their desires, and we should harness those sources that best allow us to satisfy our desires—collecting all of the benefits and costs, and all of our desires, into the calculations.

LIFE ON IRON ROCK

To see the world as a geological object is to see a hot iron rock. Geoscientists are right now scanning the subsurfaces of this rock to find where idiosyncratic minerals are hiding. Like the oil companies, mining companies are in the molecule business—often, a huge firm will specialize in just one square of the periodic table. And as with energy, humanity's history with minerals is one of growing drumbeats of demand stimulating ever more elaborate dances of supply. Metals and gems are right now being dug out with giant shovels and sifted out by hand, starting their journeys into the supply chains that will build our cities and fill them with goods. Like the chiming of slot machines within the world's casinos, the exploration, excavation, and processing of minerals rings incessantly around the globe while we are thinking of other things.

There is a real physicality to this part of our world: tunnel borers, giant dozers, smelting furnaces. If we rarely think of these, it may be because they seem just to make the props for the stages on which we perform the scripts of our real lives. Yet think of the physical infrastructure of your own body, including your brain, which supports your consciousness. And think of how much of your life you devote to absorbing and expelling matter from your body, moving your body from one place to another, keeping it fit, and dealing with disease. Humanity devotes a similar proportion of its collective life to discovering and arranging the material bases of its own complex existence. "If there were no metals," the German scientist Agricola wrote in 1556, "men would pass a horrible and wretched existence in the midst of wild beasts."[25]

Finding metals and gems has of course fired the passion of explorers for ages. Whole countries have been named for metals, like Argentina, which is silver, and Ghana, which was the Gold Coast. Still, it will be important later to keep in mind that most extractive resources are non-renewable.[26] Each ton of metal and carat of gemstones extracted from a country subtracts from its natural wealth. So it is not right to think of some country as "a platinum exporter" or "a diamond producer" in the same way as we think of countries in terms of their renewable features (like "industrialized" or "democratic"). Resource-rich nations are born with a trust fund; as Joseph Stiglitz says, "If they do not reinvest their resource wealth into productive investments above ground, they are actually becoming poorer."[27] The venerable Cyprus, for which copper is named, now produces almost none.

As mentioned in the Introduction, iron is our big metal—95 percent of global metal production makes steel.[28] At the other end of the spectrum, diamonds weigh nearly nothing but are worth more than almost everything else in nature. Anyone, without any assets beyond a bag of diamonds slung across their shoulder, could walk into any country in the world and instantly be among its one hundred richest people.[29] Many of the metals and gems spread across the geophysical spectrum are highly concentrated sources of economic value. That is what attracts such determined searches for them and—as we will see—that is what explains much of the trouble that surrounds them.

PETROWORLD

This book is mostly about oil because oil is the world's most valuable internationally traded commodity, worth more than $2 trillion in 2013. And oil is not just energy. Oil also contains chemicals that suffuse our material world. It's as though a giant petroleum geyser had erupted in the center of each continent and splashed all over it—over the roads, into the buildings, onto the people. You drive on it, and you wear it in your waistband. It may be smeared on your face, and it may be enhancing your sex life. Oil is everywhere.

Basically, if it's plastic, it's oil. And if it's synthetic, it's likely made from oil. And there's more too; a very partial list of ordinary things often made from oil includes: asphalt, aspirin, balloons, blenders, candles, car bumpers, carpets, contact lenses, crayons, credit cards, dentures, deodorants, diapers, digital clocks, dinnerware, dyes, eyeglass frames, furniture fabrics, garbage bags, glue, golf balls, hair dryers, infant seats, lipstick, lubricants, luggage, paint, patio screens, pillows, shampoo, shaving cream, slippers, syringes, tents, tires, toothpaste, toys, umbrellas, vinyl, vitamins, and wallpaper.[30] The role of oil in world food production is also significant. Modern agriculture depends on oil, not only to power farm machines but also for fertilizers and sprays. The Green Revolution of the twentieth century—which helped to double agricultural yields and the human population in a generation—grew on the nitrogen extracted from oil. As the philosopher John Gray has put it, "intensive agriculture is the extraction of food from petroleum"—yet another way in which oil today sustains the species at its size.[31]

Imagine one lifetime in today's petroworld. As a baby girl emerges, the doctor catches her in oil gloves, and nurses clean her with oil cloths. Her parents look down through oil lenses; they drive her home in an oil carriage over oil streets to the oil-furnished house where she will grow up eating oil food. All her toys are oil, and her books are written in oil ink. She buys an oil suit when she gets a job, and she spends more time looking at oil each day, in the plastic of her screens, than looking at human faces. She spends more time touching oil each day, in her keyboard, than caressing her spouse or her children. She ages; she takes oil pills; her hips are replaced with oil hips, her heart valves with oil valves. At last, she dies, lying in oil blankets. The oil tubes and catheters are removed, and the oil sheet is pulled over her. It could be any life; it could be ours.

GET THEE BEHIND ME, PETRO

We now take up a few topics that are more emotive, like the price of oil and Saudi Arabia. This will be a high-level survey: if you became President of the United States tomorrow, this is the kind of briefing on oil that your advisors might give you during your first week in office. In this section, we discuss the Middle East and world oil; in the next section, we take up the oil business and the oil companies.

The countries that have the most oil are not the countries that use the most oil: about 60 percent of the oil that is used in the world crosses an international border. The world's "artery of oil reserves" starts in Siberia, is widest in the Middle East, snakes through Africa, and then arcs up from Brazil to Canada. The Middle East has just under half of the world's proven oil reserves, and most of its production now goes to Asia.[32] The United States today imports about a third of all the oil it consumes.[33] Canada is by far the biggest source of oil imports to the United States, followed by Saudi Arabia, and then by Mexico and Venezuela. Shale in the United States has boosted domestic oil (and even more domestic gas) production remarkably since 2009, meaning that US imports have recently decreased rapidly. In 2014, many were predicting North American energy independence within a decade or so.

The United States has never been that reliant on the Middle East for oil—its dependence is now less than 10 percent, and has never been more than 15 percent, of total consumption.[34] Why then has America spent such huge amounts keeping its military in the region—and why has it shown itself so ready to use its military there, even at great cost?

This is a complex story, which we will take up again later. But as far as oil goes, there have been two basic plot lines. First, major US trade partners and allies (such as Europe and Japan) have been more heavily reliant on Middle East oil, and the United States has traditionally seen the economic vitality of these countries as favorable to its own interests.

Second, oil is a globally traded good that essentially has a single world price—everybody pays the same for a barrel of oil. The world price of oil (and so the price in the United States) is greatly influenced by what happens in the Middle East. Think of oil-producing countries as pipes of different sizes hanging down and filling up a bathtub. Think of oil-consuming countries as drains of different sizes drawing oil out from the bottom of that bathtub. The world price changes with the level of oil in the tub.[35] For price, it doesn't matter which countries are piping oil in or which countries are draining oil out: all that matters is how much is in the tub. The more oil there is in the bathtub, the lower the price for everyone in the world; the less oil there is, the higher the price for all.

Since the Middle East has the biggest "pipes," keeping oil flowing through those pipes is the best way to keep the world (and so the US) oil price down. And since the Saudi regime can open or close the valve on its huge pipe, it has traditionally had the greatest influence on the world (and so on the US) oil price. So the Middle East, and the Saudis in particular, have been important for cheaper oil, and (as can be seen from earlier on) "cheaper oil" basically means "cheaper everything"—and so more economic growth. The United States has believed that military and diplomatic engagement with the Middle East is in its overall national interests—though this is an assumption we will test in the chapters to come.

Prediction is difficult, as Niels Bohr quipped, especially about the future—and nowhere more so than with the future of oil. When the writing of this book began, the talk was about global "Peak Oil"—that the world would soon run out. Then supply curves rose, demand curves flattened—so today few speak about Peak Oil. All forecasts about energy should be taken with shakerfuls of salt. Right now, the most sensible thing to say is that the world will not soon run out of oil—but it has moved beyond cheap oil.

The giant Texan oil fields that gushed in the 1930s yielded more than a hundred times the energy it took to extract that energy—and the Middle Eastern megafields of today are likely even more generous.[36] But the world now demands much more oil than such "easy" fields provide. Deploying expensive oil platforms offshore, or evulsing the gummy oil sands of Canada and Venezuela, pushes the energy ratio down—from these new sources, one gets only a ten-to-one, or even only a four-to-one, return on the energy invested. These basic economics are what is slowly shifting the world away from oil right now—and future policies (such as on climate) could speed that shift. The Stone Age did not end because of a shortage of stones, as one commentator put it, but because new technologies were found that were better overall.[37]

COUNTRIES AND COMPANIES

Much of what is commonly believed about the big Western oil and mining companies is true. Companies like Exxon, Shell, and BHP Billiton are gigantic global firms. They are fierce capitalist enterprises wherever they operate, yet they are also powerful enough to demand large tax breaks and subsidies at home and abroad.[38] They are well connected at the highest levels of government around the world.[39] In general, these firms have been obstructionist on climate change issues. And while their investments in alternative energy and "corporate social responsibility" are not trivial, these are essentially window dressings around their core business concerns.[40]

However, some people may have a few belief weeds about these companies that it will be useful to pull out. The first surprise is that if one has heard of an oil or mining company, then it is probably better behaved than most. This is not because the familiar Western companies are altruistic, but simply because they must maintain the value of their brands. In the shadowy world of oil, there are many firms that most people never hear of—the Asian national oil companies, gigantic oil traders, small explorers—that are much worse than the Western majors when it comes to environmental safety, labor standards, and doing dodgy deals with corrupt foreign officials.[41] For firms in the extractive industries, to know them is actually to love them (at least relatively).

The second surprise is that the oil companies do not really pull all the strings in Washington, London, or Paris. These firms are well connected, they do have influence, but they represent just one business sector that lobbies among many others. And their interests are often overridden by geostrategic maneuvering. (Think, for example, of the sanctions that the American government has placed over the years on Iran, Iraq, Libya, and Sudan—these sanctions have meant that US oil companies were not allowed to make money in these big oil countries.) More, as we will see in Chapter 17, the oil and mining industries do lose political battles—sometimes even to small but well-organized NGOs. If you think of "groups that influence policy" as needles dipping into a pool of water, then the extractive industries are one large needle, but there are many other needles too.

The crucial fact that everyone needs to know about the world's natural resource trade is that it is countries, not companies, that are most important today. Countries own their natural resources—they only hire foreign companies, if at all, to get the resources out of the ground. You can think of the well-known oil companies like Chevron as star football players. A star can ask for a lot when bargaining to join a team—but it is the owners who have the money and make all the most important decisions.

The biggest oil-producing countries, like Saudi Arabia, use their own national oil companies to take their oil out of the ground—they only hire in the Western majors to do the occasional odd job. These big countries and their national companies are far more important players than any private firm. (Saudi Arabia, for example, controls close to 20 percent of the world's reserves of oil. Exxon, the largest US oil firm, controls less than 1 percent.[42]) Smaller oil-producing countries do need to hire foreign companies to extract their oil, but today, they have many foreign companies to choose from—not only the Western majors but also, for example, the deep-pocketed Chinese companies and also oil service firms like Halliburton. What the Western majors offer is world-leading technology and decades of experience in managing large, complex projects in difficult places. So the Western majors are still the top choice for the most geologically and politically challenging plays. Still, the majors have lots of competition nipping at their heels.

An oil country has oil; it needs to get that oil out of the ground. If it hires a foreign company, it will usually pay that company in oil, by letting the company keep some of the oil that it extracts. Along the way, the company will also pay money to the state (in signing bonuses, royalties, taxes, and more). These contractual arrangements often involve very large sums, and they have traditionally been kept secret. This has allowed vast corruption for decades—and, as we will see, it has also stimulated promising campaigns for greater transparency in these transactions.

Whoever gets the oil out of the ground, once the oil leaves the country it enters the global market, and it can in principle go almost anywhere. Someone will refine it and sell it to a retailer who will then sell it to consumers. The gas you buy at a Chevron station might have been extracted by Chevron and refined by Chevron—but it also might have been extracted by Kuwait, shipped by an oil trader like Vitol, refined by Marathon, and then sold to the Chevron station. The people who protested outside BP stations after the 2010 spill in the Gulf of Mexico were directly attacking only a small part of BP's business—the retail part. What these protesters were doing more effectively was piling more damage onto BP's brand.

EMERGING FROM THE MUD

The technical prowess of the extractive industries is remarkable, and what they produce is soaked into every part of our days. The scale and reach of the global resource system merits respect—here much human intelligence is realized. And taking a short-term, close-up view of the efficiency of the system shows why it seems so locked in. The politics of resources are hard because the benefits are so obvious when seen up close. It is only when we take a long-term, wide-lens view of the world's use of natural resources that we will see why changes to the system are needed. The good news is that many of the most important questions around making these changes are simply about costs and benefits. Once we become convinced of the long-term benefits of modifying the global resource system, we will have confidence that the costs of the next transition will be worth bearing.

Someday, our progeny will look back at our current primitive state, where humans propelled themselves around the planet by burning mud. But right now, if that mud suddenly became incombustible, most of the species would be dead within a year. Almost all of our energy today comes from burning long-dead plankton: when we flick a light switch or turn the ignition, we likely start or stoke a fossil fire. That will change, more quickly or more slowly, depending on the choices we make now.

Summary of the Book

This is a big book. The first part of this summary gives a preview of the book, and includes spoilers; the second part sets out the underlying philosophy. Those who don't like spoilers can skip the preview. Those who don't need philosophy can turn to Chapter 1 (and also omit the book's Epilogue). Those mostly interested in policy can read the preview and then the two policy chapters—Chapters 16 and 17.

PREVIEW OF THE BOOK

Think of the West's no-win foreign policy choices over the past forty years. Should Western countries risk removing autocrats like Assad or Gaddafi or Saddam? Or rather impose sanctions, as on Iran, while the regime continues to destabilize its region? Is it wise to back "friendly" authoritarians like the Saudis, and turn a blind eye to their human rights abuses and support for extremists? Should the United States send more aid to countries like Nigeria, where a corrupt elite rules over an impoverished and increasingly violent population? Ought Europe stand up to Russia—and endanger its own economic recovery? These have been among the West's most divisive debates: no good options exist, and much is at stake in terms of money and lives.

The questions of this book are whether some of these dilemmas can be dissolved before they form—and what opportunities would open to a less divided world. The book begins by noticing that all of these hard choices above emerge from countries rich with natural resources. In these places, oil, metals, or gems fund authoritarianism and civil wars, corruption and terrorism. All of the countries above suffer what social scientists call the "resource curse." Something in the wiring of these countries' politics keeps causing fused circuits, explosions, and fires that put Western interests at risk.

The resource curse is ingrained in Asian, African, and Middle Eastern states. Resource-enriched regimes oppress their populations, and elite networks of corruption are dug in. In fragile states, militias sell the resources they pillage to fund more violence against local people and sometimes against the government. Autocrats divide and rule, militants raid and kill, and the instabilities born of this intense coercion manifest as international aggression, civil wars, humanitarian crises, and extremist movements. The Syrian refugee crisis and Darfur, al-Qaeda and blood diamonds, all bear birthmarks of the resource curse. And the resource curse may spread: fifty-one of the fifty-four African countries, for example, are now producing or exploring for oil.[1]

The West's strategic environment would improve with better governance in resource-cursed countries, as would the prospects for peace and human rights worldwide. The promise of systemic improvements pulls this book's investigation of the resource curse down through the substratal channels of international power to find how coercive and corrupt actors in resource-cursed countries maintain their dominance despite the misery and divisions they cause. Excavating these channels of power leads through law, through history, to how Western consumers and governments help to drive the resource curse.

The Euclid moment emerges while meditating on ethical consumers in the West. Shoppers also face hard questions because of the resource curse. Blood diamonds? Why should a man looking for a beautiful gift for the woman he loves need to think about massacres in some distant war zone? An impossibly complex conflict in the Congo—an office manager pauses before she orders new computers. Didn't the newspaper say that deaths there are running into the millions?

Consumers know that they may be dirtying their hands with tainted goods that come to them through global supply chains. This book presses on how consumers come to be in *legal* relations with the coercive actors who supply those tainted goods. Supply chains are also sale chains—they make transitive legal links. Americans, for example, who have bought smart phones containing minerals pillaged by Congolese warlords own every molecule of their phones under American law. We probe how consumers come to be legally chained to distant warlords. For surely those warlords had no legal right to their plunder? Moving laterally, we consider a driver in Kansas buying a tank of gas. How, after all, does the atrocious authoritarian of Equatorial Guinea have the right to sell that country's oil so that a Kansan can buy that oil legally?

The book locates the surprising international rule that connects coercive actors in resource-cursed countries to consumers. This legal rule is called "effectiveness," which means that "might makes right." Today's international rule says that coercive control over a population ("might") will result in legal control over that population's resources ("right"). "Might makes right" is as much true for an autocrat in coercive control of an oil-rich country as it is for a band of militants who seize a mine by force. In both cases, the alchemy of effectiveness transmutes the iron of coercion into the gold of legal title. Whoever can gain coercive control sends resources down through sale chains to consumers, and consumers' cash flows back up to the coercive actors to help them maintain their power. Effectiveness puts consumers into business with bad actors abroad.

From a market perspective, effectiveness for foreign resources looks wrong. If bandits take over a warehouse, after all, no one thinks they gain the legal right to sell off the merchandise and keep the money. Yet effectiveness is the international rule for resources, and it creates incentives for coercion and crime in resource-rich regions. To see those incentives, imagine for a moment that New York declared "might makes right" for goods in New Jersey. New York declares that whoever can seize goods in New Jersey will gain the legal right to sell those goods to New Yorkers, and New York's police and courts will defend those new "property rights." One can picture what New Jersey would look like: kingpins, syndicates, turf wars, and grand theft—phenomena similar to the oppression, conflict, and corruption we see on a larger scale in resource-cursed countries today.

Coercion-based trade in resources is taken for granted now, as the slave trade once was—effectiveness is invisible in front of us. Following out the implications, however, finds that the West's situation is even worse than has been thought. Consumers may be buying goods made from tainted resources when they buy gasoline or newspapers, house paint or nail polish, laptops or game stations, sunglasses or apple pie. Money from their daily shopping will inevitably go back to the men of violence, to help fund more oppression and more war. We find that it is in fact a consumer's own government that links him in legal chains with foreign petrocrats and warlords—and that brings their injustices into his own justice system. The legal synergy between consumers and coercive actors drives conflicts and crises in resource-cursed countries, which then return to bedevil the West. By trading on coercion, we reap what we sow.

It is only when we take a historical perspective on effectiveness that the story turns from dark to light. For the long view shows humanity overcoming coercion as the basis of law many times before. In fact, the abolition of coercive rights is the arc of the narrative that most people would tell about human progress in modern times.

In the seventeenth century, effectiveness was the primary legal rule for all international affairs. Whoever could keep coercive control over a human being gained the legal right to sell that human being (the slave trade). Whoever could dominate a foreign population gained the legal right to rule that population (colonialism). Whoever could capture foreign land by force gained the legal right to rule that land (territorial conquest). Apartheid, genocide, and the abuses that we now call human rights violations were also exercises of coercive power that the international system made licit. The great moral movements of the nineteenth and twentieth centuries abolished effectiveness in all of these domains. The slave trade, colonialism, conquest, apartheid, genocide, and human rights violations are now banned by international law. Yet for natural resources, effectiveness remains the world's rule.

Once the rule that drives the resource curse is made visible, a better basis for resource trade emerges. Indeed, as a legacy of the greatest of the twentieth century's struggles, the principle needed to upgrade the global economy is already widely endorsed. This principle is popular sovereignty: the cause of Gandhi and Mandela and the democratic revolutions of the postwar era. Popular sovereignty for resources says that it is the people, not power, that should control a country's natural assets. World leaders already declare that "the people own the resources"—and 98 percent of the world's population already lives in a state that has signed a major treaty proclaiming popular resource sovereignty. For countries to reorient their resource trade from coercion to popular sovereignty will only require them to fit their policies to their principles. The penultimate part of the book shows how leading countries can do this, by changing their own laws at home.

The book describes a suite of new trade policies for resources that countries can adopt singly or together. This Clean Trade framework is ambitious, yet it is feasible, peaceful, and builds on reforms that have already gathered much strength. The policies will attract support from across the political spectrum, and they will get out in front of global megatrends like the growing power of individuals and networks. Clean Trade also gives new reasons to take decisive action on climate change—showing why, for example, most of the world's proven oil reserves cannot now licitly be tapped. The major Clean Trade policies are an American "independence from authoritarians" timetable and a European "autocrats to alternatives" plan that will disentangle the West's energy security from violent and unreliable regimes. Clean Trade states can help to end the tyranny of oil by taking themselves out of business with the men of blood abroad. This will also make other pressing global problems easier to solve.

Overturning effectiveness for natural resources will be the next stage in the history of the abolition of coercive rights. Musing on these revolutions opens space for philosophical reflections—on how moral progress changes individuals and societies, and on what kind of future we ultimately want our engagement with the world to create. Going deep into one part of today's global order, we find that it not only divides foreigners against each other but also sets those foreigners against us. Much of the war and oppression, corruption and extremism, of our times are symptoms of these divisions. If division is the problem, then unity must be the solution. Drawing on the enlightened philosophies of Immanuel Kant and John Stuart Mill, the book finishes with a vision of the free unity of humanity, which we can work to create as far as the limits of human nature allow.

THE PURE THEORY OF BLOOD OIL

This section sketches the theory underlying the book. Why do theory? Swimming in the sea can be highly satisfying, after all, while scuba means diving into water wearing heavy weights, breathing through a tube, using artificial light. Still, scuba adds a third dimension through which one can move freely—and there are wonders to see.

This book has two stories: of power and counter-power; of human divisions and human transformation. The story of power begins in countries far away, where we can imagine for a moment that money is buried under the ground—big money. These subterranean fortunes could flow up to the people of the country, like water. Instead, the money under the ground ends up in the hands of a very few men, who use it to capture more territory or even the country itself. The more cash these few men get from the ground, the better they can satisfy their own desires and dominate others. The money gives them the means to dominate in many ways: to intimidate, indoctrinate, and buy off; to persecute, imprison, and attack. All these few men need do is to keep control over the cash that comes out of those holes in the ground.

It's not really money that is buried under the ground in foreign countries, of course; it's natural resources. But let's focus on the money that ends up in the hands of these few men. The money that goes to these men wins them unaccountable power: power unchecked by law or custom or conscience. This is an old story that we know—power corrupts, absolutely power corrupts—and Part I of the book registers the divisive force of unaccountable power in the different forms of the resource curse. The few men divide and rule in various ways; sometimes they divide and kill. Part I ("Them vs. Them") shows how deep the divisions in these foreign lands can go.

Unchecked power in resource-cursed countries is so pervasive that it creates more than human divisions—it creates divisive humans. The humans we encounter in Part I are identifiable by their divisive identities: the cruel despot, the corrupt official, the executioner with his sword, the drugged-up child playing war with a loaded gun. These divisive identities have been formed within terrains of power; they are adaptations, one might say, to specific human environments.

The human environment around a person is what other people will help him to do, allow him to do, resist his doing, and try to do to him. (Think, for example, of the human environments that are a nursery school, a car showroom, a mosque, and the front lines of a battle.) A human environment can be just as important as a physical environment in defining a person's options. As Hume says, a prisoner "discovers the impossibility of his escape, as well when he considers the obstinacy of the jailer, as the walls and the bars with which he is surrounded."[2] And the human environment will be just as important as the physical environment in shaping a person's personality.

Living within a specific human environment evolves a person's character, affecting the physiognomy of his emotions, the density of his confidence, the size of his trust, as well as his proclivities, his memories, what occurs to him, and what he would never dream of. The human environments of resource-cursed countries are heavily contaminated by the unchecked power of resource-enriched men. The vicious religious policeman beating a woman on a false pretext of impiety is displaying a divisive character well-adapted to the human environment in which he has always lived.

A person's identity does not set that person's fate—a child soldier can become an Oberlin political science major.[3] And humans can change their own environments, by convening peace talks, say, or marching for civil rights. Still, unchecked power in resource-cursed countries is a strong environmental force, like floods or locusts, difficult to ignore or counteract. All of the resource curse phenomena analyzed in this book—authoritarianism, civil conflict, corruption, and so on—are manifestations of the divisiveness of this unchecked power. The divisive individuals we will encounter in Part I are acting rationally given their interests, their interests being defined by their identities, and their identities having been formed by the fractured human environments of their resource-cursed countries.

There is no karmic necessity that the coercion and instability of resource-cursed countries should spill into our countries, but they do. It's a crowded, intermingled world, and what happens there affects what happens here—not least in the West's consumer prices and financial crises. More, entrepreneurs of division in resource-cursed countries can increase their own power by focusing popular frustrations on the West. So we find the petrocrat making fiery speeches against us, and the terrorist bomb maker devising new ways to kill us. The West in turn has trained its million warriors and spies to oppose these threats. Part II ("Them vs. Us vs. Us") describes some of the divisive identities that have formed around the resource curse. These divisive identities are firmly set on both sides; many of the humans who now wear them will die, one way or another, inside of them.

There is also the deeper story of power between the West and resource-cursed countries. The narratives we see in the news are not the fundamental ones—the West installs or removes a dictator, backs one side or the other in a civil war, and so on. Those decisions may be wise or foolish, but they are ultimately just moves within the larger strategic context that is our study. This strategic context is defined by the enormous unchecked power that goes to the few men in resourced-cursed countries, which generates such strongly divisive human environments there. And the main source of that unchecked power is not in fact money buried under the ground; natural resources are buried under the ground. Ultimately, the main source of that unchecked power is the world's consumers paying money for goods made with and from those natural resources. Ultimately, the main source of that power is us. ("Us" means "us in the West"—this book is about Western countries changing their own terms of trade, putting their own houses in order, instead of telling others what they should do.)

Consumers are the main source of the unchecked power of foreigners in control of natural resources. Their unchecked power sets much of the West's international strategic context. Within that context, the West faces lose-lose choices in dealing with the oppression and instability that these divisive foreigners cause. The West can support or overthrow a dictator, support one side or another in a conflict, aim hellfire at terrorist training camps or leave them be. These are all bad options, using clumsy tools, and choosing any of them can exacerbate the problems of "Them vs. Us." Last in the story of power, "Them vs. Us" becomes "Us vs. Us" as well.

"Us v. Us" is on display daily in foreign policy debates here. Faced with endless foreign dilemmas, even well-meaning people will fight over who caused the messes, and what are now the least-bad options. Our own entrepreneurs of division then fire those fights. The strategic environment degraded by global resource trade divides us more and more from one another.

It also divides us more and more within ourselves. The theme of the divided self is explored most famously in the tradition of Jean-Jacques Rousseau. Rousseau shows that modernity implants within us desires that modernity must also frustrate. We see all of these things that we can never buy, all of these places we can never go, all of these people we can never touch or love or be. Rousseau finds the modern human a fuming heap of frustration, the energy from unsatisfiable desires coagulating in emotional disorders and self-delusions. For Rousseau, you always can't get what you want.

In this book, we find a self divided along the fault that separates public and private. The daily reality of our market life ratchets away from the desire for human unity proclaimed in our political ideals. (This was the first original discovery of the young Marx, his mind on fire.[4]) Our private consumption leads to outcomes we morally cannot stand, and this clash is palpable across many issues beyond tainted resources: with pollution, banking, sweatshops, child labor, and so on. Some people feel this public/private conflict and try to prioritize their principles by buying Fair Trade, local or organic; others give to overseas charities. The most sensitive among us experience this public/private conflict as a free-floating moral anxiety and cope by blocking out the public world, or even by disappearing into rituals or intoxication. In Goethe's tragedy, Faust cries, "Two spirits live—ach!—in my chest, Each struggles against the other."[5] That sharp exclamation in the midst of the poem conveys the pain of being constituted by contradictory lives. The public/private divide in today's resource trade is that our choices in the stores fund causes we deplore.

The story of the global resource trade is the story of how our money turns into unchecked power for a few men abroad and returns to us as danger and taint and political lies. Like some backward-plumbed neighborhood, fresh water flows away from us, and the pipes bring in filth. The unchecked power abroad forms human environments that divide foreigners against each other, foreigners from us, us from each other, and us from ourselves. The rules of this system are so embedded, the divisive identities so familiar, that this all seems to be just the way the world must be. Fortunately, the world is ready for a change.

The book's counter-narrative is a story of counter-power and transformation. Unchecked power sets the first scene of many familiar dramas that end in triumph; the victory over power has been won many times before. Some of the victories are told in our history books; others code our experience so completely now that we do not even remember—like the experiences of early childhood—what we were like before we changed. Half of the challenge of overcoming the divisions of today's resource trade is understanding their origins. The other half is recognizing where we are in the history of countering power, which can keep us from resigning in a winning position, from folding the better hand.

Think of the legal rights that can now be gained by pure power. Not the right to own a human being; no act of coercion can start a chain of title that ends in legal ownership of a human being here. Bondage still exists, but it is a shadowy, verminous thing, hiding where law cannot reach. The law now abhors slavery: the unchecked power of slave traders has been countered, and indeed, the entire identity of "slave owner"—once worn by respected, law-abiding people—has been abolished.

Three centuries ago, international law was mostly the legitimation of coercion. Captured humans became legally owned humans, captured territory became legally owned territory, defeated peoples became colonial subjects, "inferior races" could be subordinated without question, ethnic groups were licitly targeted for harassment or cleansing or extinction. In all of these domains, physical mastery created legal entitlements: might made right. The historical victories that countered power, triumphantly and at great cost, left their legacies in the laws that now block that transition.

Today's natural resource trade still runs on that old system of coercion-based legal rights. Very few men, holding coercive control over a country's resources, sell those resources through to consumers here, and the consumers' money goes back to those men in return. The transitivity of their might there to our rights here swells the unchecked power of those men, with all the attendant violence, venality, and crises. The abolition of this coercion-based right, the next stage in the history of such abolitions, will come when consumers here are no longer in this legal relation with coercive actors there and so no longer provide them with this source of unchecked power.

Power is checked by counter-power. Some forms of unchecked power are morally unredeemable, meaning the entire practice must be dismantled and its identities exploded. There is now no person who is legally a slave trader, a colonial governor, or the head of a white apartheid state. In other cases, the form of power is indispensable and can be redeemed by limiting it: by monitoring it, restraining it, subjecting it to sanction—by making it accountable. International human rights law, for example, is an attempt to make national leaders accountable to "the international community," so balancing the power of rulers over those they rule. Control over natural resources is indispensable in our crowded world, so this control must be made accountable. Popular sovereignty, a paradigm of accountability, closes the circle of power by making the rulers answerable to the ruled.

The absolute right of a few men to control resources must be abandoned, while the power of peoples to check those who control resources is increased. Citizens must become stronger: more potent, more connective, more empowered by their institutions. Part III shows what popular sovereignty over resources really means and how the counter-powerful idea of the country belonging to its people can transform international trade. Part IV sets out the practical steps that countries can take to support public accountability over resources everywhere. Confidence in the abolition of coercion-based rights over resources comes from seeing this in the long sequence of abolitions of such rights, and from seeing how close we are to taking the next step.

History has inscribed counter-power into laws that ban unredeemable power and that check power that could otherwise get out of control. Counter-power will continue to win in the future because it is now also part of the beliefs and sensibilities of ordinary people. Counter-power is the critical reason that interrogates all assertions emanating from authority, and also the conscience that checks our own temptations to abuse power with warnings of guilt and shame. Good people are now naturally appalled at plunder, religious persecution, and mass murder; it was not always so. Recall

Nietzsche: "Not so long ago it was unthinkable to hold a royal wedding or a full-scale festival for the people without executions, tortures or perhaps a burning at the stake."[6] Now, for good people, counter-powerful norms enter at the precognitive stage of their identification of the objects around them. "I know what that thing is," their perception says on encountering a human being. "That is a being that has rights against cruel treatment, and that is entitled to a certain dignity."

Unchecked power causes division; counter-power brings freedom; freedom allows people to find unity, within themselves and with each other. The dialectic of power and counter-power within this book points to the most fundamental of all goals, which is that people of integrity will unite together. The yearning for unity across persons is heard in the desire to "break down the walls" that keep people apart, and to "be part of something bigger than oneself." Popular sovereignty is more than freedom from power: it is a common life of many people together. The founders of the world's great religious traditions had supremely uniting identities; an ideal of a free human unity has inspired the most profound modern philosophy. The Epilogue of the book develops this theme of free human unity further.

PART I

Them vs. Them

To trace how today's international system distributes power, we start at the origins of global supply chains and study the resource-rich countries where consumers' spending ends up. In countries where the resource money arrived before the people were strong, we find authoritarians, corrupt officials, and militias taking the people's resources to divide and rule, divide and kill.

1

Addicted to Money

We search for riches deep within the bowels of the earth where the spirits of the dead have their abode, as though the part we walk upon is not sufficiently bounteous and productive . . . But what [the earth] has hidden and kept underground—those things that cannot be found immediately—destroy us and drive us to the depths. As a result the mind boggles at the thought of the long-term effect of draining the earth's resources and the full impact of greed. How innocent, how happy, indeed how comfortable, might life be if it coveted nothing from anywhere other than the surface of the earth.

—Pliny the Elder[1]

OIL IS ALCOHOL, DIAMONDS ARE DRUGS

Instead of starting with the idea that natural resources are a curse, think of alcohol and drugs in your own life, or in the life someone you know well. If asked whether these have been a blessing or a curse, you might say they have been both. Excesses, especially in youth, led to rash acts; maybe you took drugs at a party the night before an exam. Drinking may still be a drag on your productivity. Yet you may think that alcohol is, as George Bernard

Shaw said, the anesthesia by which we endure the operation of life. Perhaps a drink helped you to propose to your spouse. Perhaps you verged on drug addiction after the death of a parent. The impact of alcohol and drugs on a given life will be an elaborate, idiosyncratic story whose telling will turn on specific decisions and what would have happened in that life's story had those decisions been different.

Large-scale studies of both alcohol and drugs yield mildly surprising results. Even with hard drugs such as heroin, instant addiction and death turn out to be rare. Most people who use hard drugs experiment for a time, then give them up with apparently little harm done.[2] (George W. Bush and Barack Obama both used drugs but still went far.[3]) Perhaps more surprising, population-level studies show that moderate drinking is healthier than a lot of drinking or none at all. Moderate drinkers tend to live longer than both heavy drinkers and teetotalers, and they are less likely to suffer heart attacks, strokes, diabetes, arthritis, dementia, and several major cancers.[4] Indeed, studies in both the United States and Britain conclude that the health benefits of moderate consumption mean that in these countries drinking saves more lives than it costs.[5] If one were forced to choose either the "blessing" or "curse" label for alcohol overall, these studies would slightly favor "blessing."

Yet, as we know, substance abuse and addiction can be devastating. Alcohol abuse is a major factor in domestic violence, vehicle deaths, and suicide. Alcoholism increases risks to the brain, heart, liver, and immune system, in addition to its costs of lost workplace productivity, burdens on the health care system, and pressures toward family breakup. Even if drinking is not bad in a population overall, for some individuals it is catastrophic.

Common sense says that beyond a drink or two a day, the risks from alcohol increase as a person drinks more—the risks increase with the proportion of alcohol calories to total calories in one's diet. Yet history holds exceptions even among heavy drinkers—high-consuming and high-functioning individuals such as Winston Churchill. Voted "The Greatest Briton" by his countrymen, Churchill famously said that he had taken more out of alcohol than alcohol had taken out of him.[6] The economist F. A. Hayek relates a typical anecdote:

> [I] was invited to dinner with Churchill before the conferring of a degree. During the dinner, I could see him swilling brandy in great quantities; and by the time I was introduced to him, he could hardly

> speak... He was stock drunk... Half an hour later he made one of the most brilliant speeches I ever heard.[7]

Drug addiction has also ruined the careers of many. But drug addiction did not ruin the careers of John F. Kennedy or Ray Charles or the great Hungarian mathematician Paul Erdős. There are rules and exceptions, risks and those who beat the odds.

The effects of consuming alcohol or drugs will depend, at any point in a person's life, on their constitution and their self-control. Research and horse sense converge on the maxim that for most, moderation is best. Still, some people have such weak constitutions and such tenuous self-control that they will be better off avoiding these substances completely. At the other extreme, heavy drug or alcohol use will strain even the strongest constitution—yet some exceptional individuals have exceptional self-control. These individuals can take more out of these molecules than the molecules take out of them.

Extracting natural resources does not always curse a country, any more than drinking or doing drugs always curses an individual. Historically, many countries, including the United Kingdom and the United States, have done extremely well by their resources. Britain's coal and steel powered its drive to become the world's leading economy and eventually the world's preeminent nation. America's extravagant natural endowments then helped it to overtake Britain in those roles. America became the heartland of oil, the prized energy source of the twentieth century. And America's resource advantage was not just in oil; it was in everything. By 1913, "no other nation was remotely close to the United States in the depth and range of its overall mineral abundance."[8] America's resources fueled its first industrial surge through the nineteenth and twentieth centuries, and some predict that its natural gas reserves will power an industrial renaissance in the 2020s.[9]

In physical bulk, the United States today still extracts a lot of resources—if minerals were manna and oil were dew, America's 320 million people could eat and drink happily year-round. But the US economy is now huge and highly diversified, and extractives are only a small proportion of it. Mining, including oil and gas, accounts for only 2 percent of US GDP—less than the contribution of hospitals or construction or restaurants.[10] Canada, another large and diversified economy, gets 8 percent of its GDP from mining, mostly selling oil to its thirsty southern neighbor. Australia's mining industry accounts for around 10 percent of its economy: substantial enough to help Australia offset the recent global recession but still relatively modest.[11] These small-portion percentages of GDP from extractives generally benefit a country's economic health. It is like these countries have a drink or two a day, leaving them healthier overall than either the bacchanalians or the abstainers.

So extracting natural resources does not doom a nation. Nor need a nation extract natural resources to succeed. Switzerland and Singapore are as dry as Mormons when it comes to extractives, but lacking resources has not held either country back: Switzerland and Singapore have imported raw materials on their way to becoming among the richest nations on Earth. The logician says: Switzerland and Singapore show that extracting resources is not necessary for success, just as the United States, Canada, and Australia show that extraction is not sufficient for failure.

In this book, we will spend most of our time at the addicted end of the spectrum, the national equivalents of the heavy drinkers and drug addicts. These are the boozers and the hopheads among countries, who gain much, even most, of their economic energy from extractive resources and so run greater risks for trouble. Even here, in the high-risk group, there are great success stories—the national counterparts of Winston Churchill and John F. Kennedy, and we will hear one such success story soon. Yet the successes are rare: most resource-dependent countries lack the constitution or the self-control to take more from their molecules than those molecules take from them. And, as with alcohol and drug dependence, when resource dependence goes bad it can have devastating effects. Here again are some headline statistics about oil from Michael Ross:

> Since 1980, the developing world has become wealthier, more democratic, and more peaceful. Yet this is only true for countries without oil. The oil states—scattered across the Middle East, Africa, Latin America, and Asia—are no wealthier, or more democratic or peaceful, than they were three decades ago... Today, the oil states are 50 percent more likely to be ruled by autocrats and more than twice as likely to have civil wars as the non-oil states. They are also more secretive, more financially volatile, and provide women with fewer economic and political opportunities.[12]

Resource dependence in a country, like substance dependence in an individual, can blight every part of life. And as we will see, resource dependence can also make life hard for the friends and neighbors who must deal with the addict.

THE LIVES OF ADDICTS

Addicted states come from all regions and social classes. They include the world's richest state—Qatar, whose GDP per capita is more than double Switzerland's—and the world's poorest state—the Democratic Republic of the Congo, whose GDP per person is half a percent of Qatar's.[13] Addicts include Uzbekistan, with a literacy rate over 99 percent—and South Sudan, where half of the civil servants lack a primary education and where a girl is more likely to die in childbirth than she is to learn to read and write.[14]

Addicted states include ancient polities like Iran, where a national identity formed centuries ago, and also recent inventions like Iraq, where colonial powers trapped wary religious and ethnic groups together. Some addicted states seem simply bizarre. In Liberia, a presidential candidate chose as his campaign slogan "He killed my ma, he killed my pa, but I will vote for him anyway"—and won.[15] Turkmenistan's first president-for-life renamed the month of January for himself; he banned opera, ballet, and beards; he erected a fifty-foot, gold-plated statue of himself in the capital that revolved always to face the sun; and in the midst of his country's poverty, he opened a $20 million leisure center for horses, complete with air conditioning, medical facilities, and a swimming pool.[16]

Because of the variety of addicted states, daily life in them may seem quite different than life where you are. Think again of South Sudan, a country one-and-a-half times the size of California that until recently had only ten miles of paved roads.[17] What might your country be like if girls were more likely to die in childbirth than to learn to read and write?

To get a sense of daily life in other addicted states, imagine that tough young men on motorcycles ride around your town confiscating satellite dishes and arresting women for wearing the wrong clothes. Or imagine your local government does not run high schools, does not operate a clean water system, does not collect your trash, hardly pays the policemen who do not protect you, and occasionally sends in the army to open fire on your neighbors when some corrupt official has made a deal for the land under their houses.

Or imagine that foreigners make up not 7 percent of your country's population—as in the United States and the European Union—but rather 86 percent of your country's population and 94 percent of its labor force.[18] Or picture lots of suburbanites pulling their cars over and getting out—to go watch a man being publicly beheaded with a sword for the crime of sorcery.[19] Imagine that hardly anyone ever speaks of being a proud citizen of your country. When you meet a fellow citizen, you seek clues to her religion, and then her region, and then her tribe—and when someone says the name of your country, you expect to hear a story about violence or bribery.

These are scenes from different resource-dependent countries: the lives of addicted states are as diverse as the lives of addicted individuals. What addicted states have in common is that their national life turns on their resource. The Qatari population more than doubled during six years of rising oil prices, as foreign workers flooded in to become construction workers and domestic servants.[20] A single copper-gold mine in Mongolia generates one-third of the country's GDP.[21] In Angola, oil is 85 percent of the economy—and the exports that provide 80 percent of state funds recently devalued by 80 percent in four months.[22] If you live inside a big, diversified economy, then natural resources come into the news sporadically: fracking in the United States, the oil sands in Canada, a mining tax in Australia, energy prices in Britain—mostly second-order political issues. If you live in an addicted state, your country's fate depends on the unpredictable world price of some rock, liquid, or gas.

And unpredictable these prices are: every resource-dependent state is riding a restless tiger. Oil prices are more volatile than the prices of 95 percent of goods sold in the United States—averaging swings of over 25 percent per year since 1970.[23] During the period from 2007 to 2009, the price of oil went from $80 to $147 a barrel, then dropped to $32, then rose again to $60.[24] Over the eight years of the writing of this book, the price of oil doubled, then quickly collapsed to almost exactly where it had been at the outset. Extractive economies naturally go boom and bust, tempting oil states into "petromania."[25] During a boom, state spending tends to increase along with debt based on promises of future revenues; when the bust comes, the state may take on more debt to meet its expanded commitments, risking a national debt crisis (as Mexico, Venezuela, and Russia have all endured). In flush times, the economy can overheat; withdrawal symptoms can be extremely painful.[26]

Nor are unpredictable prices the only challenge for resource-dependent states. Just as large flows of chemicals gradually change the physiology of an addict's brain, making self-control more difficult, so large flows of resource revenues tend to change the structure of an addicted state's economy. Resource extraction tends to draw capital away from other sectors, tempting the economy to deindustrialize and to abandon agriculture, and so to reduce its diversification. The drinker gets more and more of his calories from alcohol.

At the same time, the large inflow of foreign cash pumps up the country's exchange rate. An inflated currency makes it harder for manufacturers and farmers to export their goods, while making foreign manufactures and food cheaper. So again the country is tempted toward more and more resource dependence, and toward less of a varied economic diet. Economists call this phenomenon the "Dutch Disease" (because of a precipitous decline in Dutch manufacturing and farming following big gas discoveries fifty years ago). The Dutch Disease means that resources take over more of the nation's economy—the addict tends to devote more and more of his life to the addictive substance.[27] In the 1960s, Nigeria had a vibrant agricultural sector and world-leading exports of palm oil and ground nuts. Once the oil came in, these exports quickly dwindled or disappeared. Nigeria, a land of exceptionally fertile soil, remains a net importer of food today.[28]

Life in addicted states is quite varied, and over the course of this book, we will drop in on many such states to observe the distinctive symptoms of their resource addictions. Three countries will get our special attention. One is Nigeria itself—a teeming land of conflict and corruption (and great potential). The second is Saudi Arabia, the biggest oil state of them all, the center of the Islamic faith, and the geostrategic crossroads of the world. Later in the book, we will stay in the dictatorship of Equatorial Guinea, an American ally that a former US ambassador called "the world's finest example of a country privatized by a kleptomaniac without a scintilla of social consciousness."[29] These three addicted states will be the major characters in the drama—other states will play supporting roles as the story unfolds.

ADDICTED TO MONEY

Alcoholics and drug addicts have better options for treatment than they used to. Research on the physiology of addiction has helped to develop pharmaceuticals like naltrexone, which block the pathways to the pleasure centers that begin the addictive cycle. Similarly, economists now understand the macroeconomics of resource dependence much better, and so can offer better prescriptions for managing price volatility and the Dutch Disease. Gifted social scientists have improved the diagnosis and treatment of the macroeconomic disorders of resource dependence, and the economist Paul

Collier has assembled an impressive group of experts to write the Natural Resource Charter, a set of strategies designed to help countries to use their resources for sustained economic development.[30]

Our study here is not the economic but the *political* pathologies risked by resource-dependent countries: authoritarianism, corruption and violence, as well as disorders like radical gender inequality. The economics do affect the politics: low-income countries, for example, are more prone to civil wars, and as we will see, the economics of oil can spell disaster for women.[31] Yet the political pathologies of resource dependence are less well understood, both in terms of causes and treatments. To see how the politics of resource-dependent states can go so badly wrong, we scan deeper into their physiologies of power.

So far, alcohol and drug use has illustrated the risks of extracting resources. Yet nations are not literally addicted to resource extraction—citizens do not wake up in the morning feeling a compulsive desire that more gas be drained from their land. What is happening in resource-dependent countries is not that the people are addicted to extraction. What is really happening is that the government is addicted to money.

The governments of oil states are not addicted to oil. The governments of oil states are addicted to oil money. The governments of diamond states are addicted to the money from diamonds, the governments of copper states to the money from copper. This is the mirror image of alcohol and drug addiction: these governments crave the money that foreigners pay, and they export their molecules to buy that money. Angola's regime drinks dollars and pays in petroleum; Zimbabwe's regime snorts dollars and pays in platinum.[32] The expert's word for unearned income is *rent*, so we call these governments *extractive-resource rent-addicted*, or *rent-addicted* for short.[33] Rent-addicted regimes vary as to how hooked they are on foreign funds. The rent-addicted regime of Guinea (not to be confused with Equatorial Guinea) gets around a quarter of its money from hawking Guinea's minerals to foreigners. The durable Sultan of Brunei gets 93 percent of his revenues from selling Brunei's oil to world markets.[34] The Sultan is the earth's thirstiest dollar dipsomaniac.

The governments of resource-dependent countries are rent addicted: their governments are addicted to the money that selling resources brings. And the fact that most explains why a government's addiction can be so devastating to its country is also the fact that is most obvious: in these countries, it is *the government* that gets the money from exporting the nation's natural assets. Addicted states mainline cash. The resource money goes right to their heads.

THE WORLD'S BEST ADDICT

Let's start with a best-case scenario for a resource-dependent nation with a rent-addicted government. This is a very rare country, like a Winston Churchill or a John F. Kennedy: a high-consuming but also high-functioning country, with an iron constitution and exceptional self-control.

Say you are a small, high-income country whose people share a remarkable solidarity. You are stable and peaceful. Your written constitution dates back to the age of Napoleon, and it was as far back as the Napoleonic Wars that your government ordered its troops to invade another country. Your democracy is one of the oldest in the world, and your civic participation rates are especially high (your citizens are 60 percent more likely to vote in national elections, for example, than either the Americans or the Swiss). Your people admire their government, expressing confidence in their national institutions at a level three times greater than the Japanese or the Czechs, and suspecting corruption only half as much as the Israelis or the Portuguese. Best of all, your people trust each other. An astonishing nine out of ten of your citizens express a high level of trust in others—overwhelmingly more than in other rich countries like the United States, where that figure is only five in ten.[35]

Now add oil to this joyful story. You are the leading oil producer in Western Europe and the third-largest gas exporter in the world.[36] Your government drinks in tens of billions of dollars a year in exchange for petroleum, leaving your national accounts in massive yearly surplus. And you can look forward to trillions more petrodollars filling your coffers in the decades to come. Hearty congratulations—you are Norway.

Norway is an anomaly because its people are unusually strong—and its people were already strong when the oil money arrived. To say that a country has a "strong" people is just to say that the ruled can control their rulers. It is the strength of the people that explains why the oil money that goes to Norway's government has furthered the country's success.

As individuals, Norwegians are multidimensionally robust. They live longer than average even compared to other rich countries, and they enjoy more good health in old age.[37] Their median income is well above the level at which people feel a basic economic security, and they average more years in school than the French, British, Canadians, or Americans.[38]

In addition to being individually robust, Norwegians are highly connective. As we have seen, they place great trust in each other. Their religious beliefs are moderate, with many professing a mild version of Lutheranism and nearly half saying that they believe not in a denominational god but in some sort of spirit or life force.[39] Large and long-standing majorities of Norwegians hold that immigrants enrich the country's cultural life and should have the same job opportunities as the native-born.[40] Combining indicators such as volunteering time, donating money, helping strangers, and relying on family and friends, one index shows Norway as having more social capital than any other nation in the world.[41]

Because they are connective, Norwegians work well together. What interests us especially is that Norwegians together form a strong people: Norwegian citizens together keep close control of the Norwegian state. Elections are free, fair, and hotly contested. The press is open and vigorous and helps to keep officials accountable to the citizenry. The people demand high levels of transparency from the government, especially regarding resource decisions. (Norway is first in the world in the leading resource governance index.[42]) Corruption is kept in check by the press, an independent judiciary, and a vibrant civil society. (Norway is top-five clean in the leading corruption index.[43]) When Norway's business tabloid discovered shady dealings within the powerful national oil company a few years ago, the country's courts acted quickly. Within the year, the company had been fined a large sum, and the company's Chairman, CEO, and Director for International Operations had all resigned.[44]

The Norwegian government is without question addicted to extractive rent: it would face serious withdrawal symptoms if it had to go cold turkey and give up the one-third of its revenues that come from petroleum sales.[45] Nevertheless, because of the people's tight control over the government, it has little choice in how to manage the oil and the oil money. The government must do what the people want. Not surprisingly, this has mostly meant that the government uses the money for public goods—for goods that benefit the people. And so far at least, Norway's public good provision has been spectacularly successful.

As the oil money began to come in, Norway's parliament set up a sovereign wealth fund—a fund to hold the wealth of the sovereign (the Norwegian people). Looking ahead to an aging population that would strain the country's finances, the parliament decided to save most of the oil money to pay pensions in the future. Today, most of Norway's oil money goes into this pension fund. Norway's sovereign wealth fund is now the largest in the world, worth almost a trillion dollars, and it is waiting to begin paying Norwegians' pensions whenever the people decide that it is time. (Americans can imagine that Social Security, instead of running a mounting deficit, is already fully funded for several *decades* to come.)

While saving most of the oil money for future generations of Norwegians, the government also uses a small percentage to pay for public goods today. Norway has the highest public health spending per person among the industrialized countries, as well as generous funding for parental leave, for public day care, and for unemployment insurance. The government devotes extra resources to women—for example, its single-parent payment system means that (unusually, even in rich countries) a woman's income does not tend to go down after a divorce.[46] Nor is the Norwegian government merely buying off its citizens with welfare-state goodies. Its targeted policies mean that it has lower unemployment than all of the major English-speaking countries.[47] Norway ranks first in the world in the Legatum Prosperity Index, which measures economic opportunities and personal freedoms as well as health, education, and security.[48]

Norway's people have made its government use the oil money for the public's good, now and in the future. Beyond public goods provision, Norway also uses its oil wealth for a further goal, which is projecting its values abroad. The main value that Norway has decided to project is corporate responsibility. Norway's huge sovereign wealth fund, which owns more than 1 percent of the world's stocks, is overseen by an ethical council that prohibits investments in companies falling short on human rights, labor rights, the environment, and peace.[49] The fund also pressures the companies that it invests in to act on climate change.[50] Norway sends tens of millions of dollars every year to poorer oil-producing states to help them build capacity to manage their petroleum. The Norwegians' use of their oil wealth shows that they are extraconnective as well as intraconnective: they seek out constructive linkages not only with each other, but across borders as well.

Norwegians are not angels; they have their corruption scandals and xenophobic spasms.[51] And Norway does, despite its best efforts, suffer symptoms from its oil dependence. Norway deindustrialized more than its peers in the 1970s, and oil may have dulled the country's entrepreneurial edge: while Finland started Nokia and Sweden grew Ericsson and Spotify, Norway has not launched any global tech brand (or indeed any global brand outside of petroleum) since major oil production started.[52] Some unwanted side effects seem inevitable: to return to the alcohol analogy, though Churchill's prodigious drinking suited his constitution overall, it also had costs—drinking may, for example, have deepened Winston's periodic depressions.

Still, like Churchill, the Norwegians are taking more out of their addictive substance than that substance is taking out of them. Not despite his drinking but helped by it, Churchill led Britain for nine years, including its "finest hour" in World War II, while also writing histories and biographies of sufficient quality to win the Nobel Prize in Literature. Not despite its petroleum but because of its excellent constitution and self-control, Norway now ranks third in the world in gender equality.[53] Not despite but helped by its petroleum, Norway has ranked first in the world in human development for over a decade—and that is during the decade when its government drank the most oil dollars.[54]

If we were to highlight one factor responsible for Norway's success, it would be that its people were strong *before* the oil came in.[55] Norwegians were well-educated, economically secure, moderate, and trusting long before they discovered their petroleum riches. And Norwegians had already taken control of their government through overlapping mechanisms of accountability: elections, the rule of law, protection of property rights, a free press, a vigorous civil society. Because of the hardy constitution of their body politic and the self-control ingrained in their civic character, when the oil money came in it made the Norwegian people stronger still.

Unfortunately, most peoples are not so strong when the resources come in. Most peoples are relatively weak economically, have no tradition of constitutional self-rule, and face serious divisions of ethnicity, religion, or tribe. Among these "shaky start" nations, some began extracting resources while subjugated by an imperial power. Others got a shaky start to resource extraction under the boot of a postcolonial strongman, or during a grim stretch of state failure. When nations with weak constitutions and low self-control start to drink great quantities of resource rents, real trouble must be feared—trouble we will see across the next three chapters.

THE CAPITAL AND CONSTITUTION OF STRONG PEOPLES

The single most important factor in explaining the success of a resource-dependent country is the strength of its people when large resource rents begin to come in: whether the ruled can control their rulers. In a modern society like Norway, the elements of popular strength include those we have seen above. Nearly all citizens are economically secure: rights of property and contract are impartially enforced, wealth and income are widely dispersed, social insurance (for health, unemployment, and old age) is provided to all as a matter of right, and state employees hold their jobs independently of their political support for superiors. Sturdy political and legal structures make rulers accountable to the public: information about state plans and actions is easily available, a free press and civil society use this information to scrutinize and sanction officials, an independent judiciary has power over the executive and legislature, and a rigorous rule of law keeps the state from targeting specific individuals and groups that challenge its power.[56]

Strong peoples also need cognitive resources to control their states. The modern state has industrial-strength ideological power at its command: the power to flood the population with its messages, the power to limit the information that citizens receive, the power even to attempt society-wide reclassifications of familiar objects (as, for example, "the master race" or "the Great Satan"). To resist this ideological power, the members of a strong people need a habitual suspicion of authority, and the critical faculties to anchor an independent intellectual stance.

Most important of all, within a strong people citizens are connective. Citizens of strong peoples are connective with each other, across divisions of family, clan, religion, race, ethnicity, and more. Connective citizens take a positive attitude toward each other: they are conditionally trusting and unconditionally trustworthy. They share information easily; they tolerate their differences; they are accustomed to bearing some costs for the common good. They form networks of civic engagement to promote their common interests, and these networks link citizens together across identity groups and status levels. The people are powerful because citizens can act together—and because they expect to act together to control their rulers.[57] (Social scientists speak of this as "social capital," which is fine—the philosopher merely notes how far the language of business has colonized thinking about human relationships.[58])

The combination of institutional accountability and high connectivity can be found in human societies throughout the world: strong peoples are everywhere. For example, in the Nso Kingdom in northwestern Cameroon, the institutions of accountability have traditionally been quite different than those of Western constitutional democracies, yet their record of checking the power of the king has been impressive.[59] The precolonial tribal institutions of Botswana emphasized broad consensual participation of the ruled to constrain the power of chiefs. These counter-powerful popular assemblies help to explain how Botswana turned its substantial diamond rents into spectacular economic growth within a steady democracy, making the country into "the miracle of Africa."[60]

Over the next three chapters, we will leave behind the strong peoples, like the Norwegians and Botswanans, to focus on the political economy of shaky-start countries: those where the people were weak when large resource rents began to flow. As we turn to these countries, it is important to emphasize that "strong" and "weak" here apply to peoples, not to individuals or smaller groups. Weak peoples may contain individuals of exceptional intelligence, talent, and energy. Indeed, individuals within weak peoples are often at least as resourceful and resilient as individuals within strong peoples, for the simple reason that they have needed to resist the coercion of their state and the predation of non-state actors.[61] For similar reasons family ties within weak peoples are often tighter than those within strong peoples: family members who can rely less on the state tend to rely more on each other.

So a weak people can be made up of hardy individuals and tight family groups: our interest is in citizens' combined strength, their capacity to control their state. The great drama of a people struggling to gain power over their government is the history of many of our own countries in the West. In these histories, a weak people first suffered from oppression and strife, then came together to resist injustice, realized their power and found their courage, and at last won a famous victory over the haughty regime. Because our own national stories are so inspiring, we may feel that peoples everywhere eventually will win, must win. And so they have won, in many lands. The people have won, they are winning today—except, as we will now see, where a source of unaccountable power allows those who seize it to reinforce their own rule, to treat the people roughly, and to keep citizens from joining their strengths with each other.

2

Power

What Big Men Want

Formula for success: Rise early, work hard, strike oil.

—J. Paul Getty[1]

THE SUN KING'S SECRET GIFTS TO THE MERRY MONARCH

Resource-dependent states mainline cash. The resource money goes right to their heads. When the people are stronger than the state, as in Norway, the people can ensure that the rents will be used to enliven the whole body politic. To explore the more common case where the people are weaker than the state, we begin with an episode in seventeenth-century England. The seventeenth century was the birth of the modern nation, so the dynamics of state power are there openly on display—as are the rules of this distant, violent time that have survived to disorder our world today.

In England's seventeenth century, the first two kings were archetypal absolutists who insisted that God had given them the right to rule. Yet England's gentry were prospering at this time, enriched by the country's burgeoning maritime trade. The result was a constitutional deadlock. The gentry in Parliament controlled the tax money, which the kings needed for their expensive armies and courts. But the kings could thwart the gentry by dissolving Parliament at will. The gentry pushed for more checks on royal power—the royals resisted, as was their divine right.

The English Civil War was the outcome of this impasse, the parliamentarians eventually capturing the king and cutting through the neck of the head of state in front of a large crowd in London. Unfortunately, the leader of the victorious parliamentary army then turned out to be an extremist with his own dictatorial tendencies. So on his death, Parliament invited the son of the beheaded king to take the throne—on condition that this new king, Charles II, behave himself.

We pick up England's constitutional story in the early reign of Charles II, who was known as the Merry Monarch because of the gaiety (some said the debauchery) of his court. With Parliament's financial support, Charles's forces won famous victories against the hated Dutch (including the capture in 1664 of New Amsterdam, which Charles renamed after his brother, the Duke of York).

The political dynamics between Charles II and Parliament at first went well. In fact, they followed what we will call a "Schumpeter Process" after the twentieth-century social scientist who described the evolution of limited government.[2] Charles hungered for money to fund his military and to pay his political supporters. Parliament doled out the cash—but only after Charles gave way, much against his will, to laws checking his powers.

In a Schumpeter Process, the executive gives political power to the representatives of citizens in exchange for the taxes that he needs to sustain his rule. Essentially, a Schumpeter Process adjusts a country's politics to its economics. The executive empowers the citizens who have the money, and in return, these citizens grant the executive enough money to sustain his (reduced) political power. The more money the executive needs from citizens, the more political power he will have to cede. A Schumpeter Process explains the evolution of limited government in England up to 1670. (This dynamic was neatly captured by the American colonists, going through their own Schumpeter Process a century later, in the slogan "no taxation without representation."[3])

In 1670, however, England's Schumpeter Process suddenly shifted into reverse. When the Dutch began to turn the tide of battle, Charles again asked Parliament for funds for his fleets. Parliament made demands that Charles said he simply could not abide. Instead, Charles dissolved Parliament. When Parliament reassembled and repeated its demands, Charles continued to dismiss and dissolve it—and finally, toward the end of his reign, he simply ruled without it. After Charles's death, his brother and successor, James II, showed an even more absolutist bent on the throne. James built up his standing army, asserted his royal right to dispense with Parliament's laws, and finally just sent Parliament packing. Had James been less arrogant, or had his opposition (including John Locke) been less able, he might have succeeded in returning Britain to the absolute monarchy of his ancestors.

How did Charles II and James II reverse England's Schumpeter Process and reassert the executive powers that Parliament had so painfully forced them to concede? How did these kings sustain their rule without opening the purse to which Parliament held the strings?

Charles and James had found a new supply of money—indeed, a large source of secret foreign funds. Louis XIV of France, the Sun King, the greatest absolute monarch in Europe, gave substantial secret payments to Charles and James from 1670 onward in exchange for the English kings' attention to French interests.[4] Confidential correspondence records how Charles and James spent their foreign bankroll.[5] Charles, for instance, spent most of Louis's secret subsidies on his armed forces. The rest he used for patronage, public works, foreign expeditions, and the maintenance of royal residences and four of his mistresses ("a seraglio item not remarkable," one historian wrote, "considering Charles's tastes"[6]).

Charles and James reversed England's Schumpeter Process by finding an external supply of money. With this money, they were able to resist limitations to their power, and indeed to reassert powers that the Crown had already given up.[7] They depended less on taxation, so they could roll back representation.

Returning to the present, we find global markets in the place where once sat the Sun King. Today, global resource markets supply foreign-source funds that enable autocrats to maintain themselves in power instead of accepting limitations on their rule. Indeed, the payments that global markets make to autocrats today encourage absolutism in just the same ways that Louis XIV did—except where they encourage it more.[8]

Like the subsidies from Louis, the resource rents that markets send to many of today's authoritarians are substantial. And they also tend to be secret. Louis once proposed to ship Charles wedges of gold hidden in bales of silk, and to send him diamonds and pearls in a way "that nobody could ever know it."[9] Similarly, global markets send autocrats hidden deliveries of dollars. This is partly due to the nature of the extractive industries. Extractive resources tend to be *enclaved*: firms bring in their own equipment and workers, dig a mine or well behind a guarded fence, and transport resources out of the country. The people have a hard time knowing the value of the resources their country is losing. (Best of all for autocrats is oil offshore, where firms extract the resource out of the people's sight.) And even if the people could get a rough idea of the quantity of the resources going out, the contracts that autocrats sign with foreign firms, which determine how many dollars are coming in, are typically state secrets. Autocratic oil states opt for opacity: these regimes allow much less press freedom, and the more oil they pump, the less transparent their budgets are.[10]

Indeed, payments from global resource markets have even stronger absolutizing effects than did the payments from Louis XIV. Louis was after all giving bribes, and bribes come with demands (mostly, Louis wanted loans of troops and pro-Catholic policies in England). Today's global resource markets are unconditional patrons of rent-addicted rulers. So long as an autocrat can keep control over the country's resource-rich territory, foreign funds will flow to him whatever his policies at home or abroad.

Moreover, the economics of resources make it harder for the people to resist the executive through a Schumpeter Process. Because of the Dutch Disease that inflates the currency, resource revenues tend to deindustrialize an economy and depress its agricultural exports, robbing the people of an economic power base with which to balance the state. So their country's international trade tends to make the people weaker. And the enclave nature of resource extraction again works against the people. Even when petroleum accounted for 90 percent of the exports of the Indonesian province of Aceh, for example, production employed less than 1 percent of its labor force.[11] In a diversified economy, factory workers, farmers, and fishermen can call a general strike to put pressure on the government. But even if every laborer in, say, Angola went on strike today, the foreign workers on Chevron's offshore platforms would extract not a drop less oil, and Angola's president would get not a penny less revenue from that oil.

Between the unconditional secret foreign payments and the corrosive economics of resources, today's rent-addicted authoritarians can throw a Schumpeter Process into reverse. Selling off resources allows autocrats to avoid accountability to the people. The result is that today's resource kings can be more absolute than even Charles or James thought they had a divine right to be.

WHAT BIG MEN WANT

In a rare country like Norway, where the people control their rent-addicted state, resource money can make the people stronger. In the more common case, where the state is an addicted autocrat, resource money can make the people weaker. This might seem to raise a puzzle. Why shouldn't all rulers want to make their people stronger? Wouldn't a strongman be stronger still if he ruled over a healthy, well-educated population that powers a vibrant, taxable economy which can sustain a larger army? Shouldn't a big fish want a bigger pond, not a smaller one?

On the question of what an autocrat should want, two of our greatest political philosophers disagree. The first, Thomas Hobbes, wrote the most important book of political philosophy in English, *Leviathan*. Indeed, Hobbes presented a manuscript of *Leviathan* to the future Charles II, then his student, while they were both in exile in Paris, having fled the parliamentary forces during the English Civil War.[12] Hobbes hoped that *Leviathan* would instruct the young prince in the best methods of ruling. In it, he wrote:

> In monarchy the private interest is the same with the public. The riches, power, and honor of a monarch arise only from the riches, strength, and reputation of his subjects. For no king can be rich, nor glorious, nor secure, whose subjects are either poor, or contemptible, or too weak through want, or dissension, to maintain a war against their enemies.[13]

In Hobbes's view, a rational monarch should make the people stronger—at least richer and healthier, if not more free.

To this view our second great philosopher—Jean-Jacques Rousseau, the author of the most important book of political philosophy in French—took great exception:

> Kings desire to be absolute, and . . . the best kings want to be able to be wicked if they please, without ceasing to be masters. A political sermonizer may well tell them that since the people's force is their force, their greatest interest is to have the people flourishing, numerous, formidable; they know perfectly well that this is not true. Their personal interest is first of all that the people be weak, wretched, and never able to resist them.[14]

In Rousseau's view, a rational monarch should make the people not stronger, but weaker. Hobbes or Rousseau—which was wiser?

We now know that it depends on the monarch's options—on his possible sources of power. What an autocrat wants first and foremost is to stay in office. An autocrat who lacks a strong desire to keep his office will likely find himself replaced. Hobbes is right that the "riches, strength and reputation of his subjects" are one possible source of power for an autocrat wanting to stay in office. Yet there are sources of power that an authoritarian will want more.

In modern times, Hobbes's wisdom best fits the first Asian Tiger countries: South Korea, Taiwan, and Singapore. In the 1950s and 1960s, the authoritarians of these countries found themselves menaced by enemies and lumbered with poor, sputtering economies. Crucially, these authoritarians had few natural resources, and so could not use resource revenues to pay their soldiers and supporters. (Singapore's only natural resource, as its leader Lee Kuan Yew often said, was its people.) So the first Tiger authoritarians took a page from *Leviathan* and decided the best chance of survival was to make their people more productive. The Tiger authoritarians secured a basic rule of law and protected property rights to attract foreign investment. They simultaneously invested in roads, irrigation, and sanitation, and they assured all their subjects primary education, health care, and access to credit. These measures required the creation of competent administrative agencies—as did collecting taxes from their increasingly productive citizens.

The Tiger autocrats' strategy worked brilliantly, transforming their economies from impoverished to advanced within a generation. All three countries rocketed through their industrial phases to high-end manufacturing, and now all three generate most of their GDP from services.[15] In 1965, the average Singaporean had only one-sixth of the income of the average American—after decades of 7 percent growth a year, he has more than caught up.[16] South Koreans used to live as long as Ecuadorians; now they live as long as Swedes.[17] The Tiger authoritarians underwrote inclusive growth, used the taxes from that growth to build up their armed forces, and enjoyed long reigns in considerable personal comfort. These autocrats gained "riches, power, and honor" by making their subjects no longer "poor . . . or weak through want." These Asian leviathans did Hobbes proud.

Unfortunately for Hobbes, and favoring Rousseau, many autocrats have sources of power to hand that they prefer to the slow, hard process of making their people more productive. Autocrats can also stay on top with aid from foreign allies, or with loans from foreign banks. Even better—indeed, their favored option—they can keep their office by selling their country's natural assets on world markets. Resource rents are the power source of choice for authoritarians. Striking oil is every dictator's dream.

Just as drinking a bottle of wine makes one feel better faster than exercising, a ruler gets richer more easily by selling off resources than by initiating economic reforms. Moreover, allowing the people to develop independent economic power is a risky long-term strategy for authoritarians who wish to pass on their jobs to their progeny. As seventeenth-century England shows, when the people get stronger, a Schumpeter Process can kick in—the eventual result being limitations on autocratic rule. The histories of the first Asian Tigers show just this: as the people's economic power grew, the autocracies of South Korea and Taiwan eventually gave way to today's democracies. And even in the easily dominated city-state of Singapore, the people have won more checks on state power.[18]

Authoritarians will much prefer resource revenues to the long and risky (for their heirs) process of making the people more productive. Of course, some authoritarians may not be able to get enough resource rents to keep themselves on top. To stay in power, these authoritarians may need a mixed strategy: some resource sales, some aid from allies, some foreign loans, some economic development. But resources will always be their first choice. The more quick-hit resource rents they can draw, the less slow-burn development they need do. Looking at the resource-rich cousins of the first Asian Tigers, like Malaysia and Indonesia, we find that their economies developed less quickly (and with Burma, much less quickly) under authoritarian rule.[19] All autocrats are addicted to money, and they will get it wherever they can—but the international resource market is their go-to dealer.

Resource rents are an easy source of power for autocrats. Getting the money often requires nothing more than signing a contract with a foreign firm and then sending some soldiers to protect the extractive site. (With offshore oil, security is even cheaper.) Broad-based economic development is a difficult source of power: it requires potentially destabilizing social transformations as well as a patience that many autocrats cannot afford.[20] Between these two in difficulty is a third source of power for authoritarians: loans from foreign banks. Bank loans bring in money even more quickly than do resources, yet they come with the distinct disadvantage that the banks expect authoritarians to pay the money back, plus interest.[21] With resource rents, an autocrat never has to pay the money back.[22]

Hobbes said, "The riches, power, and honor of a monarch arise *only* from the riches, strength, and reputation of his subjects."[23] Hobbes was wrong: a monarch can get his riches—and so power—from sources besides his subjects, like natural resources and foreign loans. And a there is a fourth source of power as well: "aid" from foreign powers, like military protection, diplomatic support, or transfers of money.

During the Cold War, many autocrats depended on such aid (or "strategic rents") to protect them from attack and strengthen their hands at home. Since the end of the Cold War, strategic rents have diminished, but by no means disappeared. The King of Bahrain, for example, belongs to a Sunni minority in his kingdom that is outnumbered two to one by restive Shia. But with Sunni Saudi Arabia as his neighbor, and as the host of US naval forces in the Persian Gulf, Bahrain's king has had all the foreign help he has needed to augment his oil rents and crush the occasional Shia uprising.[24]

Strategic rents can be vital to a king wanting to stay on his throne. But as the English kings who received strategic rents from Louis XIV knew, aid from allies always comes at a cost. The foreign power wants you to lend your troops or to change your laws—or to open your economy to American companies or your ports to the US Fifth Fleet. Moreover, foreign support can run out quickly, literally overnight. Saddam Hussein received significant strategic rents from the United States until 1990, after which he received only American invasions and sanctions.

Natural resources will be the power source of choice for the authoritarian.[25] From exploiting his country's resources, an authoritarian gets large, long-term, and secret funds with no conditions attached. And the money never has to be paid back. It is true that extractive rents are volatile, but their inflation of the exchange rate (the Dutch Disease) conveniently makes foreign luxuries cheaper for the autocrat to buy. Moreover, resources do not have long-term tendencies toward democratization. One study finds that a 1 percent increase in natural resource dependence can mean a nearly 8 percent higher likelihood of an authoritarian government.[26] Of the governments that get most of their money from resources, almost none can be considered democratic.[27]

THE TRAD SOURCES OF POWER

Let's sum up the account of authoritarian power—and make it subtler so that it better fits the versicolored world around us. The account says there are four major sources of power available to an authoritarian regime:

1. Taxes from an empowered people.
2. Resource rents.

3. Aid from allies (strategic rents).
4. Debt from foreign loans.

And the greatest of these, from the point of view of the authoritarian wishing to remain in power, is resources.

There are other sources of power for authoritarian regimes—old-fangled ones like selling flags of convenience, and new-fangled ones like selling Internet domain names.[28] Yet the ones above are the big four. Of course, a country might have had authoritarian tendencies before any of these factors became significant—just as a patient might have had asthma before she started smoking, which the smoking then intensified and complicated. And these sources of power are only determinants, not destiny. Sometimes a country with a highly entrenched authoritarian regime, like Burma, can open up with remarkable rapidity even without an obvious shift in its sources of power. Yet such cases are rare.

Some authoritarians are almost completely dependent on a single source of power, as the North Korean regime is dependent on aid from China. Most regimes rely on some mix of the four sources, and most shift their mix of power sources over time, gradually or even dramatically, in response to circumstances (as after the Cold War, when many strategic rents suddenly dried up).[29] And a single source of power can shift its points of origin: the pre-Morsi authoritarians in Egypt depended for decades on aid from the United States; the post-Morsi authoritarians have depended instead on large payments from the Saudis.

Looking more broadly, the first source of power is "internal" to a country's economy, while the rest are "external." Taxation depends on empowering the people. With the other three, the power comes from outside, and as we have seen, this generally makes the people weaker. This distinction is crucial for deciding what posture to take toward today's authoritarian regimes. The authoritarians who run China, for example, have for decades been enabling their people to become stronger economically while foregoing the external sources of power—and they may be correct that authoritarianism has been required to accomplish this, at least in the early stages.[30] This does not excuse corruption and abuse in China, but it should make us expect that the country's politics will take a different trajectory as its progressively more empowered people demand more rights.[31] As we will see in Part IV of the book, the fact that the Chinese authoritarians are following Hobbes and the Asian Tigers by making their people stronger will have major policy implications.

For the external power sources, the fact that there are three different kinds explains why resource-rich and resource-poor countries sometimes look much alike. The authoritarians of Guinea, for example, historically drew on substantial rents from exporting minerals like bauxite; in neighboring Mali, French aid was more important for keeping the autocrats in power. For the people, the results were similar—external power went to their strongmen, empowering those strongmen to divide and rule.

History will be important in explaining how far these external sources of power will allow authoritarians to divide and rule the people, because history will explain how strong (or weak) the people are. Even having had some experience of democracy before major extraction begins seems to lower the risk of autocracy—as with the Latin American resource producers. The Latin American peoples were certainly not as strong as the Norwegians when their resources revenues took off, but most had some institutions of constitutional democracy in their collective memory. Resource revenues per capita were also generally lower in Latin America, providing less fuel for authoritarianism.[32] So the Latin American producers struggled with authoritarian regimes or single-party states for some decades before finally making their transitions to constitutional democracy. (Venezuela, the largest per-capita oil producer, has gone the least far in this process—but even here, the form of authoritarianism has been populist.) One might even see the effects of a collective memory of democracy in the Gulf States—Kuwait, the Arab state with the most experience of an elected parliament before the resource money arrived, is now the Arab state where the elected parliament has the most power.

With these subtleties added to the account of the sources of authoritarian power, we can go back and emphasize how crucial the external sources of power are for explaining the persistence of coercive regimes in our day—and especially resource rents. Recall the headline figure: oil states have a *50 percent* greater risk of authoritarianism. Natural resources supercharge autocrats.

Authoritarian oil states have been much less likely to transition to democracy in the past three decades, meaning that an ever-rising proportion of the world's autocrats are petrocrats.[33] And even among leaders with some democratic credentials, resource rents bring out their heavy-handed tendencies. Resource rents are autocratizing: the more money a Chavez or a Putin got from oil, the less they needed to mind the dynamism of their economy, the liberties of their citizens, or the pressures the international community tried to exert.[34] As Thomas Friedman put it in his "First Law of

Petropolitics," as the price of oil goes up, the pace of freedom goes down.[35] Looking across recent history, we see resource rents empowering authoritarians all over.

One can take a moment to meditate on how power works in our world by calling up a list of today's authoritarian regimes, from a source like *The Economist Democracy Index* or *Polity*. *The Economist*, for example, lists fifty-two authoritarian countries, or 31 percent of all the countries in the world.[36] One can go through this list asking which of these regimes could exist without resource rents or strategic rents. A few, certainly—most significantly China. Yet one may take the occasion to muse how much further modernity would have pushed autocracy offstage were it not for petroleum and foreign support. How many authoritarians would there be today without oil and aid?

The more a regime can rely on resources, the easier it is to stay in power without risking an empowered, united people. In fact, as we'll see in the next chapter, for highly rent-addicted autocrats, Rousseau was right: "Their first personal interest is that the people should be weak, wretched, and unable to resist them."

3

Coercion, Corruption...

Wealth comes to the rulers, they dispose of it, they distribute it to cronies, they punish and overwhelm their would-be challengers at home, and they use it to sustain adventures abroad way beyond the limits of their societies.

—Fouad Ajami, *The Powers of Petrocracy*[1]

HOW TO SPEND IT

The resource-rich authoritarian is the big fish. While he may yearn for a bigger pond, his most urgent daily goal is to remain the biggest fish in the pond that he is in. He has a good deal of money at his disposal—Mother Nature has been generous, and he can afford to splash out. But his environment is murky, and there are dangers close by.

Let's open the manual for resource domination—how the big man will stay on top when he controls resources for which foreigners will pay big money. When the rent-addicted authoritarian looks out of his palace, after all, he does not see Scandinavia. Most resource-disordered countries are testaments to the human capacity for divisiveness, their cleavages running along several dimensions. The global picture shows serious divisions of race, ethnicity, and religion in the Asian and African resource exporters along the tenth parallel, as well as in colonial hybrids like Iraq and the former Soviet states, and there are large divisions of class and race in Latin America.[2]

What first strikes many in the politics of the Arab and African exporters is their tribal divisions. Naïve Westerners may hesitate to speak of modern humans in terms of their tribes, fearing a primitivism that might be politically incorrect. Arabs and Africans will chuckle. For much of the Arab world and Africa, tribal affiliation is a primary (sometimes the primary) source of self-identification. In these countries, your tribe matters—often much more than your nation does.[3]

In Saudi Arabia, there are eight major and about fifteen minor tribes; when the future King Abdullah first organized the National Guard, he did so along tribal lines. In Libya, thirty tribes have influence; Colonel Gaddafi was a master at playing them off against each other. In Equatorial Guinea, you are better off being a Fang (the president's tribe) than a Bubi, and in fact, the Fang are so dominant that it makes a large difference which of the sixty-seven Fang clans you are from (the president is an Esangui from Mongomo).

Countries with these deep differences of race, ethnicity, religion, and tribe have been sites of intercommunal violence—and again, identification with a national common good is often weak. So an authoritarian knows that enemies surround his palace, and that these enemies will be looking to get their man into power by any means available. Moreover, as the sanguinary history of monarchy shows, a king often has rivals to the throne within the palace as well; as Xenophon said, "plots and conspiracies against despotic rulers are oftenest hatched by those who most of all pretend to love them."[4] Uneasy indeed lies the head that wears a crown.

The playwright Racine, who as Louis XIV's historiographer observed an autocrat quite closely, put this speech into the mouth of one of his stage kings:[5]

> Once on the throne, our cares are so increased
> That of those cares remorse concerns us least . . .
> By vain remorse I'm undismayed;
> Of crime my heart no longer is afraid.
> They cost us dear, our first iniquities,
> But those that follow we commit with ease.

The first concern of the autocrat wanting to stay in office will be to make potential threats afraid of him; his second concern will be to make potential threats dependent on him.[6] Intimidation, then subordination, and—this is crucial—the king must always keep threats from uniting against him. Sticks first, carrots second—and always, divide and rule. If this sounds Machiavellian, we should not blame the messenger: we still read Machiavelli because he understood so well *la verità effetuale delle cose*: the actual truth of things, especially the art of authoritarian rule.

Louis XIV was of course quite Machiavellian, and there was nothing new under the Sun King. Sticks, then carrots—and always, divide and rule. We can see these eternal Machiavellian priorities equally well in Charles II's spending of the secret funds that Louis gave him. In Charles's budget, we find that the top-two categories of spending were *violence* and *clientelism*. Charles spent most on violence: his military. He also spent a great deal to pay his "clients": to give retainers to key supporters and bribes to members of Parliament. After taking care of these two necessities, Charles had money left over for more:[7]

- *Personal Luxuries*: the royal residences, "hay for deer in Windsor Forest," the four mistresses.
- *Public Goods*: public works, support for the poor of Southwark (the rough neighborhood across London Bridge).
- *Foreign Adventures*: the expeditions to Virginia and the West Indies.

We will take Charles's priorities in turn to explore how today's rent-addicted authoritarians spend the money they get from selling off their countries' natural assets. We will discover why resource rents are such potent sources of political pathologies when controlled by autocrats addicted to them. While resources are not a curse, we will see why so many have spoken of resource-diseased countries as under an evil spell.

"THEY. SHOT. THE. PEOPLE."[8]

The first personal interest of a king, said Rousseau, is that the people be weak and unable to resist him. And a king's preferred source of power for keeping the people weak is resource money. As we have seen, autocrats who control large natural resource rents have a source of funds not dependent on the people. Instead of going through the difficulty and danger of making the people productive and then taxing them, the authoritarian simply signs a contract with a foreign firm and sends soldiers protect the extractive site. The foreigners take the resources; the regime receives payments of an undisclosed sum. The people become bystanders to the economy that sustains their rulers, watching from behind fences as their national wealth disappears.

Natural resources are perfect for authoritarian divide-and-rule. A sufficiently resource-rich autocrat can coerce the people to any extent—put the whole population in chains, if he must—without blocking his main sources of money, which are literally holes in the ground. He does not need to tax the income of citizens, and indeed, many resource-rich regimes dispense with income taxes entirely.[9] What the autocrat most needs from the people of his country is that they stay out of his way. He denies the people the civil and political rights that would help them unite against him, and he orders rough treatment for trouble makers. Violence against citizens is a primary technique of governance for the resource-fueled autocrat. Sometimes the curtains drop, and we catch a glimpse of how cruel this governance can be. During the insurgency that toppled Gaddafi, journalists trailing behind the advancing rebel forces filed this report:

> ZAWIYAH, Libya—In the second-floor office of a burned-out police station here, the photographs strewn across the floor spun out the stories of the unlucky prisoners who fell into the custody of the brutal government of Col. Muammar el-Qaddafi.
>
> Some depicted corpses bearing the marks of torture. One showed scars down the back of a man dressed only in his underwear, another a naked man face down under a sheet with his hands bound. The faces of the dead bore expressions of horror. Other pictures showed puddles of blood, a table of jars, bottles and powders and, in one, a long saw.
>
> In a labyrinthine basement, workers were clearing out burned books and files. One room contained a two-liter bottle of gin. Gesturing into another room that was kept dark, a worker mimicked a gun with his hands and murmured "Qaddafi," suggesting it was an execution chamber.[10]

In 2011, the Middle East and North Africa saw a wave of popular revolutionary movements, energized by youths yearning for more opportunities and freedom. One can create one's own map of the Arab Spring, marking where popular protests failed and where they succeeded in deposing an authoritarian ruler.

Authoritarian Continued: Qatar, Kuwait, United Arab Emirates (UAE), Oman, Saudi Arabia, Bahrain, Algeria.
Authoritarian Fell: Yemen, Egypt, Tunisia, Libya.

Now add to the map a number for each country, showing how much oil income per capita the country had before the Arab Spring began.[11]

Authoritarian Continued:	Qatar	$38,160
	Kuwait	$29,840
	UAE	$21,570
	Oman	$12,160
	Saudi Arabia	$11,930
	Bahrain	$5,690
	Algeria	$2,950
Authoritarian Fell:	Libya	$9,820
	Yemen	$410
	Egypt	$400
	Tunisia	$380

The pattern you see is that (with one exception) popular protests failed in countries where the authoritarian had more oil money and succeeded where the authoritarian had less oil money. The exception is Libya, but then the Libyan revolution was exceptional: Gaddafi had a lot of oil money saved up, but the rebels had NATO as their air force. The larger pattern is that in countries with oil income of more than $2,950 per person, the autocrat survived the protests; in countries with oil income of less than $410 per person, the autocrat lost power. The larger pattern is that in the high-rent countries, the autocrat won; the low-rent countries, the protestors won. (Syria is an interesting intermediate case.[12])

We can extend this pattern to cover an earlier Middle Eastern uprising as well: the failed 2009 "Green Revolution" in Iran. When the Green Revolution began, mass marches through the streets looked like they might threaten the state. But a crackdown by the regime using the fierce Basij militia cleared the streets and left many of the protest leaders dead or in jail. Iran had $2,448 per capita of oil income when the Green Revolution began.[13]

Politics are of course more complex than one number can capture; as we have seen, for example, the King of Bahrain relies on foreign allies as well as on oil rents when he needs to shatter the protests of the Shia majority (as he did during the Arab Spring). Still, natural resources go hand-in-hand with oppression in shaky-start states. And this is true for both high-rent and low-rent countries.

It is not just that rent-addicted regimes inflict unusually severe violence on individuals. (In 2014, Saudi Arabia beheaded at least nineteen people in less than three weeks, nearly half for non-violent offenses; Amnesty International suspects that confessions of four of the executed were extracted under torture.[14]) These regimes tend systematically to deny freedom of speech, freedom of the press, and freedom to assemble—as well, of course, as the right to vote freely in fair elections. The NGO Freedom House rates countries on their civil liberties and political rights; adding up their numbers, one finds that only 16 percent of the world's proven oil reserves are in countries that are "free."[15]

Rent-addicted authoritarians also suppress civil society—the civic organizations where people come together to share information and advance their common interests. No one can join a trade union in the UAE: trade unions are banned. The Uzbek government makes membership in the government-controlled association for NGOs "voluntary but compulsory."[16] Saudis cannot organize a butterfly-collecting club, or a bicycling club—much less a political party. These are not permitted.[17] These regimes try to keep citizens within structures that are controlled by the regime—the military, the bureaucracy—instead of allowing citizens to form associations with each other. In thwarting civil society, these regimes are pursuing their strategy of keeping the people divided in order to maintain their rule.

RENTS AND CLIENTS

Rent-addicted regimes tend to spend a lot on the military—oil-exporting states spend between two and ten times more on their armed forces than others do.[18] Spending on the military makes good sense for the resource-rich authoritarian. Armies are convenient for suppressing domestic dissent, which is, as we have seen, a level-one priority for the authoritarian wanting to stay in power. The autocrat may also be nervous of the neighbors who are greedily eyeing his resource wealth. More, the great powers that provide strategic rents often make it known that, in return, they would like the autocrat to use some of his resource money to buy their military hardware. In 2011, for example, Saudi Arabia spent over 15 percent of its official budget on weapons from the United States—a larger percentage than the United States spends on its whole Defense Department.[19]

Expanding the military also makes sense to the autocrat because of the economics of extractives. As we have seen, extraction tends not to employ locals, and it weakens employment in manufacturing and agriculture. This is useful for the autocrat who wants to keep his people from gaining an independent economic power base from which to resist him. Yet it also means that the economy holds fewer jobs, and the unemployed—especially unemployed young men—have a well-known propensity to revolt. What better then but to use some resource rents to hire these men into the military? Instead of revolting, the regime pays these men to suppress revolts. Plus, the military is a rigid, hierarchical structure with the autocrat at the top. By making soldiers out of otherwise unemployed men, these men come to depend on the authoritarian for their livelihoods, their opportunities, and their social standing.

The military is not the only institution with which the autocrat establishes hierarchical relations of personal dependence—indeed, the military is not even the most of it. The governments of oil states are almost half again as large as the governments of other states.[20] The whole apparatus of the state becomes a pyramid of relations of subordination, where patronage flows downward and political loyalty flows upward. Nicholas Shaxson describes the Angolan state thus:

> You can envisage a giant network of pipes shaped like a Christmas tree, with life-giving liquid flowing in through a big pipe at the top and being subdivided at different nodes. The pipes gets smaller and more numerous on the way down, and people guzzle at their open ends. The fat cats perch at the top, sucking from the fattest pipes; at the bottom thousands jostle for access to the tiniest ones, while millions crowd around them hoping to get something. Each node has a tap, controlled by a gatekeeper, often a bureaucrat, who drizzles the liquid down to underlings, in exchange for their loyalty. This is a political structure: the relationships are between rulers and subjects; wealth is obtained from political power (one's position in the tree) and vice versa. The Angolan tree has many vertical connections but few horizontal ones; cut one link—sack a minister, for example, and a whole chain of people dependent on that link falls down.[21]

The autocrat's government expands to absorb otherwise unemployed citizens. Again, drawing citizens into state employment makes idle hands busy.

And again, these citizens become dependent on the state for their livelihoods, their opportunities, and their social status. The autocrat divides and rules the population by using the resource money to create a pyramid of vertical pipes with himself at the top. Because relationships of political power are patron-client relations, political scientists call such systems "clientelistic."[22]

In Chapter 1, we noticed that everyday life in resource-dependent countries often seems strange. Foreigners can make up 86 percent of the population, or government paramilitaries ride around on motorcycles arresting women who fraternize with men. Now we add that even when the institutions of a resource-dependent country seem familiar—one reads of a department of education, a ministry of agriculture—the reality behind these institutions is often quite different. Clientelistic states tend to have Potemkin ministries: the people behind the desks at the tourism bureau are surprised when a tourist shows up. The point of state institutions is not to collect revenues and provide public goods. The point is to employ citizens so as to make them subservient to the state, and ultimately to the autocrat himself. Whether these clients contribute to state effectiveness—indeed, often whether these clients show up to work at all—is less important than the relation of personal dependence created between them and a higher-level official.[23]

When oil was discovered in Saudi Arabia in 1938, the country had no modern institutions.[24] Saudi Arabia's founding king, Abdul Aziz, assigned a ministry (defense, interior, national guard, etc.) to each of his senior princes as a personal fiefdom. As the oil money began to flow and then flood in, these princes expanded their power by adding branches and levels to the bureaucratic pyramids below them. Indeed, with the growing oil rents, the easiest way for the king to settle a dispute between feuding princes was to give both princes more money to expand their ministries, and these expansions conveniently pulled in more of the country's expanding population as well. The resulting ministries were predictably inefficient, yet their efficiency as ministries was a lower priority than their success in keeping the princes loyal and binding citizens in personalistic hierarchies to members of the regime. Coordination between these growing bureaucracies was abysmal: departments with overlapping mandates were created within different pyramids, and Saudis often saw a "battle of the bulldozers" when two ministries ordered construction equipment to the same site to start different projects.[25]

Dividing and ruling through clientelism is no aberration in human affairs. Douglas North, John Wallis, and Barry Weingast go so far as to call clientelistic hierarchies the "natural" system in the history of governance, and they show how many states still have this structure.[26] The old Soviet state was an oil-funded clientelistic hierarchy; when we talk of *apparatchiks* toadying to the *nomenklatura*, we are speaking Soviet Russian. Entrepreneurial energy in such societies goes toward pleasing the functionaries above one instead of satisfying the desires of fellow citizens. Critically, even if a "middle class" exists in income terms, this class does not perform its classic function within free societies, which is to be a base of independent economic power that balances the power of the state. The middle class tends rather to be made up of higher-paid clients whose income depends on their remaining loyal to the regime.[27]

In these countries, the top is rich, and some riches dribble down through channels of personal dependence. What makes resource-funded clientelism astonishing is how very top-down it can be. As we've seen, resource rents can provide half, 80 percent, even 93 percent of government revenues. The regime gets its money directly from foreigners and so does not need the population for taxes. At the extreme, the people of the country rely on the autocrat for everything, and the autocrat relies on the people for nothing. Wanting hands reach upward; arbitrary power looks down. All political relations become vertical, with the authoritarian at the summit of the steep hierarchy. The resource-fueled ruler can be truly absolute.

"EVERY MAN THERE IS A BARRATOR . . . FOR MONEY, OF NO THEY MAKE AY"[28]

Talented young people often flee clientelistic countries if they can. Those who remain face career paths defined by the state. One the biggest prizes a bureaucrat can sell in a clientelist state is a job in the bureaucracy itself. In Azerbaijan, a civil service position reportedly required a $50,000 payoff—or, rather, investment.[29] In a nation of gatekeepers, the ambitious strive to keep bigger gates. In the West, rich people go into government. In clientelistic countries, people go into government to get rich.[30]

In these countries, even those who succeed in industry typically depend on the state for their success. This is true not only for the contractor getting sweetheart deals from a minister, but at the highest levels as well. Indonesia's authoritarian Suharto was famous for his "crony capitalism," doling out control of the country's industries to his generals and family. (One of Suharto's sons mismanaged the state oil company for years; another had catastrophic effects on Indonesia's spice trade.[31]) In Saudi Arabia, catching the eye of the king launched several of the world's larger private fortunes—those of Mohammed bin Laden and Adnan Khashoggi (the former "richest man in the world"), to name just two.

The government patronizes the people. Bureaucrats selectively allow citizens access to services like housing or health care or police protection.[32] Or bureaucrats sell favors: for a price, a driver's license will appear, or cooked-up jail time will disappear. Citizens become reliant on specific agents of the state to get through daily life.

Some say that natural resources breed corruption.[33] And it's true that in Transparency International's Corruption Perceptions Index, most of the countries perceived as being the most corrupt are resource dependent.[34] Yet as a Zimbabwean economist says, "We imagine corruption to be like a tick on a dog. There are some places in Africa where the tick is bigger than the dog."[35] The political economics of resource-client countries stretch the word *corruption* to the semantic breaking-point. What we see in resource-client countries is of such scale and pervasiveness that we need to ask what this word even means.

One scholar defines corruption as "the illegal use of public office . . . for private ends."[36] Yet this will not do, since much of what goes on in resource-client countries does not violate the law. Suharto gave two of his sons and a cousin the lucrative monopoly on importing plastics—which was not illegal.[37] When asked how a son of the president of a tiny African oil state could afford to buy a 101-room mansion in central Paris furnished with five works by Rodin, a $3.7 million clock, and eleven luxury cars, his lawyer said, "He earned money in accordance with the laws of Equatorial Guinea"—which is likely true.[38] If corruption required law-breaking, then for those whose word is law, corruption would simply be carelessness.[39]

Corruption within resource-disordered countries is often not illegal. The World Bank's definition of "corruption" concedes it need not be, saying rather that it is the "abuse of public office for private gain."[40] This is better, yet this definition still assumes a public-private distinction that the personalistic politics of these countries can confuse. Chile's national mining company, Codelco, has long operated some of the world's largest copper mines. President Augusto Pinochet passed a secret law giving the military 10 percent of Codelco's export revenues in a (successful) effort to keep the generals loyal to him. Was that corruption—or politics? Perhaps both?

Some of what goes on in clientelistic states, especially at lower levels, is technically against the law: it is illegal to take a bribe to grant a marriage license or to void a speeding ticket. But the government is not going to put itself in jail—as they say in eastern Africa, the big fish will not fry themselves.[41] When an official is prosecuted for corruption in a clientelistic system, this usually means that this official has fallen out of favor with his patron. Or perhaps the patron is engaging in one of the periodic shake-ups that keep clients loyal by showing that all clients are dispensable.[42] Here the enforcement of anti-corruption laws is not a check on clientelistic dependence but rather one of its tools. It may even be wise for a patron to stage a spectacular sacrifice of a powerful but unpopular official from time to time in a way that will leave ordinary people, as Machiavelli said, "satisfied and stupefied at the same time."[43]

Hillary Clinton, on a visit to Angola, said "Corruption is a problem everywhere."[44] She was being diplomatic. There is of course significant corruption within rich countries like the United States, both episodically (for example, Jack Abramoff) and systemically (such as through lobbying). But this is the difference between being soaked by storms on the one hand and being sunk in a flood on the other.[45] What is called "corruption" in clientelistic states is a primary modality of governance. For anyone expecting an impartial civil service and the rule of law, the governance of a client state *is* corruption. Officials direct money and state benefits downward at their own discretion; political support flows back up. And those in charge maximize their power by keeping secret who is doing what for whom. In 2011, the International Monetary Fund discovered that three-quarters of the Angolan state oil company's $23 billion in revenues had been spent off-budget, with no public record of where the money had gone.[46] Resource rents become like Plato's magic Rings of Gyges, allowing whoever controls them to do invisibly what they wish.[47]

Clientelism is neither episodic nor even systemic corruption—it is the system itself. This deserves attention: clientelism, which looks like corruption, is a form of governance.[48] And clientelism, when it hierarchizes a large population of a modern state, tends to be a poor form of governance. Since it is a method of divide-and-rule, it emphasizes divisions of race, religion, ethnicity, and tribe and so reinforces social fragmentation. The state encourages fewer horizontal connections between citizens, and can even accentuate antagonisms: South vs. North, Christian vs. Muslim, Sunni vs. Shia, tribe vs. tribe. Moreover, money put into clientelistic hierarchies often fails to produce public goods. It is not unknown for half, two-thirds, even 99 percent of a public budget for health or education to "leak out" before it gets to the people.[49]

Clientelistic bureaucracies are not mostly about efficient service provision. They are about relations of personal subordination. A World Bank survey concludes that even moderately less corrupt regimes have much lower infant mortality and much higher public satisfaction with health care and roads.[50] Corruption may also decrease the capacity of an economy to sustain living standards over time.[51] And heavily resource-dependent clientelism magnifies these dangers. The more an authoritarian's money comes from the top down, the less the people have the power to resist clientelism from the bottom up. Resource-fueled clientelistic states tend to have rich regimes and weak peoples.

EATING THE MONEY

Earlier, we saw how Charles II of England, in the 1670s, spent some of his foreign-source funds on his palaces and his deer (and on his dearer mistresses). In the 1970s, the Shah of Iran could afford to be grander:

> A Lufthansa airliner at Mehrabad airport in Tehran. It looks like an ad, but in this case no advertising is needed because all the seats are sold. This plane flies out of Tehran every day and lands at Munich at noon. Waiting limousines carry the passengers to elegant restaurants for lunch. After lunch they all fly back to Tehran in the same airplane and eat their suppers at home. Hardly an expensive entertainment, the jaunt costs only two thousand dollars a head. For people in the Shah's favor, such a sum is nothing. In fact, it is the palace plebeians who only go to Munich for lunch. Those in somewhat higher positions don't always feel like enduring the travails of such long journeys. For them an Air France plane brings lunch, complete with cooks and waiters, from Maxim's of Paris. Even such fancies have nothing extraordinary about them. They cost hardly a penny when compared to a fairy-tale fortune like the one that Mohammed Reza and his people are amassing.[52]

Reports of personal corruption around natural resources are as common as rust in a scrapyard. In India, a police raid on the offices of a mining baron with close ties to the state government found $1 million in cash and sixty-six pounds of gold.[53] In Bahrain a parliamentary committee reported that members of the royal court and VIPs had misappropriated state land worth almost double the kingdom's GDP—and almost 10 percent of the total area of the country.[54] Because of WikiLeaks, we know that the chief prosecutor of the International Criminal Court suspected that President Omar al-Bashir of Sudan skimmed up to $9 billion off the country's oil revenues.[55] Nigeria's General Sani Abacha is accused of having taken more than $2.2 billion of state funds during his presidency; Shell executives will tell you that one of Abacha's successors removed around $40 billion (about Larry Ellison's net worth) from the treasury, sending armored cars full of cash into a huge underground vault beneath his personal compound.[56] In 2015, Nicholas Kristof contrasted the enormous wealth of Angola's president, and his daughter, with the shocking poverty in Angola's countryside ("There are many ways for a leader to kill his people," Kirstoff wrote, "extreme corruption and negligence can be something close to mass atrocity").[57]

When leaders of resource-rich states take large amounts from the public treasury to spend on mansions and yachts, champagne and prostitutes, this seems wrong, and some of this book will be devoted to telling those stories and filling out that intuition. Still, when we look under the surface of these sensational accounts of corruption, we find that there is often more to the story. Again, the backstory is politics: much of what resource-kleptocrats steal they do not even get to use on themselves. Mobutu Sese Seko reportedly stole $5 billion from Zaire—but he needed much of this to stay in power:

> Mobutu's theft . . . was a measure not of greed but of political weakness: he needed the money to remain head of one of Africa's largest, most fractious states . . . There were bribes to be paid to Western businessmen, politicians and journalists, wages for the [presidential security force], donations to foreign guerrilla groups, gifts to generals, governors and opposition politicians . . . It was a very, very expensive business.[58]

Separate out officials' use of public funds for their own consumption. Call that "private corruption," what John Locke called a governor's use of power "for his own private separate advantage."[59] Distinguish that from officials' use of public funds, often vastly greater, for clientelism. Such "clientelistic corruption" is a taking of public funds, but it is also a giving in exchange for loyalty—as above, it is a form of governance. Clientelistic corruption is governance neither by nor for the people. It is not remediable by replacing "bad" officials with "good" officials, but only by a large-scale transition to a more accountable form of governance.

THE VIOLENCE-CLIENT MIX

An autocrat enriched by foreign money from resource sales can use different power strategies to survive. One pure strategy, as we've seen, is violence: to threaten the people physically and periodically carry out these threats. Here the regime floats above the country suspended by a balloon of money, its guards keeping their high-powered rifles trained on the masses below. The second pure strategy is clientelism: pipelines of state benefits penetrate the population and hierarchize them along its nodes, the pipes becoming progressively more articulated and the benefits smaller toward the bottom. Both violence and clientelism are "hard power" strategies, and many resource-rich autocrats are very hard indeed.[60]

Pure strategies are rare in reality, however; almost every authoritarian will pursue a strategic mix of violence and clientelism. Autocrats adept at finding the right mix can survive in power for a very long time: Gaddafi of Libya and Bongo of Gabon ruled for forty-two years, Mobutu of Zaire for thirty-one years. Obiang of Equatorial Guinea and dos Santos of Angola assumed power in 1979 and Mugabe of Zimbabwe in 1980. Those familiar with African affairs will know the repression, corruption, and strife associated with these names.

How much a regime will threaten and how much it will patronize depends on many factors (including, of course, its savvy). History will be important. To make a crude contrast: in post-Soviet countries, citizens traditionally expected much from the state—so more clientelism. In sub-Saharan Africa, citizens now expect little from the state—so more coercion. The Shah of Iran ruled relatively coercively, depending on a small coalition based around the military and large landholders. The Shah's sudden overthrow in 1979 genuinely scared the Saudi royals, who redoubled their efforts to hierarchize their population into relations of clientelistic dependence.

Violence and clientelism are required strategies for all rent-addicted autocrats. The money comes in at the top, and the ruler spends on sticks and carrots as needed to stay in office. If there is money left over, he may splurge on airplanes and penthouses. And if there is money after that, he may spend on public goods.

PUBLIC GOODS AND BADS

How much a highly rent-addicted autocrat will spend on public goods depends on how much he has left over.[61] Here our story divides into two: of the high-rent and the low-rent authoritarians. We saw earlier that the high-rent authoritarians in the Middle East and North Africa (except Gaddafi) survived the Green Revolution and the Arab Spring, while the low-rent authoritarians fell to protests. Similarly, with public goods we also find two stories. The first is of the few high-rent authoritarians that have found themselves in control of such huge sums that they can afford to coerce and patronize their citizens, indulge in luxuries beyond the dreams of Croesus—and still have a good deal left over for public goods.

If the tiny Gulf state of Qatar did not exist, we would have to invent it. Imagine 250,000 people (roughly Fort Wayne, or Hull, or Saskatoon). Now put them on top of 13 percent of the world's proven gas reserves.[62] What you are imagining is the richest country in the world. Qatar's GDP per capita is nearly twice that of the United States.[63] And that "per capita" figure is deceptive, because its denominator includes the foreign workers who are 86 percent of Qatar's population.[64] Focusing only on the country's hydrocarbon revenues, and only on its citizens, we find that the country receives the gigantic annual sum of $183,000 per Qatari citizen for its natural wealth.[65] (As a rough comparison, the entire US national income is just over $58,000 per US citizen, and total US government spending at all levels is around $22,000 per US citizen per year.[66])

Does any family—indeed, does any one man—have the right to all that money? For in reality, Qatar's hydrocarbon revenues do not get divided *per capita* or *per cives*; it all goes *ad tyrannum*. The Emir of Qatar, the head of the al-Thani family, controls the tens of billions of dollars of hydrocarbon revenues that come in to the Qatari state each year.[67] The Emir decides how much the state will spend on coercion, how much on clientelism. He also decides how much to keep for himself: the Qatari constitution states that "[t]he financial emoluments of the Emir as well as the funds allocated for gifts and assistance shall be determined by a resolution issued annually by the Emir."[68] How many billions the Emir has taken for himself, hidden in secret foreign bank accounts and invested through shell companies, we simply cannot know. The Emir and his family, though, are likely among the richest families in the world.[69] Still, even after all of this, the Emir is so exceedingly wealthy that he can afford to buy public goods.

Qatar shows that while resource-disordered countries have rich regimes and weak peoples, they do not all have rich regimes and poor peoples. Salaries in Qatar's clientelistic hierarchies are good (and foreigners do most of the work anyway). The country's cradle-to-grave welfare system is well funded. The regime spends a lot on infrastructure, and education is free. Citizens do not of course get anywhere near the value of their fair share of the oil money—but there is so much oil money that even an unfair share ends up being a fair amount being spent on them.

We will meet Qatar again later in the book, because this miniscule autocracy holds hope for the transformation of the Middle East. For now, the key point is that Qatar is a statistical blip (there are more albinos in the world than Qataris[70]). Its small neighbors, the UAE and Kuwait, get far less oil revenues per citizen every year ($98,000 and $73,000, respectively).[71] Saudi Arabia gets "only" $11,000 per citizen from its oil. Most of the world's rent-addicted authoritarians control much lower revenues per citizen than do these few high-rent regimes.

Predictably, the low-rent regimes provide far few public goods for the people—and even fewer outside of the capital city, where regime members and their supporters tend to live.[72] Indeed, the contrast between the capital city and the rest of a resource-dependent country is often stark. In Nigeria's poor, oil-producing south, civic leaders tell the story of a march on the country's capital to protest abuses by the army. Many of the protestors were astonished, never having been in such a place—the capital looked like a city in a rich country.[73] In Gabon, long ruled by the Bongo family, even the capital is only sporadically grand:

> The futuristic government palaces on Omar Bongo Triumphal Boulevard, with their flying-saucer and rocket-ship outcroppings, marbled interiors and expanses of plate glass, would make the pedestrian feel humble, if there were any. It is almost as if you could be in a prosperous city in Texas.
>
> But you are in Gabon, and behind the late ruler's palaces, which line the wide empty boulevard, are shacks and shanties stretching to the horizon, dirt roads and street vendors eking out a living selling cigarettes and imported vegetables. Most live on less than $2 a day in this little Central African country, rich in both oil and poor people. Evidence of the gulf between the haves (Mr. Bongo's extended clan) and the have-nots (everybody else) is always just around the corner . . .

> "Did you go behind the buildings? What did you see?" asked Marc Ona, an environmental activist and antigovernment dissident imprisoned under the late president for his work. "Misery is everywhere," Mr. Ona said. "Corruption is everywhere."[74]

We are heading down into the low-rent end of the resources-per-capita scale, where most resource-diseased countries linger. What one wants to avoid is being poor outside of the capital city in a country ruled by a highly addicted but low-rent regime. Here the state scrimps on giving the police a living wage, relying instead the old system used by occupying armies—letting the troops prey on the population for their incomes. Because resource extraction is enclaved, there are few jobs at the extractive sites. Because of the Dutch Disease, there are few jobs in manufacturing or agriculture. The regime lacks the cash to engage in extensive patronage—perhaps only the provincial governor gets enough to be wealthy—so government jobs are hard to come by as well. Nor is the government inclined to spend its rents on public goods. " 'We are not benefitting from this oil!' shouted Ali Mohammed, a Nigerian motorcycle-taxi driver. 'No lights, no roads, no hospitals... We are suffering in this country.' "[75]

Toward the worst extreme of the spectrum, highly addicted but low-rent rulers will even ban public goods, seeing them as a threat. In Zaire, President Mobutu issued his infamous order to "build no roads" so as to make it harder for rebels to organize against him.[76] This was disastrous for Zaire's economy, but the money from the resources kept flowing to Mobutu—and impoverished, sickly people often lack the strength to revolt. In a similar mood, King Hassan of Morocco once said, "There is no danger for the state as grave as that of the so-called intellectual. It would be better if you were all illiterate."[77]

AUTHORITARIAN LEGITIMATION

In our Dante-like travels through the afflictions of resource-disordered countries, we are just at the transition between authoritarianism and armed conflict. In the next chapter, we will explore how resources can fire civil war and incite coups. Before leaving the autocrats, however, we look at their final instrument of governance, which is the use of ideology. Every rent-addicted authoritarian must seek legitimation for his rule.

The feeble assent that is submission is a minimum for every authoritarian: the people must be coerced or co-opted enough to stay out of his way while he sells off the nation's assets. And the authoritarian will want extra leeway from the public beyond that too. All people naturally resent being coerced, and the resource rents that sustain the authoritarian's coercive power are highly volatile and so sometimes run low. Especially in the bad times, an authoritarian will need a back door into citizens' hearts and minds.

The easiest way to unite citizens behind a regime, or at least to distract their attention from their straits, is to bang the drum of nationalism: to invoke the glorious history or the national "family," to play on xenophobic fears that whip up paranoia and militarism. A war can be an excellent means for rallying popular support (as Putin did with his moves into Ukraine in 2014 and into Syria in 2015). The tactic is essentially divisive, and more so when mixed with racial or religious stereotyping of an enemy beyond or within the borders. If the regime organizes the nation's history around a victim narrative, this divisiveness will intensify.

A leader wielding a revolutionary ideology—like Ayatollah Khomeini, Saddam Hussein or Muammar Gaddafi—can be especially hazardous to his people and to their neighbors. As the political scientist Jeff Colgan shows in his book *Petro-Aggression*, revolutionary oil states are more than three times more likely to start militarized international conflicts than a typical state.[78] Hussein, for example, attacked both Iran and Kuwait, and Gaddafi picked several fights with nearby states.

Elections may seem a surprising mechanism of legitimation here, yet many autocracies today hold rigged elections for at least some offices.[79] In places where citizens can't easily share information, an election victory can make some citizens think that others do in fact support the regime.[80] And even an unfree, unfair election allows an autocrat to pose as the people's choice. As we will explore more in Chapter 10, popular sovereignty is now widely accepted as a primary source of genuine political legitimacy, and a fake poll enables an emperor at least to pretend the clothes of modernity.

Other legitimation strategies of authoritarians are more venerable. Recall the founding autocrat of Turkmenistan—the "Father of all Turkmen"—and the four-story, gold-plated statue he built in his capital that revolved always to face the sun. This attempt to construct a cult of personality would have won a smile even from a Pharaoh. In the Gulf monarchies, the royal visages are everywhere. Government buildings, banks, billboards, even businesses display idealized images of regime members, portrayed as wise and gentle. Mixed in are a few images of royals looking stern and ruthless, often in sunglasses and sometimes in uniform. "The aim here, it seems, is to demonstrate to the population that the rulers should be both loved and feared, and certainly never crossed."[81]

A different strain of ideological legitimation has been the aim of Teodoro Obiang of Equatorial Guinea, whom we will meet again in Chapter 5. As a presidential aide said of Obiang on state-run radio, "He can decide to kill without anyone calling him to account and without going to hell because it is God himself, with whom he is in permanent contact, who gives him this strength."[82] Outsiders may see Obiang as poorly cast for the role of God's lieutenant, yet one of his tactics has been to present his assaults on the people as divinely inspired.

Sometimes a legitimizing ideology is not chosen but is congenital with the regime. The best example of such an inborn ideology is in the most important oil state of them all, Saudi Arabia. The Saudi state was founded on an alliance between a political leader (ibn Saud) and a fundamentalist religious leader (al-Wahhab). Since this founding, the regime has worn the cloak of piety for its legitimacy. The Saudi king is the head of the national Sunni community, and he gains much of his luster from being *Fidei Defensor*: the Guardian of the Holy Places that are the two most sacred sites in Islam.

In 1979, this source of the king's legitimacy was severely damaged when the holiest site of all—the Grand Mosque in Mecca—was taken over by a group of violent millenarian Muslim fanatics. This was also the year of the revolution in Iran, when the Saudi king suddenly found himself next to an ayatollah pushing an antagonistic vision of Islamic fundamentalism. The king's response to these twin challenges was to reestablish his religious legitimacy by giving large amounts of oil money to the most conservative section of his clerical establishment, empowering them to spread vigorously a reactionary version of Wahhabism at home and abroad.

This the Saudi clerics did to great effect. The politico-religious conservatism of today's Saudi citizens is not an independent fact, but is partly a result of well-funded ideological campaigns of regime legitimation. More, as we will see in Chapter 6, the Saudi king's support for spreading an extreme variant of Sunni Islam abroad in the 1980s and 1990s turned into one of the most extensive ideological campaigns in world history, which had disastrous consequences that we are still living through.

THE BIG MAN AND HIS BIG HAND

Oil has a remarkable property—it can stop time. Nearly all of the world's absolute monarchies are oil states.[83] Absolute monarchy may have been an appropriate form of governance when humanity was in more primitive conditions. In ages past, when the population did not generate much economic value, when communication across distances was arduous, when hostile clans and tribes lacked sources of mutual identification, the best that might have been possible was the imposition of order through violence and patronage, supported by a legitimizing religious ideology. What is striking today is how oil money has allowed some absolute monarchs to perpetuate—even to recreate—that medieval environment.

When an authoritarian presents himself as the embodiment of national unity, he may point to a fake election. Or the unity he invokes may be bound by hate: against a national minority, against a neighboring country, against the heretics. He may set majority against minority, tribe against tribe, country against country, faith against faith. He may infect his population with a virulent nationalism or a contagious extremism. Should such an authoritarian weaken or fall—as in Syria, Iraq, and Libya—civil strife will typically be his legacy. The authoritarian divides in order to rule, and divided societies will always be liable to armed conflict—especially, as we will now see, if those aggrieved find their own sources of resource money.

4

... Then Maybe Blood

The Security Council... [is] aware that the link between the illegal exploitation of natural resources, the illicit trade in those resources and the proliferation and trafficking of arms is one of the factors fuelling and exacerbating conflicts... especially in the Democratic Republic of the Congo.

—UN Security Council, *Resolution 1653*

We have begun to see how this mineral wealth can become a curse—as it so often has been in Africa, as people are killed and communities destroyed in the fight for diamonds that will forever be marked with the blood of the innocent... Can we hear the voice of our Creator crying to us—like the blood of Abel "out of the ground" itself—"Why will you turn my gifts into an excuse for bloodshed? Why will you not use what you have for the good of the community, not for private gain or political advantage?"

—Archbishop of Canterbury, *Sermon in Zimbabwe*[1]

Before his gruesome death, Muammar Gaddafi predicted that his defeat would be the beginning of chaotic tribal infighting in Libya. He was right.[2] Western pleaders for leaders like Gaddafi often warn that only the authoritarian can "keep the lid on" hostile groups that would otherwise cause serious instability or even civil war. These apologists are also right, but like Gaddafi, their analyses come late in the story. Antagonisms among groups within resource-diseased states are not wholly independent facts; rather, these are results that the authoritarian desires and encourages. Playing tribal and religious leaders off against each other is a governing strategy characteristic of the autocrat—another means to divide and rule. Autocrats do keep the lid on the jar, but they also regularly shake that jar—and should the lid ever come off, the hornets and scorpions emerge, mad as hell.

Once petrocrats like Gaddafi or Saddam Hussein or Bashar al-Assad lose control of all or part of their countries, oil then re-enters the picture. The post-Gaddafi Libyan militias quickly began fighting with each other and with the government to control the country's oil wells and export facilities. In 2013–2014, the jihadi group ISIS seized large portions of eastern Syria and western Iraq. Oil fields in both countries were among its first targets; ISIS was soon raising up to $2 million a day selling crude oil ("It's as easy for ISIS as digging a hole and letting the oil run before siphoning it off into tankers," said one observer).[3] ISIS also enriched itself through extortion and bank robbery, and with second-hand oil money sent by sympathetic Saudis, Qataris, and Kuwaitis.[4] By mid-2014, ISIS had become "[t]he world's richest terror group" and rebranded itself Islamic State.[5]

Oil is the autocrat's power source of choice because the money is typically big, secret, unconditional, and flows even when the population is weak and divided. Oil is also highly prized by militias—for just the same reasons.

COERCION, CORRUPTION, THEN MAYBE BLOOD

Let's step back and ask the basic question of why natural resources should be correlated with strife.[6] One review found that at least 40 percent of the world's civil conflicts in the six decades after 1947 were resource fueled, in countries stretching from Indonesia to Yemen to Ivory Coast.[7] What is it about resources that adds such violent volatility to weak polities?

The process of resource extraction can itself impose heavy costs on the local community. Unless expensive measures are taken, mining is dirty work. So the mining pollutes the community's air or water. Soldiers or private security guards arrive and abuse the civilians. Rowdy bars and prostitutes then arrive to service the miners and the guards. Moreover, as we have seen, resource extraction typically creates few jobs for the locals. The community collects grievances and finds few mechanisms of accountability through which to register them with the distant government.

Poorer countries are generally more susceptible to civil conflict, either because the state is less capable or because citizens have fewer peaceful options to get money.[8] Resources make things worse: as we have seen, for instance, the governments of resource-rich states tend to be less capable than comparable governments because they get their revenues without needing to govern well.[9] And violently seizing resources is a good way for citizens to get money since resources are very valuable and easily sold. The possibility of getting richer by seizing resources or their revenues boosts the risks of civil conflict.

Extractive sites are magnets for militias, whether moved by grievances or mere greed. Unlike banks or shops, resource sites are spatially stuck: the pumps and mines can't be moved and so are easier targets for militia predation, both by direct theft and by extortion. And unlike farming, mineral extraction can usually carry on during fighting. Guerrillas extorted at least $140 million from foreign oil firms during Colombia's violent 1990s.[10] In the midst of the second Iraq war, the US government reported that armed groups were making at least $200 million a year through oil-related extortion and black marketeering and taxation. (Muqtada al-Sadr's Mahdi militia, in charge of Basra, extorted a fee for each barrel exported from the city's port.[11]) Occasionally, an embattled population can even create its own extractive sites to help its side in the fight: during Russia's second war in Chechnya, up to 30,000 Chechens were involved in illegal production from hundreds of "backyard" oil wells.[12]

Gemstones, and metals like gold and coltan, are especially attractive to militias: they have very high value relative to their weight, and they are easily sold to smugglers. Studies report that resources increase the likelihood, duration, and severity of conflicts.[13] Gems and oil far from the capital make conflicts last longer.[14] The presence of gems and oil in conflict zones more than doubles the duration of the conflicts, and secessionist conflicts in oil-producing regions are the most severe.[15] Resources correlate with more violent rebels who attack civilians more indiscriminately.[16] And resource dependence is correlated with failure in peacebuilding initiatives (the eastern Congo—sometimes called "the UN's Vietnam"—is the paradigm).[17]

Clearly, civil conflict can happen without natural resources. The Irish Republican Army and the Tamil Tigers, for instance, were funded by diasporas instead of by resources.[18] And Mexico's gangs like the Zetas and the

Sinaloa Cartel make money from narcotics and kidnapping as well as from oil theft.[19] Nor is natural resource extraction sufficient for conflict. The high-rent oil states, for example, are no more likely to see conflict than non-oil states—presumably because a rich regime can better control resistance. Low-rent oil states, however, are almost twice as likely to be at war with themselves.[20] Since low-rent oil states are growing in number and non-oil states are getting more peaceful, this has meant that the chance a civil conflict is occurring in an oil state has risen from one-in-ten to four-in-ten.[21]

The strength of the people is again crucial. We saw above that countries risk authoritarianism when oil arrives before institutions of public accountability are in place. With conflict, it's the same story: resource-rich countries that have less consensual institutions and worse enforcement of law and property rights are more prone to civil conflict.[22]

In Sierra Leone during the early 1980s, the president used his control over the diamond mining industry to foment violence in the countryside so that the clandestine commercial networks supporting him would find more opportunities to prey on the people.[23] After that president, an even less salubrious leader took over, and as we'll see in the next chapter, governance in the countryside collapsed. Into this void came militants who recruited child soldiers to help carry out a campaign of mass amputation and pillage:

> As a teenager in war-ravaged Sierra Leone, Ishmael Beah was brainwashed, drugged and forced to kill . . .
>
> "Somebody being shot in front of you, or you yourself shooting somebody became just like drinking a glass of water. Children who refused to fight, kill or showed any weakness were ruthlessly dealt with.
>
> "Emotions weren't allowed," he continued. "For example a nine-year-old boy cried because they missed their mother and they were shot."[24]

THE SPOILS OF WAR

Depending on where resources are located, armed groups exploiting them can develop separatist tendencies. Enclaved resources far from the nation's capital are most likely to be associated with a separatist conflict, since these are the easiest for a separatist group to take control of. Examples include

Indonesia (Aceh), Nigeria (Niger Delta), Sudan (South Sudan), and Iraq (Kurdistan).[25] The attraction of rebellion can also be greater when a resource-rich region is physically separated from the mainland, or is ethnically distinct, or is ruled by a government with which it has fewer historical ties (Aceh, Bougainville, Cabinda, the hill regions of Burma, Western Sahara).[26] The gems of South Asia have funded several potent military movements. In Burma, the hill tribes fought the state with the help of jade and ruby revenues.[27] For the Khmer Rouge, rubies supplemented the timber rents that enabled them to fight on after their fall from power.[28] (Pol Pot emphasized it was "imperative that we find ways to develop the natural resources that exist in our liberated and semi-liberated zones as assets to be utilized in the fight."[29])

Several of the conflicts just listed were also particularly intense because resource revenues powered more than one side. Burma's military junta remained in power in part by selling the country's natural gas to its neighbors and using that money to battle the ethnic insurgencies in the countryside.[30] In Pol Pot's Cambodia, both sides of the conflict funded themselves with timber sales. It is debatable which side won in this war, but the forests definitely lost: one study estimates that Cambodia's forest cover halved during the years of fighting.[31] And the ISIS-Iraqi-Kurdish conflict that broke out in 2014 was a war of oil against oil.[32]

Angola's ruinous civil conflict had resources on both sides. During the Cold War, Angola was a monkey puzzle of foreign intrigue. (At one point, Communist Cuban forces were defending American oil facilities, whose oil the Marxist-Leninist government sold to the United States, enabling that government to buy guns from the Soviet Union to fight American-backed rebels.[33]) After the Cold War ended, the Angolan regime supported itself with oil from wells along the coastline, and as we saw earlier, the regime used these oil rents to fund a Christmas tree of patronage sufficient to keep thousands of people (mostly in the capital) locked into hierarchies of clientelistic dependence. Yet for Angolans in the countryside, governance was all but absent. The regime got its oil money from the coast, and felt little need to keep order, much less provide public goods, in the country's impoverished interior.[34] And from the interior came trouble.

In the 1990s, the National Union for the Total Independence of Angola (UNITA) insurgency captured most of Angola's rich diamond fields, and with the money equipped a large military force that became a serious threat to the state. UNITA's control of Angola's diamond deposits was a major operation; at one point, the group imported a hundred thousand Zairean miners to boost its extractive capacity.[35] The resulting civil conflict was long, murderous, and disastrous for the population. Shaxson describes an Angolan town after a UNITA attack:

> Four story structures lay collapsed as if crushed by giant cannonballs; apartment blocks had their faces shorn off; bullet holes and the splash patterns of rocket-propelled grenades peppered once-beautiful pink walls . . . Small boys proffered damaged arms, legs and heads. "Feel my shrapnel wounds," said tiny, impish Bruno, scampering along beside me, patting his head and guiding my hand to a ridge on his scalp, which, he proudly assured me, still had metal inside. In the hospital I could see a girl's teeth through a two-inch hole in her cheek from an untreated ulcer. Nearby, pupils in a classroom studied chemistry with their AK-47s stacked outside; in the road a red-painted circle warned of an unexploded shell . . . Some of the town's residents lost their minds. An Angolan television crew filmed one injured lunatic pulling rotting flesh off his own leg and eating it.[36]

After many years, the government (the oil money) won Angola's civil war, but at great cost. By the late 1990s, three-quarters of Angolans were living on less than a dollar a day, life expectancy was only forty-five years, and over three million civilians had been displaced.[37] The war ended in 2002, and still in 2005 the UN reported that almost half of Angola's children were severely malnourished, and that less than half of adults could read and write.[38]

Regardless of who wins, a civil war is hard on the people. Roads and hospitals are destroyed; children are kept from school and parents from work. Whole communities may suffer post-traumatic insecurity. Civil conflict is "development in reverse": it can take a decade-and-a-half for a country to return to its prewar growth rate, and on average, a civil war costs a developing country thirty years' worth of economic growth.[39]

In 1999, UNICEF released a comparative report on risks to children, using figures on mortality under age five, child malnutrition, school attendance, security, and adult HIV/AIDS. The report ranked Angola, toward the end of its long civil war, as the worst country in the world to be a child. Sierra Leone, reaching the end of its bloody diamond conflict, was a close second. And still today, the data show that—in the midst of their great natural wealth—Angola is first and Sierra Leone is second in the world in the rates at which children under five die.[40]

THE WORLD'S WORST WAR

In Angola, the rebels fought the government; Sierra Leone's conflict was mostly about warlords plundering ungoverned regions of a failed state.[41] The war in the Democratic Republic of the Congo (DRC) combines both of these elements. We briefly visited this conflict in the Introduction, where we found that sirens from this distant war zone have been blasting for years, though barely audible above the din of daily life in the West. The DRC's conflict is an exceptionally complex story of refugees from the Rwandan genocide, invasions, alliances, and the splintering and merging of militias that have launched horrific onslaughts on civilians.

The great mineral riches of the eastern Congo were not the trigger for the conflict, but as the conflict progressed, minerals became an increasingly important source of finance on all sides, including for corrupt Congolese army units and militias supported by neighboring Rwanda and Uganda. At one point, an NGO estimated that conflict minerals were generating $185 million annually for armed groups, including army units.[42] Once resource extraction became part of the dynamic of conflict, the conflict itself became more entrenched, as resource revenues also became a source of personal enrichment. " 'War in this country is business,' said a UN official... 'It's like the Mafia. With every military operation, people say that the commander must be buying a new house.' "[43]

The Congo's war is marked among contemporary conflicts by its scale, duration, and ferocity. One report estimated that the conflict in the DRC caused more than 5.4 million deaths over a decade.[44] That number may overestimate the death toll during that period, which others believe closer to one million.[45] But that is still a large number. The lower number of deaths reported during that part of the Congo's war is more than all American combat deaths in all of America's foreign wars combined. The lower conflict death rate in the eastern Congo over that decade averages at 275 people per day—that's like a Boeing 757 crashing and leaving no survivors, each and every day, week in and week out, for ten years.

The war has also proved, even among modern conflicts, extravagant in its horror stories. The following scene from the war, described in Jason Stearns's *Dancing in the Glory of Monsters,* is truly disturbing:

> At least 14 people were in the chief's house when the soldiers arrived. The rebels killed all of them. Villagers who had run into the

> bushes came back the next morning and found the chief's pregnant wife eviscerated, her dead fetus on the ground next to her. The infants of the chief's younger brother had been beaten to death against the brick walls of the house. The way the victims were killed said as much as the number of dead; they displayed a macabre fascination with human anatomy. The survivors said the chief's heart had been cut out and his wife's genitals were gone. The soldiers had taken them. It wasn't enough to kill their victims; they disfigured and played with the bodies. They disemboweled one woman by cutting her open between her anus and vagina, then propped up the dead body on all fours and left her with her buttocks facing upwards. Another corpse was given two slits on either side of his belly, where his hands were inserted. Another man had his mouth slit open to his ears and was put in a chair and had a cigarette dangling from his lips when he was found. The killers wanted to show the villagers that this would be the consequences of any resistance. They would kill the priests, rape nuns, rip babies from their mothers' wombs, and twist corpses into origami figures.[46]

Amidst these death statistics and grotesqueries, a Congolese might remind us that even during the war, there have also been innumerable moments of decency, generosity, and tenderness. A Congolese might gently ask us not to think of the people of this region only as victims, but to consider that they, like we, also seek out the fullness of human life every day.

NIGERIA IS FAR FROM NORWAY

We can begin to draw together the threads of the resource disorders. The original debate among economists about a "resource curse" was whether resource dependence is bad for the growth of a country's GDP. The broad consensus today is that states which rely on resources do grow more slowly than other states, or at least more slowly than they should.[47] This is an interesting result, and given what we've seen about corruption and conflict, one might not find it surprising.

National GDP growth, however, is not what we're most interested in here. To see why, consider a parable: the story of the peripatetic president. The president of an impoverished, strife-plagued country is told that oil has been discovered offshore. Delighted, he signs contracts for its extraction, and when the oil money begins to flow into the treasury, he takes every penny of it back out. Leaving his henchmen in charge, he flies off to host a long series of gala parties in capital cities abroad. When some partygoer is indiscreet enough to ask about the wretched condition of the people back home, he produces his finance minister who explains that the country's GDP is growing by a spectacular 50 percent per annum.

Our interest here is the real condition of the people of resource-rich countries, and in the politics of those countries. Distinguishing "rich" and "poor" states by GDP per capita, as is usually done, will sometimes mislead us. By income per head, Equatorial Guinea looks as rich as a European state like Spain.[48] Yet this is an illusion: Equatorial Guinea has an extremely wealthy elite, while most of people live on less than what $2 a day would buy in the United States.[49]

When we can, it will often be more useful to look at median income: the income of the middle household in the country's income distribution. In 2005, for instance, Venezuela's oil-buoyed GDP per capita was up with middle-income countries like Turkey and Bulgaria, but its median income was down with lower-income countries like Egypt and Morocco.[50] Even the familiar distinction between "developed" and "developing" states will not suit us well. Some so-called developing states stagnate in what Collier calls a "resource trap," and others go backward by deindustrializing and becoming poorer.[51] So here we will label as "rich" those countries with both high per-capita and high median incomes (for example, Canada) and as "poor" those countries with both low per-capita and low median incomes (for example, Zimbabwe).

We began with Norway: a small, educated, rich, stable constitutional democracy with world-leading levels of civic participation, confidence in institutions, and social solidarity. The people were strong in Norway when the oil came in, and the oil money made them even stronger. Since then we have been looking at the political pathologies that can afflict countries that have been less lucky. We have seen why resource rents are the revenue source of choice for an authoritarian, how this money empowers a regime to divide and rule a population through coercion and clientelism, why resource money goes hand-in-hand with corruption of all forms, and how it can fire violent conflicts. We find all of these political pathologies together within what many think of as the archetypal state cursed by its resources: Nigeria.

Nigeria today is not among the very worst resource-disordered countries (these we will see more in chapters to come). The country is struggling toward better governance and, in 2015, elected a president with an anti-corruption agenda in its first democratic transfer of power. Still, Nigeria was not strong when the oil came in, and it has exhibited all of the resource disorders since it became one of Africa's leading exporters. Nigeria's history with its oil has been arduous and adverse.

Nigeria was a colonial creation in 1914, when the British drew a national border around 350 ethnic groups whose relations ranged mostly from indifferent to bitter (there had been, among other tensions, intertribal enslavement). The main religious divide has always been between Muslims in the north and Christians and animists in the South, with the South further divided into two major tribal regions. After independence in 1960, the country soon fell into disorder: martial law, a fraudulent election, a military takeover in a bloody coup, and then ethnic massacres leading, in 1967, to a shocking, searing civil war in a region whose name became a signifier for human suffering: Biafra. It was at this moment in the nation's history that the oil money began to come in.

Between 1965 and 2000, the Nigerian government received large rents (around $350 billion) from oil sales. Yet during this period, the percentage of Nigerians living in extreme (dollar-a-day) poverty increased. In fact, extreme poverty increased substantially: from 36 to almost 70 percent of the population. All of the oil revenue contributed nothing to the average standard of living; this period actually saw a decline in living standards. Inequality also skyrocketed. In 1970, the total income of those in the top 2 percent of the distribution was equal to the total income of those in the bottom 17 percent. By 2000, the top 2 percent made as much as the bottom 55 percent.[52]

Today, more than 80 percent of Nigerians live on what two dollars a day would buy in the United States, and nearly a quarter of children are underweight.[53] Most people still work in agriculture; the average farmer is over fifty years old, illiterate, and uses hand tools to work a few acres that yield much less food than her family needs.[54] Since independence, life expectancy in Nigeria has gone up—but only half as much as in neighboring (extractive-poor) Benin and Togo. Life expectancy is only fifty-three years now, compared with sixty-six years in nearby Ghana.[55] Astonishingly, Nigeria has just become the country in the world with the most extremely poor people. Nigeria now has even more extremely poor people than China, even more than India.[56]

As in Angola, Nigerian politics is a vertical system of descending and ever-smaller pipes of patronage. The oil money is poured in at the top, each level depends on the one above for its payments, and each level takes its portion before sending what remains down to the next level. Much energy is expended trying to capture some part of the oil money coming through the pipes. Some money makes it all the way down to ordinary people, but mostly, for example, when it is time to buy votes. Otherwise, ordinary people tend not to see their country's oil wealth but instead are harassed by underpaid policeman and bureaucrats who demand bribes for daily activities. The Nigerian government generally does a poor job of providing public services such as security and electricity, clean water and education. Public services are not the major priority of the system. Rather, the system maintains personalistic patronage relations from the top leadership down to regional and local officials and the security forces.

Nigeria's large oil rents have fostered massive corruption. One insider report says that suspicious deals and mismanagement cost the oil industry $35 billion in a decade; others think that this figure is low.[57] One way to get rich in Nigeria is through holding a position in government. In 2005, the national police chief was convicted of stealing $98 million (and was sentenced to six months in jail).[58] The head of the anti-corruption task force was removed in the middle of his term in 2007, shortly after having a wealthy ally of the president arrested.[59] A federal judge in Nigeria later cleared the wealthy ally on all 170 corruption counts.[60] In 2012, that wealthy ally, a former state governor, pleaded guilty in a British court for fraud involving nearly $77 million of public funds.[61]

Corruption suffuses the political system. In 2014, the governor of the central bank produced a trove of evidence that the Nigerian national oil company had failed to account for $20 billion of revenues during the nineteen-month period starting in January 2012—and independent analysis has found that this number may be billions too low. After the report was made public, the president asked the governor to resign.[62] Nigeria's patronage-based politics plays out what Collier has called "the survival of the fattest."[63]

The Nigerian word for oil theft is *bunkering*. A good deal of bunkering in Nigeria is poor people trying to get some money by physically breaking a pipeline in order to sell the oil they catch, or in order to file a claim for environmental damages from the resulting spill. Yet it appears that state officials are involved in bunkering too. In 2011, the national oil company admitted in the parliament that it could not account for $7 million-a-day worth of oil that it was meant to be refining.[64] A report in 2014 estimated that the country is losing $1.5 billion a month to piracy and maritime smuggling (with persistent rumors that the Nigerian Navy is complicit).[65] A major investigation recently reported that Nigeria loses more oil to bunkering than the entire exports of Cameroon: "Nigerian crude oil is being stolen on an industrial scale."[66]

In the first decade of the twenty-first century, militias in the Niger Delta, funded by bunkering, extortion, and kidnapping, caused enough instability to lock in hundreds of thousands of barrels a day. The US State Department reports that to fight the militants, Nigerian "military personnel and paramilitary mobile police carried out summary executions, assaults, and other abuses."[67] When a president from the Delta came to power, he instituted a $400 million per year amnesty program that bought off the militias in the South.[68] During that Southern presidency, however, violence shifted to the North, where inter-religious massacres and terrorist attacks became increasingly common and lethal.

Northern Nigeria has been in overall economic decline for decades, not least because the country's petroleum exports (over 90 percent of the total) have crowded out agricultural and manufacturing exports.[69] Only one girl in fourteen finishes secondary school in the North, and 70 percent of women are illiterate.[70] In 2014, the Islamist militant group Boko Haram (whose name roughly means "Western education is forbidden") kidnapped over two hundred schoolgirls; later, it began to capture and hold territory and declared itself an Islamic state.[71] Nigeria's large army was too corrupt to fight back. "Somebody is sitting comfortably in [the capital] stealing our money," lamented one corporal, "and we are here facing Boko Haram fire every day."[72]

Nigeria today has a huge population: the seventh largest in the world, easily the largest in Africa, and with more people than the United Kingdom, France, Canada, and Portugal combined.[73] It is Africa's leading oil exporter, and it exports more crude than Venezuela or Kuwait.[74] It also remains agonizingly divided and distrustful.

In the most recent poll, Nigerians showed the least trust in their political institutions among the 18 sub-Saharan countries surveyed, with more than half the people saying they trust none of their institutions.[75] A significant minority reported having to pay a bribe or do a favor for a government official in the past year to get a document, to get a child into school, to get water or electricity or phone service, to get medical attention, or to avoid a problem with the police. Only one in ten Nigerians said their national identity is more important than their ethnic identity, and over two-thirds said that they trusted people from other ethnic groups "just a little" or "not at all." While a majority said they could trust their relatives a lot, most said they could trust their neighbors just a little. When asked whether most people can be trusted, five out of six Nigerians chose the least-trusting option: "you must be very careful."[76]

As a people, Nigerians were not strong when the oil came in. And the oil has made the Nigerian people weaker.

POLITICAL PATHOLOGIES: INTERACTIONS AND ADDITIONS

Nigeria has seen coercion and civil conflict throughout its oil-producing years, while its oil money has funded patronage and personal corruption instead of public goods. All of these pathologies are risks for resource-dependent states, and as with alcohol and drug abuse, in any individual case the causal chains of pathologies may be crossed and looped. Conflict can keep a country dependent on extractive exports, which in turn increases the danger of further conflict.[77] Conflict can also be a path to authoritarianism: in what has been called the "liberation curse," a highly hierarchical rebel military organization (as in South Sudan) becomes the natural political leadership after a successful secession.[78] Resource pathologies can be contagious as well: a civil war increases the risk of civil war in neighboring countries, sometimes because of refugee flows.[79] And rent addiction can make regimes less extraconnective: oil states are less integrated into the international legal and political order.[80]

Nor, unfortunately, is that all: resource-dependent countries may suffer still further disorders. Resource-diseased states have also seen numerous coups and coup attempts. Hussein of Iraq and al-Bashir of Sudan came to power via coups. Gaddafi of Libya did also, and then backed the coup of Déby in neighboring Chad (who then backed the coup of Bozizé in neighboring Central African Republic). Hamad bin Khalifa of Qatar and Qaboos of Oman both overthrew their fathers, though more peacefully.[81]

A recent study shows correlations between more oil and more HIV/AIDS, tracing this primarily to oil-rich states investing less in public health.[82] The Organization for Economic Co-operation and Development also found a negative relationship between natural resource rents and the knowledge and skills of schoolchildren, and lamented the results:

> The total manufacturing exports of the entire Arab world have recently been below those of the Philippines (with less than one-third of the population) or Israel (with a population not much

> bigger than Riyadh's). From 1980 to 2000 Saudi Arabia, Egypt, Kuwait, the UAE, Syria and Jordan between them registered 267 patents in the United States. Over the same period South Korea alone registered 16,328 and Israel 7,652. The number of books translated into Arabic every year in the entire Arab world is one-fifth the number translated by Greece into Greek.[83]

It also seems plausible, though it is not yet proved, that authoritarianism and corruption in resource-rich states result in more damage to the environment—both locally through more pollution, and globally through higher greenhouse-gas emissions.[84]

Michael Ross argues that petroleum perpetuates patriarchy.[85] Countries that catch the Dutch Disease create fewer manufacturing jobs—especially the kinds of manufacturing jobs that draw women out of the home and into the formal economy, and which then lead to increased social networking, political participation, and eventually political empowerment. In essence, oil hinders a Schumpeter Process for women.

For example, resource-poor Korea at the turn of the twentieth century was highly patriarchal. Korean women did not even have names of their own; they were simply referred to as the daughter, sister, or wife of some man. South Korea went through a largely female-based industrialization, and has now elected a woman president. But the oil-rich Middle Eastern states never went through this cycle of female empowerment. In the greater Middle East:

> The states that are richest in oil (Saudi Arabia, Iraq, Libya, Qatar, Bahrain, the United Arab Emirates, and Oman) have the fewest women in their nonagricultural workforce, have been the most reluctant to grant female suffrage, and have the fewest women in their parliaments. States with little or no oil (Morocco, Tunisia, Lebanon, Syria, and Djibouti) were among the first to grant female suffrage, tend to have more women in the workplace and parliament, and have more fully recognized women's rights.[86]

Radical gender inequality in the Middle East, Ross says, is due more to oil than to Islam. The story of tough young men on motorcycles riding around town arresting women for fraternizing with men is from Iran, but it could have been from any number of petrostates in the region. Radical gender inequality is among the most serious of the chronic disorders that afflict resource-diseased states. One can think of the black burqa as covering a woman in crude.

As we will see, the news on the resource diseases is not all bad. In the past forty years, a series of reforms at the national and international levels—including the Foreign Corrupt Practices Act, the Kimberley Process, and the Extractive Industries Transparency Initiative—have succeeded in countering some of the worst manifestations of rent addiction. Even the Congo's mineral-fueled mayhem has been cooled by a combination of political activism and enlightened leadership. In Chapter 17, we will meet some of the determined people behind these movements and discover how they all share a common goal.

These champions will tell you, however, that there is still a very long way to go. As we've seen over the past three chapters, the pathologies of countries addicted to resource rents can be devastating. In many cases, these pathologies seem likely to remain chronic—and more countries may soon also succumb to them.

OIL IS A THREE-LETTER WORD

Before the Arab Spring, the main US aid agency sent a delegation to survey the politics of Yemen. The chapter headings of its report paint a picture of an authoritarian regime heavily addicted to oil money:

> Yemen's National Identity Deficit
> The Tribal-Military-Commercial Complex
> "There is No State": How Clientelism Works in Yemen
> The Civil Service: Capture and Corrosion
> Public Goods Not Wanted

The authors conclude, "The President holds the country together through personalized compacts with tribal leaders instead of the creation of institutions that assure all citizens basic economic and social rights." The authors go on to warn: "The members of the three most influential groups in Yemen—the tribes, the military, and the business class—all come from the same narrow set of elites. The narrowness of the bases of power in the country point to a bleak future for the country, one that is likely to be marked by tremendous instability following the passing of the current long-standing regime."[87] They were right.

There is a temptation to distil what we have seen into a catchy phrase ("resource curse") or to boil it into slogans ("Oil is a woman's worst enemy. Diamonds are a guerrilla's best friend."[88]) The reality is more subtle. Natural resources are not needed for a country to succeed, nor does extracting natural resources doom a country to failure. Even among major producers, there are success stories like Norway, where the people were strong when the resource money came in—and because the people controlled their state, that money made the people even stronger.

Most resource-rich states did not start life with a strong people but under a strongman. Natural resources are an authoritarian's power source of choice. Resource rents are large, secret, unconditional, and they never have to be paid back—a dream for the autocrat who fears dependence on an economically empowered people. With his secure source of foreign funds, the autocrat can deny rights and liberties to the people, crush any trouble makers, and make potential threats dependent on him by pouring resource money through a pyramidal hierarchy of patronage. For legitimation, he may run pretend elections or stoke ideologies of nationalism, racism, or religious extremism. The authoritarian will use up the country's natural assets to divide and rule: his *modus operandi* is to degrade the economic, political, and moral relationships of the people beneath him. In such countries, citizens may be poor and defenseless, or better-off and dependent, but in either case, they will be isolated and controlled.

The authoritarian will often be personally corrupt; some are legendarily so. The few high-rent authoritarians who control large rents per capita will have money left over to provide public goods for the population. Low-rent authoritarians are much more numerous and will have more trouble—they will not project as much coercion or patronage into the countryside, and still less public goods. Violence can combust in the ungoverned spaces of these countries, especially if there are natural resources for armed groups to plunder. For natural resources—large, secret, and unconditional sources of money available even in the midst of armed conflict—are a militia's power source of choice as well.

What most explains why resource exports can be so devastating to a country is what is most obvious. This is that an unaccountable government gets the money from selling off the country's resources—and, with civil conflict, that unaccountable militias get the money from selling off the country's resources. The essence of the problem is that natural assets flow out to the world and the world's money flows back to the despots, to the defalcators, and to the dogs of war. The consequences, blazing so intensely around our troubled world, are that resource-rich nations with weak peoples are less unified—and the unity they have is less free.

PART II

Them vs. Us vs. Us

In Part I, we diagnosed the disorders that can afflict resource-exporting states. We now start to examine the causes of those disorders that lie outside of the exporting countries themselves. By the end of Part II, we will have traced much of the trouble back to our own shores. We are vectors for, and victims of, the foreign resource diseases.

5

Might Makes Right

The Conqueror indeed will be apt to think himself master. And 'tis the very condition of the subdued not to be able to dispute their Right. But if that be all, it gives no other Title than what bare Force gives to the stronger over the weaker: and, by this reason, he that is strongest will have a right to whatever he pleases to seize on.

—John Locke

Force is a physical power; I fail to see what morality can result from its effects.

—Jean-Jacques Rousseau[1]

DIRT CHEAP

A friend tells us about a flea market at the edge of town. It's called Dirt Cheap, our friend says, and it lives up to its name. We go—we're impressed: food, clothes, cosmetics, and toys just as good as in the stores, but at great prices. We stock up. Soon we build a trip to Dirt Cheap into our weekend routine. Word spreads about the market, and it gets crowded. A second Dirt Cheap opens closer, where a car dealership used to be. High-end goods start to appear for sale: 3D televisions, smart appliances, antique furniture, and jewelry. The crowds get bigger. We hear rumors of a Dirt Cheap Superstore planned to open soon, complete with its own gas station. And lucky us, the Superstore will be a half mile from our house.

Dramatic news stories from across the border also start to appear—stories of gangs robbing trucks and stores near big cities. The gangs are wild, merciless, shooting on sight. The *Wall Street Journal* profiles one foreign hooligan who started small—just a few stickups of delivery vans—and recruited an increasingly brazen crew as his heists paid off. Now CNN runs photos of the bodies of a dozen security guards who were tied up, lined up, and shot down with automatic weapons outside a warehouse. The warehouse was storing home cinemas—the same kind that our neighbors just bought at Dirt Cheap.

The next week, the news shows a carrier truck, emptied of its Camrys and Corollas after an ambush, the truck driver sexually assaulted and left dead on the side of the road. In one suburb across the border, the gangs have started to target larger homes, executing entire families and loading vans with furniture and jewelry much like what we see on sale at Dirt Cheap. The next month, a dozen gas tanker trucks are hijacked by gangs wielding rocket-launchers and grenades, the drivers and a few bystanders left hanging from highway signs.

Now the news reports that, across the border, the rival gangs are spreading out, starting turf wars, the police helpless against their firepower. Dozens of heists of warehouses and fuel depots are being reported each week. In the capital, a gang kingpin seems to have bought off the local authorities, and the mutilated corpses of rival gang leaders are appearing in the outskirts. Social media from this city claims that this kingpin is using revenues from Dirt Cheap stores to build up a private army, with which he plans to overthrow the entire national government.

Our town is quiet and safe as always. The grand opening of the Dirt Cheap Superstore is this weekend, only half a mile from our home. Do we go?

THE ARMPIT OF AFRICA

In 1995, Exxon found oil off the shores of Equatorial Guinea, a tropical country on the bending west coast of Africa. This discovery, at a time when Western powers were searching for safe sources of oil outside the Middle East, drew Equatorial Guinea to the attention of global markets. Within ten years, Equatorial Guinea had become a leading energy exporter in sub-Saharan Africa, selling more oil per capita than Saudi Arabia.[2] Until recently, most of Equatorial Guinea's oil has been tankered from offshore platforms to the United States, Canada, and Europe through the placid waters of the Atlantic.

Because of the huge influx of oil money, Equatorial Guinea's average income grew faster than any other country's in this century's first decade, to surpass even the average incomes of Britain, Germany, and Japan.[3] Yet this average income is deceptive—almost all of the money that the state gets from oil exports (recently valued at $16 billion per year) goes to the top.[4] The World Bank reports that three-quarters of ordinary people live on less than what $2 a day would buy in the United States, as we saw in Chapter 4, and half the population does not have access to clean drinking water or proper sanitation.[5]

Equatorial Guinea has been dominated since 1979 by the strongman Teodoro Obiang, who has not shied from having state-controlled radio pronounce him to be "like God in heaven," who has "all power over men and things."[6] Nor has Obiang shied from having his guards urinate on political prisoners, slice their ears, and smear their bodies with grease to attract stinging ants.[7] The UN Special Rapporteur on torture said, after a visit to the country, "They don't even hide the torture instruments . . . I'm deeply convinced it is a governmental policy."[8] The British Foreign Office once estimated that up to a third of Equatoguinean nationals were living in exile because of "fierce political repression" over two decades.[9] The US State Department's 2014 report reads like a comprehensive catalogue of human rights—all of them violated and denied.[10]

With imagination, one can build up a picture of life in this muggy dictatorship. News of the outside world is heavily censored; the single private television and radio network belongs to the President's son Teodorín. Even basic information about government policies is secret (the last Open Budget Survey gave the country a score of 0 out of 100). Transparency International's Corruptions Perceptions Index ranks the country as one of the most corrupt in the world.[11] Only members of the ruling party get well-paid work, inside or outside the government. The police act with impunity and, when required, with brutality. People sometimes disappear without warning into the prisons; anyone joining an opposition group may be held indefinitely. Judges often check with the president before making their rulings and imposing sentences.[12]

Even in 2006, *Forbes* judged Obiang to be richer than Queen Elizabeth II, with an estimated personal wealth of $600 million.[13] (This was after Obiang had spent 55 million of his petrodollars buying one of six private jets—a Boeing 737 with gold-plated bathroom fixtures.[14]) Earlier, we heard a former US ambassador to the country calling Equatorial Guinea "the world's finest example of a country privatized by a kleptomaniac without a scintilla of social consciousness."[15] Today, life expectancy there is below the world average by eighteen years.[16] A study in *The Lancet* found that neonatal, postneonatal, and childhood death rates all increased between 1990 and 2010—that is, children died more often after the oil revenues began to come in.[17] Even as the oil raised the national income by over 400 percent, educational levels rose not at all.[18] Obiang does not need to worry about the health or education of the people, as he gets all the money he needs to sustain his rule from allowing companies such as Exxon and Hess to set up oil platforms offshore.

Teodoro Obiang's tempestuous playboy son and possible heir, Teodorín, formerly earned $7,000 a month as the country's agriculture minister, yet spent over $30 million each on a mansion in Malibu and a private jet.[19] Human Rights Watch claims that Teodorín Obiang spent almost $44 million on houses and high-end cars in the United States and South Africa between 2004 and 2006, while the total educational budget of Equatorial Guinea in 2005 was only $43 million. Part of Teodorín's wealth appears to come from a "revolutionary tax" that he imposed as minister and insisted be paid directly to him.[20]

In 2010, a US Senate Permanent Subcommittee determined that Teodorín had illegally used shell companies to shift more than $100 million into the United States; he "owned at least three dozen luxury cars, including seven Ferraris, five Bentleys, four Rolls-Royces, two Lamborghinis, two Mercedes-Benzes, two Porsches, two Maybachs, and an Aston Martin, with a collective insured value of around $10 million."[21] He has regularly been accompanied by high-priced American escorts, to whom he grants lavish shopping sprees. But 2011 was a bad year for Teodorín: he commissioned but then cancelled a superyacht costing almost three times the country's health and education budget, he lost a briefcase with $40,000 inside, and the US and French governments seized tens of millions of dollars of his assets. In 2012, the French issued an arrest warrant for Teodorín; his father appointed him to higher offices in an effort to give him diplomatic immunity. In 2014, a French court indicted him in absentia for money laundering.[22]

Teodorín is by all accounts at least as determined as his father to control the country's oil revenues for his personal use. A US intelligence officer called him "an unstable, reckless idiot."[23] Yet Teodorín might recall this reading of a speech by Mephistopheles in Goethe's *Faust*:

> I *am* ugly, but I can buy for myself the *most beautiful* of women. Therefore I am not ugly, for the effect of ugliness—its deterrent

> power—is nullified by money...I am bad, dishonest, unscrupulous, stupid; but money is honored, and hence its possessor... I am *brainless*, but money is the *real brain* of all things and how then should its possessor be brainless? Besides, he can buy clever people for himself, and is he who has power over the clever not more clever than the clever? Do not I, who thanks to money am capable of *all* that the human heart longs for, possess all human capacities?[24]

Equatorial Guinea is a nation, as a local economist put it, where "[a]n opulent minority sails in a sea of misery."[25] Given their situation, the people of Equatorial Guinea may well feel cursed by their country's resource wealth.

OUR CONNECTION TO THE RESOURCE DISORDERS

The repression of the citizens of Equatorial Guinea, and the denial to them of the revenues from the country's oil, may strike outsiders as a cause for sympathy. The situation in the country appears grim, the oppression of the people seems unjust, and something should probably be done about it. One might think of an aid program to help the Equatorial Guineans, or of Western leaders pressuring Obiang to share more of the oil money with his people. These kinds of proposals may not spark much optimism: repressive governments often capture aid money, and rich dictators can resist a good deal of foreign pressure. However, the sense remains that something should be done to help these Africans in their dire conditions.

This natural course of thinking about the situation in Equatorial Guinea overlooks something. Outsiders are already connected to its citizens' plight. Resource diseases like authoritarianism are only half about resources. Obiang could not after all overcome his political opponents by dousing them in crude oil. The other half of the equation is the foreign money that has flowed into Obiang's bank accounts as he has sold the country's oil abroad. It is this money that has increased Obiang's ability to pay his security forces, to control the channels of patronage, and to disrupt possible challenges to his rule. It is the money that outsiders have paid for the resources of Equatorial Guinea that have financed the subjection of its people. In the seventeenth century, it was payments from the Sun King that funded absolutism abroad. In our time, it is our payments to Sunoco.

The contribution of external funds to internal repression is clear enough when pointed out, and reflecting on it may cause more discomfort. We don't like to think of ourselves as funding misgovernment abroad, even indirectly. The thought that what we've paid to fuel our cars might have ended up spent in Obiang's bedchambers, or torture chambers, is not at all welcome. Yet, one might think, this is the way it often is in our world. In a globalized market economy, we pay for all sorts of goods. We do not know—indeed, we mostly cannot know—where these goods originate or where the money we use to purchase them goes. Some of the money we pay at the pump may go to tyrants, but that seems just a part of modern life. If the Equatorial Guineans have a political problem in their country, then that is very unfortunate. But it is in the end their problem, and we should try to help them (if at all) through private charity or the political influence of our government.

This way of looking at the contribution that outsiders make to the situation in Equatorial Guinea is still incomplete, and it is particularly lacking from a market perspective. Resources do not disorder countries because the inhabitants are not brave enough or bright enough to handle their own affairs. Authoritarianism in Equatorial Guinea is powered by an anti-market rule left over from the era of European empires. A flaw in the enforcement of property rights forces consumers to fund violence, coercion, and corruption when they make their everyday purchases at the gas station and the mall.

EX INJURIA JUS ORITUR[26]

A lawyer learns that physical possession and property rights are distinct. Possession is merely a physical fact: an animal possesses what it holds in its jaws, at least until a stronger animal wrenches possession away. Property is a legal relation—it need not be physical at all. As Jeremy Bentham said, "A piece of stuff which is actually in the Indies may belong to me while the dress I wear may not."[27] A thief who steals your watch takes physical possession of your watch, and might transfer physical possession to someone else, yet the thief has made no legal transfer of property rights. The watch is still your property, and the thief and his fence have merely passed possession of stolen goods.

For most natural resources in today's international order, however, possession makes property. Whoever can maintain physical control over a country's territory by any means gains the legal right to sell off that territory's resources.[28] This feature of the international trade regime violates the most basic rule of a market order, as the philosopher Thomas Pogge explains:

> A group that overpowers the guards and takes control of a warehouse may be able to give some of the merchandise to others, accepting money in exchange. But the fence who pays them becomes merely the possessor, not the owner, of the loot. Contrast this with a group that overpowers an elected government and takes control of a country. Such a group, too, can give away some of the country's natural resources, accepting money in exchange. In this case, however, the purchaser acquires not merely possession, but all the rights and liberties of ownership, which are supposed to be—and actually *are*—protected and enforced by all other states' courts and police forces.[29]

Rewarding violence with rights makes a nonsense of property. Might violates rights—it should not vest them. Yet for natural resources, might makes right. For Obiang, might vests the legal right to transfer a country's oil. Obiang gains the right to sell Equatorial Guinea's oil by keeping the country's impoverished population living in fear through intimidation, imprisonment, and torture. Nor is it only the might of foreign heads of state that makes right. What militias seize by force will also be bought legally here, as we can see by returning to the civil war that consumed Sierra Leone.

The rebels who took over Sierra Leone's diamond mines (many of them illiterate teenagers high on drugs) called themselves the Revolutionary United Front (RUF). The RUF's soldiers gave themselves names like General Babykiller, Wicked to Women, and Queen Chop Hands. This last name refers to the signature RUF tactic, which was to round up villagers (including children and infants) and hack off their limbs or lips with machetes:

> Sometimes, after capturing a village, RUF fighters would gather civilian prisoners in the town square and make them choose small strips of paper from the ground that described different forms of torture and death, such as "chop off hands," "chop off head," or simply "be killed." Soldiers would bet with one another about the sex of pregnant women's unborn children. Winners were determined after the baby had been removed from the womb with a bayonet. In one instance, a young boy was beaten and roasted nearly to death on

> a spit in front of his mother for refusing to kill her. The RUF's depravity served the military strategy: It induced tectonic population shifts away from the diamond areas.[30]

The RUF scared many of the locals away from the diamond areas and forced others to harvest the gems. The rebels then sold these "blood diamonds" to smugglers; with the cash, they bought enough weapons to seize the capital city, Freetown. The government was only able to fight back by twice trading diamond mining futures for the services of foreign mercenaries. The civil war in Sierra Leone blasted the country's infrastructure, ended around fifty thousand lives, and displaced one-third of the population. Hundreds of thousands of Sierra Leone's women appear to have suffered sexual violence, including rape and sexual slavery.[31] Even five years after the conflict, Sierra Leone ranked 177th out of 177 countries on the UN Human Development Index.[32]

Sierra Leone's diamond production is only a fraction of the global total, but its gems are highly prized because their size and quality make them ideal for luxury jewelry. The diamonds harvested at gun- and machete-point by the RUF militias flowed through international markets and into retail outlets in North America, Europe, and Australasia, where they were legally bought by shoppers. The property rights to the wedding rings and earrings made with those diamonds remain legally valid today: many wives and husbands right now fondly display Sierra Leone's blood diamonds on their bodies. Their property rights trace back to actors who, like Obiang, gained control over natural resources by physical force.[33]

AN ANCIENT, OPEN SECRET

What we are detecting here is a fragment of pre-modern international law, the rule of "might makes right," which lawyers call the rule of "effectiveness." As we will explore more in Part III, effectiveness ("might makes right") was in past ages the primary rule not only for resources but for nearly all of international affairs. For instance, in this premodern "Westphalian" era, leaders who conquered territory—who gained military control over land—also gained the internationally recognized legal right to rule that territory. Might made right. In this premodern era, a ruler with military control over territory could sell that territory, with all its inhabitants, to another ruler. Might made right. In this era, any ruler strong enough to stay in power also gained the internationally recognized legal right to abuse or neglect those he ruled, almost without limit. Which is to say that in this era, international law did not yet recognize what we now call human rights.[34]

The human rights revolution that began with the *Universal Declaration of Human Rights* in 1948 displaced the Westphalian rule that coercive control over humans legitimates their abuse or neglect. The thrust of human rights law is to insist that there are certain things that rulers must not do to the ruled (kill or arrest them arbitrarily, enforce their enslavement) and other things that rulers must do for the ruled (provide them with education and fair trials). Human rights law means that regimes can no longer assert that their abuse or neglect of the people is only a matter of "internal affairs." The treatment of their citizens is now a matter for international concern.[35] Every nation on Earth has ratified a major human rights treaty, signaling the legal death of that part of the Westphalian order.

The rule of effectiveness for natural resources is a remnant of the old Westphalian world. The contrast between this anachronism and modern ideals is vivid. It makes as little sense that coercive domination should confer the right to sell off a country's assets as it does that coercive domination should confer the right to abuse a country's people. Once the old idea of unlimited state authority is undermined, both ideas should fall together. Yet the Westphalian rule of effectiveness for resources remains lodged in the international system, and in fact is hardly noticed.

"Might makes right" for natural resources exists in the subconscious of global trade. It is an article of no treaty; judges rarely mention it, and politicians never. Working lawyers know that this rule was part of the premodern order yet have little occasion to focus on its persistence. Laymen do not notice the policy at all. Partly this is because public attention naturally goes to cross-border flows of things that (unlike resources) are illegal to sell in the country of destination, like narcotics, counterfeit goods, and human beings.[36] And partly this is a natural cognitive conservatism—this is the way that things have always been.

There is a wedge of the global resource trade in which effectiveness does not hold, which we will later use to pry open a door that leads deeper into the substructure of the world's economy. First, today's business as usual deserves emphasis. Every one of the millions of barrels of oil stolen and exported by militias in the Niger Delta since commercial production began in 1956 has been owned free and clear in its country of destination. Every one of the 32 million gallons of Equatorial Guinea's oil that arrived in the

United States in 2014 came with unquestioned legal title, with the chain of title anchored in the fact of Obiang's coercive success.[37]

Augustine asked: *Remota itaque iustitia quid sunt regna nisi magna latrocinia?* What, absent justice, is the difference between rulers and plundering gangs?[38] Cynics commonly group rulers and robbers together—the jolt here is that the international trade system officially places both above the legal line. Effectiveness for resources says "whoever can seize it can sell it." Because effectiveness persists in international trade, possession still morphs into property and gets money back. Because of effectiveness, international trade sends the products of coercion into filling stations and supermarkets in importing countries and channels consumers' dollars back to exporting countries to pay for more rifles, more spies, and more helicopter gunships. The international rule of "might makes right" puts consumers into business with some of the world's most violent and divisive men.

THE DEEPEST CAUSE OF THE RESOURCE DISEASES

It is after all consumers' money that ultimately pays for the petrocrat's secret police and for the weapons that warlords use when looting minerals. The legal connection is made through the international rule of effectiveness, which says that whoever coercively controls territory can sell the resources of that territory. This rule forces consumers to fund highly repressive and aggressive foreigners overseas. The rule also incentivizes those foreigners to steal more.

To see those incentives, imagine for a moment that New York declares "might makes right" for goods in New Jersey, declaring that whoever can seize goods in New Jersey will gain the legal right to sell those goods to New Yorkers and that the resulting "property rights" will be enforced by New York's police and courts. One can picture what New Jersey would look like: crime kings, syndicates, turf wars, fraud, and grand theft—similar to what we see on a larger scale in resource-disordered countries today.

The international rule of effectiveness generates systemic incentives toward the resource disorders described in Part I: authoritarianism, corruption, and civil conflict, with their sequelae of widespread fear and failures of human development. Authoritarians who gain the resource right will spend the revenues on violence and clientelism. Militias who seize control of resource-rich territory will get the money they need to start, or escalate, a war. Effectiveness incentivizes coercive actors to exercise unaccountable control over resources and to neutralize any resistance. Under effectiveness, the people will become the victims of those who use their country's wealth against them.

Commercial engagement with a resource-rich country is like plugging a high-voltage line into its political economy. If the country is well-wired politically and economically, it will glow brighter. If not, making the connection can cause short circuits, fires, and explosions. The current policies of importing states lead them to make commercial connections everywhere: the default is to engage with whoever can control resource-rich territory by whatever means.

As for Obiang, who seized power from his own uncle in a coup, he has been both strengthened and threatened by this international rule. In 2004, Margaret Thatcher posted $300,000 bail to get her son, Sir Mark Thatcher, out of jail. Sir Mark later pleaded guilty to bankrolling an elaborate scheme (apparently based on Frederick Forsyth's novel *The Dogs of War*) to overthrow Obiang and install a puppet ruler who would siphon the country's oil wealth back to the coup's plotters. The coup attempt misfired, and instead of being toppled, Obiang captured some of the mercenaries and allegedly had them tortured.[39] In the end, the plotters failed, but their plan understood the rule of effectiveness perfectly: hire soldiers, seize the oil, sell the oil, keep the money.

"Might makes right" is an invisible premise in all the hundreds of studies of the "resource curse." Oil-rich countries risk authoritarianism *given* that authoritarians can get so rich from selling off the resource. Minerals far from the capital increase the risk of civil war *given* that militias can trade captured minerals for serious foreign cash. Repression, corruption, and armed struggle within resource-exporting countries are enabled by consumer spending here, just as rust and fire are enabled by oxygen. When rebellion will be rewarded with large revenues, one expects more, and more violent, rebels. When repression will be rewarded with great wealth, the most repressive will rise toward the top.

EFFECTIVENESS BETWEEN HISTORY AND PRINCIPLE

Effectiveness in today's resource trade seems both peculiar and familiar. On the one hand, it seems strange that seizing a country's political capital should license selling the country's natural capital. On the other hand, everyone knows that drivers fund dictators with the money they pay at the pump. If you point out effectiveness in the resource trade, you may be met with the denial that this could possibly be true—and with the dismissal that this is obvious, even in the same conversation.

One reason for these gyrations in responses is that we now live in a halfway house between our history and our principles. As mentioned, "might makes right" used to be the main legal rule for nearly all of international affairs. The enlightened and now widespread belief is that effectiveness should be the norm for nothing. Yet the premodern policy of effectiveness zombies on in the world's resource trade. The world we've always known transgresses the principles we take for granted.

Consider, for example, how differently the news would report two similar announcements about the Angolan province of Cabinda. Like Alaska, Cabinda is an oil-rich exclave northwest of the mainland. Unlike Alaska, Cabinda has generated a series of secessionist revolts (firmly suppressed by Angola's authoritarian ruler, Eduardo dos Santos). Secessionism is perennial because while Cabinda's oil wells produce around a million barrels a day, Cabindans get little from the Angolan state besides occupying forces.[40]

If President dos Santos tomorrow announced that he was selling the province of Cabinda itself to the Chinese, he would start a front-page fracas. Powerful states would loudly protest (and perhaps actively resist) this presidential presumption. Transfer of territory without consent of its people violates a primary rule of modern international law. The international rule for transfer of territory is no longer Westphalian: a ruler's might no longer gives him the right to transfer territory at will. International law now requires that a ruler must gain the authorization of the people of the territory, ideally through a referendum.[41]

However, if dos Santos tomorrow sold all of Cabinda's *oil* to China, that story would be well down on the business page. Today, dos Santos's coercive control of Cabinda still wins him the legal right to sell off that territory's resources—even though the value of Cabinda's oil may be exponentially greater than the acres of Angolan hinterland that dos Santos cannot sell off. This is the legal halfway house we now inhabit, between the old rule of effectiveness and our modern principles that affirm the rights of the people.

The attitude one takes to the persistence of effectiveness in the international system may depend on whether one is looking forward from the past or forward from the present. One lesson that world leaders took from World War II was that effectiveness must be replaced in many domains of international affairs. For example, German and Japanese aggression convinced the postwar leaders that military might should no longer win sovereign rights over territory. They embedded this lesson in international law with a new rule making territorial conquest illegal—and as we'll see in Chapter 9, this new anti-conquest rule has replaced "might makes right" rather successfully.[42] From this past-forward perspective on overcoming effectiveness in the international system, major advances have already been made.

Projecting from the present into the future, however, the persistence of effectiveness for natural resources is a real concern. The international trade system still issues a license to sell resources to whoever is ruthless enough to commandeer those resources. The suffering and injustice engendered by this rule has been significant, and we can expect these wrongs to continue so long as the rule persists. In fact, since foreign funds are oxygen for authoritarianism, corruption, and civil conflict, these fires may burn more brightly as resource extraction begins in other weak states. Countries that may soon become significant oil exporters, for instance, include Cuba, Cyprus, Guinea, Guyana, Liberia, Mali, Mozambique, Senegal, Sierra Leone, Tanzania, and Uganda.[43]

Both the past-forward and the present-forward perspectives on effectiveness are right. Where we are now is how far we have come—this is the time in history that is ours. It is the serious suffering and injustice to which consumers everywhere will contribute that turns thoughts toward what we can do now. After the next chapter on geopolitics, we'll delve further into today's rule of effectiveness for resources to discover how that rule works, so that we can begin to see how it can be replaced. And, later in the book, we will see how the world has been turning in our favor—making it easier for us to get out of business with authoritarians like Obiang, and to disconnect our shopping from militiamen like General Babykiller, Wicked to Women, and Queen Chop Hands.

6

Curses on Us

Petrocrats, Terrorists, and Conflict

Energy revenues prop up repressive regimes by providing them with the resources to reward corrupt bureaucracies and repressive police forces. The influx of energy wealth also can destroy the impetus to diversify or reform an economy in ways that ensure the benefits flow to the people. In addition, energy wealth can fund foreign adventurism, regional mischief, and terrorism. Ultimately, an international system that weights guaranteed access to fossil fuels above law and order, adherence to international agreements, and democracy will be less safe for all countries.

—Senator Richard Lugar

And as for those who do evil deeds, the punishment of an evil deed shall be the like thereof.

—Qur'an 10:27[1]

Exporting natural resources does not necessarily curse exporting countries. "Cursed" better describes those on the other side of the trade. States that import natural resources and products made from them channel funds to hostile, repressive, corrupt, and failing regimes—and to violent non-state actors—in ways that threaten their national interests. In today's international order, "resource cursed" best fits the importers in business with resource-disordered exporters.

The story of a curse falling on those who violate principle is common to many traditions: Sisyphus and Tantalus, the Pharaoh and the Hebrews, the denizens of Dante's hell. One need not believe in cosmic balancing to see why trouble in resource-exporting states manifests as trouble elsewhere. In an interlinked world, disruption and grievances spread: the same global channels that bring the goods also bring the bombs. What we scan for in this chapter are the aftereffects of effectiveness for resources. Effectiveness for resources sends large sums to unaccountable actors who are strongly incentivized to be repressive, violent, and ideologically extreme. Our curses are blowback from our empowering foreigners to divide and rule, divide and kill.

To see today's curses on us, we turn the lens back onto the political economies of resource-diseased states—this time looking at how the West has been affected by their pathologies across the past four decades. These effects can be seen everywhere in the recent histories of the United States and other Western countries. As we move quickly through this history of economic downturns, hostile petrocrats, terrorist financing, destabilizing regional conflicts, and more, you're welcome to slow down and enrich these narratives from your own knowledge—much more can be said on every point. And as always, throughout this history, we do not forget that we live in a multivariate world.[2] Many factors beyond the resource disorders have contributed to the disasters that end up in the headlines. Nothing explains everything; human affairs have more features than any one vantage can survey.

Still, once we set our sensors to "resources," what we see is how many of the West's crises and conflicts have radiated from resource-disordered states. Natural resources have been a major contributing cause of serious threats from abroad. Resources are not everything—but they certainly are something.

In 2014–15, for example, the resource disorders helped to shape a particular pattern of headlines. After years of high oil prices, Russia's president felt strong enough to grab at territory in Ukraine while whipping up a bitter nationalism. Ebola spread through Sierra Leone, Liberia, and Guinea, partly because their health systems were still enfeebled after years of mineral-fueled conflict and repression. Civil conflict and terrorism afflicted a crescent of poorly-governed resource-exporting countries from Libya to Nigeria. Russia and the two hostile oil blocks in the Middle East—Shia Iran and the Sunni Gulf monarchies—funded a proxy war in the failed oil states of Iraq and Syria. Within this war, the bloody acts and apocalyptic Salafist ideology of the self-styled Islamic State drew in radicalized young Western Muslims. And the barbarous prosecution of this war, especially by the forces of Bashar al-Assad, helped to create a refugee crisis in the region that then burst into Europe.

You now see the headlines of today. By the time you read this, the kaleidoscope will have turned—the contribution of resource revenues to current threats will now be visible in a different pattern of crises. With each headline that we see today, we can ask this question: how much would this be happening had resource money not flowed to unaccountable foreigners with every incentive to be divisive?

A RISKY BUSINESS

The disorders of resource-exporting countries affect the citizens of other countries in many ways, most obviously in their wallets.[3] Even with the shale revolution, for instance, America still imports a lot of oil, and a lot from risky places. In 2013, over a quarter of the US trade deficit was dollars leaving the country to buy petroleum, and almost half of the barrels of crude entering the United States in a typical month in 2014 came from countries with a State Department travel warning of "long-term, protracted conditions that make a country dangerous or unstable."[4] And no matter where the barrels come from, a political risk premium gets built into the global price of oil, meaning that consumers in all countries must spend more for oil, and for what is made using it, and for what is transported with it—that is, for most everything.

To take the United States as an example of vulnerability to volatility: ten of eleven postwar US recessions were preceded by spikes in oil prices, and eleven of twelve oil price spikes were followed by US recessions.[5] And the vulnerabilities of major importing states magnify each other. Four of the last five global recessions, including the most recent one, have been preceded by a sharp rise in global oil prices. Nor is it only recession onset that may be affected by the resource disorders—it's recession duration as well. One analyst finds that the US recovery from the most recent recession stalled for a full year when Libya's oil (only 3 percent of the global trade) was taken off the market by the political instability of the Arab Spring.[6]

AID TO THE ENEMY

As we saw in Chapter 2, large resource rents supercharge authoritarians. The resource money gets poured in at the top, and authoritarians use this money to fund their police states and their clientelistic pyramids while building up their militaries and escaping accountability to their people. What has that meant for the West? Over the past four decades, Western resource payments have flowed to authoritarians counted as both friends and foes. The first big-picture fact that jumps out is just how much has gone to the foes. The West's resource payments have been a gigantic, unconditional foreign aid program to countries that it has declared enemies.

Consider the West's most serious opponent since World War II, the Soviet Union. In the 1960s, the Soviets discovered large oil reserves in Siberia and began exporting oil to the West to prop up their own impossibly inefficient economy. The Siberian oil rush, sparked by the price jump after the 1973 Arab embargo, ignited the greatest economic boom in the USSR's history. The regime had been desperately short of hard currency; after 1973, foreign funds started pouring in:

> What to do with all that cash? The Soviet leadership used its oil revenues to cushion the impact of the oil shock on its Eastern European satellites. Oil money also paid for a huge Soviet military buildup that, incredibly, enabled the country to reach rough parity with the United States. And it helped defray the costs of the war in Afghanistan, launched in the late 1970s. Oil money also went into higher salaries and better perks for the ever-expanding Soviet elite. And oil financed the acquisition of Western technology for making cars, synthetic fibers, and other products for consumers as well as Western feed for Soviet livestock.[7]

In the end, "Oil seemed to save the Soviet Union in the 1970s, but it merely delayed the inevitable... Without the discovery of Siberian oil, the Soviet Union might have collapsed decades earlier."[8] The West supported its great adversary with oil purchases throughout the final stages of their global struggle. Could the West have gotten its act together, stopped buying Soviet oil, watched its rival collapse in the 1970s, and avoided the Cold War of the 1980s? We cannot re-fight that war here. Western leaders at the time faced harrowing choices that even those alive then may now find difficult to appreciate. We are not here asking whether Western leaders should have decided differently in their foreign policies; we are only isolating effectiveness-based negatives in the recent history of the global resource trade. Here we see that the West sustained an existential threat through an extra decade of antagonism or more.

Opening this lens further makes the view no less dark. When we look at the countries that the United States has officially designated as adversaries, we find recipients of large resource rents. Five of the seven countries that have ever been on the US State Sponsors of Terrorism list have also been primary oil exporters (in italics):

Cuba / *Iran* / *Iraq* / *Libya* / North Korea / *Sudan* / *Syria*[9]

Even when the United States has imposed sanctions on these countries, the rest of the West has sent large sums to them through "might makes right." Simply in terms of cash flows, over the past four decades the West has provided a great deal of aid to its enemies in exchange for oil. And as we will see next, it is not only the West's enemies that have cursed it.

Effectiveness pressures toward a global strategic environment where all of the West's options are poor. In a world made by effectiveness, a great deal of money will go to authoritarians in resource-rich countries. Some of these authoritarians will be hostile, yet some can also be friendly—for a price. Given effectiveness, it has long seemed rational to Western leaders to form strategic alliances to keep these petrocrats onside. And yet, in country after country, the strategy of allying with petrocratic regimes has produced at best short-term benefits, with long-term damage to Western interests.[10] This strategic "short-term trap" is visible in the histories of Western relations with the three countries that have the world's largest conventional oil reserves: Iran, Iraq, and Saudi Arabia. In all three cases, the West's alliances with authoritarians has inflated giant balloons full of trouble. Two of these balloons have already burst; the third balloon has been leaking—and even still, now looks overfull.

THE CHIMERA OF STABILITY: IRAN

In 1948, Eleanor Roosevelt, "The First Lady of the World," brought an extraordinary diplomatic effort to a crescendo with the UN General Assembly's 48-0 vote to approve the *Universal Declaration of Human Rights*, which pronounced that in every country, "the will of the people shall be the basis of the authority of government."[11] Almost five years later, another American named Roosevelt slipped over the Iranian border under the false name "James Lockridge." This was Kermit Roosevelt, Jr., a CIA agent—and as it happens, Eleanor Roosevelt's first cousin once removed. Using $1 million supplied by the Agency, Kermit Roosevelt orchestrated a campaign of black propaganda and false riots against the democratically elected Prime Minister of Iran.[12] The American government, together with the British, succeeded in its objective to undermine the will of the Iranian people, and to replace the people's choice with the West's own, the Shah.[13]

The Shah of Iran was the prototype of a highly repressive ruler that the West supported politically for what it perceived as its own interests, and for twenty-five years, the West's strategy appeared to work brilliantly. The West got a steady stream of Iranian oil from the Shah, including throughout the 1973 embargo by the Arab states. The Shah also became the "policeman of the Persian Gulf," through which most Middle Eastern oil flows, sending troops, for example, to put down a rebellion in Oman.[14] The Shah not only sent oil to Israel, he supplied Israel with key votes in the UN at a time when other Islamic nations were lambasting it. Iran under the Shah became a major Western intelligence outpost for monitoring the Soviets. The Shah also extended the umbrella of his formidable military to cover Western allies, including Turkey, Iraq, and Pakistan.[15] For two-and-a-half decades, the Shah was our man in Tehran.

As we saw in Chapter 3, with the story of the airplanes flying in chefs from Maxim's of Paris, the Shah's extravagance highlighted "the contrast between the almost limitless wealth of the court and the abject poverty of much of the country."[16] Still, when US President Jimmy Carter gave tribute to the Shah in Tehran on December 31, 1977, he did not see trouble coming:

> Iran, because of the great leadership of the Shah, is an island of stability in one of the more troubled areas of the world. This is a great tribute to you, your Majesty, and to your leadership and to the respect, admiration and love which your people give to you.[17]

On that last day of 1977, Carter was looking back on an American strategy that had worked for twenty-five years—seemingly a tremendous foreign-policy achievement. Twenty-five years of autocratic stability did not then look like a short-term success, but compared to what was to come, it was.

Carter did not see that the West had inflated a huge balloon full of trouble in Iran, which was just about to burst. We can find broader lessons in the Iranian Revolution of 1978–1979 by using the account of authoritarian rule set out in Chapters 2 and 3.

The Shah ruled Iran through a small coalition of the military, major landholders, and eventually industrialists. His mix of violence and clientelism emphasized violence: after taking care of his relatively few supporters, he let his exceptionally vicious police and intelligence services take care of any threats. Labor unions were destroyed; the rural poor were ignored, or pushed off their lands into desperation. The one popular institution the Shah could not break was the mosque, which is where resistance to his rule coalesced. In the mosque, sermons hammered at the cruelty and corruption of the Shah's rule and his theft of the nation's oil wealth. With this message, the clerics eventually roused the masses to protest and then revolt. A referendum after the revolution returned 98 percent of votes in favor of establishing an Islamic republic, and Ayatollah Khomeini's rule began.

The first lesson of Iran concerns the logic of revolution against a Western-supported autocrat in a world where might makes right for natural resources. A popular revolution against a small-coalition authoritarian did not result in democracy—rather, it resulted in an authoritarian regime that was the mirror image of the one it overthrew. The Shah's pro-Western secularism was replaced by Khomeini's anti-Western fundamentalism, which has been a major source of radical Islam in the Middle East ever since. And this brings out a second lesson of the Iranian Revolution, which is that the Shah's repression made the United States a natural target for popular resentment and so for demonization by those who opposed him. Before February 1953, "the United States was by far the most beloved of Western countries in Iran."[18] By November 1979, Ayatollah Khomeini was calling the United States "The Great Satan": the number-one evil foreign threat.

The third and deepest lesson of Iran is what foreign policy experts have called "the chimera of stability offered by an autocratic status quo."[19] By supporting the Shah, the West squeezed twenty-five years of oil and geostrategic benefits out of Iran. Yet the West has since suffered thirty-five years of Iran as a hostile regional power, which has used its large oil rents to threaten core Western interests through all means at its disposal—and to grasp at nuclear capacity even in the teeth of punishing sanctions. In 2012, the State Department called Iran "the world's leading state sponsor of terrorism" and accused it of providing funding, training, and/or arms to Hamas, Hezbollah,

Islamic Jihad, the Taliban, and Shia militants attacking US forces in Iraq.[20] During the twenty-five years the Shah lasted, the West's policy of support appeared to be a success, yet those years were gestating thirty-five years (and running) of oil-powered threats to the West.

THE OPAQUE AUTOCRAT OF IRAQ

The story of the West's political support for Saddam Hussein is widely known. The West (not only the United States, but also especially France) backed Saddam as he rose to power in the 1970s and took control over the country's huge oil reserves. Saddam provided autocratic stability for oil flows out to the West and for Western business interests going into Iraq. After 1979, the West helped Saddam militarily and financially as he fought the deadly new enemy next door (though the racking Iran-Iraq War also helped Khomeini to close his grip on power). Successive Western leaders continued to view Saddam as "a thug and a bully in a neighborhood of thugs and bullies, but our thug and our bully."[21]

The alliance with Saddam was a stanchion of the West's strategy in the Middle East, and (as with the Shah) for many years this strategy paid off in oil, business, and balance of power. Yet in supporting Saddam, the West had inflated another balloon full of trouble—and, even more than Iran, this balloon burst quickly and forcibly. In the region of the world that holds by far the largest store of humanity's primary energy source, this one man transformed from stabilizer to destabilizer literally overnight—the night of August 2, 1990, when he ordered the invasion of Kuwait. The West had for years supported Saddam's divisive rule; it now reaped decades of choice points where all of its options were bad.

From 1990, Western leaders faced a series of grim dilemmas in Iraq: whether to attack a large Iraqi military force known to have used chemical weapons; having defeated that military, whether to press on to Baghdad; having left Saddam in power, whether to stand by during his ruthless suppression of Shia and Kurdish uprisings; having stood by during those uprisings, whether to tighten economic sanctions that may have led to half a million deaths of Iraqi children under five; having imposed sanctions, whether to try to alleviate their worst effects through an Oil for Food program (that went disastrously wrong); whether then to remove Saddam from power with huge costs in blood, money, and influence; having done so, whether finally to withdraw troops—and having done that, whether to go back in to fight an oil-funded, highly aggressive Salafist army called ISIS whose military leadership included many of Saddam's former officers.[22] However one judges the choices that Western leaders made at these points, all can agree that the West has paid a high price for its previous support of Saddam. Western leaders have faced many years when their options in Iraq have been consequential and terrible.

Beyond the suddenness with which a friendly petrocrat can become an antagonist, the West's political support for Saddam offers two further lessons. The first concerns autocratic opacity. Autocratic decision-making is not necessarily less rational than democratic decision-making, but its character is different because so much of it occurs within a single skull. One unaccountable, risk-taking individual at the head of state can disrupt a whole region with a single idiosyncratic bad judgment. Not only Western leaders but also closer observers like Egypt's Mubarak seem to have been entirely surprised by Saddam's 1990 invasion of Kuwait. Western leaders then ordered a counter-attack partly because they had little idea whether Saddam intended to continue his invasion into the oil fields of Saudi Arabia. Later, the West seems genuinely to have misinterpreted Saddam's claims about his weapons of mass destruction, which (it afterward emerged) may have been a ploy to deter Iran.[23] The West, it turned out, could not comprehend the ally on whom it had relied so much.

A second lesson from Iraq enhances the account of the logic of revolution and its aftermath once an authoritarian ally is removed. The Shah of Iran ruled over a 90-percent Shia majority; when he fell, he was quickly replaced by a Shia autocracy that captured the oil revenues. Saddam's Ba'ath Party, by contrast, was essentially an imposition by an Arab Sunni minority onto an Arab Shia majority and a substantial Kurdish population. Like all autocrats, Saddam divided to rule: especially in times of crisis, he inflamed antagonisms across the religious and ethnic divides. When his coercive rule ended, these antagonisms among the contending groups flared into violent strife, with resource money further firing the fight.

The post-Saddam politics of Iraq saw the Shia majority consolidating its control over the national budget and pushing its rivals out of the government, driving Sunnis into the arms of extremist groups like ISIS and the Kurds towards secession. By 2014, the conflict had turned into a petroleum battle royale, with each of the three groups in military control over an oil-producing area the size of which roughly equaled its percentage of the national population.

The postauthoritarian politics of other states in which no group is dominant are variations on this theme. In postauthoritarian Libya, the tribes that Gaddafi played off against one another engaged in open warfare, with oil money as both spoils and fuel. In Syria, the intercommunal violence that followed Assad's loss of territorial control saw several parties gaining power from oil revenues (as well as support from oil states such as Russia, Saudi Arabia, and Qatar). In all of these countries, an authoritarian kept the lid on for years. Yet because of the divisive character of their rule, when these authoritarians faltered the angry factions went for each other's throats. Among the hornets and the scorpions that emerge from the jar when a strongman loses his grip, some will form the next government, and others will be the opposition. Many will become supercharged with resource money. The legacy of these autocrats' stability has been chaos.

GLOBALIZING MEDIEVALISM: SAUDI ARABIA

The oil autocracy in the Gulf that the West has supported longest is Saudi Arabia—the third, and the biggest, balloon inflated full of trouble. As with Iran and Iraq, a great deal could be said about Western engagement with this country, and many lessons could be drawn—you may wish to add your own conclusions to those below. In this section, we discuss only one negative impact on Western interests: Saudi Arabia's use of its oil money to promote fundamentalist Islam. In the next section, we will look at the future of Saudi Arabia, and the risks should its regime falter.

The most salient fact about Saudi Arabia is the one that most people know: it holds by far the world's largest conventional oil reserves. And its basic strategic deal with the United States is also one that most people know: Saudi Arabia has used its influence over oil markets to try to stabilize the world economy, and in return, the United States has protected it militarily. The Saudis have also insisted that oil be priced in dollars, giving the United States the unique privilege of simply printing the money that buys petroleum. Yet the strategic alliance between Saudi Arabia and the United States has always been much deeper than oil-for-security, and for that reason, it has been extremely durable.[24] The American alliance with the Shah of Iran lasted for twenty-five years; with the Saudi royals, it has been seventy years—since 1945, when Franklin D. Roosevelt met modern Saudi Arabia's founding king at the Great Bitter Lake.

Despite some public ruptures—such as during the 1973 oil embargo, and immediately after 9/11—every US administration has had close ties to the Saudi monarchy. The two countries coordinated extensively in the long campaigns to counter Soviet expansion into the Middle East, Africa, and Afghanistan; the royals have also funded several presidential foreign policies that Congress has been unwilling to pay for. The vital shipping lanes in the Persian Gulf and the Red Sea run along the Saudi coasts, and the US military has depended on Saudi airspace to project force into Asian countries like Afghanistan and to protect the smaller Gulf states.[25]

As Guardian of the Two Holy Mosques, the Saudi king is a major figure within Islam; every observant Muslim in the world outside of Saudi Arabia faces that country to pray five times a day. The king is also quite influential in the Arab world: if there will ever be a peace settlement in the Middle East, Saudi Arabia will need to give its seal of approval. The Saudis have invested heavily in US assets and have directed substantial sums toward American corporations, not only in the defense industries but across the spectrum of the most respected US companies. Saudi money has meant more jobs in St. Louis and in Los Angeles. Over the electoral time horizon of any American politician, it has always made sense to continue to engage with the Saudi regime commercially and to support it diplomatically. If any one of us were to become President of the United States tomorrow, we would be urged by our advisors to maintain good relations with the House of Saud.

What interests us here are the negatives in Western political support for the Saudi regime. Many will think of the Arab oil embargo of 1973; what we will highlight is the more consequential Saudi support of fundamentalist Islam worldwide. A crucial year in this story is 1979, a pivot at which much in world history turned.[26] The Soviets invaded Afghanistan, pushing the Cold War deeper into the Muslim world. Religious extremists overthrew the Shah in Iran, scaring the Saudi royals that the same fate might await them. Most dramatically, homegrown Saudi fundamentalists captured the Grand Mosque, the heart of the Muslim faith which the royals are meant to defend. The militants were dislodged only after a bloody commando raid that left the mosque—which holds the holiest place in Islam—damaged and defiled.

The year 1979 was a great crisis for the Saudi regime. The royals' legitimacy had always rested on their leadership of the Saudi religious community and on the endorsement of its ultraconservative clerics. Now it seemed that the royals were in danger of being swept away by a populist fundamentalist revival consuming the region. The king's response was to outflank and co-opt the radicals. The regime had already been using its large post-1973 oil rents to bolster its reactionary religious establishment at home, and to empower that establishment to spread the faith abroad.[27] Now it doubled down on that strategy.

The regime sprayed out petrodollars to spread Islamic fundamentalism worldwide. Mosques, schools, "study centers"—one American think tank estimates that the Saudis spent more than $70 billion in a decade-and-a-half campaign to build institutions across Asia, Africa, and Europe.[28] Here young Muslims learned Salafism, the creed that Muslims everywhere should live according to the Islam of the seventh century, including its seventh-century laws about the punishment of crimes and the treatment of women. Young Muslims were also taught the religious duty of *jihad*. "With a population equal to only 1 percent of Muslims worldwide, Saudi Arabia funded more than 90 percent of the faith's costs, and these expenditures constituted the most expensive information campaign ever mounted."[29]

The Saudi royals' strategy of promoting Salafism at home and worldwide worked insofar as it resolved their domestic crisis and stabilized their regime. The regime's support for this pan-Islamic ideology incited thousands of young Muslims to go off to fight the godless Soviets in Afghanistan (a fight the Saudis and Americans took on in close coordination), and it encouraged many Saudis privately to support young men prosecuting violent jihads in Afghanistan and then around the world.[30] The Saudis were impressed by the success of their ideological campaign. Saudi-funded mosques and fighters rooted down in Pakistan, sprung up in the Caucasus, further balkanized the Balkans.[31] Oil money empowered the Saudis to spread a medieval understanding of Islam all over the world.

The subnarrative in this global story that many know is that of Osama bin Laden. Convinced that the royals' religious purity was not pure enough, bin Laden organized his followers around an anti-statist and globalized jihadi variant of Salafism. Bin Laden's jihadi strain of Salafism is more revolutionary than the reactionary interpretation encouraged by the Saudi regime, but his is the variant into which Salafism has often mutated under pressure, not only within Saudi Arabia but worldwide. Rejected by the regime, and prevented by its repression from organizing domestic political resistance, bin Laden vilified the "far enemy" that was supporting the corrupt Saudi royals and "stealing" the country's natural resources.[32] Fifteen of the nineteen hijackers on 9/11 were Saudi nationals, and al-Qaeda's franchises continue to threaten Western interests today. The Saudi regime has cracked down on the jihadis at home and on some "charities" that support them abroad, but Saudis continue to fund armed extremist groups through private donations that the regime is unable, or unwilling, to stop.[33]

The story of bin Laden and 9/11 is dramatic and important. Yet it can distract from the larger historical thrust. As Rachel Bronson says, "Extremism's appeal is not simply the result of a primordial clash of civilizations, nor a political response to globalization, nor even the consequence of authoritarian regimes stifling outlets for peaceful political dissent . . . Rather, Islamic radicals have been created and cultivated by political leaders for political ends."[34]

The Saudi royals, to solidify their rule, financed the spread of fundamentalist Islamic theology worldwide. That theology is not identical to the extremist jihadi theology, but it is one root from which it grew.[35] When Barack Obama addressed the UN in 2014 and encouraged Muslims to give up the ideology of Islamic State, he was in fact warning them away from Wahhabism—the version of Salafism that is the official religion of both Islamic State and the Saudi state.[36]

Let's pause to compare. The West's long struggle with Soviet communism in the twentieth century made historical sense. For all the lethality of its realization, communism was very much an Enlightenment ideology, built from the tenets of our time. Being forced into a battle of ideas with the communists pressured the West to discard practices that proved indefensible in Enlightenment terms—to pull back from colonialism, for example, and to end its harshest racial and gender biases. The Cold War was an Enlightenment civil war, and the reforms the West made during those years are welcome legacies of that struggle.

Now, in the twenty-first century, the West finds itself attacked by an ideology whose goal is to remodel the world's politics to conform as closely as possible to the convictions of seventh-century desert tribesmen. Many adherents to this ideology believe it rational to kill Westerners as part of an effort to bring down all Enlightenment institutions worldwide, and even Westerners who know nothing about jihadi Salafism are forced to spend their tax dollars and time because of the expensive measures (military campaigns, security in cities and airports) that the West has taken against this threat. Jihadi Salafism is so alien to modernity that efforts to resist it are unlikely to bring welcome reforms at home. Rather, the struggle against jihadi Salafism has so far mostly meant increased powers of secret surveillance and state coercion within Western countries, which enlightened defenders of individual freedom and democratic accountability will view with great dismay.

The jihadi Salafist threat was not inevitable; there was no necessity that the West would be "balanced" by Islamic medievalism. Of course, Islam itself deserves great respect as a faith tradition, and as the inspiration for tremendous profundity and beauty. And of course, Islam itself is not inherently violent (one study even finds that Muslim countries have lower murder rates).[37] Indeed, many Muslims, looking at their faith of forgiveness and mercy, wonder why a belligerent minority is rocketing backward through time, leaving so many corpses in its wake.

This threat is not just a historical anomaly: a black swan flying a black flag. Many elements combine to explain the origins and growth of jihadi Salafism, including Western political support for its long-time Saudi ally, the yearnings of young Muslims worldwide for more opportunities and recognition, and the encouragement of extremism from other Gulf oil states like Qatar, Kuwait, and the UAE.[38] Still, one crucial factor was that the Saudi regime chose to strengthen itself by spending from its massive petrorevenues to imprint Salafist ideology more deeply on its own people and, along with its own people, to fund Salafist schools, preachers, and soldiers throughout the world. Because of effectiveness for resources, the world's consumers unwittingly gave Saudi Arabia the financial backing to spread extremism for decades on a world-historical scale. The global jihadi movement that we now see would not exist without that oil money.

THE THIRD BALLOON

"Dictators ride to and fro upon tigers that they dare not dismount," Churchill remarked before World War II, "and the tigers are getting hungry."[39] With its commercial and political support of autocrats in Iran, Iraq, and the rest of the Persian Gulf, the West inflated balloons full of trouble. The first two of these have burst; the third, and the biggest of them all, has leaked trouble but not yet exploded. We now examine the possibility that another regime in the Persian Gulf will lose its grip, using Saudi Arabia as the study.

As we saw in Chapters 2 and 3, authoritarian regimes like the House of Saud maintain their rule by using resource rents to fund a mixture of violence and clientelism. With their huge oil bounty, the Sauds have so far been able to fund both of these activities generously. The royals maintain an efficient network of informers, police, and prisons. The princes sit atop bureaucratic hierarchies that, however inefficient, keep most Saudi citizens who work dependent on the regime for their incomes and status. The regime has also had money left over to provide public goods to most Saudis, and the country employs millions of foreign workers (about a third of the population) to do the jobs that Saudis themselves are unable or unwilling to do.[40]

Many pressures will strain the Gulf monarchies in the years to come: huge wealth gaps created by the resource revenues of the royals, the fraying of their religious legitimation, the squandering of government spending on "prestige" white elephant projects, rising energy consumption that will cut into exports, increasingly repressive forms of domestic censorship, and a citizenry that expects large state benefits without being taxed or doing meaningful work.[41] One could add to this list; for example, information technology has spread rapidly across these populations, increasing the means for people to communicate regularly, if not securely.[42] From all of these many pressures, we take Saudi Arabia's "youth bulge" as a possible source of discontent.

Saudi Arabia has one of the youngest populations of citizens in the world. While the Kingdom keeps many statistics secret, a good guess is that two-thirds of native Saudis are under thirty.[43] Before the Arab Spring, the unemployment rate for twenty- to twenty-four-year-old Saudis was nearly 40 percent. One way the king staved off trouble during 2011 was to decree nearly $50 billion of extra spending on increased wages, pensions, and bonuses for state employees and the hiring of sixty thousand new employees into the government.[44] The king bought time, but only by greatly expanding the commitments of the already bloated public sector. In 2014, a second youth bulge—the country's largest ever—started to turn eighteen.[45] In the near future, Saudi Arabia may have to deal with a generation that is "frustrated, bored [and] restless," with few avenues for meaningful work, higher status, or escape from their archaic, puritanical social world.[46] The median age of Saudi nationals is now just twenty-two years, squarely in the range most likely to protest and rebel.[47]

Pause once more to consider. In most countries, a booming generation of young people entering the workforce would stimulate decades of economic dynamism. In oil autocracies like Saudi Arabia, there are few real jobs for the youth to do, so the state views its own young people as a threat.

King Abdullah's increased spending on state employment during the Arab Spring was part of a $130 billion raft of raises, subsidies, public works, and handouts to religious organizations.[48] (During the protests, one of the king's ministers also warned, plausibly, that the regime would "cut off any finger" raised against it.[49]) The question is whether the regime will be able to hold on during a future burst of popular discontent, especially if it has lower oil revenues per citizen to sustain its rule. Although it costs the Saudis only around $5 a barrel to lift oil from the ground, the International Monetary Fund estimates that the regime needs an oil price above $100 a barrel to meet its expanded commitments.[50] Should the global oil price stay significantly below this, the regime might not be able to ride out the next uprising. There is already evidence, in the growing poverty among the native population, that the regime cannot meet its promises to its people.[51] More, as the last of the brothers who have ruled as king since 1953 finally die, the regime (which has never had clear rules for succession) will need to hold together during the struggle for power among the next generation of princes, who number in the hundreds.[52]

A major crisis for the Saudi royals has been predicted regularly for years, and still the regime endures.[53] The Saudi monarch has enormous financial resources, the backing of the Western states, and decades of success behind his dynasty. Yet so did another monarch, the Shah of Iran, until 1979.

Should the Saudi regime suddenly fail, this will be major trouble not only for the West but for the world. Instantly, there will be an unorganized citizenry, with few skills that could integrate them into a modern economy, divided by tribal affiliations and with no history of cooperation in civil society, who have no active political experience and who have been soaked in an extreme fundamentalist ideology their whole lives. This population will be living on top of the world's most valuable repository of energy, and to make matters worse, the Saudis who live closest to the largest oil fields will be the substantial and restive Shia minority that the Sunni majority has repressed for decades, intermittently quite ferociously. A major disruption to Saudi oil flows would send shockwaves through the global economy—damaging rich countries seriously and poor countries, where the poorest typically suffer the most in a crisis, even more. Saudi Arabia is a giant balloon that the world has inflated with trouble.

GIVE ME FUEL, GIVE ME FIRE

We've been looking at how the rule of effectiveness leaves the West with only bad options. We've surveyed some negative impacts on Western interests—past and possible—arising from effectiveness and Western political support for authoritarians in Iran, Iraq, and Saudi Arabia. To appreciate more fully today's real resource curse, we expand outward to vet threats to Western interests beyond these three resource-disordered countries.

Saudi Arabia is not the only Arab oil state facing a demographic squeeze. The UN has estimated that the Arab states (which are mostly oil states) will need to create 51 million new jobs by 2020 to absorb their youth bulge—an achievement scarcely imaginable.[54] Partly in anticipation of domestic unrest, the Crown Prince of Abu Dhabi gave a half-billion dollar contract to the founder of Blackwater to import a mercenary army of non-Muslims, because "Muslim soldiers cannot be counted on to kill fellow Muslims."[55]

Nor is regime instability the only threat brewing in the region. Those oppressed in oil states do notice who supports their oppressors:

> MANAMA, Bahrain—In a dark alleyway of a low-slung suburb here, two dozen protesters gathered quietly and prepared to march toward a United States naval base. A teenager wrapped his scarf close to his mouth, bracing for tear gas. A man peeked out of his doorway, holding his infant daughter above his head, to show her a ritual of defiance that has become a grinding way of life.
>
> For months, the protests have aimed at the ruling monarchy, but recently they have focused on a new target. To their familiar slogans—demanding freedoms, praising God and cursing the ruling family—the young protesters added a new demand, written on a placard in English, so the Americans might see: "U.S.A. Stop arming the killers."[56]

According to the US Military Academy, Saudi Arabia was the main source of the foreign fighters who attacked American troops during their occupation of Iraq—but Libya sent more fighters per capita, and Syria, Yemen, and Algeria all provided significant numbers.[57] The mention of Libya is a reminder that funneling huge sums to authoritarians through the policy of "might makes right" can also threaten Western interests even when those authoritarians do not receive Western political support, and even when their ideology is much less pious than the Saudis'. Muammar Gaddafi, the West's occasional ally but mostly foe, was an inventive menace with billions of petrodollars at his disposal.

Across forty years, Gaddafi sponsored terrorist attacks worldwide, from the "Munich Massacre" at the 1972 Olympics to the Berlin discotheque bombing to the destruction of Pan Am Flight 103 over Lockerbie, Scotland. He also planned attacks within the United States—including, apparently, the assassination of President Reagan.[58] Gaddafi financed Idi Amin and Robert Mugabe as they fought to stay in power, and he helped Iran to launder large sums in violation of international sanctions. Gaddafi gave haven to groups like the Baader-Meinhof Gang and the Japanese Red Army, and his own "World Revolutionary Center" has been called "the Harvard and Yale of a whole generation of African revolutionaries."[59] Among the WRC's graduates were Foday Sankoh, who led the RUF in Sierra Leone in its campaign of amputation and terror, as well as Charles Taylor of Liberia, who is (as we will see) now convicted for war crimes as well as crimes against humanity. Gaddafi supported a coup in Burkina Faso and helped to install Idris Déby in Chad.[60] His arming of Arab militias in Darfur helped the rise of the Janjaweed that terrorized civilians there, and his destabilization of regimes across the Maghreb gave al-Qaeda space to set up operations in North Africa.[61] Gaddafi sent financial support to Colombia's cocaine-dealing FARC rebels; to the Irish Republican Army, he sent shipments "estimated to include 1,000 assault rifles, a surface-to-air missile, flamethrowers, rocket launchers and three tons of Semtex plastic explosives."[62]

This was one unaccountable and highly unpredictable man who ruthlessly dominated a resource-rich country. Again, it was not inevitable that an individual like Gaddafi would get hundreds of billions of dollars to fund a global campaign of destruction over a span of decades. It is just one dimension of the effectiveness-based authoritarian resource curse on us.

FRAGILE AND FAILED

We've been assessing the drawbacks of the current system of international resource trade for Western interests, mostly examining petrocracies with substantial resource revenues per person. Some Western countries have attempted to reduce their exposure to Middle Eastern risk by supporting new production in central Asia and Africa. However, as Paul Collier observes, if these new producers are also subject to the resource disorders, then this shift will simply create "Middle East 2."[63]

Indeed, as we have seen, increasing global demand has already pushed resource exploration into many new countries even without a strategic Western shift. Fifty-one of the fifty-four African countries, for example, are now producing or exploring for oil.[64] Somalia has oil. The DRC has oil. The Middle East is also "expanding." Cyprus has oil. Lebanon has oil. In Asia, even North Korea appears to have oil.[65] These countries evidence varying degrees of authoritarianism, but what really matters is that many are fragile. Here "the most important political distinction among countries," as Samuel Huntington observed, "concerns not their form of government but their degree of government."[66]

We could visit any number of resource-rich fragile or failed states: the vast DRC, where the government has never had full control over the resource-producing regions; Sudan, where the president is trying to maintain control over fractious radical Islamists and Arab nationalists while launching new offensives against Darfur; Guinea, with its large bauxite and iron deposits, ethnic rivalry, and barely restrained security forces; gold-heavy Mali, which only recovered half its territory from jihadi Salafists and Tuareg militias with the help of the French military; or Somalia, which looks fated to produce oil before the government can exert minimal control over the country amid all the armed factions.[67]

Instead, we return to Nigeria, which we visited in Chapter 4. As we saw there, Nigeria has recently likely become the country in the world with the most poor people.[68] Also, astonishingly, Nigeria is growing so fast that by 2050 the country is projected to have a larger population than the United States.[69] Nigeria, already a giant, is a poorly governed country plagued by corruption, poverty, low trust, ethnic and regional tensions, sporadic serious violence, and deep economic dysfunctions. Now we add that Nigeria will be getting much fuller with poor people.

For all its chronic crises, Nigeria tends not to be a first- or even a second-order national security concern for Western states. Despite its elephantine corruption, alternating insurgencies in the North and South, popular protests, and frail democracy, Nigeria always seems to totter back from the brink. It's worth imagining, however, the day that Nigeria shoots to the top of the world's agenda.

A worst-case scenario for Nigeria sees a Southern assassination of a Northern president. Northerners rise in outrage; the federal government is paralyzed; amnesty payments to the Southern militias cease. Two-and-a-half million barrels of oil a day are locked in, outstripping even Saudi Arabia's capacity to compensate. The North becomes ungoverned, leaving large areas for extremists to organize. As images of mass starvation begin to fill Western television screens, huge waves of desperate Nigerian refugees take the well-traveled route across the Sahara toward Europe.[70] In this scenario, the West would suffer by being forced to inhale the smoke from Nigeria's fires.

It may be that Nigeria will not, in fact, ignite as this scenario envisions. And it bears repeating that resources do not doom exporting countries. Even large exporters like Indonesia, Mexico, and Brazil have achieved relatively inclusive growth and shaken off the worst disorders that still torment their peers. But with resource production—and so the resource disorders—spreading, the odds of fragile states failing will increase, and the West will bear the costs radiating from those states that don't beat the odds.

There is one more cost, not yet mentioned, that the world is quite likely to pay because of the workings of today's trade in resources. This is the opportunity cost of being deprived of stable, prosperous, and united countries that will instead be deranged by their resource trade. Those who know Nigerians, for instance, will have a strong sense of how extraordinary a well-governed Nigeria could be.

TOMORROW'S HEADLINES

Between allies and adversaries, the fragile and the failed, when the US Department of State drew up a list of countries a few years ago whose nationals would require extra security screening at airports before flying to the United States, nine of the fourteen countries were oil states:

Afghanistan / *Algeria* / Cuba / *Iran* / *Iraq* / Lebanon / *Libya* / *Nigeria* / Pakistan / *Saudi Arabia* / Somalia / *Sudan* / *Syria* / *Yemen*[71]

The divisiveness of resource-disordered states leaks out, through slow or sudden ruptures, to damage the interests of the West. Looking back at the examples in this chapter, what stands out is that commercial engagement on the basis of effectiveness yields highly negative results *regardless of what political strategy it is paired with*. Whether the West's political strategy has been containment, or support, or coercive intervention, or neglect, painfully hard dilemmas have been forced back on it. While critics have blasted the West's bad choices (its decisions), the deeper problem has been the West's bad choices (its options). Effectiveness poisons the wellsprings of the world's politics, and it has seriously degraded the West's strategic environment.

In this chapter, we've mostly looked at the historical negative impacts on Western interests arising from the system of international resource trade. Now, finally, we can peer as best we can into the future.

"Two great power shifts are occurring in this century," Joseph Nye recently wrote, "a power transition among states and a power diffusion away from all states to non-state actors."[72] The first transition is clearly visible in the accelerating shift of power from West to East. The National Intelligence Council (NIC) predicts that by 2030 Asia will have greater global power than North America and Europe combined.[73] Nowhere is this shift more evident than in the extractive industries, as well-funded Asian (and especially Chinese) firms have quickly increased their competence and are now competing with the Western majors in all but the most complex plays.

As Asian countries and firms have become more engaged in the global resource system, they have also experienced more negative impacts from resource-disordered countries, especially in Africa. China has supported authoritarian regimes in Sudan, Zimbabwe, and Libya—and has already lost its bet on the last.[74] A murky investment group with uncertain ties to Beijing has attempted (and mostly bungled) deals with repressive actors in Angola, Zimbabwe, and Guinea.[75] Zambian miners killed a Chinese manager during riots over pay and conditions; thousands of Chinese gold miners were forced to flee Ghana after hundreds of arrests for illegal mining.[76]

Westerners might at first welcome the resource curses descending on countries and firms they see as rivals, but their second thoughts will be more sober. As the East engages more with resource-disordered countries, the West will still be threatened by many of the curses we saw above, like terrorism and commodity price volatility, with all of its recessionary potential. Western leaders will simply have even less control over these outcomes than they had before. In the future, the West may feel increasingly like it has a hangover even though it missed the party.

Nye's second transition is the diffusion of power away from all states and toward individuals and networks. The disruptive capacity of non-state actors that has become increasingly evident in the past two decades will grow, with especially worrying implications for those hoping for stability in resource-rich regions. Imagine, for instance, an Iraq where the hostile groups have armed drones, or a Syria where all sides can mass-produce customized weapons on 3D printers, or even a Saudi Arabia where aggrieved Shia can hack into power grids. Empowered and embattled or embittered individuals will be bad news for a world that depends on natural resource flows.

More, we have already seen a future trend specific to the resource sector: the new push of production into fragile and failed states, especially in the Middle East, Africa, and South Asia. The risks of this trend will be magnified by a global "double whammy": high demographic growth in these countries will take place in the midst of increasing environmental stress. The NIC expects that by 2030 demand for food and water will increase by more than a third, while the weather becomes more extreme. The implications for conflict, migration, and state failure will be most severe in resource-rich regions: just the regions into which resource production is now pushing deeper. Resource-rich regions will become hotter, hungrier, and thirstier, which is unlikely to mean they will be more stable.

Finally, as noted in the Introduction, some of the greatest costs of the resource disorders overseas come in the divisiveness of the foreign policy choices they force upon Western states. Think of Iraq, Iran, Libya, Ukraine, Syria. Whether Western governments made the right or the wrong choices in these cases, all can agree that their range of options in each were dismal, and that the domestic debates over what to do were toxic and distracting from other priorities on the policy agenda. These debates have often started with people of good will on all sides, yet their intractability has driven even the reasonable to become more extreme, aided by our own entrepreneurs of division who intensify the spirals of acrimony. Especially in the United States, but not only there, the resource disorders abroad have incited citizens to divide against each other at home. The resource disorders mean more than Them vs. Them, and more than Them vs. Us. They mean Us vs. Us as well.

The negative effects on Western interests from authoritarianism, civil conflict and other pathologies in resource-exporting states glow through recent history, and there are serious concerns that these effects will intensify in the future. When speaking to people who seem not to care much about the disorders of resource-exporting countries, one may find it useful to paraphrase Trotsky: you may not be interested in the resource curse, but the resource curse is interested in you. The real resource curse is on us.

7

How Might Makes Right

It is the great error of reformers and philanthropists in our time to nibble at the consequences of unjust power, instead of redressing the injustice itself.

—John Stuart Mill[1]

GUNS MAKE RIGHTS

Under whose law does might make right? The answer may be unexpected. Consider, for example, a smartphone on sale in a mall in Chicago. How did the molecules that constitute that particular phone come to be buyable there?

We can view the history of this smartphone in two ways: first, as supply chains that turned raw materials into the finished good, and second, as a series of legal transactions—as sale chains—where titles changed hands as the product was created across many countries. The supply chains and sale chains have identical shapes: tributary streams combining into unifying flows. What distinguishes the two chains are the laws that govern them.

The supply chains leading to the Chicago mall are movements of molecules, governed by the laws of physics: matter and energy. These supply chains drew elements—both common and exotic—from many points under the earth's surface and fashioned them into the integral object that a teenager in the mall can hold in her hand. Supply chains are made of physical links and end in physical possession.

Sale chains are made of legal links and end in property rights: the sale chains leading to the Chicago mall are movements of property titles. Tracing the sale chain of one of the phone's components back link by link, we find the brand company's transfer of the phone's title to the retailer in the mall, then the circuit board manufacturer's sale to the brand company, then the component manufacturer's sale to the circuit board manufacturer, the refiner's sale of metal to the component manufacturer, the export company's sale to the refiner, the trader's sale to the export company, and a militia's sale of a bag of coltan, extracted from a mine in eastern Congo, to the trader.[2] At that distant anchor of the sale chain, we find a group of men keeping watch over locals bringing rocks out of the earth. These watchful men may be part of a Congolese army unit, or they may be rebels officially opposed to the army. What is certain is that these men are carrying guns.

These armed men, it is sure, have no title to the minerals—within American law, Congolese law, or any other law. The guns of these men, however, win them physical possession of the ore. The question is: in what way is the armed theft at the origin of the sale chain reflected in the law at its terminus? How the does the crime at one end affect the legal title at the other?

The answer is: not at all. Say the teenage girl buys the smartphone at the mall in Chicago. With her purchase, she gains legal title to every atom of the phone under American law, and her title is both presumptive and unassailable. Her title to the smartphone is presumptive: short of a court case, Chicago police will enforce the girl's legal right to the phone against all other claimants. And if there is a court case, her title will be unassailable. Should the owner of the Congolese mine plundered by the militia—whoever that might be—take legal action against the girl in an American court, complaining that her phone contains some of the metal stolen from the mine, this suit will fail. American law presents the mine owner with obstacles that a suit cannot overcome.[3] From the perspective of American law, the teenager has perfect title to the smartphone with the stolen Congolese mineral in it. The teenager owns the whole phone free and clear, as she would own a pint of milk with a sale chain going back to a local dairy.

It may be startling that American courts would so favor the Congolese militias responsible for the unspeakable acts, especially against women, that we saw in the Introduction (the report from the rape trauma clinic) and in Chapter 4 (the scene of the corpses after the village raid). This may be especially unwelcome since American commercial engagement with those militias not only draws stolen minerals from them into American stores, it also sends some of the money that Americans pay in those stores back to the militiamen, helping them to buy more bullets and more bayonets.

This is startling, but correct. We can, if we like, catalogue the specific American laws that legitimize the sale chain stretching from Chicago to the Congo. These American laws will use distinctive concepts and bear idiomatic names; they will differ from the specific Egyptian laws that legitimize a sale chain stretching from Cairo to the Congo, and from the specific Japanese laws that legitimize a sale chain stretching from Tokyo to the Congo. What all these specific national laws have in common is the structure of effectiveness. Every nation's laws will take the input of stolen minerals in the Congo and produce an output of perfect legal title at the point of final purchase. The laws of each country, that is, will turn a militia's might at one end of a sale chain into a pure legal right at the other.

MAKING LAW ON HIGH ISLAND

Property is a matter of everyday justice. The violation of property rights activates the familiar dramas of justice denied: of owners and thieves, police and courts, crime and punishment. Respect for property rights enables the most extraordinary coordinations of human actions. We think of a country's justice system as enforcing the property rights of its persons within its borders so as to secure expectations about who can use what when. Yet persons and things also cross borders, especially in these globalized times. Foreigners with possessions penetrate a country's perimeters, and a country's people come into possession of foreign objects. What happens then? Who defines these legal interfaces between the native and the alien? Let's imagine that we're starting anew.

Say we establish a new independent nation on a high island in the Pacific. We citizens of this new nation, High Island, have many decisions to make:

1: "Us-Here" Decisions. Each national authority determines the laws for its own persons regarding property within that nation's territory.

This is straightforward: laws by us and for us here are ours to make. Whether we will establish a common law, civil law, or novel legal code for High Island is up to us. It's also up to us, for example, whether we will manage some of our island's resources collectively or allow them to be privatized (say, through a national auction).

We must also set our property rules for foreigners who come onto our territory:

2: "Them-Here" Decisions. Each national authority determines its own laws regarding foreigners bringing property into its territory, and regarding foreigners buying and selling and using property within its territory.

At this moment, for example, the Colombian government has declared that foreigners have no right to bring used motor vehicles into Colombia. New Zealand has prohibited foreigners from importing pit bull semen. Egyptian law allows foreigners to own only two private residences, of up to 4,000 square meters each, while forbidding the sale of such private residences within five years of purchase.[4] We High Islanders will similarly decide among ourselves what property rules foreigners must follow on our island.

Finally, we must decide the rules for our persons coming to own things abroad:

3: "Us-There" Decisions. Each national authority determines the laws for its own persons regarding property transactions outside that nation's territory.

Lawyers explain this principle by saying that national authorities have personal jurisdiction in addition to territorial jurisdiction. Persons—both individuals and corporations—are under the authority of the laws of their own country, wherever they are in the world. Your country's criminal law, for instance, can follow you wherever you go. Most of the G8 countries allow prosecution of their nationals for child sex tourism if the act in question would have been a crime had it occurred at home, regardless of whether the act is a crime in the country where it took place.[5] American law condemns treason whether committed "within the United States or elsewhere."[6] One of America's homeland security laws prohibits overseas drug trafficking by any US person for the benefit of a foreign terrorist organization.[7]

The easiest way to observe personal jurisdiction over property rights is with sanctions. US sanctions on Sudan, for example, were extended in 2006 by Executive Order 13412:

> By the authority vested in me as President by the Constitution and the laws of the United States of America . . . I, George W. Bush, President of the United States of America . . . hereby order . . .

> Notwithstanding any contract entered into or any license or permit granted prior to the effective date of this order, all transactions by United States persons relating to the petroleum or petrochemical industries in Sudan, including, but not limited to, oilfield services and oil and gas pipelines, are prohibited.[8]

This executive order suspends, among other rights, the legal right of all US persons to buy Sudanese oil, no matter where in the world that US person is. That is what these oil sanctions are—a suspension of all American persons' legal rights. (Someday, a US president likely will restore to US persons the legal right to buy Sudanese oil; that will be the act which lifts these US sanctions.)

Putting all of this together (Decisions 1, 2, and 3) shows that we High Islanders must decide what legal rights our persons will have with respect to buying anything, anywhere in the world. We must settle which of us have what rights to buy what, and from whom. We could in theory require an Island-wide referendum on each proposed purchase of foreign goods. Or we might enact laws barring High Islanders from buying foreign products made with child labor—or blocking High Islanders from buying foreign ivory or great apes. It is up to us.[9]

The more general point is that there must be political decisions that define the rights of any market before transactions take place within that market. There must be a political decision on each thing: on whether each potential commodity can legally be bought and sold, and by whom, and on what terms (for example, what the laws are regarding guns, drugs, milk, gasoline, factories, passports, nuclear weapons, human beings). Politics must decide how the game is played—what the pieces are, who can move them, and how. Once the game is defined, the players can then play as they wish. The political definition of a market is an inevitable precondition—it is the step before any market can be "free."

ALL PROPERTY IS LOCAL

An Austrian who misplaces his wallet in Australia cannot file a lost property report with the global police. Should a Moroccan married to a Mexican buy a house in Monaco, no global court will decide who owns the house should they divorce. There is a World Trade Organization; there is no World Ownership

Organization.[10] No single legal order exists above national legal systems to adjudicate or enforce property rights. Property law is primarily national and subnational; little property law is supernational.[11] A property dispute with an international element that lands in some country's courts will be decided by that country's authorities according to that country's laws.

Property law cannot be seen from above; it can only be seen from within. Even the term *property law* will mislead if it's taken as a common subject studied by law students in different countries. Rather, there are as many systems of property law as there are national authorities. With limited exceptions, each national authority is decisive in setting all of its own *private law* rules: its rules regarding property, marriage, and other private relations between legal persons (individuals or corporations). Finnish private law may be structurally similar to Philippine private law—but it also may not be, and where the two systems differ, there's no higher law that decides between them. To rise to a global perspective, one must shake off all national private legality. What one then sees is many national codes—almost two hundred autonomous systems of private law.

What we're keen to know is how each national authority will set its laws for its own persons' commercial transactions with foreigners. For us, this is the crucial stitch in the tapestry of international trade. A foreigner in possession of an object offers that object for sale to one of our nationals. If the foreigner's title is morally as sound as it would be at home, then this transaction will import no injustice. (It makes no moral difference, for instance, whether milk comes from Minnesota or Manitoba.) If the foreign title is morally tainted, however, it makes all the difference in the world whether our nationals can legally buy that object or not. This legal transaction is the moment of moral transition: the moment at which foreign injustice can enter our own justice system, and where moral contamination can slip across our borders wrapped in a cloak of law.[12]

For the teenager in Chicago, all of the important laws in the sale chain of the phone in the mall are American laws. Absent American law, the Congolese minerals are to the girl *res nullius*: simply agglomerations of atoms. The presence of American law turns that matter into something she can buy. Unknown to the girl, the Congolese minerals in the phone that she covets started their superterranean existence covered in the sweat, or even the blood, of a villager forced to dig them out. For her, the crucial link in the phone's sale chain is the American law that allowed an American person to buy the metals that were stolen by the soldiers. That is the American law that will turn foreign might into her right, and which will call America's police and courts to her defense against all challengers. And that is the law that will ingrain the injustice of those conflict minerals into her daily social life.

The laws that accept armed theft in foreign sale chains are American laws—these are laws that the American government authorizes. Yet American law need not turn foreign might into domestic right, and for a few natural resources, it actually blocks such transitions. In 2008, for example, the US Congress passed an amendment to a law called the Lacey Act, with the support of a wide coalition of NGOs concerned with resource governance abroad. As amended, the Lacey Act prohibits importation into the United States of any product made with a plant exported in violation of the laws of a foreign country. The legislation's main target is timber sourced from forests in countries such as Indonesia (composed of around thirteen thousand islands), where the government can't control its territory sufficiently to prevent criminals from logging. With the Lacey Act, the United States chose against effectiveness: against legitimizing the actions of foreigners who have illegally seized foreign goods. The European Union now has similar laws regarding stolen foreign wood as well.[13]

These US and EU timber laws are attempts to block the legal domestication of thefts that occur in the world's weakly governed regions. The Kimberley Process—embedded in law in the United States and eighty other countries—attempts to do the same for rough diamonds. Nationals of countries within the Kimberley Process are prohibited from importing rough diamonds bought from civil warriors: they may only import stones that have been certified for export by the exporting country's government. The Kimberley Process, like the Lacey Act, shows that countries can stop armed robbery leading to legal property when they deem it meet to do so.

The Lacey Act and the Kimberley Process are rare exceptions. For almost all natural resources and their products, the United States affirms laws that allow might abroad to make right at home. The United States chooses a structure of law that accepts coltan theft in its sale chains instead of enacting Lacey- or Kimberley-like legislation that would treat stolen metals in the same way as stolen timber or stolen diamonds. The United States authorizes commercial engagement with the vicious Congolese militiamen by choosing laws that approve American purchase of their pillage and that send shoppers' dollars back to them. And every other country in the world does the same. For most natural resources stolen from their countries of origin, the world's nations license might to make right.

MIGHT MAKES LAW MAKES RIGHT

Raw materials stolen under the laws of the country of extraction are tainted; most people would be troubled if the global fog of wares lifted to reveal that their private property is made of plunder. Yet raw materials that are extracted in violation of foreign laws form only a small proportion of world trade. The main means by which might there makes right here passes not around foreign laws but straight through them.

You may recall Charles Taylor, a Gaddafi-trained warlord who helped to overthrow the government in Liberia and then became its president for six years.[14] Taylor's authoritarian rule was such that the judge sentencing him at a special international tribunal called him "responsible for aiding and abetting some of the most heinous crimes in human history": war crimes of terrorizing a civilian population, cruel treatment, and other inhumane acts, as well as crimes against humanity, including murder, rape, sexual enslavement, and pillage.[15] Taylor's international crimes were committed in support of the RUF militias in Sierra Leone—the militias we saw in the stories of amputations and child soldiery in Chapter 4. From the RUF, Taylor received some of Sierra Leone's blood diamonds, and Taylor then funneled some of those diamonds to terrorist groups like al-Qaeda.[16]

For his international crimes, Taylor is now serving a fifty-year sentence in a maximum-security prison. During his exceptionally coercive presidency, however, Taylor enjoyed a life of legal luxury. As president, Taylor enjoyed the legal power to sell off Liberia's natural resources, a power that all other nations accepted into their own laws.

President Taylor codified his legal power over Liberia's resource endowment by compelling the country's legislators to pass a "Strategic Commodities Act," which stated:

> The President of the Republic of Liberia is hereby granted the sole power to execute, negotiate, and conclude all commercial contracts or agreements with any Foreign or Domestic Investor for the exploitation of the Strategic Commodities of the Republic of Liberia. Such commercial agreement shall become effectively binding upon the Republic... upon the sole signature and approval of the President of the Republic of Liberia.[17]

This statute confirmed Taylor's personal legal control over all of Liberia's resources. Charles Taylor—and Charles Taylor alone—assumed the legal right to sell off the entire country's natural assets. As Montesquieu wrote, "When a man makes himself more absolute, his first thought is to simplify the laws." As a later Liberian president developed this theme, "Mr. Taylor ran this country like it was his personal fiefdom. Resources were given to people in a manner that pleased him, and there were no systems or institutions."[18] During Taylor's rule, roundwood deforestation in Liberia reportedly increased by more than 1,300 percent. Revenues from these roundwood exports allowed Taylor to buy advanced weapons from China, Libya, Nigeria, and Serbia.[19]

Yet Taylor's Strategic Commodities Act generated only half of the legal rights needed for him to sell Liberia's resources to foreigners. The other half was those foreigners' legal rights to buy those resources from him. The countries that imported Liberia's timber during his presidency (primarily France, Italy, and Turkey) echoed Taylor's Strategic Commodities Act in their own laws by authorizing their persons to buy what Taylor decided to sell.[20] Taylor's coercion made Liberian law, France mirrored Liberian law in its own law, and Taylor sold timber to French buyers and received French funds in return. For Taylor, might made law made money. For France, might made law made rights. French law was essential for the French to buy timber legally from Taylor.

French law here "echoed" Liberian law; it "mirrored" or "followed" it. The critical point is that only French law could endow French persons with the right to buy Liberian resources from Charles Taylor. We know this from the autonomy of national property systems, illustrated by the High Island example above. It was up to the French to decide whether to endow themselves with the right to deal with Taylor in ways that would generate property rights in France. For the French to buy timber from Taylor, the French government needed law in place with a structure that paralleled Taylor's Strategic Commodities Act. That parallel French law, if spelled out, would say this:

> *French persons are granted the power to execute, negotiate, and conclude all commercial contracts or agreements for the Strategic Commodities of the Republic of Liberia only with the President of the Republic of Liberia. Such commercial agreements shall vest title over Liberian resources in French persons only upon the sole signature and approval of the President of the Republic of Liberia.*

French law opened itself to receive what Taylor was putting forward. Different metaphors of bodily parts being fit together could be used here.

For example: the hand extended must be gripped by an isomorphic hand—and if there is contagion in the hand extended, it will spread to the new body.

THE LAW THAT IS NOT LAW

There's a mental short circuit that can cause a blind spot here. The short-circuited reasoning goes like this: "Passing laws is what sovereign states do. And international law requires all states to recognize other states as sovereign. So international law requires all states to respect the laws of other states within their own laws."[21]

The protection against this short circuit is a crucial fact: political recognition does not require commercial engagement. Whoever rules in a foreign country and whatever laws they pass, the international law of recognition does not require any country to align its property laws with the laws of that country.[22]

Think back to the economic sanctions on Sudan, mentioned earlier, that the United States has maintained in various forms since 1997. The United States has used these sanctions to shape commercial relations with Sudan in exquisite detail. As we've seen, under the sanctions American persons may not legally purchase Sudanese oil from anyone. The sanctions also prohibit American persons from having any commercial dealings with the President of Sudan or with named individuals and firms associated with his regime. Yet the sanctions also, for example, explicitly license US persons to buy Sudanese gum arabic—an ingredient, which Sudan has in abundance, of carbonated drinks like Coca-Cola.[23] With these sanctions, the United States decides exactly the ways it wishes (not) to engage commercially with the Sudanese. Still, throughout all the years of sanctions, the United States has recognized Sudan as an independent, sovereign state. The United States has maintained its embassy in Khartoum during sanctions, White House representatives and Sudanese representatives negotiate in climate change conferences, a US Treasury official votes on the International Monetary Fund's Sudan policy, and so on.[24]

Even during full political recognition, one state can refuse to align its property laws with those of another by forbidding its persons to buy what the foreign law says can be sold. Indeed, this point goes even deeper. In defining its own domain of law, each state has the right to pull the property laws of another state out at the roots. Any state, that is, can inform its own persons that they must regard a property statute of a foreign sovereign as having no legal validity whatsoever.

To take one example, Britain's Law Lords once considered how British law should regard an anti-Semitic Nazi statute that purported to strip fleeing German Jews of their property rights by annulling their German citizenship. Lord Cross, writing for the court, concluded:

> What we are concerned with here is legislation which takes away without compensation from a section of the citizen body singled out on racial grounds all their property on which the state passing the legislation can lay its hands and, in addition, deprives them of their citizenship. To my mind a law of this sort constitutes so grave an infringement of human rights that the courts of this country ought to refuse to recognise it as a law at all.[25]

In a later case, the British Court of Appeal contemplated a statute that Iraq passed after its conquest of Kuwait. This statute declared that all the property of the Kuwaiti national airline, including ten airliners, would thenceforth be Iraqi state property. When the Iraqi government passed this law, the Kuwaiti airliners had been flown into Iraq: the Iraqi government was here making property law for objects it possessed within its own territory. Nevertheless, the British court declared that this Iraqi law was too contrary to British principles to be used in British legal reasoning:

> Each sovereign says to the other: "We will respect your territorial sovereignty. But there can be no offence if we do not recognise your... exorbitant acts."[26]

In both the Nazi and the Iraqi cases, there was no question that the statute at issue had been approved by the government of a recognized, sovereign state (Germany and Iraq). Yet the British court decided to reject the sovereign acts of those states, so that those acts could have no consequences within British property law. For British persons, these foreign laws were simply not law. This is an even deeper way in which political recognition does not require commercial engagement.[27]

We can even find the United States switching its commercial authorization from one party to another while keeping political recognition constant, in an episode during the Arab Spring of 2011. When the year began, the

United States recognized Libya as an independent state and Muammar Gaddafi as its head of state and government. The anti-Gaddafi protests started on February 15th in Benghazi and were soon met by Libyan security forces firing into the crowds. Within ten days of the first protests, the US government issued an executive order freezing the assets of Gaddafi, two of his sons, and named members of his regime. This executive order also froze all property of the Government of Libya (Gaddafi's regime), with the effect that no US corporation could gain legal title to any of Libya's oil.[28] US sanctions, in other words, blocked US persons from buying Libya's oil from Libya's government.

The US then did something worth marking. On April 26, 2011, the Treasury Department issued General License No. 5, "Authorizing Transactions Related to Certain Oil, Gas, or Petroleum Products Exported from Libya":

> US persons are authorized to engage in transactions... related to oil, gas, or petroleum products exported from Libya under the auspices of the Transitional National Council of Libya (the "TNC"), provided that neither the Government of Libya nor any other person whose property and interests in property are blocked... receives any benefit from such transactions.[29]

With these words, the US government authorized US persons to buy Libya's oil from Libya's rebels. On this date, April 26th, the rebels had no official status under US law. It would not be until months later that the US Secretary of State would officially recognize the TNC as the legitimate government of Libya.[30] During this period, the United States recognized Gaddafi as the head of state and government of the sovereign state of Libya—yet also authorized its persons to deal only with the rebels as the legal vendors of Libyan oil. The United States ignored the law of the sovereign Libyan state that it recognized and simply announced its own law on who its persons had the right to buy Libya's natural resources from. US political recognition pointed to Tripoli; US commercial engagement pointed to Benghazi. Political recognition does not control commercial relations.

WHY MIGHT?

Authoritarians often use their power to shape their national laws, and even their constitutions, for domestic reasons: laws are leather gloves covering their grip.[31] Yet importing countries give domestic legal effect to authoritarian decisions over natural resources. And in fact, importing countries give domestic legal effect to authoritarian decisions whether these decisions are embodied in law or not. Pol Pot did not push through a law authorizing the sale of Cambodian rubies to Thai companies in the early 1990s. The Khmer Rouge simply made deals for rubies in the portion of Cambodia that it controlled, and the Cambodian gems entered the stream of international commerce. Anyone buying one of those rubies downstream gained a legal title ultimately stamped by Pol Pot's nod.[32]

Someone might object that Pol Pot should not be labeled an "authoritarian" during this period, because at this point, the Khmer Rouge was not really a "government" at all. Though the Khmer Rouge was part of a coalition that held Cambodia's seat at the United Nations until 1993, this (it might be said) was just a Sino-American geostrategic stitch-up—the Khmer Rouge really had no sovereign law-making powers but was, in fact, just an armed group in control of some territory.[33] This objection might even be correct. We need not decide, however, because what is so striking about international trade is how little commercial difference this political difference would make. Whether Pol Pot was an authoritarian ruler or a rebel leader, importing states would have validated his effective control over resources within their own laws. A ruby brooch made with a stone supplied by his soldiers would have been owned free and clear in every importing country either way. For both authoritarians and armed groups, might there makes right here.

Where a dictator's word is law, effectiveness tracks the dictator's word; where a militant's gun rules, effectiveness tracks the gun. French law echoed Charles Taylor's statute that his signature was sufficient for the sale of Liberia's timber. American law still allows Mai-Mai militiamen to start a chain of title that ends in domestic ownerships of Congolese minerals. What matters most in the laws of importing states is coercive control over natural resources. The legal default of importing states is to authorize their own persons to buy from whichever foreigners can deliver the goods. For natural resources, possession is 99/100ths of their law.

The officials of importing states need not, as we've seen, accept effectiveness as their own law—yet they do, almost reflexively, by habit. Indeed, effectiveness is so natural in law as to be nearly automatic. The French did not need to pass an extra law to make their legal code parallel Taylor's Strategic Commodities Act: their legal system was already built to do this. It's only the exceptions to effectiveness that require special measures, like the Sudan sanctions, the Lacey and Kimberley statutes, and the British court decisions above. Effectiveness is every nation's default, the assumption of all legislation. Each state spontaneously activates the alchemy that transmutes the iron of power into the gold of legal rights.

Effectiveness for resources imports injustice. Why then do importing states do this? Why do national leaders allow might abroad to make right at home? Not, presumably, because evil infects whoever occupies high office. If you had been elevated to your country's highest office yesterday, you would have been advised to continue "might makes right" for the natural resources of other countries today. One reason is that national leaders inherit effectiveness from their ancestors: as we'll see, states have converged on this rule since the great powers were blasting each other's wooden ships with cannon. Even more important, national leaders choose effectiveness in response to their citizens' relentless demands for natural resources and the products made from them.

Effectiveness sets a test that resource-rich countries can always pass. There will always be someone in the capital of an exporting country who has the most coercive power. Effectiveness makes it legal to buy resources from him. If the capital does not control the countryside, there will always be some group in the countryside that controls the mines and forests. Effectiveness drains the countryside's resources out through them. However good or bad shape a resource-rich country is in—even if it is grunting under dictatorship or torn by civil war—effectiveness always allows its resources to flow onto world markets, where one's nationals can buy those resources under color of law.

Some see effectiveness as a neocolonial policy that allows powerful countries to exploit resource-rich regions without having to bear the costs of governing them.[34] However that may be, for national leaders effectiveness will seem a no-brainer. For national leaders, the imperative to secure imports of natural resources is extremely strong. For energy resources, the imperative to secure supplies is categorical: every leader of an advanced economy must keep the lights on and the traffic moving. Consumers' demands for imports are ceaseless, they stretch into the indefinite future, and any politician's agenda will be hostage to these demands being satisfied. So today's leaders accept effectiveness as their law, as their antecessors also did.

LEGAL HOMOLOGARCHY: THE RULE OF THE SAME RULES

National leaders favor effectiveness automatically, since the rule channels resources to their people. The most coercive actors in resource-exporting regions of course also favor effectiveness, since it channels money from the importing countries to them. Many of the most powerful actors in the world are coordinated on this rule. The rule is morally unredeemable, however, so it must be changed. And the change will be fundamental: this coordination is basic for the global order.

"In anarchy," wrote the international relations theorist Kenneth Waltz, "there is no automatic harmony."[35] For the place we have now reached, Waltz is nearly wrong. In the property rules of the world's many nations, there is a harmony so nearly automatic that it may seem—if it is noticed at all—like a fact of nature instead of a coordination of choices. Indeed, the harmony is so nearly automatic that only the deviations, like sanctions, need codifying. The agreement goes without legislating.

Those impressed or distressed by "global governance" in our era often cite transnational bodies like the World Trade Organization, or intergovernmental networks such as the Basel Committee on Banking Supervision, or NGOs that provide social services across wide regions. Such global governance may be vital at its level; compared to the global governance of property, it is trivial. Harmonization on property rules is the basis of all trade—a precondition for all cross-border commerce. Agreement on property rights underlies every legal contract regarding goods. It's the infrastructure that supports the most elaborate derived instruments of international finance. It sets the groove on which a tankerful of oil sails from port to port, changing ownership dozens of times while at sea. The international harmonization of property laws is the foundation of the global market, and the global market sustains the human population at its seven-billion size.

A thing becomes a legal commodity only when it is illuminated by laws. To play its role on the stage of world commerce, a thing must be lit by the laws of several nations at once. We might here theorize how the intersubjectivity of national laws creates the legal objectivity of the international commodity. (As a Soviet legal textbook once put it: "the right of a state of one system should be related to the existence of the other system of property as to an objective fact."[36]) We might even take this moment to philosophize on "the construction of a global social reality" by the convergence of national property rules.[37] Let's leave all of that for another day, though. All we need now is this simple conclusion: the most basic structure of international markets is sustained by a nearly automatic, yet legally entirely optional, agreement of governments on "might makes right."

This is not "agreement" as in a treaty, where governments make a joint commitment.[38] This is the agreement of clocks running in sync, where each tells the same time because of the setting of its own internal mechanism. National laws are in almost complete agreement over what will count as a valid international transfer of goods.[39] Conflict of property laws is rare; what is remarkable is the concert. International trade is possible because all nations are playing the same refrains on their own legal instruments. All legal systems are tuned to effectiveness; their concert is in a minor key.

THE DICTATOR'S ENGAGEMENT

Let's take what we've discovered back to the sale of oil by Teodoro Obiang of Equatorial Guinea. Today, all nations set their own laws to validate Obiang's decisions about the sale of Equatorial Guinea's oil: all nations tell their own nationals that they must buy Equatorial Guinea's oil only from Obiang's regime. The United States identifies Obiang as the country's resource vendor by using the principle of effectiveness: as we've seen, the fact that Obiang is the president of a sovereign state does not decide whether the US government will empower Americans to buy Equatorial Guinea's natural resources from him (political recognition does not require commercial engagement). The United States uses effectiveness to identify Obiang as the legal resource vendor, which is the choice that empowers American oil companies to buy that country's oil from him, and the choice that sends American drivers' dollars back to him.

The day that US law authorized Americans to buy resources from Obiang, US commercial engagement with Obiang began. And the American consumers' contribution to authoritarian rule in Equatorial Guinea also began. The oil of Equatorial Guinea flowed into Americans' cars, clothes, and cosmetics. And Americans' money flowed back into Obiang's bank accounts. The authoritarian, first located by his power, became superpowered with American cash.

It is thus partly an American decision that has allowed Obiang to choose private jets for himself, and solitary confinement for his enemies, while neglecting the needs of his people.[40] At the time of this writing, Obiang is still in power. He is Africa's longest-ruling leader, possibly its richest, and perhaps its cruelest. US import engagement with Obiang has put Americans into business with a dictator and has driven the resource disorders in Equatorial Guinea. By the time that you read this, Obiang may be gone. But the American government's choice of "might makes right" will still be putting Americans into business with authoritarians around the world. Here the business of America is badness.

FOREIGN INJUSTICE ON HOME SOIL

Those jaded to the rude workings of foreign affairs may not yet see the further implications. The leadership of nations is a club that includes many hard men, they might think, and major changes to the membership of that club exceed the dreams of even the most enthusiastic champion of American empire. "The world is as it is," they may say. "We just do business with who is in charge." Or to phrase the thought as a question: don't we have to deal with dictators?

Perhaps. Nevertheless, we "deal with" dictators along different dimensions of foreign policy: arms control, counter-terrorism, human rights, trade, and more. And our handling of any of these areas of foreign policy will produce better or worse outcomes both abroad and at home. Yet certain areas of foreign policy have a large moral impact on the home population that the other areas lack. In many areas of foreign policy, we can treat authoritarian regimes as powerful gangs in the global neighborhood. Yet with trade, and especially with trade in natural resources, it's different. Our policies for trade in natural resources import injustice from foreign countries, ingraining their injustices into our justice system. This is a way we now "deal with" dictators that we have special reason to regret.

Contrast US commercial engagement with Obiang to US negotiations with the regime in North Korea. The authoritarians of North Korea are at least as unsavory as Obiang, willing to subject their population to extremes of regimentation, deprivation, and misinformation. The North Korean regime controls nuclear weapons and is trying to get more; the United States deals with the North Korean regime for the sake of its own national security and that of its allies. The United States signs treaties with North Korean officials, presses for them to accept inspections, offers food aid to Pyongyang in exchange for concessions, and so on. Yet notice that none of these US actions affects American law. The US government goes out of its jurisdiction to deal with the North Korean leadership, as a rancher might go off his property to deal with outlaws.

Political recognition of North Korea by the United States has almost no domestic legal effects. Should the North Korean regime rejoin the Nuclear Non-Proliferation Treaty, that will be a signal event in foreign relations, but it will not be an event that even the best-trained lawyer working in an American jurisdiction will need to notice. Similarly, if the North Korean regime decides to build roads, abolish the death penalty, hold elections, or mass troops along the border with South Korea, these will be consequential decisions for Koreans and perhaps for Americans, but they would have no consequences within American law. US political recognition of North Korea has only minor domestic legal effects: for instance, should the North Korean regime decide to pull out of the Universal Postal Union, then North Korean postage stamps will no longer be valid for delivery of mail within the United States.

Commercial engagement with Obiang by the United States is legally much more intimate. Here the United States uses its control over its own law to designate Obiang as the authoritative decision maker for resources that will be sold into America. The United States literally makes Obiang's word law: not law for Equatorial Guinea, but law for the United States. Functionally, it's as if the US government has appointed Obiang as the US Secretary for Equatoguinean Petroleum. When Obiang pushes through a new hydrocarbons law (as he did in 2006), US courts will treat that law as decisive in their own reasoning. When Obiang chooses to sell a million barrels of oil, any American will become legally empowered to buy that oil.

For a country whose courts are so reluctant to accept the relevance of foreign laws for their own reasoning, it may seem droll that the United States sets its own legal system to track the decisions of a dictator. This is, however, the current state of affairs. The United States accredits Obiang's decisions to pass title to oil to American persons, and then requires the title to that oil to be defended with the full force of the American justice system, including all its police and courts.

This means that any injustice within Obiang's control over Equatorial Guinea's oil will become injustice enforced on American soil. And injustice there is: as we'll see in Chapter 13, Obiang is literally stealing Equatorial Guinea's oil. The United States chooses not only to allow imports of this stolen oil but to declare the imports legal because they come from a powerful enough thief.

The US government's choice of effectiveness leads directly to American officials enforcing foreign injustice on home soil. To see the gravity of this choice, observe that Americans would find such enforcement intolerable in other domains. Not long ago, an Iranian official announced that three men (identified only by the initials M. T., T.T., and M. Ch.) had been executed for the crime of sodomy. Their crime appears only to be having engaged in consensual adult male sexual conduct.[41] Imagine that one of these men (say, T. T.) had somehow escaped being hanged in Iran and fled to the United

States seeking asylum. Imagine the US Attorney General saying that he was very sorry, but the Iranian government had condemned T. T. to death. Therefore, he is ordering T. T. to be hanged in Indiana.[42]

The escape in that story is fictional, but some escapes are real. In 1989, a seven-year-old boy named Francis Bok was captured in Sudan by a slave-hunting militiaman named Giemma. Giemma forced Bok to live as his slave for ten years, bullwhipping Bok when he tried to escape. Bok finally did escape from slavery, though, and made his way, with much hardship, to America. Bok was invited to tell his heroic story to Congress, he published his autobiography, and he now lives in Kansas, where he works for an anti-slavery NGO.[43] Imagine the US President at a press conference saying, "Giemma has traveled from Sudan to Kansas, and is demanding his slave back. We are very sorry, but we must enforce Giemma's property rights over Francis Bok. We must allow Giemma to keep or to sell Bok as a slave in the United States."

It may be that the United States should pressure Iran to stop executing its citizens for sodomy, and pressure Sudan to end human bondage. Yet whatever American foreign policy should be in those areas, it would be regrettable for the United States to enforce the Iranian death penalty, or Sudanese slavery, on its own territory. Foreigners may commit or allow injustices in their own countries, but the American justice system becomes tainted when it enforces those injustices within its own borders.

Once the US government grants its persons the right to buy oil from Obiang, Obiang's crimes become American law. The oil he steals in Africa becomes legally owned in America; those property rights are enforced by the American justice system. Somewhere in Kansas, a driver may be pulling into a gas station, about to pump Equatoguinean oil into his tank. Now imagine that driver looking over to see Kansas state troopers standing guard at a slave auction, underway in the lot next door. The crime of slavery is worse than a theft of a nation's resources, but the wrongness of American enforcement of these injustices on its own soil is at most a matter of degree.

THE NATURALIZATION OF RESOURCES

Trade has special potential for transmitting foreign injustice into the homeland. As mentioned, it makes no moral difference whether milk comes from

Minnesota or Manitoba—but it does matter whether oil comes from Canada or Equatorial Guinea. One way of describing the international ban on the slave trade is that nations no longer choose "might makes right" for humans: governments no longer give their people the right to buy other humans from foreigners who can maintain coercive control over those humans. Yet national authorities still grant the right to buy natural resources from foreigners who can maintain coercive control over those resources, and this policy of effectiveness magnetizes all countries to tainted goods.

Of the two main factors of production—labor and raw materials—the latter is now more likely to be a source of pure injustice imported from abroad. Foreign goods may have been produced under unhealthy or unsafe conditions, and such violations of labor rights may indeed taint the goods that consumers buy at home. These are serious moral issues and deserve full treatments of their own.[44] Yet goods produced with outright theft of labor, with slave labor, are no longer a major portion of international trade flows.[45] And even exploited foreign workers typically have some choice—they can look for another job, or return to the rural poverty from which they usually come.

Raw materials are different. Because the extractive industries are enclaved, local people often have little control over their resources. The removal of Equatorial Guinea's oil involves no African labor at all: Obiang's regime approves a contract, and foreign firms build platforms offshore and take the country's oil away. The oil is 100 percent stolen when it arrives in the ports of importing states, with no possibility of Equatorial Guineans vetoing the exports by downing their tools or destroying the machines.

A country's trade policy is not special because it has effects at home; as above, all foreign policy can have effects at home. If a government allows trade with a country that exports impure food, then its citizens may be poisoned; similarly, if a government mishandles a war abroad, then its citizens may be killed in terrorist attacks. Trade policy is special in having strong domestic *moral* effects. A country that sets its property laws to track the decisions of bad actors abroad is certain to import injustice—and to enforce that injustice with its own justice system. Consumers in these countries will find stolen raw materials within their cars and computers, their homes and telephones, their cosmetics and medicines, their glasses and dentures, even in the skin and viscera of their own bodies. Only the morally perverse would enjoy the thought that their government will defend their rights to these stolen goods against all challengers.

States' engagement by effectiveness sends consumers' cash to regimes that are as coercive as any on Earth, and to militias of barely imaginable inhumanity. It pulls in the bloody, stolen goods of other countries and declares them legally clean. Yet effectiveness also coordinates the global market that supports the human population. Our moral situation is poor. The global market that sustains our lives is harmonized on a bad rule.

8

Grasping Dirty Hands

> Let the corrupt persons return what they have corruptly obtained and let it go back to the real owners. That would make corruption a risky business. Criminalize corruption so that wherever they go, the corrupt can always be apprehended, tried and handed justice. Provide no place to hide. Let the banks and governments which keep and protect stolen wealth open their vaults. This is blood money. It leaves children dying in hospitals which have no medicine, infrastructure which has collapsed, and water unfit for human beings to drink.
>
> —Wangari Maathai

> There is no man more dangerous, in a position of power, than he who refuses to accept as a working truth the idea that all a man does should make for rightness and soundness, that even the fixing of a tariff rate must be moral.
>
> —Ida Tarbell[1]

The world outside our borders may seem like this: every foreign country has installed a government, some governments are repressive or corrupt, and at times we have propped up such governments, a regrettable necessity. Sometimes in a foreign country, a conflict breaks out: we pay for peace-keepers, or support one side or the other, or just wait to see who wins. In extreme circumstances, we may actively intervene in the internal affairs of another country, through sanctions or even militarily. In the main, however, we hope that our steady diplomatic support of human rights, and especially our trade, will over time bring democracy, peace, and prosperity to troubled foreign lands.

This picture is not wrong, but for us its frame is too small. This is the frame of "breaking news"—of journalists who accept the international order as given and report political decisions against that background. But the economies, and so the politics, of other countries are not given; they are shaped by the commercial choices of many countries, including our own. Who we engage with, and on what terms, affects who will hold power abroad, how they will exercise that power, and what conflicts their power will cause. The commercial decisions of our governments cast the actors and then set the stage on which the dramas of each news cycle play out.

Through these chapters, we've looked into the importing-state choice to engage on the basis of effectiveness, and we've seen why that choice is especially damaging. Extractive resources are highly concentrated sources of exchange value. Selling off extractive resources can yield large and secret funds. The extraction of these resources can be protected, and contested, by military force. By empowering whoever can control resources by force, importing states drive the resource diseases of authoritarianism and civil conflict, with all their political, economic, and humanitarian consequences.

The principle of effectiveness in the resource trade shapes the foundations of the global order. On top of this, but still below most of the headlines, is the topic of this chapter: the further acts of influential governments that encourage commercial relations with iniquitous figures from resource-rich countries. Our governments allow, and even assist, our firms to engage with coercive and corrupt actors abroad; and they allow, even welcome, foreigners in control of illicit resource revenues to buy goods and services from our own home markets. In this chapter, we range around the basement of global trade, finding national laws and policies that promote corruption and human rights abuses abroad.

BLOOD MONEY

Corruption around rent-addicted governments is like debauchery in a brothel. A signing bonus paid by British firms for a Ugandan oil contract failed to appear in any published Ugandan budget, and the Ministry of Finance denied any knowledge of the money's location.[2] When the head of the Russian firm Lukoil got stuck in negotiations over a giant oil field in Kazakhstan, he gave the Kazakh president a $19 million executive jet. Asked whether the jet helped Lukoil to secure the contract, he replied, "Nothing is free."[3] As we'll see in Part IV, progress in changing the rules of engagement on corruption has been made in some countries, encouraging hope for more. Yet the pressures on home-state leaders to allow their firms to engage in grand corruption continue to bulge, and officials continue to ignore, or even support, criminality by firms that are creatures of their own laws.

The World Bank has estimated that developing countries lose between $20 billion and $40 billion each year to bribery, embezzlement, and other corrupt practices—and that only $5 billion of this lost money was recovered over a fifteen-year period.[4] "Corruption is not just a moral or ethical issue," says economist Daniel Kaufmann. "We estimate that with good governance, there is a threefold increase in per capita incomes."[5] Ngozi Okonjo-Iweala makes the consequences more real:

> Every day, funds destined for schools, health care, and infrastructure in the world's most fragile economies are siphoned off and stashed away in the world's financial centers and tax havens. Corruption, like a disease, is eating away at the foundation of people's faith in government. It undermines the stability and security of nations... It also undermines the preconditions for growth and equity.[6]

Transparency International's Bribe Payers Index ranks the mining and petroleum industries as, respectively, the fourth and fifth most likely locations of bribery, and the second and third most likely locations for grand corruption of high-level officials.[7] (And to give an idea of the scale of the money that moves in these industries, in a recent year US resource firms invested over $26 billion abroad—about the same amount as America's bilateral development aid.[8]) Sometimes the laws of corporations' home states openly allow foreign corruption. Until 2006, for example, Finland and the Netherlands allowed tax deductions on bribes to foreign officials.[9] So-called "facilitation payments," which are payments to foreign officials said to fall short of outright bribery, are still permitted by under the laws of Australia, Canada, New Zealand, South Korea, and the United States.[10]

Sometimes a corporate home state will have laws against bribing exporting-country officials, but corruption passes through loopholes in those laws.[11] And sometimes anti-corruption laws are on the books, but governments decide not to enforce them. It was not until 2009, for example, that Britain successfully prosecuted a foreign corruption case against a corporation; many states still have never done so.[12] The US Department of Justice and the Securities and Exchange Commission enforce the Foreign Corrupt Practices Act; they have found serious crimes to prosecute as they have stepped up their efforts in recent years. For instance, they secured criminal convictions and fines of $579 million against Halliburton and a subsidiary for paying hundreds of millions of dollars of bribes to top Nigerian officials (including "officials of the executive branch of the Nigerian government," widely reported to include two Nigerian presidents). These bribes won $6 billion in contracts for Halliburton and associated companies to build liquefied natural gas facilities in the Niger Delta.[13]

When the Justice Department charged American businessman James Giffen with passing $78 million in bribes from American oil companies to the president and oil minister of Kazakhstan, Giffen's defense was not to deny the bribery. Rather, he claimed that his activities had been approved by the Central Intelligence Agency, the National Security Council, the State Department, and the White House. The trial judge, citing classified US documents, agreed that Giffen "had advanced the strategic interests of the United States and American businesses in Central Asia." The judge acknowledged Giffen's service to his country, gave him no prison time, and merely ordered Giffen's firm to pay a small fine for illegally providing Kazakh officials with two snowmobiles.[14]

Complaints of Chinese complicity with bad actors who control natural resources have escalated with the "going out" of Chinese firms, especially into Africa. One report claims that a single Chinese consortium (perhaps backed and at least tolerated by Beijing) transferred $100 million to a Guinean junta in a minerals deal—a month after the junta was placed under international sanctions because its soldiers killed more than 150 protesters and raped dozens of women in a sports stadium. The same Chinese consortium appears to have signed a contract directly with Zimbabwe's notorious secret police, the CIO—bypassing the rest of Zimbabwe's government—to buy diamonds from fields controlled by the CIO. These diamonds were under international embargo after repeated reports of official violence against miners, including torture, enslavement, and military attacks.[15]

These Chinese cases, like the Giffen case, exist in a liminal area of their respective governments' rules of engagement, where it is simply unclear how much the governments concerned are authorizing, or merely excusing, actions of their nationals that aggravate the resource disorders abroad. But sometimes the involvement of the state in grand corruption becomes all too clear.

For decades, the French national oil company Elf was at the center of a massive nexus of corrupt dealings in several African states. French officials secretly siphoned hundreds of millions of euros of Elf's oil money, and used some of the money to prop up authoritarian African leaders in the French sphere of influence, while French soldiers also provided these leaders military support. This dark system thwarted development where Elf was operating. For instance, an Elf representative later testified that the company was giving the head of the African country at the center of *l'affaire Elf*, Omar Bongo of Gabon, 50 million euros per year. And to take a suggestive comparison, life expectancy in Gabon today is 12 years less than in the nearby non-oil state of Togo—even though Gabon's average income is 18 times greater.[16]

Some of the rest of the illicit Elf money went for bribes to advance French diplomatic and corporate interests. And some of the money was sucked into the French political parties—mostly by the center-right Gaullists, until a Socialist president demanded that the money from the secret slush fund be evenly shared.[17] *L'affaire Elf* shows how corruption going out from a major importing country can boomerang back to damage that country's own democratic integrity.

One contemporary author devotes a book to telling lurid stories like those above: stories of opaque deals between foreign firms and African elites, which have drained off resources worth huge sums yet left the people of the countries with little or no money in return. He sums up the entire contemporary system with his title: *The Looting Machine*.[18]

OPENING THE HOME MARKET

Picture the scene. A soldier named Basher has overthrown the US government and declared himself president. Basher's militias have left everyone in Pittsburgh dead and forced the entire population of Nevada to flee their homes. Basher has put Alaska under military rule, and he has traded its oil to China for weapons and money that he is using to launch airstrikes against populations around the oil fields near the US-Mexican border. Basher has forced a law through Congress declaring that his regime now legally controls all of the natural resources in the United States, and he has sold rights to all the oil in California, again to China. Entertain what might earlier have seemed an eccentric question: should the sale of that oil be legally valid?

Now let's look at what actually happened. In Sudan, General Omar al-Bashir overthrew the government and declared himself president. When his militias first attacked in Darfur, Sudanese in numbers equal to the population of Pittsburgh were left dead, and Nevada-sized numbers fled their homes.[19] For years, Bashir traded Sudan's oil to China in what a human rights group called "a toxic oil-for-arms relationship."[20] With those arms, Bashir launched years of military campaigns into the oil-rich region that is now South Sudan. And China still buys nearly all of Sudan's oil, as part of its effectiveness-based trade.[21]

Even after the Chinese government decided to make it legal to buy oil from Bashir, it still had a further decision to make—whether to let Bashir himself into China. This China did in 2011, giving him full military honors in the Great Hall of the People in Beijing. Bashir thanked China for its "warm welcome and treatment," and he called the Chinese president his "friend and brother."[22] Bashir seemed genuinely grateful for the hospitality, as the Chinese fête came two years after the International Criminal Court issued arrest warrants for him on charges of war crimes, crimes against humanity, and genocide.[23] Before Westerners allow themselves a sense of superiority here, however, they might reflect that denying a visa to even the worst leaders is a very rare decision for any state to make. Most countries, most of the time, welcome in foreign officials who are unjustly enriched with resource money. And that includes the countries in North America and Europe.

The last chapter showed that governments use effectiveness to decide on "import engagement": to authorize their own persons to buy resources from coercive foreign vendors. As we've seen in this chapter, governments also set further "rules of engagement" for their own persons who do business in resource-rich states, which can spread pathologies such as corruption and human rights violations. The final dimension of commercial engagement is "home-market engagement." Here a state opens its own internal markets to foreigners enriched by resource sales. (Recall the "Them-Here" decisions on High Island from Chapter 7: each national authority determines its own laws regarding foreigners buying property within its territory.) If a government decides to open its home market to unsavory and unscrupulous foreigners, it will also encourage the resource disorders with the pull of its domestic goods and services.

A UN consultant estimates that the Gabonese president's family and friends misappropriated a quarter of the country's GDP for themselves. "There's absolutely no shame," the consultant said. "I would say that the people who are running the country are guilty of grand theft nation."[24] This mostly-poor African country has had the highest level of champagne consumption in the world—and it's not the poor who are celebrating.[25] Recently, the Gabonese president's wife was captured on camera sniffing at a $25 million mansion in Malibu. "I need something really big, really, really, really big," she said. "I would think for that amount of money, I would expect a bit more grandeur."[26]

The world's leading banks, hospitals, universities, arms makers, and luxury shops legally sell goods and services in exchange for resource revenues spent by highly coercive and corrupt foreign actors. Foreigners enriched with illicit resource revenues have demonstrated desires to buy munitions in Italy, to shop in Paris boutiques, to bank in London, to receive medical care in Germany, and to get their children into American universities. Each national authority determines its own laws regarding foreign purchases within its own territory. So these purchases are only legal because the Italian, French, British, German, and American governments make them so.

Allowing coercive and corrupt foreigners to spend stolen resource revenues on the objects of their desire increases their incentives to steal more. As the son of a Nigerian tribal chief said about the officials who have become rich from embezzling his country's oil money:

> These men can send their money to Shanghai or Singapore—but they don't want to go to those places. They don't like the food. They don't speak the language. And a black man will always be a second-class citizen in Asia because of the racism. These men want to fly with their family to a house in Paris. They want to take their mistress shopping in Harrods. And they want to send their children to American schools. That's where their face comes from. And when they get ill they go to the Mayo Clinic.[27]

The *Financial Times* suggested that readers could take a "Tyrant's Tour" of France, stopping at the thirty-nine French properties of the ruling family of Gabon (including an €18 million hotel in the seventh arrondissement), or the eighteen properties owned by Congo's President Sassou and his family. (The paper notes that the Sassou family's 112 French bank accounts are not open to visitors.[28]) The regulatory authority over British banks found that three-quarters of banks had leaky safeguards against money laundering by powerful foreign officials—despite a decade of legislation aimed at stopping those leaks.[29]

A bipartisan US Senate investigative committee published detailed case studies on how top officials from four oil-rich countries "used US lawyers, real estate and escrow agents, lobbyists, bankers, and even university officials, to circumvent US anti-money laundering and anti-corruption safeguards." The report names firms like Citibank, Bank of America, and PayPal as facilitating the transfer of suspect funds into the United States. Going back out of the United States were large purchases made with these funds, like armored cars and a C-130 Hercules aircraft.[30] "It's time for the US to stop allowing corrupt officials to use their countries as personal ATMs and the US as a shopping mall," says Arvind Ganesan of Human Rights Watch. "Kleptocrats need to know that the US is not open for business."[31]

Occasionally, governments do block the home-market side of their commercial engagement with a specific foreigner and his associates. In 2007, a British court seized UK assets worth £21 million from James Ibori, the powerful governor of Nigeria's Delta State. In 2010, another British court sentenced Ibori's sister and mistress to five years in prison for money laundering and mortgage fraud. Ibori himself was arrested, extradited, and in 2012 sentenced to thirteen years in prison by a London court for conspiracy to defraud.[32] In 2011, the French authorities seized eleven cars (including two Bugattis, two Ferraris, and "various Bentleys") from Teodorín Obiang's residence at 42 Avenue Foch in Paris.[33]

The US Department of Justice followed by seizing Teodorín's Malibu mansion, his private jet, and expensive memorabilia (after concluding that Teodorín's assets were derived from "misappropriation, theft, or embezzlement of public funds").[34] The US government pressed a civil asset forfeiture case, *United States v. One Michael Jackson Signed Thriller Jacket*, forcing Teodorín to sell the mansion, a Ferrari, and two life-sized statues, and to donate the money to a charity for "the benefit of the people of Equatorial Guinea."[35]

These blocks on flows of stolen resource revenues into home markets mark progress, and we'll trace them more in what follows. These are, however, rare exceptions. Most states, including the United States, welcome corrupt and coercive actors who hold resource revenues into their home markets, thinking that their dirty money is good for business. Yet, here again, this business is badness.

And indeed, for the regimes most exorbitantly endowed with resource revenues, even the goods and services we've been discussing are mere trinkets. Children and mistresses may want fancy schools and shops, yet what the richest rulers want most from the West is a stable environment in which invest their stolen wealth.[36] Consider Qatar and the UAE, both loaded with resource cash. Visitors to London will see recent Qatari investments everywhere: in Harrods, the Shard skyscraper, Canary Wharf, the Camden Locks, Barclays banks, and Sainsbury's supermarkets. Similarly, the UAE holds an investment portfolio estimated at well over half a trillion dollars, which is 60 to 85 percent held in North America and Europe.[37] Without access to the West's high-quality asset classes, these regimes would have to face the risks of investing in regions like their own.

HIDING IN THE LIGHT

Every autocrat surrounds himself with a ring of steel—the fences of his residences, the armor of his cars, the gun barrels of his guards. We can study the topology of that ring to understand the autocrat's control over his country's resources and resource money. The ring will rarely open for ordinary citizens wanting to discuss resource issues, and a true autocrat may wall out the citizenry entirely. The ring will breach to representatives of foreign resource corporations offering contracts and bribes. It will also open to foreign doctors, realtors, wealth managers, and arms salesmen. The ring of steel will open widest to the leaders of wealthy states, who can give even the most powerful autocrat what no one else can—a license to sell resources into a rich country.

States' choices on commercial engagement lead to foreigners leading worse lives: to their suffering the distress of oppressive rule, the violations of armed conflict, the indignity of an unresponsive state, the daily grinding of a filthy environment. Some of these state choices are so settled as to appear to be part of the natural order of things. They are revealed as choices when some government (usually a major power) shows that it has reserved to itself the legal flexibility to choose differently. So the United States or the

European Union will impose sanctions instead of engaging with a dictator. Or they will attempt to shore up weak states against the militias plundering their timber or diamonds instead of legalizing that plunder. Or they will close their markets to an egregious foreign kleptocrat instead of inviting him in.

These deviations from business as usual show how markets are shaped by the choices of our governments. The decisive policies of our countries, which decide the rules that run the world, are hiding in the light.

This is the inflection point; we've bottomed out. Having walked down through the infernal world created by today's trade in natural resources, we can now raise our gazes and begin to ascend. Next, history will give us confidence that effectiveness for resources can be overcome, by showing how often effectiveness has been abolished already. The history in Part III is a history that humanity has gone through together: it is a *purgatorio*—a purification, a making clean. This history shows the many giant steps that humanity has already made away from "might makes right," becoming ever stronger as it shakes off its restraints. The next step in this history is a short space in front of us—in fact, we're already almost there.

PART III

The People's Rights

Today's situation is poor, yet the prospects for reforming "might makes right" are excellent. In the brutal seventeenth century, "might makes right" was the rule not only for natural resources but for nearly all of international affairs. Since then, this international power rule has been rolled back with counter-power: with rules ending colonialism, controlling the conduct of war, banning apartheid, demanding human rights. The progress has been slow; it is still fragile and far from complete. Yet the entrenchment of counter-powerful rules has changed the ground rules of the world, and has even improved how we see ourselves.

The People's Rights

9

Counter-Power

Men who take up arms against one another in public war do not cease on this account to be moral beings, responsible to one another and to God. Military necessity does not admit of cruelty—that is, the infliction of suffering for the sake of suffering or for revenge, nor of maiming or wounding except in fight, nor of torture to extort confessions. It does not admit of the use of poison in any way, nor of the wanton devastation of a district. It admits of deception, but disclaims acts of perfidy; and, in general, military necessity does not include any act of hostility which makes the return to peace unnecessarily difficult.

—Abraham Lincoln's General Order 100
(The Lieber Code)

What an age experiences as evil is usually an untimely reverberation echoing what was previously experienced as a good—the atavism of an older ideal.

—Friedrich Nietzsche[1]

Think of the moral milestones in world history that one might teach to a child. One might say that the slave trade has been banned in international law since the nineteenth century—physically capturing human beings no longer gains the legal right to sell human beings across borders. One might continue that subjugating a foreign people or seizing their land no longer wins the right to rule those people or that land. Colonialism and conquest were outlawed in the twentieth century. The imposition of a racist state is now forbidden, as is state abuse of the individuals in its domain. Apartheid is now illegal, and we have human rights law. Each of these milestones marks a transition away from effectiveness in international law. Each of these milestones says: here might will no longer make right.

In the history of human progress, these victories over effectiveness are large markers. As we tell this history to our children, we'll add that ending "might makes right" has not magically abolished might. The slave trade has been illegal for decades—yet even today humans are trafficked across borders. Banning the slave trade has no more made slavery impossible than banning gender discrimination has meant that it no longer happens. Still, if a child asks whether the ban on the slave trade was good, we say yes. The ban has reduced this terrible wrong and signaled that respectable opinion now abhors it. The same is true for the other legal reversals of "might makes right." These milestones mark progress, both because they have furthered the value of freedom from power and because they have expanded the opportunities of so many.

A MORAL HISTORY OF PLUNDER

In modern international law, might no longer always makes right. Even war, an activity defined by the decisiveness of power, has been bound by laws limiting its excesses. The Hague Convention of 1899, a treaty that declares "the right of belligerents to adopt means of injuring the enemy is not unlimited," forbids belligerents:

- To employ poison or poisoned arms;
- To kill or wound treacherously individuals belonging to the hostile nation or army;
- To kill or wound an enemy who, having laid down arms, or having no longer means of defense, has surrendered at discretion;
- To declare that no quarter will be given;
- To employ arms, projectiles, or material of a nature to cause superfluous injury . . .
- To destroy or seize the enemy's property, unless such destruction or seizure be imperatively demanded by the necessities of war.[2]

These rules, and their successors in treaties of the twentieth century, may seem a scant achievement, overshadowed by the annihilative technologies simultaneously devised. Yet their entrenchment shows that rules to counter power can supersede "might makes right" in international affairs. The last of these Hague rules, the one prohibiting plunder, is the one we will first follow to see how moral progress happens through history. The evolution of rules on plunder illustrates in miniature how effectiveness has been rolled back, and then reversed.

VAE VICTIS

To the victors—the Roman imperialists decreed—*go the spoils*. The emperors and kings of early modern Europe, so keen to see themselves as Rome's heirs, took up this dictum with gusto. When Hugo Grotius wrote the first modern text on international law in 1625, he cited Roman authorities in support of what he called "The Right to Lay Waste an Enemy's Country, and Carry Off His Effects." Grotius affirmed the rule that an enemy's property may be wasted and plundered, even to their holy sites. "For when places are taken by an enemy, all things without exception, whether sacred or not, must fall a sacrifice" (the only minor exception being that an army should not show "wanton insult" to the ashes of the dead).[3] Grotius here codified a near-perfect law of "might makes right."

By 1796, this legal permission to plunder was in the hands of a conqueror leading a mass army and a nascent bureaucratic state. Napoleon ordered his experts to catalogue in advance the finest artworks of the Italian cities that he expected to seize; soon, hundreds of masterpieces were flowing toward the Louvre. In July 1798, the Parisian celebration of the pillage of Italy featured "a parade of art treasures—including the Apollo Belvedere, the Laocoön, Raphael's *Transfiguration*, the *Saint Jerome* of Correggio, and paintings by Titian and Veronese—on 29 carts, accompanied by troops, dignitaries, a military band and wagons with caged bears, lions and camels. Preceding the carts was a banner whose inscription explicitly placed France alongside the great ancient civilizations."[4]

Napoleon's looting of European cities fired a reaction across the continent against Grotius's pro-plunder rule. After Napoleon's defeat, the despoiled countries began a decades-long campaign to pressure France to return its booty. Abraham Lincoln strengthened the coalescing anti-plunder consensus by declaring pillage a crime in the Lieber Code of 1863.[5] By the end of the nineteenth century, France had returned most of Napoleon's loot, and the Hague Convention of 1899, with its strong anti-plunder rule, was signed by all the European powers and the United States. Judgments were converging among those with influence in international affairs on this new rule forbidding pillage.

Convergence on a rule, however, by no means ensures compliance. In the mid-twentieth century, a second mass army swept over Europe, its bureaucracy of plunder trailing behind. The guilty verdict at Nuremberg of the Nazi in charge of these thefts, Alfred Rosenberg, detailed some of the spoils: "69,619 Jewish homes were plundered in the West, 38,000 of them in Paris alone, and it took 26,984 railroad cars to transport the confiscated furnishings to Germany. As of 14th July, 1944, more than 21,903 art objects, including famous paintings and museum pieces, had been seized."[6] This time, the anti-plunder rule had an enforcement mechanism: the Nazi Rosenberg was hanged for plunder as well as other war crimes.

Yet, while prosecuting the anti-plunder rule at Nuremberg, the victorious Americans were tempted to violate it themselves. The occupying Americans took two hundred German artworks back home in 1945. Displayed in major museums nationwide, these works were seen by 10 million Americans. But then the new anti-plunder norm again kicked in: the American parading of these trophies provoked a furious response from art experts and the US government's own staff, and by 1949, the Americans had returned the German art to Germany.

These postwar episodes solidified the anti-plunder rule within American public opinion. By the time of the invasion of Iraq in 2003, a display of captured Iraqi antiquities in American art museums—much less a Napoleon-style parade of ancient Assyrian friezes through the streets of Washington—would have been blasted by the American press. Indeed, during the Iraq War, the US military was criticized not for plundering, but for falling short of its obligations under new treaties the US signed in 1954 and 1999. These new treaties require more from an occupying power than merely refraining from plundering the enemy's territory. These treaties also require an occupying power to safeguard the antiquities of the occupied country against looting by others.[7] The new rule for armies is more than anti-plunder—it is counter-plunder.

Through this centuries-long evolution of European laws, one rule has been replaced by its opposite. Since Grotius wrote in 1625, the right of victors to plunder has been negated (victors have no right to plunder) and then inverted (victors have a duty to safeguard what they formerly had a right to take). *Vae victis* has been transmuted into a requirement to care for the cultural property of the enemy. "Might makes right" has become its antithesis: "with power comes responsibility." Within this one tiny area of international affairs, at least, a rule of power has been dimmed out, and a rule of counter-power has brightened with increasing intensity.

The entrenchment of any counter-powerful rule will proceed in stages.[8] First is rule formation: someone must define a rule prohibiting plunder, as someone first framed a rule against using nerve gas or against sexual harassment. Once formed, the rule is then spread, and those bound by it increasingly converge on an understanding of what it requires and how it should be enforced.[9]

We need not be naive about the early stages of a rule's life. The motives of major players in spreading a new rule may be entirely strategic. It was politically useful, for example, for nineteenth century European leaders to do some French-bashing by repeatedly raising the issue of Napoleon's plunder in public. And while a rule is spreading, its enforcement may be inconsistent or hypocritical. We see this in America's nearly simultaneous enforcement and violation of the anti-plunder rule after World War II—first hanging Rosenberg in Germany, then hanging German paintings in museums at home.

Indeed, the acceptance of a rule often comes as a surprise to powerful actors who initially invoke it only strategically. In 1975, the Soviets were fixated on those parts of the Helsinki Accords that solidified their territorial control over Eastern Europe. The Soviets virtually ignored the human rights language of the Accords, which NGOs then used in a highly successful campaign to free Soviet Jews (this is the origin of what is now Human Rights Watch).[10] Similarly, in the 2000s, a major international oil company ran newspaper ads about its ethical conduct, which might generously be described as "incomplete." The company's leadership was later troubled by internal complaints from its own employees who were concerned that the company was not living up to its advertised principles.[11]

As a counter-power rule becomes established, there may still be waves of violations, as with the Nazi campaign of plunder after the Hague Convention had been signed. But the receding historical tide means that these waves break farther from shore. Violators stop flaunting their violations: even the Nazis, for instance, did not parade their loot as Napoleon had done. Violators instead start excusing their violations by appealing to some other important rule—as the Americans did, for example, when they said that they were merely safeguarding the German art that they had seized.

The end point of the entrenchment of any counter-power rule is internalization. During internalization, a rule becomes part of the self-image of those who accept it. The identity of the relevant actor is redefined to valorize compliance with the rule: the rule becomes a new standard of goodness ("a good boss does not sexually harass his secretaries"; "a good company does not violate human rights"). At the ultimate stage of entrenchment, identification with the rule is so complete that the relevant actor has no desire to violate the rule, the thought never occurs to transgress it. Insofar as we are what we want, and what we think, the new rule comes to define us.

Perfect internalization of any rule is never to be expected. The ban on parent-child incest, for example, is one of the strictest and most deeply internalized counter-power rules that we have. Yet you might speculate how far you would have to walk right now to discover an instance of its violation.[12] Moreover, the entrenchment of a counter-power rule, like the settling of a boulder into a river, may not keep power from reaching its destination. One insistent theme of postcolonial theory, for instance, has been the continuing subordination of former colonies even after they have won their independence.[13]

Most importantly, the progress of any rule's entrenchment—from formation to spread, from enforcement to internalization—is never inevitable. We find, in our patch of history, counter-powerful rules in every stage, from nascency to fixity. None of these rules is fated to grow further; even rules with the longest historical roots can wither at any time. The embedding of these standards, so often supported strategically and in bad faith, remains uncertain even as it nears completion. We now start all the way back at the beginning, to see the rise of the legal rule of "might makes right"—and then its supersession by new rules: rules of "might makes wrong."

THE FALL OF CHRISTENDOM

Christendom, the political formation of Europe through the Middle Ages and the Renaissance, was sustained by a consensus on the legitimacy of theocracy. In this era, all authority over men derived ultimately from God.

The Pope then had political authority. Kings had religious authority and administered their kingdoms with the help of cardinals and archbishops.

"There was not yet," as one historian put it, "any clear idea of 'the state' and much less the nation-state or the sovereignty of the people."[14] Europeans did not see themselves as divided into independent countries but rather as living within the Europe-wide domain that was Christendom. The church, led by the Bishop of Rome, distributed all dominion over men throughout this common Christian realm.

This emphasis on religious authority contrasts Christendom to our times. In its architecture of authority, Christendom more closely resembles the transnational caliphate today championed by al-Qaeda and Islamic State. In the terms used in Chapter 3, Christendom was a theocratic clientelistic pyramid. Each officeholder held authority defined by vertical relations to other officeholders within the spiritual and temporal hierarchies. Excommunication from this hierarchy was a serious threat to a ruler's legitimacy. Both ecclesiastic and royal authorities ordered the inquisition of baptized Christians who were suspected of heresy.

Basic premises of political organization were then quite different. Most Europeans were not free but belonged to the land—which itself was held either by religious institutions, such as monasteries, or by noblemen of rank from knight to king. Above that lowest level, political authority was less territorial and more personal. Trying to represent Christendom's authority relations in two dimensions would not produce anything like today's political map of Europe. Emperors, kings, and princes claimed jurisdictions that overlapped with each other (like modern Saudi princes) as well as islands of jurisdiction within larger areas ruled by others. Even within one region, religious courts and civil courts might enforce contradictory laws.

Christendom remains by far the longest-lasting European political formation. The church's domination of European institutions endured for eight centuries and deeply recoded the intellectual DNA of the West. Christendom survived low-level conflicts such as the Hundred Years War, demographic crashes from plagues and famines, and a crisis of authority that produced three claimants to the papacy by the turn of the fifteenth century. It was only across the fifteenth to the seventeenth centuries that Christendom finally cracked and then succumbed to what Locke called the flux of the world.[15]

The fall of Christendom was the collapse of the Europe-wide community of conviction on the legitimacy of theocracy. Many forces pressed toward collapse. Advances in productive (especially information) technology pushed power downward within the hierarchies, the hierarchies themselves became visibly more corrupt toward the top, and new approaches to biblical interpretation weakened the elite's ideological control. The European consensus on the legitimacy of theocracy began to collapse, and armed violence filled the void.

Armed violence in Europe increased steadily from the first peasant uprisings in the Black Forest in 1524 through to the all-consuming Thirty Years War that ended in 1648. What made these conflicts so fearsome was that no one agreed on the implications of a military victory, especially regarding rightful authority over conquered territory. Fighting became interminable because the combatants had no common standard of what should happen when one side won. Whoever won, Catholics thought that only Catholic rule could be rightful, and *mutandis mutatis* for the Lutherans and Calvinists. So the fighting, when it could, began ever again.

The Thirty Years War was a crisis of legitimation and "the most devastating European conflict after the barbarian invasion."[16] In the chaotic last stage of this European conflagration, even the ideological armies disaggregated into bands of mercenary looters (as in today's eastern Congo). Decades of violence and pestilence flayed a continent torn by contradictions. The Thirty Years War was a void of dissensus into which a quarter of the German population disappeared.[17]

THE JURISPRUDENCE OF THE JUNGLE

The worst cognitive condition is not error, but confusion. The void left by the collapse of Christendom gradually filled with a minimal structure of rules, which we now identify with the 1648 Peace of Westphalia. The rule that organized this new Westphalian consensus was effectiveness: the rule that might should make right. Grotius explained one dimension of this new rule of effectiveness in his founding text on international law—in a chapter titled "On the Acquisition of Territory and Property by Right of Conquest":

> According to the law of nations, not only the person, who makes war upon just grounds; but any one whatever, engaged in regular and formal war, becomes absolute proprietor of every thing which he takes from the enemy: so that all nations respect his title, and the title of all, who derive through him their claim to such possessions.[18]

Might, Grotius says, vests the right to rule conquered territory and the right to own captured property. All nations must recognize these titles to territory and property, which will be the foundation of all future claims that derive from them. Grotius is here setting out the more general form of the law of *vae victis*: the pro-plunder rule with which we began this chapter. In the Westphalian settlement, effectiveness became the law not just for plunder, but for everything.

Westphalia's "might makes right" rule, today so suspect in international affairs, was a step out of the void of dissensus that was the Thirty Years War. At the time, it was therefore a real moral advance. Rules like this Grotian code of conquest created grounds for agreement that could finally stop the fighting between confessional armies. By converging on effectiveness, Catholics and Protestants could agree to truces that were more than mere ceasefires; they could agree that territory was *rightfully* ruled by those who could maintain coercive control over it. Catholic princes now accepted not only that Lutheran princes had conquered a territory but that Lutheran rule was rightful, and vice-versa. So long as a leader could hold a region, he was recognized as an equal sovereign by all, no matter whether he was Catholic, Lutheran, or Calvinist.

Effectiveness eased the European crisis of legitimation. While princes still battled, they at least agreed that superior might (while it lasted) made right. The consolidation of the consensus on effectiveness marked the transition between the personalistic authority pyramids of Christendom and the modern state system of territorial sovereignty. In 1648, Pope Innocent X famously condemned this transition away from the Catholic clientelistic hierarchy which he was atop, calling the Westphalian treaties "null, void, invalid, iniquitous, unjust, damnable, reprobate, inane, and devoid of meaning for all time."[19] Those fighting the wars preferred to agree on effectiveness, and to disagree on creed. Their agreement that political authority should track force instead of faith became, as Hedley Bull called it, "a basic rule of coexistence."[20]

Effectiveness was the foundation of international law until World War II. In classic international law, European rulers held authority over territory because they were—and for so long as they remained—effective. In fact, in Westphalian international law, right tracked might along nearly all dimensions of international affairs: there was no prohibition on war against another ruler, no prohibition on the violent seizure of his territory or the property of his subjects. Effectiveness simply pronounced whatever resulted from such actions lawful. Whoever could conquer Polish territory, for example, became its rightful ruler (and that particular rule was reapplied many times). As James Crawford puts it, international law "treated its subjects, the states, as existing while they existed but it offered no guarantees as to their future. If states ceased to exist, that was as it might be. The law of nations was, in a sense, the codified law of the jungle."[21] Peace, if it occurred, was not the outcome of an international rule—it was simply an indicator of a temporary balance of power.[22]

When comparing Westphalia to the chaos it replaced, it is important that effectiveness is a genuine legal principle. The law of the jungle is codified: it is right that might makes, not just facts.[23] Effectiveness is a common standard of rightness—and often the best rule to end chaotic conflicts like wars of religion, because what is needed to end such conflicts is order through governance. Granting sovereignty to the strongest is a rule that always points not only to a definite governor, but to the one who is most likely to be able to keep order as well. Making authority track relative strength is then the rule most likely to locate an efficacious sovereign—even more than a rule that makes authority track absolute strength (as in the Arthurian "whoever can pull this sword from this stone") or a rule that tracks the will of the people (as a people may be too weak to will). Moreover, when a known actor will predictably remain the strongest, effectiveness sets a public basis for stable expectations about the future, which is highly desirable where conflict is looming (a theme of *Leviathan*, which Hobbes began writing during the English religious wars).

As a rule of legitimation in the seventeenth century, the Westphalian rule of effectiveness was literally better than nothing. However, Westphalia was hardly a charter for peace. More, it left sovereigns—identified only by their power—legally unsupervised in how they treated the people in their power. The Westphalian sovereign was a master at home and an equal abroad. Rulers remained sovereign equals to each other regardless of how they conducted their "internal affairs"—regardless of what they did within their borders. With a very few exceptions, nothing that a ruler could do to the people in his territory could be a matter of official concern to other rulers. Each ruler was the strongest in his land—that was all that other rulers needed to know. International law treated modern states as legal black boxes: what went on inside them could be of no official concern to those outside.

Effectiveness was the primary rule of European international law for the three centuries between 1648 and 1948. When we look back on this period of international law, we rightly see it as morally impoverished: as Javier Solana once noted, "humanity and democracy [were] two principles essentially irrelevant to the original Westphalian order."[24] Yet the European consensus on effectiveness was better than the discord of convictions it replaced. Convergence on effectiveness planted order in the void left by Christendom's collapse.

WESTPHALIAN EVOLUTION

In the centuries after 1648, the Westphalian international system spread spatially. Effectiveness justified Europe's gigantic colonial thrusts beyond its borders. If Poland could be rightfully ruled after conquest, how much more the East Indies or North Africa? It was not until the end of the nineteenth century that a non-Western country (Japan) fought its way into the European club of equal sovereign states. By this time, Britain, the then-dominant Westphalian imperialist, ruled one-fifth of humanity and an even larger percentage of the world's land. We will follow that story further in Chapter 10.

While the Westphalian system was being spread over (or rather forced onto) large parts of the earth's surface, within Europe itself its rules were evolving. Effectiveness is a power rule, and in the centuries after Westphalia, counter-power rules grew into European relations. We saw one minor example of this evolution earlier: the replacement of pro-plunder laws with anti-plunder laws from the seventeenth to the twentieth centuries. A more momentous evolution of international law changed the rules on how sovereigns could treat their own people. These laws redefined what a ruler could rightfully do to the ruled, and they opened up the black box that was the Westphalian state.

Westphalia had only one major rule of lawful governance of people: force. "Might makes right" transformed successful coercion of a population into sweeping permissions regarding its treatment. A ruler could violate or neglect the ruled with impunity, with no stain on his authority. With one exception (discussed below), there was nothing that a sovereign could do within his borders that could justify international condemnation, much less international intervention. A prince could abuse his people to nearly any extent, sell the land on which they lived out from under them, and ignore their material needs entirely without violating any rule of international law.

Westphalian law saw ordinary people as our laws see animals. Only sovereigns were legal persons: only sovereigns had legal rights. The common people had no legal rights, and insofar as there were any legal constraints on the treatment of the common people, these were framed as duties on rulers—not as rights of the ruled.[25] In fact, today's animals are better off legally than ordinary people were under Westphalia: animal welfare laws in most countries now require better physical treatment of animals than Westphalia required of humans. Beyond effectiveness, the Westphalian legal relation between ruler and ruled was almost entirely unstructured.

Reflecting on our ancestors, we can wonder why they accepted less-structured forms of relationships in which abuse and neglect are always dangers. For example, under Roman law, a father could legally kill his children and be subject to no official punishment or criticism of any kind.[26] In the European Middle Ages, a husband was recognized as having rights to severe "physical chastisement" of his wife. Through the nineteenth and early twentieth centuries, the legal relation between employer and employee within industrialized countries was only minimally structured (and this continues to be the case in many poor countries). Change has come as counter-powerful standards that give structure to these kinds of relations have gradually been framed and internalized—and as low-structure relations found to be unredeemable, such as the relation between master and chattel slave, have been abandoned.

Even within the Westphalian order, the legal relation between ruler and ruled was not completely unstructured. The Westphalian treaties did require one significant standard of legitimate governance, which was that rulers must tolerate religious diversity among the ruled. Sovereigns were obliged to protect the religious non-conformists within their borders—particularly the non-conformists' private worship and orderly emigration—and one sovereign could officially condemn another sovereign's lapses from this standard. Religious toleration was required by international law—toleration was not treated as merely part of the "internal affairs" of each state. The international enforcement mechanisms for this rule of religious toleration, however, were not well defined: at the limit, enforcement of this rule resembled ordinary military invasion. Even so, all sovereigns accepted that they could rightfully be criticized by other sovereigns for abusing religious dissenters, and this one exception to the rule of "non-interference in internal affairs" became a model for the growth of other counter-powerful rules within the international system.

International demands for religious toleration grew during the nineteenth century. European and American leaders decried Ottoman massacres of Christians (William McKinley ran for President in 1896 on a platform of stopping atrocities against the Armenians), and so these leaders accustomed their publics to seeing foreign abuses as matters of international concern.[27] After World War I, when the shattering of the Ottoman, Russian, Austro-Hungarian, and German empires had left eastern European ethnic minorities unsafe among the shards, the international legal rules requiring the protection of religious minorities were expanded to include ethnic minorities as well. The black boxes were becoming slightly more translucent.

Still, the fact that Westphalia's rules allowed sovereigns to condemn each other for internal abuses did not mean they always did so—and mostly, they did not. Westphalia merely permitted—it did not require—sovereigns to be officially concerned with what other sovereigns did to their people. Nor was there even a standard official language for one sovereign's condemnation of another. Mostly, sovereigns just pronounced other sovereigns to be "masters at home" and maintained an official blindness to their deeds.

One gets a sense of how recently the world was Westphalian in this respect in the diplomatic responses to the *Kristallnacht* of 1938—the Nazi outrages against German Jews that were the worst pogrom in the country since the Middle Ages. In cables back to their capitals, foreign diplomats stationed in Germany expressed their revulsion at the murders and widespread destruction. The Brazilian ambassador reported a "disgusting spectacle"; the British embassy sent London a cable on the Nazis' "Medieval barbarism." Yet no country broke diplomatic relations with Germany after the *Kristallnacht*, and only the United States recalled its ambassador (for "consultation").[28]

It was World War II, with its planetary devastations, that finally forced a thoroughgoing legal structuring of the relations between rulers and ruled. World War II is the historical pivot between the Westphalian order and our modern system of international law.

THE COUNTER-POWER OF AGREEMENT

In the eyes of the framers of the *Universal Declaration of Human Rights*, the Westphalian system of sovereignty had generated the cataclysmic instability of World War II. Westphalian sovereignty had allowed leaders to abuse and neglect their citizens on an unprecedented scale without requiring any response from outside. Moreover, as the *Declaration*'s framers saw it, Westphalia had allowed the rise of repulsive regimes in Germany and Japan, whose aggressiveness grew within and then spilled over their borders to destabilize whole continents. Modern sovereigns' capacities for coercion and propaganda—as well as the sheer destructive potential of the new weapons at their command—had dovetailed with the Westphalian blindness to internal repression to produce intolerable concentrations of power. The exercise of this power by Hitler and Tojo had undermined the entire global order through an all-involving war.

The framers of the *Universal Declaration*, led by Eleanor Roosevelt, concluded that the Westphalian rules of expansive state sovereignty legitimized too much power in the hands of sovereigns. On the one side, they saw the rulers of modern states, with all their means for efficient violence, coercion, and manipulation. On the other, they saw the inhabitants of those states, often poorly informed, subject to indoctrination, easily dispersed, and only with difficulty rallied for mutual assistance. The framers saw their challenge as setting out international standards for legitimate governance that would help to redress this great imbalance of power.

This is what human rights do. The *Universal Declaration* proclaims there are things that rulers must not do to the ruled, and other things that rulers must do for the ruled. And the securing of these rights is now to be a matter of mandatory international concern. Of course, the framers knew that regimes would still do inexcusable things to their citizens, but to do so would no longer be legal, and was to be condemned from outside. The human rights of the *Declaration* limit the rightful authority of those who hold power, denying all rulers the assertion that serious abuse and neglect of their people is only a matter of "internal affairs."

Yet how to balance the power of mighty states with mere paper? The genius of the *Universal Declaration* is in its strategy to constrain overmighty regimes. The framers sought to counter the power of sovereigns with the power of agreement. They meant for the *Declaration* to become counter-powerful through its own widespread acceptance. This brilliant strategy, leveraging what Václav Havel called "the power of the powerless," is visible in three features on the document's face.[29]

First, the framers wrote the *Universal Declaration* so that it could be maximally public—as the Preamble states, so that the document could be "a common standard . . . for all peoples and all nations," that "every individual and every organ of society" could constantly keep in mind.[30] The framers knew the ancient maxim that only power checks power, so they knew that only power could check the power of Westphalian states. Yet like Kant, they believed that a world government was neither feasible nor desirable—so they knew they could not rely on a checking power "above" the states. Their recourse was to strengthen the checks on states from the sides and from below. Their strategy was to strengthen the foreign actors surrounding an abusive regime—and to strengthen the people within that regime's borders—by uniting their strengths together.

That is was what the *Universal Declaration*'s requirement of publicity was meant to achieve.[31] A public doctrine coordinates the protests of ordinary people who live under a regime's cudgel by giving them a shared vocabulary to make their demands. When people all know that they have a "right to freedom of expression," they can put slogans on placards and go march together. A common standard of achievement also creates points of coordination for foreign governments and organizations to pressure an abusive regime from the sides: through diplomatic protests, withdrawal of aid, travel bans on leaders, economic sanctions, and more.

Moreover, foreign NGOs like Amnesty International (whose power the framers did not fully foresee) can also use human rights to coordinate pressures on regimes by focusing the protests of ordinary people in other countries. A globally public list of human rights gives all of these actors surrounding a regime a common language in which to make common demands for change. And a public list of specific, readily identifiable rights efficiently informs each human of what all humans can insist on. Human rights become, as Charles Beitz has put it, "a shared moral touchstone."[32]

Coordination through human rights has proved to be a source of counter-power that domestic leaders have often found hard to ignore. Many times since the *Universal Declaration*, human rights have facilitated resistance by focusing the power of individuals, groups, and states onto well-defined points of counter-pressure.[33] Because human rights have come to form part of what Joshua Cohen calls "global public reason," they have greatly facilitated global public action.[34]

The framers' second counter-powerful strategy was to phrase the *Universal Declaration* in terms of human *rights*. We now so naturally think of international affairs in terms of human rights—yet this is a recent development. The Westphalian era's cast list was quite short: in Westphalia's international dramas, the spotlight was always on the sovereigns; Westphalian rulers were the only actors, the ruled were just their props. To put this point in a perplexing way, in Westphalia's grammar, the sovereigns were always the subjects, and their subjects were at best their objects. To say it straight: humans then were like animals today, having no legal rights. The framers of the *Declaration* pushed the spotlight from the rulers to the ruled, and when they did so, humans appeared, for the first time, in the cast of characters of international law. Humans became persons.

Shifting the focus from the rulers to the ruled empowered individuals to resist state abuse. As Michael Ignatieff writes describing the role of human rights in the campaigns to free Soviet Jews, "Its very individualism, its affirmation that each individual human life is entitled to protection and respect, proved a powerful stimulant to civic courage and defiance in the Soviet bloc and in emerging nations with authoritarian regimes."[35] Rights are easy for humans to digest—easy for individuals to internalize and make part of their identities. Nourishing individuals with the idea that each has a right to decent treatment has everywhere quickened the civic courage that Ignatieff describes.

The third part of the framer's brilliant strategy is seen in what the *Universal Declaration* leaves out. The *Declaration* presents a public doctrine of human rights with no foundations in any particular religion or philosophy. The Preamble of the *Declaration* makes an ecumenical affirmation of the inherent dignity of the individual, as well as anodyne commitments to "freedom, justice, and peace." Beyond this, the *Declaration* leaves any deeper justification of human rights open. This silence on deeper issues is part of its strategy to gain wide acceptance, and so to become effectively counterpowerful in a world of vulnerable, but coordinable, persons.

Some philosophers mock the *Universal Declaration*'s lack of axioms, yet the framers had good reason to do it their way. The framers saw the wide diversity of the world's spiritual and speculative traditions, and they reasoned that no partisan doctrine could attract enough allegiance to empower all people everywhere through agreement. The framers believed that a consensus on the universal protection of individuals could not form around any contentious theory, so they provided no foundations for the human rights they proclaimed.[36]

The framers wrote a text for use—they created a doctrine meant to be wired into the international system and the voltage run through it. The *Universal Declaration* was approved by the UN General Assembly in 1948, three centuries after the Westphalian treaties of 1648. Slowly, unevenly, and imperfectly since then, yet to an ever-increasing extent, human rights have become entrenched as standards of legitimate rule worldwide—in institutions, in public discussions, and in individuals' self-conceptions.

Every member of the United Nations is party to at least one of the six major human rights treaties, and 80 percent of countries have ratified four treaties or more.[37] Human rights have been incorporated into many national constitutions and into the mission statements of influential NGOs. Legal adjudication of human rights is regularized across large regions, most thoroughly within Europe but also in the Americas and Africa. Unnumbered individuals and groups have converged on human rights as common standards for political resistance to persecution—for example, in the great human rights campaigns in Chile, Poland, South Africa, the Philippines, and Iran. Human rights have been wired into the international system, and compared to the darkness before, their lights now glow with unexpected brightness.

DRAWING THE MAP IN PEN

Fixing human rights as international standards of legitimate governance set one counter-powerful pivot in history. Convergence on a less-noticed rule—a rule of set borders—has raised the moral trajectory of the international system in a different way. This strangely unheralded advance beyond effectiveness has made the world safer in ways we now take almost entirely for granted.

"Might makes right" was the most that the early modern rulers of Europe could agree upon—so state borders were drawn in pencil. Back then, conquest was legitimate. War was a legal means of acquiring another state's territory under Westphalia, and the borders of European states were erased and redrawn by force of arms many times.[38] As John Vazquez writes, "Of all the possible issues states can fight over, the evidence overwhelmingly indicates that issues involving territory... are the main ones prone to collective violence."[39]

International rules to replace effectiveness by making national borders force-proof emerged only gradually. At first, these new rules were merely legalistic reactions to the victories of enemies. For example, America's Stimson Doctrine, which declared that the United States would not recognize territorial gains effected militarily, was an ineffectual response to Japan's conquest of Manchuria in 1932, and was tried again when the Soviet Union annexed the Baltic States in 1940.[40] As so often happens when we examine the entrenchment of new rules, we find expediency among the main motives.

Then, at the moment of opportunity in the post-World War II settlement, a rule of force-proof borders was wired into the whole international system at once. Article 2(4) of the UN Charter states, "All Members shall refrain in their international relations from the threat or use of force against the territorial integrity or political independence of any state." This rule made national borders legally impervious to military might: it made territorial conquest illegal. In terms of compliance, this unsung law is the most successful of all the counter-powerful rules that distinguish the modern international system from the Westphalian.[41]

These facts about compliance are not well known, yet they seed hope. Since the UN Charter was signed in 1945, there has only been one attempt by a UN member to seize all of the territory of another UN member by force. This was Saddam Hussein's invasion of Kuwait in 1990, which was quickly reversed by an international coalition.[42] Before 1946, the rate at which conflicts over territory resulted in changes in borders was 80 percent; between 1946 and 2000, the rate dropped to 30 percent. From 1976 to 2014, no UN member expanded its international borders by force.[43] That sentence merits reading again.

This rule of force-proof borders is a peacekeeper perfect for our world. The capacity of actors in the international system to solve hard problems remains extremely limited. Borders are lines, and the rule against redrawing them by violence makes them into bright lines. "No territorial conquest" is a simple rule, easily understood and monitored. Even humanity in the twentieth century—at its worst, a fairly dim collective agent—managed to follow this rule competently in the postwar period. The entrenchment of the rule since 1945 has removed a large set of explosive questions from the list of problems that international actors must solve, and so it has contributed greatly to peace, and to keeping the international agenda clearer for other issues to be taken up, The world has become robustly more stable since states have agreed to draw their borders in pen.

Accompanying the entrenchment of force-proof borders has been the phasing-in of a general presumption of stable borders (except when peoples vote to unify or secede). A rule of stable borders was championed by the leaders of the postwar anti-colonial movements, especially in Africa. These leaders turned the borders of their colonies into the borders of independent states, without taking the occasion to make boundaries track ethnicity or geography better. Leaders such as Nkrumah of Ghana and Kenyatta of Kenya judged that renegotiation of borders would spark intercommunal strife that they could not contain—and would provide more excuses for the colonial powers to meddle in African affairs. Taking borders off the table simplified state formation and eased the transition to a world of free nations.

Having noted the successes of the rule of force-proof borders, and the more general presumption of leaving borders in place, we should register some negatives—you may have thought of some already. Like the anti-plunder rule, the anti-conquest rule has been bent to the breaking point during its entrenchment and even afterward. As we saw with plunder, convergence on a rule by no means ensures perfect compliance.

In 2014, for example, Russia covertly sent soldiers into Ukraine as a prequel to a disputed referendum in which the ethnic Russian majority of Crimea voted to join Russia. Still, as with the straining of any settled rule, the offenders tried to look like they were not in violation, and afterward, they denied any breach. Putin sent Russian soldiers into Ukraine stripped of their Russian insignias, then claimed that his troops were deployed in Crimea only to ensure a fair vote. Russian media later continued to deny the presence of the Russian military in eastern Ukraine.[44]

Still, even these kinds of maneuvers are now quite rare. As the statistics above show, state borders are settled much more firmly today than they were under Westphalia. And the law itself is entirely settled: in this area of international affairs, might no longer makes right. Officially, even Putin endorsed the "no force" rule, and his ruses paid their own kind of tribute to it. Commentators were right that Putin put Russia "on the wrong side of history."[45]

Even so, the rule of force-proof borders has produced its own pathologies. Some former colonies, such as the DRC, have proved difficult to manage as unified political entities—and the borders of these states, while stable, have been porous to foreign troops. More, while set borders eased the birth of African states, they hindered national consolidation thereafter. Because borders have been force-proof, leaders in African capitals have felt less need to integrate their hinterlands as buffers against foreign invasion. And unlike their European counterparts, citizens of most African states have not bonded together as co-nationals through the experience of fighting off invaders bent on national conquest.[46] Furthermore, the presumption of stable borders that has been so useful in checking conflict has also chafed against other important values in the international system, such as self-determination. Many groups (such as the Kurds) who would prefer to have their own state have been trapped within or stretched across existing borders. The simple salience of bright lines has not helped their cause, and the "peace dividend" of set borders cannot hide these costs.

Nor, as ever, should it be thought that the rule of force-proof borders has spread only, or even mainly, from moral motives. Some part of this rule's postwar entrenchment can be put down to changes in the strategic milieu. Land is now less valuable relative to other factors of production, making territorial conquest less profitable. (Today, much of Poland's wealth would find electronic safe havens within seconds of an invasion.) Populations under occupation also have access to much better weapons and logistics, making captured territory harder to hold. And territorial incursions are riskier into nuclear-armed states and their allies.

Moreover, although stable borders are counter-powerful relative to "might makes right," settled national borders in turn establish their own configuration of power against which further counter-powerful rules may be pressed. Stable borders keep invaders out, but they also divide up the world's natural endowments in ways that some philosophers believe is unfair. Compared to Westphalia, set borders are real progress; compared to some philosophical ideal, they are themselves wanting—a theme we will return to in Chapter 18.

So the evaluation of stable borders is positive but not pure. The rule of force-proof borders has contributed to state weakness, especially in Africa, and set boundaries run skew to other principles in the international system, such as the self-determination of minority groups. The history of the entrenchment of these norms finds motives less than noble. And viewed from the perspective of an ideal of perfect justice, the shortcomings of keeping borders in place may be plain.

Still, the period of force-proof borders has seen the virtual elimination of a whole category of armed conflict—the war of territorial conquest—that has filled many pages of human history. Our era, with its assumption of set borders, has been more sturdily peaceful. And a more peaceful international system provides a platform, never to be taken for granted, for greater moral ambitions. Almost every plan for progress will be thwarted by widespread war. No justice if no peace.

AMERICAN IMPERIALISTS

The postwar success of force-proof borders rests on the acceptance of this rule by powerful actors. Studying the acceptance of this rule in the case of the most powerful postwar actor—the United States—lets us observe close-up the last stage of the entrenchment of a counter-powerful rule, which is the rule's internalization. Studying our own reactions to the conclusions we reach about American power will, in the next section, allow us to examine our own counter-powerful minds more closely.

Robert Kagan called the United States the "Cowboy Nation": "an expansionist power from the moment the first pilgrim set foot on the continent."[47] The United States continued to be territorially acquisitive even after its march of Manifest Destiny had tread over the indigenous peoples of North America, and after its soldiers had seized the Southwest from Mexico. In essence, Manifest Destiny just kept going, sailing west from California. The presence of US Marines convinced Hawaii's last queen to yield her throne; the United States then annexed Hawaii and other Pacific islands and atolls. US forces pried Guam (as well as Puerto Rico) away from Spain. Then, in 1898, they descended on their biggest prize, the Philippines.

To justify the American annexation of the Philippines, President McKinley told a delegation from the General Missionary Committee of the Methodist Episcopal Church:

> I am not ashamed to tell you, gentlemen, that I went down on my knees and prayed Almighty God for light and guidance more than one night. And one night late it came to me this way... there was nothing left for us to do but to take them all, and to educate the Filipinos, and uplift and civilize and Christianize them, and by God's grace do the very best we could by them, as our fellow men for whom Christ also died. And then I went to bed, and went to sleep, and slept soundly, and the next morning I sent for the chief engineer of the War Department (our map-maker), and I told him to put the Philippines on the map of the United States.[48]

Also in favor of annexation, Senator Knute Nelson of Minnesota announced that "Providence has given the United States the duty of extending Christian civilization. We come as ministering angels, not despots."[49]

In their civilizing and Christianizing mission, American forces prosecuted military operations against an insurgency during which hundreds of thousands of Philippine civilians perished. Nearly all of the US Army generals who fought the Filipinos had also fought the heinous wars against the Native Americans.[50] The commanding US general even thought that it might be necessary "to kill half the Filipinos in order that the remaining half of the population may be advanced to a higher plane of life than their present semi-barbarous state affords."[51] (The Filipinos were Rudyard Kipling's "new-caught sullen peoples, half devil and half child."[52]) Public figures like Mark Twain, Andrew Carnegie, John Dewey, and William James joined the

American Anti-Imperialist League to press for the withdrawal of the Philippine occupation, but their efforts were steamrolled by Teddy Roosevelt and his fellow Progressives.

American politicians during this period were infected by the European imperial self-image that was driving the feverish scramble for Africa.[53] During this stretch, the great powers fought to conquer foreign territories not only for economic gains (which were often modest), and not only to spread the faith to darker peoples, but because controlling more territory was what manly white men strove to do.

"The world," said the English imperialist Cecil Rhodes, "is nearly all parceled out, and what there is left of it is being divided up, conquered and colonized. To think of the stars that you see overhead at night, these vast worlds which we can never reach. I would annex the planets if I could; I often think of that. It makes me sad to see them so clear and yet so far."[54]

As Göring said piquantly during the Nuremberg trials in 1945, "After the United States gobbled up California and half of Mexico, and we were stripped down to nothing, territorial expansion suddenly becomes a crime."[55] With this in mind, let's step back to today and consider America's earlier imperial self-image and Americans' glorification of conquest. How much desire to expand America's borders do we detect within Americans today? How strong would we say is the desire—indeed, the felt duty—to win more territory for the nation? When is the last time we heard an American seriously suggest a forceful annexation of foreign territory, either in conversation or in the media? Are Americans still territorially acquisitive?

Critics hold that the military, economic, and cultural aggressiveness of the United States after World War II were pervasive enough, and successful enough, to speak of an "American empire"—and whether those two words should get married is a fascinating conversation.[56] Yet that question is a distraction from the tighter thesis that Americans are no longer interested in acquiring territory by force. The counter-powerful rule of force-proof borders is now entrenched—or so you might consider—within the identities of the American people and their leaders.

It's been well over a century since America's last territorial conquest, in the Philippines.[57] America's postimperial disinterest in conquest has been recognized even from great cultural distance. King Abdul Aziz of Saudi Arabia chose to ally with the United States in 1945 not least because he believed that—unlike Britain and the Soviet Union—America would never want to claim his kingdom's territory for its own.[58] American politicians no longer publicly propose expanding America's borders by force, and presidents now ritually disown territorial ambitions when describing American military doctrine.[59] Americans' collective forgetting of their own imperialist history provides even more evidence of their new self-conception—Americans of today don't recognize themselves in William McKinley. Seizing territory is no longer seen as a national interest. And the alteration of this interest indicates the internalization of a rule.

Interests are always relative to identities—what is good for you depends on who you are. We can see this by thinking laterally for a moment, about the world's shared understandings of the identities of family members—and so of the interests of family members. The world may not, for instance, share an understanding of what it means to be "a husband" deeply enough for all to agree on whether it's in a husband's interest to have sexual intercourse with a woman who is not his wife. Some in the world may think so; some may think not. But if we ask whether it's in the interest of someone who is "a father" to have intercourse with his daughter, the common response is "absolutely not." The world's shared understanding of what it is to be a father—of the identity of being a father—repels any thought of an incestuous paternal interest. Intercourse with a daughter does not make a father's life go better (while the daughter's flourishing does).

Similarly, over the past century, Americans' identities have shifted so that territorial gain is no longer seen as an American national interest. The dominant American self-understanding is now that the nation has no interest in expanding its territory by force. Indeed, as with all cases of deeply internalized rules, the thought of territorial conquest rarely occurs. Along this territorial dimension at least, Americans now form a satisfied people, seeing no reason—and in fact having no desire—to take land from other states.[60] Other countries have made this transition in self-conception as well: the former western European imperial countries have become satisfied peoples too. Rudyard Kipling wrote *The White Man's Burden* for the Diamond Jubilee of Queen Victoria in 1897; one can imagine the outrage had some poet presented an updated version to Queen Elizabeth II for her Diamond Jubilee in 2012.

Our time marks the first in modern history when the militarily dominant nation has not wanted to conquer new territory. That sounds like a success. Still, anyone who says that the United States and other powerful countries are no longer territorially acquisitive will likely be criticized. The thesis is factually correct, but some will not want to believe it—or will say that the thesis only isolates a narrow good while ignoring much worse bads. So we must recheck our reasoning. Was the move from territorially acquisitive to territorially satisfied major powers in fact a transition worthy of our support? Can we really endorse the wider international system that contains this counter-powerful rule?

CRITICAL PERSPECTIVES ON THE MODERN STATE SYSTEM

So far in this chapter, we've seen how Westphalia filled the void left by the collapse of Christendom with the rule that rights should track power. Since the Westphalian settlement, the international system has evolved more structure with the entrenchment of counter-power rules, such as human rights, force-proof borders, and the inverted rule on plunder. We may find ourselves with a natural attraction to counter-powerful rules such as these. Yet the presence of such rules may still leave us uneasy about the modern international order that they structure. Even though it is correct, for example, that the dominant American self-conception now rejects territorial expansion, we may feel loath to say so. We may believe that America advanced internally when, for example, it ended chattel slavery or banned child labor. Yet we may become reticent when asked to affirm any moral progress in American foreign policy. Why is that?

In a philosophical mood, we might reflect that it seems good that, for example, most major powers no longer view conquering territory as furthering their national interests. Yet any praise for today's anti-conquest rule may open an irresistible opportunity to criticize the modern international system as a whole—and especially to emphasize America's many blameworthy policies during the postwar period. America's transition to set borders, it may be said, resembles the penal reforms that replaced punishment by torture with punishment by detention, the objective being (as Michel Foucault described it) not "to punish less, but to punish better; to punish with an attenuated severity perhaps, but in order to punish with more universality and necessity."[61]

Such quick critical responses may greet any gestures toward advances in the international system and improvements in American foreign policy. All of the following, for example, are true. American internalization of the rule of set borders has not stopped the United States from forcefully undermining democratically elected governments—in Iran, Guatemala, Guyana, Brazil,

Chile, and Nicaragua—and replacing these governments with American-backed authoritarians in all except the last.[62] International human rights law, for all its moral appeal, has often bent to *realpolitik*, and the rise of human rights means that strong states like the United States have had a ready excuse for intervening in the affairs of weak states.[63]

Whatever else is true of the international system, we know that hundreds of millions of humans today still endure repressive governments and gender-based violence. Around one billion humans—about as many people as live in all of North America and all of South America—live each day on (at most) what $1.25 would buy in the United States.[64] Moreover, the Westphalian rule of "might makes right" still lingers in international practice, not least in the world's trade in natural resources.

As critics, we are all John Dewey's children. Our hair-trigger critical faculties, installed by modern schools and energized daily by a hyperactive media, are crucial sources of resistance to all concentrations of power, and they are especially vital for balancing the ambitions of the modern state. Our own minds are the products of counter-power campaigns so successful as to have created in us a civic second nature. As Sydney Hook wrote during the rise of the dictators in the 1930s:

> A positive requirement of a functioning democracy is an intelligent distrust of its leadership, a skepticism, stubborn but not blind, of all demands for the enlargement of power, and an emphasis upon critical method in every phase of education and social life. This skepticism like other forms of vigilance may often seem irritating to leaders who are convinced of their good intentions. The skepticism, however, is not of their intentions but of the objective consequences of their power.[65]

These critical gears in our minds generate, as Thoreau desired, "a counter-friction to stop the machine."[66] We engage these gears to put ourselves on the side of the less powerful and because we rightly believe it furthers our collective interests to do so. Taking the critical high ground also allows us to rise above the events that insult us in each day's news, so frustratingly beyond our control.

Our counter-powerful faculties are designed to critique everything, including counter-powerful rules like human rights, set borders, and restraints on the conduct of war. The suggestion that powerful states—and especially the United States—have internalized such counter-powerful rules, even to a limited extent, will trigger the most searching scrutiny. Our faculties will rightly engage fully here, as they were created to do.

Yet our critical faculties should not stop there. Going up another level, we critique the critique itself. At this meta-critical level, we may realize that criticism of counter-powerful rules can make us complicit in eroding standards that bulwark against suffering and injustice. In critiquing counter-power, we may be pulling away the blocks that keep power in check, reversing the counter-friction that slows the machine. And meta-levels of critical reflection stretch up even farther. The danger we face here is a paralysis of analysis, the mind locked up in reflecting on its own critiques instead of what we want to understand, which is the world outside.

Having sighted this mazy condition, we retreat from it to look straight at today's international system. For our purposes now, we don't need an evaluation of this system relative to some ideal standard, only a judgment of its merits relative to Westphalia. Our question is whether the counter-powerful rules of the post-Westphalian order mark overall advances worth defending—and perhaps worth extending. That will be a question both of the moral quality of these rules and of the effects of wiring them into the international system. We can approach an answer to that question with an exercise in imagination.

If humans at the end of World War II had been offered our modern state system with its counter-power rules, would they rationally have preferred it to a projected future under the Westphalian order that they knew? Even with foreknowledge of our world history after 1945—including the Indian partition, Korea, the Great Leap Forward, Vietnam, the Biafran crisis, the Khmer Rouge and the Rwandan genocide, Iraq and Syria, the mass slaughters, civilizational dictatorships, famines, and grueling civil conflicts—would survivors of the Second World War rationally have chosen a future with our modern international rules over a continuation of the Westphalian, effectiveness-based system?

We don't know the counter-factual future history of the continuation of Westphalia, but in 1945, that future would have seemed ominous. The Westphalian world had twice in a generation descended into total war—and had just added nuclear weapons to its arsenal. Almost all of the industrial economies were damaged and experiencing deprivation (which was still a widespread condition in the rest of the world). Highly authoritarian regimes were threatening to tighten their grips over most of the human population.

Could they have seen it, the future of the modern state system—our real history—would to those in 1945 have seemed nearly miraculous. In the modern state system, our forebears would see a coming age that, despite its terrible conflicts and suffering, would be the most prosperous in human history by far.[67] And also by a long way the period with the greatest increase in democracy around the world.[68] They would have seen what may be the most peaceful period in recorded human history. They would have seen what Hegel called the slaughter bench of history becoming less bloody.[69]

That thesis about "the most peaceful period in history" is naturally the hardest to believe at first, so let's take a closer look. This thesis was forcefully advanced in Steven Pinker's grandly ambitious book *The Better Angels of Our Nature*, which caused much controversy.[70] The scholarly consensus about the peacefulness of the postwar period, however, is solid. Lawrence Freedman, in a critical review of Pinker, agrees that wars between states (which cause the most deaths and injuries) have diminished from six per year in the 1950s to less than one per year over the past decade. The number of all conflicts has dropped by 40 percent since the end of the Cold War—and the number of large-scale conflicts by more than half. The decline in battle deaths per million of world population has been astonishing: by 2007, the rate of battle deaths was only 4 percent, or just 1/25th, of the rate it was in the 1950s.[71]

As Joshua Goldstein puts it in *Winning the War on War*, "We have avoided nuclear wars, left behind world war, nearly extinguished interstate war, and reduced civil wars to fewer countries with fewer casualties." Goldstein continues:

> In the first half of the twentieth century, world wars killed *tens of millions* and left whole continents in ruins. In the second half of that century, during the Cold War, proxy wars killed *millions*, and the world feared a nuclear war that could have wiped out our species. Now, in the early twenty-first century, the worst wars, such as Iraq, kill *hundreds of thousands*. We fear terrorist attacks that could destroy a city, but not life on the planet. The fatalities still represent a large number and the impacts of wars are still catastrophic for those caught in them, but overall, war has diminished dramatically.[72]

The percentage of states perpetrating or enabling mass killings of civilians is also well down since 1945, and fatalities from armed assaults on civilians (and from genocide) are down since reliable records have been kept.[73] One study reports that the ratio of civilian to military causalities has decreased since the Cold War.[74] And while the numbers on deaths from terrorism vary according to the definition of that term, all agree that the numbers of terrorism deaths are quite small compared to those caused by (increasingly rare) wars.[75]

These statistics definitely do not prove that hate or madness has ended. No decent person would deny that violence is still much too high everywhere. And there is no guarantee that any of these downward trends will continue. Still, if it really is true that the world has gotten more peaceful, prosperous, and free since 1945, could those facts get through to us? Would we even want to know?

It's always possible to wear blinders so that we see only pain. Today's seven-billion world still generates more than enough death, deprivation, and injustice to overflow our small screens, and today our small screens follow us everywhere. It's always possible to run out the clock by cataloguing the violation of the weak, the abandonment of the needy, the hypocrisy of great powers, and exceptions to even our most settled rules. It's always possible to say, "It's more complicated than that"—because that is always true.

Yet at the end of World War II, favoring a future that is now our past would have seemed easy. The big picture of our real postwar history shows significant improvements in nearly all indicators of lived human experience. Think back to some of the statistics that opened this book. The average lifespan of humans is today longer than it has ever been. A smaller proportion of women die in childbirth than ever before. Child malnutrition is at its lowest level ever, while literacy rates worldwide have never been higher. Most impressive has been the recent reduction in severe poverty—the reduction in the percentage of humans living each day on what $1.25 can buy in America. Even between 1990 and 2010, mainstream estimates show that the percentage of the developing world living in such extreme poverty shrank by more than half, from 43 to 21 percent.[76]

It would be unhealthy for our critical faculties to close our eyes to these kinds of facts. A skeptical posture, a Missourian attitude? Of course. The most thorough chewing before swallowing? Yes. But not hollow fangs. A critic so refractory as to reject all global improvements would need to defend a thesis unknown to science: a Law of Conservation of Misery. A fair challenge for such a critic is to find, as he can, any indicators of human well-being that have declined since the war—and then to compare honestly their significance to those indicators that have increased. We need critics to fight power, not to be crape-hangers at baby showers.

The "alternative futures" thought experiment favors the modern over the Westphalian system. Yet there is much this experiment doesn't do. It doesn't excuse the terrible wrongs that many countries, including the United States, have committed since 1945. Nor does the comparison show that our particular modern international system is better than other systems that might have been constructed after the war. Still less of course does it prove that we are now in the best of all possible worlds. (We will philosophize about what such a world might be like at the very end of the book.)

The overall superiority of the modern system also doesn't establish the goodness of any of its specific features. We know only that the modern system coincided with increases in peace, prosperity, and political freedom—not that any particular feature of the system helped to facilitate these goods. What the thought experiment does show is that the results of adding counter-powerful rules to the premodern international system have not been disastrous. In fact, along salient dimensions, the international system has improved significantly as these new rules bedded down. We can endorse the wider international system relative to what it was before, as we try to understand its successes and failings so that we can discover how to improve it even more.

The trick is seeing with both eyes at once. The world now is a thoroughly awful place—compared to what it should be. But not compared to what it was. Keeping both eyes open gives depth to our perception of our own time in history, and it makes us better able to see where paths to more progress may be open.

A STARFISH HISTORY

Telling the person in the seat next to you that you are interested in philosophy will often result in an uninterrupted flight. Occasionally, however, your fellow passengers will take this as a permission to discuss the big questions that interest them most. The question that the conversation most often comes around to is whether one thinks that human beings are fundamentally good or fundamentally evil.

Now as a question about individuals, this is not especially difficult. The answer must be that human beings are fundamentally pliable. Depending on the human environments in which their character develops, humans can go to either extreme and to all points in between.

On the deeper question of whether humanity as a whole is good or evil, contemporary philosophers have tended to remain quiet. If one gets an answer at all, it will likely be qualified and reserved—for example, that humanity is "good in that there is at least one possible social formation in which humans can live peacefully together under just institutions." This is not the most negative answer one can imagine, yet it's hard to draw much encouragement from such diaphanous speculations.

A more positive answer emerges if we switch to a systems perspective—evaluating humanity as we would an ecosystem or a complex machine. What happens when energy is added to this particular system—as history's progression from biomass to coal to oil and nuclear has added more energy to humanity? The encouraging answer is that with more energy the species grows like crazy. And as energy has been added to humanity, its members have generally become more tolerant, more cooperative, and more peaceful. As humans have understood ever better how to control their natural environment, they have used the knowledge to become exponentially more productive. They have also, it's true, developed energy weapons powerful enough to destroy the entire system. Yet so far, they have not used those weapons to do so. So far, at least, more energy = more humanity.

Humanity does learn, painfully and often only after thousands or even millions have died—like a giant starfish hurrying over a jagged reef, with only primitive vision, slicing off spines on its way, yet regenerating as it grows and slowly adapting its motion. Mainly, humanity learns as its members' identities alter to become less aggressive and more open, so that networks can connect their capacities more effectively and join their diverse resources together. At the individual level, where it matters, this manifests as individuals pursuing less conflictual and more coordinative interests.

Many individuals are still beyond ruthless in pursuing their own interests, yet interests are mostly more pacific than they were. The preponderance of people around you now do not want to kill you to get your phone, torture you until you profess their religion, or prey on your credulity until you join a racist gang. Some may—but not many. It makes perfect sense for an undergraduate in Manhattan to wake up on a warm Saturday, put on a few clothes and some earphones, and go for a run in Central Park—to move in close proximity to hundreds of thousands of strangers of many races and creeds—with every expectation of returning home safe and heading to the library. Contrast this with a woman of the same age in the eastern Congo, who has heard rumors of a dozen men with guns near the village, who must calculate whether it's safe enough to go to the well to get water—and who wants very much not to be assaulted, but even more wonders who will take care of the children if she does not return. Across modern history, identities have changed to make more of the world like Manhattan. If such epochal movements remain unseen, it's likely because of what we now take for granted.

What we take for granted frames the size of our concerns. We've come to expect that mayors and police chiefs will not endorse, much less order, the lynching of minorities. Within that frame, racial profiling and deaths in police custody are top priorities. After decades, we've come to expect enduring peace among the great powers. Within that frame, the invasion of a minor by a major power, or a civil war in a small state, rightly becomes top news.

We can't relax into a Whig version of history; the upward trends in time's graphs may crest at any point. Yet batting away the facts is also lazy, and requires only a lower form of intelligence. Something is happening—especially since World War II—as more energy is added to our species. What future generations might marvel at most will be if we, in the midst of it, do not see it. There are immense challenges: climate change, resource scarcity, overpopulation, and more. As we'll explore in Chapter 18, many of these are the follow-on problems of species achievement, as the world gets more crowded and productivity grows. These are the burdens of our success. But success often brings with it burdens that we accept willingly, most visibly in our personal lives. Having children brings heartaches and headaches, for instance—yet few parents regret having made this transition.

ANARCHY, STATE, AND COUNTER-POWER

In Europe since the fall of Christendom, we see three large periods. The first was the chaos of the Wars of Religion, a crisis of legitimation in which there were no common standards on who had the right to rule. This was the period of maximum division, of constant clashes between irreconcilable groups that sometimes descended into a Hobbesian *bellum omnium contra omnes.*

The second period, Westphalia, was the period of coerced order within states. The question of the right to rule was settled by giving this right to the strongest, and the strongest at least kept the peace (though with heavy hands) within the territory they controlled. The control of territory itself, however, remained up for grabs, and sovereigns contested for it across Europe during the three centuries after 1648.

Another way of describing Europe during Westphalia is as a period of coerced unity inside states. Sovereigns forcibly prevented the antagonisms of groups from breaking out into the worst forms of violence and fostered a deeper sense of national identification—though again, often by coercive means. (Even today, as we'll later see with the DRC, it may be necessary to strengthen a weak state so that it can enforce the rules that protect individuals from non-state actors.)

The rise of the modern international system is then the rise of rules that counter the power of the state—rules that limit sovereigns' potential for violence, coercion, manipulation, and deprivation. Human rights limit the power of the sovereign over those within the territory; rules of set borders limit the power of sovereigns over those in other territories—as do rules regulating the conduct of war. The hope of these counter-powerful campaigns was that an existing unity among persons—a condition of peace, toleration, and cooperation—can be preserved, while the power that formed that unity is reduced. For many of the rules of the modern system, these hopes have become reality.[77]

Our brief story of the history of Europe has had three parts: no rules, power rules, and counter-power rules. These rules were not beamed from the heavens—the rules have evolved inside persons, sometimes as felt constraints on desires and sometimes coming to constitute what is wanted and even thought. Interests are always relative to identities, and identities change as rules become entrenched in our self-conceptions. The campaign for human rights, for example, based its hope for a freer and more peaceful global order on agreement among human beings, who have come to see each other as deserving respect as such.

There is, we might reflect, no Law of Conservation of Human Misery. The human condition can get worse, or better. Along many of its most important dimensions, the modern period appears to be witnessing significant improvements. The progress may be reversible, and we definitely have not reached a morally acceptable world. Yet there is something happening that is moving the indicators of lived human experience upward, and it is crucial that we register it and further its momentum. Something is happening—we don't want to miss it.

The story of power now continues beyond Europe with a centuries-long struggle for the most counter-powerful rule of all modernity—and one holding even greater implications for how humans see themselves.

10

The Determination of Peoples

Since there is nothing greater on Earth, after God, than sovereign princes, and since they have been established by Him as His lieutenants for commanding other men, we need to be precise about their status so that we may respect and revere their majesty in complete obedience and do them honor in our thoughts and in our speech. Contempt for one's sovereign prince is contempt toward God, of whom he is the earthly image.

—Jean Bodin, *Six Books of the Commonwealth*

The Congress is unconcerned as to who will rule, when freedom is attained. The power, when it comes, will belong to the people of India, and it will be for them to decide to whom it shall be entrusted.

—Mahatma Gandhi, The "Quit India" Speech

During all the days we spent buried in the apartheid dungeons, we never lost our confidence in the certainty of our release and our victory over the apartheid system. This was because we knew that not even the hard-hearted men of Pretoria could withstand the enormous strength represented by the concerted effort of the peoples of South Africa and the rest of the world.

—Nelson Mandela, Speech at Wembley Stadium[1]

THE KING PLAYS CHESS

King James I of England, who in 1604 commissioned the Bible that bears his name, believed in witches. James's preoccupation was well-known in his day; Shakespeare began *Macbeth* with the three "weird sisters" hoping to catch his monarch's favor.[2] James said that he wrote his treatise on witches, *Daemonologie*, in response to "[t]he fearefull aboundinge at this time in this countrie, of these detestable slaves of the Devill," and he described the "unlawful charmes" that are signs of the witch's dark arts:

> Such kinde of Charmes as commonlie dafte wives uses, for healing of forspoken [bewitched] goodes, for preserving them from evill eyes, by knitting roun trees, or sundriest kinde of herbes, to the haire or tailes of he goodes: By curing the Worme, by stemming of blood, by healing of Horse-crookes, by turning of th riddle, or doing of such like innumerable things by wordes, without applying anie thing, meete to the part offended, as Mediciners doe.[3]

James had firm Biblical support to worry about sorcery. As readers of the Old Testament know, Pharaoh's magicians matched God plague for plague until they failed to bring forth lice. And shortly after the Ten Commandments, God himself decrees, "Thou shalt not suffer a witch to live." Saul's séance with the Witch of Endor is the Bible's first intimation that the soul lives on after the body dies.[4]

James could also cite solid Scripture for his views on his own political authority, which he set out in a speech to Parliament in 1610:

> The state of monarchy is the supremest thing upon earth; for kings are not only God's lieutenants upon earth, and sit upon God's throne, but even by God himself they are called gods... Kings are justly called gods, for that they exercise a manner or resemblance of divine power upon earth; for... they make and unmake their subjects, they have power of raising and casting down, of life and of death, judges over all their subjects and in all causes and yet accountable to none but God only. They have power to exalt low things and abase high things, and make of their subjects, like the men at chess,—a pawn to take a bishop or a knight—and to cry up or down any of their subjects, as they do their money. And to the

> King is due both the affection of the soul and the service of the body of his subjects.[5]

James I (whose grandsons Charles II and James II we saw earlier taking Louis XIV's secret funds) believed that absolute political authority belonged to kings. It is worth pausing to affirm that this is not true. Absolute power does not descend from God to monarchs. (And there are no witches.) This will become important in Chapter 13, when we return to Saudi Arabia and oil.

POWER TO THE PEOPLE?

The modern model of political authority is popular sovereignty: the people of the country should control their country. This is Jefferson, not James: "I consider the people who constitute a society or nation as the source of all authority in that nation." As Benjamin Franklin put it, "In free governments the rulers are the servants and the people their superiors and sovereigns."[6]

Popular sovereignty is a rule of authority: a rule of who rules. It looks good from many angles. Power should be reduced for the sake of freedom, and one means to reduce power is to divide it. Popular sovereignty disperses power among many individuals who will be affected differently by any policy. In a democracy, the checks and balances live all around you: your fellow sovereigns.

Such checking and balancing produces better results. War between modern democracies happens either rarely or never (depending on the definitions of "war" and "democracy").[7] Democracies are also more likely to comply with international treaties, and to participate in international institutions.[8] Democracies are more likely to protect basic individual rights, such as the rights not to be tortured, arbitrarily imprisoned, or murdered by the state.[9] Democracy also prevents large-scale crises like famines.[10] Behind all of these results is a citizenry holding ultimate authority, checking the passions and limiting the ambitions of rulers. "A dependence on the people is," as Madison put it, "the primary control on the government."[11] The king no longer plays his subjects as men at chess; now citizens also make moves, including the move of removing their king.

Counter-power explains much of popular sovereignty's pull. Power can be reduced by being dispersed. That is a counter-powerful norm for authority—for the "input" to law (who decides). Counter-power also explains the attraction of popular sovereignty's modern twin: human rights. Human rights reduce power by constraining how it may be exercised. Human rights are counter-powerful norms for governance—for the "output" of law (what may be decided). When paired with popular sovereignty, human rights limit what the people can rightly do. The complete modern political ideal is that the people have the ultimate, but not an absolute, power to rule their country. Only citizens ultimately decide what will be done (dispersal of power), but there are some rights even the citizenry must respect (limitation of power). The combination of popular sovereignty and human rights, dispersed authority and limited governance—the ideal of constitutional democracy—is the most counter-powerful political ideal ever to attract a majority of humanity.

Across the next three chapters, we'll test the principle that the people should have the ultimate (but not the absolute) authority to rule their country. Our framing question will be whether the people have the right to rule in all countries. Do we believe in popular sovereignty—and not only for our own country, but as a principle that should be realized everywhere? Assume for the moment that the transition to popular sovereignty could be made peacefully and with respect for all persons and national traditions. Do we support the *principle*?

We will take several perspectives on what popular sovereignty means—and on what it means for natural resources. We will look at how well the principle has rooted across the globe, what we should make of today's failures to achieve it, and whether popular sovereignty is still an ideal that can guide us in the future. The aim is to discover whether we can affirm that popular sovereignty is right, and with the clarity and the force with which we affirm that the divine right of kings is wrong. Are we willing to support "power to the people" everywhere, even after thinking through all we know about the world?

WESTPHALIA VS. SAN FRANCISCO

The old international system, identified with the treaties of Westphalia, was the game of the Club of Europe. The players of the game were the sovereigns of Europe, and then later Europe's white-ruled former colonies, and then also Japan. Effectiveness was the foundation of this international system, the core principles of which were as follows:

1. *Non-Interference*: Sovereigns could rightly govern populations under their effective control in any way whatsoever, without interference from other sovereigns, subject only to constraints of religious toleration.
2. *Effective Jurisdiction*: Any sovereign who could seize control over territory—including the territory of another sovereign—gained authority over that territory and its population.
3. *Free Disposition of Territory and Populations*: Sovereigns could freely cede or sell territory to each other, thereby transferring authority over the people in that territory without their consent.
4. *Pacta Sunt Servanda*: Sovereigns were to keep their treaty obligations.

These Westphalian principles legitimized the many wars within Europe as well as the gigantic European conquests of foreign lands. They legitimized imperial and colonial rule as well as minority white rule, and later apartheid. They allowed France to cede Canada to Britain, for example, and Spain to cede the Philippines to the United States, without consulting the populations of these places—populations could be, as Woodrow Wilson said, "bartered around from sovereignty to sovereignty as if they were mere chattels and pawns in a game."[12] The members of the Club of Europe were to tolerate religious minorities and keep their agreements; otherwise, might made right.

If we identify the modern international system with a location of comparable significance to Westphalia, it should be San Francisco, where the Charter of the United Nations was signed in 1945.[13] San Francisco is an American city—fitting since the United States, of all nations, has been the lead architect of the international system since 1945. Yet San Francisco is also the major American city geographically most distant from American power—the farthest from the short-term *realpolitik* of the White House, Capitol Hill, and Foggy Bottom.[14] (For those fond of cartographic symbolism, San Francisco is roughly equidistant from Beijing, Brussels, Brasilia, and Banjul as well.) The new international system was made in America, yet assembled from materials of many nations. And the primary principles of the modern system are quite different from those of Westphalia:

1. *Colonial Independence*: Peoples under colonial rule or military occupation must be freed from it.
2. *Force-Proof Borders*: States may not gain territory through conquest. Borders may only change through colonial independence, secession, or the voluntary union of peoples.

3. *Non-Interference*: States have a qualified right to govern their jurisdictions without external interference, and especially without threats to their territorial integrity.
4. *Human Rights*: States must, in governing their jurisdictions, respect human rights.
5. *Popular Sovereignty*: "The will of the people shall be the basis of the authority of government; this will shall be expressed in periodic and genuine elections which shall be by universal and equal suffrage and shall be held by secret vote or by equivalent free voting procedures."[15]
6. *Pacta Sunt Servanda*: States are to keep their treaty obligations.

Compared to Westphalia, the San Franciscan international system has more structure. Under Westphalia, the pliant borders of countries expanded and shrank as sovereigns wrestled over European territory. European state power also ballooned into the places where no Europeans lived, and Europeans then began wrangling over that territory as well. Internally, each sovereign's domain was legally amorphous: however the sovereign pushed around his subjects, this could hardly be a matter of international concern. As the legal scholars James Crawford and Susan Marks put it, Westphalia accepted "a de facto approach to statehood and government, an approach that followed the facts of political power and made few inquiries into how that power was established."[16]

The modern international system is more ordered: it draws a grid of borders on the earth's surface, and that grid is drawn in pen. Moreover, the modern system also builds more structure inside state borders, erecting legal barriers against violations of human rights. Under Westphalia, political authority was a few blobs stretched over the earth's surface; now it is a large number of baffle boxes.

Modernity's rules—colonial independence, set borders, human rights, popular sovereignty—all disperse and limit power. The ideal of the modern system envisions the peoples of the world, governing themselves with limited powers, within assured borders, and dealing peacefully with each other on a basis of legal equality. As a system, this is further toward an ideal of the free unity of humanity than Westphalia was, and real improvements have accompanied its entrenchment in international affairs. The modern world is more peaceful and prosperous than the old world, and political power is more dispersed, and more checked, than it was. Humans are now freer and more united than their ancestors were.

Still, the modern ideal is only imperfectly realized in the real rules of international relations. We come to the law like we come to the dinner table: there is a knife, fork, spoon, napkin, and plate. We rarely consider that each of these tools has a distinct origin, and that these different tools became socially accepted for dining in different centuries, even different millennia, of our history. When we come to the table, it's already set with "a bride's good luck" of tech. Similarly, when we look at the surface of our law, what we are seeing is many historical layers.

Modern international law is a palimpsest, with Westphalian effectiveness still showing through in several areas. As we have seen, we've only come so far. The persistence of effectiveness in some parts of law keeps the modern world at a distance from the modern principles that most states endorse.

As we've seen, for instance, effectiveness still haunts international trade in natural resources. Effectiveness also sets the rules for the struggles within states that crash into the news, like civil wars and revolutions. Today's legal rule remains that outside states should let power decide these internal struggles, and then grant diplomatic recognition to whoever wins. The persistence of Westphalian effectiveness in these international rules shows how our world is still far from its own ideal—and painfully so during punishing internal conflicts like those in Sri Lanka and Syria. Better rules in these areas have been put forward, but they have not yet been put onto the global agenda.[17]

Popular sovereignty presents the gripping drama of an imperfectly realized ideal. Popular sovereignty is the world's aspiration, affirmed in founding documents of the modern international system like the *Universal Declaration of Human Rights*, and in most of the world's national constitutions. As we will see, the "external" half of popular sovereignty has been hammered into international law and made real around the world. Popular sovereignty's "internal" half is now nearly universally affirmed as well: fine words demanding it abound in international treaties. And it is real in many states—but not all.

For all its successes, popular sovereignty has had a "last mile" problem. The drive of popular sovereignty to replace effectiveness in the international system has traveled remarkably far, but it still has not yet arrived. Scanning over the progress of popular sovereignty during the past four centuries allows us to reflect on why this principle has not traveled that last mile, and to think through how it might.

THE WINNERS OF WORLD WAR III

The principle of popular sovereignty says that the people of a country should rule the country. This principle is the combination of two principles—of external and internal self-determination:

> **External Self-Determination:** Outsiders should not rule the people.
> **Internal Self-Determination:** The people should rule themselves.

The "shot heard 'round the world" in 1775 was fired for the principle of external self-determination. "A history of repeated injuries and usurpations, all having in direct object the establishment of an absolute Tyranny," America's *Declaration of Independence* explained, made it necessary "for one people to dissolve the political bands which have connected them to another and to assume among the powers of the earth, [a] separate and equal station... We, therefore, the Representatives of the united States of America... do, in the Name, and by Authority of the good People of these Colonies, solemnly publish and declare, That these united Colonies are, and of Right ought to be Free and Independent States, [and] that they are Absolved from all Allegiance to the British Crown."[18] This declaration of external self-determination by a subject people that they "of Right ought to be Free and Independent" echoed around the world—because the subjection of peoples was so familiar, and so ferocious, worldwide.

There have in fact been three world wars. The third was a slow-motion war, its battles flaring up around the planet across half a millennium. In the 1400s, Europe began its invasion of Earth. Europe was everywhere victorious; it defeated every civilization it engaged in battle. During this epochal offensive, Europe asserted coercive control over nearly all of the planet's dry land. Then, fitfully, mile by mile and continent by continent, Europe was defeated, surrendering its gains to the denizen peoples. Some of these denizen peoples—like the Americans and the Japanese—themselves later joined the European imperial offensive, only to surrender their gains in their turn.

One reason we read less about this third world war is because its histories were mostly written by the losers—the imperialists. Another reason is that memories of our imperialism no longer fit our identities. We cannot wear those old adolescent clothes; we discard them; morally, we are bigger now. Still, this is our past. Those of us from formerly imperialist countries might recall that our countries ended up on the losing, and also the unjust, side of World War III.

The history of the European imperial war would be years in telling. One episode will serve as the exemplar for the extremes of its violence. This is an account, written by a Mexica in the sixteenth century, of Cortés's *conquistadores* and their surprise attack on a celebration in the main temple:

> [The Spaniards] ran in among the dancers, forcing their way to the place where the drums were played. They attacked the man who was drumming and cut off his arms. Then they cut off his head, and it rolled across the floor. They attacked all the celebrants, stabbing them, spearing them, striking them with their swords. They attacked some of them from behind, and these fell instantly to the ground with their entrails hanging out. Others they beheaded: they cut off their heads, or split their heads to pieces. They struck others in the shoulders, and their arms were torn from their bodies. They wounded some in the thigh and some in the calf. They slashed others in the abdomen, and their entrails all spilled to the ground. Some attempted to run away, but their intestines dragged as they ran; they seemed to tangle their feet in their own entrails. No matter how they tried to save themselves, they could find no escape.[19]

Popular resistance to the European invasion will also be pictured in a single episode, from nearly four hundred years later: the 1908 *puputan* of the Balinese *Klungkung* nobility, who preferred mass suicide to subjection by the ruthless Dutch:

> The [Dutch] soldiers reached Klungkung by early afternoon, having encountered no one during their slow and hot march. Heavy field ordnance was rolled into the crossroads, just across from the high brick walls of the royal residence known as Smarapura, abode of the god of love. It was only then that a cluster of Balinese men and boys appeared, all dressed entirely in white. They charged forward, brandishing lances and *keris* (wavy-bladed daggers). As rifles and howitzers loosed volleys of fire, the Balinese fell in bloody and mangled heaps before managing to so much as scratch an enemy soldier with their weapons. Moments later they were replaced by other white-clad figures, intent upon the same end. Among them were women, resplendent in gold and jewels, many leading children by the hand or carrying them in arms. They too fell before the

> relentless guns as they advanced toward the Dutch troops, and so the massacre continued until nearly two hundred Balinese lay dead or wounded on Klunkung's main road. At last the king himself appeared, together with his remaining lords. One more round and it was over.[20]

Pulses of violence emanated outward from Europe for five centuries. Because of European colonization, today's linguistic map of the Americas roughly parallels the west coast of Europe: English in the north, French in the north and center, and Spanish in the center and south, with a pocket of Portuguese.

Resistance to European rule stiffened in the Americas, among colonists and indigenes, during the early centuries of the third world war. The United States won independence in 1783, then Haiti in 1804; by 1825, nearly all of Latin America was free from Europe's fist. European attempts thereafter to exert political domination westward broke on the rocks of these new nations (although regarding the economic domination of Latin America, a new chapter had just begun). Still the Europeans continued to radiate violence to the east, forcing their coercive control over South, Southeast, and East Asia, including the two giant civilizational prizes, India and China. Finally, during the most intense imperial era, the decades surrounding the turn of the twentieth century, the steamship and the machine gun allowed Europe to project its power into the interior of Africa and divide a new continent among its members.

Words from the European attack on the world evoke the basest humanity: the reprisals for the Indian Revolt, the punishments for the Boxer Rebellion; King Leopold's Congo. Of course, human life is complex: there was cruelty on all sides of this long world war, Europeans also performed millions of acts of kindness and self-sacrifice, and the encounter in many ways benefited both sides.[21]

Yet there can be no case for Europe's war as a just war, not by any standards that we would accept today. Rationalizations of European imperium now seem so risible: the slogan of the Belgian Governor-General of the Congo in the 1930s and 1940s was *Dominer pour servir*, "Dominate in order to serve."[22] And this change in our attitude has come quickly: it was only the grandfathers—even the fathers—of Europeans now alive who were imperialism's shock troops:

> Take up the White Man's burden—
> The savage wars of peace—

Fill full the mouth of Famine,
And bid the sickness cease;
And when your goal is nearest
(The end for others sought)
Watch sloth and heathen folly
Bring all your hope to nought.[23]

The peoples subjected by the Westphalian empires, some only recently, won their freedom. This is freedom in its oldest sense: the political independence of a community from external domination, as the freedom of the ancient Greeks from the Persian superpower. The victory of the world's peoples over empires was a remarkable event, and its crescendo was the most significant political transition of the twentieth century.

A mere century ago, most of the earth's land was ruled by the few great powers. Their empires claimed one-quarter of the Americas, more than half of Asia, 90 percent of Africa, and nearly all of the South Pacific.[24] Tiny Britain ruled a population ten times greater than its own, and territory one hundred times larger than the United Kingdom itself.[25] (To match this feat, America today would have to rule close to half of the world's people—and the land of six-and-a-half Earths.)

Many of the subject peoples of Europe gained their freedom as the empires smashed each other in World War I: the end of the German, Russian, Austro-Hungarian, and Ottoman empires spelled freedom for the Finns, the Baltic peoples, the Ukrainians, and the Poles. The Irish fought the British well enough to gain dominion status within the Empire in 1922, and within a decade, all of Britain's white-ruled dominions (Ireland, Canada, Australia, New Zealand, South Africa, and Newfoundland) had won their legislative independence.

Still, the new freedom of white peoples did not convince leaders in Europe (or Japan) that they should cede rule over the "inferior races." It took another war to weaken the imperial grips of the Westphalian sovereigns, and to harden resolve in their colonies, sufficiently to make possible the 1945 declaration in San Francisco that all national peoples should be free: "We the Peoples of the United Nations," says the UN Charter, set as a founding purpose "to develop friendly relations among nations based on respect for the principle of equal rights and self-determination of peoples."[26]

This principle of external self-determination in the UN Charter was, at its signing, quite aspirational: only three African states were charter members of the United Nations, and only eleven in Asia and the Middle East combined. In 1945, one-third of all human beings were still colonial subjects. Over the next fifteen years, thirty-seven national peoples won their freedom. Over the following three decades, the number of member states in the United Nations tripled. Gandhi's leadership of India from under British rule was one turning point in the history of external self-determination, as was Algeria's searing, shocking defeat of France. More peoples, behind the adamant leadership of national heroes like Aung San, Sukarno, and Nkrumah, pressed for independence.

In 1954, Britain executed what was likely the largest cordoning and mass detention action in the history of its empire—Operation Anvil, in which over twenty-four thousand Kikuyu were detained without trial in Nairobi in an effort to defeat the Mau Mau insurgency in what would become Kenya.[27] Yet history was flowing against them. Once the British realized that independence was inevitable, they at least tried to prepare their colonies by helping to build some national institutions in the last few years. By contrast, the Belgians, having exploited the people and resources of the Congo for decades, and having viewed professional education for the natives as potentially subversive, abandoned their giant colony over the course of weeks, leaving behind not a single Congolese lawyer, doctor, or officer in the police—and one lone agricultural engineer.[28]

The greatest success of the United Nations as an institution is the part it played in the anti-colonial movement. In 1960, the General Assembly simply declared, in an unusually firm resolution, that imperial rule must stop:

> 1. The subjection of peoples to alien subjugation, domination and exploitation constitutes a denial of fundamental human rights, is contrary to the Charter of the United Nations and is an impediment to the promotion of world peace and co-operation.
> 2. All peoples have the right to self-determination; by virtue of that right they freely determine their political status and freely pursue their economic, social and cultural development…
> 5. Immediate steps shall be taken…to transfer all powers to the peoples of [dependent] territories, without any conditions or reservations, in accordance with their freely expressed will and desire, without any distinction as to race, creed or color, in order to enable them to enjoy complete independence and freedom.[29]

The UN's clarity allowed no more excuses. As late as 1974, the Portuguese authoritarians were pleading that Angola and Mozambique were not colonies but merely parts of Portugal separated from the mainland by an ocean. Yet the day for such evasions had gone. By 1995, Portugal itself was asserting the right of all peoples to self-determination in the International Court of Justice, and the Court responded by acknowledging self-determination as "one of the essential principles of contemporary international law."[30] The last European empire, the Soviet Empire, dissolved into its constituent parts in the early 1990s. The United Kingdom ceded its final colonial territory in 1997. Even the Saudi leadership, whose dogged resistance to its own people's rights we will study later, now invokes a people's right to external self-determination in the international system's highest court.[31]

The right of external self-determination "requires a free and genuine expression of the will of the peoples concerned" as to their desired political status.[32] If a people dominated by a foreign power expresses a desire for independence (historically, often through a UN-supervised vote), then it must be allowed to form its own state. If a subject people votes to integrate with a foreign state (as Hawaii did with the United States and the Keeling Islands with Australia), then it must be allowed to do so. If a people chooses to associate, but not integrate, with the foreign power (as Puerto Rico does with the United States and Gibraltar with the United Kingdom), then it has the right periodically to reassess that relationship through referenda on independence, integration, or continued association.

The principle of external self-determination has triumphed in the international system. And as it has become fully integrated into the system, it has been adjusted to fit with the system's other principles. For example: the principle of external self-determination may not be used to justify invasion, as Hitler had attempted in central Europe.[33] Equally important (and a point to which we will frequently return) in the General Assembly's declaration that "peoples" must be free, the meaning of the term *peoples* is crucial. The right of external self-determination in the international system is a right of colonial peoples against foreign domination. It is not a right of minority groups to secede from an existing state.[34]

Given the huge number of minorities in the world that could claim a right to independence, a secessionary right to self-determination would overwhelm the modern system's ability to settle disputes. (In Africa, for example, only Somalia, Botswana, and the two South African microstates are ethnically homogenous.) So while minority groups do have rights under modern international law, these are not the dramatic rights of colonial subjects to independence from foreign domination.

The principle of external self-determination has been built into the international system, and in a way that allows the system to continue to work. Understood as an anti-imperial principle, external self-determination is now what lawyers call *jus cogens,* and its obligations are *erga omnes*. That is, its requirements are paramount in international law, and they bind all states.[35]

The shot heard 'round the world has now been fired 'round the world. Subject peoples have gained their independence and have fixed the principle of external self-determination firmly into the international order. Between 1945 and 2000, the number of independent states swelled from 51 to 192—though our "great forgetting" erases how recently the empires passed.[36] Dutch men today, to our eyes seemingly so civilized, could easily be the grandsons, even the sons, of Dutchmen who sailed to Indonesia and executed the suicidally desperate Balinese in Klungkung. Britain's King George VI included "RI" ("Rex Imperator") in his signature—and his daughter Elizabeth II, ruler in the twenty-first century, would have been Empress of India had her father died just five years earlier.

Independence was the biggest political transition in the twentieth century, and the transition was not only political but also conceptual, and identity-altering. We can do a quick introspection to show how far this is true. Observe your own reactions as you imagine that your government today makes laws, enforced by your army, for India's 1.3 billion people—and calls this rule natural because Indians are racially inferior to white people.

The liberation of subject peoples from empires is modernity's greatest saga—the victory of a hundred dark horses. Afterward, in our time, even this great story comes to be taken for granted. A few words come to stand for the titanic determination of peoples who, day by day and decade by decade, finally won their freedom.

HERE THE PEOPLE RULE

Outsiders should not rule the people; the people should rule themselves. Entwined with the global movement for external self-determination has been the struggle for internal self-determination in its fullest sense: that the people should have the final authority over their land and each other. The popular revolts in our time against authoritarians in every region of the world hint that this idea has universal appeal. But the story of internal self-determination in international law, at least to now, has a different ending. External self-determination is now fully entrenched in law and real in fact; internal self-determination is only partially so.

The idea that the people should rule was given mouth honor even by Roman emperors: "A law is what the Roman people enact…for the people…make a concession to [the emperor] of their whole power."[37] The formulation that the people are the principal whose agent is the government dates to at least the thirteenth century.[38] The idea of popular sovereignty was then for a time buried under the dogma of absolute monarchy. We heard that dogma of absolute monarchy at the start of the chapter in King James I's address to Parliament in 1610. We hear it still, over a century later, in the hauteur of France's King Louis XV:

> As if anyone could forget that the sovereign power resides in my person only…that public order in its entirety emanates from me and that the rights and interests of the nation, which some dare to regard as a separate body from the monarch, are necessarily united with my rights and interests, and repose only in my hands.[39]

The Bastille was stormed for internal self-determination. By 1787, revolutionary France had a National Assembly—an assembly of the representatives of the nation—which asserted a new principle in its *Declaration of the Rights of Man and of the Citizen*:

> The principle of all sovereignty resides essentially in the nation. No body, no individual may exercise any authority that does not emanate expressly from the nation.[40]

Most countries now have their own stories about the people's struggle for sovereignty; together, these stories narrate the triumph of the idea. Chapters in this saga were written in many lands: the Chartists' brave fight for votes for the English working man, the Suffragette's courage in winning the vote for women, the European "Springtime of Peoples" in 1848, the glorious victory over apartheid in the 1990s. This saga can be shortened into the drama of three small words, set together in America in 1789: *We the People.*[41]

More fully: "We the People of the United States…do ordain and establish this Constitution." Those first three words declare that it is the people of the country who will have the ultimate authority over their country. And as empires collapsed in the twentieth century, more and more peoples took these words for their own.

After Gandhi's historic leadership to independence, the Indian people began their new constitution with these words ("We the People of India..."). The Japanese, among the ruins of their totalitarian militarism, also opted for popular sovereignty ("We, the Japanese people..."). As new states struggled free in the decades after World War II, these three words became the most widely shared constitutional opening of all time ("We the People of Egypt, Bangladesh, Samoa, Micronesia..."). The three words were the legacy of Nelson Mandela's leadership of South Africa to internal self-determination ("We the People of South Africa..."), and their momentum has carried them into the world's newest state, founded in 2011 ("We the People of South Sudan..."). Even groups of countries are now declaring the words to themselves and the world ("We, the Peoples of the Member States of the Association of Southeast Asian Nations [ASEAN]...") In this, they are following the founding document of the modern international system, the Charter of an organization which declares that its legitimacy is derived from popular sovereignty ("We the Peoples of the United Nations...").

Half of humanity now lives in a democracy, and a large majority of countries have a written constitution that proclaims popular sovereignty.[42] In some constitutions, the divine right of kings has been replaced, literally, with the divine right of peoples:

> In the Name of the Most Holy Trinity, from Whom is all authority and to Whom, as our final end, all actions both of men and States must be referred, We, the people of Éire [Ireland], Humbly acknowledging all our obligations to our Divine Lord, Jesus Christ...Do hereby adopt, enact, and give to ourselves this Constitution.

> In the name of God...We, the people of Sudan, with the help of God...have made this Constitution...God, the creator of all people, is supreme over the State and sovereignty is delegated to the people of Sudan by succession, to be practiced as worship to God, performing his trust.[43]

Popular sovereignty is the declared ideal of nearly all states, including those in which the people are far from sovereign. Nowhere is this more poignant than in the People's Democratic Republic of Algeria (motto: "By the People and For the People"), where the military regime prosecuted a bruising, ten-year crackdown when it lost elections in 1991.[44]

Popular sovereignty is also the ideal proclaimed in the remarkable first paragraph of the Chinese constitution:

> China is one of the countries with the longest histories in the world. The people of all nationalities in China have jointly created a splendid culture and have a glorious revolutionary tradition. Feudal China was gradually reduced after 1840 to a semi-colonial and semi-feudal country. The Chinese people waged wave upon wave of heroic struggles for national independence and liberation and for democracy and freedom... After waging hard, protracted and tortuous struggles, armed and otherwise, the Chinese people of all nationalities led by the Communist Party of China with Chairman Mao Zedong as its leader ultimately, in 1949, overthrew the rule of imperialism, feudalism and bureaucrat-capitalism, won the great victory of the new-democratic revolution and founded the People's Republic of China. Thereupon the Chinese people took state power into their own hands and became masters of the country.[45]

Some may find the language of these declarations, constitutions, and speeches inspiring. Some may find it insipid. For most of us, the affirmation of popular sovereignty is just sleep talking. As Mill feared, we only register these words with "a dull and torpid assent."[46]

"All good ideas have already been thought," Goethe once said, "one must only strive to think them again."[47] We now find ourselves naturally allied to the principle of popular sovereignty—indeed, perhaps even to the point of boredom. Of course, the people should rule; that's a real commitment in our own lives, and not just on paper. (Consider most people's reaction to a man at a party who brags that he just can't be bothered to vote.) To the democratic citizen, "power to the people" may be so present as to be undetectable: the taste of one's own saliva.

Yet politics is about power—its use is a matter of life, death, and events even more important. It would be an error to dismiss popular sovereignty as ideology, or to fall into the "deep slumber of decided opinion."[48] The matters are of too much moment.

State action—the decisions of a few, named individuals—can be an extraordinarily potent force. The state authorizes and prohibits, regulates and educates, protects and provides, spies and lies. The state may force citizens not to buy things they want (a healthy kidney or drugs) and force them to pay for things they don't want (old-age insurance, profane art, or nuclear weapons). The state may forbid a citizen to practice his religion or to marry the person she loves. The state might order citizens into certain death, during a war, or kill them itself, during peacetime. It may enforce rules that exacerbate inequalities along a dozen dimensions. It may seize the nation's assets for itself, leaving citizens to starve or worse. The decisions of a few named individuals will shape everyone's freedoms and opportunities, rights and resources—and also their intimate relations, their convictions, and over time, their characters.

Popular sovereignty makes those few named people accountable to those they rule. To evaluate popular sovereignty, we need bear no illusions that citizens, as a group, could control their own governance in any detail, even under favorable conditions. Day to day, political decisions will be made and enforced by the few. The people's ultimate authority is to examine the outcomes of the rule of those few, and to change any personnel or policy in the government that produced those outcomes. Again, we needn't paper over most citizens' ignorance of the mechanics of their political systems, nor their indifferent understanding of major policies.[49] The people live directly under the mechanisms of the state, and they experience the effects of its operations. They've shown that they know well enough what is done to them and for them, enough to throw out those they distrust. The people can't have daily control over their rulers, but they have found a feasible alternative—ultimate authority, which counters power and makes them more free.

THE UNITED STATE

The fervency of peoples' demands for sovereignty reaches beyond even a dream of freedom. Such a dream of freedom was shared by all the counter-powerful movements that displaced Westphalia: by the movements against the slave trade, against colonialism, against conquest and apartheid, and more. These "movements against" were all negative in nature: by countering power, they hoped to open up free space for ordinary people to live as they like.

As important as this negative freedom is, popular sovereignty also has a positive thrust. Freed from violence, coercion, and manipulation, individuals want to decide their own fates together, to have their own fights and reconciliations, to fail and succeed while they make a common life as a people. Individuals want to contribute more than their daily grind, to further projects past their own small allowance of years, to "be part of something bigger than themselves." Say the name of the country you identify with, and then imagine how disorienting it would be if that country disbanded. If you are American, for example, imagine that next month you will have no fellow Americans because there will be no such thing as America. In our era, popular sovereignty has given many what Mill called "the feeling of unity with our fellow creatures."[50]

Human unity takes many forms: there are unities of beliefs, of judgments, of feelings, of sentiments, and the highest of these—for which the others are stanchions—the unity of action. When citizens become responsible for the decisions of their state, they create a people that acts politically instead of being objects that are acted upon. Citizens become united into a single actor with its own unique biography—the wars and the dark times, the great reforms and the mistakes—and so achieve an active mutual identification that is possible in no other way. This is like being in a marriage—a political marriage—with millions. The subjects of authoritarians like the Saudis may feel related, much as young siblings do, but they cannot be co-creators of a common life. And creating such a common life has been a strong desire across modern history. The people should rule themselves.

Popular sovereignty is not, as we know, all the world's reality. Yet it is the world's ideality. As Amartya Sen says, "While popular sovereignty is not yet universally practiced, nor indeed universally accepted, in the general climate of world opinion democratic governance has achieved the status of being taken to be generally right."[51] Even in the Arab countries, support for democracy ranges between 83 and 96 percent.[52] Of course, people understand "democracy" in varying ways, and they want to use democracy to further different ends.[53] Yet on popular sovereignty itself there is a broad consensus.

Holding aside a few countries that we will look into later, popular sovereignty is now a basic principle of political authority throughout the world. This is true within nearly every nation. Popular sovereignty is the idea of political legitimacy that almost all elites (even the unaccountable ones) offer to their own people. It is the frame of every democratic constitution, and the façade of every façade constitution. This is even more true in international affairs: popular sovereignty is the only permanent principle of legitimate authority affirmed in the primary documents of international law.

Over the many centuries of their struggle to rule together, citizens have won that argument at least.

DESIGN CONSTRAINTS ON THE INTERNATIONAL SYSTEM

As an absolute ruler, the king is nearly dead. Only one man in Europe is now taken seriously when he claims to be an absolute monarch, and he claims only one neighborhood in Rome. Across the centuries, nations countered the conceits of kings, forcing them to confess that they are agents not of God but of man. Humanity is now most of the way through its own Schumpeter Process, adjusting its politics to the rising power of its peoples.

And still, there is the last mile. As we wonder whether we can affirm popular sovereignty, we test our convictions against what we see in the world. If popular sovereignty really is a universally valid principle, why is it so lacking in some countries? Even our own leaders, who talk the talk in public, rarely take the steps required to support popular sovereignty as international law. Indeed, our own state leaders often walk away from popular sovereignty, allying with dictators and cold-shouldering democratic movements.[54] And then, when some state does take action (allegedly) to promote popular sovereignty, such as the US-led invasion that overthrew Saddam Hussein, strong protests of injustice are heard worldwide. Why is this? Perhaps our imagined solidarity with the peoples of the world is illusory?

Clearly, some elite resistance to popular sovereignty is merely self-interest. Authoritarians want to keep power over their people; they do not want to become accountable to their people. And some of our own elites' support for authoritarians has been, as we've seen, raw corruption. This kind of self-interest gives us no reason to doubt popular sovereignty—rather, popular sovereignty provides the grounds for criticizing what these elites do.

Some of our own elites will justify their neglect of popular sovereignty with geostrategy. Throughout its postwar history, for example, the US government has gone to great lengths to keep authoritarians in power in Islamic countries from Egypt to Pakistan. For the French elite, it was the dictators of West Africa, from Burkina Faso to the Republic of Congo, who were backed by any means necessary. There are narratives in which Western support for these authoritarians has been required to safeguard democracy—first against communism, then against terrorism. We need not now judge how far those narratives are right. We need only say that these claims of necessity give no reason to doubt the desirability in principle of popular sovereignty—only, at most, the feasibility of supporting it in a dangerous world.

There is a far weightier reason why we don't see consistent international action in support of popular sovereignty. And this is a more compelling reason, because it would remain even if our own leaders were entirely uncorrupt and exceedingly wise. As we saw in the description of the San Franciscan international system, popular sovereignty is a major modern principle, yet it is only one principle. And any principle, given too much emphasis, can be dangerous. Popular sovereignty can overwhelm other important principles—even its twin principle, individual human rights. Hitler's rule was, after all, endorsed by the people—at least in the early days—as was Mao's. The international system is constituted by not just one but many major principles, and they do press against each other.

The most contentious struggle between international principles in recent times has been between popular sovereignty and non-intervention. One of the two justifications given for the 2003 Iraq invasion, a justification especially emphasized by George W. Bush, was the sovereignty of the people of Iraq. "We have no ambition in Iraq except to remove a threat and restore control of that country to its own people," Bush said, and "[t]o tear down the apparatus of terror" so that the Iraqi people could "set an example to all the Middle East of a vital and peaceful and self-governing nation."[55]

One can see why intervention for the sake of popular sovereignty raises the world's nerves. A general permission to invade for the sake of democracy would license interventions likely to be counter-productive even in democratic terms—as well as risking wider, destabilizing conflicts. The global protests at the idea of invasion for the sake of democracy have come especially from nations historically on the sharp end of interventions by powerful states. Peoples in these places have learned that "democracy" in foreign mouths may be followed by the sound of warplanes headed toward their capitals. The modern international system hears these concerns and prioritizes peace. Once the colonies have become free, states are generally to refrain from military action toward each other.[56] In accepting the priority of peace, supporters of democracy are left to hope that eventually it will grow behind hard foreign borders, with respectful encouragement from outside. We may endorse popular sovereignty heartily—yet not wholeheartedly, if that endangers a heartfelt commitment to peace.

Here we reach a deeper theme about today's international system, and one that will stay with us. In evaluating the modern international system, we need to be alive to the complexity of its construction. The modern system is made not from one but from several principles, concerning treaties, borders, human rights, popular sovereignty, and more. These principles can press against one another. When we ask whether we can affirm the principle of popular sovereignty genuinely, on full reflection, it's in the midst of other principles that we value. The international system is made of many parts; in falling short on popular sovereignty, the system might be hitting its design constraints.

Consider the design constraints on shipbuilding. Good shipbuilding follows two principles: first, that the ship should safeguard the crew and cargo, and second, that the ship should move speedily to its destination. A ship that fails to float will drown its crew and lose its cargo. A ship that moves too slowly may starve its crew and spoil its haul. To stay afloat, a ship's design should maximize the water's upward pressure against the hull: the hull should be bowl-shaped. For maximum speed, the design should minimize pressure against the hull in the direction of travel: the hull should be knife-shaped. All shipbuilding is a compromise between floating and speeding, between bowl-shaped and knife-shaped. All ships' hulls are wedge-shaped. The two principles of floating and speeding cannot both be fully realized at once, so even in the best ships, each principle will be, to some extent, "violated."[57]

The ideal of the modern international system is the peoples of the world governing themselves with limited powers, within assured borders, and dealing peacefully with each other on the basis of legal equality. The ideal is complex, and the tensions among its principles would persist even if we assumed (which we cannot) that all foreign policy is made honestly and with the best intentions. The ship cannot maximally float and speed at the same time—the international system gives priority to staying afloat, and we hope that it will take us to our destinations quickly enough. We see a similar tension between the principles of peace and of individual human rights, where again the international system chiefly favors peace.

This prioritization of peace is apt, but not because peace is in absolute terms a higher value. Popular sovereignty and human rights—including other people's—can be worth fighting for.[58] The prioritization of peace is plausible because it fits the cognitive limitations of the agent that now runs the international system. "Keep the peace" is a rule that humanity, feeble-minded from its many myths and distrusts, has a chance of enforcing successfully. All sighted eyes can see bombers and tanks crossing a border—even the billion-and-a-half human eyes that still cannot read.[59] The international community has shown it can see violations of peace, well enough at least to differentiate unprovoked aggressions from the military actions meant to reverse them (as when Iraq was forced to release Kuwait). By contrast, what would count as successful international enforcement of popular sovereignty, or human rights, is often much less obvious—with exceptions such as interventions to stop genocide, which "shocks the conscience of mankind."[60]

Here we find a final reason why we do not see consistent international action in support of popular sovereignty. We lack consensus on what popular sovereignty requires, and so we lack agreement on where it is real and where it is not. Nor is this disagreement just an artifact of human obtusity: we also lack good theory. What does it mean for the people to be the ultimate authority in their country, and how can outsiders tell when they are not? These questions can make us hesitate in supporting popular sovereignty as a principle for all nations. Answering those questions, along one dimension of popular sovereignty, is the agenda of the next three chapters.

11

Popular Resource Sovereignty

Popular sovereignty! Everlasting popular sovereignty! [Laughter and continued cheers.] Let us for a moment inquire into this vast matter of popular sovereignty.

—Abraham Lincoln

The land of Ireland, the land of every country, belongs to the people of that country.

—John Stuart Mill

This country belongs to the people. Its resources, its business, its laws, its institutions, should be utilized, maintained or altered in whatever manner will best promote the general interest. This assertion is explicit. We say directly that "the people" are absolutely to control in any way they see fit, the "business" of the country.

—Theodore Roosevelt[1]

1. All peoples have the right of self-determination. By virtue of that right they freely determine their political status and freely pursue their economic, social and cultural development.
2. All peoples may, for their own ends, freely dispose of their natural wealth and resources.[2]

These words begin Article 1 in both of the two main human rights treaties. These two human rights treaties—the *International Covenant on Civil and*

Political Rights and the *International Covenant on Economic, Social, and Cultural Rights*—are the codification of the *Universal Declaration of Human Rights*, and almost everyone on Earth lives in a country that has accepted one of these treaties (and so the text above) as law.[3] The *Charter of the United Nations* is sometimes called the Constitution of the modern international system; these Covenants are its Bill of Rights.

In this chapter, we dig into the meaning of these principles of popular sovereignty, and especially the principle for natural wealth and resources. One initial point of interest is that the principles above enjoy pride of place in the Covenants—they are showcased in Article 1 of both. So popular sovereignty is a human right.[4] The human rights of both peoples and individuals counter the power of the modern state to abuse and neglect those within its domain, leaving them more free, as individuals and together.

ROYALTIES

A sovereign makes laws for the people and for the land: a sovereign has both "personal" and "territorial" jurisdiction.[5] When the people are sovereign, citizens make laws for themselves (regarding, for example, voting and marriage) and laws for the territory (regarding, for example, national parks—and our subject, natural resources).

The history of the struggles of peoples to control the natural resources of their countries is part of the wider struggle for popular sovereignty that we surveyed in the last chapter. These struggles over natural resources are again stories of kings and queens, of emperors and empresses, who called their rule right and extended it by might, until peoples, in an epochal struggle, won sovereignty over the natural wealth of their territories—at least on paper.

From their earliest days, European kings and queens grasped the value of their realms' minerals. Royals announced their ownership of those minerals by decree as early as the twelfth century.[6] The tight link between monarchs and minerals is visible in the two senses of the English word *royalty*, meaning both "the position or office of a monarch" and "a payment made to a landowner for the privilege of working a mine."[7] Monarchs invested themselves with the natural resources of their own lands—and then seized resource-rich lands from each other under the principle of "might makes right." In 1740, Frederick the Great of Prussia wrestled iron-rich Silesia from Maria Theresa, Queen of Bohemia and Hungary. In 1870, Frederick's great-grandnephew, Wilhelm I, ordered the invasion of France and demanded iron-laden Alsace-Lorraine from Napoleon III.

As popular sovereignty replaced monarchical sovereignty across Europe, the mineral holdings of kings and queens passed to the control of democratic legislatures, which sometimes granted the property back to the monarch in qualified form. In Britain, for example, Parliament has granted to the Crown a complex property portfolio, including the North Sea oil reserves, all of Britain's silver and gold, all of its seabed and most of its shoreline, as well as Windsor Great Park and (until recently) Scotland's wild oysters. The British monarch, however, cannot transfer the rights over any of these holdings, and all of the revenues from the properties go directly into the national treasury.[8] The people's grant of resources to the Crown is today mostly symbolic.

While European countries were slowly putting their own natural resources under democratic control, as imperial powers they were grabbing the lands of militarily and immunologically weaker peoples overseas. Most infamously, in 1885, King Leopold of Belgium claimed the gigantic territory of the Congo as his personal property. (To get a sense of Leopold's territorial presumption, imagine claiming to be the individual who privately owns all of New England, the mid-Atlantic States, the Upper South, and the Deep South—or all of California and Mexico—or all of Ontario, Manitoba, and Saskatchewan—or all of New South Wales, Victoria, and the Northern Territory—or all of Britain, France, Germany, Spain, Italy, and Norway.)

The natural resources of the colonies received special attention from their imperial masters. In 1914, for example, when the United Kingdom created Nigeria, it also passed an ordinance "to regulate the right to search for, win and work mineral oils" in the subject territory:

> No lease or license shall be granted except to a British subject or to a British company with its principal place of business within Her Majesty's dominions, the chairman and the managing director (if any) and the majority of the other directors of which are British subjects.[9]

By 1946, the British had become even more appreciative of the natural wealth of Nigeria, and simply declared themselves owners of all of it:

> The entire property in land and control of minerals and mineral oils, in or under or upon any lands in Nigeria, and of rivers, streams

> and watercourses throughout Nigeria, is and shall be vested in the state.[10]

This is an imperial ordinance: "vested in the state" means "vested in the British state." If we take the monarch as the holder of colonial property in trust for the British state, then this act alone gave Queen Elizabeth II, on the day of her coronation, title to Nigerian minerals worth trillions of today's dollars. It was not until 1963 that an independent Nigeria removed the British Queen as its head of state. The Nigerian constitution of that year reads:

> We the People of Nigeria, by our representatives here in Parliament assembled, do hereby declare... all property which, immediately before the date of the commencement of this constitution, was held by the Crown... [shall] vest in the President and be held by him on behalf of... the Government of the Federation.[11]

POPULAR RESOURCE SOVEREIGNTY

Popular resource sovereignty is part of popular sovereignty. The first article of the human rights Covenants says, "All peoples may, for their own ends, freely dispose of their natural wealth and resources." France belongs to the French; America's natural resources belong to the American people; the resources of Nigeria belong to the Nigerian people; and so on.

Saying that the people own the resources of their country pulls on a few cognitive knots, which we will soon untie. First, we can just register how natural it is to talk this way. As Bob Graham, former Senator and Governor of Florida, said not long ago, "There is a fundamental fact that the oil and gas off our shores is an American asset. It belongs to the people of the United States of America."[12] If it were found that Cuba had drilled a long diagonal pipeline through the Gulf of Mexico and was now siphoning American oil, the American people would immediately (and perhaps literally) be up in arms. The oil within the territory of the United States belongs to the American people, and foreigners must not take it without permission.

Popular resource sovereignty also explains why Americans would be outraged by private theft of the country's resources. In the years leading up to the Reagan administration, companies like Shell discovered large oil deposits off the coasts of Louisiana and Florida. One can imagine the public response had President Reagan sold this oil to Shell, then put the profits into his private bank account and ordered the FBI to silence any objections. America's natural resources start out owned by the American people, and these resources must not be disposed of in ways that wholly bypass their approval. (What Congress actually did in 1982 was to start a system of public auctions for drilling leases in America's coastal waters. These auctions send the proceeds from resource sales into the national treasury, and that auction system is still in place today.)

The principle that the people of the country own the resources of the country is affirmed in many national constitutions and laws—even in nations where the principle is flouted in fact. For example:

> All deposits of liquid and gaseous hydrocarbons which exist underground or on the continental shelf within the national territory...belong to the Angolan People.
>
> The land, forests, rivers and lakes, water sources, underground natural resources, resources in the territorial waters, on the continental shelf and in the air space...fall under the ownership of the entire [Vietnamese] people.
>
> The fundamental Law of the Republic of Equatorial Guinea consecrates and designates as the property of the people of Equatorial Guinea all resources found in our national territory...It is by the mandate and delegation of the people, to whom these resources legitimately belong, that the Government undertakes to manage them.[13]

The Iraqi constitution declares, "Oil and gas are owned by the people of Iraq in all the regions and provinces."[14] The second President Bush and many in his administration emphasized this principle ("The oil belongs to the Iraqi people. It's their asset.")[15] Britain's Tony Blair asserted the more general principle ("Iraq's natural resources remain the property of the people of Iraq.")[16] Indeed, there is an extraordinary consensus among national leaders on popular resource sovereignty, at least at the rhetorical level. And this consensus unites leaders of completely different political persuasions:

> What we say is that when it comes to the mineral resources of Australia, the Australian people own those resources. (Rudd of Australia)

> The oil belongs to 190 million Brazilians, and we will show everyone that the oil is ours. (Lula of Brazil)
>
> All hydrocarbons will remain the property of the Mexican people. (Peña Nieto of Mexico)
>
> The oil belongs to the Venezuelan people. (Chavez of Venezuela)
>
> The oil belongs to the people of Azerbaijan. (Aliyev of Azerbaijan)
>
> The oil belongs to the people. (Khamenei of Iran)
>
> There is no ruse here. People cannot be fooled. This oil belongs to the Libyans. (Gaddafi of Libya)
>
> The [oil] resource belongs to the people of Ghana. (Mahama of Ghana)
>
> Norway's petroleum resources belong to the Norwegian people. (Parliament of Norway)[17]

Like popular sovereignty in general, popular resource sovereignty is all the world's ideal. Elites tell their people that the people own the resources, and elites tell each other's people that the people own the resources. Yet popular resource sovereignty is not, as we saw in Part I, all the world's reality.

Why not? For three reasons, already familiar. First and most obviously is self-interest: political elites have the most direct control over the international system, and many in those elites do not want to give power (instead of words) to the people of their own and other countries. Second, like any principle, popular resource sovereignty can, if overweighted, strain at the design constraints of the international system. Third and most important, the meaning of the principle of popular resource sovereignty is not settled—it is not certain what it would require as a matter of law. The first reason cycles through the other two: it's in the interests of elites to muddy the meaning of popular resource sovereignty as much as possible, and then to intimate, even to fulminate, that the principle contains dangers.

Here we find ourselves at a fortunate point in history. We've inherited texts that explain in a straightforward way the meaning of popular resource sovereignty and how it meshes with the other principles of the international system. With these texts, we can cut these three reasons down to one: the self-interest of elites. The texts that history has given us are none other than the Covenants that we started with. History, through its cunning, has already given us the legal texts that should be law. All that needs adding is belief in their plain meaning.

Our good fortune with texts is captured by Hegel's famous *Doppelsatz*: "What is rational is actual; and what is actual is rational."[18] What is rational is actual: the most plausible principle of popular resource sovereignty is embodied in the international legal documents that most states are already party to. And what is actual is rational: there is a natural, even obvious, interpretation of the international legal documents that explains popular resource sovereignty and integrates it with other priorities in the international system. The world already has the doctrine that it needs.

The rest of this chapter will describe our happy Hegelian situation. In Chapter 12, we will glance through the curious distorting lenses which international elites use to read these documents. And in Chapter 13, we will listen to what the texts have to say about today's most difficult cases to check whether we really do believe that all peoples should control their resources.

THE ALPHA AND OMEGA OF THE COVENANTS

Here again is the text from common Article 1 of the human rights Covenants:

1. All peoples have the right of self-determination. By virtue of that right they freely determine their political status and freely pursue their economic, social and cultural development.
2. All peoples may, for their own ends, freely dispose of their natural wealth and resources.

More than six out of seven states are already party to at least one of the Covenants. This includes all of the countries in the Americas, Europe, and Africa (except South Sudan and small islands) and nearly every country in Asia, including China and India. The rejectionist countries are mostly absolute monarchies like Saudi Arabia and microstates like Tuvalu. Holding aside countries of less than a million finds 95 percent of states are party to one of the Covenants. Counting persons instead of nations finds that a full 98 percent of humanity is living in a country that has accepted the text above. As a matter of law, nearly everyone on Earth is part of a people that has the human right to self-determination.[19]

The principle of popular resource sovereignty in paragraph 2 is what we want to understand. It's significant that this principle appears in the very first article of the Covenants. It's also useful that the principle is affirmed again in the last substantive article of each treaty:

> Nothing in the present Covenant shall be interpreted as impairing the inherent right of all peoples to enjoy and utilize fully and freely their natural wealth and resources.[20]

Popular resource sovereignty is stated at the beginning and at the end—it is the alpha and the omega of the Covenants. The people's right to control their resources is the *only* right in the two main human rights treaties that is declared twice, as if for extra emphasis. As for the meaning of the principle, the treaties helpfully supply these two different formulations. If we ask the treaties what it means to say that the people "may, for their own ends, freely dispose of their natural wealth and resources," then the treaties themselves answer that the people have an inherent "right... to enjoy and utilize fully and freely their natural wealth and resources."

The meaning of these passages is what we want to understand, and the natural first assumption is that they mean what they say.[21] The people of each country have the right freely to control the resources of their country. Our method for expanding our understanding of these words will be to flashlight the darkness that some have tried to wrap around them. There are lawyerly myths encircling Article 1 that are easy to dispel.[22] Our targets will be thicker obfuscations: elite attempts to say that Article 1 means something different than what it seems to—or that it contains hidden threats.

POWER TO THE CITIZENS

"On the surface it sounded reasonable," huffed a British administrator sent to the colony of Ceylon. "[L]et the people decide. In fact it was ridiculous because the people cannot decide until someone decides who are the people."[23] Maurice Cranston is even more mordant on the meaning of "peoples": the Covenants, he says,

> increased confusion by introducing as Article I the old stalking horse of German nationalists, Victorian idealists, and President Woodrow Wilson: "All peoples have the right of self-determination"... But what

> constitutes a "people"? Are the inhabitants of Provence or Quebec or Wales or Brittany a people? Each is undoubtedly an ethnic group, distinct in some ways from the other inhabitants of the political society to which it at present belongs. Do the inhabitants of those areas have a right to independence that the governments of France, Canada, and the United Kingdom ought to concede?[24]

Mention of the rights of "the people" can start a stampede of such ill-tempered critiques. Yet while some will try to buffalo us on popular sovereignty, we need not panic. The word *people* has various applications, but so do many words—including the word *state*. And *state* is a word that all in the international elite claim to understand. So elite attempts to make mischief around the meaning of *people* merely rebound back onto them. Is the *state* system ridiculous, because *states* cannot decide until someone decides who are the *states*? Are Taiwan, Kosovo, Somaliland, and Donetsk states? And who exactly is the *someone* who decides?

Luckily, there is no call to obfuscate at all. In our fortunate point in history, "people" in Article 1 just means the people of an independent country. And the people of an independent country consists of all of its citizens. So it is the citizens of the country who should have the ultimate authority over their country. This simple answer is the right one: that is popular sovereignty.[25]

The question of "who is a people" was harder before the independence of the colonies. Before decolonization, no one knew, for example, that Tanganyikans and Zanzibaris would shortly become citizens of a new country, Tanzania. With the independence of the colonies, these questions have now been settled. Once the colonies became independent, the question of who belongs to which fully self-determining people becomes the question of who is a citizen of which state—not a trivial question, but a tractable one.

To make popular sovereignty work today, international actors still need to agree on who is a citizen during military occupations, but this they can do. (No one doubted, for instance, who was an Iraqi citizen during the US occupation of 2003–2004.) International actors need to keep track of unifications (East and West Germany) and secessions (South Sudan from Sudan), which they've also shown they can do. The plight of stateless persons is of great moral concern, deserving much more international attention than it gets. Yet statelessness is a second-order problem of indeterminacy, within a first-order system that is 99.8 percent determinate regarding which individuals are citizens of which states.[26]

This leaves us with Cranston's question of whether the inhabitants of Quebec or Wales or Brittany are a people. And we can happily say they are. We can gladly accept that the Ijaw of Nigeria are a people, as are the Cofán of Ecuador and the Uighurs in China. These are "peoples within a people"—just as federal systems like the United States, Germany, and Malaysia have "states within a state." (Q: How many states are within America's borders? A: Fifty-one—the fifty states plus the United States.) Many subnational peoples enjoy special rights within their national political systems: for example, the people of Quebec have crafted distinctive laws regarding the public use of the French language, and the Welsh have their own parliament. The rights of such peoples are quite varied across countries, but a few generalizations can be made. There has been some progress in the recognition of indigenous people's rights in North America and Australia, and there has been movement in Western Europe toward greater autonomy for national minorities such as the Scots and the Catalans.

The question then is which rights should international law ascribe to subnational or cross-national peoples. Cranston's suggestion that all such peoples might be internationally recognized as having a right to complete independence has been repeatedly rejected. Why? Because it raises the specter of multiple and conflicting claims to independent territory—claims that are well beyond the international system's capacity to resolve. The human rights Covenant on civil and political rights sets a more modest baseline, which is to secure the rights of minority groups against serious forms of discrimination and harassment:

> In those states in which ethnic, religious or linguistic minorities exist, persons belonging to such minorities shall not be denied the right, in community with the other members of their group, to enjoy their own culture, to profess and practice their own religion, or to use their own language.[27]

The international system's first-order ideal is to distribute power to the people of independent states—that is, to all of their citizens. The system has made progress in addressing the second-order problems of the rights of indigenous peoples and national minorities, and experts like Will Kymlicka recommend continuing to work within this system to make more progress.[28] We don't yet have proposals for a different first-order system of distributing political power among the world's individuals that gives reasonable assurance of securing weighty values like peace, human rights, individual political autonomy, and minority rights. So responsible actors will affirm the rights of the peoples of independent states, while also looking to win more rights for subnational peoples where they can be won.

SCARE STORIES

Popular resource sovereignty—that "all peoples, shall for their own ends, freely dispose of their natural wealth and resources"—is one dimension of popular sovereignty. We continue to cut through to the real meaning of this principle by asking what are the "natural wealth and resources" that peoples may dispose of, and what it means to say that these resources are "theirs." Again, we start by whetting our blade with vinegary warnings from elites as they try to sour us on ascribing real rights to peoples.

In 1948, a man named Frank Holman was the President of the American Bar Association, the main organization representing America's lawyers. As the UN General Assembly was preparing to vote on the *Universal Declaration of Human Rights*, Holman took the opportunity to address the State Bar of California. In a speech titled "Human Rights on Pink Paper," Holman explained how the *Universal Declaration* "is a proposal for worldwide socialism to be imposed through the United Nations on the United States and on every other member nation." Holman continued:

> If it became the supreme law of the land by virtue of the adoption of the Covenant as a treaty, our various states would be prevented from passing laws or enforcing existing laws relating to such matters as compulsory vaccination, sterilization of the insane, treatment of sexual psychopaths and the like... Sterilization of the criminally insane should be properly left open for states and nations to decide for themselves upon the basis of population, the number of the criminally insane, etc.[29]

In 2012, the Dominican economist Fabio Fiallo similarly summoned an image from *The Communist Manifesto*:

> A new specter is haunting Latin America. It is inducing States to chase away foreign firms from, and to assume themselves the management

> of, the natural resources of their countries... It is at work in a handful of countries ruled by so-called "progressive" (read: left-wing) governments... The specter has a name: "resource nationalism."[30]

In other words, human rights are an international socialist plot. A national property right in natural resources is too. Do these fears seem strained? The decades since the United States voted in favor of the *Universal Declaration* have not seen the United Nations imposing socialism on the world. And we might recall from the quotations above that President George W. Bush (a man rarely described as a socialist) went out of his way to affirm the principle of popular resource sovereignty, that the people of the country own the oil of the country. Ideologists like Fiallo have tried to muddy popular resource sovereignty—we can enjoy making it clear.

PRESENT YOUR TERMS

Elites can make mischief out of the relation between a people and their resources because the concepts here are all a jumble. "The central core notion of a property right in X," wrote Robert Nozick, "is the right to determine what shall be done with X."[31] Yet this is also the central core notion of a *sovereignty* right in X. Property or sovereignty, ownership or rule, economics or politics—which, for example, did Lincoln mean when he said, "This country, with its institutions, *belongs* to the people who inhabit it"?[32] And there are conundrums concerning "this country" too. If "this country" belongs to the people, does that mean the country's land, its resources, its institutions, something else?

One might also think that *territory* is a purely political term: that territory is the area over which a sovereign exercises political authority. But then what to make of the italicized terms in the Territory Clause of the US Constitution: "The Congress shall have power to dispose of and make all needful Rules and Regulations respecting the Territory *or other Property* belonging to the United States"?[33]

The concepts make a mare's nest, and the tangle of words can conceal the stratagems of those who are trying to obscure the people's rights. So we just cut through by defining clearly all the terms we need—*sovereignty*, *jurisdiction*, *territory*, *property*, and *natural resources*. We also nail down how these terms are related so that they express the meaning of "popular resource sovereignty."

Sovereignty, Jurisdiction, and Territory

To have sovereignty is to have jurisdiction: the right to authorize laws. A modern sovereign has personal jurisdiction: the right to authorize laws valid for citizens, wherever they are. A modern sovereign also has territorial jurisdiction: the right to authorize laws valid for everyone within a specified physical space. A sovereign's territory is the physical space over which that sovereign has the right to authorize laws. Territorial jurisdiction—the right to authorize laws that are valid in a space—is the core of modern political authority.[34]

Jurisdiction and Property

One dimension of territorial jurisdiction is the right to authorize property laws. Property laws define property rights and establish property entitlements. The paradigm of a property right is an alienable and waivable right to the exclusive use of some non-bodily object or to the exclusive occupation of some space.[35]

Sovereignty and Natural Resources

Within any territory, there will be natural resources: non-manufactured and unprocessed, non-human objects with a value in use. One part of a sovereign's territorial jurisdiction is the right to authorize laws for natural resources. For example, a law may specify, as in the United States, that rights to extract oil under public land will be auctioned off to private bidders, with the revenues going into the national treasury. Or rights over oil can be granted to a national oil company, as in Mexico in 1938. Or the law may vest title to oil in the Crown, as in Britain, while management of the resource is assigned to a government ministry. Or the law can require that oil be left in the ground. Any of these laws, and many others, are possible: a sovereign has the right to free disposition of the resources of its territory.

Popular Sovereignty

When the people are sovereign, they hold all of these rights. The country's laws and institutions "belong" to the people in the sense that the people have the ultimate jurisdiction over persons and territory, which they use (as in Article 1 of the Covenants) to "freely determine their political status and freely pursue their economic, social and cultural development." Citizens together have the ultimate authority over which laws will be in effect for each citizen and which laws will be in effect over every person within the borders of their territory.

Popular sovereignty over land and resources

When the people are sovereign, the land (the country) "belongs" to the people in the sense that the people have the ultimate right to authorize laws for that territory. All of the country's natural resources also "belong" to the people in this sense: the people have the jurisdictional right (as the Covenants say) to "freely dispose of" these resources—the right "to enjoy and utilize" them "fully and freely." One implication of "free disposition" is that without a valid law, no one can gain ownership of resources—and with a valid law, the people can create any property rights they choose over the resources.

Popular property in land and resources

The land (the earth's surface and subsurface) also "belongs" to the people in the sense that the land is a natural resource. All of a territory's natural resources are property originally vested in the people; as the Covenants say, these are "their" resources. The resources originally belong to the people; at independence, the resources start out in the people's hands. The natural resources of a country are, as the UN General Assembly once put it, the people's "birthright."[36]

WE THE OWNERS

All of this conceptual untangling should seem straightforward. It is simple to show, for example, that a sovereign people have original property rights in their natural resources. It would be odd to say that natural resources within a national territory are originally unowned. In 1975, Shell discovered the Cognac oil field in US territorial waters, one hundred miles offshore from New Orleans. No one ventured that Shell's discovery was an "original acquisition" of unowned resources—what Shell found was of course a resource that already had an owner. The American people's original property right explains why Shell had to ask the US government for permission to drill into Cognac, and why Shell had to pay into the US national treasury for each barrel of oil extracted from it. (Recall Senator Graham: "There is a fundamental fact that the oil and gas off our shores is an American asset. It belongs to the people of the United States of America.")

It would be even odder to posit that a country's natural resources are originally owned by someone besides the people—like the officials of the country's government. If Scotland someday becomes an independent country, no one will think that the new Scottish prime minister will own the offshore oil, holding rights to sell that oil and spend the revenues even against all the wishes of the Scottish people.

The natural assumption is that the sovereign people originally own the country's resources, and that their government manages those resources for them. This is again the assumption that shows up in ordinary talk. For instance:

> In the early 1900s, the United States was trying to encourage people to populate areas—mainly out west—that it considered to be unpopulated... Mining speculators who recognized the value of oil were gobbling up the petroleum-rich property relatively cheaply. On September 17, 1909, the director of the Geological Survey sent a report to the Secretary of the Interior concluding that oil lands were passing into private control so rapidly that it would "be impossible for the people of the United States to continue ownership of oil lands for more than a few months. After that, the Government will be obliged to repurchase the very oil that it has practically given away."[37]

The people start off owning the nation's resources, and thereafter, the people have the right to freely dispose of them. Without law that the people authorize, no one can rightly own the nation's resources but the people. With law that the people authorize, anyone can come to own them. We see the people exercising their right to dispose of their natural resources differently within different national laws. For example, according to the Mexican constitution:

> The Nation has an original right of property over the land and waters within the boundaries of the national territory. The Nation has and will have the right to transfer its property's domain to private individuals in order to create private property rights.[38]

Zambia's constitution, on the other hand, sets itself against privatization:

> The State shall devise land policies which recognize ultimate ownership of land by the people. The management and development of Zambia's natural resources shall not bestow private ownership of any natural resource.[39]

Papua New Guinea's Land Act designates the great bulk of the country's land (currently 97 percent) as "customary land": "owned by the Indigenous People of Papua New Guinea whose ownership rights and interest are regulated by their customs."[40] Each country's people has original rights to their natural resources, and as they exercise their sovereign rights to dispose of those resources for their own ends, quite different ownership arrangements will result.

O PETRÓLEO É NOSSO: THE OIL IS OURS

Jacques Maritain, one of the framers of the *Universal Declaration of Human Rights*, said that many different kinds of music can be played on the document's strings.[41] This is certainly true for the principle of popular resource sovereignty in Article 1 of the Covenants. In all, 169 UN member states with quite different political systems, including the United States, Brazil, India, and South Korea, are party to at least one of these treaties. All of these countries' constitutions are compatible with popular resource sovereignty. The principle is compatible with laws allowing private development of natural resources (as in the United States and Canada), with laws establishing national resource companies (as in Norway and Venezuela), or with mixed systems (as in Indonesia).[42]

The United States and Canada are unusual in having laws that allow subsurface minerals to become privately owned.[43] And indeed, US federal law allows the individual states to experiment with different systems of private mineral ownership. Texas developed its own special state laws for private ownership of oil: the landowner owns the oil beneath his or her land, but any adjacent landowner who drains that oil out gets title to it—one neighbor can "drink the other's milkshake."[44] George W. Bush's family made much of its fortune under those rules, and President Bush had nothing to fear when he endorsed the principle of popular resource sovereignty that validated those Texan oil laws.

So one of Putin's former economic advisors erred when he said (in response to the Clean Trade policies that will be set out in Part IV) that the principle of popular resource sovereignty "really means that resources must be nationalized, government-owned, and government-managed."[45] Concerns about nationalization, government ownership, excessive statism, and "resource nationalism" are real and important, but they're downstream from the basic political principle we've been exploring.

Resource nationalism is a downstream concern within investment law. Foreigners invest in a country and come to own property under its laws. Sometimes what foreigners build are facilities like oil rigs and liquefied natural gas plants—assets that can be worth billions of dollars. The state then decides it would rather own these things and attempts to nationalize the assets. Resource nationalism denotes an aggressive use of state powers to take control of resource assets belonging to foreigners.[46]

To affirm popular resource sovereignty is not to affirm resource nationalism.[47] More importantly, to affirm popular sovereignty is not to affirm absolute sovereign rights. To be sovereign is to have *ultimate* jurisdictional rights and *original* ownership rights, not necessarily to have *unlimited* rights of these kinds. And in the modern international system, none of the people's rights could be unlimited.

We see this in the human rights Covenants themselves: the group rights of popular sovereignty in Article 1 are limited by the human rights of individuals in the articles that follow. Peoples must respect the human rights of individuals as they authorize laws—as the German Basic Law states clearly:

> **Article 1.** (1) Human dignity shall be inviolable. To respect and protect it shall be the duty of all state authority. (2) The German people therefore acknowledge inviolable and inalienable human rights as the basis of every community, of peace and of justice in the world.[48]

The people's sovereign rights over their resources are limited not just by human rights but also by other principles of the international system as well. In his book on resource sovereignty, Nico Schrijver lists many legal duties that now accompany these sovereign rights, including the duty to respect the rights and interests of indigenous peoples, the duty to take due care of the environment, and the duty to settle transborder resource issues equitably.[49] Moreover, it may be that the future is being plundered by the present—that the current generation of people in many countries is wrongly using up assets that should instead be saved for future generations.[50] An international law that required peoples to save resources for the future would not violate popular resource sovereignty—only limit it.

Indeed, even speculative proposals to further "global justice" often involve nothing more than qualifications on popular resource sovereignty. For example, Thomas Pogge's proposal for a Global Resource Dividend assumes that nations have full discretion over when and how to exploit their resources, but it also requires them to pay into a fund for the world's poor whenever they extract those resources.[51] Whether these kinds of "global justice" reforms are feasible and desirable we'll check in Chapter 18; as a matter of principle, they are fully compatible with peoples' sovereign rights over their resources.

IT'S CLEAR ENOUGH—BUT IS IT TOUGH ENOUGH?

Like popular sovereignty, popular resource sovereignty is all the world's ideal—and some of the world's reality. World leaders everywhere talk it up, and it has pride of place in international legal documents to which almost all nations have committed. There is a natural, even obvious, interpretation of these treaties that explains the principle, and that integrates it with other priorities in the international system. In unpacking the ordinary meanings of the terms in these texts, we have found powerful ideas that are clear and precise, yet also quite flexible. The great good fortune of our place in history is that for natural resources, the world already has the principle that it needs.

The meaning of popular resource sovereignty is now out in the open. To become rugged enough for use in the rough-and-tumble of real international politics, however, we must be sure that we know it when we see it—a fascinating challenge that we will take up after unmasking some devious elite doublespeak in Chapter 12.

12

The State of the Law

With respect to this, and other fictions, there was once a time, perhaps, when they had their use. With instruments of this temper, I will not deny but that some political work may have been done, and that useful work, which, under the then circumstances of things, could hardly have been done with any other. But the season of Fiction is now over.

—Jeremy Bentham[1]

LIFE, LOGIC, LAW

This is a short chapter on how to read treaties. Treaties like the human rights covenants are a primary source of international law, and the great majority of states are party to at least one of them. Nevertheless, the plain meanings of the words on the page are not regarded as law by everyone. The main problem is that the elites who run states do not act as though they have any obligations arising from the words "All peoples may, for their own ends, freely dispose of their natural wealth and resources." Why not?

The life of the law has not been logic, as Oliver Wendell Holmes said, and to outsiders, international law can seem a bit Dada.[2] International law can, for example, deny the principles that seem to motivate the rules that it recognizes—as the following thought experiment will illustrate.

A white racist regime is a violation of international law—apartheid is now illegal.[3] Yet imagine that South African history went very differently than it in fact did. Imagine that toward the end of apartheid in South Africa, a large, extended family of black South Africans seized power. Just by chance, the surname of this family is White (they are Emmanuel White, Nadine White, etc.). Once in power, the White family does nothing more to change the apartheid legal code than to capitalize all occurrences of the word *white* in it: the rule of whites in South Africa is replaced by a legally identical rule of the Whites. Under the revised laws, only a member of the White family can be prime minister, many public accommodations are Whites-only, and so on. The new code is indistinguishable from the apartheid code in its inequality and discrimination—except that racial rule is replaced by family rule. Would White rule violate international law?

It would not. International law is quite rigid in its reasoning: it resists generalizing beyond the specific rules supported by state practice. When apartheid became illegal, that was the only change that registered in international law—no broader conclusions about inequality of political power or discrimination were reached.

International law tends to be limited in a second way too. As Holmes also said, "The law is the witness and external deposit of our moral life. Its history is the history of the moral development of the race."[4] The contents of international law are often more of a reflection of inequalities between nations than they are a tool for reforming those inequalities. As legal scholars such as Antony Anghie have detailed, much of international law has been the rationalization of power relationships that, through the colonial and postcolonial periods, have been quite unequal.[5]

International lawyers may be progressive in their political views, yet in their professional work, most are quite hidebound. They characteristically see their professional virtue as faithfulness to the law as it has been given to them—limited and perhaps even morally objectionable though it may be. Most see their job as focused on the law as it is, not as it should be: on *lex lata* instead of *lex ferenda*.

We might therefore feel some sympathy for the typical international lawyer looking at the human rights treaties. This lawyer sees the words of common Article 1 that plainly assert the rights of peoples to control their resources—and also the words that reaffirm those rights at the end of the treaties as well. But when he raises his eyes and looks at state practice—what regimes actually do—he sees no consistent efforts by regimes to enforce the people's rights. So he follows the leaders, and he reads the texts in ways that may seem to outsiders peculiar, even outlandish.

In this chapter, we look at how international lawyers do it—how they read ringing declarations of popular sovereignty so that these give no meaningful rights to peoples. These lawyerly interpretations open a window on how global elites think, and they reveal a kind of doublespeak that the officials of our own governments use when speaking to their citizens—a doublespeak that is by no means benign.

By the end of this chapter, the lawyers' readings will turn out to be a bust: clearly in conflict with settled international law. Yet the failure of these interpretations can't ultimately be blamed on the lawyers who devise them. These lawyers are only trying to bridge the abyss between what states say and what states do, where their profession encourages them to cling to the rocks of the latter. Exposing this lawyerly language will remove one resource that state leaders now use for doublespeak—and so give these leaders one more reason to do what they say.

THE MASK OF STATE

Thus far, an international lawyer may have watched the unfurling of our interpretation of popular sovereignty placidly, untroubled by any thought that the doctrine set out so lucidly in the human rights texts could impose obligations on states. "Full points for getting this far," he might say, "but you do not have law—at least not in the way you hope could make a difference. For you still have not appreciated the law's understanding of the relation between the people and the state. Once you have understood this, you will see why what look like strong statements of popular sovereignty in the treaties require no change at all to the world as it is."

The drama here is the relation between the people and the state, and to stage it, we need to understand the actors. For all the elite fulminations about the "people," the people are well known to us. Indeed, the people *are* us: the citizens of independent countries. It is the other part in the play that is not what it seems—at least from the audience's perspective.

Open any textbook on international law and you'll find the traditional gloss on the word *state*: a state has a defined territory, a permanent population, and an effective government.[6] This tells us what constitutes a state—its elements, as it were. Yet this does not tell us how these elements are configured. What, exactly, is a state? The US Department of State (where presumably they know) publishes on its website that it recognizes 195 independent states. It also declares:

> In this listing, the term "independent state" refers to a people politically organized into a sovereign state with a definite territory recognized as independent by the United States.[7]

The State Department is saying that it regards "a state" as being, first and foremost, "a people." In saying this, it is misleading visitors to its website—it is doublespeaking. International elites tell their publics that they mean one thing by "state," but among themselves, they use the word to mean something quite different. The word *state*, which we have ourselves used innocently up to now, is a mask word. For those in the know, a state is not a people. A state is a regime.

Within political elites, "state" means "regime": the officials who rule, the dominant coercive power in the territory. Elites see "state" as a word from Westphalia. To put the traditional elements in their unmasked order, elites believe that a state is an effective government—effective in the sense of having coercive control over the permanent population of a defined territory. As one historian summarizes the elite usage, when elites speak about the state, they are "merely referring to a prevailing system of legal and executive power, together with an associated apparatus of bureaucracy and coercive force."[8]

When leaders speak to each other, they speak in the Weberian language of power. When a government speaks to its own public, it says the same words but switches to a Jeffersonian dialect. Within elite circles, "state" means "regime"; when elites talk publicly, "state" means "people." This slipperiness with words is not innocent. Indeed, this doublespeak can burden a whole country for a generation.

Today, when an international lender makes a loan to a foreign "state," the money goes straight to that country's regime. The people of the country may have no control over the regime that's taking out the loan—the people may not even know that the regime is borrowing the money. In fact, regimes sometimes use the money from loans to pay soldiers to repress the people—or simply spend the money on themselves. And here is where the elite doublespeak kicks.

By law, the state (regime) gets the money—but the state (people) gets the debt. The beneficiary of the loan (regime) can spend all the money on paramilitaries or on palaces. Yet should the state (regime) collapse, the state (people) must still repay the old debt as they struggle to establish a new political system. Debt incurred by a non-representative regime—by a Mobutu or a Marcos—is known as "odious debt," and "odious" describes the elite doublespeak that works to conceal it.

After being elected President of South Africa, Nelson Mandela came under heavy international pressure to use his new government's revenues to pay back the debts of the apartheid regime that had imprisoned him. In the Republic of Congo, the regime used money from a loan to buy weapons to fight a large and eventually successful insurgency; as one observer later said, "Thousands of Congolese died, and now the survivors must pay for the arms that killed their loved ones."[9]

To keep ourselves from speaking double, from now on we will speak like the elites speak to themselves. The word *state*, as the subject of any verb, will mean only the regime—and *the regime* will mean the officials with effective coercive power over a permanent population in a defined territory.[10] In this sense, there is a Swedish regime, just as there is a Sudanese regime. But to protect ourselves from elitism, we will reserve the word *government* for those regimes that have not only the coercive power but also the rightful authority to rule that flows from popular sovereignty.[11]

PEOPLES MEANS REGIMES

International lawyers speak the elite language of states, which is one reason that the international treaties read so differently to them. Indeed, sometimes international lawyers become so state-centric that they can only see regimes as the bearers of legal rights, no matter what words they see on the page.

For instance, the UN Charter says that one of the United Nations' guiding purposes is "[t]o develop friendly relations among nations based on respect for the principle of equal rights and self-determination of peoples."[12] What do you think those words mean? Probably not what they meant to Hans Kelsen—a very distinguished jurist indeed. Kelsen looked at the word *peoples* in that passage and said that it "means probably states, since only states have 'equal rights' according to general international law... so 'self-determination of peoples'... can mean only 'sovereignty of states.'" That's how many lawyers think.[13]

To support an insistence that in law "people" can only mean "state," an international lawyer may cite texts in which the rights of peoples seem interchangeable with the rights of states. For example, the African Charter on Human and Peoples' Rights begins with robust affirmations of peoples' rights:

> **Article 20**
>
> 1. All *peoples* shall have the right to existence. They shall have the unquestionable and inalienable right to self-determination. They shall freely determine their political status and shall pursue their economic and social development according to the policy they have freely chosen...
>
> **Article 21**
>
> 1. All *peoples* shall freely dispose of their wealth and natural resources. This right shall be exercised in the exclusive interest of the people. In no case shall a people be deprived of it.
> 2. In case of spoliation [plunder] the dispossessed *people* shall have the right to the lawful recovery of its property as well as to an adequate compensation...[14]

Yet then, a lawyer might point out, the Charter's language slips back into statism:

> 4. *States* parties to the present Charter shall individually and collectively exercise the right to free disposal of their wealth and natural resources with a view to strengthening African unity and solidarity.

In fact, our lawyer might press, while the original UN General Assembly resolution on "Permanent Sovereignty over Natural Resources" ascribed these sovereign rights to "peoples and nations," by the time the resolution was reaffirmed nine years later, the sovereign rightholder had changed to "states."[15] "Peoples," the lawyer will repeat, can really only mean "states." And "states," as we have seen, to the international elite really means "regimes."

PRINCIPALS AND AGENTS

As a matter of political principle, the difference between regime sovereignty and popular sovereignty over natural resources is momentous. One might try speaking with conviction each of the following principles:

A: Regime sovereignty. Each country's regime has the right freely to dispose of the country's natural resources for its own ends, even against the wishes and interests of the country's people.

B: Popular sovereignty. Each country's people has the right freely to dispose of the country's natural resources for its own ends, even against the wishes and interests of the country's regime.

The choice is easy: A is hideous; B is obvious. Yet an international lawyer, as always, does not work on *lex ferenda*; his job is *lex lata*. He only reads legal texts so that they express the law as it is—which in this case, he says, is captured by *A*.

We can begin to push the lawyer away from his unfortunate approach to reading treaties by showing him that for the human rights treaties, at least, it would produce absurdities. Taking "peoples" to mean "states" would contradict the object and purpose of those treaties and so would violate the prime directive of interpretation.[16]

The object and purpose of the human rights treaties is to limit the power of states (meaning, as always now, regimes). Human rights are, uncontroversially, rights that constrain state action—they are rights *against* the regime. And the self-determination of peoples is a human right.[17] But if "people" means "state," then the treaties would be ascribing to states a right against themselves—which makes no sense. Reading the human rights treaties this way would turn Article 1 to applesauce and make the text incapable of legal effect, which no drafter could have intended. The lawyer's interpretation can't fly.

Fortunately, it's not necessary to read "peoples" as "states" in any legal text. There's an easy reading that captures an ordinary understanding of the relation between the two, which is in fact the straightforward reading that will come to the mind of anyone who has not come under the influence of the legal profession. This is the "ultimate/agent" reading. On this interpretation, when a legal text refers to a people's rights over resources, it is identifying the *ultimate* authority over the country's natural wealth. Final rights over resources are vested in citizens: these are citizens' rights against colonial powers, kleptocratic regimes, and other rapacious threats to their natural assets. It is the people who are ultimately sovereign over the country's resource wealth.[18]

However (this reading continues) a good deal of law relating to resources is naturally concerned not with timeless authority, but with day-to-day administration. Here the texts need no longer affirm deep sovereignty but instead will take up mundane management. In these contexts, the documents will rightly present governments as holding rights over resources. On this reading, the people have the *ultimate* authority over resources, and delegate day-to-day authority to the government as their managing *agent*. As one nation's law expresses this idea, "It is by the mandate and delegation of the people, to whom these resources legitimately belong, that the Government undertakes to manage them."[19] This ultimate/agent reading gives solid, common-sense results when applied to any legal text.

Yet even here, an international lawyer may not be convinced. Even having lost all the tricks so far, our lawyer might play what he has always taken to be his trump card. In fact, he may say that in setting out an "agency" reading of the legal texts, we have given the game away.

THE DOCTRINE OF STATE UNITIES

The international lawyer might now abandon the literal statement that "people" actually means "state." But, he may say, the law exists for practical purposes—and for all practical purposes to refer to a people must be to refer to a regime. For how could a people possibly act independently of a regime? Who can speak for a people but their state? What would it even mean for a people to control natural resources, except that the state exercises control "in the people's name"? Even if he admits that, in some abstract way, the people have rights, our lawyer will insist that in reality, the state is always presumed to speak for the people. Any control over resources must be entirely exercised by the state.

The lawyer is saying that the people can have no rights independent of their regime. The state will always be seen as exercising the rights of the people—no matter if it is a police state, and no matter what the police do to the people.[20] Whatever the state is like, whatever it does, the state will be interpreted as acting for the people. The two entities are legally one person, with the regime as the head.

Any lawyer tempted toward this interpretation of the international legal texts may merit a gentle reproof. Even for a conservative profession, this interpretation is very conservative indeed. This principle of interpretation resembles nothing more than the ancient "doctrine of unities" between a husband and his wife, famously summarized in the eighteenth century by William Blackstone in his *Commentaries*:

> By marriage, husband and wife are one person in law: that is, the very being or legal existence of the woman is suspended during the marriage, or at least is incorporated and consolidated into that of the husband: under whose wing, protection, and cover, she performs everything... A man cannot grant anything to his wife, or enter into covenant with her: for the grant would be to suppose her separate existence; and to covenant with her, would only be to covenant with himself... If the wife be injured in her person or her property, she can bring no action for redress without her husband's concurrence, and in his name, as well as her own: neither can she be sued, without making the husband a defendant.[21]

Likewise, our international lawyer is proposing a doctrine of state unities. Once a regime and a people are married at independence, the legal existence of the people is suspended, or at least incorporated and consolidated into that of the regime. A regime cannot, as a matter of logic, enter into legal relations with the people, nor can the people bring any legal action independently of the regime. The regime and the people are one, and the regime necessarily acts for them both.

This doctrine of state unities is clearly an inheritance from an earlier age. (In 1603, King James I, who tilted against witches, used the Pauline language of matrimonial unities to explain his sovereign rights over Britain: "What God hath conioyned [sic] then, let no man separate. I am the Husband, and all the whole Isle is my lawfull Wife; I am the Head, and it is my Body."[22]) To maintain this doctrine of state unities in modern times, a lawyer would have to give up the idea of popular sovereignty as a human right. For a people to have rights against its regime makes no more sense than for a Blackstonian wife to have rights against her husband. Yet some modern lawyers are tepid about peoples' rights as human rights anyway, so this may be a sacrifice that these lawyers are willing to make in order to preserve their doctrine of state unities.

While we might look with sadness at a lawyer whose interpretative strategy drags him ever further into the dark politics of the past, the best means of resetting the discussion is not to dispute those politics. We can just take this lawyer back to his own grounds. The doctrine of state unities is simply legally incorrect: it is straightforwardly incompatible with modern international law. Under settled international law, a population can act independently of its state. Under settled international law, a state is not always taken as acting for its citizens. And under settled international law, a state can violate the rights of a population, which the population holds separately from the state. The leading examples of settled law here concern territorial transfer and apartheid:

- *Territorial Transfer:* A state may not legally transfer territory to another state without the consent of the population of that territory.[23] The citizens living on the territory must give their explicit consent to any transfer of that territory to another state, ideally through a referendum. Recall our earlier hypothetical about the Angolan president wanting to sell the territory of Cabinda to China. International law firmly forbids the president to claim to speak on this matter for the people of Angola, or for the people in Cabinda. The people in Cabinda must themselves explicitly agree to any such transfer for it to be legally valid. The distinct right of a population within an independent state here constrains state action. Populations can no longer, to recall Woodrow Wilson's words, be "bartered around from sovereignty to sovereignty as if they were mere chattels and pawns in a game." Populations have their own rights, which they exercise independently of the regime. And we also see these rights in status referenda, like those periodically held by Puerto Rico and Gibraltar.
- *Apartheid*: A state may no longer legally impose an apartheid system.[24] Apartheid is a violation of international law, because it violates the right of the people to internal self-determination. Again, here we cannot presume that the state speaks for, or represents, the people, when it passes what would otherwise be valid legislation: an apartheid code cannot be valid from the perspective of international law. The people have rights independent of the state, and these rights constrain what the state may do. In order not to violate the independent rights of the people, a state must show by its actions that it is "a government representing the whole people belonging to the territory without distinction as to race, creed or color."[25]

In sum, as Cassese says about the main human rights treaties:

> To hold that peoples as such are not entitled to any legal claim proper means to gloss over the significance of the step taken in 1966

> by Member States of the UN when adopting Article 1—a step designed to *upgrade* peoples to the status of *co-actors* in the world community, of participants in at least some international dealings.[26]

It can no longer be said that for all practical purposes "people" means "state." International law cannot be read to say that regimes exercise the rights of peoples regardless of what the regimes are and do. Rather, international law grants to groups of citizens rights against their regime, and sometimes requires that groups of citizens exercise their rights independently of their regime. Within today's law, skepticism about the people's rights, and the old-school doctrine of state unities, cannot be sustained. Like the other attempts to read the rights of peoples out of declarations of popular sovereignty, this last one is a wash.

FULLY FURNISHED, AVAILABLE NOW

Recall Hegel's *Doppelsatz*: "What is rational is actual; and what is actual is rational." As we saw in Chapter 11, what is rational is actual: the most plausible principle of popular resource sovereignty is already embodied in the international legal documents. And what is actual is rational: there's a natural, even obvious, interpretation of the international legal documents that expresses popular resource sovereignty and that integrates it with other principles in the international system. The doctrine we need, we have.

International elites mostly dismiss the people's resource rights because of their own self-interest and for "reasons of state." Still, one small reason why international elites continue to grant unlimited control over extremely valuable resources to the most atrocious regimes is that they lack a clear understanding of the alternative—of what popular resource sovereignty would really look like. Even when they admit that they understand the common sense of what the principle means, they may say they still don't know what popular resource sovereignty would require "on the ground."

And here our lawyer's questions return as genuinely urgent questions of politics. How could a people actually "dispose freely of their natural wealth and resources"? Who can possibly exercise authority over resources, except a regime? What would it even mean for a people to control natural resources, except that the state exercises control in their name but for its own ends?

To answer these questions, we now probe deeper into what it looks like when the people have power over resources. Really to understand popular resource sovereignty, we now need theory—and, to be useful, not just any theory. Philosophers have already designed many theories of popular sovereignty—liberal theories, republican theories, radical theories, and many others. For a philosopher to add a theory of popular resource sovereignty would be no harder than it would be for an architect to fill in the floor plan for the wing of a building he has designed already. Yet what we need now are not blueprints for superluxury condos, much less for floating skyscrapers.

The challenge is to find good theory for those who will need to use it. The main actors in the international system often have real difficulties working together. Their interests conflict, their trust runs out quickly, and their mutual comprehension is often genuinely low. These are the actors who will have to understand a theory of popular resource sovereignty and use it to redefine their relationships. We need a mental structure suited to those who will live in it, and one that is ready for them to move into tomorrow. We need a political theory of popular resource sovereignty.

13

Popular Philosophy

[It is a] happy truth that man is capable of self-government, and only rendered otherwise by the moral degradation designedly superinduced on him by the wicked acts of his tyrants.

— Thomas Jefferson

Find out just what any people will quietly submit to and you have found out the exact measure of injustice and wrong which will be imposed upon them, and these will continue till they are resisted with either words or blows, or with both. The limits of tyrants are prescribed by the endurance of those whom they oppress.

—Frederick Douglass

I will be the father to the young, brother to the elderly. I am but one of you; whatever troubles you, troubles me; whatever pleases you, pleases me.

—Fahd bin Abdul Aziz Al Saud,
public message after being
proclaimed King of Saudi Arabia[1]

California is one of many states where criminal cases are called *The People v. X*—where "The People" are both plaintiff and respondent. And speaking about the people is as old as the nation; both of America's founding documents star that same protagonist. The people take the lead role from the first sentence of the *Declaration of Independence* ("When in the Course of human events it becomes necessary for one people to dissolve the political bands which have connected them with another..."). The people also authorize the US Constitution ("We the People of the United States...do ordain and establish this Constitution"). As we saw above, "the people" are also the now the champion of the Chinese constitution, and the invocator of a great many other national constitutions too.

So even Americans—so individualistic—are on familiar terms with this group called "the people." As Danielle Allen lyrically describes a famous colonial American almanac from 1758, it "expresses the unity of peoplehood as joining heart and hand in common cause."[2] Yet is it really respectable to speak about peoples and what they do—or is that just fancy talk? This chapter shows that speaking of peoples is not just respectable, it is vital. Peoples exist, they can act, and what is crucial, in certain conditions the people can authorize its government's plans—or can choose not to.

Here we start from simple intuitions and build up practical tests for citizens' power over resources. We ask: can the American people control their country's resources? What about the Russian people, or the Iranian people? The first half of this chapter draws on philosophy and law to set out an account of popular resource sovereignty; the second half asks where in the world we see popular resource sovereignty today—and where we don't.

PEOPLES EXISTING AND ACTING

The early, philosophical stages of our enquiry into peoples are easy (the harder questions will come when we get to Saudi Arabia). A people is a group, and philosophers are relaxed about the existence of groups.[3] Groups have their own interests and can bear their own rights.[4] Nor need talk about groups acting cause excitement. Couples go on cruises, after all; corporations pay their dividends; churches change their doctrines; governments change their laws.

After Pearl Harbor, the American people supported war with Japan; after the war, the British people supported the creation of a national health service; in 1989, the Polish people rejected their Communist regime. All of this is natural to say, and perfectly right. A people learns as its citizens learn; a people deliberates as its citizens talk; a people decides when its citizens make up their minds.

A people acts, we might say, when most of its relevant members act as citizens with the same intention.[5] So we say "the Finnish people resisted the Russian invasion" when most Finns who could resist the Russians did so, and "the Irish people considered the referendum" when Irish voters discussed the referendum with each other in the weeks leading up to the vote. We can hold groups responsible, while also holding individuals responsible for their contributions to the group.[6]

So peoples can act—in fact, groups such as peoples are often more efficacious actors than individuals: they live longer, they have more information, and they can call on powers beyond any single person's.[7] Which is not to say, of course, that all peoples can always act. To do something like resisting an invasion or amending the constitution, for example, citizens must be able to coordinate by sharing information and talking over options. That's how a people deliberates and then decides. When citizen coordination is impossible, however, a people may be unable to act at all. Citizens may be (in conditions we will examine) like neurons in a sedated brain: in close proximity, but unable to send signals to each other in ways that produce coherent thought.[8]

THE STATE AGENT

Where the people are sovereign, they have original property rights in their country's resources and the ultimate right to authorize the laws for those resources. We now look at the relationship between the people and a regime that enables the people to exercise those rights: that allows citizens "for their own ends, freely to dispose of their natural wealth and resources." Simple legal concepts will be all we need.

The foundations of popular resource sovereignty are ownership and authorization. As we've seen, a people may use its sovereign powers to authorize different kinds of laws for their resources—from "privatize them" to "let the state manage them" to "leave them in the ground." And we now add that the people's sovereignty is permanent. If citizens first authorize a law allowing the privatization of resources, they may later (as the Bill of Rights says) authorize a law calling the resources back for "public use."[9] If citizens authorize a law entrusting the regime to manage resources, they may later change those arrangements or countermand any of the regime's decisions.

The only conceptual limit to the people's sovereign power is what we might call Rousseau's Thesis, which holds that the people can't permanently cede law-making rights to the regime without negating its own sovereignty: "If, then, the people promises simply to obey, by that very act it dissolves itself... the moment a master exists, there is no more sovereign, and the body politic is destroyed forthwith."[10]

A sovereign people authorizes the laws—it does not write them. (Your authorized biography will not be the one you write, but the one whose text you approve.) The legal relation envisioned since ancient times is that the citizens are the principal, and the state is their agent. As Jefferson said:

> I consider the people who constitute a society or nation as the source of all authority in that nation; as free to transact their common concerns by any agents they think proper; to change these agents individually, or the organization of them in form or function whenever they please; [and] that all the acts done by these agents under the authority of the nation are the acts of the nation.[11]

A sovereign people may relate to its authorized agent within different legal forms. Today's national constitutions typically choose one of two forms for natural resources. First is a principal-director relationship in which the principal retains full ownership of the resources and the agent undertakes to manage them. This is the arrangement envisioned, for example, in the Sudanese constitution, where it says that natural resources remain public property and the state should prepare plans to exploit them.[12] This form is familiar from joint-stock companies, where the shareholders own the assets and the board of directors takes charge of administering those assets.

A second agency relation is described in the Ghanaian constitution, which says that all minerals in the territory "shall be vested in the President on behalf of, and in trust for the people of Ghana."[13] This is a trust model: in common law jurisdictions, we say that the regime is given legal title to the resources as a trustee while the people have equitable ownership.[14]

Whatever its legal form, the people's relation to the regime demands little of citizens. Citizens need not be involved in, or even aware of, the management of the country's natural resources. Like shareholders of a corporation or beneficiaries of a trust, most citizens will not be interested in tracking the management of their assets. Popular resource sovereignty only requires that citizens be able to find out what those in power are doing with the country's resources—and that citizens be able to influence these decisions collectively if they choose. To take the analogy: There's nothing unusual about shareholders who don't know about or try to influence how a company's assets are managed. There would be something seriously wrong, though, if shareholders couldn't possibly find out about mismanagement of the company, or had no way to affect what the directors do.

While the people's attention to the regime's resource management may be slack, a regime's obligations to the people are tight. In all legal forms, the regime is a fiduciary of the people, and a fiduciary's guiding duty (as anyone who has been one knows) is to manage the principal's affairs for the principal's benefit—not for any benefit to the fiduciary.[15]

The main rule is that a fiduciary must not profit from his or her position without the principal's approval. So the duty of a president (fiduciary) entrusted with a country's natural resources is to manage the people's resources for the benefit of the people (principal)—not for any benefit to the president. A president may not profit from being the manager of the people's resources without the people's approval, but instead must direct all revenues from resource transactions to the people. All payments gained by the president through managing the people's resources must go to the people—as must all bribes, kickbacks, and secret commissions, unless the people approve otherwise. For all of these rules, a fiduciary's liabilities are strict. The president cannot offer the excuse that he intended no harm, or that his deals left the people better off than they were.

Lawyers and judges naturally assume that state officials are fiduciaries of the people in just this sense. For instance, Justice Peter Smith of the English High Court of Justice ruled not long ago that the President of Zambia and his subordinates had defrauded the country of $46 million. Justice Smith said that these Zambian officials

> owed fiduciary duties to act in good faith, to act in accordance with the powers and authority vested in them, not to place them in a position of conflict, not to make any secret profit or receive any secret payment and have a duty to account. These... are familiar duties and none of the Defendants disputed such duties. [The President] clearly owed those duties when he carried out the functions that are vested in him by virtue of... the Constitution.

Noting that over the course of a decade the President of Zambia had spent ten times his official income at a single designer clothing shop in Switzerland, Justice Smith declared, "*The people of Zambia will know that whenever [the President] appears in public wearing a smart handmade suit or a pair of his 'signature' shoes that they were acquired by stealing money from the people.*"[16]

Throughout all of this law, the people's authorization is the key. In a fiduciary relationship, the baseline is that the principal (here the people) receives all of the money. A fiduciary (here the regime) may profit from managing the principal's assets—so long as the principal (the people) authorizes this. A fiduciary can collect a reasonable fee, with the reasonableness of the fee being decided by the legal authority of that jurisdiction—again ultimately the people.

Indeed, the people must authorize the regime's management of its resources, whatever form that management takes. A regime's resource management can take a shareholder model or a trust model, or any variation on these models—so long as the people authorize it. Or the regime may privatize certain resources, taking them out of public ownership—so long as the people authorize it. Rousseau famously asked the sovereign people to answer a double-layered question when authorizing its regime, which we can adapt for resources:

> Does it please the Sovereign to preserve the present form of resource management?
> Does it please the Sovereign for the regime to manage resources as it is doing?[17]

The people can only answer those questions—can only authorize the regime's decisions—when citizens are in conditions that make such authorization possible. Those conditions are our next study, and good theory is again in easy reach.

CONDITIONS FOR AUTHORIZATION

Call all of a regime's decisions regarding the country's resources its "management" of those resources. So in Liberia, when Charles Taylor's regime passed the Strategic Commodities Act 2000, which ascribed to Taylor the sole right to sell any of the country's natural resources, that was an act of management.[18] Management also includes decisions to sell resources under current laws. So the decision of the US government in 2013 to auction off exploration leases for oil acreage off the shores of Texas was an act of management. Intuitively, Taylor's Strategic Commodities Act could not have been authorized by the then oppressed and strife-torn Liberian people; for the US auction, popular authorization seems at least possible. What must be true for a regime rightly to claim the people's authorization while it manages a country's resources?

For X to authorize, X must have the capacity to authorize. Lawmakers have already developed useful accounts of capacity, since they have needed these for important topics like consent to medical procedures. So for instance, under the English Medical Capacity Act 2005, an individual is taken to have the capacity to make a decision affecting his or her own health when he or she:

1. Can understand and retain information relevant to the decision;
2. Can use that information in a process of deliberation leading to a decision;
3. Can communicate his or her decision.[19]

In explaining the first condition, courts have required that a person must be able to understand "in broad terms the nature of the procedure which is intended."[20] The second condition requires that the person to be able to weigh this information in a rational process leading to a decision.[21] The third condition requires that the person be able to convey his or her decision to the relevant authority. If these three conditions obtain, then the law considers that person to have the capacity to authorize.

Contract law sets out a further condition for an individual to authorize. Valid consent cannot be given with a gun to the head or, as British law has it, where the consenter is under "duress or undue influence."[22] Authorization can only be given by an individual who is at least minimally free.

These conditions—about information, deliberation, communication, and freedom—are easy to transpose from individuals to peoples. They give intuitive shape to the account of when citizens can authorize a regime's management of their resources.

What kind of authorization are we looking for from the people? In pleading that it has the people's authorization, a regime may claim that the people *asked* the regime to sell off resources. Or a regime may claim that the people explicitly *agreed* that the regime should do these things. The claim that a regime is most likely to make is that the people signaled their acquiescence to its management of the country's resources by remaining silent as the regime made its decisions.

Any regime's most likely appeal, that is, is to the people's *tacit approval*: that the people could have objected, but didn't. This can be a plausible appeal. Many citizens may not be interested in tracking the management of the country's natural assets, and may have only very general ideas about what the regime is doing with the country's resources. (Polling of Ghanaians, for instance, suggested that they overwhelmingly supported the general idea of creating of a fund to save some of the country's oil money for future generations.[23])

Tacit approval can be real approval: under the right conditions, silence can be just as much a signal of approval as shouting "Aye."[24] To take an example from personal finance: Your financial manager trades stocks for you, perhaps dozens of times a year, with your tacit approval. You chose this manager as your agent, and you could change his investment strategy for your portfolio from conservative to aggressive if you liked. You're in the right conditions to change your financial manager's strategy, but you don't. So your financial manager rightly claims your tacit approval for the trades that he makes in your name.

It would of course be unrealistic to expect this kind of personal relationship in politics, between ruled and rulers. So, what then? We need an account of public authorization that describes uncontroversially the circumstances where citizens could not possibly be approving—even tacitly—a regime's resource management. And this theory must not only be correct, it must be useful and natural for those who will apply it—for politicians, and for members of the public too.

Combining all of the points so far yields four political conditions for popular authorization of resource management that should be beyond doubt. These are minimal conditions for authorization, formulated simply so that they are clear:

1. *Information:* Citizens who can't find out about the management of their resources can't approve that management, even tacitly. At the very least, the average citizen should be able to obtain reliable general information about who is getting the revenues from resource

sales and how these revenues are being spent. Citizens need not have the details of all commercial arrangements (any more than, say, shareholders do). But there must be some systems in place that will reliably alert citizens to what they would regard as gross mismanagement of their assets.

2. *Independence:* To be authorizing, approval must not be forced. Citizens who are brainwashed, relentlessly propagandized by the regime, or subject to extraordinary psychological manipulation do not authorize the management of their resources even if they remain silent as those resources are being sold. North Korea may have oil, but the comprehensively dominated people of that country could not now give tacit approval to the regime selling off their oil, even if the regime were inclined to do this.
3. *Deliberation:* For the people to be able to approve the regime's resource management, citizens must be able to discuss that management with each other. Ordinary citizens must be able to pass information to each other about resource laws and policies without reasonable fear of suffering major harms like serious injury, loss of employment, imprisonment, torture, disappearance, or death. And citizens must be able to debate the regime's resource policies with each other, in public or in private, without reasonable fear of such harms.
4. *Dissent:* To approve the regime's resource management, citizens must be able to dissent from that management without risking severe costs. Any regime claiming that it has the authority of the people for its resource management must allow the people to disagree with that management. Citizens must be able peacefully to express their dissent, alone or together, inside or outside of formal mechanisms, without justified fear of major harms. (This is what Natan Sharansky calls "the town square test."[25]) And the people's dissent must work: if a majority of citizens strongly oppose the regime's resource management, that management must, within a reasonable time, change to reflect the people's opposition.

In concrete political terms, these conditions require that citizens must have at least bare-bones civil liberties and basic political rights. For civil liberties, there must be enough press freedom for citizens to have access to information about the regime's resource decisions and about possible gross mismanagement. The state must not be so deeply opaque that it's nearly impossible for citizens to find out who is getting the revenues from resource sales and how these revenues are being spent. All citizens (including women, as well as members of religious and ethnic groups that are not in power) must be able to discuss the regime's resource management with each other without fear of serious injury, loss of employment, imprisonment, torture, disappearance, or death. There must be enough rule of law that citizens who wish to protest resource decisions publicly and peacefully may do so without fear of arrest, dismissal, or worse.

Citizens must also have basic political rights, to ensure that the regime's management of resources will change to reflect the majority's views within a reasonable time. A deep exploration of the meaning of democracy would not be useful here. For politics, we need signs that all can see. The people cannot possibly control their resources under a highly authoritarian regime: a military junta or a personalistic dictatorship, an autocratic theocracy or a single-party state. Nor can a people control their resources if the state is so failed that it lacks control over large parts of the populated territory. (In Part IV, we'll see how these civil liberties and political rights are already measured by reputable metrics, for all of the countries in the world.)

If these minimal conditions don't obtain within a country, then the silence of citizens while their resources are sold off can't signal authorization. Absent minimal civil liberties and political rights, the people's silence is just silence. Either citizens can't find out about resource sales, or they are too scared or oppressed to discuss and protest them. Where citizens can't learn about what is happening with their resources, where they can't debate what the regime is doing, or where they can't conceivably say no to their resources being sold off, they can't possibly be authorizing those resource sales.[26]

Popular resource sovereignty says that the natural resources of a country belong to the people of that country. The rights of a people are violated whenever someone gains control of this property through deception, force, or extreme manipulation. The oppressed citizens of Equatorial Guinea, for example, could not possibly have been authorizing Obiang to sell off their oil. These citizens could not find out what sales Obiang was making or where the money was going, and they've been either unable to protest his sales or too fearful to try. In no case can the citizens of Equatorial Guinea have approved Obiang's deals.

Obiang has taken control of the oil because he can, without authorization from the people. The capacity to threaten a people should not confer the right to sell off their resources, nor should the capacity to deceive or overbear them. Obiang cannot rightly sell the country's oil, so the corporations that have signed contracts with him could not have gotten title to what they have transported in the holds of their tankers. If we believe in popular resource sovereignty, these international resource corporations have been carrying away stolen goods.

THE EPISTEMOLOGY OF AUTHORITY

In 1947, the United Nations asked dozens of the world's leading intellectuals—including Gandhi, Benedetto Croce, and Aldous Huxley, as well as leading Confucian and Muslim scholars—which human rights should be included in its universal declaration. When these distinguished thinkers returned their lists of human rights, many were surprised at how similar they were.[27] Cross-cultural consensus is sometimes waiting for us, if we ask, and it should be well within reach for popular resource sovereignty too. There's nothing particularly controversial in the theory set out so far. As so often in politics, the main challenge comes not in finding good theory, but in finding good theory that can be used by the people who will have to apply it.

In fact, it could seem that so far we have been straining to swallow a gnat. We've now proved to ourselves that popular resource sovereignty is incompatible with authoritarianism? Big, it might be said, deal. We needed a theory for that?

Our account of popular resource sovereignty must be useful by politicians and ordinary citizens in countries like ours, to explain to each other why authoritarians and militias have no right to sell off their countries' natural resources. The theory must also be solid enough to resist attacks from powerful interests that are heavily invested in business as it is. These powerful interests will throw everything they have at our theory to bring out any latent uncertainties, any lingering doubts. They will, like Iago, play on our hesitations. The strategy of the inevitable opponents of popular resource sovereignty will be to intimate that while gulping at our neat little theory, we have inadvertently swallowed a camel.

The strongest ploy of the enemies of popular resource sovereignty will be epistemology: to say that even if the account above is sound, its application to the real world requires more information than we can be sure that we have. Can we really (they will whisper) know what happens far away, in places that seem so strange to us? Who, after all, are we to judge what deals are made between distant peoples and their leaders? Such apprehensions are captured with real skill by Michael Walzer:

> The state is constituted by the union of people and government... Foreigners are in no position to deny the reality of that union, or rather, they are in no position to attempt anything more than speculative denials. They don't know enough about its history, and they have no direct experience, and can form no concrete judgments, of the conflicts and harmonies, the historical choices and cultural affinities, the loyalties and resentments, that underlie it. Hence their conduct, in the first instance at least, cannot be determined by either knowledge or judgment. It is, or it ought to be, determined instead by a morally necessary presumption: that there exists a certain "fit" between the community and its government and that the state is "legitimate." It is not a gang of rulers acting in its own interests, but a people governed in accordance with its own traditions. This presumption is simply the respect that foreigners owe to a historic community and to its internal life...
>
> There is no point at which foreigners can point to a tyrannical regime and say, "Self-determination has clearly failed..." For revolution often comes unexpectedly, as it came to the Iran of the Shah, a sudden upsurge of previously invisible political currents.[28]

This is a potent pattern of ideas. The phrases that radiate from Walzer's words are "Foreigners... don't know enough" and "the respect that foreigners owe." These phrases may capture our own thoughts when we feel mystified by events in other countries, when we wonder how much the people there are reconciled to their rulers. Walzer's words may also come back to us when we see what he calls "previously invisible political currents" suddenly surge up, as we saw in the popular revolutions of the Arab Spring.

Walzer's own example of the revolution against the Shah of Iran is excellent. As we've seen, in late 1977 that charismatic, modernizing leader—the darling of a superpower, in command of great wealth, a huge army, and a savagely efficient secret police—had ruled for decades and faced no obvious challengers or crises. In little over a year, he was gone, replaced to great public celebration by ultraconservative Shia clerics who were politically his mirror image. Which outsiders can know what accommodations citizens make with their leaders, Walzer asks, and who can know the people's plans to change their country's fate? Those who don't know should not judge, and should assume a fit between the people and the state—until the people themselves show otherwise through their own actions. Above all, peoples should respect each other, and assume except in the most extreme circumstances that each people is tacitly approving what its rulers do.

As we consider Walzer's challenge, we need to isolate it from any thoughts about the rightness or wrongness of outside interventions, like invasions or sanctions. We are now only thinking through what outsiders can *know* about popular authorization within a culturally distant country. For now we can just forget about interventions: we first need to know what to think, before thinking about what (if anything) to do. Our interest is the epistemological issue raised by Walzer's words, which is how sure outsiders can be about whether a people is tacitly approving its regime's actions.

ARABIA, OIL, AUTHORITY

Saudi Arabia has the largest conventional oil reserves in the world. Are the citizens of Saudi Arabia authorizing what the Saudi regime is doing with the country's oil? This question directs the full force of Walzer's concerns onto our theory of authorization, since Saudi Arabia is a country about which many Westerners feel very much in the dark. Walzer would say that we must presume a union between people and regime because we do not know enough to say otherwise. But even if we are neutral instead of presuming, we may be unsure of what to say next. Saudi Arabia certainly does not seem to meet the minimal conditions for popular resource sovereignty. Yet things are so different there; perhaps the best we can do is to suspend judgment about the people's views altogether?

The problem with Saudi Arabia is not about knowing the basics of its politics or about citizens' daily lives. Saudi Arabia is not Mars. You can go there—with your embassy's help, you could be in the capital, Riyadh, this time tomorrow. Saudi has superhighways and the Internet, reformers and reactionaries, loving parents and child prostitution, Dunkin' Donuts and drug addicts, soccer games and silly rumors about the politics of other places. Because of its great geopolitical significance, there's a lot of excellent analysis of the country, both scholarly and journalistic, and Western governments and think tanks keep close watch on what happens there.[29]

The difficulty for Westerners is that much of what they discover is so different from what they're accustomed to. The three dramatic impressions of the country are the apparent devotion of the majority of Saudis to a very conservative interpretation of Islam, the segregation and inequality of the sexes, and the radiation of public authority into areas of life that in the West would be protected as private. In many ways, these impressions are disorienting, yet the country also seems quite stable. To fill the cognitive void, we may grasp at the idea that perhaps the Saudi people like things, more or less, as they are.

Saudi Arabia is also difficult because it is one of the few countries left where popular sovereignty is not the public philosophy. Unlike most states, the Saudi regime has never signed the treaties that would commit it to popular sovereignty. Saudi Arabia is, quite explicitly, an absolute monarchy. Were James I of England brought back to life and made the Saudi king, he would not care for the clothes or the climate, yet he would find much of the country's constitution quite congenial. The Saudi king is the head of the Saudi *ummah*, the body of believers that is the national population. In this role, he orders the promotion of virtue and the punishment of sin (including—as James might be pleased to see—the public beheading of witches) so as to help guide the souls entrusted to his care to heaven instead of hell.[30] The king commands piety, the people obey piously—that is the ideology.

Arabia is the name of a place; Saud is the name of a family. Referring to the place by the family should be striking—it would be like officially renaming the United Kingdom "The Windsors' Britain." Speaking of "Saudis" should be equally striking; imagine that Americans are instead called "Clintonians" or "Bushies" after being ruled by that family continuously for generations.

The House of Saud has been extraordinarily successful in keeping its kingdom its own. For decades, the Sauds have controlled fractious tribes across a territory as big as the Louisiana Purchase, they have maintained a united front through many palace intrigues, and so far they have guided their theocracy through all the gales of modernity. The regime has weathered long periods of low oil prices, and it has secured the greatest terrestrial energy source in history from jealous neighbors and covetous great powers across eighty years of crises in the Middle East.[31] Simply in terms of dynastic survival skills, the Sauds must be ranked with the Medicis, if not (yet) the Ming.

The main source of the Saud family's power has been oil money. The Sauds have controlled gigantic oil revenues (over $300 billion in 2013); African and Asian petrocrats are poor cousins by comparison.[32] The Sauds have pushed this money through a classic clientelistic political system, with the vertical pipes of patronage topped by senior royals. They have used the oil money to waive taxes and to provide benefits for citizens: to subsidize food and housing, to provide free education and health care, and to create many pointless government jobs for Saudis who would otherwise be unemployed. The Sauds have also built a secret police and informant network that the East German *Stasi* would have admired, and have generally kept a loose leash on the fearsome *Mutaween* religious police. As we saw in Chapter 6, when internal discontent has threatened, as in the Arab Spring, the regime has characteristically dialed up both benefits and repression.

The Sauds have also drawn legitimacy from Wahhabi Islam. A body of Wahhabi religious scholars, the *ulema*, is integral to the Saudi regime. The Saudi *ulema* approve important royal decrees, form the judiciary of the country's main (*sharia*) courts, and strongly influence the educational system and the enforcement of public morals. The *ulema* are ultraconservative in their social views, to the right of even the most extreme American fundamentalists, and their politics support the monarchy. The *ulema* teach that the Sauds are the legitimate Islamic authority of the country, and that any public protest against them is a sin and a crime (these concepts are closer there than elsewhere).

Members of the *ulema* sometimes show up in Western news stories when they make public pronouncements, such as issuing *fatwas* against soap operas or all-you-can-eat buffets, or declaring Mickey Mouse to be a "soldier of Satan."[33] But their influence on Saudi society is much more profound than these chucklesome stories show. Insofar as the *ulema* differ from the Saudi royals on social issues, they pressure toward more conservative policies such as greater restrictions on women: on their dress, interactions with men, and activities outside the house. When a *sharia* court sentenced a woman to two hundred lashes for being alone with a male non-relative shortly before she was gang-raped, it was the king who pardoned the woman.[34] The royals also intervened to increase the punishment of a well-known cleric when a religious court sentenced him to just a few months in jail and the payment of a fine—for torturing and killing his five-year-old daughter because he suspected her virginity.[35]

Within all the fascination of Saudi politics, our question is only one: could the Saudi people be tacitly approving how their regime is managing the country's oil? Outsiders might express genuine uncertainty about, for example, how thoroughly the majority of Saudis accept the state's official ideology. Citizens can't authorize the state's management of the people's resources, it might be said, if they don't believe that the resources ultimately belong to the people. And recalling Rousseau's Thesis, citizens can't give their authorization as part of a sovereign body if they believe that they must obey the state, whatever the state decides.

We might imagine a public poll in which Saudi citizens are asked, with assured anonymity, whether they generally approve of the ways in which the regime is managing the country's oil, given that the oil belongs ultimately to the Saudi people. It might well be that the average citizen would express puzzlement at the question—at the idea that the resources belong to the people, or that a Saudi subject should sit in judgment over the king's policies instead of supporting the king as a matter of religious duty. We cannot know: the regime will never allow such a poll.

Outsiders might also wonder how independent the views of citizens are from the regime. The state closely supervises schools, mosques, the media, and public spaces, so whether the regime controls citizens' beliefs at the level of "extraordinary psychological manipulation" is an open question. When the regime made a rightward shift in social policy in 1979, for example, there appeared to follow a corresponding shift in social attitudes; yet many Saudis, especially in relatively progressive urban centers like Jeddah, would scoff at the idea that they had been brainwashed by the state.

SAUDI: *SAPERE AUDE*[36]

Doubts surround the issues just discussed, and having given them space, we can return to what we know. The answer to our original question is the obvious one we started with: Saudi Arabia has a highly authoritarian regime; the citizens cannot control the country's oil. Saudi citizens do not have the minimal civil liberties and political rights required for their silence to signal valid tacit approval of the regime's management of the country's resources. Since 2003, the Kingdom has been in a reformist phase and has reversed some of the most reactionary trends of the 1979–2003 period. Like an addict attempting to clean up and fly right, the regime has also made efforts to diversify the country's economy away from oil, to modernize the educational system, and to make enforcement of *sharia* law more predictable. But most of the political conditions necessary for popular authorization are still far from met.

Information

Saudi citizens cannot get reliable information about how the country's oil is being managed, and crucial facts about the national budget (like how much oil money the royals are taking for themselves) are state secrets.[37] The media environment remains "extremely restrictive," with the authorities holding broad "powers to prevent any act that may lead to disunity or sedition." Journalists are closely monitored, all newspapers must be licensed, and citizens need a license to post on YouTube.[38] Reporters Without Borders gives Saudi Arabia its worst rating for press freedom as well as the designation "Enemy of the Internet."[39] No critical reporting on royal corruption is permitted. For example, when the British media were full of stories of the one billion pounds sterling that a British defense firm allegedly kicked back to a Saudi prince, the Saudi press was limited in its coverage to a single story, in an English-language daily, devoted to the prince's categorical denials of impropriety.[40]

Deliberation

Citizens cannot deliberate together in public about the regime's management of resources without risking severe consequences. Political parties do not exist in Saudi Arabia; neither do licensed trade unions or human rights organizations. Any public debate can be closed down by the regime for raising "sensitive" issues; indeed, scholars debate how far civil society should be said to exist at all.[41] On resource issues, the Saudi people are like a sedated brain, the neurons fully alive but the connections blocked so that the signaling between them cannot produce coherent thought.

Dissent

"Ministers," as Jefferson said, "cannot in any country be uninfluenced by the voice of the people."[42] The Saudi regime is not deaf to public discontent; indeed, like all successful authoritarian regimes, it is sensitive to murmurs on the street. Interior Ministry informants at mosques and universities report on incidents; monitors brief the royals regularly on the trend of broadcast media (and especially call-in shows); the *Majalis*, where citizens appeal to officials to solve local disputes, also help alert the regime to trouble spots.[43] The regime responds, as all regimes must, to public unease. What the regime does not allow is the Saudi people to protest its resource decisions. The regime does not allow itself to be held accountable by the people.

The royals do not welcome petitions. The main consultative body is appointed by the king and can only express views on matters referred to it by the king. Most seriously, in Saudi Arabia, public protests are prohibited. The US State Department reported that in the year of the Arab Spring, "no government-permitted, peaceful political demonstrations" occurred:

> The law requires a government permit for an organized public assembly of any type, and it was a crime to participate in political protests or unauthorized public assemblies... The Basic Law does not provide for freedom of association, and the government strictly limited this right in practice. The government prohibited the establishment of political parties or any group it considered as opposing or challenging the regime. All associations must be licensed by the Ministry of Social Affairs and comply with its regulations. Groups that hoped to change some element of the social or political order reported that their licensing requests went unanswered.[44]

During the Arab Spring, some Saudis tried to organize Egypt- and Bahrain-style protests via social media:

> On March 11, the day of the planned demonstrations, things were quiet. Helicopters flew low in the skies over Saudi cities, mirroring the intimidation of protesters in Tahrir Square and Pearl Roundabout. Security forces spread through every corner and street. An unannounced curfew loomed over Riyadh and Jeddah. At noon, Saudis prayed as usual, then they got into their cars to drive home for lunch and the usual siesta. One man dared to defy the curfew. The lone demonstrator, Khalid al-Johani, told BBC journalist Sue Lloyd Roberts and her camera crew, "The royal family don't own us... I need freedom; all the country is a jail... We need a parliament." Al-Johani anticipated that he would be arrested. "I demonstrate because it is worth it," he said, "I am doing this for my four children." He gave Roberts his mobile number, but after that day, al-Johani stopped answering his phone... [H]e disappeared.[45]

The regime does not allow informed citizens to deliberate together on whether they approve of the regime's resource decisions—or to demand changes, individually or collectively, if they do not approve. The king, as Rousseau says, "exploits the silence which he prevents men breaking, and the irregularities which he makes them commit, to assume in his own favor the tacit consent of those whose mouths are closed by fear and to punish those who dare to speak."[46] An average Saudi citizen—and even more, a group of them—would fear serious consequences for dissenting to the regime's resource management. An informed observer of Saudi Arabia will predict high risks for anyone who tried to spread this message: "The oil belongs to the people. The royals must tell us how much of our oil money they are taking for themselves—or we should give them none of our oil money, at all."

The Saudi regime has survived by pushing a mixture of violence and clientelism down to the household level. Each household is effectively offered benefits for obedience and punishments for dissent, all against a background of limited information and, most significantly, serious blocks to combining with other households for greater bargaining power. The regime varies this mix across households and as conditions change, but the overall goal has been to make it appear to each family that there is no rational alternative to the regime's rule.

The strategy has so far been successful. Faced with the overwhelming resources of the state, most citizens have stayed quiet. Citizens have not been powerful enough in themselves, or in the limited alliances they can make with each other, to challenge the regime. But neither can the citizenry in such conditions authorize the regime's management of the country's resources. The people are not free to balance the regime's power. And this is one major reason that Saudi Arabia has become a balloon full of trouble.

BENEVOLENT DESPOTISM

We've been asking whether the Saudi people could, by their silence, be authorizing the regime's management of the country's resources. The epistemological barriers have turned out to be low: we know the people cannot be doing so. In this way, Saudi Arabia is like Equatorial Guinea. Neither country comes close to meeting the minimal conditions for popular resource control.

"Look into the Absolute Monarchies of the World," said John Locke, "and see what becomes of the Conveniences of Life, and the Multitudes of People."[47] Locke was, as it turns out, wrong about Saudi Arabia. Saudi Arabia is different from countries like Equatorial Guinea in a way that's apparent to all observers—and the powerful enemies of popular resource sovereignty might use this difference to try to sow further doubts in our minds.

The average citizen of Equatorial Guinea is materially badly off, these opponents might say, while the average Saudi is not. Saudis receive many more benefits from the country's oil wealth than their Equatoguinean counterparts, both in public and in private goods. Infant mortality is fairly low in Saudi Arabia; life expectancy is a respectable seventy-four years; literacy is slightly above the world average.[48] A crude way to measure how well a regime is transforming "national income" into "human development" is to compare the country's world ranking in national income per capita to the country's world ranking in the Human Development Index. Saudi's income is only twenty-two ranks higher than its human development score; Equatorial Guinea's is ninety-six ranks higher.[49] As we've seen, Saudi citizens cannot now actually approve the deal they're getting from their oil: their monarchy is one of the most authoritarian regimes in the world. Yet, opponents may suggest, Saudis should be satisfied with the benefits that they get.

This kind of thought may be lingering as we ponder the Saudi regime's resource sales. It resembles the public poll we imagined above, yet its philosophical orientation points in a different direction. The thought is not that Saudi citizens are approving, only tacitly; the thought is that Saudi citizens should rationally approve because they are getting a good enough deal from the regime's management of their oil. Hypothetically (the argument goes), if Saudis were adequately informed, if they could discuss the matter freely together and then express their views, most would endorse the status quo. In a philosopher's parlance, we are considering authorization not by tacit but by *hypothetical* popular approval.

In speculating about hypothetical approval, we might tell different stories about what benefits the average Saudi should want from the oil. One story is that Saudis are devout: the average Saudi gets all that a good Muslim should want, and he or she does not begrudge the royals—who lead the Arab and the Sunni worlds and protect the holy sites—their palaces. Indeed, the average Saudi enjoys a bit of royal celebrity, much as the average Canadian or Spaniard does.

Or we could tell this story: the average Saudi doesn't like the royals so much, living their lavish, jet-set, and extremely debauched lifestyles while imposing strict *sharia* on the people. The average Saudi wants his or her children to develop their socially useful talents and to enjoy the satisfactions of meaningful work, instead of being unemployed or trapped in an inane state job. The average Saudi worries that when the oil money runs out, the foundations of the country's economy will cave in. Their grandchildren may be taking crowbars to the abandoned palaces, and loading up camels with scrap.

Such speculations are useless for grounding responsible policy toward Saudi Arabia; they reveal more about the speculator than about the Saudis. We might try instead to rigorize our thoughts about hypothetical approval by using more scientific comparisons between resource-exporting countries, to see in which countries the citizens are getting more benefits from their resources. For example, we might look at the country scoring system developed by the World Bank that measures resource depletion against environmental quality and investment in human capital.[50] Or we could deploy the "sustainable development" measures of Kenneth Arrow and his colleagues to evaluate how well different regimes have used natural capital to build up human and manufactured capital in ways that can sustain standards of living across generations.[51] The Saudi regime has in recent years gained a reputation for more prudent resource management, so it would not be surprising if the Kingdom came out well in such comparisons to other authoritarian countries.

We should, however, resist making the question of "enough benefits" a technical one. The entire discussion is misconceived from the start. Recall Walzer on what foreigners can know about the relations between a people and a regime. It's extremely difficult for outsiders to know whether citizens in culturally distant countries are happy with the deal they're getting from their regime. Statistics about economic performance are not helpful. Before the revolution against Ben Ali in Tunisia, the head of the International Monetary Fund (IMF) called his economic model a miracle.[52] Egypt's economy grew at 2.6 percent in the decade before the Arab Spring, and Tunisia's grew at 3.4 percent—higher rates of growth than in Europe or the United States.[53] A month after the Syrian uprising started, the IMF forecast 3.1 percent growth for that year and 5.1 percent for the year to come.[54] "Revolution often comes unexpectedly," as Walzer said, "a sudden upsurge of previously invisible political currents." We would need to see those currents to form a judgment about hypothetical popular approval, but we cannot.

Nor should we be hypothesizing about approval at all. Tacit approval is real approval; hypothetical approval is not. As Ronald Dworkin says, "A hypothetical contract is not simply a pale form of an actual contract; it is no contract at all."[55] The only approval that can authorize a regime's actions is actual approval—the actual approval of the citizenry. For outsiders to think otherwise, to make a technical exercise out of the level of benefits they believe the people should agree to, would be a kind of cognitive colonialism.

Popular resource sovereignty is about the *control* that peoples should exercise. Peoples "may for their own ends, freely dispose of their natural wealth and resources"; they have a "right . . . to enjoy and utilize fully and freely their natural wealth and resources." Foreigners respect a people not by computing what they believe those citizens should want, but by respecting the decisions they make. The only way for outsiders to judge popular resource sovereignty by a "benefit" standard would be if the citizens themselves had actually endorsed a weighted list of benefits—jobs, welfare provisions, an undamaged environment, political stability, etc.—that they wanted as priorities for spending the resource money. And this the people cannot do, either in Saudi Arabia or Equatorial Guinea.

We have now cornered a final thought, a final sentiment about sovereignty in Saudi Arabia. This thought may bubble up from our memories of childhood stories—stories that we inherited from the many centuries when our own ancestors could only muse on whether they had been given a good king or a bad king, one blessed or hard. When expressed, this thought is that Obiang is a brutal despot, while the Saudi king is benevolent.[56] A good king confers benefits on his people; a bad king cruelly deprives them.[57]

If we have this thought, it can serve as a touchstone for our convictions about popular resource sovereignty. If we believe in popular resource sovereignty, there can be no such thing as a ruler who is benevolent with resource revenues. No one can be generous by giving someone what they already own. The citizens of a country are entitled to all the value of their resources; the regime is entitled to not a penny. All of Saudi Arabia's oil belongs to the Saudi people, and the royals can only have their superyachts and palaces—indeed, anything bought with the oil money—at the people's sufferance. A king's right is not to "all," it is to "nothing." And the same holds for all dictators, supreme leaders, and big-man presidents. The next time someone says that Saudi citizens are happy with what the king gives them, ask if they wouldn't be happier still if they controlled all of the oil money.[58]

One agent steals the assets he's been entrusted with, sells them, and uses some of the proceeds to keep the principal bound and drugged, wasting in pain. Another agent steals the assets he's been entrusted with, sells them, and uses some of the proceeds to keep the principal bound and drugged, yet also decently nourished and in what seems a not unpleasant (though perhaps ultimately fatal) condition. The second agent is morally better than the first; that—and not "benevolent"—is the most we can say of him.

The reason that hypothetical approval seemed attractive is not because it is a plausible account of political authorization, but because it seemed to take a posture of respectful international relations—it seemed a way to check whether the people are getting what they want. Yet outsiders do have real difficulties understanding the political dynamics of distant countries, and they can do great damage when taking it on themselves to judge what a people "really" wants.

What respectful outsiders can do instead is to check whether a people can possibly authorize their regime's actions—and if a people can authorize, to assume that they do authorize. When citizens can change—but don't change—the "deal" they're getting for their resources, outsiders should accept that the deal is what the citizens want. This is the real power of Walzer's words—that assuming a fit between a people and their government "is simply the respect that foreigners owe to a historic community and to its internal life." The respectful posture is to assume that the citizens are authorizing their regime when they can do so: that the necessary conditions for the people's tacit approval are sufficient to signal their assent.[59] One tragedy in our world is that in so many states such approval is impossible: the people cannot possibly authorize what is being done with their assets.

LINE-DRAWING

For a people to authorize a regime's management of its resources, citizens must be able to learn what the regime is doing, to discuss this freely among themselves, and to dissent in ways that change the regime's policies. This requires that citizens enjoy at least minimal civil liberties and political rights. The practical philosophy of popular resource sovereignty is no more than that. The theory that we needed, we knew already—it was just a matter of spelling it out. In Part IV, we'll find metrics to make this account even more precise, so that popular resource sovereignty can guide real lawmaking. Still, having made our knowledge explicit, we can already say with conviction that certain regimes do not respect their people's resource rights.

What about countries in the West—do these countries meet the four conditions of information, independence, deliberation, and dissent? Say you're American, and you want the federal authorities to ban fracking, or to boost it—or perhaps to save some of the country's oil revenues for future generations. You can find out what the current government's policies are, you can discuss your plans for change with other Americans, and you can advocate your views in public without fearing severe consequences. So America passes the "town square test."[60] And it seems unlikely that the American authorities are so relentlessly controlling citizens' thoughts that you can't come to independent views about the country's resources (evidence your reading this book).

If there's a real question here, it's about dissent. If a determined majority of your fellow citizens wanted to ban fracking in America, for example, would fracking be banned? If more than one hundred million Americans repeatedly voted with this ban as a top priority—or if most Americans supported a general strike until fracking was illegal—would fracking be banned within a reasonable time? Critical faculties engage fully here, as they were designed to, yet any lingering doubt about positive answers can be dispelled by asking someone who works in national politics what they could do with that kind of support.[61] Americans today control their resources well enough to change national resource policy if most really want to; to that extent, at least, the people's sovereignty is real.

Still, knowing what we know, and looking again around the world, we must make a melancholy survey. There is no pleasure in confirming that the Saudi people lack control over their natural resources. It's true that some Persian Gulf states are now at least better than they once were. In recent years, some regimes have taken steps to build up the educational system, to diversify the economy, to grant the people a few more political rights. Friends of popular resource sovereignty can only wish these efforts success. Still, these countries are a considerable distance from satisfying the minimal conditions for popular authorization, and experience advises caution in thinking that these regimes can quickly cure themselves of the chronic pathologies caused by their long addictions to oil rents.

Looking further afield gives some grounds for hope. Indonesia, formerly authoritarian and the world's largest Muslim country, beat its addiction to oil and is now well along its democratic transition. Islam itself is obviously compatible with popular resource sovereignty.[62] (Perhaps even Wahhabism is: the Qatari regime is also Wahhabi, but it is closer to constitutional monarchy than is Saudi Arabia, and it even went out of its way to create Al Jazeera.) Nigeria is still very troubled but is better than it has been. For example, in 2012, widespread public protests and a general strike forced the Nigerian government to reverse course on oil subsidies, suggesting that the country satisfied the minimal conditions for popular authorization (at least regarding those subsidies, in that year). And the Arab country farthest down the road of reform, Morocco, does nearly satisfy the minimal conditions for popular resource sovereignty.[63] Yet—less hopeful—the one topic about which Moroccans are least free to discuss and dissent (besides the dignity of the king) is a topic tightly connected to the country's primary resource export (phosphates).[64]

And sadly, overall, the global situation is dire. Looking around the world for oil, we see big Middle Eastern producers, like Saudi Arabia, Iran, Iraq, UAE, and Qatar, as well as major producers elsewhere, like Russia, Kazakhstan, Algeria, and Angola. That's already half of the world's proven oil reserves, and none of these countries meets the minimal conditions for popular resource sovereignty.[65]

Mankind's primary energy supply is mostly controlled by a roomful of men. These few men are—financially, militarily, geostrategically—heavily entrenched. Some of them have used their oil money to inculcate authoritarian ideologies in their populations, and some, like the Saudis, have also spread those ideologies vigorously abroad. The citizens of these countries—many poorly educated, most askant-eyed with distrust, some the descendants of generations of oppressed people—are usually in bad shape for taking control over their country's resources. Popular resource sovereignty is the ideal, but not the reality, of today's international system.

What it takes for a people to be able to control their resources is clear, as it should be. Spelling this out reinforces what we already knew, and gives confidence that we can know what we need to about even culturally distant countries like Saudi Arabia. The Saudi people cannot control their resources, and debating whether their regime is generous enough to them is disrespectful of them. The right question is not whether we believe citizens are getting enough benefits from their resources, but whether citizens can control their resources well enough to approve the deal they are getting.

After all, if "benefits" were our standard, rather than "control," then we would have no principled objection to imperial rule: a foreign emperor could be as benevolent as any native king.[66] Yet that is not popular sovereignty. Neither outsiders nor authoritarians should rule the people. Once free, the people should rule themselves.

14

Our Corruption

Why Leaders Must Lie

A nation that is afraid to let its people judge the truth and falsehood of ideas in an open market is a nation that is afraid of its people.

—John F. Kennedy[1]

Every store is Dirt Cheap. The cross-border robberies and raids, gangs and kingpins, in that fictional story from Chapter 5 are as nothing compared to the real crimes in our real world right now. Today, huge regions, even whole nations, are being run as criminal enterprises, their natural resources taken by force to make the goods on our shelves. In one country, heavily armed militias are plundering the gems and minerals that go into our jewelry and electronics. In another, a tyrant is selling off the country's petroleum to sustain his repressive regime, and that petroleum is being used to make everything from our toys to our shoes to our perfumes. Each and every product we find on the shelves right now might have been made from, made with, or transported using that stolen oil. And when we buy any of those products, we may be putting more money in the pockets of some of the most merciless men on earth.

"Might makes right" violates property rights—the property rights of each people to their natural resources. As in neighborhoods where properties are constantly burgled, the failure to enforce citizens' rights makes those citizens poorer and weaker. At the same time, the violators strengthen themselves through success. Pay ransom to pirates who have taken an oil tanker hostage, and tomorrow sailors will face more potent pirates. Pay royalties to a president who has taken an oil country hostage, and tomorrow the people will face a more potent president. Occupying armies used to live off the land by seizing farmhouses and killing livestock; indigenous militias can now live off the land more profitably.

Where property rights are not enforced, markets fail; when the violations are widespread, genuine markets do not even exist. The worldwide web of supply chains circulates stolen goods around the planet, and we have no choice but to consume this endless pillage. Wherever we look right now, we may see the products of theft—including when we look straight down.

IT SHOULD BE SO EASY

It should be so easy: we buy products made with other people's raw materials, our money makes them better off—win/win. We want horizontal relations of trade, ultimately with ordinary people in other countries. Our governments instead force us to send our money upward, and diagonally, to coercive men who then use our money to hold themselves above ordinary people, to tear their resources away from them. When trade is hard like this, what we buy will always be tainted with coercion, often with distress, and sometimes with death.

But aren't some of these regimes respectable? Don't the Arab royals own American treasures like the Chrysler Building, and don't they sponsor top European teams like Manchester City and Paris Saint-Germain? Don't the West's great universities like NYU and the Sorbonne also take their money? And yet—what do these connections really prove? Consider that in the nineteenth century it was profits from the slave trade that built up the skylines of Liverpool and Bristol. And as for our universities, we might cast our minds back to 1902, when the African diamonds plundered by the shockingly racist and imperialist Cecil Rhodes began to fund the scholarships to Oxford that bear his name.[2] Most in our own elites do not owe their places to their moral perceptiveness or courage. Mostly, like most of us, they just take the money. The deals done between our elites and regimes illegitimately enriched by resources are to the credit of neither.

For a few chapters, we have entertained elite concerns that popular resource sovereignty is too difficult to understand, or too dangerous to use. But popular resource sovereignty turns out to be simple and safe. Citizens should control their country's resources, and no one should sell off that property without their OK—that's it. If we believe this, then we believe that international oil and mining companies are flying, trucking, and sailing away billions of dollars of stolen wealth every day.

Popular sovereignty lives in the minds of our own people—it is the ideal of our own countries. To get into office, our leaders must praise the people's rights incessantly. How then can they explain to their own people why they choose "might makes right"? We have, over many pages, worked through the international elite's fulminations and obfuscations. We have unmasked the masking words with which they use the language of peoples to affirm the privileges of power. Have we been too hard on our leaders? Would they doublespeak to us if we asked them directly?

Let's give them one last chance, and ask one leader to explain why he or she so consistently chooses the rules of resource trade that violate the people's rights. We could ask any number of leaders—of Britain, Germany, Australia—about trade with any number of countries—with Algeria, Angola, Azerbaijan. Here, let's ask the US Secretary of State about America's resource trade with Equatorial Guinea.

PRESSING THE SECRETARY OF STATE

Consider the US government's decision to engage commercially with Obiang: its decision authoritatively to identify the individual Obiang as the person from whom Americans have the right to buy Equatorial Guinea's oil. Imagine we ask the US Secretary of State, "What is the US government's justification for putting the American people into business with this dictator?"

As we heard in Chapter 5, a regime radio station in Equatorial Guinea once declared that Obiang is "like God in heaven," who has "all power over men and things."[3] No American official could endorse that justification for Obiang's authority over resources. Americans believe that all men are created equal, that no one has more divinely granted political authority than any other. The Secretary of State can't simply close the discussion by saying that Obiang is President of Equatorial Guinea, so of course we have to buy from him. As current US sanctions show, the US government reserves for itself the right not to make a commercial connection between the American people and any foreign regime. Nor can the Secretary just say that every country has the right to choose its own political arrangements. That would be sloppy thinking, exposed by asking what is meant by "country"—whether it is Obiang or the people who have the right to choose the country's political arrangements.

By the self-evident truths of the *Declaration of Independence*, the US government must hold that it is the citizens of Equatorial Guinea who have the ultimate right to control the natural resources of their country. As we saw in Chapter 11, the principle that "the people own the oil" is so mainstream in American thought that politicians like George W. Bush and Bob Graham apply it both to the American people and the people of other countries. And the US government has ratified a major human rights treaty that proclaims popular resource sovereignty as its alpha and omega—more often than it proclaims any other right.

To justify putting Americans into business with Obiang, the Secretary of State might point to the hydrocarbons law that his regime enacted in 2006, allegedly making Obiang the country's resource vendor. Yet as we've seen, the citizens of Equatorial Guinea could not possibly have approved that law, even tacitly, so buying resources under that law violates their resource sovereignty.

To frame this in a different way: popular resource sovereignty is an American principle and a human right—and American officials are not required to give their legal authority to foreign laws that violate American principles and human rights. In Judge Benjamin Cardozo's words, US courts may ignore a foreign law when it "would violate some fundamental principle of justice, some prevalent conception of good morals, some deep-rooted tradition of the common weal."[4] And so President Wilson: "If [America] stands for one thing more than any other it is for the sovereignty of self-governing people."[5]

The Secretary of State, so pressed to justify giving Americans the right to buy oil from Obiang, might broaden the discussion. Popular sovereignty is one principle of the international system, the Secretary might say, as it is one principle in America's public philosophy. But as any diplomat knows, it is not the only principle. Peace is also a major aim of the international system, and so are the political independence and territorial integrity of states. We can't push popular sovereignty too far without risking other principles, the Secretary might continue, which are of such great weight that we must sometimes give them priority.

This reply is cogent, it can be granted in its entirety, and it merely makes things worse. We could even allow that the other principles of the international system have absolute priority over the principle of popular resource sovereignty—and still, we ask the Secretary why the United States decides to engage commercially with Obiang. The other principles of the international system do not require it, or even speak particularly to this decision. Should the United States disengage with Obiang commercially, he would not launch a military attack. Stopping oil sales would not violate the political independence or territorial integrity of Equatorial Guinea, or of any other country. The US decision to engage commercially with Obiang is not the high politics of war and peace; it is the low politics of trade policy. Its only justification is America's economic gain.

The American government violates American principles for the sake of American economic gain. The Secretary of State cannot say this, cannot admit to putting economic interest over principle, cannot affirm that all men are created equal—unless we can raise GDP by 0.1 percent. This is why American commercial engagement with Obiang seems even more dishonest than, say, Richard Nixon's crimes in Watergate, which were at least guided by a political goal. When it engages with Obiang, the US government exercises its authority to violate popular sovereignty for the sake of Americans' private advantage. And it sells out its principles depressingly cheaply: in 2014, Equatorial Guinea accounted for less than 0.2 percent of US oil imports, an amount that could have been imported from other sources with only the slightest financial sacrifice.[6]

The Secretary of State might grab at a final straw: the popular sovereignty of the American people. The American people are the final authority over America's laws, the Secretary might say, and if the people want to authorize themselves to buy Equatorial Guinea's oil from Obiang, it is their own sovereign right to do so. Yet that straw sinks in the grip. The right of choice in one people cannot be used to justify the violation of that same right in another, as Thomas Jefferson said when he was Secretary of State:

> We surely cannot deny to any nation that right whereon our own government is founded, that every one may govern itself under whatever forms it pleases, and change these forms at its own will, and that it may transact its business with foreign nations through whatever organ it thinks proper, whether King, Convention, Assembly, Committee, President, or anything else it may choose. The will of the nation is the only thing essential to be regarded.[7]

Our Secretary's last stratagem is not only wrong intellectually, it is wrong in trying to shift the blame for engaging with Obiang onto American citizens. Some Americans might conceivably believe the kinds of justifications that the State Department offers publicly for engaging with Obiang. As we'll see, however, the Secretary of State cannot.

THE IMPOSSIBLE WEBPAGE

In October 1959, the US Ambassador to Thailand cabled back to the State Department:

> There can be no quarrel with the basic proposition . . . that the US Government must work with authoritarian military governments in the less developed countries of Free Asia and Africa. As the Department has pointed out, "authoritarianism will remain the norm in Free Asia for a long period." This being the case, the problem of explaining to the American people and to friendly nations which are not sympathetic toward an authoritarian form of government why we support such governments becomes a matter of public relations, not of policy. We need not, for example, feel self-conscious about our support of an authoritarian government in Thailand based almost entirely on military strength . . . Aside from the practical matter of Thailand's not being ready for a truly democratic form of government, it can be pointed out that the United States derives political support from the Thai Government to an extent and degree which it would be hard to match elsewhere.[8]

This candid statement from a diplomat may well have been correct as *realpolitik*. The world is as it is, and our governments must sometimes deal with the authoritarian regimes that are out there. Some of these regimes are hostile, as North Korea's is, and our governments know they have nuclear weapons. Other such regimes are friendly, as Thailand's was, and our governments might have to use their support to further larger strategic aims (at the time of this cable, checking the spread of communism). It's vital that the US government chooses its strategic aims wisely, and that when it does deal with authoritarians, it does so well. Yet as we've seen, such US dealings with authoritarians have few effects on the laws enforced within the United States.

The US government's decision to engage commercially with Obiang is legally different and quite intimate. The United States literally makes

Obiang's word law: not law for Equatorial Guinea, but law for the United States. This means that any injustice within Obiang's control over Equatorial Guinea's resources will be naturalized: it will become injustice enforced on American soil. And injustice there is: as we now see, Obiang is literally stealing a nation's oil. The United States chooses not only to allow imports of this stolen oil, but to declare these imports legal because the exporter was strong enough to steal them.

This makes much harder "the problem of explaining to the American people and to friendly nations which are not sympathetic toward an authoritarian form of government" why the United States engages commercially with Obiang. The "public relations" challenge to the State Department is to explain publicly why the US government has authorized oil purchases from Obiang since oil exports began in 1995. This a very specific challenge: it doesn't ask whether Equatorial Guinea is an independent state, whether Obiang is the president of that state, or whether his regime can rightly defend the country's borders, or issue currency or postage stamps. The challenge can't be avoided by saying that the United States is legally required to accept Obiang as Equatorial Guinea's resource vendor, or that some other agency makes this decision. No appeals to peace, territorial integrity, political independence, or other priorities in the international system will help. What then?

The way that US officials now respond to this challenge—the way that actually appears on the State Department webpage "U.S. Relations with Equatorial Guinea"—again makes matters worse:

> Three major U.S. foreign policy issues form the cornerstone of the bilateral relationship with Equatorial Guinea—good governance and democracy; the protection of human rights; and U.S. national security, especially access to energy resources. The United States seeks to encourage improved human rights, the development of a working civil society, greater fiscal transparency, and increased government investment in Equatorial Guinea's people in areas such as health and education.[9]

The appeal to national security sounds the most plausible here, at least until it's spelled out: The United States of America authorizes the theft of the main asset of some of the world's poorest and most oppressed people, so that it can use these stolen goods to boost its own economy, for the sake of its own national security. That can't go onto the website.[10] Beyond this, we see the familiar appeal to engagement for development, both political and economic. The United States engages with less-than-perfect countries in the hope that, over the long term, the engagement will improve the freedom and prosperity of their citizens. This appeal is disingenuous, at least for Equatorial Guinea, in ways that State Department officials already know.

US Secretaries of State know about the "resource curse." Speaking on the importance of transparency and accountability in South Sudan, Hillary Clinton said, "We know that [oil] will either help your country finance its own path out of poverty, or you will fall prey to the natural resource curse, which will enrich a small elite, outside interests, corporations, and countries, and leave your people hardly better off than when you started."[11] And the State Department knows that this is what has happened in Equatorial Guinea. The independent think tank that the State Department uses to rate countries' level of freedom has given Equatorial Guinea its lowest possible score, "worst of the worst," through all the years of Obiang's oil sales.[12] And the State Department knows from its own human rights reports how much progress US engagement with Obiang has made toward the goals, stated on its website, of "good governance and democracy... protection of human rights... civil society, greater fiscal transparency, and increased government investment in Equatorial Guinea's people in areas such as health and education." Here is the latest summary from the State Department itself:

> The most significant human rights abuses in the country were disregard for the rule of law and due process, including police use of torture and excessive force; denial of freedom of speech, press, assembly, and association; and widespread official corruption. Other human rights abuses included: inability of citizens to change their government; arbitrary and unlawful killings; abuse of detainees and prisoners; and poor conditions in prisons and detention facilities. Arbitrary arrest and detention, incommunicado detention, harassment and deportation of foreign residents without due process, and lack of judicial independence were problems. The government restricted the right to privacy, freedom of movement, and political party activity. Restrictions on domestic and international nongovernmental organization (NGO) activity, violence and discrimination against women and children, and trafficking in

> persons occurred... The government did not take steps to prosecute or punish officials who committed abuses, whether in the security forces or elsewhere in the government, and impunity was a serious problem.[13]

As we saw in Chapter 5, the country's health and education scores have not risen even over the years when floods of American cash went to Obiang. No honest Secretary of State could assert that the US decision to channel hundreds of millions of dollars to Obiang in exchange for the oil he his stolen has been good for governance, development, democracy, or human rights—for any of the goals on the State Department's webpage.

This is not hyperbole: by America's own principles, Obiang has stolen the country's oil from its people, and the US government has authorized Americans to buy that stolen oil from him. There is no way to paint this in the colors of "development." The people of Equatorial Guinea were extremely poor when their oil started flowing in 1995. Their oil has now been stolen, has been sold off, and has gone up in smoke while its value skyrocketed. And that oil is not a renewable resource. All of the value from the oil produced so far has been spent by Obiang's clan: the value has gone to realtors in Paris, Maryland, and Malibu; to Gulfstream Aerospace and Maserati; through the clan's patronage networks and through their digestive systems. Only a fraction has been spent on the citizens, and in ways they never approved. Much of the total value of the country's oil endowment is now gone, and today's revenues continue to be misappropriated.

The Secretary of State might make one last try: a tough-love justification. The people of Equatorial Guinea are not (as the Thai ambassador said in 1959) "ready for a truly democratic form of government." Obiang is the best we can do; we must suffer him as the people get on their feet and become capable of ruling themselves.

Here the United States would be declaring that Obiang is the agent of an incompetent principal. But could the Secretary look us in the eye and say this? Let the State Department put on its webpage that it does not consider the people of Equatorial Guinea competent to make their own decisions. Let it include that it does not consider Obiang to be keeping the citizenry incompetent by denying them education, information, and opportunities for political participation. Finally, let it publish that it does not believe that Obiang is using his control over the people's resources to further his private interests instead of the interests of the people—that he is not taking resource revenues for himself and his family. Recall from Chapter 1 the State Department's own ambassador to Equatorial Guinea, who said that the country is "the world's finest example of a country privatized by a kleptomaniac without a scintilla of social consciousness."[14] That is what State Department officials know from their own reports, and why they face so acutely a problem of public relations.

The primary challenges of the "resource curse" are, just as Secretary of State Clinton said, transparency and accountability: the transparency and accountability of the American government to the American people. The American government can't publicly explain its trade policy toward Equatorial Guinea. If forced to focus on why it authorizes Americans to buy oil from Obiang, American officials must evade or lie. And this is not evasion or lying justified, for example, by the need to keep troop movements secret in time of war. America's trade policy toward Equatorial Guinea is entirely discretionary, and it undermines the popular sovereignty of a foreign people for the sake of Americans' private gain. The webpage describing this policy is impossible. The US government can't come clean about its foreign policies toward Equatorial Guinea—or about its policies toward many other resource-disordered countries.

If you're curious, we do know what a US Secretary of State actually said to Obiang himself after all the years of repression and impoverishment, of rigged elections and censorship, that are documented in the State Department's own reports. At a joint press conference, Secretary of State Condoleezza Rice said:

> Welcome. I'm very pleased to welcome the President of Equatorial Guinea, President Obiang... Thank you very much for your presence here. You are a good friend and we welcome you.[15]

If you go to the Web, you can find the photo of Secretary Rice posing with Obiang at that press conference, shaking his hand.[16] That same year, the State Department revealed that the American taxpayer was paying $17,500 a month to rent the American embassy building in Equatorial Guinea—and paying that money to Obiang's uncle, a security chief who tortured an opposition leader to death.[17] And showing favor to Obiang is not a partisan policy. On the Web, you can also see President Barack Obama and his wife, smiling while the pose for a staged photo with Obiang and his wife.[18]

One definition of corruption is "the abuse of public office for private gain." By this definition, our politicians are corrupting us. They are abusing their public office for our private gain.

THE STATE'S PREDICAMENT

The US Supreme Court heard a property dispute back in 1856. An owner from State A had traveled to State B with his property. Yet States A and B had different laws, and under State B's, laws the owner could not have title to that property. The question for the Court was which property laws should prevail in this case: State A's or State B's. The Court ruled—in perhaps its worst decision across all its long history—that the slave state's law should prevail in the free state: Dred Scott belonged to his master's estate, and moreover, the ban on slave owning in the free state was unconstitutional.[19]

The US government is in a difficult situation over Equatorial Guinea, yet its problem is more about its own principles than about the oil from that country. The United States could disengage commercially from Obiang without much difficulty: this would be a temporary headache for the Assistant Secretary in charge of the Bureau of African Affairs, the American oil companies involved would need to be placated, and the story might get a few headlines in US media. The United States has not gotten that much oil from Equatorial Guinea in absolute terms, the place is otherwise of no strategic significance, and its ruling family is a minor public relations liability. In itself, Equatorial Guinea doesn't matter much to the US government.

The government's predicament is that, as in the Dred Scott case, it finds itself deeply committed, and committed on the wrong side of its own national principles. Were the United States suddenly to uphold the principle that the people of Equatorial Guinea own that country's oil, and announce publicly that Obiang is stealing that oil, Americans might start to wonder about the other authoritarians that the US government is authorizing its people to buy resources from, like the Saudi royals. And Saudi Arabia matters a lot.

As we've seen, Saudi Arabia matters in many ways to the US government. Saudi supplies around 6 percent of US oil consumption.[20] Yet US-Saudi relations are not only—and not even primarily—about US oil imports. Rather, as we saw in Chapter 6, the US government has relied on the Saudi leadership as a key strategic ally across several high-priority policy areas, such as global economic stability, arms sales, and inward investment. Over the electoral time horizon of any American politician, it's always made sense to continue to engage with the Saudi regime commercially, and to support it diplomatically.

The US Secretary of State therefore wishes not to—indeed, cannot—answer the question of why the US government authorizes Americans to buy oil from the Saudi regime. The answer can't be the one from the Saudi Basic Law that we glimpsed in the Introduction: that the king derives his authority from the Holy Qur'an, that his regime owns all of the oil, and that Saudi citizens must obey him in good times and bad.[21] Nor can the Secretary's answer be the principled American answer that the people are sovereign over Saudi Arabia, including its resources, and that any king can only be the agent of those people. For the US Secretary of State, the truth about Saudi Arabia is unspeakable.

OUR PREDICAMENT

When, in the eighteenth century, a small group of Quakers began their campaign to end the Atlantic slave trade, the British elite were thoroughly entwined in the slave economy. The Lord Mayor of London was the richest absentee plantation owner of the day. Dozens of Members of Parliament owned Caribbean plantations, and a certain Lord Hawkesbury even had a slave ship named in his honor.[22] As for the Church of England, it owned slaves through

> [t]he church's missionary arm, the Society for the Propagation of the Gospel in Foreign Parts, whose governing board included the Regius Professors of Divinity at Oxford and Cambridge and the head of the church, the Archbishop of Canterbury. The estate's brand, burned onto the chests of slaves with a red-hot iron, was SOCIETY. The clerics on the society's board noticed the plantation's high death rate, but made no move to change how it operated. "I have long wondered & lamented," wrote the Archbishop of Canterbury to a fellow bishop in 1760, "that the Negroes in our plantations decrease, & new Supplies become necessary continually. Surely this proceeds from some Defect, both of Humanity & even of good policy. But we must take things as they are at present."[23]

Slavery was then entirely accepted—indeed, it was a large source of wealth for many of Britain's richest people. While the anti-slavery movement's leaders struggled for decades, seemingly in vain, to convince the Members of Parliament and the bishops in London, ordinary people in the provinces—and especially women—took matters into their own hands. They organized the first modern boycott: a boycott against the slave-harvested sugar that was a mainstay of the British economy. Elizabeth Heyrick, a former schoolteacher from Leicester, later wrote in a powerful pamphlet called *Immediate, not Gradual, Abolition*:

> The perpetuation of Slavery in our West India colonies is not an abstract question, to be settled between the Government and the Planters. It is a question in which we are *all* implicated; we are all guilty (with shame and compunction let us admit the opprobrious truth) of supporting and perpetuating slavery. The West Indian planter and the people of this country, stand in the same moral relation to each other, as the thief and the receiver of stolen goods. The planter refuses to set his wretched captive at liberty, treats him as a beast of burden, compels his reluctant, unremunerated labour under the lash of the cart whip—why?—because WE furnish the stimulant to all this injustice, rapacity, and cruelty—by PURCHASING ITS PRODUCE. Heretofore, it may have been thoughtlessly and unconsciously, but now this palliative is removed; the veil of ignorance is rent aside.[24]

The theft of a country's oil may not be as opprobrious as slavery in Barbados, but our own lives are much more deeply enmeshed with oil than Heyrick's was with sugar. What percentage of the miles we drive, the clothes we wear, the lotions we smear on, is injustice? How much of what we eat was grown and shipped with stolen oil; what proportion of our bodies is plunder; what portion flows from breast and bottle? The taint of stolen resources is engrained in our lives; it is perhaps part of the story of every object you will taste, touch, and see today.

The daily reality of our market life ratchets away from our political ideals. Our private consumption leads to outcomes we morally cannot stand, and our choices in the stores send our money to causes we deplore. We find our selves divided.

OUR FORTUNATE CIRCUMSTANCE

Our town is quiet and safe as always. The stores full of tainted goods are not far from our home. Do we go? What else could we do?

We're in more fortunate circumstances than our forebears who faced off against slavery. We're better off materially than they were, by a long way, and so more able to accept costs for the sake of our principles. We don't need to invent the slogans for popular sovereignty, or to scandalize polite company by speaking them. The fight for the people's rights has been fought and mostly won—the gun muzzles have been faced and the prisons endured—by men and women possibly braver than we. Our surprise is how much we contribute to the violation of people's rights, but when this is noticed, we don't doubt which side is right.

Our identities, that is to say, are already transformed. In the twentieth century, it was a shock for many whites when they realized that their belief in their own innate racial superiority was wrong.[25] That belief had supported their understanding of the justifiability of the social order they grew up in, and it was a significant source of their self-esteem. Giving up the belief in their racial superiority meant coming to terms with the injustice of the system they had accepted—which was difficult enough—and also finding other sources of belief in their own goodness. These are not our problems. We identify strongly with popular sovereignty already. We may feel guilt for helping to violate our own rules, and shame for not having lived up to our standards, but we don't need to replace our principles—in fact, we may be energized by the possibility of furthering them.

The tools we have for realizing popular resource sovereignty are exceptionally sturdy. The world has already converged on the principles needed; as we've seen, all of the law required is already in place, ready to go. We don't need to fret the politics of getting the United States, or China, or any other country to say the right words—nearly every country, including all of the major powers, has signed on to the right principles. So much of the hard work has already been done for us by others.

Which leaves the politics and the economics. Yet even here, as we've seen, our long-term interests are damaged by the current system of global trade in natural resources. We've been resource cursed our whole lives: mired in an unstable global economy, living in fear of war, terrorists, and diseases that threaten in part because of the short-term fixes our politicians chose ten, twenty, or thirty years ago. The only permanent cure for the pathologies of power is to counter that power, and the sources of accountability over resources are just the people that we see and that we are.

Switching our policies deliberately to empower peoples will mesh with the great shifts in power now taking place the world over. Even in the worst resource-disordered countries, national populations are becoming increasingly potent: more numerous and youthful, better educated, better armed, better informed, and more connected. They're aware of their strengths, and they expect to have more political power than they do. Confronted with repressive and corrupt elites, they will increasingly use their power in ways that undermine these elites: through street protests, strikes, and vandalism, or through terrorism, sabotage, kidnapping, and armed rebellion. The people will gain more power, one way or another. It's time to get on their side.

The end of the Atlantic slave trade was once unimaginable to the Archbishop of Canterbury who profited from it. Apartheid was permanently entrenched, until it collapsed. Containing the Soviet Union was the strategic priority for decades, until the Soviet Union was suddenly gone. The only justification for not living by our principles would be that we lacked feasible policies to replace our current ones. And it's to exploring feasible policies that we turn in Part IV. We in the West have the opportunity to end our corruption, and to lead the world through its next moral revolution.

PART IV

Clean Trade

Today's resource trade makes many peoples weaker (Part I). That's not only bad for them, it's bad for us as well (Part II). We choose for might to make rights, which violates popular resource sovereignty (Part III). Trade based on the people's rights will make all peoples stronger, including our own.

15

Principles for Action

Above all, our Nation is strong in its support of principle: we espouse the cause of freedom and justice and peace for all peoples, regardless of race or flag or political ideology. Though in this strength we have reason for confidence, we likewise have need for wisdom, and the caution that wisdom enforces...

By caution, I mean: a prudent guard against fatuous expectations that a world, sick with ignorance, mutual fears and hates, can be miraculously cured by a single meeting...

By wisdom, I mean:...a persevering resolution to explore every decent avenue toward a just and lasting peace, no matter how many and bitter our disappointments. I mean an inspired faith that men's determination and capacity to better their world will in time override their ability to destroy it; and that humanity's hunger for peace and justice is a mightier force than a few men's lust for power.

—Dwight Eisenhower, Address at West Point, 1955[1]

ALMOST THERE

Oil is the most valuable good traded across borders, and seven of the eleven largest public companies in the world by sales are oil companies.[2] These companies are significant transnational actors, and they are not charities. Their priorities are to extract as many resources as they can and to send those resources on to consumers. Any action that might limit their business will need to be grounded in deep principles that cannot easily be dismissed. These principles will need natural allies who will defend them when they come under attack. When one adds that these principles will also be enforced for international sales of other extractable resources, such as iron, copper, and diamonds, the need for them to be strong increases.

Indeed, some countries might resist reform even more than the companies will. Many Western countries import large quantities of extractive resources from authoritarian and failed states. (Some European countries, for example, are highly dependent on authoritarian natural gas.) Resource-hungry countries such as China must also be persuaded to end imports of stolen oil and minerals, and the West is often thought to have little political leverage on China—or on rich petrocracies such as Saudi Arabia and Qatar. In fact, much leverage goes the other way because of the trade, investment, and debt relations that these countries have with the West.

The challenges of change will be substantial. Nevertheless, by our own principles, oil and minerals exported from authoritarian and failed countries are stolen goods. We—and the world—should no longer buy them.[3] And we have been here, at the beginning of a movement against effectiveness, many times before. In 1787, a dozen men met in a small room in London and solemnly pledged themselves to a preposterous campaign to end the Atlantic slave trade. Britain was then the greatest international power. Her empire was already intercontinental; her navy ruled the waves. Britain was also the world's leading slaving nation—before she stopped, her wooden ships would carry over three million captured human beings to the New World (with many others dying along the horrific Middle Passage). And as we saw in the last chapter, her political, military, and religious establishments were heavily invested in slavery.

Parliament, the Church of England, and London's gentlemen's clubs all counted plantation owners among their members. The slave trade employed thousands of sailors, shipbuilders, blacksmiths, and merchants; financial houses like Barclays and Lloyds grew richer on slave profits; slavery even gave Britain its first millionaire—a Member of Parliament named William Beckford, who owned more than 22,000 acres of plantations in Jamaica.[4] Demand from the slave regions hugely boosted Britain's industrial growth.[5] By the early 1800s, slave-harvested sugar from the West Indies by itself accounted for almost 5 percent of British national income, and the growing slave-based trade was the most valuable trade in all the empire.[6]

In short, when reform started, slavery seemed essential to the economy. The practice made some uneasy, yet few in the elite saw it as a serious moral problem. Still, within twenty years, the British people had abolished their slave trade.[7] And three decades, later they had gone further and emancipated all of the slaves within their empire. Alexis de Tocqueville wrote in 1843:

> Sixty years ago, if the foremost maritime and colonial nation of the globe had suddenly declared that slavery would disappear from its vast domains: what shouts of surprise and admiration would have broken out everywhere! With what concerned and passionate curiosity the eyes of civilized Europe would have followed the development of that immense enterprise! What fears and hopes would have filled every heart! This bold and remarkable task has just been undertaken and completed before our own eyes. We have seen something unprecedented in history... Open the annals of all peoples, and I doubt you will find anything finer or more extraordinary.[8]

Britain's anti-slavery leaders were an eclectic group of brilliant characters who insisted on one principle of freedom: that chaining a human should not mean owning that human, that might should not make right. These leaders worked incessantly to persuade the British elites to unwind themselves from the trade in which they were so thoroughly entangled. Lord Castlereagh, the British Foreign Secretary, first thought that the abolitionists were "left-wing agitators or sentimental idealists." After thinking long on their words, however, he concluded that "the trade was in truth a terrible evil, and that it was the duty of Great Britain to use her moral influence, her wealth, and her maritime power to secure its general abolition."[9]

Leadership was crucial in pressuring the British elites to end the slave trade. Yet if we no longer much remember names like William Wilberforce and Thomas Clarkson, it is because they were not in the end the main force for change. However brilliant the leaders, brilliance cannot beat interest for sixty years. It was the British people who demanded that slavery be stopped. Up and down the country, year after year, the people organized and rallied, boycotted and petitioned, prodded and supported politicians. They did so throughout liberal and conservative governments, war and peace, fat years and lean years, as well as through constitutional revolutions at home and shifts in allies abroad. They did so even after the deaths of their gifted leaders, and often at cost to their own jobs and families. Then, as now, the people are the main wellspring of principled action—and especially of action that counters power.

POPULAR SOVEREIGNTY AND PROPERTY

As far as the human race has heroes, they are champions of popular sovereignty: Gandhi and Mandela. Popular sovereignty is already the world's ideal, and property rights live within that ideal—the people own their nation's resources. The importance of protecting property rights is vivid to most people in their daily lives (think again of the most valuable thing you own, and then think of finding it gone). So already what we see is promising—the movement to abolish effectiveness for natural resources begins with most people instinctively committed to its two major principles: popular sovereignty and property rights.

Protecting property rights is the also the mantra of many powerful global actors. All companies rely on the protection of property rights as owners, buyers, and sellers. No property, no business. More, the protection of property is the daily demand of the world's largest investors, a group that today includes the major oil companies, private equity funds, and China. All market participants insist on property rights; for them, this is an existential concern.

Property rights are the foundation of free trade—so long as the rights themselves are justified. Within Westphalia, human beings could be owned; today, we know they cannot be. Within Westphalian politics, coercive domination won the right to sell resources; under modern principles, resource sales need the people's authorization. Once we know what property rights are justified, we can see which trade is really free. The transportation of captured *Homo sapiens* could once be considered "free trade in humans," but no longer. The transportation of coercively extracted petroleum could once be considered "free trade in oil," but again, no longer. In both cases, we now see that the "trade" is invalidated by coercion—in one case the wrongful coercion of Africans, in the other the wrongful coercion of citizens, and in both the forceful appropriation of a valuable asset. Against property owners, might makes wrong. Trade in resources will only be free when its foundations are the people's rights.

Popular sovereignty and property rights are unbeatable together. Politicians oppose popular sovereignty at their peril; for firms and investors, fighting property rights would be fatal. And these two principles are not all—the case against effectiveness can also call on other modern principles with widespread appeal, such as human rights, which counter the power of the state. As we've seen, popular resource sovereignty is already the first and the last right in the main human rights treaties. So free trade needs—in order really to be free—to be based on this human right.

The rule of law is a further principle that enlists against "might makes right." The rule of law requires that all state officials be accountable. It also demands that basic rights should be secured against self-dealing elites. So the rule of law is, in an interesting alliance, the call of both the foreign investor and the domestic oppressed.

Finally, and greatest of all, the case for the abolition of effectiveness will be joined by the principle of peace. Peace is the word invoked by nearly everyone, and also a condition that many genuinely desire.

Popular sovereignty and property, human rights, the rule of law and peace. These are not ideas that the world needs to be converted to; these are the world's stated principles, and the declared ideals of the world's most important actors: individuals, firms, investors, and politicians. Some of their support for these principles is of course hypocritical, but not all. To a large degree, each of these actors also affirms these principles from their own interests, from their own identities. Attacking these principles would be self-destructive; advancing these principles will suit their self-image.

In contrast, effectiveness is no one's ideal. Effectiveness exists subliminally, hiding in the light of the international system. "Might makes right" is the rule of coercive and corrupt actors who subsist on dead ideologies and the money that the world unwillingly sends them. Supporters of the world's ideals will discover endless alliances to make with each other. Partisans of effectiveness will rally support only through fear and bribery—and will always be tempted to defect to the rules of modernity and to the side of the majority. While effectiveness may hold out for a time, determined action on principle must win.

THE PRICE OF PRINCIPLE

The chapters ahead will set out policies for ending today's trade in stolen resources. Since today's system is all we've known, some skepticism is natural that such change is possible. The proof will be in the doing. Still, history shows that three kinds of concerns often emerge during the early stages of campaigns against effectiveness, and the rest of this chapter is devoted to discussing them. The three concerns are that people will not bear costs for change, that no nation can afford to start the reforms, and that short-term thinking will always swamp long-term plans. We can call these concerns "costly action," "first-mover fear," and "short-termism."

Acting on principle can be costly, as anyone who volunteers or gives to charity knows. And people do bear costs for the sake of principles. If principles are entrenched within their identities, people will see such action as being true to themselves, as an expression of who they are. There are many well-known cases we could explore here, like the Allied home fronts during World War II or the American civil rights movement. Let's continue instead with the less-known abolition of the slave trade in the early nineteenth century.

The ending of the Atlantic slave trade cost thousands of ordinary Britons their jobs and their businesses. Yet the British were so committed to abolition that even as they were dismantling their own slave trade, they also began the huge task of persuading other nations to end their trade as well. Britain exhorted, implored, and paid the other great powers to stop slaving. It also used its huge navy to patrol the Atlantic and to turn back slave-laden ships.

All of this required real sacrifices of blood, treasure, and power.[10] The Royal Navy's West Africa Squadron spent fifty years devoted almost entirely to suppressing the slave trade; in the end, five thousand Britons perished in the campaign (fifty-five thousand would be the proportionate number of Americans today). The other major maritime nations (especially France and the United States) deeply resented Britain's "moralism," and the disputes at sea escalated into several serious diplomatic incidents. Britain's sugar-based trade plummeted, as its competitors' trade skyrocketed.

In ending bondage within their own domains and suppressing it in others, the British people also imposed large and uncompensated economic losses on themselves. Chaim Kaufmann and Robert Pape describe the damages:

> Virtually all elements of British society suffered net economic costs from the anti-slavery efforts... British taxpayers paid for government efforts against slavery; consumers paid higher prices for sugar and other tropical produce; and manufacturers, shippers, merchants, and bankers who traded with the West Indian colonies or with Africa lost business... [As for compensating benefits,] anti-slave trade efforts did not yield Britain any noticeable material benefits, either in wealth or power.[11]

Imagine the equivalent today: in one year, the British government spent *40 percent* of its budget on ending slavery.[12] We even have an estimate of the total economic cost to the nation. Britain's anti-slavery campaign cost nearly 2 percent of national income, each and every year, for sixty years.[13] That's a gigantic sum, to be added on to the cost in lives and in strained international relations.

Britons today may well be poorer because of their ancestors' determination to end the Atlantic slave trade. Again, nearly 2 percent of national income sacrificed, every year, for sixty years—consider which politicians would have the courage to stand behind such a campaign today. Determined people accepted these costs for the sake of their principles. The question for us, thinking of them, is whether we believe that the British people did the right thing.

Today, the countries of the West will face costs as they transition away from authoritarian oil and conflict minerals. These costs will differ from those the British paid—there will be, for example, no military expenses—and there will be many compensating benefits. Still, the shift from effectiveness in the resource trade comes with a price tag. We'll go through the costs in the chapters that follow; here we can reflect on one reason why those costs are worth bearing.

COSTLY ACTION AND TRUST

Reforming the resource trade may impose costs, yet "might makes right" may be more costly still. In Chapter 6, we surveyed the resource curses on the West that flow from effectiveness: hostile authoritarians, unpredictable allies, the spread of extremism, empowered terrorists, higher prices, economic crises, and more. If we stick with it, "might makes right" will keep exacting its sacrifices. One big concern is that effectiveness will, because of its logic, continue to set foreigners against us. One benefit of reforming effectiveness is that this will allow the West to build trust instead.

This is a delicate point, or perhaps it is a truth that needs to be faced. Many in the West have a sense that the rest of the world views the West with some suspicion. Americans, for example, can see on television that ordinary people in places like the Middle East and Asia do not seem to place much credence in what the American government says. The hard truth is that things are much worse than most Westerners (and especially most Americans) think. To generalize, much of the world just does not trust Westerners to act rightly, and much of the world does not believe what Western governments say. Here are a few statistics:

- In 2011, Pew did a survey of Muslims in Muslim countries; it found majorities in all countries said that Westerners are "Selfish," "Violent," "Greedy," "Immoral," "Arrogant," and "Fanatical."
- The same survey asked who carried out the 9/11 attacks. In no Muslim country did even 30 percent of Muslims say they believed that Arabs carried out the 9/11 attacks. Even in large non-Arab countries that are American allies, like Indonesia (20 percent) and Turkey (9 percent), the percentages connecting Arabs with 9/11 were quite low.
- When Robert Keohane and his colleagues analyzed the Twitter postings of Arabs during 2012–2013, they found that anti-American tweets outnumbered pro-American tweets by three to one. After the Boston Marathon bombing of 2013, Arab tweeters were twice as likely to speculate that the US intelligence agencies were behind the bombing as they were to express sympathy for its victims.
- These are not just Muslim and Arab attitudes. A 2013 Pew survey found that clear majorities of ordinary Chinese also believe that Americans are "Aggressive," "Violent," "Arrogant," and "Greedy." And just over half added "Selfish."[14]

There are many causes of this lack of trust: the West's troubled history of militarism and its exploitation of foreigners' resources, the anti-Western rhetoric of foreign demagogues and extremists, and other causes too. There's enough blame to go around, if we're interested in blame. Yet even after we understand the causes of this distrust of the West, we will still need to know what to do now. When we look forward, our questions will be whether this distrust will get better or worse in the future, and what can we do now so that future surveys will show more trust.

Reformers must accept that the rest of the world will not at first believe an announcement from a Western nation that it's determined to put its own house in order, and that it no longer plans to buy natural resources from the autocrats and militants who are stealing those resources from the people. If one Western nation makes this announcement, foreigners will spin it as a plot; when others join, it will be said to be a conspiracy. Still, one can think of how trust builds in personal relationships. We come to believe those who do what they say, who carry through on their commitments, who keep their promises even when this is hard for them. We come to think well of people with integrity—and integrity is shown by what a person will and will not do.[15]

Principled action is the best way for Western countries to counter the conspiracy theories and charges of hypocrisy that now echo all over the world. To take one important instance of this, principled action is the best way for Western countries to counter the jihadi victimization narrative that now attracts thousands of young Muslims toward radicalization and then toward extremism. Every Western killing of a Muslim abroad can be spun to strengthen this jihadi narrative. Western countries must establish a counter-narrative that is much more compelling. Only by showing its willingness to bear costs for the sake of people abroad can the West drain the swamps of suspicion that mire it in its resource curse. Trust is the moral measure of all human relations. Acting on principle is the best way to build trust.

THE FEAR OF MOVING FIRST

To end effectiveness in the international resource trade, some nation or nations must be the first to take action against stolen imports. Statesmen should relish the chance to champion action that will further long-term national interests and contribute to a better world. Still, making a first move can take steady nerves, even if the move is in the right direction. Do countries ever really move first when this requires short-term costs?

They do; here is one example of many. After Watergate, Americans were fed up with corruption. While pursuing several post-Watergate prosecutions, the Securities and Exchange Commission found that hundreds of American companies had given bribes to foreign officials worth hundreds of millions of dollars. It issued a report saying that the bribery of foreign officials by US corporations was "serious and sufficiently widespread to be a cause for deep concern."[16] The Senate opened its own hearings, and heard testimony that many major American companies—especially oil companies like Exxon, Mobil, and Gulf—were heavily implicated in this practice.

Many senators expressed their disgust, and not least at the violation of basic market principles. One Senate report said, "There is a broad consensus that the payment of bribes to influence business decisions corrodes the free-enterprise system. Bribery short-circuits the marketplace. Where bribes are paid, business is directed not to the most efficient producer, but to the most corrupt."[17] Senators also expressed their concern about the sacrifice of long-term national interests to short-term business imperatives:

> There is also little doubt that widespread corruption serves to undermine those moderate democratic and pro-free-enterprise governments which the United States has traditionally sought to foster and support. Several oil companies testified before the subcommittee that they had made huge political contributions... supporting the democratic forces who are friendly to foreign capital in those countries, but in fact, they were subverting the basic democratic processes... [W]hile bribes and kickbacks may bolster sales in the short run, the open participation of American firms in such practices can, in the long run, only serve to discredit them and the United States. Ultimately, they create the conditions which bring to power political forces that are no friends of ours.[18]

Late in these Senate debates, however, first-mover fear kicked in. When it looked like sentiment toward anti-corruption legislation was swelling, some Senators noted that it wasn't just American firms that were bribing foreign officials. Bribery, it was said, is universal. Indeed, many European countries even encouraged foreign bribes, by allowing firms to write them off as a business expense. So even if America banned bribery, this would not end the practice. A ban would not reduce foreign corruption. It would only mean that American firms would lose business.

This first-mover fear was also deployed against the British campaign to ban the slave trade. As one resident of Bristol wrote to a newspaper, "To abandon [the slave trade] to our rivals the French would be to stab the vitals of this nation as a trading people, and leave our posterity to be in time Slaves themselves."[19] The poet William Cowper even wrote some satirical verse on the popular boycott of slave-harvested sugar:

> I own I am shock'd at the purchase of slaves,
> And fear those who buy them and sell them are knaves;
> What I hear of their hardships, their tortures, and groans
> Is almost enough to draw pity from stones.
>
> I pity them greatly, but I must be mum,
> For how could we do without sugar and rum?
> Especially sugar, so needful we see;
> What, give up our desserts, our coffee, and tea!
>
> Besides, if we do, the French, Dutch, and Danes,
> Will heartily thank us, no doubt, for our pains:
> If we do not buy the poor creatures, they will:
> And tortures and groans will be multiplied still.
>
> If foreigners likewise would give up the trade,
> Much more in behalf of your wish might be said;
> But, while they get riches by purchasing blacks,
> Pray tell me why we may not also go snacks?[20]

In the end, the US senators overcame their first-mover fear, as the nineteenth-century British had. Senator William Proxmire saw the soft-power benefits of moving first on corruption:

> If we have a reputation of being the one country that enforces the law and everything that we sell is sold on the basis of merit and competition and not on the basis of bribery, it seems to me that's an enormous advantage that shouldn't be overlooked. I would think unilateral action wouldn't isolate us. It would give us a great advantage and other countries would perforce be constrained to follow.[21]

Senator Harrison Williams sensed a "first-mover advantage" in being able to set standards that could then be spread to other countries too:

> Action by our Government will facilitate, what I believe is generally agreed is necessary, an international solution. Once the bill

> becomes law our Government will be in a position to argue forcefully, with integrity and credibility, for bilateral and multilateral agreements.[22]

Was this just hypocrisy? Maybe—but they did it. Congress passed the Foreign Corrupt Practices Act (FCPA) in 1977. And international agreements did follow. The Organization for Economic Co-operation and Development (OECD), a club of developed countries, pushed a treaty requiring all members to implement FCPA-like legislation. The anti-bribery rule was gradually adopted across all rich countries—finally, in 2009, Poland became the last country explicitly to prohibit tax deductions on foreign bribes.[23] The rule was becoming entrenched. As it happened, this left Britain as the laggard in passing strong anti-bribery legislation, and British leaders were teased about this at OECD meetings.[24] This goaded Britain to leapfrog the other OECD members and to pass an anti-bribery act in 2010 that is significantly tougher than the FCPA.[25] What we see in the history of anti-bribery laws is a slow but steady race to the top for better standards against foreign corruption.

As the stories from Chapter 8 showed, bribery is still with us. But then, so is some international trade in enslaved human beings. These anti-bribery laws have been significant steps toward their goals, as the abolition laws were steps toward theirs. Prosecutions for corporate bribery, such as the gigantic one against a Halliburton subsidiary for its bribery in Nigeria, have grown across rich countries (and especially in the United States). The threat of prosecution for bribery is now a significant constraint on Western business activities worldwide.[26] Even international arbitration panels are today becoming reluctant to enforce contracts won through corruption.[27] Western firms are still far from saintly, but any oil man who remembers the old days will tell you that foreign bribery is now much riskier, and that the old "business as usual" is now gone. US leadership overcame the fear of moving first, and so moved international affairs a step forward.

THE LONG RUN

Western countries that change their policies can promote popular resource sovereignty peacefully—by reforming their own laws, enforced within their own borders, and showing by example what sovereign peoples can do. Declaring principle as the basis of policy is also the best way to build international coalitions for reform. On the Clean Trade website, you will find a *Declaration on Trade in Natural Resources*, written by an international team of lawyers. By passing legislation based on this declaration, countries can announce that they are ready to cooperate in supporting popular resource sovereignty everywhere.[28] "Sign the *Declaration*" can be a strong demand of citizen campaigns encouraging national leaders to make principled change.

A commitment to principle will be needed for leaders to keep their resolve when the going gets tough, as it will. The authoritarians and warlords enriched by today's rule of effectiveness are entrenched in the system as it is, and as we've seen, they're rich and ruthless. We now add that they're also clever and adaptive. Whatever actions are taken that endanger their power, today's authoritarians and warlords will respond dynamically. The big fish do not fry themselves. Here's one scenario of many: the cruelly cunning Algerian regime might stage a serious terrorist incident within its own country or in a neighbor's, so as to present itself as the best guarantor of regional stability and to offer its promise of stability in exchange for Western concessions. There may be many critical situations like this one while the West turns away from effectiveness, and politicians' spines must keep firm throughout them.

The most significant, sustained challenge to principled action is short-term thinking. When headlines yell, the temptation is to forget the future and act only on the now. We can imagine a dialogue where the short term and the long term can talk to one another:

> SHORT TERM: Yes, we know that oil money has for decades funded the spread of extremism worldwide—but there's just been a terrorist attack. What should we do right now?

> LONG TERM: Right now, in 1977, America should act on the goal in President Carter's Freedom Plan to cut US oil imports in half by 1985. Then we'd likely not face these terrorist threats.[29]

> SHORT TERM: No, no—oil-fueled militiamen are beheading hostages in the Middle East and taking "infidel" women as sexual slaves.[30] What should we do right *now*?

> LONG TERM: Right now, in 1992, America should use the peace dividend from the end of the Cold War to heed President George

> H. W. Bush (and all presidents after Johnson) by reducing its dependence on foreign oil. Then we wouldn't face many of today's lose-lose strategic choices…[31]
>
> SHORT TERM (FOUR YEARS FROM NOW): No, no—a lethal epidemic is spreading fast out of poor mineral-exporting countries. What should we do *right now*?

The resource curse on the West is like poison ivy: one symptom is a compulsive desire to do in the short term what will make the affliction last longer.[32] Western countries must of course act on short-term crises quickly and skillfully. But this shouldn't distract them from the commitment to make the long term better, by ending effectiveness for resources. Calling here on "our children's futures" would be right—yet this is perhaps too trite to be heard. Put it another way then: we were once the children of the future—and how do we feel that past leaders ignored the "long term" that is now our lifetimes for the sake of short terms past?

DEEP KNEE BENDS

"All politics must bend its knee before right," said the great philosopher Immanuel Kant. "Right must never be fitted to politics, but politics must always be fitted to right."[33] Kant has been thought utopian, even crazy, for saying this. Yet Kant is correct if he is read more subtly. Determined, long-term action in support of popular resource sovereignty is essential. Still, right also requires peace as a goal, and right requires maintaining a global economy that can sustain our species at its size. Earlier, we saw that the international system is built with several principles, and that its design constraints mean that no single principle can be pressed too hard. Now we say even more firmly that action on the resource trade would be self-defeating were it to trigger a war, or to collapse the global trade that all peoples depend on. Reform must be responsible as well as implacable. Right is sovereign, but it is not singular—politics must serve the many principles that rule over it.

So determined action to reform the global resource trade must choose its tools wisely. The sharp-edged tool of military action to force democratic change is, as we've seen, not fit for this work. Even putting aside the efficacy of bombing for democracy, this is too much like the colonizing campaigns of the past to build the trust that the West now needs. Western nations should instead work to align their policies to fit their own principles—first by powering down their own destructive laws like effectiveness for resources. The first tools the West needs are not those for state-building; first turn off the West's machines that are now state-razing.

The design constraints of the international system will also require reformers to have patience. Abolishing effectiveness for resources can start today, but it won't be finished tomorrow. This won't take sixty years, like abolishing the slave trade—yet resistance will be significant, and setbacks will happen.

And once more, the world is not monocausal or even oligocausal. Resources are something, but not everything. (Will you live to one hundred just because you stop smoking unfiltered cigarettes? No. Should you stop smoking if you want to live longer? Yes.) Even the best policies will fall far short of magic. The resource-diseased countries that we've studied, such as Saudi Arabia and Equatorial Guinea, have many weaknesses beyond resources; they may not become stable constitutional democracies even in the medium term. We should also remember that in many resource-disordered countries, corruption is not a fault in the system, it is the system—so changing the basic structure of governance will take time. More, there are many important global challenges—such as nuclear proliferation and banking secrecy—that resource reforms by themselves will not meet. The finale of our journey is not an earthly *Paradiso*; we press on.

THE FLUX OF THE WORLD

The best policies to end effectiveness will be adaptive. The principles we engrave; the policies we pen. The British people demanded to be taken out of business with slavery across the decades of the nineteenth century—through the deaths of their leaders, through boom and bust, through peace and war. They learned that circumstances must always be seized upon—but never relied on—to further the cause. They gripped their principles and adjusted their policies; their ends endured, their means evolved. And in the end, they won.

During the years of the writing of this book, several events shifted the global resource picture significantly. A big spill in the Gulf of Mexico tarred the oil industry. The Arab Spring wounded, but did not remove, most of the high-rent Middle Eastern petrocrats. Uprisings left a Gaddafi-less mess in

Libya, and an Assad-ISIS morass across Syria and western Iraq. A reactor disaster in Japan ended nuclear power—but in Germany, not Japan. Russia flexed its well-oiled muscles toward Europe. A supercycle in mining and metals waxed and then waned; a bad crash in the financial sector slowly and unevenly eased.

Action against effectiveness can't be diverted by events like these. Grotius was codifying effectiveness four hundred years ago. The ink dried in Westphalia in 1648. We're nearing the end of the long struggle to overcome "might makes right" in all of international affairs; this is not a campaign of a day or a decade. Principle is the pole star, and that's why we have to this point in the book not relied on recent events to make the case for reform—even when recent events have been favorable. And favorable they have been. During the last decade, one change in the global resource picture has shrunk a major obstacle to reform. The world has started to turn faster toward us, even as we stride toward the goal. We can seize on this change to strategize, but we ought not depend on it to seal the deal for reform.

In 2006, the talk was of Peak Oil. US crude oil production was continuing its decades-long decline; oil imports were continuing their decades-long rise. American officials had declared African oil to be a growing national strategic interest: they predicted that African oil could rise from 15 to 25 percent of US imports by 2015, and they were planning US naval patrols off west Africa to protect tankers.[34] Even in 2010, the International Energy Agency's *World Energy Outlook* was forecasting two decades of flat US oil production.[35]

By 2013, the *Outlook*'s first line was "Many of the long-held tenets of the energy sector are being rewritten."[36] By 2014, US crude oil production was up 80 percent since 2008; oil imports had fallen by a quarter since 2005.[37] The joke used to be that one could walk from America to Nigeria without getting one's feet wet, just by jumping from one tanker to another. But during 2014, Nigerian imports of crude zeroed out—the United States imported not one drop of oil from Nigeria.[38] Defying all the forecasts, African oil imports overall were down 90 percent in only four years.[39] And America was, astonishingly, passing Saudi Arabia as the world's leading liquid petroleum producer.[40] In 2010, a former head of Shell in the United States titled a book chapter "Energy Independence? Keep Dreaming."[41] Three years later, US officials were saying that "North American energy independence is within our grasp."[42]

All of this brings the goal of ending Western imports of authoritarian oil much closer. When this book was started, many thought it would be impossible for the United States to end its dependence on Middle Eastern imports; now many think this is inevitable even without policy changes. The world is turning ever faster toward the end of effectiveness. In fact, lower imports are better whether one's priorities are energy security, geostrategy, deficit reduction, or action on climate change. Petrocrats now have less leverage; the West now has more flexibility. We may still be over a barrel, but increasingly, it's our own barrel that we are over.

This opens opportunities that can be taken—yet again, we must not say that recent events make the case for reform. For the world will keep turning. Low oil prices might scuttle US production, fracking might be banned, the Secretary of State might be tempted again to extend Obiang a welcoming hand in exchange for imports. Or perhaps high-temperature superconductivity and nuclear fusion will spin the world even faster our way.[43] Resource markets are too volatile for us to make our principles hostage to them. Effectiveness must be ended, one way or another way. A tide that is now flooding in the affairs of man should be ridden as far as it will go. Still, commitment to principle will be required to stay upright through all of the flux of the world.

THE PRIZE

The goal is to end effectiveness for the world's natural resources. The tremendous power that resources bring can no longer remain unaccountable. This is too dangerous, too unjust. The Soviet Union, Iran, Iraq, Saudi Arabia, Libya, Syria, Russia, Sierra Leone, Liberia, the Congo—unaccountable resource power has not worked out well for them, or for us. Resource power must become accountable, to the people who are literally on the ground. Citizens must be the ultimate authority over the resources of their country. That is how it works in Norway, in Botswana, and—if we allow it—how it can work the world over as well.

This commercial world is diagonal; we can make it flat. Consumers are now forced to send their money diagonally upward to unaccountable actors in exporting countries. Those unaccountable actors then descend back down onto our territory to sate their desires with our real estate and our escorts, our goods and our services. Better trade relations would be horizontal: consumers freely exchanging their money for resources ultimately under citizens' control. This kind of horizontal exchange allows more broad-based, more gradual adjustments in relations—for slow tectonic shifts instead of earthquakes. Trade can build trust between nations so long as it is level trade, ultimately connecting ordinary people.

The main means by which we can level global trade is through our own self-control. Since it is our own governments that are putting us into business with unaccountable actors abroad, the challenge is to summon our own powers of accountability, to make our own governments change their ways. The aim is to make our leaders live up to what they always tell us, to make our nations speak with one true public voice. Much of the prize will be the daily, tangible benefits of life without our current resource curse. But what we'll win is also larger than stability and security. Every day, we are divided within ourselves, our private consumption in violation of our public principles. And our societies are divided as we fight over which awful foreign policy option we must choose. Principle must win: the principles of popular sovereignty, property, human rights, the rule of law, and peace. The prize is self-mastery, so we keep our eyes on the unity within ourselves that will enable greater unity with others.

"The specific problems we face," said Einstein, "cannot be solved using the same patterns of thought that were used to create them."[44] Can we, like him, allow ourselves to imagine, to unlock the mind? Is it too much to imagine a Middle East where the people are sovereign and at peace? Is it too much to see a Congolese ex-militiaman calling at a woman's home, politely asking her parents whether he might accompany her to help fetch the water? Can we conceive of American soldiers plundering Toronto, setting fire to the legislative assembly building—and the British army torching the White House and the Capitol in retaliation? There's no need to invent the last; it happened in 1814, within the lifetime of a constitution—still healthy, now one of many—that countered unaccountable power, and established the people's rights.

16

Clean Trade Policy I

Protecting Property

The purpose of foreign policy is not to provide an outlet for our own sentiments of hope or indignation. It is to shape real events in the world.

—John F. Kennedy[1]

The goals of the policies here are to end the global trade in stolen natural resources and to support public accountability over resources everywhere. Countries adopting these policies will disengage commercially from resource-exporting countries where public accountability is absent and will support public accountability in countries where it is weak. The global trade in resources that is today based on the rule of effectiveness can be shifted, carefully and responsibly, onto a better foundation.

As we saw in Part III, the scale of today's resource theft is immense. Looking around the world for oil, we found large Middle Eastern producers, such as Saudi Arabia, Iran, Iraq, UAE, and Qatar, as well as major producers elsewhere, like Russia, Kazakhstan, Algeria, and Angola. That is already half of the world's proven oil reserves, and none of these countries meets the minimum conditions for popular resource sovereignty. All of the resources exported from these countries are stolen from the peoples of those countries. The rule of "might makes right" then transforms these violations of property rights into trade as usual as the resources enter international markets.

The transition in the rules of trade from effectiveness to popular resource sovereignty will mind both principles and results. For the sake of positive results, this transition must respect principles such as those that protect peace; and many aims will be weighty, such as the health of the global economy. These design constraints on the international system have shaped the policies set out here. Adopting these policies will not challenge the political legitimacy of any state. Popular resource sovereignty should not be furthered by military action, and it cannot be demanded all at once. Yet even within these limits, a safe and prudent transition is in sight, and this transition will open opportunities to make progress on important issues beyond resources.

This chapter first sets out policy tools. Some of these tools have dramatic aspects—they taper off oil imports from the Middle East, for example, and impose duties on trade partners like China. Just as important as the tools themselves are the plans for their use. Even the best tools can be dangerous if used foolishly, and some tools work mostly by being displayed as ready for use if needed (think of a police officer's handcuffs).

The dramatic tools discussed below are designed to be used within strategies that leverage the persuasive power of commitment to principle. Clean Trade countries will make strong commitments to ordering their own affairs by the principles of popular sovereignty and property rights as well as human rights, the rule of law, and peace. By committing to these principles, these countries will demonstrate their willingness to bear costs for better relations with the peoples of other nations, which will in turn advance their own national interests. The sharper-edged tools here are merely means. The real power of this framework is that of democratic leadership—the power of free peoples committing to self-disciplined action on behalf of the freedom of peoples everywhere.

All policies of course have unintended consequences—including the established policy of "might makes right" for natural resources. As we saw in Chapter 6, commercial engagement on the basis of effectiveness has consistently produced grave foreign policy dilemmas for the West, and these dilemmas have emerged no matter what political strategy effectiveness has been paired with. Western leaders did not intend for effectiveness to contribute to lengthening the Cold War with the Soviet Union, to the generational hostility of the Iranian people, to the worldwide funding of extremism by Saudi Arabia, to the fighting following the falls of authoritarians in Iraq and Libya, to the civil conflicts in Sudan and Syria, to recessionary global oil price shocks or to any of the other phenomena that we have studied.

The unintended consequences of "might makes right" have already been adverse, and these adverse effects will multiply as resource production expands into more fragile and failed states. The reforms below will dissolve the no-win foreign policy choices that effectiveness would otherwise force on us, and will expand the capacity for future cooperation across borders.

ENFORCING PROPERTY RIGHTS: A CLEAN TRADE ACT

Clean Trade policy divides into two parts. This chapter sets out policies related to exporting countries where citizens cannot possibly be controlling their natural resources, such as fossil fuels, metals, and gems. In the next chapter, we will look at policies toward exporting countries where there is at least some public accountability. Most of the attention will be on oil, the big resource, but the discussion will apply to the other resources too. (As always here, the term *oil* can include both oil and natural gas; later we will split the two out.)

A Clean Trade Act

A Clean Trade Act replaces the trade policy of effectiveness with laws that respect the ultimate right of peoples to control their countries' resources. Passing a Clean Trade Act will disengage commercially from resource vendors in countries that do not meet the minimal conditions for popular resource sovereignty. As we saw in Chapter 13, these conditions require that citizens have bare-bones civil liberties and basic political rights. To review:

> For civil liberties, there must be some press freedom for citizens to have access to information about the state's resource decisions and about possible gross mismanagement. The state must not be so deeply opaque that it's nearly impossible for citizens to find out who is getting the revenues from resource sales and how these revenues are being spent. All citizens must be able to discuss the regime's resource management with each other without fear of serious injury, loss of employment, imprisonment, torture, disappearance, or death. There must be enough rule of law that citizens who wish to protest resource decisions publicly and peacefully may do so without fear of arrest, dismissal, or worse.

> Citizens must also have basic political rights... The people cannot possibly control their resources under a highly authoritarian regime: a military junta or a personalistic dictatorship, an autocratic theocracy or a single-party state. Nor can a people control their resources if the state is so failed that it lacks control over large parts of the populated territory.

If these minimal conditions do not obtain, then the silence of citizens while their resources are exported is just that: silence. Either citizens cannot find out about resource exports, or they are too scared or oppressed to discuss and protest them. Where citizens cannot learn what is happening with their resources, where they cannot debate what the regime is doing, or where they cannot conceivably say no to their resources being sold off, they cannot possibly be authorizing those sales.

A Clean Trade Act enforces the property rights of the peoples of these countries by disengaging commercially from those who would sell off their resources:

- The Act makes illegal the purchase of resources from a disqualified country, and sets out legal penalties for making purchases or facilitating imports.[2]
- The Act denies all commercial and financial facilities of the home jurisdiction to vendors of a disqualified country's resources. Regime members and militants from disqualified countries will be barred from entering the home jurisdiction. Sale of real estate to them will be prohibited, as will be sale of any domestic goods and services (including financial services). No regime-controlled businesses will be permitted to list on enacting-country stock exchanges, and no inward investment will be permitted from the wealth funds of disqualified countries.
- The Act declares all judicial venues of the home jurisdiction closed to the actors in a disqualified country who control the country's resources. Any resource contracts to which these actors are party will be unenforceable in home-country courts.[3]

These policies are dramatic. Ending imports from traditional suppliers will be a significant change. Resource-enriched regime members will protest the loss of access to countries where they get their "face"—and even more the loss of opportunities to keep resource revenues safe by investing them in stable democracies. Some regimes might retaliate by selling off their existing investments in countries that adopt the Act, or by ending their purchases of military hardware and dialing down their foreign policy cooperation.

Yet a Clean Trade Act is less dramatic than more familiar foreign policy options. A country passing this Act will be changing its own laws, enforced on its own soil, regarding its own terms of trade. Not a single bomber or soldier need be sent abroad to implement these policies.

Moreover, a Clean Trade Act does not challenge the right of any regime to rule its country. An enacting state need say nothing about the legitimacy of foreign leaders, and need make no changes in the list of states receiving its diplomatic recognition.

This was discussed in Chapter 7. Political recognition and commercial relations are distinct, and passing a Clean Trade Act only alters commercial relations. Leaders of a Clean Trade country can say that who holds the presidency of a resource-exporting country is "none of our business," while also saying that today its president qualifies for "none of our business."

Bright-Line Metrics

A state or states passing a Clean Trade Act will implement it with rules-based standards for identifying countries where the conditions for public accountability are not met. Reliable, robust, and bright-line standards are essential so that exporting states can understand how to end or avoid disqualification. They are also important for firms and funds that need predictability for their long-term investment decisions.

Standards of qualification for resource trade can be set by metrics of governance that evaluate civil liberties and political rights. A variety of respected metrics already exist, including the World Bank/Brookings Institution Worldwide Governance Indicators, the Resource Governance Index, the Transparency International Corruption Perceptions Index, the Fund for Peace Fragile States Index, the Social Progress Index, as well as those produced by Polity, Freedom House, the *Economist*, and so on. To minimize bias and to protect against political pressures, a transparent "index of indices" should be agreed among Clean Trade states. Such composite indices are already in use (for example, by the United States, to draw bright lines for countries to qualify for development aid).[4]

Illustration of a Clean Trade Act

Solely for illustration, we can use a single index to draw bright lines: the index from Freedom House, an independent NGO established in 1941 by Eleanor Roosevelt and Republican presidential candidate Wendell Willkie. Since 1973, the organization has published *Freedom in the World*, an annual evaluation of civil liberties and political rights in countries around the world. This index identifies countries as "Free," "Partly Free," and "Not Free" according to the civil liberties and political rights actually enjoyed by individuals. Freedom House's "Not Free" countries can be taken as those in which the minimal conditions for popular resource sovereignty are not met.

Here are the "Not Free" resource-dependent exporters at the time of this writing: Algeria, Angola, Azerbaijan, Bahrain, Brunei, Cameroon, Chad, DRC, Equatorial Guinea, Gabon, Iran, Iraq, Kazakhstan, Oman, Qatar, Republic of Congo, Russia, Saudi Arabia, South Sudan, Sudan, Syria, Turkmenistan, UAE, Uzbekistan, Vietnam, Yemen, and Zimbabwe.

A Clean Trade country will disengage commercially from resource vendors in all of these countries. Yet it need not disengage from all at once. To take the United States as the example, it would be too politically and economically disruptive to stop oil imports from all of these countries overnight. In 2014, these countries accounted for about one-eighth of US oil consumption—a significant (if declining) share—and several of these countries are geostrategically important as well.[5] A Clean Trade Act should instead be set to taper off engagement with "Not Free" exporters, and in a way that encourages them to rise out of that category.

There are many options for tapering. An ultraminimal Act could disqualify only one minor, "worst of the worst" regime, such as the one in Equatorial Guinea, while leaving further disqualifications open to later decision. A more committed Clean Trade Act would disqualify any country that remains "Not Free" after a certain number of years (say, five years).

Another way to taper would be to link disqualification to a country's current share of imports. To take the United States and oil, tapering could, for example, allow one year for every one percent of US oil consumption on the date the Clean Trade Act is passed. This would give Saudi Arabia, which supplies six percent of US consumption, six years before disqualification.[6] Angola's window would be one year, while a supplier like Equatorial Guinea would be disqualified immediately or within a matter of months. Any exporter that rises out of the "Not Free" category during the tapering period will not be disqualified. And even after disqualification, any exporter that rises to "Partly Free" or "Free" will be commercially re-engaged.

Popular Support

Leadership from many sources will be critical for passing a Clean Trade Act, and especially to explain publicly why it is wise and right to get out of business with the authoritarians and militias who are empowered by resource revenues. Ultimately, citizens themselves will be decisive in driving policy change. As with the end of the Atlantic slave trade discussed earlier, only a determined citizenry can ensure that a major transition in trade policy will be sustained. Citizens can vote, pressure their representatives, support advocacy organizations, circulate petitions, and educate others through conversations at work, school, and online. Citizens can also take advantage of their personal opportunities and skills; the key will be for everyone to do what they do best.

For example, citizen action can encourage corporations to support Clean Trade by putting pressure on firms' reputations and access to capital:

- Investors in mutual funds can tell their funds to "Make my portfolio Clean Trade"—to replace companies that operate in disqualified countries with companies that do not, while maintaining the portfolio's risk profile.[7]
- Those enrolled in institutional pension funds have even more leverage over firms' access to capital. One model is the "Investors Against Genocide" campaign that convinced TIAA-CREF, which at the time had $400 billion under management, to divest from firms operating in Sudan.[8]

Could even major oil companies be persuaded to take a neutral, or a positive, posture toward a Clean Trade Act? The Clean Hands Oil Company Index (CHOCIX) has been developed for Clean Trade by the industry analyst Laurent Ruseckas (it is available on the Clean Trade website).[9] The CHOCIX scores the major oil companies on how much public accountability there is in the countries where they produce oil. Firms that do more business with authoritarian regimes and in failed states score lower on the CHOCIX; firms that do more business in countries that respect popular resource sovereignty score higher.

Investors can use the CHOCIX to bring pressure onto the oil majors that score lowest. And drivers can use the CHOCIX to buy gasoline from the stations of higher-scoring companies—while using social media to tell the lower-scoring companies with stations nearby that they just lost business. Oil companies can respond to this investor and driver pressure by staying out of authoritarian and failed countries and by working to improve governance in the countries where they operate. Oil companies can also reduce their competitive pressure to operate in the most resource-disordered locations by supporting a Clean Trade Act, which will level the playing field by keeping all home-listed firms from doing business in disqualified countries.

Citizens are endlessly inventive in coming up with ideas to drive progress. Students might create Clean Trade divestment campaigns (compare today's "Fossil Free").[10] Frequent fliers might organize "Clean Trade offsets," where air passengers donate money equal to the stolen oil used in their flights to the campaign for a Clean Trade Act. Lawyers might bring suits against oil companies for transporting stolen petroleum into the home jurisdiction.[11] The best ideas will come from citizens themselves, convinced of the need for change.

ENFORCING PROPERTY RIGHTS: RELATIONS WITH TRADE PARTNERS

By passing a Clean Trade Act, a country will get itself out of business with vendors of stolen resources. The people of a country adopting the Act will end their complicity with bad actors—and reduce their own resource curse—by blocking direct imports of tainted goods.

Still, even if some countries enact a Clean Trade Act, others may not. And the authoritarians and militias will still sell the stolen resources elsewhere. We see this already. The United States has had oil sanctions on Sudan for years, but this has meant that Sudan's oil has gone to Asia instead, and Asian money has been more than sufficient to keep the authoritarian Bashir in power even after his indictment for genocide and the loss of South Sudan.

If all of the countries in the West simply stopped buying oil from authoritarians, the authoritarians would then sell that oil to China and other Asian countries. We would see an "Asian-authoritarian embrace." The authoritarians would remain in power, and the Clean Trade countries would still be tainted with stolen oil—when they import Asian goods (it will be hard to know which) that are made from or with that oil. So the resource disorders would continue in the exporting countries, the West would still be affected by the instability and extremism that emanates from resource-diseased countries (though less so), and the West's hands would still be dirty (though again, less so).

Clean Trade countries need to go beyond their own commercial disengagement to encourage their trade partners also to stop buying stolen resources. The challenge here is substantial. The Chinese state, for instance, is responsible for hundreds of millions of people who are extremely poor and who want to pull themselves up to a decent standard of living. China also has a rising middle class that demands ever more prosperity. Chinese leaders will at first be suspicious of any suggestion that they should cut off the resource imports on which they rightly believe their growth depends. And clearly, it would be mad to try to "make" the Chinese enact a Clean Trade Act, either through military action or sanctions.

What the West needs are tools to persuade China to reconsider its long-term plan—it needs policies that shift China's economic incentives and that take a consistent, hard-to-resist stand on principle. We look at some such tools now. Whether the West will ever need to use these tools—and indeed, whether the Chinese will in the end need to change their resource suppliers—we will discuss in the *Strategy* section. The tools must first be shown to be sturdy, so that (like police handcuffs) they can influence behavior just by being displayed.

These tools are, again, measures to enforce property rights. They work by encouraging trade partners to respect property rights, the fundamental rights of any genuine market order.

Clean Hands Trusts

The first tool is Clean Hands Trusts. Any country that passes a Clean Trade Act can set up these trusts to protect the property rights of the peoples whose resources are being stolen. The idea is illustrated with a US Clean Hands Trust for Equatorial Guinea.

As we've seen, Equatorial Guinea is an oil-rich African country dominated since 1979 by its authoritarian president Teodoro Obiang. Obiang's regime allows no significant political opposition, press freedom, or judicial independence. International observers have reported many cases of detention, torture, and extrajudicial killing of political opponents. Obiang's sales of Equatorial Guinea's oil are entirely beyond the control of the country's citizens, who have no means to "freely dispose of their natural wealth and resources." This means that Obiang's regime cannot be a legitimate vendor of the country's resources.

Passing a Clean Trade Act will not in itself improve the situation in Equatorial Guinea. The United States now buys little, if any, oil from Obiang, and in any case, Obiang would just sell to China instead (as he is already doing). The resource diseases in Equatorial Guinea would continue. Moreover, as the Equatorial Guinea-Chinese sales went through, American consumers would continue to pay for this stolen oil because of America's trade with China. The stolen oil would percolate through the Chinese economy and so become a factor in producing goods exported from China to the United States. Even after the United States had blocked direct deals with Obiang's regime, American shoppers would still end up paying for Equatorial Guinea's stolen oil when buying Chinese-made electronics, clothing, and toys.

With a Clean Hands Trust, the US government can treat Obiang's shipments of oil to China as what they are: the passing of stolen goods. Say, for example, that China buys $3 billion worth of oil from Obiang. The US government's response will be to establish a Clean Hands Trust for Equatorial Guinea. This trust is a bank account that the US government will fill until it contains $3 billion. The money to fill the trust will come from duties on Chinese imports as they enter the United States. The $3 billion in this trust will then be held for the citizens of Equatorial Guinea, the owners of the stolen assets, until a minimally accountable government is in place there.

This Clean Hands Trust will protect the American people from the taint of the stolen oil that China buys from Obiang. The duties will extract from Chinese imports the value of the oil taken from Equatorial Guinea, and the trust will hold this money until it can be returned to Equatorial Guinea's citizens. With the duties in place, American consumers can buy Chinese imports with clean hands because the duties subtract from those imports the value of the oil stolen by Obiang's regime. And with the duties in place, the Chinese will have an economic incentive not to buy more oil from Obiang. If China buys another $1 billion worth of oil, the United States will impose another $1 billion worth of duties on its goods. The people of Equatorial Guinea, for their part, will know that a large sum of money is waiting to be turned over to them if they can replace the regime that is stealing their assets. Everyone within and outside of the country (and even Obiang) will have an economic incentive to improve governance in Equatorial Guinea.

Clean Hands Trusts can be opened by several countries at once. Any state that passes a Clean Trade Act may set up a Clean Hands Trust once the Chinese buy from Obiang. Each state that creates such a trust will then regularly update its public report of how much money its trust is holding. All governments will stop filling their trusts once the combined global total of the trusts equals the value of the Chinese purchase ($3 billion). This gives the "clean" countries a competitive incentive to announce and fill their trusts as quickly as possible while limiting the duties on the Chinese to the value of the stolen goods they have imported.

Enforcing property rights is hard on those who make their living by violating those rights, and it changes the incentives of those who do business with the violators. A Clean Hands Trust can be set up for the people of any disqualified country—that is, for any country where the people cannot control their natural assets. There are questions still to be answered about these trusts, of course—how to return the money in the trust to the people, for instance.[12] We leave these for now to discuss further tools to encourage trade partners to respect property rights over resources.[13]

Popular Campaigns

At the turn of the nineteenth century, the British elite began to face determined popular protests against the Atlantic slave trade. One pro-slavery Member of Parliament, contemplating these protests, conceded that the slave trade "was not an amiable trade." Still, he said, "neither was the trade of a butcher an amiable trade, and yet a mutton chop was nevertheless a very good thing."[14]

Some foreign leaders might similarly be inclined to concede that today's trade in stolen resources is not an "amiable" trade. And yet, they might think, cheap resource imports are nevertheless a very good thing. The Chinese leadership, for example, might at first be disinclined to support measures to enforce the rights of peoples in exporting countries. In the nineteenth century, abolitionist boycotts of "slave sugar" were pivotal in changing the minds of the British elite. Today, public campaigns can help to convince foreign elites to end their complicity in resource theft.

Boycotting all Chinese goods would be infeasible, disproportionate, and unnecessary. (Even while the British abolitionists boycotted slave-grown sugar, they did not target slave-grown coffee or cotton.) Action should be consequential enough that the Chinese cannot ignore it, and it should make the point of principle in compelling ways. In the spirit of "all do what they do best," citizens of Clean Trade countries can lead different kinds of boycotts. The best ideas will again come from creative people with conviction; here are a few possibilities:

- *The Baby Boycott:* New parents can resolve not to buy "Made in China" clothes or food for their babies. The campaign encourages parents to show solidarity with the parents of newborns in resource-disordered countries that suffer from authoritarianism, civil war, and corruption. Parents can encourage each other not to clothe or feed their babies with products tainted by stolen raw materials.
- *The Toycott:* Plastic toys are made almost entirely from hydrocarbons—and parents should not let their children play with stolen goods. A widespread toycott has the potential to focus China's attention. "Toys and Sporting Goods" is the fourth-largest category of Chinese imports to the United States, worth tens of billions of dollars a year.[15]
- *The Washed Clean Campaign:* Many personal care products, such as soaps, shampoos, and lotions, are scented with fragrances made from petroleum. A campaign against using Chinese-made personal care products can encourage consumers not to clean up with dirty oil. Celebrities and young people can wear "Washed Clean" clothing and accessories to show their commitment.[16]

Boycotts work by combining economics with ideals—they show that consumers are willing to sustain costs to take a stand on principle. The consumer boycott on blood diamonds, for instance, drove reforms in the international diamond trade. And such campaigns need not be only negative: after the blood diamonds movement began, jewelry companies sprang up offering ethically sourced gems.[17] (Similarly, one can now buy a good conflict-free smartphone.[18]) Positively marked Clean Trade products will take Fair Trade to a deeper level and empower the public to support genuine trade over theft worldwide.

QUESTIONS AND ANSWERS

So far we have laid out some of the tools of the Clean Trade framework. Plans for using these tools are to come. Before getting to strategy, however, we can quickly look at the questions that are most frequently asked about these tools.[19]

Measuring Freedom

The Clean Trade policies will rely on metrics to identify the countries where the people cannot approve resource sales. A lot of weight will be put on these metrics—the scores will have significant implications for trade, investment, and relations between states. Are these metrics really up to the job? And wouldn't political and commercial pressures be put on the authors of these metrics to raise or lower certain countries' scores?[20]

Every importer must use some standard or other to determine who it has the right to buy resources from. The standard that countries use today is "whoever is in coercive control over resource-rich territory." Our "metric" today is "might makes right," and we can do better than that.

Clean Trade will rely on metrics like those listed above because the organizations that produce them are insulated from external pressures. The alternative is to leave disqualification to politicians, which is risky. Letting the US State Department or the UK Foreign Office decide which states qualify for resource trade would leave the policies hostage to short-term strategic thinking—and to foreign complaints of coercive political manipulation. The success of the framework requires building trust wherever possible. Fortunately, the independent metrics that are available have established track records that will make any deviations from trend easier to detect. They tend to reach similar conclusions, and as mentioned earlier, an "index of indices" can be constructed that cancels out their biases.[21] For Clean Trade, only those indices whose data and methods are open to public scrutiny should be included.

Could countries wanting to go Clean Trade ever agree with each other on a common set of metrics? Yes. Even large groups of countries like the OECD have already shown they can do so in other areas.[22] And the enormous economic pressure to establish a predictable system of trade rules will incentivize countries to reach a sensible agreement on metrics for resource sales.[23]

Any standards that draw a bright line on a spectrum can be challenged. Yet consider an analogy. The question of whether a people is in sufficiently good conditions to approve resource transfers is structurally similar to the question of whether a woman is in sufficiently good conditions to consent to sex. The relevant conditions (like "degree of intoxication" and "degree of developmental impairment") will be along spectrums that range from "none" to "extreme." Simply because these are spectrums—and because it is sometimes hard for outsiders to know where a woman was along these spectrums—does not mean that society should avoid laws on rape, nor that the clearest and worst cases of rape should be ignored.

Rather, the law should set bright-line standards for sexual consent, and the justice system should prosecute violations firmly and consistently. Drawing bright lines on a spectrum is much better than having no lines at all, which is today's standard for resource sales. Effectiveness is like having no laws against forced sex: states today say that coercive actors in resource-rich countries may take what they will. If the bright lines for sexual consent have any residual ambiguity, then prudent men will stay well clear of the danger zone—and similarly for resource vendors under the reformed rules for the resource trade. Any state wanting to sell off a country's resources should keep its country well clear of the zone of disqualification.

This last point highlights that bright-line standards will have positive effects above the line as well as below it. A leader with authoritarian tendencies will be less tempted to curtail political liberties and civil rights if this will drive his country into the zone of disqualification. Potential rebels will be less likely to seize resources to fund a rebellion if doing so will result in those revenues being shut off. Bright lines will incentivize everyone to make governance better in resource-rich countries.

Interference in Internal Affairs

A different kind of question is whether implementing a Clean Trade Act would wrongly interfere with the internal affairs of sovereign states. Clean Trade countries will, after all, be judging which foreign countries are governed well enough to trade with. The Chinese authorities have been particularly energetic in invoking the rule of "non-interference in internal affairs." Could they use it to object to the policies above?

We first met the international "non-interference" rule in Chapter 9, at the origin of the Westphalian international system around 1648. Recall that during Westphalia, almost nothing a sovereign could do to his people could license interference by another sovereign. Countries were "black boxes" to each other, and inside these boxes, rulers could abuse and neglect the ruled to almost any extent without legal consequences.

The modern international system has modified this old Westphalian rule, especially with human rights. Human rights now set limits on what regimes may rightly do inside their borders, and outsiders are now allowed—even required—to take action when a regime violates human rights. Popular resource sovereignty is a human right. It is repeatedly affirmed in major human rights treaties to which countries (including China) that hold 98 percent of the world's population are already party. Leaders of Clean Trade countries can say that their new trade policy is required to uphold a human right, in the violation of which their countries no longer wish to be complicit. International action to support popular resource sovereignty is, at the least, justifiable "interference" to protect human rights.

And would Clean Trade really be interference at all? The Chinese have been generous in characterizing other countries' actions as "interference." For example, the Chinese have complained about Western "interference" in their internal affairs when:

- The United States called for the Tiananmen Square demonstrators to be released from prison.
- The United States criticized a state crackdown on a religious group.
- The United States released a report on Chinese human rights violations.
- The United States released a report on China's military capacities.
- The President of the United States met the Dalai Lama.
- The Norwegian Nobel Committee awarded the Peace Prize to a Chinese citizen.[24]

Which of these things is genuinely an "interference in internal affairs"?

What counts as "interference" depends on what is the right expectation. Take an analogy to what counts as "good health" and what counts as "disease." In 1851 a certain Dr Samuel Cartwright reported in the *New Orleans Medical and Surgical Journal* that he had discovered a new disease in local slaves. He called it "drapetomania"—an addiction to running away from one's master.[25] If slavery was the right expectation, then repeatedly running away could be thought of as pathological. As with "disease," what counts as "interference" depends on what is the proper course of events—which can be controversial. As Abraham Lincoln said, "The shepherd drives the wolf from the sheep's throat, for which the sheep thanks the shepherd as his liberator, while the wolf denounces him for the same act as the destroyer of liberty... Plainly the sheep and the wolf are not agreed upon a definition of the word liberty."[26]

Whatever decisions Western countries make on trade will have major implications for foreigners. Would a Clean Trade nation be "interfering in the internal affairs" of a country whose regime it stopped buying resources from? Say you've been shopping at a neighborhood grocery store for years. Now you decide to stop after discovering that the owner donates to racist political parties. Does your decision to stop shopping with him interfere with his business?

It is true that when you stop buying from the grocer, you will be judging him. But then you were judging him before—you were judging that he was all right to do business with. There is no action without judgment; you are just changing your judgment. The grocer could only charge you with "interference" if he had a right that you shop with him. And similarly with regimes in disqualified countries: these regimes could only charge a Clean Trade country with interference if they have a right that other countries buy resources from them. Holding World Trade Organization (WTO) issues aside for the moment, there is clearly no such right. "Free trade" includes "free not to trade." The grocer has no right that you shop at his store; no regime has a right that other countries buy resources from it. No one thinks, for example, that sanctions on the Sudanese regime violate Sudan's "right to be traded with."

The Chinese might pull back from a strict charge of "interference" and instead make a weaker charge of "political meddling." Powerful states, they might say, that decide not to trade with weaker states exert wrongful pressure on the weaker states' politics: this is imperialism by another means. In contrast, the Chinese leadership may advertise its own trade policy as "no politics—just business." The Chinese may praise their own trade as coming with "no political strings attached."[27]

It would be dark humor for any country with an effectiveness-based trade policy to charge a Clean Trade country with "political meddling." For translate a Chinese "just business" claim into plain English:

> *Today, we choose to take Equatorial Guinea's oil. In exchange, we choose to give hundreds of millions of dollars to a brutal dictator, knowing that the money will help him to keep power by paying for soldiers and secret police and torture chambers for political prisoners. However, if mercenaries are tempted by our money and can assassinate Obiang*

tomorrow, we will buy oil from whoever hired the mercenaries and assumes the presidency. We are not meddling in the politics of Equatorial Guinea. It is those who buy no oil who are meddling.

This is not compelling. There is no action without judgment, and buying resources means making a political judgment on who ultimately owns those resources. It is countries that send large sums to "whoever can be most coercive" that are interfering in the internal affairs of other nations and meddling in their politics. Countries that refuse to send large sums to authoritarians and militias are the ones that are not interfering, not meddling. And this point applies not only to the Chinese. After all, today all countries choose effectiveness to decide from whom to buy foreign natural resources.

The WTO

Wouldn't Clean Trade policies violate WTO rules? Those rules require that WTO members not discriminate against the goods of other members—and discriminating against the resources of authoritarian and failed member states is what Clean Trade policies do.

Leading WTO scholar Lorand Bartels has detailed how Clean Trade is compatible with WTO rules.[28] Here we only note that WTO rules apply to trade, not to stolen goods. Clean Trade does not restrict free trade—rather, it enables free trade by enforcing property rights.

Again, there is no action without judgment, and to rule against a Clean Trade country, the WTO would have to make some quite challenging judgments. To rule against Clean Trade, the WTO would have to affirm that violence creates property rights: that seizing a country's political capital should gain the right to sell off its natural capital. It would also need to insist that countries must trade even in violation of their own most settled principles of public morals, such as the principle of popular sovereignty. The WTO would need to insist, that is, that countries must buy goods that they regard as stolen.[29]

Clean Trade goes to the heart of who has the right to sell property. It is thus more internal to the trade system than, for example, proposals based on environmental or animal welfare concerns. And the principles of Clean Trade are much deeper than the grounds that disqualified countries or their trade partners could offer in support of retaliatory measures. Clean Trade is WTO-compatible; retaliatory action is not.

Bad Effects on Disqualified Countries

Some questions about Clean Trade policies are about their effects. Clean Trade policies will, for example, greatly reduce the funds going into countries like Equatorial Guinea, where there are many poor people. So wouldn't the policies be bad for these countries' citizens, who will not only be tyrannized but will also be more destitute as well?[30]

Those wondering this might remember Part I—the analysis of the resource diseases. When the resource diseases set in, the money from resource sales strengthens authoritarian rulers, raises the dangers of civil war, and empowers corrupt officials. The money works to lock the people into their fate, and this is apparent in the cases we have seen. Life was bad enough for people in Equatorial Guinea before oil, when they were poor and oppressed by a megalomaniacal despot. Now that Obiang can sell off their oil, the people are poor and oppressed by a megalomaniacal despot who has hundreds of millions more dollars with which to cement his personal hold on power. Worse, much of the country's natural "trust fund" has now been drained away and spent beyond the people's control. They are still in poverty, but now their country is itself much poorer.

What of failed states like the DRC? As Jason Stearns says, "Since the 1970s the Congolese state has not had an effective army, administration or judiciary, nor have its leaders been interested in creating strong institutions. Instead they have seen the state apparatus as a threat, to be kept weak."[31] Indeed, the Congolese state has now failed so completely that in 2013, two seasoned Africa experts concluded "the Democratic Republic of Congo does not exist."[32] Here the power that needs countering is not that of an overmighty state, but rather the power of militiamen—backed by the state, or backed by neighboring states, or freelance—who use mining revenues to prey on the people across large, lawless regions.

When discussing policies toward the DRC, expectations must be moderate. The country has been a mess for decades, and progress will require hard work on many fronts for many years. The key for resource exports is to find policy that will reverse the incentives of "might makes right," which the Clean Trade policies do.

To see how Clean Trade reverses incentives, picture the day when all importing states have adopted its policies. On that day, the main players in Congolese politics will have real incentives to improve the country's governance. Resource revenues will only flow to Congolese leaders—and to the elites of "involved" neighboring states, like Rwanda and Uganda—once the Congolese state can protect the basic civil liberties and political rights of all its citizens. Natural resources will only flow to manufacturing and consuming countries when the Congolese state is sufficiently competent and accountable. And the people in all regions of the Congo will have reason to unite in supporting governance that will secure their common rights. Greater popular control over resources has the potential—along with other conditions, like basic security and the rule of law—to unite citizens across their divided identities.

Progress in the Congo is already encouraging. Backed by determined public pressure in the West, a range of tracing, transparency, and certification initiatives have reduced the money that militias now get for selling stolen minerals. This, along with better peacekeeping, has contributed to reductions in armed conflict in the DRC.[33] A recent American law requiring that firms perform due diligence in their supply chains was a significant step forward (though again by no means sufficient).[34] If these positive trends continue, the Congo will no longer host "The World's Worst War." And the progress so far suggests that reducing the resource revenues of armed groups can help the people take greater control of their country.

Bad Effects on the Poor Elsewhere

Even if Clean Trade policies are good for the people of exporting countries, might they be bad for the poor elsewhere? After all, blocking raw material exports may raise prices for consumers here, and some consumers here are struggling. And putting duties on Chinese exports to fill a Clean Hands Trust might hurt workers in Chinese industries too. When the idea of a US Clean Hands Trust for Sudan was presented at a conference in Beijing, one prominent Chinese intellectual asked politely, "How many people are there in Sudan?" On being informed that there are about 40 million, he said, "Ah, but there are 1.3 billion Chinese—and many of them are very poor."[35]

It may be that choosing no longer to buy coercively extracted resources will make some consumers and workers worse off. But this would be for just the same reason that buying a car from a dealer's showroom costs more than buying one from carjackers. It is sometimes possible to become better off by stealing, or by buying what someone else has stolen. This does not justify doing so.

Let's pause to reflect. If assets really do have to be stolen for the sake of consumers here or workers in China, are the impoverished and oppressed people of Sudan and other resource-diseased countries the most suitable victims? Why not steal the assets of the rich here (or of the rich in China) instead?

No one's property should be stolen for the sake of the prosperity of others. In a sound market economy, prosperity comes from mutually advantageous trades based on secure property rights. Peoples have rights, and there are things no one may do to them without violating their rights.[36] If consumers and workers face costs during a transition away from trade in stolen resources, then their national leaders should look for policies that will avert those costs or compensate for them.

Are the People Ready?

By using the Clean Trade policy tools described above, countries will be shaping their own laws to open space for the peoples of exporting countries to gain more power over their resources. And "power to the people" is such a compelling principle. Still, some may have concerns. Power really is power, and some peoples in exporting countries seem ill-prepared to use power responsibly—in ways that are safe for us or that are even good for themselves. Perhaps some peoples are just not yet ready to handle the power of popular resource sovereignty. For example (as a skeptical Egyptian columnist recently asked), can the Arab peoples really be relied on to make good decisions?[37]

We might be circumspect with this concern. During the twentieth century, in country after country, even poor and ill-educated peoples threw off colonial or authoritarian rule and established stable self-government. Before these transitions, the people (for example) of India, South Korea, Taiwan, Argentina, Chile, and South Africa looked "unready" to handle political power. Even in Europe not so long ago (when ABBA and Elton John were topping the charts), both Spain and Portugal were poor countries dominated by long-ruling autocrats who were supported by a reactionary religious elite. Today, all of these countries are consolidated constitutional democracies.

And yet, even those who grant past successes may be nervous about today. Recall the discussion of Saudi Arabia in Chapter 6. The Saudi people are today divided by tribal affiliations and by fissile Sunni-Shia relations. Ordinary Saudi citizens have no history of cooperation in civil society and no active political experience. Most have been immersed in an extreme fundamentalist and anti-democratic ideology for their entire lives. In fact, it is possible that the Saudi political leadership is somewhat less reactionary than the average Saudi citizen. On full consideration, do we want to take a chance on the Saudi people?

One way or another, we may have no choice. Saudi Arabia is a balloon filled with trouble (and many of its troubles are common to the other Gulf monarchies, which are at least as likely to destabilize). So far, Saudi Arabia has only leaked trouble, spreading extremism and funding jihadi Salafists worldwide. Unlike Iran and Iraq, this third balloon has not yet burst. Even so, when we wake up tomorrow, we will need to have a policy toward the country. We can continue the policy that has helped create today's explosive situation, empowering an exceptionally repressive absolute monarchy that relies on a medieval ideology for its legitimacy, through a coming era in Saudi Arabia that will see a restless young population, increasingly unbalanced finances, an unstructured generational transfer of leadership, and sectarian discord within the country and the region (as in Iraq and Bahrain). Alternatively, we can begin a policy that aims, slowly and deliberately, to let the air out of the balloon.

It would be imprudent for the West to continue commercial engagement with the Saudi authoritarians forever. Yet it would be equally imprudent for that regime to be delegitimized all at once. A sudden power vacuum in the country would be highly destabilizing for global markets. And a monarchical overthrow would be dangerously disorienting for Saudis. We can recall that despite all the divisiveness of their reigns, Saddam Hussein and Muammar Gaddafi represented their own persons as the embodiments of their respective states (*l'état c'est lui*). When these two autocrats met their bitter ends, it looked like a delegitimization of the entire national project. No one should look forward to a day when the Saudi king is dragged from a spider hole or a sewer pipe; on that day, the Saudi people would not even know their country's name.

Clean Trade does not deny any regime's right to rule. It is a declared and deliberate tapering off of resource purchases from regimes that remain authoritarian. Announcing these policies will embolden the movements, present in all countries, that favor a gradual transition to greater popular sovereignty.[38] A new generation of princes is now contending for Saudi leadership; the West's policies can encourage those who are favorable to the aspirations of Saudi youth and to a gradual opening up of political space.

The people need to develop out of their enforced political disability to become responsible actors on the world stage; outsiders can assist by treating them as equals already.[39]

Friends of liberty may look forward to the day when Saudi Arabia becomes the Arabian Republic (al-Jumhūriyyah al-ʿArabiyyah).[40] The question is how to help create conditions for positive change instead of maintaining "might makes right"—and praying that there will be no explosion tomorrow. The country is now kinetic with divisiveness, both within and across its borders, not least because of the financial energy we have overfilled it with. As far as changing our policies toward Saudi Arabia and other resource-disordered exporters, we are damned if we don't. A final question is whether we are also damned if we do.

Will We Have Enough Energy?

A country or region that adopts Clean Trade will be announcing that it plans to taper off supplies from some of the world's largest energy repositories. Is this realistic? Where will our energy come from?[41]

North America and Europe can safely transition away from authoritarian oil and gas (we now split these out). In fact, this will not be excessively difficult. Oil and gas are global markets. Should demand shift, supply will shift to meet it. The physical transition (like building pipelines and adapting refineries) is simple engineering. The real issue is economics, and looking at the economics shows feasible paths forward.

Nick Butler, the energy columnist for the *Financial Times*, was asked to evaluate the time and cost of North American and European transitions away from authoritarian oil and gas.[42] (The authoritarian countries were those listed above.) Butler concluded that North America imports would present few problems: these could be switched away from authoritarian oil and gas in a matter of months. Europe could also make a quick transition for its oil. In these cases, imports could easily be substituted on the open trading market, while the oil excluded from Europe and North America could find ready buyers elsewhere.

The hardest part of a transition will be European gas, because parts of Europe currently are heavily dependent on Russia for supply through pipelines. Even here, Butler predicted that supplies could adjust within a few years. Norway and other non-authoritarian countries would boost production, new pipelines would be laid, the European gas grid would be joined up, and more use would be made of underutilized import capacity for liquefied natural gas. Moreover, the cost of these changes would be manageable.

Indeed, Butler thought the problem with the transition was not that it would be too costly but that it would be ineffectual. It would merely speed up an "Asian-authoritarian embrace"—with Russia developing its trade to the East and through Turkey—and so would have little effect on the authoritarians. This is a point we will return to in the *Strategy* section.

Other analysts may differ on the specifics of timing and costs, but not with the overall thrust. For each analyst, there will be some number of months (call it M) over which North America and Europe can transition away from authoritarian oil and gas at a reasonable cost. The consensus range for M then sets the time frame over which these two regions can make the transition. The main message is that this time frame will not be excessive. North America and Europe will have enough energy even without the authoritarians.

GREEN TRADE

Garrett Hardin's classic article "The Tragedy of the Commons" identifies a class of particularly difficult problems in which the short-term rationality of each actor leaves all worse off.[43] For example, it is rational for each herdsman to graze more animals on the commons, but then all herdsmen become poorer as the commons are overgrazed. It is rational for each parent to have more children (Hardin's focal problem), but then all suffer in an overpopulated world. It is rational for each person to "free ride," but a system of free riders crashes.

The problem of climate change has this structure. It is rational for each nation to emit more carbon, but a world of higher emissions eventually leaves all worse off. The "commons" here is the absorptive capacity of the Earth's atmosphere, which is being substantially overburdened. Fossil fuels are a primary cause: all nations should reduce their use, yet it is rational for each to resist reforms. Call it the Tragedy of the Carbons.[44]

The subtitle of Hardin's essay is sometimes forgotten: "The population problem has no technical solution; it requires a fundamental extension in morality." By "morality," Hardin did not mean "the rules of conscience" but rather collective action to enforce common rules. Since collective action is quite difficult at the international level, enforcing (even formulating) common rules on climate has proved difficult.[45] The principles that guide Clean Trade, such as popular sovereignty and property rights, are already well understood and widely endorsed. Can Clean Trade be part of the solution to this particularly difficult problem?

Climate change is a set of highly complex issues with their own dynamics. Clean Trade is compatible with any responsible long-term plan to address these issues. While Clean Trade is not the solution to the Tragedy of the Carbons, it can become part of the solution by adding momentum toward collective action with two of its own lines of reasoning. The first adds immediate emphasis to the imperative to leave hydrocarbons in the ground. The second sets precise, significant, and independently justified targets for import-dependent regions to reduce their use of fossil fuels.

First, Intergovernmental Panel on Climate Change reports have said that avoiding dangerous anthropogenic climate change will require decarbonizing energy supplies.[46] Many have interpreted these reports to mean that most of the world's fossil fuels are "stranded assets"—that they will have to be left in the ground.[47] However, the idea of stranded assets has not so far gained traction outside of the academic and activist communities. One reason is that, to anyone with a market orientation, the idea of leaving assets stranded sounds counter-intuitive, even perverse.

The idea of taking action to protect property rights, however, is familiar to all market actors. Clean Trade says that today, over half of the world's oil production, and over half of the world's oil reserves, cannot be exported without violating property rights.[48] This oil is "stranded" in the sense that no one can rightly sell it: it is stranded because it cannot be sold without passing stolen goods. On strict market principles, more than half the world's oil is right now not available to be exported at all.

Now this is an argument whose force will decay as oil-rich countries transition away from authoritarianism. Until that transition happens, however, Clean Trade offers a high-impact, market-based argument that a large proportion of the world's oil should right now be staying in the ground.

Second, Clean Trade sets reduction targets for fossil fuel importers, such as the European Union. Clean Trade offers two different plans for such importers to taper off stolen oil. In one plan, the European Union would announce "After M months, we will accept no more oil from any country which is at that point authoritarian." The climate change impact of this first plan will vary depending on how many countries remain authoritarian during and after the tapering. Alternatively, the European Union could lock in its reductions. It could calculate the percentage of oil it now imports from authoritarian countries (call it Y), and announce "After M months, we will accept no more oil from any country that is at that point authoritarian. *And* by this future date D, we will have reduced our oil use by Y."

This "locked-in" plan has a solid rationale and many advantages. It will provide welcome predictability for investors inside and beyond Europe. It will immediately stimulate investment in alternative energies, incentivizing human ingenuity to focus on the fuels of the future. And it will help Europe to overcome its internal divisions on climate by setting reductions targets that it has independent and decisive reasons to meet.[49]

How much difference would this make? In the last year for which records are available, the European Union imported just over half of its crude oil and just over a third of its natural gas from "Not Free" countries.[50] A locked-in Clean Trade plan would require reductions in oil and gas use by those amounts. These are significant targets for fossil fuel reductions in themselves. European resolve to meet these targets could also ease some of the more recalcitrant deadlocks in broader international climate negotiations.

Of course, as climate specialists will already be thinking, this entire transition path must be set so as not to increase use of coal, which produces higher emissions than the other fossils. Clean Trade can add momentum to the coal-reduction argument by showing that approximately 25 percent of today's European coal imports also violate property rights.[51] Proportionate reductions in coal use should be added to the tapering targets.[52] So overall, Clean Trade sets Europe, today, the target of reducing its use of oil by half, gas by one-third, and coal by one quarter.

The locked-in Clean Trade plan can add momentum to progress on climate by immediately nailing down specific goals that importers like Europe have strong reasons to reach. Europe has long stood for the peaceful support of popular sovereignty. It is also the "greenest" region of the developed world. Clean Trade can help to move both agendas forward together, by becoming part of a European "Authoritarians to Alternatives" plan. Clean Trade can be clean in multiple and mutually reinforcing ways.

STRATEGY

The goals of Clean Trade are constant; the strategies for using its tools will be specific. The Norwegian Prime Minister and an American ride-share group will have different opportunities to help end the global trade in stolen resources. New opportunities for advancing the goals may open with a drop in the price of oil, or with the rise of an anti-authoritarian movement in Russia. The diplomacy of explaining Clean Trade to current allies and trade partners will depend very much on the politics of the day. Here are some general notes about the strategies that will be successful.

Successful strategies for Clean Trade will welcome all to join—and will always keep the door open. Even a major oil company, even the Chinese, indeed even the head of a Persian Gulf oil state, may become receptive to these reforms sooner or later. This may seem inconceivable at first. Yet there may come a day, a crisis, or a leadership challenge when Clean Trade policy is just what these actors need. And even if they demur at first, they may join later.

Ultimately, it is the ideas that will win. The tools discussed above, like the Clean Trade Act and the boycotts and the Clean Hands Trust, bring out the issues of principle. Once the principles are on the table, those taken aback by the proposals will find themselves torn—for these are their own avowed principles too. Popular sovereignty, property rights, human rights, the rule of law, and peace are public commitments of everyone with influence on resources, except for the most incorrigible absolutists and jihadis. These ideas have already won their battles; they are already alive even inside those not yet convinced of the need for policy change. In time, the skeptics will convince themselves. The overall strategy is to act positively, and so to attract doubters to come over to their own side.

First Movers

The most natural Western first movers on Clean Trade will be countries that see themselves as moral leaders, and that are also large energy producers (and so already less dependent on authoritarian oil). Norway, for example, could do "proof of concept" by passing a Clean Trade Act tomorrow, without the slightest change in its energy mix. Norway receives zero barrels of oil from "Not Free" countries, and it will need zero barrels from them for the indefinite future.[53] (Nor will Norway need natural gas—it has its own abundant supplies, and already produces 97 percent of its electricity with hydropower.) Indeed, Norway, as the largest oil exporter in Western Europe, and the third-largest gas exporter in the world, is a natural supplier for less hydrocarbon-rich countries that want to disengage from authoritarian regimes.

Canada and Australia are also natural leaders on principled action and on resources.[54] For Britain, Clean Trade will continue the leadership it has already shown, for example, with its transparency and anti-corruption initiatives.[55] Brazil could make a powerful statement of its arrival at the highest global level by moving first. North America as a whole is also quite a plausible early adopter, as its looks like it will achieve energy independence in the medium term even without reforms.[56] Clean Trade would be an excellent foreign-policy initiative for a North American alliance.[57]

The United States can lead—as we will see in the next chapter, it has been leading already. A plan to disengage from authoritarians can be a vote-winner in domestic politics. A campaign to "End the Tyranny of Oil" could unite a strong coalition, including liberal, conservative, libertarian, and progressive groups.

A *Declaration on Trade in Natural Resources* is now available on the Clean Trade website. The declaration is available for national adoption, and for diplomats to use in discussions on details (such as metrics) in preparation for their countries to coordinate their own Clean Trade policies. The advantages of being an early adopter of this *Declaration* will come from taking global leadership, and from shaping global standards that can then be spread further.[58]

Oil-Rich Authoritarian Defectors

During the transition away from authoritarian oil, some authoritarians may themselves transition to become qualified for commercial engagement. The possibility of today's authoritarians "defecting" to greater freedom is real and should be anticipated. Russia, for example, would only have to return to being as well-governed as it was in 2004 to rise out of the "Not Free" category.[59]

And the world is full of surprises. Small, ultrarich Qatar (which we visited in Chapter 3) is the Gulf monarchy most likely to lead the Middle East to popular resource sovereignty. The ruling family of Qatar sees itself as the progressive leader of the Arab world and has repeatedly promised constitutional reforms. The family is popular enough with Qatari citizens that its rule seems unlikely to be damaged by allowing citizens to have a genuine say on the country's resource management. And the example that the Qataris could set for the region would be transformational, not least because the country, like Saudi Arabia, is officially Wahhabi.[60] Qatar could raise the trajectory of all Arab peoples, peacefully and single-handedly, with a single referendum.

The Asian Challenge

The strategic touchstones for Clean Trade are transparency, inclusiveness, and trust. Advocates say: These are our principles; we think that you support them too. We will show you why these reforms are in our long-term interests; we think that they are in yours as well. We are prepared to move first and to bear costs, to make these reforms and to build trust. It will be better for all of us—it will avoid conflict and lower everyone's costs—for us all to move together. We want to work with you to make this transition easier and quicker. We do not want to use these sticks against you—which, as you can see, will be bad for us too. But here are the sticks, so that you can predict what will come next. And even if you do not at first agree to move with us, our door will always be open.

This strategy should never presume enemies. In foreign countries and in large companies, change agents are often waiting for openings to push a new agenda. As long as advocates for reform have their policies ready to go, windows of opportunity will open—sometimes in the most unexpected places. Reformers have no permanent adversaries, only a permanent interest in moving to the next stage of history beyond Westphalia.

Questions about strategy today often cluster around China, since it may seem that China has reasons to resist Clean Trade. Skeptics will say that should the United States, for example, propose these reforms, China will play hardball with American debt and investments and dig in its heels against other international initiatives.

Yet perhaps not. For three decades, much of the legitimacy of the Chinese leadership has depended on delivering greater prosperity to the Chinese people. And for prosperity, trade talks are much better than trade wars. The Chinese people have broadly supported the national leadership during China's rise; still, as the people are becoming richer, they are also demanding more political power. China is just about to pass the threshold of average income that typically triggers demands for democratization.[61] And China—like America—is after all officially a people's republic. Both countries' constitutions are defined by popular sovereignty. (Recall the Chinese constitution's Preamble: since the revolution, "[t]he Chinese people have taken control of state power and become masters of the country."[62]) The Chinese leadership may judge it unpropitious to start a public fight against peaceful international efforts to promote popular sovereignty just as its own people are demanding a greater voice. The wiser path might be to claim leadership in the campaign for a more harmonious international society.

More deeply, in discussing China it is crucial to recall the political economy of natural resources and the analysis of different sources of power in Part I (the disagreement between Hobbes and Rousseau). Clean Trade is not about authoritarianism as such. It challenges regimes that are escaping accountability through resource revenues and that are ruling by making their people weaker. The Chinese leadership, by contrast, has for decades been following the first Asian Tigers by cultivating its internal sources of power. It has been enabling the Chinese people to become economically much stronger. This does not excuse corruption and abuse in China, but it does mean that Clean Trade contains no principled objection to China's current form of governance.

Clean Trade is by no means a Western campaign against China. Rather, it is a set of solutions for problems that the West and China face together. As it rises, China is beginning to feel its own resource curse. It is suffering from the instabilities of the global economy in which it is becoming ever more integrated, and it is becoming burdened with the risks of unreliable authoritarians and unpredictable civil conflicts in the places where it does business. China has already, for example, lost its bet on Gaddafi, and it holds the nervous position of being the largest investor in Iraq's oil.[63] As Elizabeth Economy and Michael Levi report:

> China's experience in countries where there has been a significant government transition—particularly from a friendly authoritarian to a more democratic ruling party, as in Burma—is contributing to a debate... Some Chinese business leaders, as well as NGO activists, are reassessing the trade-off between the short-term economic gain from working with unpopular authoritarian governments and the longer-term damage to China's reputation and ability to do business when those regimes fall.[64]

The Chinese leadership prides itself in planning for long-term success. Examining the West's experience with effectiveness should lead it to prefer a more solid foundation for its resource trade.

China and the West working together to manage a fundamental transition in the greater Middle East would be highly mutually advantageous. In this transition, the West could ramp down its extravagantly expensive military support for the extreme and unreliable regimes that its citizens find odious. China could preempt its greatest future vulnerability, which will be primary energy dependence on a region whose security is guaranteed by the United States. If this transition in the Middle East were combined with a long-term climate deal, Chinese and Western leaders could plausibly present themselves to their publics as having saved the world from some of its gravest threats.

The ideal would be for all the major powers to agree to move first together. Were China to commit along with the West to taper off imports of authoritarian oil, the game would be up for rent-addicted authoritarians—at least as authoritarians. They would instantly lose the future revenue streams they need to sustain their divide-and-rule regimes, and their people would have huge incentives to demand the minimally accountable governance required for resource exports to continue. These transitions might even be accomplished without regime change. The major powers could say to the Saudi king: we will be happy to continue buying oil from you, as soon as we see the signs that your people approve of your selling it. The Saudi kings (as well as other monarchs in the region) have over the years floated their own plans for transitions toward constitutions with greater civil liberties and political rights. The prospect of losing their most important markets would give them a decisive reason to take those plans off the shelf.

It is even conceivable that China will by itself be the first mover on Clean Trade in some indigenized form. (That may sound impossible, yet how many "impossible" political changes have occurred within your lifetime?) The Chinese leadership knows that to become a world-historical power, it must become a moral leader. During its rise, Britain stood for antislavery and free trade. America has stood for individual freedom and opportunity. Even with their many transgressions, the British and American "empires" were admired as they rose to world leadership, and this won them many allies and imitators.[65]

So far, China's allies have mostly been grudging or repulsive states. For its own success, China needs to champion a global vision. The "Chinese Dream" of prosperity with sustainability is one contender for this vision.[66] Green technologies, less wasteful consumption, peaceful international relations that strengthen peoples through trade—that is a vision to win China both friends and emulators. Clean Trade can help to make this distinctively Chinese dream real, especially when it is presented as the ultimate noninterventionist foreign policy.

Or perhaps this is just a dream. It may well be that China will not move first, or indeed—at first—at all. The West may need to take the lead, to push forward the principles of popular sovereignty and human rights. The harder-edged tools of the framework like the Clean Hands Trusts and boycotts may need to be deployed. These may spur action from those whose trade is disrupted, who will respond by imposing costs on those making the reforms. These costs may be substantial, and they may increase the better the tools work.[67]

In assessing the costs of Clean Trade policies, it is important to lift the discussions out of the "energy" and the "trade" silos. National leaders know that security often takes priority over these issues, and also that the costs of security are quite large. A recent academic estimate for the economic cost of America's intervention in Iraq put the figure at over $2 trillion.[68] Another study put the cost to the United States of maintaining military force in the Persian Gulf for three decades at $7 trillion.[69] Even if not precise, these are very big numbers. And these costs are just part of the degraded, no-win foreign policy environment created in large measure by the current policy of effectiveness. The costs of Clean Trade may catch our attention because we are so accustomed to paying the price for business as usual. And even Clean Trade's costs can become part of its success, since the West can gain the world's trust by showing that it really does stand by its principles.

Think again of the moral milestones of modern history that one would teach to a child: the abolition of slavery, the liberation of the colonies, the outlawing of territorial conquest, better rules for the conduct of war, demands for human rights, the ending of apartheid. All of these marked a transition away from "might makes right" in international affairs, and all of them required the bearing of costs. As we saw in the last chapter, the West should welcome the opportunity to absorb costs to continue this history. The West needs more trust, especially on resources; indeed, for its long-term success, it needs trust much more than it needs any economic or military buildup. A willingness to bear costs can change minds. Acting on principle is the best way to build trust.

OPEN DOORS

Just before becoming Prime Minister at age twenty-four, the British statesman William Pitt made a famous speech against a policy that was said to be required by necessity. "Is it not necessity," Pitt asked, "which has always been the plea of every illegal exertion of power, or exercise of oppression? Is not necessity the pretense of every usurpation? Necessity is the plea for every infringement of human freedom. It is the argument of tyrants: it is the creed of slaves."[70]

Pitt was right: necessity is always a plea made against change. One can imagine being an idealistic young reformer eighty years ago, sitting in a cold marble room in London, Paris, or Amsterdam, as a fixture of the establishment tells you that the colonies are vital to the economy, that it is simply impossible to contemplate their loss. In South Africa just eighteen months before the release of Nelson Mandela, a poll of prominent Afrikaners found most saying that black majority rule would increase communist influence and end in dictatorship.[71] Progress may appear impossible, until the day it comes.

In this chapter, we have looked at policies regarding exporting countries where citizens cannot possibly be controlling their natural resources. In the next chapter, we will turn to policies toward exporting countries where there is at least some public accountability. Again, the touchstones will be inclusiveness, transparency, and trust. The doors of reform should always be open, so that new allies can come through.

17

Clean Trade Policy II

Supporting Accountability

I will say then that I am not, nor ever have been in favor of bringing about in any way the social and political equality of the white and black races, [applause]—that I am not nor ever have been in favor of making voters or jurors of negroes, nor of qualifying them to hold office, nor to intermarry with white people; and I will say in addition to this that there is a physical difference between the white and black races which I believe will forever forbid the two races living together on terms of social and political equality.

—Abraham Lincoln, 1858[1]

In 1993, three young friends saw the resource diseases: how coercive and corrupt actors empower themselves worldwide by selling off natural resources. Since they couldn't find an NGO focused on these issues, they decided to start one themselves, in London, where they lived. They borrowed money from friends and family, stood outside of Underground stations at 5 a.m. collecting coins in cans, scraped together enough to rent a small office, and—a bit of luck—found a usable computer in the trash bin outside the door. A lawyer friend donated his time to help them fill out the legal registration papers for their new organization, which they christened "Global Witness."[2]

The resource-diseased country in the news at the time was Cambodia, where a huge international effort had not dislodged the atrocious Khmer

Rouge army from the forests along the border with Thailand. One of the three friends later said:

> The UN was brokering elections in Cambodia. It was the most expensive UN intervention ever. It was in the news quite a lot. Cambodia had been in a state of war for thirty-odd years so it was quite a big news story. We read that timber from areas controlled by the Khmer Rouge was being traded along the border. There was very scant information. We thought, well, the rain forest is being cut down, which is bad. And the money is being used to fund possibly one of the nastiest rebel organizations ever, and a war. Why doesn't somebody stop that? And we said, "Hell, why don't we?"[3]

They raised money for a year, then two of the friends set off for the Cambodia-Thailand border. They drove 2,000 hazardous miles, following every road they could, pretending they were timber buyers and talking to loggers and drivers. They took photos of trucks and shipping documents, followed up leads with multiple sources, and kept detailed records.

Then they broke the story: the Khmer Rouge was making $10 million to $20 million a month selling timber from Cambodia (where there was officially a logging ban) into Thailand (which had officially closed the border) with the connivance of top officials on both sides. Western and domestic media amplified the story—this illicit timber trade was obviously undoing the expensive international efforts to end the conflict in Cambodia. The friends showed their photos and documents to Western governments, and those governments (especially the United States) pressured Thailand to cut off the illegal timber trade. Global Witness had, incredibly, scored a victory against the Khmer Rouge.

Knowing this would not be enough; the friends kept going. The next year, they got hold of leaked documents showing that Cambodia's prime ministers had secretly sold a million cubic meters of timber to Thailand's prime minister—a deal that would have made the Khmer Rouge $90 million richer. Using the leaked documents, they published a report proving complicity throughout the highest levels of both countries' governments. International pressure grew to the tipping point: the IMF withdrew from Cambodia; Thailand really did close the border. Within eighteen months, the Khmer Rouge's remaining soldiers had defected—its army had run out of money. The courage and hard work of these three young friends had helped to defeat the Khmer Rouge.

In the years that followed, Global Witness became a counter-narrative to many of the stories of tyranny, war, and corruption that we've seen in this book. The grotesquely violent Angolan civil war (which we visited in Chapter 4) was their next investigation. The friends reported a connection that others had not seen. By buying Angolan gems, the international diamond industry was funding the right-wing rebels who were fighting the oil-fueled left-wing government, the result being a blasted countryside as well as hundreds of thousands of maimings and deaths.

In 1998 Global Witness alerted the world to blood diamonds. UN members immediately saw how diamonds were thwarting their peacekeeping efforts in Angola—and how diamonds were also enriching the RUF militias in Sierra Leone, who (as we've also seen) were using child soldiers to prosecute a campaign of killings and amputations, and who were selling some of these blood diamonds to the strongman of neighboring Liberia, Charles Taylor.

The Security Council asked Global Witness for a briefing; the UN commissioned a report. And Global Witness found the US and British governments receptive to ideas for stemming the flow of money to the rebels in the conflict zones. From this early activism a global campaign against blood diamonds began to grow. Giant diamond firms like De Beers came under increasing pressure as Western consumers became more aware of the war zones where their gems were coming from. (One executive was said to have had nightmares where De Beers' famous advertising slogan "A Diamond is Forever" was changed to "Amputation is Forever."[4])

In 2000, Global Witness led a group of NGOs promoting a fundamental reform in the international diamond trade—a certification scheme in which all rough diamonds would be bagged and tagged by exporting states, and importing states would impose legal penalties on anyone importing diamonds without a certificate. The Kimberley Process was born. (The meeting in Kimberley, South Africa, is the finale of the 2006 Leonardo DiCaprio film *Blood Diamond*.[5])

To come into force, Kimberley needed to be made law in both importing and exporting countries. Momentum built. The UN General Assembly passed a resolution supporting Kimberley. Early in 2001, Presidents Clinton and then Bush signed executive orders banning importation of rough diamonds from Sierra Leone and Liberia. The enacting legislation for the

Kimberley Process passed the US House of Representatives—but the political will was not yet there; the bill kept stalling in the Senate.

Then the window of opportunity opened. The *Washington Post* broke the story that al-Qaeda had bought Sierra Leone's blood diamonds from Charles Taylor before 9/11. Al-Qaeda had converted its cash into blood diamonds in anticipation that its bank accounts would be frozen.[6] Overnight, blood diamonds became a US national security priority. On the next vote, the bill implementing the Kimberley Process passed the House by 419-2, and then passed the Senate unanimously. Kimberley became US law in April 2003.[7] Three US congressmen nominated Global Witness for the Nobel Peace Prize.[8] Kimberley has since become law in eighty-one countries, including nearly all of the major diamond producers and importers.[9]

Global Witness grew with its success. The three friends won some more grant money, took on staff, and moved out of their one-room office into a small suite that the Body Shop Foundation lent them rent-free. They also attracted ever-more NGOs, funders, and government agencies to focus on the cash-coercion-corruption nexus around resources.

Since 2000, Global Witness has broken many of the bad-news stories we've seen in this book—and has advanced many initiatives for reform. Global Witness next teamed with Liberian activists to reveal how Charles Taylor was making large sums by selling off the country's forests (recall Taylor's Strategic Commodities Act from Chapter 7). Their sustained advocacy was successful; the Security Council imposed sanctions on Liberian timber in 2003—after which Taylor ran out of money, fled the country, and was captured and then convicted of war crimes and crimes against humanity. He is now in prison.

Moving up to the bigger global picture, Global Witness began a determined campaign for greater transparency throughout the opaque world of natural resources. They called for laws requiring extractive firms to make their payments to states public, so that citizens could learn more about the resource deals their leaders were making. In 2002 Global Witness was joined in this campaign by George Soros (a strong force for reform of the resource trade for many years). Their joint creation was a coalition called "Publish What You Pay," which was soon joined by influential NGOs such as Oxfam and Transparency International. At the same time Global Witness worked with the British government to design and (again helped by Soros) to launch the Extractive Industries Transparency Initiative (EITI). The EITI is a club that states can join when they agree to make their resource revenues public, publishing their payments from corporations for everyone to see. By 2015, the EITI had forty-eight member countries, thirty-one of which had achieved enough transparency to be compliant with its standards.[10]

In 2003, Global Witness helped Ken Silverstein of the *Los Angeles Times* to break the first big story about Obiang's money-laundering in the United States. Riggs Bank, a venerable Washington institution, was allowing Obiang to use Equatorial Guinea's oil revenues as if they were in his personal bank accounts. The US Senate opened an investigation that resulted in substantial fines on the bank. Riggs (which had been the bank of Lincoln, Grant, and Eisenhower) was exposed as having become a secret facilitator of foreign corruption. Riggs vanished as its assets were bought at a large discount by another bank.[11]

Turning to Libya, Global Witness published leaked documents showing that Gaddafi's regime kept hundreds of millions of dollars of state funds in secret accounts secured by the West's biggest financial institutions, like HSBC and Goldman Sachs. (As the prosecutor of the International Criminal Court said, "In his position of absolute authority, Gaddafi has control of vast financial resources derived, primarily, from oil revenues. Gaddafi makes no distinction between his personal assets and the resources of the country."[12]) The Libya story was part of a growing Global Witness campaign to focus attention on the murky global financial infrastructure that facilitates the theft of resource revenues by corrupt officials.

Across its many successful campaigns, Global Witness has built a reputation for resisting co-optation by the rich and powerful, and for caring more about results than its own glory. In 2011, Global Witness walked away from its most famous co-creation, the Kimberley Process. Kimberley has helped to limit diamond-fueled wars—nothing like Angola or Sierra Leone has been seen since 2003. But the Kimberley Process has itself become deadlocked, as members have been unable to agree on condemning state-sponsored violence and other human rights violations. (While the diamond industry has found a form of words to assure consumers that the gems it sells are "conflict-free," some of the stones that you see in an average jewelry shop may really be blood diamonds.[13]) So Global Witness left the Kimberley Process—and began pressuring it from the outside.

The biggest initiative that Global Witness helped to push, the EITI, raised the bar for transparency in the extractive sector and now boasts compliant countries worldwide. Still, the EITI is a voluntary scheme: resource-rich states can sign up or not, and many have not. In the first decade of this century, many thought that the next step forward—mandatory transparency requirements on the West's largest energy and mining corporations—was still many years away. Yet Global Witness and other Publish What You Pay members, supported by the savvy Revenue Watch Institute, kept preparing the ground for the next step—just in case a window of opportunity opened.[14] They worked to persuade influential members of the US Congress that opacity in the extractive industries harmed core US national interests. Led by Republican Senator Richard Lugar and Democratic Senator Ben Cardin, the powerful Senate Foreign Relations Committee published a report declaring that "[t]he 'resource curse' damages US foreign policy and humanitarian interests abroad, [and] it also negatively impacts Americans at home."[15] In 2009, Lugar introduced a bill requiring extractive industry transparency. It did not even get out of committee. Oil was strong.

Then, in 2010, the window of opportunity opened. In April, the Deepwater Horizon platform exploded off the coast of Louisiana. A silver lining of that huge spill for the campaigners was that it made oil lobbyists toxic all summer. Washington stopped returning their calls, and when they could get a message through, their only plea was for the industry's top business priority: to be allowed to resume work in the Gulf of Mexico. That summer, the industry could not fight a bill requiring it to become more transparent. The Cardin-Lugar amendment, mandating that all US-listed oil and mining companies report their payments to foreign states, was passed in July 2010. The transparency that had seemed far-off was suddenly law.[16]

The sequel to Cardin-Lugar is especially instructive on the issue of whether countries should fear moving first. Once the United States did move first, other countries moved quickly to follow in requiring transparency in their resource sectors. Norway soon adopted similar mandatory reporting requirements. The European Union passed a directive requiring all EU members to enact even stricter legislation—and the United Kingdom, France, and Germany fast-tracked their own bills into law. Canada, home to many world-leading mining firms (and with a government long resistant to regulation) enacted mandatory reporting legislation in 2015. And one Irish oil company, Tullow, has already gotten a publicity jump on the rest of the industry by disclosing all its payments to foreign governments before it was legally required to do so.[17]

The US first-mover fear turned into a first-mover advantage. By being the first big country to pass legislation, the United States was able to define the global standard and to boost its soft power through leadership. No one expected America to take the lead on regulating its oil and mining corporations—once it did, however, transparency quickly became the new normal in the West.[18]

The three friends, working with many others, have helped to change the world. Their approach has been to talk with everyone, work with anyone who will be net positive, be rigorous, keep focused, and don't let up. The Global Witness ethos is that any recognition is a resource for future campaigns. In the end, it's not about you; it's about progress. And this is, perhaps not coincidentally, the advice for good living recommended by the sages of the ages—to unify one's own life around action with others and for others.

EVERYONE HITS THE SAME TARGET

Over the past forty years, determined people have advanced dozens of initiatives that bear on the global trade in natural resources. Many of these initiatives have succeeded; others are just now making their move into the spotlight. Those pushing these initiatives have come from importing and exporting countries, civil society, government, indigenous communities, and corporations. These change agents have had quite different priorities and motivations. And while they have sometimes coordinated their campaigns, mostly they have been working on their own issues.[19]

Even without coordination, these initiatives have tended to fall into a few specific categories:

- *Anti-Corruption:* Laws, like the US Foreign Corrupt Practices Act, that penalize bribes to officials.[20]
- *Transparency:* Mechanisms for making information about resource revenues publicly available. The EITI and the mandatory corporate reporting laws just mentioned are examples.[21] Others include campaigns for oil contract transparency and Publish How You Spend.[22]
- *Resource Validation:* The Kimberley Process is the resource-validation scheme for diamonds; there are proposals to strengthen Kimberley, as well as to extend resource validation to other gems and metals.[23] Also in this category are US laws requiring corporations to perform due diligence on their supply chains if they have reason

to believe that their products may contain conflict minerals from the DRC.[24]

- *Commercial Disengagement:* Embargoes and sanctions cut off commercial connections. For example, the UN Security Council has ordered an arms embargo on all non-state entities operating in the eastern DRC, and has announced travel bans and asset freezes on named individuals and entities there. The United States has longstanding sanctions on Sudanese petroleum; the European Union once banned imports of Burmese timber and mined goods.
- *Revenue Distribution:* Prominent figures have recommended that resource revenues be divided equally among all of a producing country's adult citizens. Revenue distribution would require governments to get their money through taxation instead of directly from foreigners—and so to become more responsive to their people. Alaska and Mongolia already do some revenue distribution; Iraq and Nigeria have been two countries often discussed for this reform.

These different initiatives target different activities with different techniques, yet they share one major objective. It is as if the smart, determined people working on their own issues had all reached the same conclusion. All of these initiatives aim to increase public accountability over resources and resource revenues. That is, all aim to increase the power of citizens of exporting countries to check the decisions of actors who control resource exports and resource money. What the champions of these and many other initiatives have seen is that the resource diseases make a people weaker. In their different ways, their initiatives all aim to help peoples make themselves stronger:[25]

- *Anti-corruption* measures discourage outsiders from making secret (unaccountable) resource deals with export-country officials.
- *Resource validation* decreases the power of unaccountable armed groups like militias.
- *Commercial disengagement* from resource-disordered countries stops foreign revenues from empowering unaccountable actors, either state or non-state.
- Both *transparency* and *revenue distribution* policies increase citizens' power of control over resources—by giving citizens more information about resource deals, or by putting the money from resource deals directly into their hands.

This unplanned convergence of initiatives also converges with the analysis of this book: that the risks of the resource diseases increase when foreign demand for natural resources connects to actors insufficiently accountable to citizens. This is the core conclusion that everyone, from different angles, has reached. The profusion of initiatives aimed at reducing this risk is also a bonanza for Clean Trade. The world has already created a giant toolbox of policies for supporting public accountability in resource-exporting countries. And public accountability can be encouraged even more by putting these tools together.

SUPPORTING PUBLIC ACCOUNTABILITY

The Clean Trade framework in the last chapter sets policies toward the worst resource-diseased exporters: toward exporters where civil liberties and political rights are so poorly respected that the people have no control over their resources. Happily, most exporting countries are not so badly off. In most exporting countries, citizens are at least partly free—they have some, but not enough, power over their natural assets. Among the countries in this categories are, for example, Nigeria and Venezuela.

The second half of the Clean Trade framework crafts trade policy toward such countries using the tools already available to sustain and encourage public accountability. By implementing the second half of the framework, a country will change its laws and policies so that they stop working against, and start working for, the peoples of exporting states.

This part of the framework has two spaces into which specific policies fit. The first sets out the rules for the companies and agencies of the enacting country that do business in exporting countries. We call these "Rules of Engagement." The second organizes responses to increases and decreases in public accountability in exporting countries. Policies geared to developments in exporting countries form a "Public Power Spectrum."

Rules of Engagement

A country's Rules of Engagement will set uniform standards for all "home" oil and mining companies (those that are domestically incorporated or listed). These Rules will bring the policy tools described above together so that they reinforce each other. For example, an enacting country may combine a robust anti-bribery law with transparency laws that require disclosure of payments to foreign officials, and with money-laundering laws that oblige banks to perform due diligence on foreign officials who may have embezzled funds. When combined, such laws can change the basic business posture that home firms will take toward officials abroad.

Each Clean Trade country will determine for itself which Rules work best and which best suit its own circumstances. At the same time, an enacting country should keep an eye on creating Rules that can be easily shared with other countries, since its own firms will much prefer to compete with other countries' firms when all are on an internationally level playing field.

A Clean Trade country should do more than join up its laws in areas like those described above, where there has already been much progress. It should also adopt Rules that require its companies to maintain high standards while they operate on the ground to extract resources in foreign countries.

Clean Trade emphasizes that it is our own countries' laws that create our resource companies; it is our own laws that create these legal persons. These companies can have great influence over whether people overseas can control their resources and lead decent lives. Yet to a great extent, the laws that today keep our resource firms in check when they operate abroad are in the hands of the officials of those corrupt and weak exporting states. Without better Rules of Engagement, what countries that are home to resource firms will continue to say every day is:

> *We hereby sustain the life of a person—a person of potentially unlimited power and not subject to mortal death. We have endowed this person with many of the rights of natural persons, yet fewer liabilities. We will protect this person when it goes abroad with the force of our law. Whether this person can be deterred or disciplined by the laws of the weaker countries where it may go—that we neither know nor will attend to. Should our creation violate the most basic rights of those abroad, that we will not see.*

The big recent initiative on corporate conduct has been the UN Guiding Principles for Business and Human Rights, developed by John Ruggie (who is also a top political theorist).[26] As we saw in Chapter 4, the extractive industries are especially prone to endangering people in exporting countries. And as Ruggie writes:

> Extractive companies have had adverse impacts on a broad array of human rights, such as resettlement of communities without adequate consultation and compensation; environmental degradation and its effects on health, sources of livelihood and access to clean water; as well as charges of forced labor, rape and even extrajudicial killings by security forces protecting company assets, with some cases meeting the legal definition of corporate complicity.[27]

Under Ruggie's Guiding Principles, all firms are expected to take responsibility for their direct and indirect impacts on human rights—including the human rights of the people in the communities where they operate. The Guiding Principles also encourage firms to ensure that remedies are available to anyone whose human rights may have been violated by their activities.

Ruggie's Guiding Principles were unanimously accepted by the UN Human Rights Council—and were also welcomed by large companies and industry associations in oil and mining. One reason for this positive reception is that extractive firms have realized that ignoring human rights can be expensive. Such firms can be spurned by "ethical" investors. They become vulnerable to consumer pressure campaigns, lawsuits, NGO whistle-blowing, and parliamentary scrutiny. An abusive or negligent firm may forfeit its "social license to operate" in a particular community or country. A firm's recruitment, and its employees' morale, may also suffer if it or its industry is perceived as bad. Ruggie cited an example of a major oil company that was losing billions annually because of poor relations with community "stakeholders," and he found mining companies losing millions every day to delayed production.[28] Extractive firms can suffer their own resource curses.[29]

Ruggie's Guiding Principles took a significant step forward by establishing meaningful international human rights standards for corporations. Clean Trade countries can take the next step by making these voluntary standards legally binding on their own firms—especially for the most egregious corporate behavior abroad. The Guiding Principles are not legally binding on corporations, so today, a company or its employees may be guilty of plunder, extortion, racketeering, torture, rape, enslavement, or murder—or do business directly with those who are guilty of these crimes—and face no legal consequences whatsoever. If the justice system of the country where the crimes take place is weak (or is influenced by the company), the company may face no accountability at all.[30]

The Rules of Engagement of a Clean Trade country will establish legal standards of criminality and complicity for its own firms working abroad. These Rules should also set standards for home government agencies, such as any export-credit agencies that finance the extractive projects of home firms in other countries.

The gold standard of Clean Trade is a country that holds its firms and agencies to the same legal standards whether they are doing business at home or abroad—and across the board on bribery, money-laundering, transparency, and human rights. Australia, for example, is well known for the high legal standards of accountability it imposes on mining firms operating at home—and for the execrable business practices of some of its mining firms abroad. The Rules of Engagement of Clean Trade Australia would move the rules for Australia's firms abroad closer to the rules for its firms at home—and in the ideal, to parity. One can imagine the statesmanship—of both political and corporate leaders—that would be on display in an announcement of a move to this gold standard. And as we have seen with earlier initiatives, when countries move first, they often lead other countries to follow to the new, higher level.

The Public Power Spectrum

What then of Nigeria, and other exporting countries of great potential, where our countries' current trade policies are contributing to the resource disorders? As we've seen, governance in Nigeria is a dysfunctional, oil-funded, clientelistic pyramid. Corruption, grand and petty, is widespread, and it is especially egregious throughout the oil sector. Serious conflict has flared in both the South and the North. Citizens' identification with the nation is weak; trust runs low. Countries like Nigeria are not so bereft of public accountability that their exports should be treated as stolen goods. Yet repression, conflict, and corruption frustrate the people's control over their resources, and foreign trade today works to ratchet down these disorders. In this category are also the many fragile countries just starting out as producers, where the resource trade is beginning to cause serious problems.

Nigeria's problems are, quite obviously, for Nigerians to solve—and the same is true for all exporting countries. Outsiders can help by reversing the forces now generated by their own terms of trade. A Clean Trade country will change its own laws so that they are no longer geared against public accountability in exporting countries, but instead work to support it. These policies will incentivize exporting-country officials to move up a Public Power Spectrum by allowing more control over resources to their people. A Clean Trade country will say to these officials: "We want to trade with your country very much, and we now want to do it in ways that will help your people to empower themselves."

Structuring trade policies with conditionalities is already widespread. For example, the US African Growth and Opportunity Act allows extra trade privileges to African countries that score higher on the rule of law, political pluralism, and anti-corruption indices. A Clean Trade country will set out a scale of commercial connections to resource-exporting countries that tracks the level of public accountability over resources that those countries achieve.[31] More public accountability will mean more commercial connections; less public accountability will mean fewer. Clean Trade countries can design their conditionalities to be easily shared by other countries, since uniform standards across many countries will magnify their effects.

All trade policies will generate incentives for those with power in other countries, one way or another. The art of crafting conditionalities is arranging them so that the short-term incentives of those with power in exporting countries will point toward the long-term empowerment of the people. Recall the Nigerian, quoted in Chapter 8, who described what the members of the country's governing elite want: "These men want to fly with their family to a house in Paris. They want to take their mistress shopping in Harrods. And they want to send their children to American schools. That's where their face comes from. And when they get ill they go to the Mayo Clinic." He continued:

> An American is caught bribing a Nigerian big man. If America puts travel bans on that big man, that would very bad for him. And also if Europe did the same thing. You can hit these corrupt men even more by banning their children to go to your schools. But with every travel ban, America should also give a good ruler an invitation to Washington. And for every child of a corrupt man who is blocked from going to an American school, America should give a scholarship to a Nigerian child.[32]

Conditionalities will match exporting-country events to responses by the Clean Trade country. Figure 17.1 gives examples of events in exporting country (left) that could be paired with responses in the Clean Trade country (right). Many different pairings of events on the left with responses on the

Higher or lower scores on independent metrics of public accountability (like the Resource Governance Index).	Increase or decrease direct foreign investment or foreign aid.
Implementation of transparency initiatives (like EITI) or laws (like a freedom of information act).	Increase or decrease access to home educational institutions, banks, etc.
(Lack of) externally certified free and fair elections in a region or nationally.	Diplomatic invitations, scholarships, cultural exchanges.
Export-country official named as receiving a bribe in a successful corruption case against the bribe-payer (e.g., under the FCPA).	Travel bans or fast tracks (individual or family).
Implementation of a resource validation scheme for exports.	Asset freezes.
Implementation of a revenue distribution program.	Capacity building in the judiciary, the anti-corruption agency, higher education, etc.

FIGURE 17.1 Conditionalities: Events in the Exporting Country (Left) Paired with Responses from the Clean Trade Country (Right).

right are possible—and there are many more possible events and responses beyond those listed. Which events to match with which responses is a matter for political judgment informed by the best empirical research. The options above are planks with which good policy can be built.

All those involved in framing conditionalities should remain alive to the fact that different policies will suit countries in different conditions.[33] For example, the information revealed by transparency laws will be more empowering in countries with a stronger, more independent civil society that can use the information to pressure the state. Transparency is most useful where there is also a focused light source—where there are many bright people trained and motivated to set their eyes on the data. A structure of policy incentives should recognize that greater transparency will be more empowering in Ghana, say, and less so in Guinea.

A Clean Trade country might set out a single schedule of conditionalities for all exporting countries. Or a Clean Trade country can instead invite exporters to join a club where decisions on conditionalities and review procedures will be made by the members. During a club summit, an exporting country could, for example, identify a need for the training of its judiciary, while agreeing to submit its progress on transparency to a peer review panel that can trigger positive actions.[34] Such a club could be regionally based—for example, the African Great Lakes countries could commit to share more in each other's good governance, in league with a Clean Trade country or countries. This club model is more participatory, and more adaptable to export-country circumstances, than a single schedule.[35]

GIVING CITIZENS THEIR MONEY

Let's take a closer look at one promising policy that Clean Trade could encourage in exporting countries: revenue distribution. As we saw at the outset, many of the afflictions of resource-disordered countries arise because the resource money goes straight to their heads. Sending resource revenues to officials can fund clientelistic and personal corruption, and thwart formation of an economically independent citizenry that balances the state's power. This in turn hinders a Schumpeter Process, in which leaders must give greater political rights to citizens in exchange for the tax revenues that they need to stay in power.

Distributing resource revenues to the people reverses the effects of rent addiction. When citizens get the resource money, the state must tax them to get its revenues—and so must become more responsive to their needs. Citizens in turn have reason to scrutinize the state's resource management more closely, since they will get more money when the state manages the resources well. State power is balanced; accountability gets built in to the system.

One model for revenue distribution is known as Oil-to-Cash, or Minerals-to-Cash: the government of the exporting country sends revenues from resource sales directly into citizens' bank accounts. This model has been championed for years by Nancy Birdsall, Alan Gelb, Arvind Subramanian and Todd Moss at the Center for Global Development; by Martin Sandbu; and recently by Larry Diamond.[36]

Another model for distribution is to transfer revenues from resource sales into a mutual fund known as a "People's Fund." Nobel economist Vernon Smith, advocating such a fund, wrote that a country's resources "should first be declared transferred to the accounts of the citizens, recognizing the birthright of each citizen to a personal, empowering property right in the land and assets of the country of their birth. All citizens should have an equal share in this fund."[37]

Resource revenues are, in a very real sense, the citizens' money. These are not handouts; these are birthrights—the proceeds from the sale of the citizens' property. ("Iraqi oil belongs to all Iraqis" as the Iraqi Prime Minister said in December 2014.[38]) In resource-rich states, revenue distributions could constitute a basic income or a "citizen share."[39]

Basic income and citizen shareholding have been endorsed for many years, for reasons of both justice and prosperity, by reformers with different political agendas: by Thomas Paine and the British Green Party, for example, and by Martin Luther King and Milton Friedman.[40] Here is a rather sweeping pronouncement from Friedman on citizen shareholding in Iraq:

> Almost every country in the Middle East that is rich in oil is a despotism [for] one reason, and one reason only—the oil is owned by the governments in question. If that oil were privately owned and thus someone's private property, the political outcome would be freedom rather than tyranny. This is why I believe the first step following the 2003 invasion of Iraq should have been the privatization of the oil fields. If the government had given every individual over 21 years of age equal shares in a corporation that had the right and responsibility to make appropriate arrangements with foreign oil companies for the purpose of discovering and developing Iraq's oil reserves, the oil income would have flowed in the form of dividends to the people—the shareholders—rather than into government coffers. This would have provided an income to the whole people of Iraq and thereby prevented the current disputes over oil between the Sunnis, Shiites and Kurds, because oil income would have been distributed on an individual rather than a group basis.[41]

The numbers show that revenue distribution will have significant anti-poverty effects in many resource-rich countries.[42] Some have worried that transferring cash to the poor will increase laziness or dependency—and this may occur in some cases, especially at first. Yet the data from large countries where cash transfers have been tried are quite encouraging. In the main, poor people use the money to save against illness, to start a business, and to keep their children in school.[43] New technologies such as mobile phone banking and biometrics can also cut down on fraud.[44]

Moreover, having an independent source of income frees citizens from manipulation by officials: revenue distribution can liberate the poor from the pyramids of clientelistic dependence under which they jostle for a few drops from the pipes coming down from above.[45] And, as an extra benefit, a policy that distributes money equally to citizens—regardless of their region, religion, race, or tribe—can also reinforce a sense of national unity.[46]

A Clean Trade Public Power Spectrum can make the implementation of revenue distribution a trigger for positive responses. The United States, for example, could make this offer to Nigerian officials:

> *If you commit to distributing most of the oil revenues to citizens, we will work with your agencies and banks to build technical capacity for implementation. We will facilitate cooperation between our countries' firms to roll out the needed biometric, mobile banking, and citizen registration facilities. And we will line up investments from these ten companies outside of the extractive industries to help create jobs in the North and the South.*

Vote-conscious leaders in exporting countries will be attracted by such offers, which Western countries are well placed to make. The returns on these Western investments will be more stable, peaceful, and unified countries that will spread their prosperity regionally as they realize more of their great potential.

ONE HAND DIRTY, ONE HAND CLEAN?

The principles we engrave; the policies we pen. Choosing specific Rules of Engagement for home actors, and conditionalities for a Public Power Spectrum, will be decisions for a Clean Trade country to make in consultation with experts and with other countries. This part of the framework holds two flexible spaces that combine policy tools which support public accountability in exporting countries; you might consider what rules and conditions you believe would work best today. In this last part of the chapter, we turn to some larger strategic questions for Clean Trade and consider its longer-term goals.

One abiding debate among those who act on principle is whether to collaborate with interest. Should reformers make alliances with those who have different agendas—even with those motivated only by money or votes or their own narrow issues? For instance: setting up a Clean Hands Trust for some exporting country might involve duties on imports of Chinese goods. If the US government announces that $3 billion needs to be raised through import duties on China, American industries from electronics to machinery to apparel will lobby to have those duties imposed on Chinese imports within their sector. Should principled supporters of Clean Trade join forces with these protectionists if needed to get a Clean Hands Trust set up?

Of course. Many interests and agendas are aligned with the policy framework discussed above, and reformers should be open to working with all of them. In Clean Trade, protectionists will see a way to insulate domestic industries from foreign competition. Environmentalists will be attracted to reducing environmental damage in resource-diseased countries, and to making progress on decarbonizing the global economy. Those who prioritize national security will see measures that weaken hostile petrocrats and strengthen failed states where terrorism can incubate. Humanitarians will favor the policies for bettering the opportunities of some of the most impoverished and oppressed people in the world. The framework is aligned with many powerful interests, and it will be broadly appealing across the political spectrum from right to left.

Promising coalitions of interests and agendas are also present in many exporting countries where public accountability is lacking. There are supporters of reform waiting in every country, even in the royal palaces. Ambitious industrialists in places where resource production is just starting will want to fight against the bad governance that they see in the older exporters. In exporting countries with elections, anti-corruption is often a vote-winner, and revenue distribution could be even bigger. The resource trade today concentrates power in the few, so many will want to reform it.

Even international resource firms will have some interests aligned with Clean Trade. If regulation is inevitable in one jurisdiction, they will have both cost and competitive grounds to work for the quick spread of these same regulations across all jurisdictions. And these firms have reason to support reforms that will genuinely improve state governance in fragile exporting countries, since this will help to lift their resource curses. Better state governance will relieve firms of having to provide remedial governance (security, environmental regulation, etc.) that forces them well beyond their core competences, and that ends up endangering their reputations, their social license to operate, and over time, their morale and recruitment. A real corporate statesman who sees the long-term advantages of Clean Trade could change the image of the whole sector within a single career.

The presence of interest is not the absence of justice.[47] Nearly all successful movements in history have been driven by a coalition of principles and interests, some just along for the ride and some downright cynical. The movement to abolish child labor in America, for example, started in earnest in 1904. Several attempts in succeeding years to make the federal government regulate child labor (including two attempts at a constitutional amendment) fell short. It was only in 1938, in the depths of the Great Depression, when cheap child labor was taking work away from adults, that the landmark legislation was finally passed.[48] After the Depression ended, the reforms stuck—the rules had become entrenched. This is a common story of success. There were interests behind the triumphs of decolonization, of human rights, and of the anti-apartheid movement too.

Interests will do what they do; how much the better if they can be harnessed for justice and the permanent interests of all. Moreover, as we've seen, action on interest is often the gateway to identity change. What is at first expediency eventually leads to internalization of a new outlook. This is, after all, the story of our own personal histories from early childhood onward—for example, with education: the prizes and punishments that initially incentivized us to study were gradually replaced by a genuine desire to learn.

The right ethos of reform is the one we saw earlier, with the three friends from Global Witness. Talk to everyone, work with anyone who will be net positive, be rigorous, keep focused, and don't let up. This is the ethos that has already won success for principled reformers—and that promises much more.

WIN^X

The shape of the policies needed for progress on resources is evident: brilliant reformers have converged on the core idea of supporting public accountability without even trying. And it is encouraging how much progress has been made by relatively small players already. Most change agents on resource issues so far have been striplings in global terms: Davids surrounded by towering Goliaths. Still, they have won striking victories—on blood diamonds and conflict minerals, on country and corporate transparency, against abusive militias and unscrupulous rulers. These victories have been aided by a wider sense of conscience, which has drawn many to the side of change. The world appears to be set up for more success.

It is sometimes said that the Western powers will soon be eclipsed by others. If so, what better final act than to build popular resource sovereignty into the machinery of the global economy? Our grandchildren—who will in this scenario be overshadowed by foreigners—will thank us for leaving them that legacy. Yet there is no reason to see the future as zero-sum in this way.

If you ask Americans which post-World War II foreign policies the United States can be really proud of, many may be momentarily stuck. (Let's agree that the moonshot does not count as "foreign policy.") A leading contender must be the Marshall Plan: America's effort to help reconstruct a devastated Europe after the war. Food, fuel, and raw materials were scant. Rationing was everywhere; hunger was widespread. Greece's democracy was threatened by a civil war, and with several economies failing, many feared revolution or even anarchy spreading across the continent.

On hearing Marshall's 1947 speech announcing the Plan, the British Foreign Secretary said that it was "[a] lifeline to sinking men. It seemed to bring hope where there was none. The generosity of it was beyond belief."[49] The United States was itself facing shortages of the goods that Europe needed most, and economists warned that the Plan would push up inflation. But President Truman made a personal appeal to Americans, asking them especially to eat less poultry and eggs and to observe "meatless Tuesdays" so that extra grain could be sent to avert starvation in Europe.

The response was overwhelming. Letters of support from all over the country flooded the White House. Children pledged to clean their plates. Bakers and distillers found clever ways to use less grain. Farm, restaurant, and hotel owners all offered to boost the Plan, and the airlines and merchant marines promised to do their part. Managers in major American industries even reached out to share new technology and techniques with their European counterparts—even though the Europeans were their competitors.[50]

The Plan, which assisted both wartime enemies and allies, succeeded spectacularly. European productivity increased dramatically; economies that had been in decline turned around. National income per capita grew by one-third in Europe during the first three of the four years that the Plan was in effect.[51] As growth took off across Europe in the succeeding decades, the American economy was enriched as well through its increasingly extensive European trade. Perhaps more importantly, the Plan also raised European good will toward Americans, and trust in American intentions, which served their alliance and the cause of democracy well in the years that followed.

The Marshall Plan greatly aided democracy in Europe. It was also an exemplary exercise of democracy in America. A Democratic President and a Republican Congress coordinated their efforts to pass the Plan; business and labor leaders formed committees that circulated petitions and praised the Plan through the media. Most of all, citizens, through their political support and personal commitment, ensured that the Plan would be carried through (and even paid for millions of CARE packages to be sent in addition).[52] The collective enterprise was an other-directed initiative that required short-term sacrifice, but it also helped to bring people together by asking for extra efforts. The long-term results were hugely positive—politically, economically, and even for greater unity among Americans and between them and peoples across the sea.

Tomorrow's movement for popular sovereignty will require self-control more than it will require sending aid. All the coordination points for this campaign are ready to go—the treaties, policies, and slogans are waiting. What is needed is coordinated leadership from many sources, and especially from citizens themselves. A determined campaign to take the next step for popular sovereignty abroad will also strengthen democracy at home by showing the power of citizens working together.

ALMOST THERE

During the American Civil War, the people of Manchester, England, were confronted with a choice. Over the decades, they had accepted serious costs on themselves for the abolition of slavery within the British domains and for the suppression of the Atlantic slave trade. Yet the Civil War raised a new question: what stand would the people of Manchester take on slavery within a foreign country—the United States—now that they were forced to take sides?

In the 1860s, cotton was king, and Manchester's many mills turned cotton into the fabric that clothed the world. But Manchester's economy was heavily dependent on slave cotton from the Confederate States of America. Lincoln's blockade of the South—though only partially effective—was already causing great suffering to Manchester's working people. More than half of the city's looms had no cotton to weave. Unemployment was becoming critical; starvation was setting in.[53]

On the last, cold day of 1862, citizens of Manchester crammed into the Free Trade Hall to share their views on importing cotton from the Confederate States. The crowd was impassioned. A motion was offered, a show of hands asked. The vote was overwhelming: Manchester would buy no more of the South's slave-picked cotton. Moreover, a letter should be sent to President Lincoln, expressing the people's fervent hopes for victory in America's struggle against the evils of human bondage.

The cotton boycott deepened the already desperate circumstances of Manchester's working class. Still, month after month, the people stood firm. In 1863, Lincoln wrote an open letter thanking the people of Manchester for their vote. "I cannot but regard your decisive utterance upon the question," he wrote, "as an instance of sublime Christian heroism which has not been surpassed in any age or in any country. It is, indeed, an energetic and reinspiring assurance of the inherent power of truth and of the ultimate and universal triumph of justice, humanity, and freedom."[54] Soon afterward, relief ships bearing provisions for the people of Manchester began arriving in port, sent by Americans in the North grateful for their solidarity.

Many of the great movements for moral progress in the past three centuries have been morally simple. All humans should be free: the hard work was ending slavery. All nations should be free: the hard work was fighting the empires. Effectiveness for resources is also morally simple: it violates rights on a massive scale, and it causes enormous suffering. Yet reforming the resource trade should be much easier, as both principle and prudence advise the same course.

"Might makes right" was the rule of slavery and of imperialism. It is still our rule for resources, and the policies to abolish it are already close at hand. We need only affirm our own principles and allow them to guide our actions. Here, as with other enlightened causes, results come from resolve. Act on principle, progress will follow.

PART V

All United

We now look ahead at new challenges that will emerge for humanity and what it will take to meet them. We also test the principles that we have chosen to guide us. Will these really lead us toward greater justice? (And should we care?)

Today, oil divides us. Because we still say that "might makes right," what should be win-win exchanges in a free market instead produce a lose-lose world of hostile authoritarians, endless civil wars, and extremists maddened by hate. The great philosophies of Kant and Mill share the vision of transcending such divisions. These philosophies project an ideal of the free unity of humanity, which (depending on one's optimism about human nature) manifests as international peace, cooperation, and solidarity. Reforming the natural resource trade will be one step toward solving the problems of our day. Thinking through these reforms allows us to meditate on how good we hope the world can become.

18

The Future

What strange views of the world there are among clever people!

—Otto von Bismarck[1]

THE CRISES OF OUR INVENTION

We've visited the seventeenth century several times in the pages past. In it, we've found the divine right of kings, a treatise on witches, and the rise of the rule of effectiveness. In this chapter, we step back twice more into that dark age.

London, 1665. The capital smelled of death in its last large outbreak of the Plague, the worst since the Black Death of the fourteenth century. The diarist Samuel Pepys mourned, "Every day sadder and sadder news of its increase. In the City died this week 7,496; and of all of them, 6,102 of the Plague. But it is feared that the true number of the dead this week is near 10,000—partly from the poor that cannot be taken notice of through the greatness of the number."[2]

As the deaths mounted and the streets filled with uncleared waste, Londoners noticed that dogs and cats were everywhere in the city. And so the order went out from the Lord Mayor.

Kill the dogs and cats.

The Chamberlain of the City paid the huntsmen, and the huntsmen slaughtered more than four thousand animals.[3] But the dogs and cats were chasing the rats that were feeding on the waste—and the rats were carrying the fleas that transmitted the Plague.[4] Now spared from their canine and feline predators, the rats spread the affliction even more fiercely. The medical advice from the College of Physicians—to press a live hen hard on the swellings until the hen died—did not actually help.[5] In the end, the Plague of 1665 is thought to have killed almost 20 percent of London's population (what would be roughly a million-and-a-half people today).[6] A great fire then consumed a third of the city.

In the seventeenth century, people thought that dogs and cats—not rats and fleas—spread the Plague. Many humans and animals died in this crisis of ignorance. Now that we understand the transmission mechanisms—and, indeed, the Plague bacterium itself—we know which procedures and medicines will keep the disease from becoming epidemic. Ignorance, we might say, no longer plagues us.

Today, pestilence threatens not so much because of our ignorance but because of our industry—because of the spacious reach of our systems. Our transport networks are now so fast and far-flung that they transmit diseases worldwide before vaccines and cures can catch up. The next epidemics will play on our strengths, not our weaknesses—fighting them will mean canceling flights, not killing fleas. This Horseman of the Apocalypse has dismounted and now travels coach.[7]

The twentieth century marked an inflection point, the beginning of humanity's transition from its ancient crises of ignorance to its modern crises of invention. Our science is now so penetrating, our systems are so robust, that we are mostly endangered by our own creations. The Horseman of War is now armed with particle physics. Our computers have become so sapient, so present, and so vigilant that we can scarcely keep anything from them.

In 1665, perhaps half a billion humans sweated to sustain the species near subsistence with their crude implements. Now our global life machine is so productive that a double-doubled-doubled-doubled number of humans will soon be alive, most never having known such poverty. The pale Horseman of Scripture killed with the beasts of the earth; now humans are more threatened by diabetes mellitus.

Indeed, our machines have multiplied so much that a new crisis looms because of all the smoke coming off of them as they combust. Future food crises, if they come, will be driven by anthropogenic climate change. Famine will descend not from the wrath of God but from the growth of GDP. We ourselves are outfitting the Horsemen of the future, or perhaps it's better to say that we are creating them.

Our new crises of invention are so challenging because the bads are so tightly bound with the goods. This is where we began: breaking the world's slave chains was a moral triumph; breaking the world's supply chains is not an option. Fighting these new crises means disciplining the creations of which we are so proud. Climate change is a crisis of invention. So many more humans, living longer, eating better, traveling more to see the world and each other—how poignant that all of this avalanches into a mortal danger.

Both self-control and ingenuity will be needed to limit the threats that rise with our success. And we can be sure that new threats will emerge as our invention climbs asymptotically upward. The Industrial Revolution of the nineteenth century came when we started to use machines to make machines. Today, we use computers to make machines. Tomorrow, computers will program computers—and we may find ourselves dependent on, and menaced by, our grand brain-children. Molecules are heavy and expensive; bits are fast and cheap. So if the past was about scarcity, the future should be about abundance—but the future may also be abundant with trouble.[8]

It would be ungenerous to be impatient with humanity, which—like everyone—needs time to learn. It was quite a shock for humankind to wake one day with atomic weapons suddenly in its midst, especially as a world war was then ablaze. In 1945, humanity had little idea how to handle this novel existential threat. But it learned, through death and nightmares, and at least so far, it has done better than many first feared. With ever more threats of invention emerging, humanity will need to learn again, and it will need to learn quicker and better. The currents are pushing the starfish faster, the reefs ahead are sharper—humanity must become sharper too.

Two factors will determine the success of the species in meeting the challenges ahead. The first is how much humanity will be able to limit the spread of divisive identities. Put simply: how many people will there be who very much want to kill large numbers of their fellow humans? The US National Intelligence Council, a well-resourced group of "wise men and women," forecasts the megatrends that will most shape the world in the decades to come. In its latest report, the first megatrend it identifies is "Individual Empowerment":

> Individual empowerment is the most important megatrend because it is both a cause and effect of most other trends—including the expanding global economy, rapid growth of the developing countries, and widespread exploitation of new communications and

> manufacturing technologies. On the one hand, we see the potential for greater individual initiative as key to solving the mounting global challenges over the next 15–20 years. On the other hand, in a tectonic shift, individuals and small groups will have greater access to lethal and disruptive technologies (particularly precision-strike capabilities, cyber instruments, and bioterror weaponry), enabling them to perpetrate large-scale violence—a capability formerly the monopoly of states.[9]

Many individuals, determined to kill, can cause enough local crises to distract from global, long-term threats—and might be able to trigger their own global crises as well. The odds for the human future worsen as more individuals wear divisive identities: the suicide bomber, the radical preacher, the ultranationalist. Political and economic systems generate human environments, and these human environments will form identities. As we've seen, today's effectiveness-based international trade in natural resources generates human environments defined by divide-and-rule and divide-and-kill. Effectiveness will proliferate divisive identities just as individuals will be handed more potent means of destruction. Individuals may get worse as weapons get better.

The more hopeful note in the quote above is that individuals will become more empowered to meet the coming global challenges of invention. This is the second critical factor in species success: Will individuals become more connective as they become more connected by technology? Will they become more open to cooperating across boundaries of nationality, religion, race, and tribe? Will they have enough beliefs in common to agree on the problems that face them? Will they be secure enough in themselves to take the first steps to build trust?

Think of all the children in South Asia and sub-Saharan Africa, where more than a third of humanity lives. In these regions, the average child now gets less than five years of schooling, and that schooling is often poor.[10] Education, of course, is a priority. Which regimes and religious groups will be doing the teaching? What will be taught? As these countries rise out of enervating poverty, will the curriculum be set by those who legitimate themselves through xenophobia or anti-modern exhortations? Resource-funded authoritarians, militias, and corrupt officials have reasons to make people weaker. Only leaders whose strength depends on the strength of their people will have reason to empower their youth to be more knowledgeable, more tolerant, more autonomous, more open—more connective.

IS HUMANITY GETTING SMARTER?

Human connectivity will decide whether we will meet the coming crises of invention. A simple version of Moore's Law says that computer processing power doubles every two years.[11] We will need a social Moore's Law of connections among humans to keep up.

What about humanity itself, looking at this very large group as a single intelligence, like a corporation or a country? Is humanity getting smarter, more able to solve the problems that it will face? It might be that an IQ test of humanity would show ever-rising scores over the decades—but maybe not. We know of no natural law that ensures the line on that graph always goes up. Even more and abler individuals might form a less and less intelligent group—if those individuals are less able to work together. (The Neanderthal brain had more neurons than the modern human brain does—but our neurons hook up in ways that make us smarter.)

Human connectivity will be the primary determinant of the trajectory of species intelligence. A second major factor will be the quality of international institutions: the rules, networks, and bodies that coordinate (or fail to coordinate) relations across borders. These institutions will greatly influence how capable humanity will be at the species level, and here we face one of the most intriguing crises of our own invention.[12]

Today's familiar international institutions have been largely successful in achieving the aims of those who laid their foundations after World War II. Those aims were economic growth and the prevention of major wars. With all of the collapses and catastrophes of the postwar period, the framers of the international system would be gratified if they could see the future that is now our past. Yet success, as so often, brings new challenges. Several of today's hardest challenges are side effects of the progress made within the postwar institutional order.

For example, the postwar system was designed to stop wars of conquest by making borders force-proof. This design has worked well—the anti-conquest rule is now entrenched in the international system and has contributed to significant reductions in armed conflict. Yet a side effect of this success is that that some states have been frozen in failure. At its independence in

1960, the giant DRC had almost no chance to succeed as a well-governed political entity. In the days of Westphalia, it would have been divided up, sooner or later, by conquering sovereigns better able to control its territory. Because of the modern anti-conquest rule, however, the DRC has survived in a sickly and near-comatose state as crooks, militias, and its neighbors have drained its blood away and so made it even weaker. This doesn't mean that the world should revoke its anti-conquest rule—a rule the world only learned after centuries of wars over territory. It does mean that we should redouble our efforts to counteract its unwanted consequences.

The same is true of the global institutions of trade and finance. With the exception of the United States, the world's major economies emerged from World War II seriously damaged. Even in Britain, which was on the winning side, food and fuel were rationed for years afterward. Women in the north of England still remember repairing worn-out shoes with cardboard; an elderly Welshman might tell you he grew up so hungry that he would jump over a farmer's fence before dawn each morning to suck some milk from the udder of a cow. The world needed growth, and got it, in part, through the Bretton Woods institutions designed by John Maynard Keynes, Henry Morgenthau, and Harry Dexter White in 1944 and rebuilt by many hands thereafter.

This global system of trade and finance has been spectacularly successful in boosting growth. In fact, production and consumption have expanded so much that they now endanger the environment: this is the system spewing the fumes that will worsen the weather. (The original "world trade" agreement in 1947 aimed at "developing the full use of the resources of the world." Our age would surely replace "full" with "prudent."[13]) A parallel story of growth in the postwar economy has been the extraordinary enlargement of corporations. Some of these artificial persons have now become so monstrous as to be dreadful to their creators. In the end, these are all predicaments born of our institutional success.

The international system has slowly started to address some of the side effects of its achievements.[14] Peacekeeping has improved and now substantially reduces the risk of armed conflict within countries.[15] International bodies are becoming incrementally more inclusive, as seen in the move from the G7 to the G20. Transgovernmental networks on issues from the environment to banking are becoming more robust. Above them are "meta-networks" such as the Financial Stability Board; below them are private bodies of technocrats such as the International Accounting Standards Board. There are also public-private hybrids such as the Global Fund to Fight AIDS, TB, and Malaria, as well as legions of civil society organizations that hold states accountable for (and sometimes provide services in lieu of) governance. As we saw in the last chapter, human rights norms for businesses are slowly solidifying too.[16]

Still, the old, familiar institutions of the international order are locked in and looking increasingly less functional. The UN Security Council still allows vetoes only to five countries from the winning side of World War II. The international financial institutions still mostly serve the West. The WTO strains to move at all. As new powers rise—both state and non-state—they are making demands that these old structures resist. This is again a crisis of invention: the institutions that aided the expansion of peace and prosperity are cemented and so can't adjust themselves to the results. These institutions now force international relations into shapes that waste a lot of brainpower. Dealing with climate change, financial instability, nuclear proliferation, terrorism, pandemics, and inequality will mean reimagining the postwar institutions.[17] If an apocalypse does charge down on us during the twenty-first century, its horse may be named Gridlock.[18]

"THE EARTH HATH HE GIVEN TO THE CHILDREN OF MEN."[19]

By now, this book's position on the reform of international institutions will be familiar. It is to counter the power of unaccountable actors who have incentives to sow divisions, and to do so in ways that build trust by emphasizing the principles that most of the world has in common. The reform of trade in natural resources will do this. And reform, though by no means sufficient in itself, will preempt some of the intractable crises that now congest the international agenda. This will open more space to ease today's gridlock and speed the birth of institutions that will make better use of all of humanity's abilities.

We've reached a point of reflecting on the long-term future of global institutions. Much could be said about, for instance, whether India should become a permanent member of the Security Council, or even whether we should think of the Security Council itself as permanent. Let's instead ask the deeper question about the principles that should guide global institutional reform, and whether we've chosen the best principles to go forward with. The guiding principles of this book are popular sovereignty and property, human rights, the rule of law, and peace. Some philosophers have suggested quite different principles, and this opens an opportunity to check our moral compass. What we want to discuss with these philosophers are the most basic questions of justice. As we better achieve these guiding principles, will we really be furthering the cause of a more just world? Are there points on the moral horizon that we should recommend humanity to sail toward instead?

This book has highlighted the principle of popular resource sovereignty, that "all peoples may, for their own ends, freely dispose of their natural wealth and resources." There are philosophers today who have looked to supplement, or even to replace, that principle. Some philosophers have said that "the people own the resources" is insufficient for justice, or even misguided. These philosophers advance a new principle—in fact, a new old principle—which is that the world's natural resources belong to humanity as a whole. On this principle, America's resources belong not only to Americans but to all humans equally. And so—these philosophers say—for all natural resources, everywhere. What shall we make of this alternative principle, of the common ownership of the Earth?

The idea that God has given the Earth "to mankind in common" is most familiar from the seventeenth-century philosophy of John Locke.[20] Those who have studied political philosophy will recall that Locke used this principle of common ownership to imagine an original "state of nature," and that many philosophers since Locke have tried to develop "state of nature" arguments into more complete theories of justice. It is now known that such arguments are highly sensitive to the specification of their initial conditions—what exactly common ownership is and what moves are allowed starting from it—about which we only have weak intuitions.[21] So it is doubtful that we can ever have enough confidence in the premises of any "state of nature" argument to support comprehensive and controversial conclusions about what institutions we should have now.

John Locke himself deployed his property arguments in a more modest way—not to construct ideal societies but to constrain real politics. Locke's property arguments are essentially counter-powerful. For Locke, who was himself a fugitive from the king's men, the power that needed countering was that of royal absolutism. Locke was opposing the divine right of kings, as asserted by Charles II and James II, whom we met in Chapter 2 taking secret payments from Louis XIV. In his book, Locke first counters their claims to divine right by arguing that even if God did give the whole world to Adam, this could not be a basis of absolute political power today because *property rights cannot be that strong.*[22] Locke then shows that political power cannot be absolute today because, starting from common ownership of the Earth, we can prove that in society *no one's property can rightly be taken without the consent of the people or their representatives.*[23]

Locke's property arguments were influential because they were counterpowerful. His was a philosophy to embolden the rising Parliamentary forces in their Schumpeter process, to assert their rights against the high-handed monarchs. Locke's philosophy was then taken up by the American colonists, who fought their own battle against "absolute Despotism" in the century following.[24] Locke continues to inspire those who oppose excessive state power today.

More cautious contemporary philosophers, such as Mathias Risse and Thomas Pogge, invoke "the common ownership of the Earth" much in the spirit of Locke—as a principle that should constrain institutions, only this time international ones. Accepting that nations should control their natural resources, they say, the common ownership of the Earth requires that the international system should also work to meet the basic needs of all persons. For Risse, common ownership grounds a human right: the right of each person to have opportunities to meet his or her own basic needs.[25] For Pogge, common ownership requires that nations should be forced to pay into a global fund whenever they extract natural resources, with that fund being used to meet the basic needs of the world's poor.[26] For both of these philosophers, popular resource sovereignty need not be replaced—it needs to be constrained by a "common ownership" principle so that the international system works for the good of the poor everywhere.

The values that these philosophers emphasize are weighty ones. Satisfying basic needs will indeed be a priority for any justifiable international system; this is not controversial. Moreover, "common ownership" might well be a useful principle for guiding institutional design in some areas—especially for uninhabited regions such as the deep seabed and outer space, where ideas like "the common heritage of mankind" already appear in treaties.[27] The common ownership of the Earth's atmosphere is also a promising starting point for property-based proposals to reduce greenhouse-gas emissions.[28]

Principles that countered power in centuries past, however, may not do so now. And principles that countered power within English-speaking countries may not do so when stretched over the Earth. It all depends on the reality: on who has too much power and how the opposition can claw some away. "Common ownership of the Earth" will not be a counter-powerful principle for natural resources right now; in fact, invoking it may be counter-productive. What is crucial is that we attend to the world as it is now.

"DON'T THINK; LOOK."[29]

Between World War II and the end of the twentieth century, philosophers forgot the world—at least mainstream English-speaking philosophers did. With a few noble exceptions, there was very little sustained attention to issues affecting what was then called the "Third World."[30] Indeed, insofar as international issues were discussed by English-speaking philosophers at all, the discussions centered on Western preoccupations. Philosophical hawks scrutinized the confrontation with the Soviets; doves worried about human rights and the famines seen on television.

What no leading English-speaking philosopher theorized was the main narrative of most of humanity: the struggle of peoples to gain control over their own countries, and not least over their natural resources. The determination of peoples to control their own fates was, for most of the world, the most important political story of the twentieth century—much more important than the rise of human rights, more important even than the Cold War. Yet this great drama of the century hardly registered in Anglophone philosophy. For philosophers in America and other former British colonies, "victory over the empire" was very old news. For the British, a sense of imperial loss kept eyes down and lips shut.

This is part of the "great forgetting" of how recent the victories of popular sovereignty have been—and how aspirational this step away from Westphalia still remains for many peoples. One can hear both the pain of the battle and the yearning for popular sovereignty in the Namibian constitution of 1990:

> We the people of Namibia—have finally emerged victorious in our struggle against colonialism, racism and apartheid; are determined to adopt a Constitution which expresses for ourselves and our children our resolve to cherish and to protect the gains of our long struggle; desire to promote amongst all of us the dignity of the individual and the unity and integrity of the Namibian nation among

> and in association with the nations of the world; will strive to achieve national reconciliation and to foster peace, unity and a common loyalty to a single state; committed to these principles, have resolved to constitute the Republic of Namibia as a sovereign, secular, democratic and unitary State securing to all our citizens justice, liberty, equality, and fraternity.[31]

And also in the South African constitution of 1996:

> We, the people of South Africa, Recognise the injustices of our past; Honour those who suffered for justice and freedom in our land; Respect those who have worked to build and develop our country; and Believe that South Africa belongs to all who live in it, united in our diversity.
>
> We therefore, through our freely elected representatives, adopt this Constitution as the supreme law of the Republic so as to: Heal the divisions of the past and establish a society based on democratic values, social justice and fundamental human rights; Lay the foundations for a democratic and open society in which government is based on the will of the people and every citizen is equally protected by law; Improve the quality of life of all citizens and free the potential of each person; and Build a united and democratic South Africa able to take its rightful place as a sovereign state in the family of nations.[32]

To these two nations, which have so recently overcome the worst manifestations of their Westphalian disorders, one can add the anguished bravado of a third nation that has not. This is the Iraqi constitution of 2005.

> We the people of Iraq, who have just risen from our stumble, and who are looking with confidence to the future through a republican, federal, democratic, pluralistic system, have resolved with the determination of our men, women, the elderly and youth, to respect the rules of law, to establish justice and equality, to cast aside the politics of aggression, and to tend to the concerns of women and their rights, and to the elderly and their concerns, and to children and their affairs and to spread a culture of diversity and defusing terrorism.[33]

The triumph of most peoples in the past century was winning sovereignty over their countries from the powers that had oppressed them and gaining control of the resources that those powers were so shamelessly taking.[34] The headline of the 20th century was the victory of the Third World in the Third World War. In this context—in our world as it is now—an attempt to weaken peoples' resource sovereignty with "the common ownership of the Earth" will not counter power.

Think of being a citizen inside a former colony such as Algeria or Indonesia or Zimbabwe, where the national identity hardened in bloody struggles to wrestle national territory and its resource wealth away from relentless empires that clothed their exploitation in the colors of morality. Westerners now come to you saying that you do not entirely own your country's resources, because the British and French, the Dutch and Japanese, and even the Americans partly own them too. However worthy are the derivations from this principle, the principle itself will be hard for many to hear. There just is not enough trust for it to sound in their ears.

A proposal such as Pogge's, which uses "common ownership of the Earth" to argue for a tax on resources that countries extract, may be especially silent. Imagine living in South Sudan, one of the poorest countries in the world, and being informed that because of the oil, your country owes a debt to the Swiss.[35]

Demands like Pogge's would also be counter-productive because they would set peoples in resource-rich and resource-poor developing countries against each other. Many of the leaders of resource-rich countries are strongmen who still wear the clothing of the anti-colonial revolution. They would cry to their peoples, "The big powers want to take from us what we have won at such a price, and give it to strangers." And they would be right.

Pogge's goal is "global social justice." Yet social justice requires that people have shared beliefs about the world and the moral problems that face them. It requires that people are willing to compromise and sometimes sacrifice for each other. Social justice needs trust, and trust across borders is today sadly quite low.

"The common ownership of the Earth" resonated with Locke's readers in the seventeenth century, and with colonial Americans in the eighteenth century, because of its scriptural source and their shared Christian faith. In countries like India and China, common ownership has never had that kind of resonance—and in countries that have recently escaped empire (including these), it may today seem like a Western Trojan horse. By contrast, popular resource sovereignty is the principle that peoples everywhere have actually insisted upon across the decades to counter the powers that have oppressed them, and it's the principle that can counter the powers that continue to hound them today.

In the big picture, the world's transition to popular sovereignty is going well. In 1973, democratic countries were outnumbered by almost three to one. Today, the democracies form a majority.[36] Progress is good—except, as we know, in the authoritarian oil exporters, where the regimes survive on an external source of power. Few highly rent-addicted, oil-exporting regimes have ever transitioned to democracy.[37] The struggle of these countries to overcome Westphalia continues.

The institutions of popular sovereignty may feel like old news to some in the West, but to many elsewhere, they remain aspirations. Remnants of the Westphalian version of the state system are still with us, and the damage that these remnants cause—especially around natural resources—should not be confused with failures of the system itself. For centuries, peoples everywhere have fought hard to entrench the counter-powerful principle of popular sovereignty. There's still work for us to do to finish theirs.

GRINDING TOGETHER OR GROWING TOGETHER?

Philosophers enjoy an intellectual knockabout, and what's been said will provoke some to climb back into the ring and announce no holds barred. Take the worldwide distribution of natural resources itself, these philosophers will say. Isn't it just luck that some are born in countries rich with mineral bounties, like Botswana, while others are stuck with empty plains, as in Paraguay?[38] Justice (these philosophers say) demands the redistribution of resource wealth away from the lucky peoples in resource-rich countries toward the unlucky peoples in resource-poor countries. The baseline should be that each person in the world has a claim to an equal share of the world's resources. We should in the future see humans not as citizens of lucky or unlucky countries but instead as "cosmopolitans"—as equal citizens of a common world.[39] This is a fundamental challenge to the idea of popular resource sovereignty.

Now thinking back to Part I of this book, we know that many of those born in resource-rich countries would not think themselves lucky. Natural resources are not necessarily a curse, but they are dangerous enough to pause any argument that assumes they are necessarily a blessing to be divided equally.[40]

Philosophers of a cosmopolitan bent may express impatience with such details. It's incontrovertible (they may say) that great wealth is gained from natural resources, and that peoples do not deserve the natural wealth they just happen to have. Those Norwegians and Qataris, so rich and smug in their luck. Surely their natural windfalls can be taken and used to help individuals regardless of nation—to feed the poor, to cure disease, to fund education. We should stop seeing natural resources as rightly owned by peoples (they conclude) and start seeing them as resources for all of humanity, considered as a United Persons.

Again, the moral seriousness here is admirable; the causes that these thinkers favor are important. And the ideal of humans uniting across borders is undeniably attractive. The difficulty is not in finding good causes to support globally. That's easy—in a sense, there are too many. The questions, as always, surround principles and power: finding the paths that will actually achieve these worthwhile ends. The real difficulty is finding cosmopolitan principles that it would be reasonable to press hard enough to achieve the ends that all agree are good.

Taking the broadest view, what the world has now is a decent consensus on principles for good governance within countries: principles such as popular sovereignty and human rights. There is also relatively firm agreement on what should happen in relations between countries, such as that territorial conquest is wrong and keeping treaties is right. These agreements are by no means univocal, but they are substantial. In coming to consensus, it's been quite useful that modernity has generated a small, globally shared vocabulary to describe human beings and what should happen to them. "Human rights" and "genocide" are in this shared vocabulary; "capabilities" is making a bid for inclusion; "responsibility to protect" may not make it.[41]

What remains absent as yet are substantive shared principles and concepts for relations among individuals as such, considered not as citizens of nations but as "citizens of the world." Philosophers have imagined many cosmopolitan alternatives, yet in the absence of agreement, the question is how power could responsibly be used to realize any one of them.

At this transnational level, collective thinking today is still turbid—much like it was within Europe during the Middle Ages. After a long review of early European politics in his masterful *General History of Civilization in Europe*, the French politician François Guizot offers this summary:

> I have now run over all the great attempts at political organization which were made in Europe, down to the end of the fourteenth or beginning of the fifteenth century. All these failed. I have endeavoured to point out, in going along, the causes of these failures; to speak truly, they may all be summed up in one: society was not yet sufficiently advanced to adapt itself to unity; all was yet too local, too special, too narrow: too many differences prevailed both in things and in minds. There were no general interests, no general opinions capable of guiding, of bearing sway over particular interests and particular opinions. The most enlightened minds, the boldest thinkers, had as yet no just idea of administration or justice truly public.[42]

On "cosmopolitan" issues, the world is now in a condition similar to what Guizot describes here. "There were no general interests, no general opinions" is vivid enough today. Imagine, for example, that you are the cosmopolitan who has been chosen to present a case to Venezuela or Kuwait to submit itself to a global resource-redistribution regime. A tough job.

Given the divergences in interests and opinions, the issue becomes one of power. Picking up Guizot's passage again:

> The most enlightened minds, the boldest thinkers, had as yet no just idea of administration or justice truly public. It was evidently necessary that a very active, powerful civilization should first mix, assimilate, grind together, as it were, all these incoherent elements; it was necessary that there should first be a strong centralization of interests, laws, manners, ideas; it was necessary, in a word, that there should be created a public authority and a public opinion.[43]

The question for cosmopolitan philosophers is how much "grinding together" they are proposing in order to impose their controversial principles. Redistributions must be enforced; entreaties will not suffice. All of the important questions surround the agency that will implement any cosmopolitan ideal. What is the nature of this agency's coercive power? Will anyone suggest that it be backed by armed force? Yet if not, how does a global redistributive agency require compliance? How, for instance, to make the petrocrats give up their source of power?

At their least edifying, cosmopolitans use a passive voice to insist on aggressive reforms. Something—something even quite difficult—must be done, yet who does this difficult thing, and how, remains hazy. Occasionally, a gesture may be made to some hypothetical body, like a widely trusted and incorruptible global panel of experts, or a world citizenry willing to accept majority decisions for the sake of humanity as a whole. Yet what is meant to happen when some powerful group—say, the Russians or the Saudis—rejects the ideal is left unsaid. It is no use planning tea parties for tigers. If some pattern will be imposed across the planet, the power that does this cannot be passive.

While waiting for the "grind together" proposals to become more complete, we might revisit the virtues of popular resource sovereignty, which works instead on a "grow together" model. One great advantage is that popular sovereignty is already the world's ideal: peoples have won that battle. The treaties have been signed; elites and mass movements reflexively speak its language; there is already a place for the principle in the hierarchy of international principles. Policies to support popular resource sovereignty will require the creation of no coercive world bodies, and they are compatible with responsible national foreign policies. These policies work within the design constraints of the system that today secures the preconditions for moral progress of any kind.

The great promise of popular sovereignty is that self-determining nations do grow together. Popular sovereignty makes peoples more extraconnective as well as more intraconnective. Democracies are less likely to go to war with each other. They are also more likely to create and participate in international institutions and more likely to respect international treaties.[44] Even better, national democracy is the best school that we know to make individuals capable of connecting across borders too.

To whatever extent a cosmopolitan future will arrive, it will require individuals who are able to act together despite the features that distinguish them. For that to be possible, individuals in today's resource-disordered countries will have to become more democratically capable than they now are: more knowledgeable about the safe use of political power, more accustomed to the give-and-take of life within a self-ruling group. The surest way we know for these individual capacities to develop is within the institutions of popular sovereignty, which now exist in all regions of the world.[45]

The most judicious cosmopolitans praise the value of individuals freely associating to determine their common future.[46] Moving power over resources away from authoritarians and militias, toward sovereign peoples, will advance that weighty goal. Those who wish to see power spread still further can see popular resource sovereignty as a stage along their way.

Enabling peoples to control their fates and to grow together will make humanity smarter, and so better able to choose for itself the principles that might someday constitute a United Persons. Peacefully promoting popular sovereignty will encourage the kinds of relations across borders that may eventually allow justice to emerge in some richer form. In the meantime, strengthening peoples will enhance humanity's ability to meet the challenges that will soon come. If we can now succeed in taking the next step in the three hundred year progress against "might makes right," we can then leave it to our more democratic, more trusting, and more united descendants to decide for themselves what forms of justice they want to achieve, given the relations they have formed and the conditions of the world that they will see much better than we now do.

PEOPLE OVER PATTERNS, RELATIONS OVER ALLOCATIONS

Let's stay with our friends the philosophers for just a while longer, as they can help us in our cosmomeletics—our meditations on the world. Philosophy can help us to think about general principles, and about what basic orientation we might take toward the reform of institutions over the longest term. It can assist us in developing our *Weltanschauung*, which Heidegger grandly describes as "a self-realized, productive as well as conscious way of apprehending and interpreting the universe of beings."[47]

Those coming to academia from outside may be surprised to find that some of those inside do a kind of political philosophy without politics—a sort of "powerless" theory. These philosophers will say that they are less concerned with *what to do* (about power, say). Their real interest is only in *what is true* (about justice, say). Outsiders might think that what is true about justice must include facts about power because of its potential to warp characters and wreck relations—but this isn't the kind of truth that these thinkers seek. They say they are looking for the ideal form, the perfect description of what justice *is*.[48]

For those coming from outside, it may take a moment to get into the mood to think like this. Imagine that you take your job to be to describe an ideally just world. And what this means is listing the most important rights that people have—like rights over their bodies, rights over property, rights to do what they really want to do—and saying who should have rights to how much of what. At the end of a good day of work, you will have argued for a principle like "Everyone should have rights to equal ___" or "Everyone should start their adult lives with the same rights to ___."

The final truth about justice, all of these philosophers agree, is that the world should first realize a just distribution of rights. In a just distribution, these rights will be allocated so that everyone has exactly what they're really entitled to: each person will start with precisely the right rights—and starting from there, everyone can be free to do whatever they want (so long as they respect the rights of others). What these philosophers debate vigorously is how to fill out the key terms, like what counts as a "just distribution," and which rights are really the most important. Those disagreements need not concern us here.[49]

When doing this kind of philosophy, questions about the power that enforces the perfect pattern (or even about how goods like food are produced) fade away. The goal is to find the truth about the ideal—as it's said, the ideally just distribution of rights. And yet, we might ask, if we really are permitted to abstract away from all of the problems of politics, and if we are really allowed to imagine any ideal of human life that we like, would any such vision top our lists? For after some reflection, one might notice that none of these ideals talks about what people will actually do with the rights that they're given. These ideals merely take, as Rousseau would say, "people as they are." And people as they are—they are not what they might be.

Whatever a philosopher's "ideally just distribution" might be, it will allow frightful social failures. All such ideals permit the most appalling selfishness and cruelty, arrogance and petulance, insecurity and duplicity, delusions, betrayals, and hate. All of these ideals are concerned only with what individuals get—not with what kind of people they are, or how they relate to each other. In terms of what matters most in most human lives—including in philosophers' lives when they leave the study—these philosophers may be designing ideally just hells.[50]

If we're really allowed to imagine any ideal that we like—if we really don't have to worry about keeping the peace, or keeping the lights on—then we are unlikely to choose any of these ideals. We would rather just go for "universal love" and be done with it. So long as "universal love" includes each having a justified love of self, this is a much more attractive ideal of human life than any mere distribution of rights could be.

It's true that universal love is not an ideal of *justice*. Yet what of that? Ought we take "justice" as a priest's incantation? Why did we start talking about justice at all? What is justice *for*? What, after all, do just institutions mean for human life?

There is an older tradition of thought about just institutions that speaks about distributions, but not for their own sakes. What this tradition emphasizes is the effects that institutions have on people, and especially on their relations with one another. This is the tradition of Plato and Aristotle, of Montesquieu and Burke, of Rousseau and Wollstonecraft and Marx. In this tradition, institutions do more than distribute what people desire—they influence the desires that people have. A modern philosopher in this tradition writes that a country's social system

> shapes the wants and aspirations that its citizens come to have. It determines in part the sort of persons they want to be as well as the sort of persons they are. Thus an economic system is not only an institutional device for satisfying existing wants and needs but a way of creating and fashioning wants in the future. How men work together now to satisfy their present desires affects the desires they will have later on, the kind of persons they will be.[51]

This tradition looks to "people as they are, and laws as they might be"—and so, as this passage says, to "the kind of persons they will be."[52] In this tradition, what is ultimately worth caring about is what kinds of people there are and how they relate to each other—whether men and women are shallow, capricious, and mean, or whether they are beings of integrity, generosity, conscience, and joy.

In this tradition, the best institutions form human environments that foster positive identities and allow individuals freely to express them: identities that are more integrated, open, cooperative, and uniting. This is the tradition that will be the most rewarding as we orient ourselves toward reforming institutions over the longest term. And this brings us back again to the first thesis of this chapter. The success of humanity will ultimately depend on how connective the people of the future will be.

YOU ARE THE ENLIGHTENMENT

The Enlightenment is all around you, shining from your screens, the molecules of many nations united to keep you warm while speeding 35,000 feet above the Earth. The Enlightenment is in your body: nutrients, vitamins, a vaccine keeping your blood clean, a stent keeping your heart clear. The Enlightenment has changed your tools and rulers and religions. Most of all, it has changed your mind. You demand and examine, absorb and analyze, bite and chew. You stand for progress and principle. You are the Enlightenment.

You critique the Enlightenment. After the Revolution comes the Terror. Einstein delivered the atom bomb; Mozart did not stop Germany from attacking the world. You expose false calls for unity, like demagogues who offer glory for obedience, and entrepreneurs of division who build up by cutting out. You see through political fantasies born of insecurity and wrapped up in myths. Uniformity bores you. You do not fear difference.

At your best, you are conditionally trusting, and unconditionally trustworthy. Hard-headed and soft-hearted, a pessimist of intelligence and an optimist of will.[53] You reach confidently across boundaries to join your energies with others so that together you are stronger and free. You are powerful and counter-powerful. You are connective. You should rule the world.

Epilogue

The Philosophy of Unity

There is this basis of powerful natural sentiment... This firm foundation is that of the social feelings of mankind—the desire to be in unity with our fellow creatures, which is already a powerful principle in human nature, and happily one of those which tend to become stronger, even without express inculcation, from the influences of advancing civilization.

—John Stuart Mill

Almost every nation represented at this table is composed of disparate elements of populations that have been combined in one way or another into a unified or federated political system. Here differences among formally separate peoples either have been or are being submerged and new and larger peoples are emerging. This process of evolution and merger is still going on. It is a trend which diminishes the possibilities of conflict. Must we not exercise the greatest care lest anything we do here tend to freeze the pattern of peoples along present lines and thus instead of promoting the unity of mankind, emphasize certain obstacles to such unity?

—Eleanor Roosevelt[1]

Successful movements to counter Westphalia's rule of "might makes right" have included the abolition of the slave trade, the liberation of the colonies, the end of white rule, and the many campaigns for human rights. The reform of "might makes right" for natural resources will be the next of these movements. Going deep into one part of today's global economy, we've found that it divides foreigners against each other. It also sets those foreigners against us, and it sets us against ourselves as well. Much of the war and oppression, the corruption and the extremism of our times are symptoms of these divisions. If division is the problem, then unity must be the solution.

COUNTER-POWER AND FREEDOM

Power rules legitimize advantage for those with more power; counter-power rules demand more for those with less. Today, effectiveness is a rule of power; the rule of law is counter-power. Nepotism is a power rule; it is countered by making careers open to talents. Why do we feel such a strong natural attraction toward rules that counter the ancient connection between might and right?

Let "political power" encompass violence, threat, and manipulation through institutions. Then power should be countered for the sake of freedom. On this the many heirs of the Enlightenment agree, differing in where they find power and what kind of escape from power they foresee.

So Foucault saw the modern task as requiring "a patient labor giving form to our impatience for liberty."

> We know that the great promise or the great hope of the eighteenth century... lay in the simultaneous and proportional growth of individuals with respect to one another. And, moreover, we can see that throughout the entire history of Western societies... the acquisition of capacities and the struggle for freedom have constituted permanent elements... What is at stake, then, is this: How can the growth of capacities be disconnected from the intensification of power relations?[2]

And Hayek, who calls power "coercion by the arbitrary will of another."

> We are concerned in this book with that condition of men in which coercion of some by others is reduced as much as is possible in

> society. This state we shall describe throughout as a state of liberty or freedom… The task of a policy of freedom must therefore be to minimize coercion or its harmful effects, even if it cannot eliminate it completely.[3]

And Engels, the optimist:

> As soon as there is no longer any social class to be held in subjection; as soon as class rule, and the individual struggle for existence based upon our present anarchy in production, with the collisions and excesses arising from these, are removed, nothing more remains to be repressed, and a special repressive force, a state, is no longer necessary… State interference in social relations becomes, in one domain after another, superfluous, and then dies out of itself; the government of persons is replaced by the administration of things… It is the ascent of humanity from the realm of necessity into the realm of freedom.[4]

The common trajectory is toward social worlds in which human relations track power less and less, leaving more and more space for spontaneous action, both individually and together. At utopia, power is unnecessary: human desires will at least not conflict irremediably and will at best converge freely on the same ends. That ideal may be distant, perhaps permanently so—in our lives, power will always be with us. Our attraction to counter-power rules draws from this ideal of freedom, from the desire to diminish the power that cannot (yet) be dispensed with.

At this very high level, we see strong agreement on the value of countering power. Liberals and conservatives, libertarians, socialists, and anarchists agree, in the abstract, on the value of buffers against violence, threat, and manipulation. Whether they will agree on the value of counter-powerful rules like human rights or set borders—or even on the desirability of laws or nations in the long run—depends on their confidence in existing institutions and the potential for their transformation. The high-level consensus among political philosophies holds only that power should be opposed, leaving spaces for human action, individually and together, that is free from its operation.

The countering of power is always accompanied by the puncturing of ideology. Critique has made it harder to endorse, for example, hoary theories of racial superiority and divine right. In the fourteenth century, Marsilius refused the pope's political supremacy, as the Taoists had earlier opposed the Chinese elite's apologetics for its rule.[5] The *Sermon on the Mount* is pure counter-power: its valorizations of the merciful and the meek, the persecuted and the peacemakers, were outrageous inversions of the Roman Empire's ideology of effectiveness. This perennial resistance to power is aroused by an ideal deep in our understanding—deep enough to be called foundational in our evaluations of human relations.

THE FREE UNITY OF ENDS

"One need not go around the world," said Goethe, "to grasp that the sky is blue everywhere."[6] One need not go to the antipodes to know how others judge the goodness of human relations. Conflict is less desirable than toleration, and toleration less desirable than cooperation. We all appraise forms of human relations on a continuum, marking their degree of convergence or divergence in ends. Conflictual ends are incompatible; their mutual achievement is impossible. With toleration, people at least agree to forbear the pursuit of incompatible ends. In cooperation, ends are aligned enough that people may act positively together.

At their core, most of our moral concepts indicate degrees of convergence or divergence in ends. They thereby locate forms of human relations along a continuum of value. Compare cruelty with rivalry. Cruelty is worse than rivalry because cruel desires are more divergent than rivalrous ones. A rival merely opposes what the other desires as an obstacle to his own ends. In cruelty, one person opposes what the other desires simply because the other desires it. To be cruel is to thwart what the other wants because the other wants it: to aim at the other's unhappiness. Torture is a species of cruelty where one person aims to thwart desires that the other cannot help but have.[7] The concept of evil adds to the core idea of cruelty an associated attitude: to be evil is to take pleasure in cruelty. Evil occupies the negative pole of the spectrum of value where ends are maximally divergent.[8]

Toward this continuum's positive pole, ends converge more and more: persons increasingly will the same ends, and increasingly for the same reasons. Forbearance, reciprocity, alliance and solidarity describe relations of increasing convergence in ends, with the associated positive attitudes. As Aristotle and Kant saw, what we now think of as moral relations in a narrower sense are continuous with personal relations like community, friendship, and intimacy.[9]

At the positive extreme of the continuum of value are ideals of unity, such as Kant's "realm of ends": a "whole of all ends... in systematic connection."[10] Mill's ideal rests upon "a powerful principle in human nature": "the desire to be in unity with our fellow creatures." As Mill explains further:

> In an improving state of the human mind, the influences are constantly on the increase, which tend to generate in each individual a feeling of unity with all the rest; which, if perfect, would make him never think of, or desire, any beneficial condition for himself, in the benefits of which they are not included.[11]

What an individual thinks of, and desires, is a function of his identity. The perfect human identity that Mill describes is that of an individual who thinks only of self-benefits that are also other-benefits: an individual who only wants goods that are common goods.[12] Such an individual pursues these common goods freely, not because of force; his acts toward unity express his own identity. A community of such individuals is the end point of all ideals like Mill's, which are, with the appropriate sentiments added, nothing other than ideals of universal love.[13]

REDEEMING POWER

Let's look again at this continuum of convergence of ends, this time to locate power within the relations that spread across it. Relations defined by power, broadly construed, gravitate toward the negative pole of the continuum. Violence, threat, and manipulation are, in their essence, means for one party to achieve his ends at the expense of another's: power presumes divergent desires. Both domination and indoctrination, for instance, are defined in terms of divergent ends, as are deception and fraud. Harassment, bullying, and molestation again have divergence at their core, with their conceptual peripheries tailored to specific interpersonal contexts.

While relations of power gravitate toward the negative pole of the continuum, these relations can be redeemed by—they can be justified because of—the value that they also engender or embody. Hobbes's argument is that the coercion of a Leviathan is redeemed by the great goods of peace.

Leviathan's domination in itself has negative value—coercive ends are necessarily incompatible with others' ends. Yet the coercive success of Leviathan stops the antagonism that defines the state of war, and thereby creates an environment where many peaceful and cooperative projects can succeed. Power is redeemed by the greater unity it facilitates.

A great many arguments in politics have this structure, turning on the redemption of power. The punishments of criminal justice are said to be redeemed by the maintenance of public order. The coercive enforcement of private property rights is said to be redeemed by the productivity that such a system enables. The soundness of such arguments depends on empirical facts—what we notice is that they all have the right form to register an overall increase in value.

Now power can be redeemed by the value of what it engenders, but excessive power—by definition—cannot be. The domination by Leviathan is redeemed by the great goods of peace—if the only alternative really is endless war *omnium contra omnes*. Yet Leviathan can also be condemned, as Locke and Rousseau condemned him, should a peaceful and less coercive commonwealth be feasible. The feasibility of peace without absolutism was a discovery of human social capacity: a discovery of a freer form of unity.

The philosopher works with concepts at high levels of abstraction. A philosopher's political ideal will be framed in general terms that describe non-conflictual conditions (peace, toleration, non-domination) or convergent ends (a social contract, a general will). When philosophers speak of power, they will describe a high-level goal: that the exercise of power be minimized, for instance, or that power be redeemed as far as possible by convergences of ends that are chosen while free (that is, while confident, focused, with good mental faculties, provisioned with information, unburdened by falsehood, unforced by man or need, etc.).

Yet we don't live at a high level of abstraction. When we assess the social formations around us, our judgments will turn on what alternatives are available. What to do now depends on what is possible now. Greater unity, like greater happiness, is radically indeterminate without information about what people's ends are, and how they can be achieved and changed. This is why these political philosophies will be most alive when evaluating real human circumstances. To become action-guiding, the imperative to increase free unity must be contextual, with the context being especially crucial for rules of counter-power.

Power is suspicious because it always enables some to achieve their ends at the expense of others. This explains our natural attraction to rules of counter-power. Forms of power vary greatly across time, however, and therefore also what counts as counter-power. Power and counter-power are relative concepts, like cold and warm. Codes of chivalry limited violence against women in feudal times and so counted as counter-powerful; later, these codes reinforced gender subordination. The rule prohibiting plunder during war was counter-powerful in the nineteenth century; in the twentieth century, the rule requiring the safeguarding of an enemy's antiquities was more counter-powerful still. Our discussions of counter-power in Chapter 9 were so concerned with the actual entrenchment of rules, and with the emergence of specific identities, because the value of rules and identities depends on the context of power within which they exist.

Each human lives within an environment of convergent and divergent ends, facing the threats and opportunities of his or her exact social location. What is practically significant is the actual achievement of valuable relations among people of flesh, now and in the future. So what actual relations should be preserved, reformed. and rebelled against today depends on which rules are entrenched and what identities are present today. What matters for action is what relations of unity and disunity exist around us and how a greater free unity of ends can be created. The primary evaluation of any act, rule, role, or identity is how it contributes, at its time, to promoting or hindering the achievement of freely harmonized ends over the long term. The promulgation of a counter-powerful rule that's attractive in the abstract may be counter-productive on the day.

Even pushes for peace can be untimely. The Kellogg-Briand Pact of 1928 required nations to renounce all war; it likely increased the time that Hitler was given to build Germany's military. John Maynard Keynes was impressed in 1918 with the rhetoric of President Wilson's Fourteen Points, yet Wilson "had no plan, no scheme, no constructive ideas whatever for clothing with the flesh of life the commandments which he had thundered from the White House. He could have preached a sermon on any of them or have addressed a state prayer to the Almighty for their fulfillment; but he could not frame their concrete application to the actual state of Europe."[14] Policies, treaties, institutions, offices, traits, even what are conceived of as basic rules of interpersonal morality are ultimately to be evaluated by their contribution in their time, within a specific social world, to increasing or decreasing free unity among individuals' ends.

This is an ideal-based consequentialism—a theory that judges everything by its contribution to the ideal, and with the ideal set by the maximum achievement of freely unified ends.[15] The theory has many levels, including acts, rules, roles, principles, and identities.[16] And the rule ordering these multiple levels is again unity. A person should reason on these levels as will result in the greatest free unity.[17]

As in all consequentialist theories, here the ends justify the means. Yet to a great extent, the ends justify the principles that constrain the means. Principles solve collective action problems and prioritize long-term reasoning. Supporting principles within a context is especially propitious when these principles have proved their worth already, when the mechanisms to enforce them are at hand, when they have gained widespread adherence, and when coordination on their realization is as yet incomplete.

In this theory, there can be tension between ends and means, but that is not where the real action is. Rather, the action is where the ideal justifies the ends. The foundries of actions are the roles and relationships at the core of every identity, which make options salient to individuals and set the ends they take as final. Identities are the foundations of free unity. Their unification can also be a basis for reconciliation. Reconciliation to being an individual who is inevitably defined by so many divisions (of labor, gender, generation, and so on) comes from seeing oneself as contributing to a larger whole, both in one's time and across time.[18]

POWER AND THE PROMOTION OF UNITY

Popular sovereignty is counter-powerful, as it gives the citizenry the authority to hold the state to account. Yet popular sovereignty also contains within itself a positive ideal of unity. The hope of popular sovereignty transcends a coerced peace, where citizens benefit from the exercise of a political power they see as alien. The hope is that citizens will exercise power together, toward their shared ends and as a shared end. The hope is that sovereign citizens will have not only their particular wills, but that they will together form a general will.

Here citizens want what politics bring, and they also want a political relationship with each other. They want to make a common life, to join with other citizens in creating the history of a nation that they've inherited and will pass on. When this ideal is realized, citizens give a certain priority to the political over the personal. Citizens will be reasonable, willing to be guided by shared values and institutions even at some cost to their own private advantage. Such citizens will see political values as "very great values and hence not easily overridden: these values govern the basic framework of social life—the very groundwork of our existence."[19]

The ideal of popular sovereignty is of a higher-order unity, a unity of citizens wanting to decide their rules together and willing to abide by what is decided. This unity may contain great diversity. Unity does not mean uniformity; a unification of varied elements may contain more value than the same of sames. Diversity allows persons of various constitutions to pursue their favored ends. Different rites and styles will also suit different lives. The diversity itself allows citizens to enjoy and learn from each other, and so to have richer experiences than in a monoculture. And a more diverse community, like a more robust immune system, may also have more human resources with which to meet the challenges that fate sends its way.

More, pluralism can also be the product of valuable action: "the outcome of the free exercise of free human reason under conditions of liberty."[20] So within unity theory, pluralism can be valuable in itself, and it can result from, and also lead to, valuable states of affairs. Yet as theorists of all stripes have concluded, diversity will always be most valuable when it's set in a context of unity.

The "Renaissance man" is universally admired: complexity contains more value than simplicity—so long as there is a unity holding it all together. The ideal of popular sovereignty is that each citizen endorses the common political values firmly and freely, so that amidst diversity, each has an identity in which the shared ends are integral. Here each citizen is internally unified, in a distinctive way, around ends that unite all citizens together. This ideal is common to many different theories of popular sovereignty. Even agonistic pluralists look for the mediation of perpetual contestation by democratic politics.[21] In a Rawlsian "social union of social unions," all have the "common aim of cooperating together to realize their own and one another's nature."[22] All of these accounts of popular sovereignty are essentially Rousseauian—all envision how citizens' identities can be unified around commitments that unite difference.[23]

IDENTITIES AND FREE UNITY

The evaluation of acts, rules, and institutions is relative to their effects in their context. And this evaluation attends not only to their immediate implications for unity, but also to their effects at a deeper level, on the identities of future humans: literally on who will come to exist, "the kind of persons they will be."

Rules of conduct that constrain the pursuit of interests are ultimately less significant than shifts in identities that alter what people perceive their interests to be. As we've seen with the international rules on conquest and human rights, such rules are the gateways to identity change. Rules first adopted for self-interest then change the self, and so the self's interests. The wider benefits of compliance become evident, and the narrative, cultural, and spiritual colorings of the new identities get filled in.[24] Here is Mill, in the passage leading up to the quotation above:

> Not only does all strengthening of social ties, and all healthy growth of society, give to each individual a stronger personal interest in practically consulting the welfare of others; it also leads him to identify his feelings more and more with their good, or at least with an even greater degree of practical consideration for it. He comes, as though instinctively, to be conscious of himself as a being who of course pays regard to others. The good of others becomes to him a thing naturally and necessarily to be attended to, like any of the physical conditions of our existence...
>
> This mode of conceiving ourselves and human life, as civilization goes on, is felt to be more and more natural. Every step in political improvement renders it more so, by removing the sources of opposition of interest, and leveling those inequalities of legal privilege between individuals or classes, owing to which there are large portions of mankind whose happiness it is still practicable to disregard. In an improving state of the human mind, the influences are constantly on the increase, which tend to generate in each individual a feeling of unity with all the rest; which, if perfect, would make him never think of, or desire, any beneficial condition for himself, in the benefits of which they are not included.[25]

In the development of desires that Mill describes, human relations migrate toward the positive pole on the continuum of value, from opposition and disregard, to attentiveness, to mutuality. The emotional bases of the desires that Mill praises are robust in most people. Experiences of unity—most obviously in the womb, and thereafter in familial and romantic love—are some of the most profound.[26] The loss of a person with whom one identifies is often the deepest loss. More, as Rousseau and Hume also emphasized, human desires have a tendency to unify through the mechanism of sympathy, which reason can extend and smooth.[27] We see the living results of these human desires for free unity in the history of moral progress surveyed in Part III—in the campaigns against the slave trade, against colonialism, for human rights, and for popular sovereignty. The circle of moral concern, as Peter Singer says, has continued to expand.[28]

How far Mill's "improving state" of the human mind can achieve its perfect orientation toward unity has been differently imagined by different thinkers. In the Rawlsian well-ordered society, citizens raised under just institutions develop a strong desire to cooperate with their fellow citizens. In the Marxist ideal of free social production, each wants to labor in ways that satisfy the true needs of others. Earthly utopias such as Thomas More's approach an ideal of spontaneous universality as closely as the constraints of human nature allow. With the constraints of human nature removed—in the scientific utopias by technology, in the Christian utopias by death—utopian ideals converge in describing beings who by nature desire what others desire, all freely acting toward their universal common good.

We can elaborate visions of the free unity of ends to whatever limits our skepticism permits. Kant's own realm of ends is a utopia of unity. Kant holds that the realization of a realm of ends will always be hindered by the imperfections of human nature that he describes in his anthropology, yet his vision is continuous with the superhuman relations that he describes in his religion. Kant's mistake in moral theory was to disqualify actions whose success depends on disunified ends (hence the rigorism on deception and coercion) instead of seeing the unity of ends as a collective cause to be furthered, arduously and approximately, with whatever means we have on hand. Kant's realm of ends, though, correctly expresses a common utopian vision of voluntary volitional coalition.

THE VALUE OF POWER

Our impatience with such ideals flows from suspicion about the degree of unity of which humans are capable, as well as from two further sources. The first source is a justified fear of power itself, when it has the word *unity* in its mouth. Demagogues always call for unity when enforcing their own (racial, religious, nationalist, class-based) ideology. So Lenin:

> Concerning the significance of individual dictatorial powers from the point of view of the specific tasks of the present moment, it must be said that large-scale machine industry—which is precisely the material source, the productive source, the foundation of socialism—calls for absolute and strict *unity of will*, which directs the joint labours of hundreds, thousands and tens of thousands of people... But how can strict unity of will be ensured? By thousands subordinating their will to the will of one... *Unquestioning subordination* to a single will is absolutely necessary for the success of processes organised on the pattern of large-scale machine industry... [The] revolution demands—precisely in the interests of its development and consolidation, precisely in the interests of socialism—that the people *unquestioningly obey the single will* of the leaders of labour. [29]

History forever replays this very same move.[30] As a result of this history, even those who know little of it will hear invisible klaxons whenever unity is praised. Our ancestors, instructed in the dire lessons of demagoguery, have designed our minds to sound alarms upon any presentation of unification as an ideal. Yet here the resistance really reinforces the ideal. These mental alarms are themselves counter-powerful, and so can be guides toward a free unity of ends that, it deserves emphasis, has no violence, coercion, or manipulation within it.

The valorization of power poses a second and more direct challenge to unity as an ideal. Can free convergence of ends really be taken as a foundational standard for the evaluation of human relations when power-based rules and identities are so widely and loudly praised? The peacemakers may be blessed, but within our nations, it's the war makers that get the lion's share of the spending. The first *Song of Moses* says that the Lord himself is a man of war; by the last *Song of Moses,* God's sword devours flesh, and his arrows are drunk with blood.[31] Ideals of free unity are not the only ideals, and the valorization of power may seem to put paid to the whole theory here described. There must, after all, be rules of power (the fullness of papal authority, the divine right of kings) for rules of counter-power to balance.

And rules of power trumpet standards of value that are unlike ideals of free mutual identification.

A unity created by violence, coercion, or manipulation can be more desirable than no unity at all. Life under Leviathan is preferable to chaos in conflict. The text leading up to *Leviathan*'s most famous quote describes the dystopia compared to which absolute rule is good:

> A time of war, where every man is enemy to every man, the same consequent to the time wherein men live without other security than what their own strength and their own invention shall furnish them withal. In such condition there is no place for industry, because the fruit thereof is uncertain: and consequently no culture of the earth; no navigation, nor use of the commodities that may be imported by sea; no commodious building; no instruments of moving and removing such things as require much force; no knowledge of the face of the earth; no account of time; no arts; no letters; no society; and which is worst of all, continual fear, and danger of violent death; and the life of man, solitary, poor, nasty, brutish, and short.[32]

The Thirty Years War approached Hobbes's nightmare. The Westphalian consensus on effectiveness in international affairs was, as we saw in Chapter 9, an advance over the political void it replaced. Power is redeemed by a common desire for the effects of its exercise. Power will always assert its necessity for creating peace, and sometimes rightly so.

Where there is chaos, we call for order. Power can create peace, which is a species of unity and a step toward more. Where there is peace, we call for freedom. Once order is established, counter-powerful campaigns will begin, promising that unity can be preserved under conditions of greater liberty. Sometimes what those campaigns promise is true.

Which side should prevail in any struggle between power and counter-power is a question of consequences, and how far one believes that counter-power can ultimately progress will again turn on one's confidence in how far institutions and identities can be remade. Rawls's international ideal, for example, is a liberal compromise between power and counter-power. In this "realistic utopia," there is still significant coercion in the international system, especially at national borders.[33] Yet in this utopia, all nations are inherently satisfied with their place in the world order, and the great evils of human history ("unjust war and oppression, religious persecution and the denial of liberty of conscience, starvation and poverty, not to mention genocide and mass murder") no longer occur.[34]

Power is rightly praised above chaos, and partial unities are better than none. The valorization of power derives from the desire to protect a partial unity perceived as under threat. God's strong arm protected the Hebrews from their tormentors; our modern warriors work for the Department of Defense. We will always prefer partial unities so long as no reasonable alternative is in sight. And again, we have only come so far in a historical movement toward greater free unity. The capacity for collective reasoning remains poor; divisive identities are widespread.

Still, looking from the past toward ourselves, the scope of our current partial unifications is remarkable. Imagine what Rousseau—much less Aristotle—would have said of the chances that 65 million (United Kingdom), 320 million (United States), or even 1.3 billion humans (India) could unite in political formations that maintain civil peace, political rights, and personal liberties, as well as high levels of mutual identification. When the planes crashed into the towers in New York, Alaskans cried—and not only out of sympathy, but from the pain of their own injury. Current valorizations of power are inevitable in the circumstances of partial unities, and they will endure so long as progress toward the free unity of ends remains incomplete. Still, philosophy begins in wonder—and one may be full of wonder at how much humanity has achieved.

SEEK UNITY

In the chaotic seventeenth century, Hobbes wrote that the fundamental law is to "Seek Peace." We can now see that this is a theorem of a more basic law—"Seek Unity": the unity of identities, freely expressed. The use of power is only justified to the degree that this leads to a greater free unity of human ends; otherwise, power should be countered. This is because value is itself relative to the unity of ends. Mill was correct that the yearning for unity is a strong principle of human nature; where he erred was thinking that value can be measured independently of that unity. The achievement of ends is better the more the ends are freely shared.

Value is intersubjective, and a value based on a partial unification will never be as good as we can imagine. The common good comprises the shared ends of persons insofar as their common identities define their common interests. The best goods are common goods; realizing a universal common good would be the *summum bonum*, the best of all.

Notes

INTRODUCTION

1. BIS/DFID Trade Policy Unit 2011, 3. Figure is for 1980–2008.

2. European Aluminium Association 2014. Based on this 2013 figure, global consumption was 3,509 pounds of aluminum per second. The figure includes recycled material.

3. World Steel Association 2014, 16. Based on this 2013 figure, global steel consumption was 48.93 tons per second.

4. International Tropical Timber Organization 2012, v.

5. London Metal Exchange 2012. The specific figure for 2011 is 21.8 million tons.

6. Pilling 2011b.

7. Stanford Graduate School of Business 2012.

8. Life Expectancy at Birth, Maternal Mortality Ratio, Malnutrition Prevalence Height for Age, and Literacy Rate Adult Total from World Bank 2015b.

9. Ravallion 2013, 145. Even more optimistic improvements in poverty relief are reported in Chandy and Gertz 2011. The UN reports that the Millennium Development Goal of halving severe poverty was met five years early. United Nations 2012a, 1. For criticisms of these mainstream numbers, see Pogge 2010a.

10. Deaton 2013, 218, 219, 13, 59.

11. Richard J. Durbin quoted in Polgreen 2008.

12. John Prendergast in US Senate Committee on Foreign Relations 2013.

13. Margot Wallstrom quoted in BBC 2011a.

14. Pole Institute 2010, 42–43.

15. Gettleman 2007.

16. "The World's Worst War" is from Gettleman 2012. The number of conflict-related deaths in the Congo is difficult to ascertain and disputed. See Chapter 4, note 45.

17. Conrad 2010, 14.

18. The next paragraph summarizes Ross 2012, 1–2. Ross's measure for resource dependence uses oil income per capita. In the text, "oil state" will follow Ross's usage; "resource dependent" will follow the IMF definition: that resources provide at least 25 percent of exports or fiscal revenues or GDP.

19. The natural resources most associated with a "curse" in the literature are oil and gems, with metals and timber also getting some attention. (As in many texts, here the term *oil* often includes natural gas; when it matters, we will split the two out.) The literature focuses on the resources above because these are high-demand commodities, with a high value to weight, that often require little or no free domestic labor for their extraction (in contrast, for example, to fish).

The social scientific literature on the resource curse is large. Ross 2014 is a literature survey on the "political" resource curse; Frankel 2012 surveys research on the "economic" resource curse. Instead of reproducing the citations in these surveys, here we cite leading or recent work on a topic. All researchers agree that causal claims are difficult to establish in this area with social-scientific techniques. The analysis in this book draws on the resource curse literature and also goes beyond this literature in its conclusions. Reaching judgments beyond the range of current empirical techniques is one role of the theorist (as in Kant 1991).

20. Freedom House 2014a; BP 2014, 6.

21. On corruption, see Leite and Weidmann 1999, Arezki and Brückner 2011, Andersen et al. 2014. On institutional quality, see Karl 1997, Isham et al. 2005, Wiens 2014. On trust, see Kolstad and Wiig 2012, which finds an indirect influence of natural resources on trust, mediated by inequality, corruption, and civil war.

22. On resources and conflict, see Collier et al. 2009, Ross 2012, Le Billon 2012.

23. Kaufmann 2012, Kaufmann 2013.

24. Smith 1904, IV.7.18; Marx 1977, 917.

25. US Energy Information Administration 2013. "Authoritarian" here indicates a country rated as "Not Free" in Freedom House 2012.

26. *Forbes* 2014b. Ranking is by market value.

27. Fox 1792, 3.

28. Seventy-five years of one handshake per second would span 2,365,200,000 seconds; the number of people living on $2.00 a day or less is approximately 2.4 billion. World Bank 2014f.

29. Personal communication, Port Harcourt, June 2010. Jello Biafra quoted in Naylor 2007.

30. On complicity, see Lepora and Goodin 2013.

31. For example, Sourcemap (free.sourcemap.com).

32. On Zimbabwe, see Andersson 2011, BBC 2011b.

33. Jamieson 2014, Chapters 1 and 2.

34. Smith 1904, I.2.1.

35. Marx 1992, 379.

36. *Saudi Arabia Basic Law* 1992, Chapter 2, Article 7.

NEED TO KNOW BASIS

1. Yergin 2008, 167.

2. Calvin Coolidge quoted in Hughes 2014, 46.

3. Chomsky 1999, 31.

4. Yergin 2008. For much more on the big picture of global energy today, see Yergin 2011.

5. See www.cleantrade.org.

6. IPCC 2014, 111.

7. Geology 2014.
8. Brown 2012.
9. Crooks 2013.
10. Lossan 2014.
11. Victaulic 2009.
12. NOIA 2013, Sandbu 2009.
13. RT.com 2014b, Maritime Connector 2014, US Navy 2014.
14. For overviews of the history, technology, and economics of oil, see Bridge and Le Billon 2013, Smil 2008.
15. Shah 2004, 3–4; calculations corrected by Michael Tucker.
16. Bryce 2013.
17. Dukes 2003.
18. Sartre 2004, 154.
19. Dukes 2003.
20. Marx 2008, 119. Now see Smil 2010. For a provocative recent statement of the materialist position, see Morris 2015.
21. Emerson 2003, 46 (italics suppressed).
22. Johansson et al. 2012, 34.
23. BP 2014, 42.
24. Calculation derived from Berners-Lee and Clark 2013, 204.
25. Agricola 1950, 6.
26. The main exception is timber, which is renewable.
27. Stiglitz 2012.
28. *Economist* 2012b.
29. *Forbes* 2014a. On today's global diamond industry, see Smillie 2014.
30. After Oilandgasinfo.ca 2014.
31. Quoted in Pilling 2011a.
32. BP 2014, 8.
33. US Energy Information Administration 2014a.
34. Luft and Korin 2013.
35. The metaphor is from Nordhaus 2011.
36. Hall et al. 2003, 320. It is important that these "energy return" figures do not include the cost of, for example, military expenditure to protect oil sources or of environmental policies.
37. Former OPEC minister Sheik Yamani, quoted in Friedman 2008, 250.
38. See, for example, Kocieniewski 2010, Bast et al. 2014. On Exxon, see Coll 2012.
39. To give one small example: when a federal agency decided to stop insuring the US company Freeport on its huge Indonesian gold mine—because of reports of human rights abuses and environmental damage—Freeport got its board member Henry Kissinger to lobby in Washington, and then got former CIA director James Woolsey to argue its case in arbitration. See Bryce 1995, Ballard and Banks 2009.
40. Frynas 2009.
41. The Swiss oil trading firms—some very large indeed—have reputations for doing secret deals with ethically challenged regimes. One study finds that these firms' payments to the top-10 oil-exporting states in sub-Saharan Africa over a two-year period topped $55 billion—more than double these states' receipts from development aid. See Gillies et al. 2014.
42. ExxonMobil 2010.

SUMMARY OF THE BOOK

1. Brown 2013, xi and Appendix.
2. Hume 1975, 86 (substituting "jailer" for "gaoler").
3. Gumbel 2007.
4. Marx 2000.
5. Goethe 1997, 43 (author's translation).
6. Nietzsche 2006, 75 (substituting "burning at the stake" for *auto-da-fe*).

CHAPTER 1

1. Pliny the Elder 1991, 286.
2. Goode 2014, Chapters 8–11.
3. Gibbs 1999; Obama 2004, 138.
4. Hanson 2015b.
5. Hanson 2015a, though now see Casas et al. 2014.
6. BBC 2002a; Kresge and Wenar 1994, 106.
7. Hayek 1994, 94.
8. Wright and Czelusta 2002, 4.
9. See, for example, Motavalli 2012.
10. US Census Bureau 2012b. Forestry and fishing add a very small amount (less than 0.2 percent) to the US national GDP.
11. Government of Canada 2014, Colebatch 2012.
12. Ross 2012, 1.
13. CIA 2014, GDP per Capita (PPP) 2013 figures.
14. CIA 2014, Uzbekistan; *Economist* 2011e.
15. Cooper 2012. The candidate was Charles Taylor, whom we will see again in Chapter 6; many Liberians voted for Taylor from the justified fear that he would restart the country's bloody civil conflict if he lost the election.
16. Cheung 2012.
17. Myers 2010. In 2012, South Sudan opened its first paved highway, 120 miles long. USAID 2012.
18. US Census Bureau 2012a, 2; Rogers 2010; QNB 2014, 4.
19. Bradley 2006, Chapter 7.
20. Hyslop 2010.
21. Hume and Hook 2013.
22. CIA 2014, Angola; Leigh et al. 2009.
23. Ross 2012, 50, 51; volatility in the period since 1970.
24. Naim 2009.
25. Karl 1997, 67.
26. Robinson et al. 2006, Arezki et al. 2012.
27. Ebrahim-Zadeh 2003. Some countries start large-scale resource production before they develop a significant industrial or modern agricultural economy. In these countries, resource production does not reduce economic diversification but pressures against it emerging.
28. Bevan et al. 1999, Part 1; Ross 2008; Okoh 2011.
29. Maass 2009, 32.
30. For surveys of the literature and policy options, see Frankel 2012. For the Natural Resource Charter, see Natural Resource Governance Institute 2015.

31. Hegre and Sambanis 2006.

32. Most resource contracts today are denominated and settled in US dollars.

33. Mahdavy gave the focal definition of a "rentier" state as one that takes in substantial funds from "foreign individuals, concerns or governments." Mahdavy 1970, 428. An extractive-resource rent-addicted state is a rentier state that depends on resource revenues to maintain its form of governance and major policies.

34. IMF 2013.

35. OECD 2011a, Trust, Confidence in Social Institutions. The last time the Norwegian government ordered the invasion of another country was during the Dano-Swedish War of 1808. Norway has been invaded since 1808 (by the Swedes and the Germans), and Norwegian troops have recently fought under the command of various international coalitions (UN, NATO, ISAF, etc.).

36. US Energy Information Administration 2014c.

37. OECD 2014b, Mortality: Life Expectancy, Total Population at Birth, Morbidity: Health >= Good, Total.

38. CIA 2014, OECD 2014a.

39. European Commission 2005, QB2.

40. Statistics Norway 2012.

41. Legatum Institute 2014, Social Capital.

42. Revenue Watch Institute 2013, 4. The website of the Norwegian sovereign wealth fund shows a complete list of all its equity holdings and updates the total value of the fund several times per second. See Norges Bank Investment Management 2015.

43. Transparency International 2014.

44. Alexander's Gas & Oil Connections 2004.

45. Garton and Gruen 2012.

46. Sollund 2010.

47. World Bank 2014g. OECD 2012, 23, shows that Norway's labor participation rate is also at least as high as those of the major English-speaking countries.

48. OECD 2012, graph 8; Legatum Institute 2014.

49. In practice, this means that the fund shuns companies that make nuclear, chemical, or cluster weapons; that cause severe environmental damage; or that produce tobacco.

50. The environmentally conscious may be cheered to hear that despite Norway's gigantic petroleum production, its domestic power generation comes almost entirely from renewables, especially hydroelectric—hydro power is even cabled out to power undersea oil and gas platforms. Nearly all of the carbon dioxide associated with offshore production is reinjected to the ground instead of being released into the atmosphere. Also, unusually, Norway does not subsidize domestic gasoline consumption; rather, the government imposes one of the highest gasoline taxes in the world, making drivers pay up to $10 per gallon at the pump. See Persily 2011.

51. For example, the 2011 bombing and mass shooting in and near Oslo by the xenophobe Anders Breivik.

52. Grytten 2005, Listhaug 2005.

53. World Economic Forum 2014a.

54. Norway is also a highly egalitarian country and ranks first in the UNDP's Inequality-Adjusted Human Development Index. United Nations Development Programme 2014, Tables 1 and 3.

55. Mehlum et al. 2012, Al-Ubaydli 2012, Robinson et al. 2006. For an analysis of authoritarian resilience that emphasizes the timing of the appearance of oil revenues, see Smith 2007.

56. So far, it may seem as though speaking of a strong people is just a folksy way of speaking about strong institutions. For example, what has been said so far about strong peoples could be translated into Daron Acemoglu and James Robinson's categories of centralized, "inclusive" economic and political institutions, "which make power broadly distributed in society and constrain its arbitrary exercise." Acemoglu and Robinson 2012, 82.

Yet strong peoples may have features that outstrip any institutional analysis—and they need these to control their rulers. In premodern societies, for example, the ruled may need physical possession of weapons like knives to counter the power of their rulers, and physical possession of weapons is not an institution. In modern societies, the ruled may need critical faculties—which are encouraged by institutions like good schools and free media, but which are features of individuals, not institutions.

57. Social scientists have sometimes gone beyond institutional analysis to discuss the importance of citizen connectivity in fostering good governance. For example, Douglas North, John Wallis, and Barry Weingast take up the connective aspects of citizens within what they call an "open access order": "citizens in open access orders share belief systems that emphasize equality, sharing and universal inclusion." North et al. 2009, 111.

58. As Francis Fukuyama puts it, "Social capital is what permits individuals to band together to defend their interests and organize to support collective needs; authoritarian governance, on the other hand, thrives on social atomization." Fukuyama 2002, 26. Social capital is a second concept (along with "good institutions") with which social scientists can identify strong peoples. Glaeser et al. 2004 finds human and social capital to be the prime drivers of economic performance, with institutions secondary. For the importance of trust to democracy and social justice, see Miller 1995, 90–99. For the importance of trust to prosperity, see Fukuyama 1995.

59. See Wingo 2004, 455. As Wingo describes these institutions, they develop characteristics in the Nso similar to those necessary for liberal democracy: "individual autonomy and group cohesion, autarky, consensus through thoughtful deliberation and debate, honesty, tolerance, mutual respect and organized, enthusiastic participation." It should be noted, however, that the Nso formal institutions of accountability are filled only by males.

60. Robinson 2013.

61. Barack Obama's grandfather Onyango, who lived under British colonial rule in Kenya, apparently gave a good deal of thought to what accounted for British domination of his country. Filtering out the racial essentialism, we can see in Onyango's words the idea of "vulnerable individuals, strong people": "He would say that the African could never win against the white man because the black man only wanted to work within his own family or clan, while all white men worked to increase their power. 'The white man alone is like an ant,' Onyango would say, 'He can be easily crushed. But like an ant, the white man works together. His nation, his business—these things are more important to him than himself.'" Obama 2004, 417.

CHAPTER 2

1. The Getty line is widely quoted; the source remains elusive.

The mostly gendered pronouns in this book are intentional, since most who are endowed with unaccountable power over resources are male. There are many strongmen—there are no strongwomen. There are many warlords, but few warladies. One might say that the resource diseases show man's inhumanity to humans (only corruption appears to be an equal-opportunity affliction).

2. See Schumpeter 1991, 102ff; Ross 2004, 230–36.

3. Haber and Menaldo 2012 shows that a Schumpeter Process is not the only route to democratization.

4. Grose 1929. Through this period, Louis was also spreading smaller secret bribes around Parliament, though much less successfully.

5. Grose 1929, 201–3.

6. Grose 1929, 203.

7. In the end, the Stuarts overplayed their hand. The money from Louis was not sufficient to match the growing power of the English gentry, much less the armies of the Scots. James was chased from the country in a bloodless coup, and Parliament invited in a king and queen (William and Mary) who accepted substantial limitations on royal prerogative. England's Schumpeter Process resumed.

8. Huntington 1991, 64–65.

9. Grose 1929, 193. For secrecy around oil revenues, see Ross 2012, 58–62.

10. Ross 2012, 80–83. See also Heuty and Carlitz 2009.

11. Schulze 2007. When resource production can be performed with local unskilled labor, as with alluvial diamonds, the laborers have sometimes been forced to work in highly coercive conditions, as in Sierra Leone during its civil war and more recently in Zimbabwe's Marange fields. BBC 2011c.

12. Charles II thanked his former tutor Hobbes immediately on ascending the throne by granting the philosopher a pension and access to court. See Noel Malcolm's biographical sketch in Hobbes 1994, 817–20.

13. Hobbes 1996, 131 (spellings modernized).

14. Rousseau 1997, 137.

15. CIA 2014, Singapore, South Korea, Taiwan.

16. CIA 2014, Country Comparisons: GDP per Capita (PPP). In these terms, Singapore's average income surpassed America's around 2004.

17. World Bank 2014d; comparing 1965 and 2012.

18. For differences in the fate of democracy in these states, see Slater 2012.

19. Malaysia did become more authoritarian under Mahathir as extractives became a bigger share of the Malaysian economy, but Mahathir never gained the political control that Suharto did over Indonesia. On Malaysia's use of its natural resources (including non-extractives like rubber and palm oil) for development, see Abidin 2001, 147–64.

20. The thesis that resource rents hinder democratization must be sensitive to the level of rents that governments actually receive from oil production. As Ross has emphasized, before the 1960s most of the rents generated by oil production outside the West were captured by the West's "Seven Sister" oil companies—so one sees more of an anti-democratic effect from resource production after this period. Ross 2012, see Andersen and Ross 2013. Jones Luong and Weinthal 2010 argues that the pernicious effects of oil are most pronounced when the government dominates the oil industry.

21. Loans can also come from allies or the international financial institutions. Yet loans from private creditors are larger than official (bilateral or multilateral) loans by an order of magnitude—in 2011, the ratio was $434 billion to $30 billion. World Bank 2013b, 3.

22. This does not necessarily mean that resource-rich regimes will in the end have a lower debt burden than comparable resource-poor regimes. Many regimes look to take out all the loans they can get, and banks will be more willing to lend to regimes that have the higher expected revenue streams that resource endowments promise. Loans taken

out by authoritarian regimes generate what is called "odious debt," a subject we will return to in Chapter 12.

23. Emphasis added.

24. Many have noticed that development aid, and especially budget support, is structurally similar to resource rents, and they have wondered whether both shift a state toward political dysfunctions. See, for example, Collier 2006, Morrison 2009, Morrison 2012. Development aid does have some characteristics that distinguish it from resource rents, and its complexities mean we cannot consider it responsibly here. However, those comparing states with and without large resource revenues should keep in mind the possibility that official aid might be playing a similar role in the latter.

25. Haber and Menaldo 2011 attempts to throw the resource-authoritarian link into question. Andersen and Ross 2013 and Wiens et al. 2014 expose weaknesses in their methods and data. Prichard et al. 2014 use an improved data set and econometric techniques to show consistent associations between greater non-tax income and less democracy.

26. Wantchekon 2002.

27. The possible exceptions are Nigeria and East Timor, though whether these are exceptions depends on how one understands "democratic" (*The Economist Democracy Index*, for instance, categorized Nigeria as "authoritarian" in 2013). Venezuela, another controversial case, gets slightly less than half of its state revenues from petroleum. CIA 2014, Venezuela: Economy.

28. Taiwan paid Charles Taylor, the strongman of Liberia, over $20 million to maintain its diplomatic recognition. After Liberia became democratic, one group of drug traffickers offered the son of its president, who was also its national security chief, $1.6 million to accept four tons of cocaine from Colombia's FARC rebels. Carvajal 2010; Weiser and Rashbaum 2010.

29. The Castro regime, for example, first depended on the Soviets for strategic rents; starting in 2000, it benefitted from highly subsidized oil imports from Venezuela. Cuba's opening to America in 2014 came as the Venezuelan oil ramped down.

30. Part of the Chinese economic miracle may have been the regime co-opting market-based institutions that developed independently of its control after the Cultural Revolution. See Nee and Opper 2012.

31. See Glaeser et al. 2004 for a model of economic growth and eventual democratization under authoritarians who build up human and physical capital.

32. For a theory of resources and democratization in Latin America, see Dunning 2008.

33. Ross 2012, 71–76.

34. On Chavez, see Corrales and Penfold 2011. On Putin, see Stoner 2012, Sakwa 2014. Compare these more recent analyses to Stephen Holmes's description of the weak Russian state before oil prices rose after 2001, in Holmes 2001.

35. Friedman 2006. Larry Diamond linked the worldwide "democratic recession" of the mid-2000s to the escalating prices for commodities in Diamond 2008, 56–87.

36. Economist Intelligence Unit 2013. For the Polity index, see Center for Systemic Peace 2014.

CHAPTER 3

1. Ajami 2007.

2. Griswold 2010.

3. See, for example, Manea 1998, 205–18.

4. From Xenophon 2009, 13.
5. Racine 2010, 69.
6. For a formal model of authoritarian priorities, see Wintrobe 2007.
7. Grose 1929, 203–4.
8. Text message from Muhammad al-Maskati, founder of the Bahrain Youth Society for Human Rights, after the Bahraini army opened fire on peaceful protestors in March 2011; quoted in Slackman 2011.
9. In one index, the six states with the lowest tax burdens are all oil states; Heritage Foundation 2014. See also Ross 2012, 30–31.
10. Kirkpatrick 2011b.
11. Oil income per capita figures from Ross 2012, 20–23; updated to 2011 with an oil price of $94.87 per barrel. Note that these figures are per capita; as explained below, the revenues per national are substantially higher in states with large foreign populations.
12. Syria's oil revenues, which helped to sustain the regime for years, had by 2011 diminished to around $690 per capita. The Syrian revolt that started in 2011 was not strong enough to depose the authoritarian, yet neither was the authoritarian strong enough to keep control over all of the territory of his country.
13. Figure is from Ross 2012, 20; updated to 2011. Morocco is an intriguing marginal case. In 2011, Morocco had a mildly authoritarian king. The milder nature of the Moroccan regime may be partly explained by its smaller resource rents as well as by the less-enclaved nature of its resource. While Morocco controlled 75 percent of the world's phosphates, in 2011 it got only sub-Tunisian levels of resource income per head ($203), and its phosphate industry employed tens of thousands. The popular protests in Morocco during the Arab Spring were relatively restrained, and in response to them, the king made a few concessions, limiting his powers. Phosphate figure from Daragahi 2012.
14. Gladstone 2014. After a beheading, the corpse is sometimes left "crucified" in the public square. Killalea 2014.
15. Freedom House 2014a, BP 2014, 6. None of the 12 OPEC Members (which claim 81 percent of all oil reserves) are rated "free." OPEC 2013b.
16. Freedom House 2011, Uzbekistan.
17. Haykel 2008.
18. Humphreys et al. 2007, 13.
19. Saudi military spending figure from Keating 2012. Saudi 2011 budget figure from Gamble 2011, 6. Projected 2015 US Defense Department spending from US Government Printing Office 2014, 94. In 2012, Saudi Arabia spent 8.7 percent of GDP on its military and internal security, almost twice the percentage of the second-highest military spender, the United States. Perlo-Freeman et al. 2012, 2.
20. Ross 2012, 5.
21. Shaxson 2007, 44.
22. On the tendency of rent-addicted regimes to spend on patronage (like public-sector jobs) instead of on economically more productive investments, see Robinson et al. 2006. The text folds clientelistic politics together with patrimonial administration under the name "clientelism." For distinctions and relations between these two, see Brinkerhoff and Goldsmith 2002.
23. Anderson 1987.
24. For example, the American advisor tasked with setting up the central bank had to send an assistant to a local *souk* to check prices so that he could construct a simple price index. Hertog 2011, 78.

25. Hertog 2011, 138. The exceptions to this rule of inefficient ministries will typically be the institutions along the path of rent-flows into the state. The Angolan state oil company, for example, has a reputation for driving hard bargains with foreign firms; the Saudi central bank is now widely admired.

26. North et al. 2009, 35ff. See also Fukuyama 2011.

27. See generally Auty's theory of rent cycling, which argues that sustained economic growth requires the creation of wealth by the people through markets instead of merely the distribution of wealth through patronage by the state. Auty 2010.

28. Alighieri 2005, Canto XXI. In the fifth pit of the Eighth Circle, devils keep corrupt officials submerged in boiling pitch.

29. Kaldor 2007, 169–70.

30. Robinson and Verdier 2013; Van de Walle 2007, 50–67. On patronage and rent seeking in resource-dependent states, see Mehlum et al. 2006, Kolstad and Wiig 2009.

31. Meyer 1998. See generally Vatikiotis 1993.

32. Hicken 2011, 291.

33. Leite and Weidmann 1999, Kolstad and Søreide 2009.

34. Transparency International 2014 ("most corrupt" as index scores < 20). For natural resource discoveries and increased corruption among politicians and bureaucrats, see Vicente 2010.

35. Dowden 2008, 220.

36. Theobald 1990, 16.

37. Robertson-Snape 1999, 594.

38. de la Baume 2012. As Teodorín Obiang noted in testimony in South Africa, "Cabinet ministers and public servants in Equatorial Guinea are by law allowed to own companies that, in consortium with a foreign company, can bid for government contracts," and when the contract is awarded, the "cabinet minister ends up with a sizable part of the contract price in his bank account." Maass 2009, 43. The next chapter will discuss Teodorín Obiang and his father in more detail.

39. Al-Kasim et al. 2008, 14. See Dolan and de Morais 2013 for an investigation into the sources of the wealth of the daughter of the President of Angola.

40. World Bank [n.d.].

41. Dugger 2009.

42. See Turner and Young 1985, 165–66.

43. Machiavelli 1998, 27. Compare Voltaire 2006, 65: "In this country it is found good, from time to time, to kill one Admiral to encourage the others."

44. Gettleman 2009.

45. Chabal and Daloz call Western corruption "horizontal": "Such practices generally occur at the top, where deals are struck between, on the one hand, the main industrial and financial sectors and, on the other, the political classes...By contrast, corruption in Africa concerns the whole population and operates essentially according to vertical relations of inequality." Chabal and Daloz 1999, 102.

46. Human Rights Watch 2012.

47. In *The Republic*, Plato uses the story of the enchanted Ring of Gyges to discuss the idea that no one would be just if they could become invisible at will. Plato 1991, 2.359a–2.360d.

48. Sarah Chayes, writing about the clientelistic Afghan government, calls it a "vertically integrated criminal syndicate." Chayes 2015, Chapter 5.

49. Moss 2011, 10.

50. World Bank 2004.

51. Aidt 2009.

52. Kapuscinski 2006, 62–63.

53. Kumar and Yardley 2011.

54. England 2010.

55. Simons 2011.

56. *New York Times* 2004; personal communication with Shell concerning the total taken by Olusegun Obasanjo during his 1999–2007 presidency. Using the midpoint of Obasanjo's period in office, 2003, and converting into 2015 dollars finds $51.5 billion. Larry Ellison's net worth at the start of 2015 was $54.7 billion. *Forbes* 2015.

57. Kristof 2015a. See Kristof 2015b and 2015c.

58. Wrong 2000, 294–97.

59. Locke 1988, 399.

60. "Hard" and "soft" power definitions from Nye 2011, 20–22.

61. The one public good that most autocratic oil states do provide is one that requires the least administrative capacity, and the one based on the resource they must control: oil states give oil subsidies. In Kuwait in 2012, the price of premium gasoline was 89 US cents a gallon; in Venezuela, it was nine cents a gallon. Randall 2012. Oil subsidies are a highly inefficient use of the public resources, and since the rich tend to spend a larger share of income on fuel, they are also regressive. Nevertheless, once a regime puts oil subsidies in place, they are very difficult to withdraw. In a poignant episode in 2012, Nigerian technocrats finally persuaded the country's top officials to roll back Nigeria's ruinous oil subsidies, estimated to cost $8 billion annually. A nationwide strike forced the government to restore subsidies, as Nigerians protested the withdrawal of one of the few benefits they receive from their country's oil riches.

62. BP 2014, 6, 20. At the end of 2013, Qatar had 1.5 percent of proven global oil and 13.3 percent of proven global gas reserves.

63. CIA 2014, GDP per Capita (PPP); 2013 figures.

64. For every Qatari citizen, that is, there are six foreign workers living in the country. Qatar population from QNB 2014, 2. As mentioned above, Qatar's small population more than doubled in the six years after 2004, the increase almost entirely due to foreigners arriving for employment. Most workers were unskilled or low-skilled laborers from South Asia, brought in for infrastructure projects, but Western and Arab professionals, such as bankers, doctors, and teachers, also flooded in. The expat labor force is itself tightly controlled: all expats must have a Qatari sponsor and can be expelled at will; no labor unions exist. US Department of State 2013. There have been persistent reports of the exploitation and bad treatment of the foreign workers from poor countries, for example, Booth 2014.

65. Qatar net oil export figure ($55 billion in 2012) from US Energy Information Administration 2014e. Hydrocarbon revenue per national figure is for 2012 and from QNB 2014, 2.

66. Taking US GNI per capita PPP from World Bank 2014b to be $53,960, and taking 92.7 percent of the US population to be citizens. Grieco et al. 2012, 2. GDP per head for 2012 from OECD 2014b, GDP per Head, US $, Current Prices, Current PPPs. Taking the total US government expenditure at all levels as $6.25 trillion (OECD 2014b, Government Expenditure by Function) divided into the 2011 population of 310 million US citizens.

67. IMF 2014b, 28.

68. *Constitution of Qatar* 2004, Article 17. (This resolution is apparently not publicly available.)

69. Davidson 2012, 127. A small indication of the al-Thani family's wealth: the main London residence of a former prime minister (a relative of the Emir's) cost more than three times the value of Haiti's annual budget for education.

70. Grønskov et al. 2007 estimates the prevalence of albinism as 1 in 17,000.

71. QNB 2014, 2. These figures are on a PPP basis, and so differ from p. 34.

72. The president's home town can also get lavish spending. Mobutu famously turned his home village into the "Versailles of the Jungle," building three palaces and an airport runway that could accommodate the Concorde for his chartered flights to Paris.

73. Personal communication.

74. Nossiter 2009.

75. Nossiter 2012.

76. Collier 2010a. Dunning 2005 describes conditions in which elites will fail to invest in diversification, for fear that it will raise the probability of a revolt, and applies this model to Zaire's development. For a model of kleptocratic divide-and-rule applied to Mobutu, see Acemoglu et al. 2004.

77. Quoted in Herb 1999, 12.

78. Colgan 2013.

79. Magaloni 2010, 752–53. For Angola, see Marques de Morais 2012.

80. Authoritarian elections can also have other functions: providing the regime with opportunities for patronage, with a means to co-opt opposition, and with information about which regime members and policies are more publicly palatable. See Gandhi and Lust-Okar 2009, Miller 2013.

81. Davidson 2012, 67.

82. BBC 2003.

83. The tiny exceptions are Vatican City and the Swaziland microstate.

CHAPTER 4

1. *UN Security Council Resolution 1653* 2006, Williams 2011.
2. Kirkpatrick 2011a, Stephen 2014.
3. McElroy 2014.
4. Rogin 2014. Hubbard 2013 reports on money going to the al-Nusra Front, from which ISIS splintered.
5. Lakshmanan and DiPaola 2014, McElroy 2014. See also Abdelaziz 2014.
6. Collier et al. 2009, Le Billon 2012, Koubi et al. 2014, Ross 2014.
7. UN Environment Programme 2009, 8.
8. Fearon and Laitin 2003, Collier and Hoeffler 2004.
9. See Besley and Persson 2011.
10. Renner 2002, 150.
11. Maass 2009, 164.
12. Jamestown Foundation 2008.
13. Le Billon 2012, 15–16 and *passim*.
14. Buhaug et al. 2009.
15. Lujala 2009, Lujala 2010.
16. Weinstein 2007.
17. Doyle and Sambanis 2000.

18. Victor 2007.

19. Corcoran 2012. In Ivory Coast, a UN Panel of Experts reported that rebels were using non-extractive resources (like cocoa and cotton) as well as diamonds as sources of military and personal funds. Global Witness 2007a.

20. Ross 2012, Chapter 5.

21. Ross 2012, 159–60; increase is relative to the period 1960–2006. See also Le Billon 2012, 66–67.

22. Besley and Persson 2011.

23. Reno 2003, 78.

24. Barnett 2012.

25. Le Billon 2001.

26. Ross 2007, 200.

27. Smith 1999, Lintner 2000.

28. UN Environment Programme 2009, 12.

29. Pol Pot quoted in Le Billon 2012, 143.

30. Turnell 2011.

31. Bottomley 2000.

32. Lakshmanan and DiPaola 2014.

33. Shaxson 2007, 49.

34. Le Billon 2007.

35. Paes 2009, 151–52.

36. Shaxson 2007, 58–59.

37. Global Witness 2006, 17.

38. World Food Programme 2005.

39. This paragraph follows DFID et al. 2011, 2.2–2.3. See also Collier 2007, Chapter 2.

40. UNICEF 1999, A Promise Renewed 2015 (using the latest data, from 2013). See Kristof 2015a.

41. The rebels in Sierra Leone also attacked the capital Freetown. They captured it once, and a second time coerced the government into appointing a rebel leader as vice president and as chairman of the body in charge of the country's diamond mining.

42. Enough Project 2009, 3.

43. York 2012.

44. Gettleman 2012; Coghlan et al. 2007, 16.

45. Human Security Report Project 2011, 131, estimates excess deaths in the DRC from 2001 to 2007 to be 863,000. For the debate over the IRC's figure, see *Science Insider* 2010. All reports agree that most excess deaths have been civilian and non-violent (for example, child deaths from disease and malnutrition).

46. Stearns 2011, 257.

47. The pivotal papers were Sachs and Warner 1995, Sachs and Warner 2001. See also Frankel 2012.

48. CIA 2014, Country Comparisons: GDP per Capita (PPP).

49. Freedom House 2013, Equatorial Guinea.

50. 2005 medians from Branko Milanovic, personal communication.

51. Collier 2007, Chapter 2.

52. Sala-i-Martin and Subramanian 2003. The oil revenue figure is in 1995 dollars. The $1 per day figure is the World Bank 1993 PPP standard for extreme poverty.

53. Income figure from Masetti 2014, 3; the report uses the 2014 rebased Nigerian GDP figures. Child nutrition percentage from CIA 2014; using the latest (2011) figure.

54. UN Development Programme 2008–09, 37.
55. CIA 2014, Ghana, Life Expectancy at Birth, 2014 estimates.
56. Chandy and Gertz 2011, 6, 8.
57. Allison 2012.
58. BBC 2005; Human Rights Watch 2005, XI.
59. Last 2007, Kennedy 2010.
60. *Economist* 2012a. The judge's ruling has since been overturned on appeal.
61. BBC 2012a.
62. Wallis 2014.
63. Collier 2007, 42–46.
64. *Economist* 2011d.
65. DefenceWeb 2014, WikiLeaks 2009.
66. Katsouris and Sayne 2013, 1.
67. US Department of State 2011a. A book-length account of the militias in the Niger Delta is Peel 2009.
68. Many militia members in the Delta appear to have turned from violence to larger-scale bunkering and refining operations, placing further burdens on the local environment. *Economist* 2012b.
69. Nigeria National Bureau of Statistics 2014, 3.
70. Afripol 2013.
71. BBC 2014.
72. Abdul'Aziz and Mbachu 2014.
73. CIA 2014, Population.
74. OPEC 2013a, 11; figures are for 2012.
75. Lavallée et al. 2008, 4.
76. Lavallée et al. 2008, 6.
77. Collier 2007, Chapters 2–3.
78. Copnall 2014.
79. Hegre and Sambanis 2006, Salehyan and Gleditsch 2006.
80. Ross and Voeten 2013 argue that oil states are less likely to be integrated into the international order, both legally (in terms of acceptance of international judicial bodies) and politically (in terms of memberships in international organizations, number of treaties signed, number of peacekeepers contributed per capita, and number of foreign embassies).
81. Collier finds no increased risk of coups in resource-dependent states, perhaps because he did not separate out low-rent states or perhaps because almost all resource-enriched rulers can afford stepped-up personal security. Collier 2007, 33–37. However, we can be confident that capturing a resource-rich government has motivated at least some coup attempts, not least because the coupists themselves have explained their motivations in detail. The best explanation of the actions of the mercenaries and financiers in the "Wonga coup" attempt in Equatorial Guinea is that they were doing what several have said they were: trying to overthrow the ruler of a resource-rich regime so as to replace him with a puppet who would funnel the country's rents to them. See Roberts 2006. See also Le Billon 2005, 37–38, on the Republic of the Congo (not to be confused with the Democratic Republic of the Congo) in the 1990s. These are good illustrations of cases where "causation is not correlation": we can be nearly certain that capturing oil rents was a major explanatory factor in some coup attempts, regardless of whether there are any overall correlations. ("Causation is not correlation" from personal communication with Paul Segal.)

82. de Soysa and Gizelis 2013.

83. *Economist* 2009. Gylfason 2001 finds that public education relative to national income, years of schooling for girls, and enrollment in secondary school is inversely related to the share of natural capital in a country's national wealth.

84. See cleantrade.org.

85. Ross 2012, Chapter 4; Park 1990. On the gender-specific harms of resource dependence, see Wisor 2014a.

86. Ross 2012, 125.

87. Root and Bolongaita 2008, i, 2, ii. President Saleh was forced out of office in 2012.

88. Malaquias 2001.

CHAPTER 5

1. Locke 1988, 392; Rousseau 1997, 44.
2. US Energy Information Administration 2014a, Total Oil Supply (2005).
3. US Department of State 2012b; *Economist* 2011c; IMF 2014c, GDP per Capita (PPP) 2005.
4. World Bank 2013a estimates the value of hydrocarbon exports at $15 billion to $17 billion in 2012.
5. World Bank 2013a.
6. BBC 2003.
7. US Department of State 1998.
8. Nossiter 2011. See also UN Human Rights Council 2008.
9. UK Foreign and Commonwealth Office 2003, 55.
10. US Department of State 2014c.
11. Transparency International 2013 (the country was not rated in 2014). In a 2009 interview, Obiang said, "I ask myself, where is this corruption, how is it found, where is it discovered? I don't have any knowledge of that. There is none whatsoever." Faul 2009b.
12. Freedom House 2014a, Equatorial Guinea.
13. Kroll 2006. Even at the time, the $600 million figure may have been an understatement: a 2004 US Senate investigation found that Obiang personally controlled up to $700 million in one bank, as well as owning two mansions in the Washington, DC area.
14. Roberts 2006, 51.
15. Maass 2009, 32.
16. World Bank 2014d.
17. Rajaratnam et al. 2010, Table 2.
18. UN Development Programme 2014 shows no change in expected or mean years of schooling since 2000, the year when these data series start. In previous years' reports, the Expected Years of Schooling data series goes back to 1980 and shows a decline after 1995 (the oil years).
19. Global Witness 2011.
20. Johnson 2006, Human Rights Watch 2009, Urbina 2009. For a profile of Teodorín, see Silverstein 2014, Chapter 2.
21. Silverstein 2011.
22. Silverstein 2011, Faul 2011, BBC 2012c, Human Rights Watch 2014.
23. Birrell 2011.
24. Marx 1959, Third Manuscript, Section 42.
25. Rademayer 2004.

26. *Lat.*: A right may originate from injustice.

27. Bentham 1896, 112.

28. The main exception is when the party in physical control is in violation of international law—for example, during an illegal occupation or territorial incursion, or when a state has nationalized resources without adequate compensation of the foreign owners. In such cases, the principle being violated (self-determination, territorial integrity, etc.) takes precedence over the principle of effectiveness for resources.

29. Pogge 2008, 119.

30. Campbell 2002, xv, 71.

31. Human Rights Watch 2003, 25–26.

32. UN Development Programme 2007/2008, 232.

33. The Kimberley Process, discussed more in Part IV, has had some success in reducing the flow of conflict diamonds onto world markets. The scheme does not aim to control gems beyond diamonds; it has had no effect, for example, on the emerald and gold trade controlled by mafias and guerrillas in Colombia.

34. Here the Westphalian system is identified with systems of state sovereignty that lasted from the mid-seventeenth to the mid-twentieth centuries, with its high point in the nineteenth century. As we will see, several significant Westphalian rules persist within today's modern state system. (There is a different usage of "Westphalian" in which the term refers to the state system as a whole, including both its classic and modern phases.) See Held 2003. Westphalia did contain some protections for individuals: for foreign nationals (mainly investors) and, as we will see, regarding religious non-conformity.

35. See Beitz 2009. There were mentions of human rights before the *Universal Declaration*—for example, in the UN Charter.

36. Naím 2006. World Economic Forum 2014b, 1, estimates that the global value of illicit trade in narcotics and counterfeit goods plus human trafficking is between $1.42 trillion and $1.67 trillion.

37. US Energy Information Administration 2014b, US Net Imports by Country. There is a happy fact about Equatorial Guinea's exports in 2014 that experts will know—we will take up such facts in Part IV, when discussing oil policies for the future.

38. Augustine 1955, 101.

39. Amnesty International 2005, 14–15. Journalist Adam Roberts gives full treatment to the 2004 coup attempt involving a group of international businessmen and mercenaries in Roberts 2006. A seaborne attack on Obiang's presidential palace in 2008 also failed. Faul 2009a. At one news conference, Obiang mused that having oil money was a mixed blessing since so many people want to take it away. Wines 2004.

40. The money that dos Santos's forces gained from Cabinda's oil was a major factor in their victory over the diamond-funded UNITA rebels in Angola's long civil war, noted in Chapter 4. The Angolan government has agreed to give 10 percent of Cabinda's oil revenues to the people; whether it does so is disputed. See Iob 2012. Oil production figure in 2012 from *Africa Confidential* 2012.

41. "Self-determination renders null and void treaties providing for the transfer of territories whenever such treaties do not include provision for any prior and genuine consultation of the population involved." Cassese 2001, 63.

42. *Charter of the United Nations* 1945, Article I.2.4: "All Members shall refrain in their international relations from the threat or use of force against the territorial integrity or political independence of any state."

43. This list of countries updates Ross 2012, 10.

CHAPTER 6

1. Lugar 2006; *The Holy Quran with English Translation* 2011; cf. Galatians 6:7, Job 4:8.

2. The phrase "multivariate world" is taken from remarks by Gerald Gaus, University of Arizona, March 30, 2013.

3. Marshall and Cole 2009, 15.

4. Gross 2013. June 2014 import figures from US Energy Information Administration 2014d. US Department of State 2014b.

5. Hamilton 2011, 26. Now see Rasmussen and Roitman 2011, Kilian and Vigfusson 2014.

6. Blair et al. 2014; BP 2012, 3. Oil prices and shocks also appear to be negative for stock returns. Wang et al. 2013.

7. Kotkin 2008, 15–16. See also Gaidar 2007.

8. Kotkin 2008, 16, 15.

9. Sloan and Anderson 2009, 640; US Department of State 2015b. South Yemen is a debatable case and so omitted; its oil exports began halfway through its time on the list.

10. Hilton Root argues that the United States suffers an "alliance curse" in much the same way that this book argues that it suffers from a "resource curse." In Root's view, American strategic rents to authoritarians have promoted long-term economic failure, political instability, and popular resentment that end up damaging US security interests. Root 2008.

11. See Glendon 2002.

12. Black propaganda is misinformation that appears to come from a source that is not its true source. Roosevelt disseminated materials that appeared to come from Mohammad Mossadegh's party, and that made it seem that Mossadegh, the elected prime minister, was a communist who intended to suppress Islam.

13. Kinzer 2003.

14. Rubinstein 1981.

15. Root 2008, 124.

16. Sick 1985, 12.

17. Carter 1977.

18. Diamond and Milani 2006, 10–11.

19. Asmus et al. 2005, 7.

20. US Department of State 2012a, 172.

21. Thomas Friedman quoted in Kirk and Wiley 2003.

22. On sanctions, see Gordon 2010.

23. Johnston 2004.

24. A good single volume on this topic is Bronson 2006.

25. Bronson 2006.

26. See Caryl 2013.

27. Kepel 2006, Chapter 3.

28. Maass 2009, 172.

29. Maass 2009, 172.

30. For a genealogy of the Hijazi pan-Islamist ideology, see Hegghammer 2011. For a less subtle overview of Saudi charitable funding of foreign fighters and international terrorists, see Burr and Collins 2006.

31. See Hegghammer 2010 and, for example, Armstrong 2014, Poggioli 2010.

32. Gerges 2009; Klare 2009, 48.

33. For Saudi terrorist financing to 2007, see the summary in Blanchard and Prados 2007. There is also a good deal of journalism; see, for example, Daou 2012.

34. Bronson 2006, 9.

35. Esposito 2010, 167.

36. White House 2014, Kirkpatrick 2014.

37. Fish 2011, 109–32.

38. See, for example, European Parliament 2013.

39. Churchill 2015, 128.

40. Population figure is the official 2010 number from Saudi Arabia Central Department of Statistics & Information 2013.

41. Davidson 2012, Chapters 4–6.

42. Kumar and van Welsum 2013.

43. Sfakianakis et al. 2011, 1. Nolan 2011, 5, has an 80 percent figure for the under-30 population.

44. Al-Sheikh and Nuri Erbas 2012, 20, 24.

45. Murphy 2013, 15.

46. Davidson 2012, 118.

47. Murphy 2013, 15 (citing Richard Cincotta); Dabbs Sciubba 2011, Chapter 2.

48. MacFarquhar 2011.

49. BBC 2011d. See Diamond 2010, 100.

50. Lifting figure from *Economist* 2014c; IMF 2014a, 5. See also Plumer 2012.

51. Sullivan 2013.

52. *Economist* 2015, Collinson 2015.

53. See, for example, Rouleau 2002.

54. UN Development Programme 2009, 108–9.

55. Mazzetti and Hager 2011. Blackwater is now called Academi.

56. Fahim 2012.

57. Fishman and Felter 2007.

58. On Gaddafi's funding for Black September, see *Time* 1972. On the presidential plot, see *Belfast Telgraph* 2012.

59. Zoli et al. 2011; on money laundering for Iran, see Lichtblau et al. 2011.

60. See Farah 2011.

61. Gettleman 2011.

62. Will 2001.

63. Collier 2007, 252.

64. Brown 2013, xi and Appendix.

65. Whether North Korea has commercial oil, and whether anyone will actually be willing to produce it, are far from certain. Byrne 2014.

66. Huntington 1968, 1.

67. On Sudan, see Natsios 2012. On Somalia, see Manson 2013.

68. Chandy and Gertz 2011, 6.

69. United Nations 2012b.

70. For the Sahara human trafficking route, see Baxter 2002.

71. Lipton 2010.

72. Nye 2011, xv.

73. National Intelligence Council 2012, 15.

74. China had to evacuate thirty-five thousand workers from Libya during the revolution of 2011; one report says that China offered Gaddafi's regime $200 million worth of arms as late as July 2011 (Gaddafi was killed in August). Smith 2011.

75. *Economist* 2011a. See also Deborah Brautigam's insightful and evolving analyses of the 88 Queensway group on her blog *China in Africa* (www.chinaafricarealstory.com).

76. BBC 2012d, Fox News 2013.

CHAPTER 7

1. Mill 1909, 959.

2. Coltan is the ore from which tantalum is extracted; tantalum is used to make the capacitors for many kinds of electronics, including smart phones. At the time of this writing, a third of the tin, tantalum, and tungsten mines surveyed in eastern Congo were reported as having armed groups present (and the artisanal gold mining trade was still under the control of armed groups, including groups officially in the Congolese army). Bafilemba et al. 2014, 2.

3. Within American law the processing of the coltan along the supply chain would, for example, be sufficient to block the owner's suit against the girl. For specialists it may be noted that the "Conflict Minerals" Section 1502 of the US *Dodd-Frank Act* 2010 does not change the conclusions reached here. Greater due diligence in supply chains does not affect the law's underlying structure of effectiveness.

4. US Department of Commerce 2011, 20; *Dog Control Amendment Act* 2003, Part 4, Section 17; World Trade Organization 2005, 16–17.

5. US Department of Justice 2007.

6. *Treason* 2006.

7. *Controlled Substances* 2005.

8. *US Executive Order 13412* 2006, Preamble and Section 2 (the minor exceptions to the prohibition have been omitted).

9. If High Island becomes a member of the UN, and if the UN Security Council imposes mandatory sanctions on some country (as it did on, for example, apartheid South Africa), then our national authority will not have discretion over sanctioning that country. If High Island becomes a member of the WTO, then it may or may not (depending on how Article XX of the GATT is interpreted) remain the choice of its authorities to impose a restriction such as the one on the products of child labor described. WTO law will be discussed more in Chapter 16.

10. More, the WTO is explicit that "[t]he WTO does not regulate ownership of natural resources." WTO 2010, 16.

11. Property law is subnational; for example, the several US states have their own systems, which sometimes differ substantially. Also, European efforts to harmonize the private international laws of member states sometimes make it convenient to think of Europe as a single legal entity. We leave these complexities aside. International law does constrain domestic property law in such areas as intellectual property, foreign investment, deep sea minerals, cultural objects, and satellite orbits. Globalization is adding to these constraints: in John G. Sprankling's metaphor, international property law is like a coral reef gradually emerging from the ocean to create a new legal category. See Sprankling 2014, vii.

12. It may be that American property law has a structure that would also wash domestic armed robbery out of entirely domestic sale chains, yet this does not reduce the concern about international trade adding substantially to domestic injustice. Few minerals from within the United States, for example, pass into production from the hands of coercively exploitative militiamen.

13. The Lacey Act as amended is unusual for being fact-based and not document-based. The law turns on the fact that foreign wood has been sourced in violation of the laws of another country, not on the presence or absence of any particular certification for the wood. It differs in this way from the Kimberley Process. The EU now has similar legislation for foreign source timber, *(Illegal) Timber Regulation* 2010.

14. Helene Cooper gives a poignant account of the impact of Taylor's troops in the civil war in Cooper 2012.

15. BBC 2012b, BBC 2011a.

16. Farah 2004. Taylor also apparently sent diamonds one night to the model Naomi Campbell. *Daily Mail* 2010.

17. Global Witness 2007b, 7; see also Williams 2002, 447. On the coercion of Liberia's parliament, see Johnston 2013, 31.

18. Montesquieu 1989, 75. President Ellen Johnson Sirleaf quoted in Carvajal 2010.

19. World Rainforest Movement 2002; Global Witness 2003, 20–23. The UN banned Liberian diamond exports in 2001 and timber exports in 2003 (which contributed to Taylor's exit from power).

20. Global Witness 2001.

21. State recognition is a delightful mess of international law, domestic law, and politics. For instance, the attributes of statehood are neither sufficient nor necessary for an entity to be recognized as a state. Somaliland declared independence decades ago; its government controls its territory and issues currency and passports. Yet Somaliland is internationally unrecognized—while Somalia, for years an entirely failed state, has received universal recognition. There are different theories of how recognition is meant to work; for convenience, we follow the leading theory: that the existence of a state is a wholly factual matter, and that recognition acknowledges that fact. On this theory, recognition of other states is not optional; it is a requirement of international law. See Grant 1999. States sometimes announce that they recognize only states, not governments. Even when this distinction is legally meaningful, however, it does not affect the argument here, as the argument works for both sides.

22. There are qualifications that do not affect the argument: for example, when country A nationalizes a foreign investment from country B, international law requires country B to accept that taking of property provided just compensation is paid.

23. *US Executive Order 13067* 1997; *US Public Law 106-476* 2000, Section 1464a–b.

24. The United States suspended its embassy operations in Sudan from 1996 to 2002 because of the country's links with international terrorist organizations. US Department of State 2014e.

25. *Oppenheimer v. Cattermole* 1976. For ease of exposition, the law of England and Wales is here called "British."

26. *Kuwait Airways Corporation v. Iraqi Airways Corporation* 2001, 318. Lord Justice Brooke's analysis continues at 320: "The rule whereby there is a principle of judicial restraint insofar as a sovereign acts within his own territory is only a prima facie rule. It is subject to certain exceptions. One exception we have already mentioned is that a penal or discriminatory act of a foreign sovereign cannot be made the basis of a claim in our courts. This is perhaps one aspect of a general exception to the effect that these courts will not recognize the act of a foreign sovereign which is contrary to English public policy. The existence of this exception is not in doubt."

27. It may also be noticed that international law distinguishes between states acting in a sovereign and in a commercial capacity, with the first being governed by public and the second by private international law. See Cassese 2001, 98–101.

28. *US Executive Order 13566* 2011.

29. *General License No. 5* 2011.

30. Wan and Booth 2011. The United States did not recognize the TNC as Libya's government in May 2011 when the American refiner Tesoro bought Libyan oil sold by the TNC, although other countries were already doing so. US Department of State 2011c, CNN 2011. After its eventual diplomatic recognition of the TNC, the United States had to issue a further order unblocking transactions with "the Government of Libya," since in its view the TNC had now become the Government of Libya. *General License No. 6* 2011.

31. In 1975, the Sultan of Oman (who is also the minister of foreign affairs, the minister for defense, the director of the central bank, and the chief of staff of the armed forces) decreed that he is simply "the source of all laws." See Davidson 2012, 39.

32. McCullough 1990. For the history of the Thai-Khmer Rouge resource trade, see Rungswasdisab 2010.

33. See Harding 1992, 180–83.

34. Pogge 2008, 5–6.

35. Waltz 1959, 186.

36. Soviet property law was obviously quite different from property law in the West, yet the two sides continued their trade even through the chilliest years of the Cold War. Here is a Soviet legal textbook on how the coordination of property rules looked from the perspective of the USSR: "From the principle of legal equality of the two systems of property flows the recognition—on the part of the USSR and the other socialist states in their mutual relations with the capitalist world—of the capitalist system of property, and of the rights of individual owners of capitalist firms. At the same time, the Soviet Union and other socialist states demand that capitalist countries recognize socialist property and the rights that arise on the basis of the laws of the socialist states... In this way the right of a state of one system should be related to the existence of the other system of property as to an objective fact." Boguslavskiĭ 1982, 117–18.

37. Searle 1995.

38. Gilbert 2006, 134–45.

39. The domestic property laws of weak states, like the DRC, do not form part of this consensus—as above, rebels in the eastern DRC are violating Congolese law when they seize minerals by force. Yet officials of these weak states are quite unlikely to attempt to break the international consensus on effectiveness by launching international legal actions. This is not only because these states are weak but because, as we saw in Chapter 3, officials in these states often benefit, directly or indirectly, from the illegal resource trade in their jurisdiction.

40. Nowak 2010, 2.

41. Taylor 2011. Previous Iranian capital convictions for sodomy came under a charge suggesting an element of coercion or violence in the act. The charges against these three men, however, contained no such suggestion.

42. The US federal death row is at the prison in Terre Haute, Indiana.

43. Bok 2003.

44. For ambitious proposals to improve labor standards, see Reddy and Barry 2008.

45. The International Labour Organization estimates that almost twenty-one million persons worldwide are subject to forced labor in some form. International Labour Organization 2015. This is a scandalously large number in terms of human suffering, yet in a global labor force of over three billion, this does not represent a significant percentage.

CHAPTER 8

1. Maathai 1999; Tarbell 1911, 364.
2. Lay and Minio-Paluello 2010, 7.
3. Maass 2009, 190.
4. Brun et al. 2011, xi. To put that first figure in context, the GDPs of both Jamaica and Latvia are in the range of $20 billion to $40 billion. CIA 2014, GDP per Capita (PPP).
5. Stodghill 2006.
6. Okonjo-Iweala 2011, ix.
7. Hardoon and Heinrich 2011, 15, 18. Public works contracts and construction are reported as the most likely locations of grand corruption.
8. OECD 2014a, FDI Flows by Industry > United States > Mining and Quarrying, 2011; USAID 2011.
9. OECD 2011b.
10. Wrage 2010.
11. Moran 2011, 13.
12. UK Government 2010, 4.1.
13. US Department of Justice 2009, PBS 2009.
14. Glovin 2010, Neumeister 2010. Giffen was the model for the character of Danny Dalton in the film *Syriana*.
15. *Economist* 2011a; *Economist* 2011b; see Chapter 6, note 76; Partnership Africa Canada 2009; McDougall 2009.
16. *Times (South Africa)* 2009. Life expectancy figures from CIA 2014; GDP per capita (PPP) figures from IMF 2014c, using the estimate for 2015.
17. Shaxson 2007, Chapters 3–5; Ignatius 2002.
18. Burgis 2015.
19. Degomme and Guha-Sapir 2010, UN Secretary-General for Sudan 2009.
20. Herbst 2008, Andersson 2008.
21. US Energy Information Administration 2014b, Sudan and South Sudan. Bashir's forces and proxies continued attacks on southerners after South Sudan became independent in 2011.
22. Moore 2011.
23. Bashir's response to the first announcement of these international warrants was to call a rally in the capital at which he danced onstage in defiance. Martell 2009. In 2013, the United States denied Bashir a visa to enter the country to give a speech at the UN.
24. Ross and Schecter 2011.
25. Joselow 2012.
26. Ross and Schecter 2011.
27. Personal communication, July 2010, Abuja.
28. Kuper 2011.

29. Financial Services Authority 2011, 26. The report notes that only two cases have resulted in corporate convictions for corruption (one of which was squashed by the British government). See generally O'Murchu 2014.

30. Levin and Coburn 2010, 1. The university officials were those of the American University in Washington, DC, whom the report says accepted $14 million in consulting services from corporations connected to Nigeria's then-vice president without inquiring where those corporations got their money.

31. Human Rights Watch 2010.

32. Tran 2011.

33. Kuper 2011, Allen 2011.

34. Global Witness 2011, Urbina 2009.

35. *United States v. One Michael Jackson Signed Thriller Jacket* 2014, [26–31].

36. A representative from Britain's development agency has said that its main leverage over Joseph Kabila, the President of the DRC, has been his desire to have mining companies with which he is connected listed on London's AIM stock market. Personal communication, London, June 2014.

37. Bazoobandi 2013, 80–87.

CHAPTER 9

1. Adjutant General's Office 1863, Article 16; Nietzsche 1998, Section 49.

2. *Hague Convention* 1899, Article 23.

3. Grotius 1901, Book III, Chapter 5.

4. Sandholtz 2007, 51. The historical material in this section draws heavily on Sandholtz's work.

5. Adjutant General's Office 1863, Article 28.

6. Avalon Project 2008.

7. Sandholtz 2007. The requirement of occupying powers to protect the cultural property of the occupied territory was codified in a later Hague Convention (1954, and expanded in 1999), which the United States ratified and supports diplomatically.

8. Power rules legitimize advantage for those with more power; counter-power rules legitimize advantage for those with less power. In Philip Pettit's terms, successful counter-powerful rules enhance anti-power, which is a kind of freedom. See Pettit 1996. The philosophy of counter-power is most associated with the republican tradition; the major contemporary statement is Pettit 1997. Now see Pettit 2014.

9. There are rich literatures on norm-change within law and international relations; see, for example, Lessig 1995, Sunstein 1996, Finnemore and Sikkink 1998, Koh 1998, Wendt 1999, Sikkink 2011.

10. Korey 1987.

11. Personal communication, 2010.

12. Leventhal 1998.

13. Ashcroft et al. 2005.

14. Jackson 2007, 25. This section follows Jackson's exposition on Christendom.

15. Locke 1988, 372.

16. Nussbaum 1962, 116.

17. War mortality figures are, as always, estimates. Outram 2001, 163–64, concludes that the German population ended the war approximately 23 percent smaller than it would have been.

18. Grotius 1901, 335. As Krasner says, the Westphalian treaties are often misunderstood as themselves effecting a change to the modern system of state sovereignty, when in fact they only marked one significant step in this process. Krasner 1999, 73–82.

19. Davies 1996, 568.

20. Bull 2012, 33.

21. Crawford 2001, 12.

22. Article 124 of the Treaty of Münster, which formed part of the Westphalian settlement, did require signatories to join in a system of collective security against "an Infringer of the Peace"; however, this attempt to generate a norm of peace within the Westphalian system did not gain traction.

23. Recall that Grotius framed the Westphalian pro-plunder norm in terms of entitlements: "The *Right* to Lay Waste an Enemy's Country, and Carry Off His Effects."

24. Solana 1998.

25. Malanczuk 1997, 91.

26. Nicholas 1962, 65–68.

27. Balakian 2003, 64; Lauren 2011.

28. Wiegrefe 2013. For "consultation," see Kennedy 1999, 416.

29. Havel 2010.

30. *Universal Declaration of Human Rights* 1948, Preamble.

31. As the Preamble to the *Universal Declaration* states, "A common understanding of these rights and freedoms is of the greatest importance" for the "promotion of universal respect for and observance of human rights and fundamental freedoms."

32. See Beitz 2009, 44.

33. Simmons 2009, Risse et al. 1999, Risse et al. 2013. New democratic governments may also join a human rights regime to "lock in" democratic institutions against non-democratic threats. Moravcsik 2000.

34. Cohen 2010, Part 3.

35. Ignatieff 2002, 56.

36. "Jacques Maritain, a member of the UNESCO Committee on the Theoretical Bases of Human Rights reported a colleague's remark that, 'We agree about the rights *but on condition no one asks us why*'... He went on to describe human rights as 'practical conclusions which, although justified in different ways by different persons, are principles of action with a common ground of similarity for everyone.'" Beitz 2009, 21. In this sense, the framers of the *Universal Declaration* were Rawlsians before Rawls.

37. This summary is taken from Nickel 2007. Moyn 2010 provides a compelling counter-narrative to the standard history of the rise of human rights.

38. In the Westphalian system, a transfer of territory might require a treaty, but given that the conquered could legally be forced to sign a treaty under threat, this is a distinction without a difference.

39. Vazquez 1993, 293.

40. The Stimson Doctrine was itself foreshadowed by Woodrow Wilson's "Fourteenth Point" on political independence and territorial integrity, which became embodied in Article 10 of the Covenant of the League of Nations in 1924. The League of Nations in turn supported the Stimson Doctrine after the Japanese incursions into China.

41. Raic 2002, 67–68.

42. Boutros-Ghali 1996, 3.

43. Zacher 2001. See also Hensel et al. 2009.

44. RT.com 2014a, Sputnik 2014.

45. Miller 2014.

46. Herbst 2000; Tilly 1990; Krasner and Pascual 2005; Fukuyama 2011, especially Chapters 7 and 22; Roberts 2014.

47. Kagan 2006.

48. Rusling 1903. See also Millis 1931.

49. Bowden 2009, 227–28.

50. Williams 1980.

51. Woods 2006, 50.

52. Kipling 1994, 334.

53. During the Senate debates over the Treaty of Paris, by which Spain was to cede Puerto Rico, Guam, and the Philippines, Henry Cabot Lodge claimed that failure to ratify would mean the United States "being branded as a people incapable of taking rank as one of the greatest world powers." Bowden 2009, 227–28.

54. Stead 1902, 190.

55. Gilbert 1947, 66.

56. See, for example, Keohane 1991, Hardt and Negri 2000, Ignatieff 2003, Walzer 2003.

57. In the twentieth century, the United States added to its territory by purchase (the Virgin Islands) and through bilateral treaties (settling minor boundary disputes with Canada and Mexico). It also administered several Micronesian islands as Trust territories after World War II.

58. At one of the lowest points of US-Arab relations, the 1973 oil embargo, it appears that top US officials considered an invasion to take control of major Saudi and Kuwaiti fields. The plans, however, seem never to have gone beyond the discussion stage. Bowcott 2004.

59. For example, in setting out the "Bush Doctrine," which asserted the right to use preemptive military force in Iraq, George W. Bush emphasized that "[w]e have no territorial ambitions, we don't seek an empire." Bush 2002, 2060. Speaking to troops returning from Iraq in 2011, Barack Obama said, "Because of you, because you sacrificed so much for a people that you had never met, Iraqis have a chance to forge their own destiny. That's part of what makes us special as Americans. Unlike the old empires, we don't make these sacrifices for territory or for resources. We do it because it's right." BBC 2011f.

60. Rawls 1999, but see Wenar and Milanovic 2009.

61. Foucault 1995, 82.

62. Rosato 2003, 590–91.

63. On the first point, see Goldsmith and Posner 2005, Chapter 4. Goldsmith and Posner admit that human rights law can coordinate state expectations in mildly beneficial ways.

64. The poverty figure is the World Bank's 2011 figure, based on $1.25 a day in 2005. World Bank 2015a, 36.

65. Hook 1939, 39. See also Piaget quoted in Elkind 1968, 80: "The principal goal of education in the schools should be creating men and women who are capable of doing new things, not simply repeating what other generations have done; men and women who are creative, inventive and discoverers, who can be critical and verify, and not accept, everything they are offered."

66. Thoreau 1983, 396.

67. To take just one indicator of growth, the Maddison Project estimates that the world's GDP per capita grew more than three-and-a-half times larger between 1950 and 2010 in constant dollars. Nor was this just the rich getting richer—even the region that ended up poorest per capita (Africa) saw its GDP per capita more than double. Maddison Project 2013.

68. Again, to take one of many indicators, according to the Polity IV scores, in 1945 only one in five humans lived in a democracy; by 2009, well over half did. (Before 1945, the percentages living in democracies were of course even smaller.) Center for Systemic Peace 2014.

69. Hegel 1861, 22.

70. Pinker 2011, 189–377. Pinker relies especially on the work of John Mueller, such as Mueller 2009. See also Lebow 2010, Gat 2013.

71. Freedman 2014, 658. In the most thorough review of the recent evidence, the Human Security Project concludes: "Claims that the number of interstate wars has decreased dramatically since the 1950s, and that civil war numbers have declined since the end of the Cold War, are now uncontroversial within the mainstream conflict research community, though they still occasion surprise and sometimes skepticism among non-specialists." The report also says, "Wars between states have almost completely disappeared, while the overall number of major wars of all types being waged around the world—civil wars as well as wars between states—has more than halved since the end of the Cold War." Human Security Report Project 2014, 3, 32.

72. Goldstein 2011, 328, 4.

73. Pinker and Mack 2014; Human Security Report Project 2014, 80.

74. Melander et al. 2009, 529.

75. For comparisons of terrorism deaths, see most recently Mueller and Stewart 2014.

76. See notes 8 and 9 in the Introduction for citations. Using a different (non-comparable) line for extreme poverty, Bourguignon and Morrisson 2002, 732–33, estimate that 72 percent of humanity lived in extreme poverty in 1950. Those looking for dynamic charts showing improvements across a wide range of indicators of well-being can visit the "Wealth and Health of Nations" page at gapminder.org.

77. Morris 2014 tells much the same history at greater length, and comes to many of the same conclusions about the relative benefits of being born today.

CHAPTER 10

1. Bodin 1992, 46; Proctor 2013.

2. Wortham 1996, 112–15.

3. James I 1597, Preface, Chapter 4. The "countrie" in the text is Scotland, which James then ruled as James VI.

4. Exodus 7–8, Exodus 22:18; 1 Samuel 28:7–25.

5. Houston 1995, 21–22.

6. Jefferson 1999, 554; Franklin 1965, 398.

7. For a recent literature review on the "democratic peace," see Hayes 2012.

8. Simmons 1998.

9. Christiano 2011 gives a good summary of the literature supporting the empirical claims about democracy in this paragraph.

10. Sen 1999b.

11. Hamilton et al. 1999, 319.

12. Wilson 1925, 182.

13. Just as the principles of the classic international system did not emerge fully formed from Westphalia in 1648, so the principles of the modern international system did not emerge fully formed from San Francisco in 1945. The locations are appropriately associated with the systems insofar as they identify where the most significant treaties were signed.

14. San Francisco is farther from Washington, DC than any other major American city, including San Diego, Los Angeles, Portland, and Seattle. (Honolulu and Anchorage are not in the US top-fifty metropolitan areas by population. US Census Bureau 2013.)

15. *Universal Declaration of Human Rights*, Article 21(3).

16. Crawford and Marks 1998, 72.

17. The most prominent rights-based proposal for the international law of secession is in Buchanan 2004a. For an alternative rights-based view, see Wellman 2005.

18. *Declaration of Independence* 1776.

19. Leon-Portilla 1992, 74–76.

20. Wiener 1995, 3.

21. Ferguson 2002, Lal 2004.

22. Welch 1980, 115.

23. Kipling 1994, 334.

24. MacQueen 2007, 23–24.

25. MacQueen 2007, 26.

26. *Charter of the United Nations* 1945, Preamble and Article 1.

27. French 2011, 115–16.

28. Jacobson 1964, 78: "Using the broadest definition of a university education . . . the number of Congolese who had received training at this level as of June 30, 1960, was at most several hundred, with priests predominating. Only 17 Congolese had received European university education."

29. *Declaration on the Granting of Independence to Colonial Countries and Peoples* 1960. The UN followed in 1970 with the even more resolute *Friendly Relations Declaration*, which insisted that all states have a duty "[t]o bring a speedy end to colonialism, having due regard to the freely expressed will of the peoples concerned; and bearing in mind that subjection of peoples to alien subjugation, domination and exploitation constitutes a violation of the principle [of equal rights and self-determination of peoples], as well as a denial of fundamental human rights, and is contrary to the Charter." *Friendly Relations Declaration* 1970.

30. *East Timor (Portugal v. Australia)* 1995, [29]. This is the case in which the Court declared that self-determination is *erga omnes*: a duty owed by each state toward the community of states as a whole.

31. *Public Sitting CR 2009/26* 2009, [34].

32. *Western Sahara [Advisory Opinion]* 1975, [32]. See also Crawford 2001.

33. Cassese 1995, 40.

34. The General Assembly defined foreign domination as pertaining to a people on "a territory which is geographically separate and is distinct ethnically and/or culturally from the country administering it," especially if the relationship is an arbitrary one of subordination. This definition, though rough and ready, has served well enough to distinguish between anti-colonial independence and secession from an independent country. *Non-Self-Governing Territories* 1960, Annex Principle IV.

35. See, for example, Crawford 2013, 578–83, 594–96; Cassese 1995, 133–40.

36. Hochschild 1998, Chapter 19.

37. Justinian 1812, 8, 9.

38. Purdy and Fielding 2007.

39. Quoted in Rothney 1969, 177.

40. *Declaration of the Rights of Man and of the Citizen* 1789, Article 3.

41. The phrase was conceived by Governour Morris, a New Yorker who also helped to devise the street grid of Manhattan.

42. Economist Intelligence Unit 2013, 2. The constitutions of at least 135 countries guarantee the right to vote and to be represented at all levels of government. And this figure undercounts the countries that claim to be democratic. For example, the United States is the world's oldest democracy, yet as the US Supreme Court emphasized in *Bush v. Gore 2000*, the US Constitution does not ascribe to US citizens a right to vote. See Raskin 2001.

43. *Constitution of Ireland* 1937, Preamble; *Constitution of the Republic of Sudan* 1998, Preamble, Article 4.

44. See also *Constitution of the Socialist Republic of Vietnam* 1992, Article 2: "The State of the Socialist Republic of Vietnam is a State of the people, by the people, for the people. All State power belongs to the people."

45. *Constitution of the People's Republic of China* 1982, Preamble.

46. Mill 1989, 42.

47. Goethe 2014, 103 (author's translation).

48. Mill 1989, 44.

49. See, for example, Carpini and Keeter 1996.

50. Mill 2001, 27. For an exemplary contemporary exploration of the value of self-determination, see Stilz 2015.

51. Sen 1999a, 5.

52. Tessler et al. 2012, 90.

53. Dalton et al. 2008, Diamond 2010.

54. "It is difficult to discern any consistent action taken in the international arena to protect the rights of peoples subjected to authoritarian or despotic governments, and based on the principles that such governments are in violation of their people's right to self-determination." Cassese 1995, 102.

55. CNN 2003a, CNN 2003b.

56. The main exception to the ban on military action is a response to a threat to peace.

57. Note that the designs which further the two goals will be relative to the ship's medium of travel; the optimal shapes will be different for, say, seaships and airships and spaceships. This analogy can be returned to political systems, with the ship of state negotiating the flows of history.

58. "Peace is generally good in itself," said Teddy Roosevelt, accepting the Nobel Peace Prize, "but it is never the highest good unless it comes as the handmaid of righteousness." Roosevelt 1910. Given Roosevelt's imperialist past, the award of the Peace Prize bemused even him; it was given for his brokering of a peace treaty between Russia and Japan.

59. UNESCO 2013.

60. *The Crime of Genocide* 1946. There is now also an uncertain expansion of the genocide norm into an international "responsibility to protect" populations, even militarily, against mass atrocities. Evans 2008, Bellamy 2011.

CHAPTER 11

1. Lincoln 2015, 136; Mill 1909, II.10.4; Roosevelt 1911.
2. *ICCPR* 1966, *ICESCR* 1966.

3. The *Universal Declaration of Human Rights* was a declaration of the UN General Assembly. As such, it is not legally binding, though many lawyers hold that parts of it have become binding as customary international law.

4. Self-determination is not the only group right mentioned in the treaties: the family is said to be entitled to protection, and the crime of genocide is a crime against a group. The rights of states are also of course group rights in just the same way as the rights of peoples are.

5. See Cassese 1995, Chapter 7.

6. Ross 2012, 33.

7. Ross 2012, 33. Definitions from *Oxford English Dictionary* 2014.

8. The Crown's public holdings are managed by different organizations: oil, for example, is handled by the Department of Energy and Climate Change, while precious metals are managed by the Crown Estate. The British monarch receives an annual grant for expenses from the treasury, now called the Sovereign Grant. The British monarch also owns properties such as Balmoral Castle in a personal capacity. On UK mineral rights, see Morgan 2005. Parliament transferred Scotland's naturally occurring oysters and mussels to Scotland in 2014.

9. *Mineral Oils Ordinance* 1914, 6(1a).

10. *The Mineral Act* 1946, 47.

11. *Constitution of the Federal Republic of Nigeria* 1963, Preamble and Article 158.

12. E&E TV 2011.

13. *Petroleum Activities* 1978; *Constitution of the Socialist Republic of Vietnam* 1992, Article 17; *Hydrocarbons Law* 2006, Preliminary Recitals.

14. *Constitution of Iraq* 2005, Article 111.

15. Bush 2006, 1119; see also CNN 2003. Several Bush administration officials asserted the Iraqi people's resource sovereignty, including Colin Powell. Walsh 2003.

16. *Telegraph* 2003.

17. Australian Government 2010; Blount and Brasileiro 2009; Rathborne and Garcia 2013; AP 2005; President of Azerbaijan 2012; BBC 2002b; World Bulletin 2008; John and Kpodo 2010; Norwegian Ministry for Petroleum and Energy 2011, 5.

18. Hegel 1991, 20. On interpreting this passage, see Stern 2006.

19. UN Treaty Collection 2013; CIA 2014, Population.

20. *ICCPR* 1966, Article 47; *ICESCR* 1966, Article 25.

21. This assumption is supported by the general rule for interpreting treaties as set out in the Vienna Convention of 1969: "A treaty shall be interpreted in good faith in accordance with the ordinary meaning to be given to the terms of the treaty in their context and in the light of its object and purpose." *Vienna Convention* 1969, Article 31.

22. Speaking to the lawyers for a moment. Article 1 is not a relic of the New International Economic Order. It does not express a "third-generation" right of solidarity. (Though it is contained in declarations of such rights, e.g., in the *Declaration on the Right to Development* 1986). It is justiciable in principle through the interstate complaints procedure under Article 41 of the *ICCPR*. It does not merely ascribe rights to peoples under colonial rule or military occupation. Higgins 1994, 115ff.

23. Buchheit 1978, 9. See also Beitz 1999, 106.

24. Cranston 1984, 8.

25. See Cassese 1995, 59–61.

26. The UN Refugee Agency estimates that there are ten million stateless persons worldwide, within a global population of about seven billion. UNHCR 2014.

27. *ICCPR* 1966, Article 27.

28. Kymlicka 2010, 377–96. Kymlicka's survey of recent attempts to gain more rights for minority groups is instructive, because it shows that their failures did not derive from a lack of good intentions, ideas, or opportunities. Rather, advocates became concerned about the implications of their proposals for igniting armed conflict and for the protection of human rights of "minorities within minorities." Even the progress made on securing rights for indigenous peoples may be temporary, Kymlicka says, because the incentives created by this progress threaten to draw too many claimants into the category of "indigenous peoples" for the system to be stable. See Wenar 2016.

29. Holman 1949, 19, 23.

30. Fiallo 2012.

31. Nozick 1974, 171.

32. Lincoln 2015, 232 (italics added).

33. *Constitution of the United States of America*, 1787, Article IV, Section 3 (emphasis added). On the relations between these concepts, with historical background, see generally the Australian High Court's judgment in *Mabo v Queensland* 1992 and the International Court of Justice's *Western Sahara [Advisory Opinion]* 1975.

34. A sovereign also has meta-jurisdictional rights over its territory. One meta-jurisdictional right is the right to control the territory's borders: to determine who can enter and exit the territory. Another meta-jurisdictional right is the right to change the borders: to abandon, or transfer, or acquire territory. When we speak of jurisdictional rights from now on, we include these meta-jurisdictional entitlements. See Buchanan 2003.

35. "Non-bodily" means "not presently part of a human body" (one can sell one's cut hair). For an erudite exploration of the many values that bear on and flow from property rights in a liberal society, see Purdy 2010.

36. *Question of Namibia* 1979, [3].

37. Epstein et al. 2003, 131.

38. *Constitution of Mexico* 1917, Article 27. Article 27 further specifies: "The Nation owns what follows: all natural resources at both the continental platform and the islands' seafloor . . . all the oil and all solid, liquid and gaseous hydrocarbons." The Mexican constitution carefully distinguishes "the Nation" (*la Nación*) from "the State" (*el Estado*).

39. *Constitution of Zambia* 1996, Article. 10v, 339f.

40. Anaya 2011, 2.

41. Glendon 2002, 230, summarizing Maritain in UNESCO 1948, 16.

42. Radon 2005, 61–62. See generally Bastida et al. 2005 and more generally McHarg et al. 2010.

43. In Canada, only minerals under land purchased before the early twentieth century (depending on jurisdiction) can be privately owned; the remainder (now covering 90 percent of Canada's land) are owned by Canadian governments. Natural Resources Canada 2015. The US federal government only has rights in minerals offshore and under federal public lands like national parks. Still, the US government directly owns nearly 30 percent of the entire territory of the United States—including more than 40 percent in states like California and Arizona, and nearly 85 percent in Nevada. On the history of US mineral law, see Wright and Czelusta 2002.

44. Anderson 2006, 129.

45. Illarionov 2008.

46. "Resource nationalism" can also denote increased taxation of resource-derived assets, whoever owns those assets, as in the Australian "supertax" on all firms mining in Australia. See, for example, Blas 2011.

47. In the past, there was a question as to whether a state has the right to nationalize foreign-owned property, and in our fortunate historical era, this question has been settled in international law: it does. However, it is also settled in international law that this right is limited. There is an international Takings Clause: foreign property may only be taken for domestic use upon payment of prompt, adequate, and effective compensation to the foreign owners. This limitation on nationalization is indicated in the Covenants. The full first sentence of Article 1(2) is "All peoples may, for their own ends, freely dispose of their natural wealth and resources without prejudice to any obligations arising out of international economic co-operation, based upon the principle of mutual benefit, and international law." The language beginning at "without prejudice…" concerns nationalization. See Schrijver 1997, 392 and *passim*.

48. *Basic Law for the Federal Republic of Germany* 1949, Article 1(1–2).

49. Schrijver 1997, 391–92.

50. Collier 2010b, 114.

51. Pogge 2008, 202–21.

CHAPTER 12

1. Bentham 1838, 268–69.

2. Holmes 1881, 1.

3. Cassese 2001, 65, 202.

4. Holmes 1997, 992.

5. See, for example, Anghie 2004.

6. *Montevideo Convention* 1933, Article 1. A fourth element, the capacity to enter into relations with other states, is sometimes added but is not agreed as being necessary for statehood.

7. US Department of State 2015a.

8. Harold Laski quoted in Skinner 2010, 42. Laski was echoing John Austin: a state is "the individual person, or the body of individual persons, which bears the supreme powers in an independent political society." Skinner 2010, 41. "Supreme powers" in Austin's quotation is a descriptive term, with no overtones of morally rightful authority.

9. Kremer and Jayachandran 2003; Howse 2007, 13; Boyce and Ndikumana 2011, 17.

10. When speaking this way, the "self-determination" of a state can only carry its external sense: a self-determining state is a regime politically independent from other regimes.

11. When referring to spaces instead of regimes ("within the borders of a state"), the word *territory* will be used instead of *state*.

12. *Charter of the United Nations* 1945, Preamble. See also Alston: "The symbolism of the term 'peoples' was prominently, even ostentatiously enshrined in the UN Charter by the proclamation of the Charter in the name of 'We the Peoples.'" Yet in the end, he continues, the invocation of peoples was merely a "rhetorical flourish." Alston 2001, 260.

13. Kelsen 1950, 52.

14. *Banjul Charter* 1982 (emphases added).

15. *Declaration on Permanent Sovereignty over Natural Resources* 1963, [1]; *Declaration on Permanent Sovereignty over Natural Resources of Developing Countries* 1972, [1].

16. Recall the directive from the Vienna Convention (the "treaty on treaties"): "A treaty shall be interpreted in good faith in accordance with the ordinary meaning to be given to the terms of the treaty in their context and in the light of its object and purpose." *Vienna Convention* 1969, Article 31.

17. See, for example, *Vienna Declaration and Programme of Action* 1993, I.2.

18. As Cassese says, "The drafting history of Article 1 shows that self-determination was generally considered to afford a right to be free from an authoritarian regime." Cassese 1995, 59–60. Internal self-determination, as set out in common Article 1 of the human rights covenants, "requires that the people choose their legislators and political leaders free from any manipulation or undue influence from the *domestic* authorities themselves... In short, there is no self-determination without democratic decision-making." Cassese 1995, 53–54. He continues: "Article 1(2) can have an impact in extreme situations, where it is relatively easy to demonstrate that a government is exploiting the natural resources in the exclusive interest of a small segment of the population and is thereby disregarding the needs of the vast majority of its nationals. Similarly, it may be invoked with some success where it is apparent that a government has surrendered control over its natural resources to another State or to foreign private corporations without ensuring that the people will be the primary beneficiaries of such an arrangement. Either of these situations would constitute a clear violation of Article 1(2) of the Covenants." Cassese 1995, 56.

19. *Hydrocarbons Law* 2006, Preliminary Recitals.

20. See, for example, Arangio-Ruiz 1974, 562–65.

21. Blackstone 1803, I.15 (spellings modernized). At the end of his chapter on marriage, Blackstone writes: "These are the chief legal effects of marriage during the coverture; upon which we may observe, that even the disabilities, which the wife lies under, are for the most part intended for her protection and benefit. So great a favorite is the female sex of the laws of England."

22. James I 1918, 271–72, recalling the language of Ephesians 5:22–23: "Wives, submit yourselves unto your own husbands, as unto the Lord. For the husband is the head of the wife, even as Christ is the head of the church: and he is the saviour of the body."

23. Cassese 1995, 132–33, 189–90.

24. Cassese 2001, 65, 202.

25. *Friendly Relations Declaration* 1970.

26. Cassese 1995, 144 (italics in original).

CHAPTER 13

1. Jefferson 1903–07, VI, 130; Douglass 1986, 204; Bashir 2005.

2. Allen describing the *Almanac* of Nathaniel Ames in Allen 2014, 117.

3. For example, even the more robust ontology of groups in List and Pettit 2011 does not posit any "mysterious social forces" (3); see their Part I.

4. See, for example, Raz 1986, 166, 176; Raz and Margalit 1990, 449–50.

5. Individuals act "as citizens" when they vote, march in protest, go off to war, write letters to the newspaper, and so on. "Acting" can also include helping or even passively supporting those who act more directly, so long as the relevant intention is present. This account of collective action is more permissive than those in the literature that require, for example, that members act toward some goal to which they are jointly

committed (see Gilbert 2006, 101–47) or that each member have beliefs about the beliefs of other members regarding everyone doing their part (see Tuomela 1989).

6. Miller 2007, Chapter 5.

7. Nickel 1997.

8. See List and Koenig-Archibugi 2010 on the distinction between a compositional and performative conception of a group agent.

9. The Takings Clause of the Fifth Amendment requires that private property may only be taken for public use on payment of "just compensation."

10. Rousseau 1997, 57.

11. Jefferson 1903–07, III, 227. See also Purdy and Fielding 2007.

12. *Constitution of the Republic of Sudan* 1998, Article 9.

13. *Constitution of the Republic Of Ghana* 1992, Article 257(6).

14. That is, the people, not the trustee, are regarded as having the beneficial rights in the trust property and thus are the beneficiary of the trust. James Penner, personal communication 2014.

15. Munday 2010, Chapter 8.

16. *Zambia v Meer Care & Desai (a firm) & Ors* 2007, [95], [62], [465–67] (italics in original, bold suppressed).

17. Rousseau 1997, 120.

18. See Chapter 7 above.

19. *UK Mental Capacity Act* 2005, Section 3(1). See also Herring 2012, 149ff.

20. Herring 2012, 159–61, 166–67. The person must be capable of understanding the procedure in broad terms when treatment is not misrepresented and no information is deliberately withheld.

21. Herring 2012, 157, 163.

22. McKendrick 2013, 293–303.

23. Amoako-Tuffour 2010, 16.

24. After Simmons 1979, 80.

25. "Can a person walk into the middle of the town square and express his or her views without fear of arrest, imprisonment or physical harm?" Sharansky and Dermer 2004, 40–41.

26. Popular sovereignty is constituted by civil liberties and political rights. In this way, the theory of popular sovereignty builds in the idea that the people have the *ultimate* but not an *unlimited* authority. The people cannot violate fundamental civil and political rights without undermining the conditions for their own sovereignty.

27. Jacques Maritain in UNESCO 1948, 10.

28. Walzer 1980 at 212, 222. Walzer is using the word *state* to mean "the political formation of a country."

29. See, for example, Bronson 2006, Hegghammer 2010, Hertog 2011. There is also, unfortunately, a great deal of cartoonish caricature and conspiracy theorizing about the country, especially since 9/11.

30. Amina bint Abdulhalim Nassar was the second person beheaded for witchcraft in 2011 (and the seventy-third overall), having been charged with tricking people into paying for cures for illnesses. BBC 2011e.

31. It is sometimes forgotten that Saddam's forces invaded Saudi Arabia during the first Gulf War, and that several Arab states supported this invasion. Nasser's Egypt also bombed Saudi Arabia repeatedly during the Yemeni civil war in the 1960s.

32. OPEC 2014, 8.

33. Worth 2014, Withnall 2014.

34. Zoepf 2007. (Not all gang-rape victims are fortunate enough to get a royal pardon; see Shabrawi 2009.)

35. The cleric had admitted to using cables and a cane to burn his daughter's skin and to break her arm, ribs, back, and skull; he may also have raped her. Evans 2013, Hall 2013, Usher 2013.

36. *Lat:* Dare to know. (Kant's motto for the Enlightenment.)

37. Revenue Watch Institute 2013 reports that "revenue management policies are opaque" and gives the country 0 out of 100 for "Government disclosure of conflicts of interest," "checks on fund spending," and "fund disclosure of conflicts of interest."

38. Freedom House 2014b, Norman 2013.

39. Reporters Without Borders 2014.

40. Leigh and Evans 2007, Ghafour 2007.

41. Montagu 2010, Al-Rasheed 2012.

42. Jefferson 1903–07, V, 452.

43. Lacey 2009.

44. US Department of State 2011b, 15, 16.

45. Al-Rasheed 2012. Al-Johani was held without trial for nearly a year, then charged with support of demonstrations, presence at the location of a demonstration, and communications with the foreign media in a manner that harmed the reputation of the Kingdom of Saudi Arabia. Amnesty International 2012.

46. Rousseau 1968, 147.

47. Locke 1988, 170.

48. CIA 2014, Saudi Arabia, Literacy.

49. UN Development Programme 2014, Table 1.

50. Hamilton and Clemens 1999. See also World Bank 2014a.

51. Arrow et al. 2012.

52. Ryan 2011.

53. Milanovic 2011.

54. Bakri 2011.

55. Dworkin 1975, 17.

56. Or, to be more agnostic about his motives, at least beneficent. When the Saudi regime announced tens of billions of extra spending on housing, salaries, unemployment, and other benefits during the Arab Spring, a White House official described this spending as "safety valves the Saudis open when pressure builds"; another official called the money "stimulus funds motivated by self-preservation." Sanger and Schmitt 2011.

57. It should be noted that under any interpretation, the Saudi regime has often not been particularly kind to the Shia minority that is 10 to 15 percent of the Kingdom's citizenry, and it has not been magnanimous to many of the expat workers who constitute more than a quarter of the country's population.

58. "It is sometimes suggested that the citizens of the oil monarchies feel gratitude to their rulers for giving them the money, and that this gratitude translates into political support. Yet gratitude results from the receipt of a gift. The Gulf Arabs, however, think that they themselves, as citizens, own the oil, *not* the ruling families... Few are particularly grateful on receipt of something they think is theirs in the first place." Herb 1999, 241.

59. There are also practical difficulties in going beyond presumed tacit approval and drawing a bright line around what might count as a people's "explicit" approval.

Consider a spectrum of institutions that provide citizens increasing control over the resources of their country. On one end of the spectrum are the four conditions for tacit assent set out above. On the other end, citizens approve every decision made regarding the country's resources (every contract, every privatization, etc.) through a referendum. In between these two points are all the existing and possible institutions of representative governance. Those who want to judge a country's resource sales by whether the people have "actually authorized the sale" will need to draw a bright line somewhere on this spectrum, and it must be a line that is visible and rugged enough for use in international politics. *Pace* Pogge 2010b, 224–30.

60. The United States ranks second only to Norway in the latest Resource Governance Index, which measures transparency, accountability, disclosure, oversight mechanisms, and more. Revenue Watch Institute 2013. (America is evaluated on the Gulf of Mexico).

61. One might also ask a resident of New York, where the governor not long ago banned fracking—to a significant degree because of public opposition.

62. Muslim-majority democracies include large countries like Bangladesh and Turkey and small countries like Senegal and the Maldives. See also Diamond 2010, 94.

63. Comoros is a member of the Arab League, and Comorans are in more control over their resources than Moroccans are over theirs. But Comoros, as a small set of islands with a more diverse population, is a less interesting comparison for our purposes here.

64. Moroccans are below the minimal conditions for authorizing their regime's management of resources in Western Sahara. An average citizen protesting the regime's control over Western Sahara's phosphates (a large part of the country's export revenues) would rationally fear serious consequences from the regime. The regime's restrictions on citizens' deliberation and dissent on Western Sahara are tightly focused; without them, Morocco could meet the minimal conditions for popular resource sovereignty.

65. Oil reserve figures from BP 2014, 6.

66. Nili 2011a.

CHAPTER 14

1. Kennedy 1963b, 163.

2. In his 1877 "Confession of Faith," Rhodes wrote, "I contend that we [the English] are the finest race in the world and that the more of the world we inhabit the better it is for the human race. Just fancy those parts that are at present inhabited by the most despicable specimens of human beings, what an alteration there would be if they were brought under Anglo-Saxon influence... Africa is still lying ready for us, it is our duty to take it." Flint 1974, 248–52. It may be thought that enough time has passed to wash the taint out of the money that now funds the Rhodes Scholarships. Maybe so. Yet why not now use that money to fund young Britons, Americans, Canadians, Australians, and New Zealanders to learn from Africans at African universities?

3. BBC 2003.

4. *Loucks v Standard Oil Co of New York* 1918, 202.

5. Wilson 1981, 28.

6. US Energy Information Administration 2014b, Crude Oil, Monthly. As before, there is a happy fact about Equatorial Guinea's exports to the United States after August 2014 that experts will know—we will take up such facts in the next chapter.

7. Jefferson 1903–07, IX, 36–37.
8. US Department of State 2014a.
9. US Department of State 2014d.
10. Nor is the appeal to national security factually plausible. Equatorial Guinea provides a little if any of US total oil supply; if access to energy resources were as critical as the webpage suggests, the United States could not have disengaged commercially from Sudan, Libya, and Iran, whose proven oil reserves are, respectively, 4, 44, and 143 times greater. US Energy Information Administration 2014a.
11. US Department of State 2011d.
12. See the Freedom House *Freedom in the World* reports for 1995 through 2014.
13. US Department of State 2014b.
14. Maass 2009, 30.
15. US Department of State 2006.
16. Reed 2006.
17. Maass 2009, 48.
18. US Department of State 2009.
19. *Dred Scott v. Sandford* 1857. The history of the case is complex. In the text, State A can be taken as any of the states or territories under which the laws recognized the Emersons' ownership of Scott, and State B can be taken as any of the states or territories in which slavery was prohibited.
20. US Energy Information Administration 2014a, US Imports and Consumption through November 2014.
21. *Saudi Arabia Basic Law* 1992, Articles 6 and 7.
22. Hochschild 2005, 15, 137, 153.
23. Hochschild 2005, 67–68.
24. Heyrick 1824, 4 (punctuation modernized).
25. See, for example, the powerful account in Buchanan 2004b.

CHAPTER 15

1. Eisenhower 1959, 575.
2. *Forbes* 2014b. Not counting Glencore as an oil company, which would make it 8 out of 11.
3. Shmuel Nili was the first philosopher to propose limiting resource trade among democracies. See Nili 2011b, Nili 2013.
4. Darity 1990, 127; Martin 1999, 55–56; Martin 2011; Ackrill and Hannah 2001, 28. The Barclays were Quakers who publicly supported abolition.
5. Walvin 2001, 270–71.
6. Kaufmann and Pape 1999, 631, 634.
7. The United States abolished the slave trade in the same year, 1807. Slaves continued to arrive in the United States for many years after, but most of the growth of the US slave population after 1807 was from what was then called the "natural increase" of the slave population already in the country.
8. de Tocqueville 2001, 199.
9. Weinert 2007, 124.
10. Kaufmann and Pape 1999, 635.
11. Kaufmann and Pape 1999, 636, 638.
12. Manning 2013.

13. Kaufmann and Pape 1999, 631, 636–37. The cost they estimate is 1.8 percent of national income annually.

14. Pew Research Center 2011; Jamal et al. 2014; Carnegie Endowment 2013, 12.

15. For a masterful meditation on trust, see O'Neill 2002.

16. US Department of Justice 2011.

17. Quoted in Koehler 2012, 947. See also US Senate Committee on Banking, Housing, and Urban Affairs 1977, 3–4.

18. Koehler 2012 at 940, 942–943.

19. Hochschild 2005, 140.

20. Cowper 1843, 197–98.

21. Koehler 2012, 949.

22. Koehler 2012, 949.

23. OECD 2011b.

24. Personal communication 2012.

25. *UK Bribery Act* 2010.

26. See, for example, Henning 2013, Ashcroft and Ratcliffe 2012.

27. Moran 2011, 14.

28. See www.cleantrade.org.

29. PBS 2014.

30. *Economist* 2014b.

31. Kedrosky 2010.

32. Compare Naim 2009: "Countries that already have all these institutional strengths need not worry. For the rest, like an autoimmune disease, the curse undermines the ability of a country to build defenses against it. Indeed, we've learned in recent years that concentrated power, corruption, and the ability of governments to ignore the needs of their populations make it hard to do what it takes to resist the resource curse."

33. Kant 1923–55, XXIII, 380; VIII, 429 (author's translation).

34. Katzenellenbogen 2002; Blas 2014a.

35. International Energy Agency 2010, 128.

36. International Energy Agency 2013, 1.

37. Crooks and Raval 2014, US Energy Information Administration 2014d.

38. Blas 2014b.

39. Philips 2014.

40. Crooks and Raval 2014.

41. Hofmeister 2011, Chapter 2.

42. Energy & Commerce Committee 2013.

43. Randhawa 2014.

44. Einstein quoted in Brant 2011.

CHAPTER 16

1. Kennedy 1963a, 736.

2. Sometimes it is said that oil is sold onto world markets, so it might be difficult to trace where it comes from and where it goes. In response, it might be noted that the US Energy Information Agency website already publishes monthly data on oil imports, with each shipment matched by country of origin. More broadly, there are several feasible schemes for certificates of origin that could be required for tankers to dock. Finally, those impressed by the complexities of oil title transfers also sometimes forget

that oil tankers have measurable displacements and are easily tracked from port to port—indeed, some commercial intelligence services already collect this information. Extending the prohibition on crude oil imports to refined product is discussed in Gerecht and Dubowitz 2011.

3. Commercial disengagement can be strengthened with other measures, for example by denying government procurement or correspondent accounts or shipping insurance to commercial entities that do business with disqualified resource vendors. A Clean Trade Act need not effect commercial disengagement with a country beyond its resources and resource vendors—it would still be legal, for instance, to hire workers from the country or to invest in it outside of the extractive sectors. Care must be taken with rules for the latter, however, because in highly authoritarian countries it is often difficult to do business with anyone without actually being in business with the regime.

4. The US Millennium Challenge Corporation (MCC) decides on eligibility for aid using an index based on several indicators. The MCC says that it "favors policy indicators developed by independent third party institutions that rely on objective, publicly available data and have an analytically rigorous methodology. [The] MCC seeks indicators that have broad country coverage, cross-country comparability, and broad consistency in results from year to year." US Millennium Challenge Corporation 2014. The MCC often picks indicators that are the relevant components of metrics that are themselves aggregated from several components, as Clean Trade will also. For example, it might use only the "Governance" and "Personal Freedom" indicators from the Legatum Prosperity Index, or even subindices from these.

5. US Energy Information Administration 2014a, US Imports and Consumption through November 2014.

6. US Energy Information Administration 2014a, US Imports and Consumption through November 2014.

7. One model is the "Terror Free" divestment campaign for Iran. Elis 2009.

8. Journalists can help by drawing attention to such divestment campaigns, as *New York Times* columnist Nicholas Kristof did for the Sudan anti-genocide campaign: "Is your pension fund helping to finance the Janjaweed militias that throw babies into bonfires in Darfur?" Kristof 2007.

9. See cleantrade.org.

10. A Clean Trade divestment campaign might be a potent complement to "Fossil Free," as it gives oil companies positive goals of improving governance in producing countries instead of asking them to go out of business. See Wisor 2014b.

11. Speaking for a moment to the lawyers: even post-*Kiobel*, there may be openings for suits in the United States or the United Kingdom (for example, for a tort of conversion against a firm transporting oil from a highly authoritarian regime into the domestic jurisdiction). For some pre-*Kiobel* scoping of the issues, see the brief by Cecily Rose on the Clean Trade website.

12. The United States faced this question in its 2014 civil action against Teodorín Obiang, *United States of America v One Michael Jackson Signed Thriller Jacket*, cited in Chapter 8. In this civil forfeiture case, the US government (which had concluded that Teodorín's assets were derived "from misappropriation, theft, or embezzlement of public funds") forced the sale of Teodorín's mansion in Malibu and other assets. The settlement stipulates that the money from the sale of the mansion will be held in an escrow account, then given to a charity that will use it for the benefit of the people of Equatorial Guinea—

with strict provisions that none of the money will go to the Obiangs. *United States of America v. One Michael Jackson Signed Thriller Jacket* 2014; Global Witness 2011.

13. See the Q&A section of cleantrade.org for more discussion of this and many other issues.

14. Hochschild 2005, 85.

15. US Trade Representative 2014. The 2013 figure for Chinese toys and sporting equipment was $21.7 billion.

16. Catholics can start their own Washed Clean campaign against petrocrat-sourced shampoo. As the Psalmist says, "Never let the oil of the wicked anoint my head." Psalm 141:5. (This is the translation of the verse in the *New Revised Standard Version Catholic Bible* 2008; other translations vary.)

17. See, for example, www.brilliantearth.com.

18. See www.fairphone.com.

19. Since 2006, the Clean Trade policy framework has been presented in over 60 lectures across five continents and 14 countries, including at the World Bank, the Peace Palace in The Hague, and many academic conferences. It has, for instance, been discussed by policy experts in China, Australia, and Ghana; at multistakeholder roundtables in Washington, DC and Stanford; at the major international law conference in London; after hours at a high-level IMF seminar in Algiers; and in innumerable private conversations with politicians, advocates, journalists, and country specialists. The book you are reading has also been the focus of interdisciplinary workshops at four universities in three countries. The questions here have been the ones raised most often in these discussions.

20. During a policy makers' meeting in Washington, DC, one of the delegates suggested only half-jokingly that Clean Trade would require organizations like Freedom House to be relocated inside of the Pentagon to protect them from attack.

21. On the reliability of the metrics, see, for example, Seawright and Collier 2014, Armstrong 2011.

22. OECD countries, for example, have since 1999 harmonized their country risk categories so as to avoid damaging competition among their export credit agencies. OECD 2014c.

23. Moreover, failure to agree on metrics would force officials to face the press essentially with this message: "We regret that our countries must continue to pay billions of dollars each day for stolen resources to maintain a system that ends up harming our national interests—yet we simply cannot agree on which measures of repression and chaos to use."

24. *Indian Express* 2010, Chinese Embassy 2010, *China Daily* 2011, *Guardian* 2009, Blanchard and Mason 2011, *China Daily* 2010.

25. Foddy and Savulescu 2010, 9.

26. Lincoln 2015, 340 (italics suppressed).

27. Ng'Wanakilala and Obuslutsa 2013. It is widely believed that the Chinese leadership actually works behind the scenes politically in many countries—for example, that it pressured the President of Sudan to allow the South Sudanese people to vote peacefully on secession in 2011. If the Chinese did pressure Bashir, they were praiseworthy—though not for their consistency in upholding a "just business" policy.

28. Lorand Bartels of Cambridge University discusses the compatibility of Clean Trade policies with WTO rules in an article on the Clean Trade website.

29. It is not merely a theoretical possibility that the WTO will permit exceptions to its general rules when trade in resources is causing serious international "public bads."

The WTO granted a waiver to the Kimberley Process in 2003 and renewed the waiver in 2006 and 2012. This precedent for "blood diamonds" could be part of an argument for a similar waiver for "blood oil."

30. As mentioned earlier, objections to reforms tend to recur. Elizabeth Heyrick, the British abolitionist quoted in Chapter 15 who recommended a boycott on slave-harvested sugar, included in her pamphlet her own "objections and replies": "But (it will be objected) if there be no market for West India produce, the West Indian proprietors will be ruined, and the slaves, instead of being benefited, will perish by famine. Not so..." Heyrick 1824, 5.

31. Stearns 2011, 126.

32. Herbst and Mills 2013.

33. Enough Project 2014. See also Global Witness 2015.

34. See Enough Project 2014.

35. Personal communication, Beijing 2012.

36. After Nozick 1974, xix.

37. *The National* 2013, quoting Imad Eddine Adeeb in *Asharq Al Awsat*.

38. Indeed, as seen with Saudi Arabia's accession to the global trade rules, more progressive forces within the country can use international standards of transparency and rule of law as justifications for drawing their more conservative co-nationals forward. See Aaronson and Abouharb 2011. See also the dynamic of how multilateral institutions can enhance domestic democracy in Keohane et al. 2009.

39. As Pettit writes, treating an agent as responsible can itself be "responsibilizing." Pettit 2007.

40. It might be said that in Arabic "Arabian Republic" sounds too much like a truncated form of Jumhūriyyat Miṣr al-ʿArabiyyah, "Arab Republic of Egypt," and other country names that have the pattern "Arab Republic of X." The official new name of the country could thus be "The Republic of the Arabian Peninsula," Jumhūriyyat Shibh al-Jazīrah al-ʿArabiyyah, جمهورية شبه الجزيرة العربية.

41. To continue the previous point briefly, the question of where our energy will come from should also be put to those who want to continue current policy. They can be asked: "What is your confidence in secure energy supplies without a major disruption, say from the Middle East, over the medium term?" Effectiveness will continue to send very large amounts of money to coercive actors, both state and non-state, who support antagonistic versions of extreme religious and nationalist ideologies and who are now engaged in either proxy or direct hostilities. Resource money is the fuel of those fires. Western governments do have contingency plans for major disruptions in Middle East—for the Persian Gulf being closed off, or for Iraq or even Saudi Arabia going offline—but these are highly negative scenarios both for the West and for the rest of the world. "No change" is an uncomfortable position from which to object to reform.

42. Nick Butler, personal communication, December 2014.

43. Hardin 1968.

44. Climate change is not all about carbon: there are, for example, non-carbon greenhouse gases and important land-use issues as well.

45. See Jamieson 2014, Chapters 2 and 3.

46. IPCC 2014, 111.

47. In the 2014 report, the IPCC estimated that only one trillion additional tons of carbon can be emitted to stay within the 2°C warming boundary—but that proven reserves of fossil fuels in 2011 were already about four to seven trillion tons (with an

additional 28 to 43 trillion tons of fossil fuels likely under the ground but not yet proven). IPCC 2014, 67–68.

48. BP 2014, 8, 6; matched with the Freedom House 2014a ratings.

49. The "locked-in" import reductions would reward authoritarian defectors by once again accepting their oil, but it would do so without changing the path to the climate targets. This would still incentivize authoritarian countries to rise out of the zone of disqualification, though less so. Since Europe, for example, will have locked in its reduced demand, this will likely mean lower oil prices than if Europe simply bought oil from whatever countries become qualified.

50. Eurostat 2014.

51. Eurostat 2014; US Energy Information Administration 2014a, Total Coal Exports (Thousand Short Tons) 2012. The European imports referred to are all from Russia. The US Energy Information Administration data show that around 15 percent of coal imports worldwide are from "Not Free" countries.

52. On coal, see Jamieson 2014, 236.

53. US Energy Information Administration 2014b.

54. Even so, both Canada and Australia currently import more oil from authoritarian countries than many of their citizens suspect. See Statistics Canada 2013, Australian Government 2014.

55. For transparency, see the Extractives Industry Transparency Initiative in Chapter 17. Britain has also been innovative in fighting corruption: the capture and conviction of the corrupt Nigerian governor James Ibori (described in Chapter 8) was accomplished primarily by the Metropolitan Police, funded by the British development ministry.

56. North American energy forecasts have grown strongly optimistic in recent years, with US production taking off and new potential in Mexico as the country opens up its investment laws and offshore areas. "North American energy independence" has already been foreseen by 2020 by respected analysts. See, for example, BP 2015.

57. See Petraeus et al. 2014.

58. Conditional commitment is a lower-cost option for states that cannot summon the political will to move first. A state can commit to conditional implementation of Clean Trade, leaving the choice of metrics, for example, to a later multilateral agreement. A state can also commit to conditional enactment: for example, it can commit to enact the framework when states accounting for a certain percentage of global trade have also committed, or when a certain number of EU members have also committed.

59. Again using the Freedom House metric, and again noting that this is solely for the purpose of illustration in this chapter.

60. It is sometimes thought that Wahhabi Islam is politically reactionary by its very nature. Yet the Qatari leadership has proved much more progressive than the Saudi leadership in the past decade, hosting several important international peace initiatives and creating the Al Jazeera network.

61. The threshold is $15,000 per capita at purchasing power parity. See World Bank 2014b; National Intelligence Council 2012, vii.

62. *Constitution of the People's Republic of China* 1982, Preamble.

63. Bozorgmehr and Hornby 2014.

64. Economy and Levi 2014, 192.

65. On moral transformation within China, see the compelling account in Appiah 2010, Chapter 2.

66. See the remarks by Wang 2013. See also JUCCCE 2015.

67. Even if the Chinese are "all business" and an Asian-authoritarian embrace occurs, the cunning of history may still work to achieve some of the project's goals. If Asian countries come to be the main buyers of authoritarian oil, they will have much greater power to set prices. (In economic terms, they will become "oligopsonists.") They will be able to demand lower prices from high-cost suppliers, and they may even demand prices lower than is needed to keep those regimes in power. It will be harder to remain the autocrat of Angola or Equatorial Guinea when China is one of the few places you can sell to.

68. Crawford 2014. The figure includes veterans' benefits but not interest. It also does not include the large human costs to the United States, or any of the very substantial human and economic costs to the Iraqis.

69. Stern 2010.

70. Pitt 1806, 90–91. (The past-tense verbs in the reporter's text have silently been changed back to the present tense it seems likely that Pitt spoke.) See Hague 2005, 140.

71. Manzo and McGowan 1992. Of prominent Afrikaners, 78.2 percent said that black majority rule would be bad for democracy; most seemed to believe that the country would devolve into a dictatorship like some other black-ruled African countries.

CHAPTER 17

1. Lincoln 2015, 158.

2. The Global Witness material in this section is collected from personal communications, from the Global Witness website (www.globalwitness.org), and from Center for Global Development 2007.

3. Center for Global Development 2007.

4. Campbell 2002, 115.

5. For a personal account of the activist origins (and later fate) of Kimberley, see Smillie 2010.

6. Farah 2004.

7. Clean Diamond Trade Act 2003.

8. The Nobel nomination was shared by Partnership Africa Canada, another NGO that had done pioneering work on African conflict diamonds.

9. Kimberley Process 2015.

10. Iraq has many problems, but transparency in its tender of national oil contracts is not one of them: the country is EITI-compliant. See Ruseckas 2009.

11. Silverstein 2003. See also Maass 2009, 38–47. Global Witness has also doggedly documented the profligate ways of Obiang's son, Teodorín (see Chapter 8).

12. Stuart 2011.

13. Gooch 2011. See also Miklian 2013, Kerr and England 2013.

14. The Revenue Watch Institute has now joined with the Natural Resource Charter to become the Natural Resource Governance Institute.

15. US Senate Committee on Foreign Relations 2008.

16. The material in this paragraph and the next comes from personal communications in 2010–2014 with several sources who were involved in the passage of the Cardin-Lugar amendment.

17. Publish What You Pay 2014, Burgis 2014. The Hong Kong Stock Exchange in fact made a significant move on corporate transparency even before the United States did, enacting rules in June 2010.

18. The US-listed oil firms did regroup and launch a lawsuit to block Cardin-Lugar's requirements, claiming these would require illegal activity and damage their competitiveness. The widespread international adoption of similar transparency standards weakened the industry's arguments, but at the time of this writing, the legal challenge remains undecided.

19. For an overview and analysis of many of the initiatives discussed in this chapter, see Simons and Macklin 2014.

20. Also, for example, *OECD Anti-Bribery Convention* 1997, *United Nations Convention Against Corruption* 2004, and *UK Bribery Act* 2010.

21. More examples of transparency initiatives (like Publish How You Extract and Publish How You Spend) can be found at the Publish What You Pay website (www.publishwhatyoupay.org).

22. Publish What You Pay 2015.

23. See, for example, BGR 2013.

24. *Dodd-Frank Act* 2010, Section 1502.

25. Many other initiatives could be added to this list—for example, national and multilateral Stolen Asset Recovery schemes; the Free, Prior, and Informed Consent standard for resource extraction from the land of indigenous communities; human rights standards built into export-credit agency financing procedures; environmental monitoring initiatives; and many others.

26. Ruggie 2012, 1. See also Ruggie 2013.

27. Ruggie 2006.

28. Ruggie 2013, 138.

29. See Clarke 2007, 278.

30. For proposals for reforms in these areas, see Global Witness 2010. In June 2014, the UN Human Rights Council adopted a resolution (sponsored by Ecuador and South Africa) to begin the process to turn the Voluntary Principles into a binding treaty.

31. The compatibility of conditionalities with international trade rules is well understood. On conditionalities and WTO rules, see, for example, Tangermann 2002.

32. Personal communication, Abuja, 2010.

33. Economists like Joseph Stiglitz, Jeffrey Sachs, and Paul Collier have also emphasized this point for macroeconomic policies: these must be appropriate for the country's circumstances. Humphreys et al. 2007, Collier 2010b.

34. One example of such peer review is the African Peer Review Mechanism.

35. The club model has been described by Reddy and Barry 2008, 81–85. The schedule and club models can also be combined. For example, an importing state could announce a schedule of negative conditionalities while offering positive conditionalities to countries that join a club. Or an importing state could announce that a schedule of negative and positive conditionalities will be in effect for all countries that are not members of the club, while country-specific plans will be negotiated by members.

36. For an overview of research and proposals, see the Center for Global Development, Oil-to-Cash webpage (www.cgdev.org/initiative/oil-cash-fighting-resource-curse-through-cash-transfers). See also Moss et al. 2015, Sandbu 2006, Diamond and Mosbacher 2013.

37. Smith 2003.

38. Al-Abadi 2014.

39. For basic income, see Van Parijs 2000. See also www.basicincome.org.

40. Paine 2000, 319–37; King 2010, 171–74; Green Party 2014.

41. Arnn 2006.

42. See Segal 2011.

43. Hanlon and Barrientos 2010. For the latest studies, search for "cash transfers," looking especially at studies on large, established programs like those in Brazil and Mexico.

44. Nigeria, for instance, is rolling out a biometric voter identification card that links to prepaid financial services provided by MasterCard and Nigerian banks. Geuss 2014.

45. Root 2008, 61, 206.

46. Giugale 2011.

47. "In designing and reforming social arrangements one must, of course, examine the schemes and tactics it allows and the forms of behavior which it tends to encourage. Ideally the rules should be set up so that men are led by their predominant interests to act in ways which further socially desirable ends. The conduct of individuals guided by their rational plans should be coordinated as far as possible to achieve results which although not intended or perhaps even foreseen by them are nevertheless the best ones from the standpoint of social justice." Rawls 1971, 57.

48. The National Child Labor Committee was formed in 1904. Attempts at amending the US Constitution were made in 1924 and 1937. The Fair Labor Standards Act was passed in 1938.

49. Newell 1982, 122–23.

50. Sanford 1982, 8, 15.

51. Sanford 1982, 17.

52. CARE, founded in 1945, was originally the Cooperative for American Remittances to Europe.

53. There are many tellings of Manchester's great cotton famine during the American Civil War; for a journalistic account, see Rodrigues 2013. The People's History Museum in Manchester has a permanent display of artifacts from the events in the text.

54. Lincoln 1953, Volume 6, 64.

CHAPTER 18

1. Quoted, apparently without irony, in Heidegger 1988, 5.

2. Pepys 2000, 170.

3. Jenner 1997, 49.

4. A new study says that gerbils and marmots—not rats—spread the Black Death into Europe. See Sarchet 2015.

5. Jenner 1997, 54.

6. Twigg 1993. There were actually three diseases concurrent: bubonic, pneumonic, and septicemic plague.

7. Which of the Four Horsemen brings what aspect of the Apocalypse is ambiguous in Revelation 6 and has been differently imagined over the centuries. Here we interpret freely.

8. See Diamandis and Kotler 2014.

9. National Intelligence Council 2012. We have already seen this megatrend in Chapter 6, in Joseph Nye's "power diffusion away from all states to non-state actors." Nye 2011, xv. (It is possible that the NIC report and Nye's book share a common source.)

10. Schaffnit-Chatterjee 2013, 11. Population figures from World Bank 2014e, South Asia and Sub-Saharan Africa (Developing Only).

11. Moore's Law is, more exactly, about the number of transistors that can be fit inexpensively onto an integrated circuit.

12. The analysis in this section derives from and tracks that in Hale et al. 2013.

13. *General Agreement on Tariffs and Trade* 1947, Preamble.

14. Slaughter and Hale 2010.

15. Fortna 2008; Bellamy and Williams 2010, 1–3.

16. See also the Business and Human Rights Resource Centre at www.business-humanrights.org.

17. For analysis of the history of global inequalities and reflections on their current significance, see the work of Branko Milanovic at www.gc.cuny.edu/liscenter-branko-milanovic.

18. Hale et al. 2013.

19. Psalm 115:16 (King James Version).

20. Locke 1988, II, Section 25.

21. Wenar 1998.

22. Locke 1988, I, Sections 41–43.

23. Locke 1988, II, Section 140.

24. Bailyn 1992.

25. Risse 2012, 89–151. Risse also deploys the common ownership premise within arguments relating to immigration, future generations, and climate change.

26. Pogge 1994; Pogge 2008, Chapter 8; Pogge 2011. See also Wenar 2010. Though Pogge offers his proposal for a Global Resource Dividend as fulfilling a modern Lockean proviso, it is not clear that he endorses the Lockean approach, all things considered.

27. *United Nations Convention on the Law of the Sea* 1982, Article 136; *Outer Space Treaty* 1967, Article 1.

28. See www.skyshares.org.

29. Wittgenstein 2003, Section 66 (author's translation).

30. The noble exceptions include Peter Singer, Michael Walzer, Charles Beitz, Henry Shue, Onora O'Neill, James Nickel, and Thomas Pogge.

31. *Constitution of the Republic of Namibia* 1990, Preamble.

32. *Constitution of the Republic of South Africa* 1996, Preamble.

33. *Constitution of the Republic of Iraq* 2005, Preamble.

34. "Third World" countries were the prime movers in getting Article 1(2) into the human rights covenants as well as in pushing other declarations of permanent sovereignty over natural resources. Schrijver 1997, Part I.

35. "Nations (or persons) may appropriate or use resources, but humankind at large still retains a kind of minority stake which . . . confers no control but a share of the material benefits." Pogge 1994, 200.

36. Here extending Larry Diamond's series to 2014, see Diamond 2008, 372. According to *The Economist Democracy Index*, cited earlier, almost half of countries are democracies.

37. As Ross notes, some countries like Indonesia and Ecuador have transitioned to democracy as their oil rents per capita have declined. Ross 2012, 74–75, 238. As we saw in Chapter 2, in the discussion of the TRAD sources of power, some authoritarians who are not on a path of democratic transition also stay in office through strategic rents or "aid."

38. Paraguay currently produces a little iron and not much else. As in many poor countries, however, natural riches may yet be discovered. A country's resource revenues

are a function not only of natural endowment but also of the investment put into exploration and extraction.

39. This is "political" cosmopolitanism, which is distinct from the ethical and cultural cosmopolitanism of Anthony Appiah. See Appiah 2006.

40. For this reason, Charles Beitz later qualified a premise on which rested his argument for a globally redistributive principle for resources. Compare pages 137–43 of the 1979 text of Beitz 1999 with page 206 of the 1999 edition.

41. For capabilities, see Sen 1999b, Nussbaum 2000, www.hd-ca.org.

42. Guizot 1838, 311.

43. Guizot 1838, 311–12. Guizot's centralizing force was the nation-state, which became progressively more powerful over the succeeding centuries.

44. See Christiano 2011.

45. For a rich account of popular sovereignty in the creation of cosmopolitan agency, see Ypi 2011, Chapter 6.

46. For example, Beitz 1999, 92–104; Caney 2005, 177–81.

47. Heidegger 1988, 5.

48. The great philosopher Sidgwick once gently teased this manner of theorizing: "It is told of Socrates that he once met a professional teacher of Wisdom, who informed him that he had discovered the true definition of Justice. 'Indeed,' said Socrates, 'that is a splendid discovery. Now we shall have no more contests in the law-courts, and nations will not have to go to war any more. Every one will have his rights and there will be no more wrongs.'" Sidgwick 1893, 3.

49. The positions described encompass what philosophers call ideal theories such as luck egalitarianism and both right- and left-libertarianism.

50. One might say that no truly inspiring philosophical ideal could be the premise of a reality-television show.

51. Rawls 1971, 259. It is sometimes thought that Rawls is the "distributive" philosopher *par excellence*, but this is a mistake. Rawls's just distribution gives public assurance to each citizen of their equal worth to society, so supporting the self-respect that everyone needs to pursue their plan of life "with zest and to delight in its fulfillment." Rawls 1971, 178. Rawls's just distribution also enables an especially intense form of social unity—in this society, citizens live together within institutions that allow them to "share one another's fate" at a very deep level. Rawls 1971, 102.

52. Rousseau 1826, 25 (author's translation).

53. Gramsci 2014, December 19, 1929 (translation by Pietro Maffettone).

EPILOGUE

1. Mill 2001, 31–32; Roosevelt 1999, 177–78.

2. Foucault 1984, 47–48; translating *capacites* as "capacities."

3. Hayek 2011, 57, 59.

4. Engels 1892, 128–29, 135; translating *l'humanité* as "humanity" and *règne* as "realm."

5. Clarke 1999.

6. Goethe 2014, 221 (author's translation).

7. Sussman 2005.

8. There are forms of negative relations not representable on this continuum in which one party does not even recognize the other as a human having ends. In the

report from the Congolese civil war in Chapter 4, militiamen disemboweled their victims and posed their stiffened corpses like mannequins.

9. Korsgaard 1996, Chapter 8; Velleman 1999.

10. Kant 1998, 45; substituting "realm" for "kingdom."

11. Mill 2001, 32, 33.

12. See also Adam Smith: "Hence it is, that to feel much for others and little for ourselves, that to restrain our selfish, and to indulge our benevolent affections, constitutes the perfection of human nature; and can alone produce among mankind that harmony of sentiments and passions in which consists their whole grace and propriety." Smith 2002, 30.

13. "I know that it is the achievement of universal love—but is it good?" Philosophers might consider how well this ideal answers Moore's open question argument. See Ridge 2014.

14. Keynes 1920, 39.

15. Sinnott-Armstrong 2014. Classic utilitarianism is sometimes defined as consequentialism plus welfarism plus maximization; the view here substitutes "free unity of ends" for the middle term. ("Unitarianism" would be a good label for this view, were it not already taken.)

16. For the value of personal attributes, consider what Rawls says about the "excellences": "Imagination and wit, beauty and grace, and other natural assets and abilities of the person are goods for others too: they are enjoyed by our associates as well as ourselves when properly displayed and rightly exercised. They form the human means for complementary activities in which persons join together and take pleasure in their own and others' realization of their nature." Rawls 1971, 443.

17. One of the most sensitive expositions of the resources of a sophisticated consequentialist theory remains Railton 1984.

18. See Rawls 1971, 565, on the idea of a social union ("the self is realized in the activities of many selves"). For reflections on the great importance of seeing one's projects as continuous with others' across time, see Scheffler 2013.

19. Rawls 2005, 139. The parallel in Hobbes to Rawls's "reasonable" is the fifth law of nature, "compleasance": "that every man strive to accommodate himselfe to the rest." Hobbes 1996, 106. Scanlon's "reasonable" plays an analogous role in his contractualism.

20. Rawls 2005, 144. Rawls is here describing reasonable pluralism.

21. Honig 1993.

22. Rawls 1971, 527.

23. Interpersonal unity is one of the three dimensions of unity that guide our evaluation of value. Intrapersonal unity—the free unification of a single life over time—is also fundamental in our evaluation of the goodness or badness of persons. (Compare, for example, saying that a person has integrity to saying that a person is deranged.) The existentialist tradition studies this dimension of value; its exemplar is Nietzsche, who yearned for individual lives unified by self-given ends.

The third dimension of value is extrapersonal: the unity between the self and the world. This encompasses the scientific, religious, and aesthetic ideals of understanding the world perfectly, reacting to it aptly, and controlling it effortlessly.

The ultimate ideal of value is maximization along all three dimensions: internally unified individuals, who are also united with each other, and who have full appreciative mastery of their environment. Working on all three dimensions of value at once is a hard but familiar challenge—think, for example, of today's designers of "smart" self-driving cars who are aiming to create reliable machines that coordinate perfectly with each other and navigate their surroundings so as always to reach their destinations safely. The same tridimensional maximization is the aim, *mutatis mutandis*, of primary and secondary schooling.

24. Compare the transition from a *modus vivendi* to an overlapping consensus in Rawls 2005, 158–67.

25. Mill 2001, 32–33 (italics suppressed).

26. One might wonder whether the contemporary fixation on sex in popular culture is partly a result of a frustration over the difficulty of achieving deeper forms of unity among thick-walled, complex, modern selves.

27. We seem headed toward a future where these natural affective bases favoring unity cannot be taken for granted. Some people are now using technology to implant horns on their foreheads and give themselves forked tongues; imagining the equivalent genetic manipulations of the affective bases of behavior makes it all the more important to appreciate the value of the natural mechanisms of sympathy.

28. Singer 1981.

29. Lenin 1965, 268–69 (italics in original).

30. So Hitler in September 1938 after the *Anschluss*: "Soldiers of the German *Wehrmacht*! . . . For the first time, you stand here as soldiers of the Greater German Reich! . . . We acknowledge the necessity of the existence of the Movement, the Movement which in less than two decades' time succeeded in liberating the German *Volk* from its greatest inner confusion and chaos and leading it to the unity which we see today. The teachings of National Socialism and of the Party are guarantors of this inner German *Volksgemeinschaft*." Hitler 1922–1945, 473.

31. Exodus 15:3, Deuteronomy 32:42. Power is also valorized in the popular music, black and white, following in the venerable tradition of folk songs giving life to the fantasies of the frustrated.

32. Hobbes 1996, 89.

33. As Joseph Carens memorably put it, "Borders have guards and the guards have guns." Carens 1987, 251.

34. Rawls 1999, 6–7.

References

LEGAL TEXTS

Banjul Charter. 1982. African Charter on Human and Peoples' Rights. 21 I.L.M. 58.
Basic Law for the Federal Republic of Germany. 1949.
Bush v. Gore. 2000. 531 US 98.
Charter of the United Nations. 1945.
Clean Diamond Trade Act. 2003. 19 USC 3901.
Constitution of Ireland. 1937.
Constitution of Mexico. 1917.
Constitution of Qatar. 2004.
Constitution of the Socialist Republic of Vietnam. 1992.
Constitution of the Federal Republic of Nigeria. 1963.
Constitution of the People's Republic of China. 1982.
Constitution of the Republic of Ghana. 1992.
Constitution of the Republic of Iraq. 2005.
Constitution of the Republic of Namibia. 1990.
Constitution of the Republic of South Africa. 1996.
Constitution of the Republic of Sudan. 1998.
Constitution of the United States of America. 1787.
Constitution of Zambia. 1996.
Controlled Substances. 2005. 21 USC 960a.
The Crime of Genocide. 1946. UNGA Res 96 (December 11).
Declaration of Independence. 1776.
Declaration on Permanent Sovereignty over Natural Resources. 1963. UNGA Res 1803 (November 18).
Declaration on Permanent Sovereignty over Natural Resources of Developing Countries. 1972. UNGA Res 3016 (December 18).
Declaration on the Granting of Independence to Colonial Countries and Peoples. 1960. UNGA Res 1514 (October 14).
Declaration on the Right to Development. 1986. UNGA Res 41 (December 4).
Declaration of the Rights of Man and of the Citizen. 1789.

Dodd-Frank Act. 2010. Dodd-Frank Wall Street Reform and Consumer Protection Act. Pub. L 111-203.
Dog Control Amendment Act. New Zealand. 2003.
Dred Scott v. Sandford. 1857. 60 US 393.
East Timor (Portugal v. Australia). 1995. ICJ Rep 90.
Friendly Relations Declaration. 1970. UNGA Res 2625 (October 24).
General Agreement on Tariffs and Trade (GATT). 1947. 55 UNTS 194.
General License No. 5. 2011. US Department of the Treasury. April 26.
General License No. 6. 2011. US Department of the Treasury. August 19.
Hague Convention. 1899. Convention with Respect to the Laws and Customs of War on Land. July 29.
Hydrocarbons Law. 2006. Equatorial Guinea. Hydrocarbons Law No. 8/2006. 3 November.
ICCPR. 1966. International Covenant on Civil and Political Rights. 999 UNTS 171.
ICESCR. 1966. International Covenant on Economic, Social, and Cultural Rights. 993 UNTS 3.
(Illegal) Timber Regulation. 2010. Regulation (EU) No 995/2010.
Kuwait Airways Corporation v Iraqi Airways Company. 2001. Nos 4 and 5. 3 WLR 1117.
Loucks v Standard Oil Co of New York. 1918. 224 NY 99.
Mabo v Queensland. 1992. No 2. HCA 23.
The Mineral Act. 1946. Nigeria. To Amplify Mineral Industry Legislation (Reserving Minerals of Special Importance to the State for Licensing). February 15.
Mineral Oils Ordinance. 1914. Nigeria. To Regulate the Right To Search for Win & Work Mineral Oils. December 31.
Montevideo Convention. 1933. The Rights and Duties of States. 165 LNTS 19.
Non-Self-Governing Territories. 1960. UNGA Res 1541 (December 15).
OECD Anti-Bribery Convention. 1997. OECD Convention on Combating Bribery of Foreign Public Officials in International Business Transactions.
Oppenheimer v Cattermole. 1976. AC 249 (HL).
Outer Space Treaty. 1967. Treaty on Principles Governing the Activities of States in the Exploration and Use of Outer Space, Including the Moon and Other Celestial Bodies.
Petroleum Activities. 1978. Angolan Law No 13/78. August 26.
Public Sitting CR 2009/26. 2009. International Court of Justice.
Question of Namibia. 1979. UNGA Res 3492 (12 December).
Saudi Arabia Basic Law. 1992. The Basic Law of Governance, Royal Order No. (A/91), 27 *Sha'ban* 1412H.
Treason. 2006. 18 USC 2181.
UK Bribery Act. 2010.
UK Mental Capacity Act. 2005.
UN Security Council Resolution 1653. 2006. January 27. UN Doc S/RES/1653.
United Nations Convention Against Corruption. 2004. A/58/422.
United Nations Convention on the Law of the Sea. 1982. 18 UNTS 3.
United States of America v. One Michael Jackson Signed Thriller Jacket. 2014. CD Cal 13-9169-GW-SS.
Universal Declaration of Human Rights. 1948. UNGA Res 217 A (III). December 10.
US Executive Order 13067. 1997. Blocking Sudanese Government Property and Prohibiting Transactions with Sudan.
US Executive Order 13412. 2006. Blocking Property and Prohibiting Transactions with the Government of Sudan.

US Executive Order 13566. 2011. Blocking Property and Prohibiting Certain Transactions Related to Libya.

US Public Law 106–476. 2000. 114 Stat. 2101. Amending the Harmonized Tariff Schedule of the United States.

Vienna Convention. 1969. Vienna Convention on the Law of Treaties.

Vienna Declaration and Programme of Action. 1993. World Conference on Human Rights.

Western Sahara [Advisory Opinion]. 1975. ICJ Rep 12.

Zambia v Meer Care & Desai (A Firm) & Ors. 2007. EWHC 952 (Ch).

OTHER TEXTS

A Promise Renewed. 2015. "Under-Five Mortality Dashboard." www.apromiserenewed.org/dashboard/ (Accessed May 11, 2015).

Aaronson, Susan Ariel, and M. Rodwan Abouharb. 2011. "Unexpected Bedfellows: The GATT, the WTO and Some Democratic Rights." *International Studies Quarterly* 55(2): 379–408.

Abdelaziz, Salma. 2014. "Group: ISIS Takes Major Syrian Oil Field." www.cnn.com/2014/07/03/world/meast/syria-isis-oil-field/ (Accessed April 25, 2015).

Abdul'Aziz, Ibrahim, and Dulue Mbachu. 2014. "Nigerian Troops Say Corruption Saps Will to Fight Islamists." *Bloomberg Business*, July 16.

Abidin, Mahani Zainal. 2001. "Competitive Industrialization with Natural Resource Abundance: Malaysia." In *Resource Abundance and Economic Development*, ed. Richard M. Auty. New York: Oxford University Press, 147–64.

Acemoglu, Daron, and James A. Robinson. 2012. *Why Nations Fail: The Origins of Power, Prosperity and Poverty*. New York: Random House.

Acemoglu, Daron, James A. Robinson, and Thierry Verdier. 2004. "Kleptocracy and Divide-and-Rule: A Model of Personal Rule." *Journal of the European Economic Association* 2(2–3):162–92.

Ackrill, Margaret, and Leslie Hannah. 2001. *Barclays: The Business of Banking, 1690–1996*. Cambridge: Cambridge University Press.

Adjutant General's Office. 1863. *General Orders No. 100*. Washington, DC.

Africa Confidential. 2012. "Angola: Hope of Peace for Cabinda." April 13.

Afripol. 2013. "93% of Northern Girls Lack Secondary Education—Sanusi." www.afripol.org/afripol/item/1116-93-northern-girls-lack-secondary-education-%E2%80%93-sanusi.html (Accessed January 25, 2015).

Agricola, Georgius. 1950. *De Re Metallica*. Trans. Henry Clark Hoover and Lou Henry Hoover. New York: Dover.

Aidt, Toke S. 2009. "Corruption, Institutions and Economic Development." *Oxford Review of Economic Policy* 25(2):271–91.

Ajami, Fouad. 2007. "The Powers of Petrocracy." *US News & World Report*, December 19.

Al-Abadi, Haider 2014. "Council of Ministers Decides to Approve Oil Agreement between Federal Government and Kurdistan Regional Government." pmo.iq/pme/press/2-12-2014en.htm (Accessed February 14, 2015).

Al-Kasim, Farouk, Tina Søreide, and Aled Williams. 2008. *Grand Corruption in the Regulation of Oil*. Bergen: U4 Anti-Corruption Resource Centre.

Al-Rasheed, Madawi. 2012. "No Saudi Spring." *Boston Review*, March 1.

Al-Sheikh, Hend, and S. Nuri Erbas. 2012. "The Oil Curse and Labor Markets: The Case of Saudi Arabia." Working Paper 697. Giza, Egypt: Economic Research Forum.

Al-Ubaydli, Omar. 2012. "Natural Resources and the Tradeoff Between Authoritarianism and Development." *Journal of Economic Behavior & Organization* 81(1):137–52.

Alexander's Gas & Oil Connections. 2004. "Iran's Statoil Affair Is Awaiting Outcomes of Probes." www.gasandoil.com/news/2004/06/cnm42400 (Accessed January 23, 2015).

Alighieri, Dante. 2005. *Inferno*. Trans. Charles Eliot Norton. Stilwell, KS: Digireads.

Allen, Danielle. 2014. *Our Declaration: A Reading of the Declaration of Independence in Defense of Equality*. New York: Liveright.

Allen, Peter. 2011. "Embarrassing Moment: Playboy Son of an African Dictator (Whose People Live on £1.50 a Day) Has £5 million in Supercars Seized from Outside His Home." *Daily Mail*, October 1.

Allison, Simon. 2012. "Nigeria: How to Lose $35 Billion." *Guardian*, November 13.

Alston, Philip. 2001. "Peoples' Rights: Their Rise and Fall." In *Peoples' Rights*, ed. Philip Alston. Oxford: Oxford University Press, 259–93.

Amnesty International. 2005. *Equatorial Guinea: A Trial With Too Many Flaws*. London.

Amnesty International. 2012. "Saudi Arabia: Trial of Riyadh Protester 'Utterly Unwarranted.'" www.amnesty.org/en/articles/news/2012/02/saudi-arabia-trial-riyadh-protester-utterly-unwarranted/ (Accessed February 6, 2015).

Amoako-Tuffour, Joe. 2010. *How Ghana Plans to Manage Its Petroleum Revenues: A Step Towards Transparency, Accountability and Governance Standards*. Accra: Institute of Economic Affairs, Ghana.

Anaya, James. 2011. "Urgent Request. Violation of Indigenous Peoples' Property Rights and the Right to Effective Remedy." Office of the High Commissioner for Human Rights. Geneva.

Andersen, Jørgen J., and Michael L. Ross. 2013. "The Big Oil Change: A Closer Look at the Haber–Menaldo Analysis." *Comparative Political Studies* 20(10):1–29.

Andersen, Jørgen Juel, et al. 2014. "Petro Rents, Political Institutions, and Hidden Wealth: Evidence from Offshore Bank Accounts." www.nielsjohannesen.net/wp-content/uploads/2014/08/Oil_submission.pdf (Accessed April 25, 2015).

Anderson, Lisa. 1987. "The State in the Middle East and North Africa." *Comparative Politics* 20(1):1–18.

Anderson, Paul Thomas. 2006. *There Will Be Blood*. cinemascopian.com/pics/2008oscars/TWBB.pdf (Accessed December 1, 2014).

Andersson, Hilary. 2008. "China 'Is Fuelling War in Darfur.'" news.bbc.co.uk/1/hi/world/africa/7503428.stm (Accessed January 29, 2015).

Andersson, Hilary. 2011. "Soldiers Tell of Zimbabwe Diamond Field Massacre." www.bbc.co.uk/panorama/ (Accessed January 19, 2015).

Anghie, Antony. 2004. *Imperialism, Sovereignty and the Making of International Law*. Cambridge: Cambridge University Press.

AP. 2005. "Chavez: Our Oil Reserve Does Not Belong to Mr. Bush." March 8.

Appiah, Kwame Anthony. 2006. *Cosmopolitanism: Ethics in a World of Strangers*. New York: Norton.

Appiah, Kwame Anthony 2010. *The Honor Code: How Moral Revolutions Happen*. New York: Norton.

Arangio-Ruiz, Gaetano. 1974. "The Normative Role of the General Assembly of the United Nations and the Declaration of Principles of Friendly Relations." In *Collected Courses of the Hague Academy of International Law, 1972-III*. Vol. 137. The Hague: Hague Academy, 419–572.

Arezki, Rabah, and Markus Brückner. 2011. "Oil Rents, Corruption and State Stability: Evidence from Panel Data Regressions." *European Economic Review* 55(7):955–63.

Arezki, Rabah, Kirk Hamilton, and Kazim Kazimov. 2012. "Resource Windfalls, Macroeconomic Stability and Growth: The Role of Political Institutions." Working Paper 11/142. Washington, DC: International Monetary Fund.

Armstrong, David A. 2011. "Stability and Change in the Freedom House Political Rights and Civil Liberties Measures." *Journal of Peace Research* 48(5):653–62.

Armstrong, Karen. 2014. "The Deep Roots of Islamic State." *New Statesman*, November 21, 24–31.

Arnn, Larry. 2006. "Free to Choose: A Conversation with Milton Friedman." *Imprimis*, July.

Arrow, Kenneth, et al. 2012. "Sustainability and the Measurement of Wealth." *Environment and Development Economics* 17(3):317–53.

Ashcroft, Bill, Gareth Griffiths, and Helen Tiffin, eds. 2005. *The Post-Colonial Studies Reader*. 2nd ed. Abingdon: Routledge.

Ashcroft, John, and John Ratcliffe. 2012. "The Recent and Unusual Evolution of an Expanding FCPA." *Notre Dame Journal of Law, Ethics and Public Policy* 26:25–38.

Asmus, Ronald D., et al. 2005. "A Transatlantic Strategy to Promote Democratic Development in the Broader Middle East." *Washington Quarterly* 28(2):5–21.

Augustine. 1955. *De Civitate Dei Contra Paganos*. Corpus Christianorum, Series Latina. Vol. 47. Turnhout, Belgium: Brepols.

Australian Government. 2010. "Prime Minister Transcript of Doorstop Interview, Geelong Hospital 7 May 2010." pmtranscripts.dpmc.gov.au/browse.php?did=17284 (Accessed February 1, 2015).

Australian Government. 2014. "Australian Petroleum Statistics." www.industry.gov.au/industry/Office-of-the-Chief-Economist/Publications/Pages/Australian-petroleum-statistics.aspx (Accessed February 12, 2015).

Auty, Richard M. 2010. "Elites, Rent-Cycling and Development: Adjustment to Land Scarcity in Mauritius, Kenya and Cote d'Ivoire." *Development Policy Review* 28(4):411–33.

Avalon Project. 2008. "Judgement: Rosenberg." avalon.law.yale.edu/imt/judrosen.asp (Accessed November 27, 2014).

Bafilemba, Fidel, Timo Mueller, and Sasha Lezhnev. 2014. *The Impact of Dodd-Frank and Conflict Minerals Reforms on Eastern Congo's War*. Washington, DC: Enough Project.

Bailyn, Bernard. 1992. *Ideological Origins of the American Revolution*. Cambridge: Harvard University Press.

Bakri, Nada. 2011. "Sanctions Pose Growing Threat to Syria's Assad." *New York Times*, October 10.

Balakian, Peter. 2003. *The Burning Tigris: The Armenian Genocide and America's Response*. New York: Harper Collins.

Ballard, Chris, and Glenn Banks. 2009. "Between a Rock and a Hard Place: Corporate Strategy at the Freeport Mine in Papua, 2001–2006." In *Working with Nature Against Poverty: Development, Resources and the Environment in Eastern Indonesia*, eds. Budy P. Resosudarmo and Frank Jotzo. Singapore: ISEAS, 147–78.

Barnett, Errol. 2012. "Ex-Child-Soldier: 'Shooting Became Just Like Drinking a Glass of Water.'" edition.cnn.com/2012/10/08/world/africa/ishmael-beah-child-soldier/ (Accessed January 24, 2015).

Bashir, Abdul Wahab. 2005. "Unwavering in His Commitment to the Cause of Islam." *Arab News*, August 2.

Bast, Elizabeth, et al. 2014. *The Fossil Fuel Bailout: G20 Subsidies for Oil, Gas and Coal Exploration*. London: Overseas Development Institute.

Bastida, Elizabeth, Thomas Wälde, and Janeth Warden- Fernández, eds. 2005. *International and Comparative Mineral Law and Policy*. The Hague: Kluwer.

Baxter, Joan. 2002. "Mali's Dangerous Desert Gateway." news.bbc.co.uk/1/hi/world/africa/2063526.stm (Accessed January 27, 2015).

Bazoobandi, Sara. 2013. *Political Economy of the Gulf Sovereign Wealth Funds: A Case Study of Iran, Kuwait, Saudi Arabia and the United Arab Emirates*. Abingdon: Routledge.

BBC. 2002a. "Churchill Voted Greatest Briton." news.bbc.co.uk/1/hi/entertainment/2509465.stm (Accessed January 21, 2015).

BBC. 2002b. "Iran Wields Oil Embargo Threat." news.bbc.co.uk/1/hi/business/1912795.stm (Accessed January 26, 2015).

BBC. 2003. "Equatorial Guinea's 'God.' " news.bbc.co.uk/1/hi/world/africa/3098007.stm (Accessed January 26, 2015).

BBC. 2005. "Nigerian Ex-Police Chief Jailed." news.bbc.co.uk/1/hi/world/africa/4460740.stm (Accessed January 25, 2015).

BBC. 2011a. "The Charges Against Charles Taylor." www.bbc.co.uk/news/world-africa-12391507 (Accessed January 29, 2015).

BBC. 2011b. "DR Congo Rape Study 'Questionable.' " www.bbc.co.uk/news/world-africa-13448513 (Accessed January 30, 2015).

BBC. 2011c. "Marange Diamonds: Zimbabwe Denies Torture Camp.' " www.bbc.com/news/world-africa-14468116 (Accessed January 19, 2015).

BBC. 2011d. "Saudi Arabia Prepares for 'Day of Rage' Protests." www.bbc.co.uk/news/world-middle-east-12708487 (Accessed January 27, 2015).

BBC. 2011e. "Saudi Woman Executed for 'Witchcraft and Sorcery.' " www.bbc.com/news/world-middle-east-16150381 (Accessed February 5, 2015).

BBC. 2011f. "Transcript: President Obama Iraq Speech." www.bbc.co.uk/news/world-us-canada-16191394 (Accessed January 31, 2015).

BBC. 2012a. "Former Nigerian Governor James Ibori Jailed for 13 Years." www.bbc.co.uk/news/world-africa-17739388 (Accessed April 25, 2015).

BBC. 2012b. "Liberia Ex-Leader Charles Taylor Gets 50 Years in Jail." www.bbc.co.uk/news/world-africa-18259596 (Accessed January 29, 2015).

BBC. 2012c. "Teodorín Obiang: 'Arrest Warrant' for E Guinea Leader's Son." www.bbc.co.uk/news/world-africa-18832045 (Acessed January 25, 2015).

BBC. 2012d. "Zambian Miners Kill Chinese Manager During Pay Protest." www.bbc.com/news/world-africa-19135435 (Accessed April 25, 2015).

BBC. 2014. "Boko Haram Declares 'Islamic State' in Northern Nigeria." www.bbc.co.uk/news/world-africa-28925484 (Accessed January 25, 2015).

Beitz, Charles R. 1999. *Political Theory and International Relations*. Princeton: Princeton University Press.

Beitz, Charles R. 2009. *The Idea of Human Rights*. Oxford: Oxford University Press.

Belfast Telgraph. 2012. "Gaddafi 'Planned to Kill Reagan.' " December 28.

Bellamy, Alex J. 2011. *Global Politics and the Responsibility to Protect: From Words to Deeds*. Abingdon: Routledge.

Bellamy, Alex J., and Paul Williams, eds. 2010. *Understanding Peacekeeping*. 2nd ed. Cambridge: Polity.

Bentham, Jeremy. 1838. *Works*. Vol. 1. Ed. John Bowring. Edinburgh: William Tate.

Bentham, Jeremy. 1896. *Theory of Legislation*. Trans. R. Hildreth. London: Kegan Paul, Trench, Truebner.

Berners-Lee, Mike, and Duncan Clark. 2013. *The Burning Question: We Can't Burn Half the World's Oil, Coal and Gas. So How Do We Quit?* London: Profile Books.

Besley, Timothy, and Torsten Persson. 2011. *Pillars of Prosperity: The Political Economy of Development Clusters*. Princeton: Princeton University Press.

Bevan, David, Paul Collier, and Jan William Gunning. 1999. *Nigeria and Indonesia*. New York: Oxford University Press.

BGR. 2013. "Mineral Certification at the BGR." www.bgr.bund.de/EN/Themen/Min_rohstoffe/CTC/Home/CTC_node_en.html (Accessed February 14, 2015).

Birrell, Ian. 2011. "The Strange and Evil World of Equatorial Guinea." *Guardian*, October 23.

BIS/DFID Trade Policy Unit. 2011. *Global Context—How Has World Trade and Investment Developed, What's Next?* London.

Blackstone, William. 1803. *Commentaries on the Laws of England*. 14th ed. London: Cadell and Davies.

Blair, Dennis, et al. 2014. "Transcript: Fracking Revolution Transforming the Global Energy Landscape." www.cfr.org/energy-and-environment/fracking-revolution-transforming-global-energy-landscape/p32598 (Accessed November 26, 2014).

Blanchard, Ben, and Jeff Mason. 2011. "China Slams U.S. 'Interference' After Obama Meets Dalai Lama." www.reuters.com/article/2011/07/17/us-usa-obama-dalailama-idUSTRE76E6UK20110717 (Accessed April 25, 2015).

Blanchard, Christopher M., and Alfred B. Prados. 2007. *Saudi Arabia: Terrorist Financing Issues*. Washington, DC: Congressional Research Service.

Blas, Javier. 2011. "'Resource Nationalism' Returns to Commodities." *Financial Times*, June 14.

Blas, Javier. 2014a. "US-African Oil Trade Wanes after Shale Revolution." *Financial Times*, August 3.

Blas, Javier. 2014b. "Victim of Shale Revolution, Nigeria Stops Exporting Oil to US." *Financial Times*, October 12.

Blount, Jeb, and Adriana Brasileiro. 2009. "Tupi Oil Imperiled as Price Drop Unravels Energy Plan." www.bloomberg.com/apps/news?pid=newsarchive&sid=aszdg.tiMLMs (Accessed February 1, 2015).

Bodin, Jean. 1992. *On Sovereignty*. Trans. Julian H. Franklin. Cambridge: Cambridge University Press.

Boguslavskiĭ, Mark Moiseevich. 1982. *Private International Law: The Soviet Approach*. Dordrecht: Martinus Nijhoff.

Bok, Francis. 2003. *Escape from Slavery: The True Story of My Ten Years in Captivity and My Journey to Freedom in America*. New York: St. Martin's Griffin.

Booth, Robert. 2014. "Qatar: Migrants Bear the Brunt of Price of Progress." *Guardian*, July 29.

Bottomley, Ruth. 2000. *Structural Analysis of Deforestation in Cambodia*. Tokyo: Institute for Global Environmental Strategies.

Bourguignon, François, and Christian Morrisson. 2002. "Inequality Among World Citizens: 1820–1992." *American Economic Review* 92(4):727–44.

Boutros-Ghali, Boutros. 1996. "Introduction." In *The United Nations and the Iraq-Kuwait Conflict*. New York: United Nations, 3–125.

Bowcott, Owen. 2004. "UK Feared Americans Would Invade Gulf During 1973 Oil Crisis." *Guardian*, January 1.

Bowden, Brett. 2009. *The Empire of Civilization: The Evolution of an Imperial Ideal*. Chicago: University of Chicago Press.

Boyce, James K., and Léonce Ndikumana. 2011. *Africa's Odious Debts: How Foreign Loans and Capital Flight Bled a Continent*. New York: Zed.

Bozorgmehr, Najmeh, and Lucy Hornby. 2014. "China Offers to Help Iraq Defeat Sunni Extremists." *Financial Times*, December 12.

BP. 2012. *Statistical Review of World Energy*. London.

BP. 2014. *Statistical Review of World Energy*. London.

BP. 2015. *Energy Outlook 2035*. London.

Bradley, John R. 2006. *Saudi Arabia Exposed: Inside a Kingdom in Crisis*. Basingstoke: Palgrave Macmillan.

Brant, Steven G. 2011. "Russell Ackoff, 'Einstein of Problem Solving,' Has Died." www.huffingtonpost.com/steven-g-brant/russell-ackoff---the-eins_b_341349.html (Accessed April 25, 2015).

Bridge, Gavin, and Philippe Le Billon. 2013. *Oil*. Cambridge: Polity.

Brinkerhoff, Derick W., and Arthur A. Goldsmith. 2002. *Clientelism, Patrimonialism and Democratic Governance: An Overview and Framework for Assessment and Programming*. Cambridge, MA: Abt Associates.

Bronson, Rachel. 2006. *Thicker than Oil: America's Uneasy Partnership with Saudi Arabia*. New York: Oxford University Press.

Brown, David E. 2013. *Africa's Booming Oil and Natural Gas Exploration and Production: National Security Implications for the United States and China*. West Point, NY: US War College Strategic Studies Institute.

Brown, Eliot. 2012. "Tower Rises, And So Does Its Price Tag." *Wall Street Journal*, January 30.

Brun, Jean-Pierre, et al. 2011. *Asset Recovery Handbook*. Washington, DC: World Bank.

Bryce, Robert. 1995. "International Business: U.S. Cancels Indonesian Mine's Insurance." *New York Times*, November 2.

Bryce, Robert. 2013. "The Tyranny of Oil." *National Review*, March 11.

Buchanan, Allen. 2003. "Boundaries: What Liberalism Has to Say." In *States, Nations and Borders: The Ethics of Making Boundaries*, eds. Margaret Moore and Allen Buchanan. Cambridge: Cambridge University Press, 231–61.

Buchanan, Allen. 2004a. *Justice, Legitimacy, and Self-Determination: Moral Foundations for International Law*. Oxford: Oxford University Press.

Buchanan, Allen. 2004b. "Political Liberalism and Social Epistemology." *Philosophy & Public Affairs* 32(2):95–130.

Buchheit, Lee. 1978. *Secession: The Legitimacy of Self-Determination*. New Haven: Yale University Press.

Buhaug, Halvard, Scott Gates, and Päivi Lujala. 2009. "Geography, Rebel Capability, and the Duration of Civil Conflict." *Journal of Conflict Resolution* 53(4):544–69.

Bull, Hedley. 2012. *The Anarchical Society*. 4th ed. New York: Palgrave Macmillan.

Burgis, Tom. 2014. "Tullow Steps Up Transparency in Reporting." *Financial Times*, March 23.

Burgis, Tom. 2015. *The Looting Machine: Warlords, Oligarchs, Corporations, Smugglers and the Theft of Africa's Wealth*. New York: PublicAffairs.

Burr, J. Millard, and Robert O. Collins. 2006. *Alms for Jihad: Charity and Terrorism in the Islamic World*. Cambridge: Cambridge University Press.

Bush, George W. 2002. *Public Papers of the Presidents of the United States*. Book 2. Washington, DC: US Government Printing Office.

Bush, George W. 2006. *Public Papers of the Presidents of the United States*. Book 1. Washington, DC: US Government Printing Office.

Byrne, Leo. 2014. "North Korea Takes First Steps toward Oil Exploration." *Guardian*, July 1.

Camp, David. 2006. "President's Remarks to the Travel Pool After Meeting with Interagency Team on Iraq." georgewbush-whitehouse.archives.gov/news/releases/2006/06/20060612-6.html (Accessed February 7, 2015).

Campbell, Greg. 2002. *Blood Diamonds: Tracing the Deadly Path of the World's Most Precious Stones*. Boulder: Westview.

Caney, Simon. 2005. *Justice Beyond Borders: A Global Political Theory*. Oxford: Oxford University Press.

Carens, Joseph H. 1987. "Aliens and Citizens: the Case for Open Borders." *Review of Politics* 49(2):251–73.

Carnegie Endowment. 2013. *US-China Security Perceptions Survey*. Washington, DC.

Carpini, Michael X. Delli, and Scott Keeter. 1996. *What Americans Know About Politics and Why It Matters*. New Haven: Yale University Press.

Carter, Jimmy. 1977. "Tehran, Iran Toasts of the President and the Shah at a State Dinner." www.presidency.ucsb.edu/ws/?pid=7080 (Accessed November 26, 2014).

Carvajal, Doreen. 2010. "Hunting for Liberia's Missing Millions." *New York Times*, May 30.

Caryl, Christian. 2013. *Strange Rebels: 1979 and the Birth of the 21st Century*. New York: Basic.

Casas, Juan P, et al. 2014. "Association Between Alcohol and Cardiovascular Disease: Mendelian Randomization Analysis Based on Individual Participant Data." *British Medical Journal* 349:g4164.

Cassese, Antonio. 1995. *Self-Determination of Peoples: A Legal Reappraisal*. Cambridge: Cambridge University Press.

Cassese, Antonio. 2001. *International Law*. 2nd ed. Oxford: Oxford University Press.

Center for Global Development. 2007. "Q&A with Patrick Alley, Co-Founder of Global Witness." www.cgdev.org/article/qa-patrick-alley-co-founder-global-witness-winner-2007-commitment-development-ideas-action (Accessed February 14, 2015).

Center for Systemic Peace. 2014. "The Polity Project." www.systemicpeace.org/polityproject.html (Accessed January 31, 2015).

Chabal, Patrick, and Jean-Pascal Daloz. 1999. *Africa Works*. Oxford: James Currey.

Chandy, Laurence, and Geoffrey Gertz. 2011. *Poverty in Numbers: The Changing State of Global Poverty from 2005–15*. Washington, DC: Brookings.

Chayes, Sarah. 2015. *Thieves of State: Why Corruption Threatens Global Security*. New York: Norton.

Cheung, Helier. 2012. "The Dictator: Why Do Autocrats Do Strange Things?" www.bbc.co.uk/news/magazine-17990615 (Accessed January 21, 2015).

China Daily. 2010. "China Opposes to US Resolution on Nobel Peace." December 9.

China Daily. 2011. "China: US Meddling Not Welcomed." April 9.

Chinese Embassy. 2010. "U.S. Senate Urged to Stop Interfering in China's Internal Affairs." www.china-embassy.org/eng/zt/ppflg/t36574.htm (Accessed April 25, 2015).

Chomsky, Noam. 1999. *Profit over People: Neoliberalism and Global Order*. New York: Seven Stories.

Christiano, Thomas. 2011. "An Instrumental Argument for a Human Right to Democracy." *Philosophy & Public Affairs* 39(2):142–76.

Churchill, Winston. 2015. *While England Slept: Political Writings 1936–1939*. London: Bloomsbury Academic.

CIA. 2014. *The World Factbook*. www.cia.gov/library/publications/the-world-factbook/ (Accessed November 18, 2014).

Clarke, Duncan. 2007. *Empires of Oil: Corporate Oil in Barbarian Worlds*. London: Profile.

Clarke, John J. 1999. "Taoist Politics: An Other Way?" In *Border Crossings: Toward a Comparative Political Theory*, ed. Fred Dallmayr. Lanham, MD: Lexington, 253–65.

CNN. 2003a. "Bush Declares War." edition.cnn.com/2003/US/03/19/sprj.irq.int.bush .transcript/ (Accessed February 1, 2015).

CNN. 2003b. "Bush: 'Leave Iraq within 48 Hours.'" edition.cnn.com/2003/WORLD/meast/03/17/sprj.irq.bush.transcript/ (Acessed February 1, 2015).

CNN. 2011. "Libyan Rebel Group Sells First Oil to US." edition.cnn.com/2011/US/06/08/libya.rebels.oil/ (Accessed March 15, 2015).

Coghlan, Benjamin, et al. 2007. *Mortality in the Democratic Republic of Congo: An Ongoing Crisis*. New York: International Rescue Committee.

Cohen, Joshua. 2010. *The Arc of the Moral Universe and Other Essays*. Cambridge: Harvard University Press.

Colebatch, Tim. 2012. "Our Economic Irrationalism." *Sydney Morning Herald*, March 13.

Colgan, Jeff D. 2013. *Petro-Aggression: When Oil Causes War*. New York: Cambridge University Press.

Coll, Steve. 2012. *Private Empire: ExxonMobil and American Power*. New York: Penguin.

Collier, Paul. 2006. "Is Aid Oil? An Analysis of Whether Africa Can Absorb More Aid." *World Development* 34(9):1482–97.

Collier, Paul. 2007. *The Bottom Billion: Why the Poorest Countries Are Failing and What Can be Done About It*. New York: Oxford University Press.

Collier, Paul. 2010a. "Why Bad Guys Matter." *Foreign Policy*, June 15.

Collier, Paul 2010b. *The Plundered Planet*. New York: Oxford University Press.

Collier, Paul, and Anke Hoeffler. 2004. "Greed and Grievance in Civil War." *Oxford Economic Papers* 56:563–95.

Collier, Paul, Anke Hoeffler, and Dominic Rohner. 2009. "Beyond Greed and Grievance: Feasibility and Civil War." *Oxford Economic Papers* 61(1):1–27.

Collinson, Stephen. 2015. "Washington Sighs Relief at Saudi Succession." *Washington Post*, January 24.

Conrad, Joseph. 2010. *Last Essays*. New York: Cambridge University Press.

Cooper, Helene. 2012. "On Day of Reckoning, Recalling Horror that Swallowed Liberia." *New York Times*, April 26.

Copnall, James. 2014. "South Sudan Peace Talks Must Include All Parts of Society." *Guardian*, January 27.

Corcoran, Patrick. 2012. "Oil Theft Is Big Business for Mexican Gangs." *InSightCrime*, March 20.

Corrales, Javier, and Michael Penfold. 2011. *Dragon in the Tropics: Hugo Chávez and the Political Economy of Revolution in Venezuela*. Washington, DC: Brookings.

Cowper, William. 1843. *Complete Poetical Works*. New York: D. Appleton.

Cranston, Maurice. 1984. "Are There Any Human Rights?" *Daedalus* 112(4):1–15.

Crawford, James. 2001. "The Right to Self-Determination in International Law: Its Development and Future." In *Peoples' Rights*, ed. Philip Alston. Oxford: Oxford University Press, 7–67.

Crawford, James. 2013. *Brownlie's Principles of Public International Law*. 8th ed. Oxford: Oxford University Press.

Crawford, James, and Susan Marks. 1998. "The Global Democracy Deficit: An Essay in International Law and its Limits." In *Re-Imagining Political Community: Studies in Cosmopolitan Democracy*, eds. Danielle Archibugi, David Held, and Martin Köhler. Stanford, CA: Stanford University Press, 72–90.

Crawford, Neta C. 2014. "US Costs of Wars Through 2014: $4.4 Trillion and Counting." unpublished manuscript, Costs of War Project.

Crooks, Ed. 2013. "Cost of Australia's Gorgon LNG Project Rises to $54bn." *Financial Times*, December 12.

Crooks, Ed, and Anjli Raval. 2014. "US Poised to Become World's Leading Liquid Petroleum Producer." *Financial Times*, September 29.

Dabbs Sciubba, Jennifer. 2011. *The Future Faces of War: Population and National Security*. Santa Barbara: Praeger.

Daily Mail. 2010. " 'They Gave Me Some Dirty Looking Pebbles': Naomi Campbell Tells War Crimes Tribunal She Received Blood Diamonds from African Dictator." August 5.

Dalton, Russell, Doh Shin, and Willy Jou. 2008. "How People Understand Democracy." In *How People View Democracy*, eds. Larry Diamond and Mark Plattner. Baltimore: Johns Hopkins, 1–15.

Daou, Marc. 2012. "How Saudi Petrodollars Fuel Rise of Salafism." www.france24.com/en/20120929-how-saudi-arabia-petrodollars-finance-salafist-winter-islamism-wahhabism-egypt/ (Accessed January 27, 2015).

Daragahi, Borzou. 2012. "Morocco Secures $250m Loan to Upgrade Phosphate Industry." *Financial Times*, May 15.

Darity, William. 1990. "British Industry and the West Indies Plantations." *Social Science History* 14(1):117–49.

Davidson, Christopher M. 2012. *After the Sheikhs: The Coming Collapse of the Gulf Monarchies*. London: C. Hurst.

Davies, Norman. 1996. *Europe: A History*. Oxford: Oxford University Press.

de la Baume, Maia. 2012. "A French Shift on Africa Strips a Dictator's Son of His Treasures." *New York Times*, August 23.

de Soysa, Indra, and Theodora-Ismene Gizelis. 2013. "The Natural Resource Curse and the Spread of HIV/AIDS, 1990–2008." *Social Science & Medicine* 77:90–96.

de Tocqueville, Alexis 2001. *Writings on Empire and Slavery*. Trans. and Ed. Jennifer Pitts. Baltimore: Johns Hopkins.

Deaton, Angus. 2013. *The Great Escape: Health, Wealth, and the Origins of Inequality*. Princeton: Princeton University Press.

DefenceWeb. 2014. "IMB Warns of West Africa Piracy Threat." www.defenceweb.co.za/index.php?option=com_content&view=article&id=33914:imb-warns-of-west-africa-piracy-threat&catid=108:maritime-security (Accessed January 25, 2015).

Degomme, Olivier, and Debarati Guha-Sapir. 2010. "Patterns of Mortality Rates in Darfur Conflict." *Lancet* 375(9711):294–300.

DFID, Foreign & Commonwealth Office, and Ministry of Defence. 2011. *Building Stability Overseas Strategy*. London.

Diamandis, Peter H. and Steven Kotler. 2014. *Abundance: The Future Is Better Than You Think*. Updated ed. New York: Simon & Schuster.

Diamond, Larry. 2008. *The Spirit of Democracy: The Struggle to Build Free Societies Throughout the World*. New York: Holt Paperbacks.

Diamond, Larry. 2010. "Why Are There No Arab Democracies?" *Journal of Democracy* 21(1):93–112.

Diamond, Larry, and Abbas Milani. 2006. *Democracy and the Middle East: Prospects and Problems.*

Diamond, Larry, and Jack Mosbacher. 2013. "Petroleum to the People." *Foreign Affairs*, September/October.

Dolan, Kerry A. and Rafael Marques de Morais. 2013. "Daddy's Girl: How an African 'Princess' Banked $3 Billion In a Country Living on $2 a Day." *Forbes*. August 14.

Douglass, Frederick. 1986. *The Frederick Douglass Papers*. Series 1. Vol. 3. New Haven: Yale University Press.

Dowden, Richard. 2008. *Africa: Altered States, Ordinary Miracles*. London: Portobello.

Doyle, Michael W., and Nicholas Sambanis. 2000. "International Peacebuilding: A Theoretical and Quantitative Analysis." *American Political Science Review* 94(4):779–801.

Dugger, Celia W. 2009. "Battle to Halt Graft Scourge in Africa Ebbs." *New York Times*, June 9.

Dukes, Jeffrey S. 2003. "Burning Buried Sunshine: Human Consumption of Ancient Solar Energy." *Climatic Change* 61(1–2):31–44.

Dunning, Thad. 2005. "Resource Dependence, Economic Performance, and Political Stability." *Journal of Conflict Resolution* 49(4):451–82.

Dunning, Thad. 2008. *Crude Democracy: Natural Resource Wealth and Political Regimes*. Cambridge: Cambridge University Press.

Dworkin, Ronald. 1975. "The Original Position." In *Reading Rawls*, ed. Norman Daniels. New York: Basic, 16–52.

E&E TV. 2011. "Oil & Gas: Spill Panel Releases Offshore Drilling Recommendations." www.eenews.net/tv/videos/1264/transcript (Accessed February 7, 2015).

Ebrahim-Zadeh, Christine. 2003. "Dutch Disease: Too Much Wealth Managed Unwisely." *Finance & Development* 40(1):50–51.

Economist. 2009. "All Change, No Change." July 23.

Economist. 2011a. "China International Fund: The Queensway Syndicate and the Africa Trade." August 13.

Economist. 2011b. "Does the Government in Beijing Control the China International Fund?" August 12.

Economist. 2011c. "GDP Growth: Hares and Tortoises." June 13.

Economist. 2011d. "Nigeria's Subsidies: End Them at Once!" December 31.

Economist. 2011e. "South Sudan: Now for the Hard Part." February 3.

Economist. 2012a. "Corruption in Nigeria: Hard Graft." April 29.

Economist. 2012b. "Iron Ore: The Lore of Ore." October 13.

Economist. 2012c. "The Niger Delta: Still An Oily Dangerous Mess." August 11.

Economist. 2012d. "Oil Prices: Keeping it to Themselves." March 31.

Economist. 2014a. "The Saudi Succession: Next After Next." April 5.

Economist. 2014b. "Slavery in Islam: To Have and to Hold." October 18.

Economist. 2014c. "Why The Oil Price Is Falling." December 8.

Economist. 2015. "Saudi Arabia's Gerontocracy: Ail The King." January 10.

Economist Intelligence Unit. 2013. *Democracy Index*. London.

Economy, Elizabeth C., and Michael Levi. 2014. *By All Means Necessary: How China's Resource Quest Is Changing the World*. New York: Oxford University Press.

Eisenhower, Dwight D. 1959. *Dwight D. Eisenhower: Public Papers of the Presidents of the United States 1955*. Washington, DC: US National Archives.

Elis, Niv. 2009. "The Pension Fund Attack on Iran." *Forbes*, October 16.

Elkind, David. 1968. "Giant in the Nursery—Jean Piaget." *New York Times Magazine*, 25–80.

Emerson, Ralph Waldo. 2003. *Collected Works*. Cambridge: Harvard University Press.

Energy & Commerce Committee. 2013 "On the Path to North American Energy Independence: U.S. Oil Output Highest in Two Decades." energycommerce.house .gov/blog/path-north-american-energy-independence-us-oil-output-highest-two-decades (Accessed February 7, 2015).

Engels, Frederick. 1892. *Socialism: Utopian and Scientific*. Trans. Edward Aveling. Chicago: Charles H. Kerr.

England, Andrew. 2010. "Row Over Land Deals Unsettles Bahrain Election." *Financial Times*, October 22.

Enough Project. 2009. *A Comprehensive Approach to Congo's Conflict Minerals*. Washington, DC.

Enough Project. 2014. *Conflict Minerals: A Broader Push for Reform Is Essential*. Washington, DC.

Epstein, Lita, C. D. Jaco, and Julianne C. Iwersen-Niemann. 2003. *The Complete Idiot's Guide to the Politics of Oil*. New York: Penguin.

Esposito, John. 2010. *The Future of Islam*. New York: Oxford University Press.

European Aluminium Association. 2014. "Primary Aluminium Consumption 2011–2013." www.alueurope.eu/consumption-primary-aluminium-consumption-in-world-regions/ (Accessed January 16, 2015).

European Commission. 2005. *Social Values, Science and Technology: Special Eurobarometer 225*. Brussels.

European Parliament. 2013. *The Involvement of Salafism/Wahhabism in the Support and Supply of Arms to Rebel Groups around the World*. Brussels.

Eurostat. 2014. "Main Origin of Primary Energy Imports, EU-28, 2002–12." ec.europa .eu/eurostat/statistics-explained/index.php/File:Main_origin_of_primary_energy_imports,_EU-28,_2002%E2%80%9312_(%25_of_extra_EU-28_imports)_YB14.png (Accessed February 12, 2015).

Evans, Becky. 2013. "Celebrity Saudi Preacher 'Raped' and Tortured His Five-Year-Old Daughter to Death." *The Daily Mail*, February 4.

Evans, Gareth. 2008. *The Responsibility to Protect: Ending Mass Atrocity Crimes Once and for All*. Washington, DC: Brookings.

ExxonMobil. 2010. "2009 Largest Oil and Gas Companies (Percent of Worldwide Reserves)." www.exxonmobilperspectives.com/wp-content/uploads/2011/04/Largest-oil-companies-by-reserves.png (Accessed December 10, 2014).

Fahim, Kareem. 2012. "As Hopes for Reform Fade in Bahrain, Protesters Turn Anger on United States." *New York Times*, June 23.

Farah, Douglas. 2004. *Blood from Stones: The Secret Financial Network of Terror*. New York: Broadway.

Farah, Douglas. 2011. "Harvard for Tyrants." *Foreign Policy*, March 4.

Faul, Michelle. 2009a. "Eq. Guinea Leader Expected to Win Near 100 Percent." *Seattle Times*, November 27.

Faul, Michelle. 2009b. "Eq. Guinea Vote to Reinstall Leader Denying Graft." *San Diego Union-Tribune*, November 29.

Faul, Michelle. 2011. "African Dictator's Son Orders Luxury Superyacht." *San Diego Union-Tribune*, February 27.

Fearon, James D., and David D. Laitin. 2003. "Ethnicity, Insurgency, and Civil War." *American Political Science Review* 97(1):75–90.

Ferguson, Niall. 2002. *Empire: The Rise and Demise of the British World Order and the Lessons for Global Power*. London: Penguin.

Fiallo, Fabio Rafael. 2012. "The Dismal Economics of Resource Nationalism." *Commentator*, May 11.

Financial Services Authority. 2011. *Banks' Management of High Money-Laundering Risk Situations*. London.

Finnemore, Martha, and Kathryn Sikkink. 1998. "International Norm Dynamics and Political Change." *International Organization* 52(4):887–917.

Fish, M. Steven. 2011. *Are Muslims Distinctive? A Look at the Evidence*. New York: Oxford University Press.

Fishman, Brian, and Joseph Felter. 2007. *Al-Qaeda's Foreign Fighters in Iraq*. West Point, NY: Combating Terrorism Center.

Flint, John E. 1974. *Cecil Rhodes*. Boston: Little Brown.

Foddy, Bennett, and Julian Savulescu. 2010. "A Liberal Account of Addiction." *Philosophy, Psychiatry, & Psychology* 17(1):1–22.

Forbes. 2014a. "The Richest People in America 2014." www.forbes.com/forbes-400/ (Accessed December 10, 2014).

Forbes. 2014b. "The World's Biggest Public Companies." www.forbes.com/global2000/list/ (Accessed November 18, 2014).

Forbes. 2015. "The World's Billionaires: Today's Winners and Losers." www.forbes.com/pictures/efik45eklkh/carlos-slim-helu-3/ (Accessed January 23, 2015).

Fortna, Virginia Page. 2008. *Does Peacekeeping Work? Shaping Belligerents' Choices After Civil War*. Princeton: Princeton University Press.

Foucault, Michel. 1984. *The Foucault Reader*. Ed. Paul Rabinow. New York: Pantheon.

Foucault, Michel. 1995. *Discipline and Punish: The Birth of the Prison*. 2nd ed. Trans. Alan Sheridan. New York: Vintage.

Fox News. 2013. "4,500 Chinese Leave Ghana After Illegal Mining Crackdown." www.foxnews.com/world/2013/07/12/4500-chinese-leave-ghana-after-illegal-mining-crackdown/ (Accessed April 25, 2015).

Fox, William. 1792. *An Address to the People of Great-Britain, On the Propriety of Abstaining From West-India Sugar and Rum*. 9th ed. Boston: Samuel Hall.

Frankel, Jeffrey A. 2012. "The Natural Resource Curse: A Survey of Diagnoses and Some Prescriptions." www.hks.harvard.edu/centers/cid/publications/faculty-working-papers/cid-working-paper-no.-233 (Accessed April 25, 2015).

Franklin, Benjamin. 1965. *The Political Thought of Benjamin Franklin*. New York: Bobbs-Merrill.

Freedman, Lawrence. 2014. "Steven Pinker and the Long Peace: Alliance, Deterrence and Decline." *Cold War History* 14(4):657–72.

Freedom House. 2011. *Freedom in the World*. Washington, DC.

Freedom House. 2012. *Freedom in the World*. Washington, DC.

Freedom House. 2013. *Freedom in the World*. Washington, DC.

Freedom House. 2014a. *Freedom in the World*. Washington, DC.

Freedom House. 2014b. *Freedom of the Press*. Washington, DC.

French, David. 2011. *The British Way in Counter-Insurgency, 1945–1967*. Oxford: Oxford University Press.

Friedman, Thomas L. 2006. "The First Law of Petropolitics." *Foreign Policy*, October 16.

Friedman, Thomas L. 2008. *Hot, Flat and Crowded: Why We Need a Green Revolution—and How It Can Renew America*. New York: Allen Lane.

Frynas, Jedrzej George. 2009. *Beyond Corporate Social Responsibility: Oil Multinationals and Social Challenges*. Cambridge: Cambridge University Press.

Fukuyama, Francis. 1995. *Trust: The Social Virtues and the Creation of Prosperity*. New York: Simon & Schuster.

Fukuyama, Francis. 2002. "Social Capital and Development: The Coming Agenda." *SAIS Review* 22(1):23–37.

Fukuyama, Francis. 2011. *The Origins of Political Order: From Prehuman Times to the French Revolution*. New York: Farrar, Straus and Giroux.

Gaidar, Yegor. 2007. "The Soviet Collapse." www.aei.org/feature/the-soviet-collapse/ (Accessed November 26, 2014).

Gamble, Paul. 2011. *Saudi Arabia's 2012 Budget*. Riyadh: Jadwa Investment.

Gandhi, Jennifer, and Ellen Lust-Okar. 2009. "Elections Under Authoritarianism." *Annual Review of Political Science* 12:403–22.

Garton, Phil, and David Gruen. 2012. "The Role of Sovereign Wealth Funds in Managing Resource Booms: A Comparison of Australia and Norway." www.treasury.gov.au/PublicationsAndMedia/Speeches/2012/The-role-of-sovereign-wealth-funds-in-managing-resource-booms (Accessed April 25, 2015).

Gat, Azar. 2013. "Is War Declining and Why?" *Journal of Peace Research* 50(2):149–57.

Geology. 2014. "Magnolia Tension Leg Oil Platform—Is It the World's Tallest Structure?" geology.com/stories/13/magnolia-oil-platform/ (Accessed December 10 2014).

Gerecht, Reuel Marc, and Mark Dubowitz. 2011. "The Case for an Iranian-Oil-Free Zone." *Wall Street Journal*, May 31.

Gerges, Fawas A. 2009. *The Far Enemy: Why Jihad Went Global*. 2nd ed. Cambridge: Cambridge University Press.

Gettleman, Jeffrey. 2007. "Rape Epidemic Raises Trauma of Congo War." *New York Times*, October 7.

Gettleman, Jeffrey. 2009. "Clinton Praises Angola, but Urges More Reform." *New York Times*, August 9.

Gettleman, Jeffrey. 2011. "Libyan Oil Buys Allies for Qaddafi." *New York Times*, March 15.

Gettleman, Jeffrey. 2012. "The World's Worst War." *New York Times*, December 15.

Geuss, Megan. 2014. "Mastercard-Backed Biometric ID System Launched in Nigeria." *Ars Technica*, September 3.

Ghafour, P. K. Abdul. 2007. "Bandar Says BAE System Funds Went to Govt." *Arab News*, June 13.

Gibbs, Nancy. 1999. "'I've Made Mistakes': Bush Says He's Been Drug-Free for Seven—No, 25 Years. You Got a Problem with That?" edition.cnn.com/ALLPOLITICS/time/1999/08/23/bush.html (Accessed January 21, 2015).

Gilbert, G. M. 1947. *Nuremberg Diary*. New York: Farrar, Straus and Giroux.

Gilbert, Margaret. 2006. *A Theory of Political Obligation*. Oxford: Oxford University Press.

Gillies, Alexandra, Marc Gueniat, and Lorenz Kummer. 2014. *Big Spenders: Swiss Trading Companies, African Oil and the Risks of Opacity*. Washington, DC: Natural Resource Governance Institute.

Giugale, Marcelo. 2011. "Give Africans a Stake in Their Own Wealth." www.huffingtonpost.com/marcelo-giugale/give-africans-a-stake-in-_b_882266.html (Accessed April 25, 2015).

Gladstone, Rick. 2014. "Saudi Arabia: Executions Draw Rebukes." *New York Times*, August 21.

Glaeser, Edward L, et al. 2004. "Do Institutions Cause Growth?" *Journal of Economic Growth* 9(3):271–303.

Glendon, Mary Ann. 2002. *A World Made New: Eleanor Roosevelt and the Universal Declaration of Human Rights*. New York: Random House.

Global Witness. 2001. *The Role of Liberia's Logging Industry*. London.

Global Witness. 2003. *The Usual Suspects: Liberia's Weapons and Mercenaries in Cote d'Ivoire and Sierra Leone*. London.

Global Witness. 2006. *The Sinews of War*. London.

Global Witness. 2007a. *Hot Chocolate: How Cocoa Fueled the Conflict in Côte d'Ivoire*. London.

Global Witness. 2007b. *Taylor-Made: The Pivotal Role of Liberia's Forests and Flag of Convenience in Regional Conflict*. London.

Global Witness. 2010. *Simply Criminal: Targeting Rogue Business in Violent Conflict*. London.

Global Witness. 2011. "U.S. Takes Welcome Action to Seize Dictator's Son's Haul." www.globalwitness.org/archive/us-takes-welcome-action-seize-dictators-sons-haul/ (Accessed May 1, 2015).

Global Witness. 2015. "The Current Situation in Eastern Congo." www.globalwitness.org/campaigns/democratic-republic-congo/current-situation-eastern-congo (Accessed May 4, 2015).

Glovin, David. 2010. "Cold War Patriot Defense Helps Giffen Beat Bribe Case." *Bloomberg Business*, December 16.

Goethe, Johann Wolfgang. 1997. *Faust: Der Tragödie erster Teil*. Ed. Sybille Demmer. Munich: Deutscher Taschenbuch.

Goethe, Johann Wolfgang. 2014. *Wilhelm Meisters Wanderjahre oder die Entsagenden*. Berlin: Holzinger.

Goldsmith, Jack L., and Eric A. Posner. 2005. *The Limits of International Law*. New York: Oxford University Press.

Goldstein, Joshua. 2011. *Winning the War on War: The Decline of Armed Conflict Worldwide*. New York: Dutton.

Gooch, Charmian. 2011. "Why We Are Leaving the Kimberley Process." www.globalwitness.org/library/why-we-are-leaving-kimberley-process-message-global-witness-founding-director-charmian-gooch (Accessed February 14, 2015).

Goode, Erich. 2014. *Drugs in American Society*. 8th ed. New York: McGraw-Hill.

Gordon, Joy. 2010. *Invisible War: The United States and the Iraq Sanctions*. Cambridge: Harvard University Press.

Government of Canada. 2014. "Gross Domestic Product at Basic Prices, by Industry." www.statcan.gc.ca/tables-tableaux/sum-som/l01/cst01/econ41-eng.htm (Accessed January 21, 2015).

Gramsci, Antonio. 2014. *Lettere dal Carcere*. Milan: LediPublishing.

Grant, Thomas D. 1999. *The Recognition of States: Law and Practice in Debate and Evolution*. Westport, CT: Praeger.

Green Party. 2014. "Economy." policy.greenparty.org.uk/ec.html (Accessed February 14, 2015).

Grieco, Elizabeth, et al. 2012. *The Foreign-Born Population in the United States: 2010*. Washington, DC: US Census Bureau.

Griswold, Eliza. 2010. *The Tenth Parallel*. New York: Farrar, Straus and Giroux.

Grønskov, Karen, Jakob Ek, and Karen Brondum-Nielsen. 2007. "Oculocutaneous Albinism." *Orphanet Journal of Rare Diseases* 2:43–51.

Grose, Clyde L. 1929. "Louis XIV's Financial Relations with Charles II and the English Parliament." *The Journal of Modern History* 1(2):177–204.

Gross, Daniel. 2013. "U.S. Closing Trade Deficit with Better Oil Numbers." www.thedailybeast.com/articles/2013/06/05/us-closing-trade-deficit-with-better-oil-numbers.html (Accessed April 25, 2015).

Grotius, Hugo. 1901. *The Rights of War and Peace*. Trans. A. C. Campbell. New York: M. Walter Dunne.

Grytten, Ola Honningdal. 2005. "The Economic History of Norway." eh.net/?s=grytten (Accessed November 19. 2014).

Guardian. 2009. "China Condemns US Military Report As 'Interference.'" March 26.

Guizot, François M. 1838. *General History of Civilization in Europe*. 2nd ed. Oxford: DA Talboys.

Gumbel, Andrew. 2007. "Long March to Normal Life for a Former Child Soldier." *New Zealand Herald*, January 24.

Gylfason, Thorvaldur. 2001. "Natural Resources, Education, and Economic Development." *European Economic Review* 45:847–59.

Haber, Stephen, and Victor Menaldo. 2011. "Do Natural Resources Fuel Authoritarianism? A Reappraisal of the Resource Curse." *American Political Science Review* 105(1):1–26.

Haber, Stephen, and Victor Menaldo. 2012. "Natural Resources and Democracy in Latin America: Neither Curse nor Blessing." In *The Oxford Handbook of Latin American Political Economy*, eds. Javier Santiso and Jeff Dayton-Johnson. Oxford: Oxford University Press, 367–80.

Hague, William. 2005. *William Pitt the Younger*. New York: Harper Collins.

Hale, Thomas, David Held, and Kevin Young. 2013. *Gridlock: Why Global Cooperation Is Failing When We Need It Most*. Cambridge: Polity.

Hall, Charles, et al. 2003. "Hydrocarbons and the Evolution of Human Culture." *Nature* 426(6964):318–22.

Hall, John. 2013. "Saudi Royal Family Intervenes over Preacher Released Despite Raping and Killing Daughter." *The Independent*, February 12.

Hamilton, Alexander, James Madison, and John Jay. 1999. *The Federalist Papers*. New York: Signet.

Hamilton, James D. 2011. "Historical Oil Shocks." Working Paper 16790. Washington, DC: National Bureau of Economic Research.

Hamilton, Kirk, and Michael Clemens. 1999. "Genuine Savings Rates in Developing Countries." *World Bank Economic Review* 13(2):333–56.

Hanlon, Joseph, and Armando Barrientos. 2010. *Just Give Money to the Poor: The Development Revolution from the Global South*. Sterling, VA: Kumarian.

Hanson, David J. 2015a. "Benefits of Drinking Outweigh Harm from Abuse." www2.potsdam.edu/alcohol/HealthIssues/1098893243.html#.VL7DMEeDkyo (Accessed January 21, 2015).

Hanson, David J. 2015b. "Health." www2.potsdam.edu/alcohol/AlcoholAndHealth.html#.VL7Az0eDkyo (Accessed November 18, 2014).

Hardin, Garrett. 1968. "The Tragedy of the Commons." *Science* 162(3859):1243–48.

Harding, Henry. 1992. *A Fragile Relationship: The United States and China Since 1972*. Washington, DC: Brookings.

Hardoon, Deborah, and Finn Heinrich. 2011. *Bribe Payers Index 2011*. Berlin: Transparency International.

Hardt, Michael, and Antonio Negri. 2000. *Empire*. Cambridge: Harvard University Press.

Havel, Václav. 2010. "The Power of the Powerless." In *The Power of the Powerless: Citizens against the State in Central-Eastern Europe*, ed. John Keane. Abingdon, UK: Routledge, 10–59.

Hayek, F.A. 1994. *Hayek on Hayek: An Autobiographical Dialogue*. Eds. Stephen Kresge and Leif Wenar. Chicago: University of Chicago Press.

Hayek, F. A. 2011. *The Constitution of Liberty*. Definitive ed. Ed. Ronald Hamowy. Chicago: University of Chicago.

Hayes, Jarrod. 2012. "The Democratic Peace and the New Evolution of an Old Idea." *European Journal of International Relations* 18:767–91.

Haykel, Bernard. 2008. "Islam in Saudi Arabia's Politics." www.carnegiecouncil.org/studio/multimedia/20080221/index.html (Accessed April 25, 2015).

Hegel, Georg Wilhelm Friedrich. 1861. *Lectures on the Philosophy of History*. Trans. J. Sibree. London: Henry G. Bohn.

Hegel, Georg Wilhelm Friedrich. 1991. *Elements of the Philosophy of Right*. Trans. H. B. Nisbet. Ed. Allen W. Wood. Cambridge: Cambridge University Press.

Hegghammer, Thomas. 2010. *Jihad in Saudi Arabia: Violence and Pan-Islamism since 1979*, Cambridge: Cambridge University Press.

Hegghammer, Thomas. 2011. "The Rise of Muslim Foreign Fighters: Islam and the Globalization of Jihad." *International Security* 35(3):53–94.

Hegre, Håvard, and Nicholas Sambanis. 2006. "Sensitivity Analysis of Empirical Results on Civil War Onset." *Journal of Conflict Resolution* 50(4):508–35.

Heidegger, Martin. 1988. *The Basic Problems of Phenomenology*. Trans. Albert Hofstadter. Bloomington: Indiana University Press.

Held, David. 2003. "The Changing Structure of International Law: Sovereignty Transformed?" In *The Global Transformations Reader*, ed. David Held. Cambridge: Polity, 162–76.

Henning, Peter J. 2013. "Dealing with the Foreign Corrupt Practices Act." *New York Times*, March 4.

Hensel, Paul R., Michael E. Allison, and Ahmed Khanani. 2009. "Territorial Integrity Treaties and Armed Conflict over Territory." *Conflict Management and Peace Science* 26(2):120–43.

Herb, Michael. 1999. *All in the Family*. Albany: State University of New York Press.

Herbst, Jeffrey. 2000. *States and Power in Africa: Comparative Lessons in Authority and Control*. Princeton: Princeton University Press.

Herbst, Jeffrey, and Greg Mills. 2013. "The Invisible State." *Foreign Policy*, June 24.

Herbst, Moira. 2008. "Oil for China, Guns for Darfur." *Bloomberg Businessweek*, March 14.

Heritage Foundation. 2014. *Index of Economic Freedom*. www.heritage.org/index/ (Accessed November 20, 2014).

Herring, Jonathan. 2012. *Medical Law and Ethics*. 4th ed. Oxford: Oxford University Press.

Hertog, Steffen. 2011. *Princes, Brokers, and Bureaucrats: Oil and the State in Saudi Arabia*. Ithaca: Cornell University Press.

Heuty, Antoine, and Ruth Carlitz. 2009. "Resource Dependence and Budget Transparency." www.resourcegovernance.org/news/resource-dependence-and-budget-transparency (Accessed May 11, 2015).

Heyrick, Elizabeth. 1824. *Immediate, Not Gradual Abolition*. London: Hatchard and Son.

Hicken, Allen. 2011. "Clientelism." *Annual Review of Political Science* 14:289–310.

Higgins, Rosalyn. 1994. *Problem and Process: International Law and How We Use It*. Oxford: Oxford University Press.

Hitler, Adolf. 1922–1945. *Collection of Speeches*. Trans. Aubrey Durkin. Google e-book.

Hobbes, Thomas. 1994. *The Correspondence of Thomas Hobbes*. Vol. 2. Ed. Noel Malcolm. New York: Oxford University Press.

Hobbes, Thomas. 1996. *Leviathan*. 2nd ed. Cambridge: Cambridge University Press.

Hochschild, Adam. 1998. *King Leopold's Ghost: A Story of Greed, Terror, and Heroism in Colonial Africa*. New York: Houghton Mifflin.

Hochschild, Adam. 2005. *Bury the Chains: Prophets and Rebels in the Fight to Free an Empire's Slaves*. New York: Houghton Mifflin.

Hofmeister, John. 2011. *Why We Hate the Oil Companies: Straight Talk from an Industry Insider*. New York: Palgrave Macmillan.

Holman, Frank E. 1949. "Human Rights on Pink Paper." *American Affairs* 11(1):18–24.

Holmes, Oliver Wendell. 1881. *The Common Law*. Boston: Little, Brown.

Holmes, Oliver Wendell. 1997. "The Path of the Law." *Harvard Law Review* 110(5):991–1009.

Holmes, Stephen. 2001. "What Russia Teaches Us Now." *American Prospect*, December 19.

The Holy Quran with English Translation. 2011. Trans. Maulawi Sher Ali. 2nd ed. Surrey: Islam International Publications.

Honig, Bonnie. 1993. *Political Theory and the Displacement of Politics*. Ithaca: Cornell University Press.

Hook, Sidney. 1939. "Democracy as a Way of Life." In *Tomorrow in the Making*, eds. John N. Andrews and Carl A. Marsden. New York: McGraw-Hill, 31–46.

Houston, S. J. 1995. *James I*. 2nd ed. Abingdon, UK: Routledge.

Howse, Robert. 2007. "The Concept of Odious Debt in International Law." Discussion Paper 185. Geneva: UNCTAD.

Hubbard, Ben. 2013. "Private Donors' Funds Add Wild Card to War in Syria." *New York Times*, November 12.

Hughes, Llewelyn. 2014. *Globalizing Oil*. New York: Cambridge University Press.

Human Rights Watch. 2003. *We'll Kill You if You Cry: Sexual Violence in the Sierra Leone Conflict*. New York.

Human Rights Watch. 2005. *"Rest in Pieces"—Police Torture and Deaths in Custody in Nigeria*. New York.

Human Rights Watch. 2009. "Equatorial Guinea: Account for Oil Wealth." www.hrw.org/news/2009/07/09/equatorial-guinea-account-oil-wealth (Accessed January 25, 2015).

Human Rights Watch. 2010. "US: Adopt Anti-Corruption Proposals." www.hrw.org/news/2010/02/04/us-adopt-corruption-proposals (Accessed April 25, 2015).

Human Rights Watch. 2012. "Angola: IMF Should Insist on Audit." www.hrw.org/news/2012/07/11/angola-imf-should-insist-audit (Accessed January 23, 2015).

Human Rights Watch. 2014. "Equatorial Guinea: Indictment of President's Son in France." www.hrw.org/news/2014/03/20/equatorial-guinea-indictment-president-s-son-france (Accessed November 26, 2014).

Human Security Report Project. 2011. *Human Security Report 2009/2010: The Causes of Peace and the Shrinking Costs of War*. New York: Oxford University Press.

Human Security Report Project. 2014. *Human Security Report 2013*. Vancouver.

Hume, David. 1975. *Enquiries Concerning Human Understanding and Concerning the Principles of Morals*. 3rd ed. Oxford: Oxford University Press.

Hume, Neil, and Leslie Hook. 2013. "Rio Says Mongolia Mine Remains on Track." *Financial Times*, January 31.

Humphreys, Macartan, Jeffrey D. Sachs, and Joseph E. Stiglitz, eds. 2007. *Escaping the Resource Curse*. New York: Columbia University Press.

Huntington, Samuel P. 1968. *Political Order in Changing Societies*. New Haven: Yale University Press.

Huntington, Samuel P. 1991. *The Third Wave: Democratization in the Late Twentieth Century*. Norman: University of Oklahoma.

Hyslop, Leah. 2010. "Qatar Population Booms As Economy Grows." *Telegraph*, July 19.

Ignatieff, Michael. 2002. "Human Rights, Sovereignty and Intervention." In *Human Rights, Human Wrongs: The Oxford Amnesty Lectures*, ed. Nicholas Owen. Oxford: Oxford University Press, 49–88.

Ignatieff, Michael. 2003. "The American Empire; The Burden." *New York Times*, January 5.

Ignatius, David. 2002. "True Crime: The Scent of French Scandal." *Legal Affairs*, May/June.

Illarionov, Andrei. 2008. "To Punish the Guilty." www.cato-unbound.org/2008/05/21/andrei-illarionov/punish-guilty (Accessed April 25, 2015).

IMF. 2013. "IMF Executive Board Concludes 2013 Article IV Consultation with Brunei Darussalam." www.imf.org/external/np/sec/pn/2013/pn1371.htm (Accessed January 28, 2015).

IMF. 2014a. *Middle East, North Africa, Pakistan and Afghanistan: Turning the Corner?* Washington, DC.

IMF. 2014b. *Qatar: 2014 Article IV Consultation—Staff Report, Country Report No. 14/10*. Washington, DC.

IMF. 2014c. *World Economic Outlook Database*. www.imf.org/external/pubs/ft/weo/2014/01/weodata/index.aspx (Accessed November 18, 2014).

Indian Express. 2010. "China Accuses US of 'Rude Interference' in Internal Affairs." June 6.

International Energy Agency. 2010. *World Energy Outlook*. Paris.

International Energy Agency. 2013. *World Energy Outlook*. Paris.

International Labour Organization. 2015. *Forced Labour, Human Trafficking and Slavery*. www.ilo.org/global/topics/forced-labour/lang--en/index.htm (Accessed May 1, 2015).

International Tropical Timber Organization. 2012. *Annual Review*. Yokohama.

Iob, Emilie. 2012. "Oil-Rich Cabinda Still Waits for Independence from Angola". www.voanews.com/content/cabinda-still-waits-for-independence/1515340.html (Accessed January 27, 2015).

IPCC. 2014. *Climate Change 2014: Synthesis Report*. Eds. Rajendra K. Pachauri and Leo Meyer. Geneva.

Isham, Jonathan, et al. 2005. "The Varieties of Resource Experience: Natural Resource Export Structures and the Political Economy of Economic Growth." *World Bank Economic Review* 19(2):141–74.

Jackson, Robert. 2007. *Sovereignty*. Cambridge: Polity.

Jacobson, Harold Karan. 1964. "ONUC's Civilian Operations: State-Preserving and State-Building." *World Politics* 17(1):75–107.

Jamal, Amaney, et al. 2014. *Anti-Americanism and Anti-Interventionism in Arabic Twitter Discourses*. Unpublished manuscript.

James I. 1597. *Daemonologie*: Edinburgh.

James I. 1918. *Political Works*. Cambridge: Harvard University Press.

Jamestown Foundation. 2008. *Oil in Chechnya: A Brief History*. www.jamestown.org/single/?tx_ttnews%5Btt_news%5D=4870#.VMOI3EeDkyo (Accessed January 24, 2015).

Jamieson, Dale. 2014. *Reason in a Dark Time: Why the Struggle Against Climate Change Failed—and What It Means for Our Future*. New York: Oxford University Press.

Jefferson, Thomas. 1903–07. *Writings*. Washington, DC: Jefferson Memorial Association.

Jefferson, Thomas. 1999. *Political Writings*. Cambridge: Cambridge University Press.

Jenner, Mark S. R. 1997. "The Great Dog Massacre." In *Fear in Early Modern Society*, eds. William G. Naphy and Penny Roberts. Manchester: Manchester University Press, 44–61.

Johansson, Thomas B., et al. 2012. *Global Energy Assessment: Toward a Sustainable Future*. Cambridge: Cambridge University Press.

John, Mark, and Kwasi Kpodo. 2010. "Ghana Bids to Break Africa's Oil Curse." www.reuters.com/article/2010/05/26/us-frontiers-ghana-idUSTRE64P1HU20100526 (Accessed April 25, 2015).

Johnson, R. W. 2006. "Playboy Waits for His African Throne." *Sunday Times*, September 3.

Johnston, David. 2004. "Saddam Hussein Sowed Confusion about Iraq's Arsenal as a Tactic of War." *New York Times*, October 7.

Johnston, Patrick. 2013. "Timber Booms, State Busts: The Political Economy of Liberian Timber." In *Conflict and Security in Africa*, ed. Rita Abrahamsen. New York: Boydell & Brewer, 25–40.

Jones Luong, Pauline, and Erika Weinthal. 2010. *Oil Is Not a Curse: Ownership Structure and Institutions in Soviet Successor States*. New York: Cambridge University Press.

Joselow, Gabe. 2012. "Can New Oil States in Africa Avoid the 'Resource Curse'? www.voanews.com/content/can-new-oil-states-in-africa-avoid-resource-curse/1211081.html (Accessed February 6, 2015).

JUCCCE. 2015. "China Dream." juccce.org/chinadream (Accessed February 12, 2015).

Justinian. 1812. *The Institutes*. Trans. Thomas Cooper. Philadelphia: P. Byrne.

Kagan, Robert. 2006. "Cowboy Nation." *New Republic*, October 23.

Kaldor, Mary. 2007. "Oil and Conflict: The Case of Nagorno Karabakh." In *Oil Wars*, eds. Mary Kaldor, Terry Lynn Karl, and Yahia Said. London: Pluto, 157–82.

Kant, Immanuel. 1923–55. *Kants Gesammelte Schriften*. Berlin: W. de Gruyter.

Kant, Immanuel. 1991. "Perpetual Peace." In *Political Writings*, trans. H. B. Nisbet, ed. H. S. Reiss,. Cambridge: Cambridge University Press, 93–130.

Kant, Immanuel. 1998. *Groundwork of the Metaphysics of Morals*. Trans. and Eds. Mary Gregor and Jens Timmermann. Cambridge: Cambridge University Press.

Kapuscinski, Ryszard. 2006. *Shah of Shahs*. Trans. Christopher de Bellaigue. London: Penguin.

Karl, Terry Lynn. 1997. *The Paradox of Plenty: Oil Booms and Petro-States*. Berkeley: University of California Press.

Katsouris, Christina, and Aaron Sayne. 2013. *Nigeria's Criminal Crude: International Options to Combat the Export of Stolen Oil*. London: Chatham House.

Katzenellenbogen, Jonathan. 2002. "United States Eyes West African Crude." *Business Day*, December 10.

Kaufmann, Chaim D., and Robert A. Pape. 1999. "Explaining Costly International Moral Action: Britain's Sixty-Year Campaign Against the Atlantic Slave Trade." *International Organization* 53(4):631–68.

Kaufmann, Daniel. 2012. "Poverty in the Midst of Abundance: Governance Matters for Overcoming the Resource Curse." www.brookings.edu/research/opinions/2012/09/13-poverty-governance-kaufmann (Accessed January 17, 2015).

Kaufmann, Daniel. 2013. "Era of Big Oil Secrecy Is Over." www.brookings.edu/research/opinions/2013/04/24-big-oil-secrecy-kaufmann (Accessed January 17, 2015).

Keating, Joshua. 2012. "Saudi Arabia's Military Shopping Spree." *Foreign Policy*, August 27.

Kedrosky, Paul. 2010. "Foreign Oil Dependency by U.S. Presidential Exhortation." seekingalpha.com/article/201014-foreign-oil-dependency-by-u-s-presidential-exhortation (Accessed February 7, 2015).

Kelsen, Hans. 1950. *The Law of the United Nations: A Critical Analysis of Its Fundamental Problems*. New York: Praeger.

Kennedy, David M. 1999. *Freedom from Fear: The American People in Depression and War, 1929–1945*. New York: Oxford University Press.

Kennedy, John F. 1963a. *John F. Kennedy: Containing the Public Messages, Speeches, and Statements of the President, January 20 to November 22, 1963*. Washington, DC: Office of the Federal Register.

Kennedy, John F. 1963b. *Public Papers of the Presidents of the United States, John F. Kennedy*. Washington, DC: US Government Printing Office.

Kennedy, Sam. 2010. "Nuhu Ribadu: Nigeria's Relentless Corruption Hunter." www.pbs.org/frontlineworld/stories/bribe/2010/01/nuhu-ribadu-nigerias-relentless-corruption-hunter.html (Accessed January 25, 2015).

Keohane, Robert O. 1991. "The United States and the Postwar Order: Empire or Hegemony?" *Journal of Peace Research* 28(4):435–39.

Keohane, Robert O., Stephen Macedo, and Andrew Moravcsik. 2009. "Democracy-Enhancing Multilateralism." *International Organization* 63(1):1–31.

Kepel, Gilles. 2006. *Jihad: The Trail of Political Islam*. New ed. London: Taurus.

Kerr, Simeon, and Andrew England. 2013. "Mugabe in the Money with Gems Lifeline." *Financial Times*, April 5.

Keynes, John Maynard. 1920. *The Economic Consequences of the Peace*. London: Macmillan.

Kilian, Lutz, and Robert J. Vigfusson. 2014. "The Role of Oil Price Shocks in Causing US Recessions." Discussion Paper 114. Washington, DC: US Federal Reserve.

Killalea, Debra. 2014. "Beheadings at Record Levels: Saudi Arabia Executes Dozens in Deadly August." www.news.com.au/world/middle-east/beheadings-at-record-levels-saudi-arabia-executes-dozens-in-deadly-august/story-fnh81ifq-1227037172765 (Accessed May 4, 2015).

Kimberley Process. 2015. "About." www.kimberleyprocess.com/en/about (Accessed April 25, 2015).

King, Jr., Martin Luther. 2010. *Where Do We Go From Here: Chaos or Community?* Boston: Beacon.

Kinzer, Stephen. 2003. *All the Shah's Men: An American Coup and the Roots of Middle East Terror*. New York: Wiley.

Kipling, Rudyard. 1994. "The White Man's Burden: The United States and the Philippine Islands (1899)." In *Collected Poems*. Ware: Wordsworth Editions, 334–36.

Kirk, Michael, and Louis Wiley, Jr. 2003. *Frontline: The Long Road to War*. www.pbs.org/wgbh/pages/frontline/shows/longroad/etc/script.html (Accessed April 25, 2015).

Kirkpatrick, David D. 2011a. "Hopes for a Qaddafi Exit, and Worries of What Comes Next." *New York Times*, March 21.

Kirkpatrick, David D. 2011b. "Photos Found in Libya Show Abuses Under Qaddafi." *New York Times*, April 5.

Kirkpatrick, David D. 2014. "ISIS' Harsh Brand of Islam Is Rooted in Austere Saudi Creed." *New York Times*, September 24.

Klare, Michael. 2009. "There Will Be Blood: Political Violence, Regional Warfare, and the Risk of Great-Power Conflict over Contested Energy Sources." In *Energy Security*

Challenges for the 21st Century: A Reference Handbook, eds. Gal Luft and Anne Korin. Santa Barbara: ABC-CLIO, 44–65.

Kocieniewski, David. 2010. "As Oil Industry Fights a Tax, It Reaps Subsidies." *New York Times*, July 3.

Koehler, Mike. 2012. "The Story of the Foreign Corrupt Practices Act." *Ohio State Law Journal* 73(5):929–1014.

Koh, Harold Hongju. 1998. "The 1998 Frankel Lecture: Bringing International Law Home." *Houston Law Review* 35:623–82.

Kolstad, Ivar, and Tina Søreide. 2009. "Corruption in Natural Resource Management: Implications for Policy Makers." *Resources Policy* 34(4):214–26.

Kolstad, Ivar, and Arne Wiig. 2009. "It's the Rents, Stupid! The Political Economy of the Resource Curse." *Energy Policy* 37(12):5317–25.

Kolstad, Ivar, and Arne Wiig. 2012. "Testing the Pearl Hypothesis: Natural Resources and Trust." *Resources Policy* 37(3):358–67.

Korey, William. 1987. "Helsinki, Human Rights, and the Gorbachev Style." *Ethics & International Affairs* 1(1):113–33.

Korsgaard, Christine M. 1996. *Creating the Kingdom of Ends*. Cambridge: Cambridge University Press.

Kotkin, Stephen. 2008. *Armageddon Averted: Soviet Collapse, 1970–2000*. Updated ed. New York: Oxford University Press.

Koubi, Vally, et al. 2014. "Do Natural Resources Matter for Interstate and Intrastate Armed Conflict?" *Journal of Peace Research* 51(2):227–43.

Krasner, Stephen D. 1999. *Sovereignty: Organized Hypocrisy*. Princeton: Princeton University Press.

Krasner, Stephen D., and Carlos Pascual. 2005. "Addressing State Failure." *Foreign Affairs* July/August.

Kremer, Michael, and Seema Jayachandran. 2003. "Odious Debt: When Dictators Borrow, Who Repays the Loan?" www.brookings.edu/research/articles/2003/03/spring-development-kremer (Accessed February 3, 2015).

Kristof, Nicholas D. 2007. "Death by Dollars." *New York Times*, February 11.

Kristof, Nicholas D. 2015a. "Deadliest Country for Kids." *New York Times*, March 19.

Kristof, Nicholas D. 2015b. "Two Women, Opposite Fortunes." *New York Times*, March 21.

Kristof, Nicholas D. 2015c. "An Unsettling Complicity." *New York Times*, March 26.

Kroll, Luisa. 2006. "Fortunes of Kings, Queens and Dictators." www.forbes.com/2006/05/04/rich-kings-dictators_cz_lk_0504royals.html (Accessed November 26, 2014).

Kumar, Hari, and Jim Yardley. 2011. "India Charges Mining Baron with Fraud." *New York Times*, September 5.

Kumar, Krishna B., and Desiree van Welsum. 2013. *Knowledge-Based Economies and Basing Economies on Knowledge: Skills a Missing Link in GCC Countries*. Santa Monica: RAND.

Kuper, Simon. 2011. "Tyrant's Paris: The Tour." *Financial Times*, October 14.

Kymlicka, Will. 2010. "Minority Rights in Political Philosophy and International Law." In *The Philosophy of International Law*, eds. Samantha Besson and John Tasioulas: New York: Oxford University Press, 377–98.

Lacey, Robert. 2009. *Inside the Kingdom: Kings, Clerics, Modernists, Terrorists, and the Struggle for Saudi Arabia*. New York: Viking.

Lakshmanan, Indira A. R., and Anthony DiPaola. 2014. "Islamic State: Oil Magnates of Terror." *Bloomberg Businessweek*, September 4.

Lal, Deepak. 2004. *In Praise of Empires: Globalization and Order*. Basingstoke: Palgrave Macmillan.

Larmore, Charles. 1987. *Patterns of Moral Complexity*. Cambridge: Cambridge University Press.

Last, Alex. 2007. "Nigerian Ex-Oil Governor Arrested." news.bbc.co.uk/1/hi/world/africa/7141047.stm (Accessed January 25, 2015).

Lauren, Paul Gordon. 2011. *The Evolution of International Human Rights: Visions Seen*. 3rd ed. Philadelphia: University of Pennsylvania Press.

Lavallée, Emmanuelle, Mirielle Razafindrakoto, and François Roubaud. 2008. *Corruption and Trust in Political Institutions in Sub-Saharan Africa*. Working Paper No. 102. Abuja: Afrobarometer.

Lay, Taimour, and Mika Minio-Paluello. 2010. *Contracts Curse: Uganda's Oil Agreements Place Profit before People*. London: Platform.

Le Billon, Philippe. 2001. "The Political Ecology of War: Natural Resources and Armed Conflicts." *Political Geography* 20(5):561–84.

Le Billon, Philippe. 2005. *Fueling War: Natural Resources and Armed Conflicts*. Oxford: Oxford University Press.

Le Billon, Philippe. 2007. "Drilling in Deep Water: Oil, Business and War in Angola." In *Oil Wars*, eds. Mary Kaldor, Terry Lynn Karl, and Yahia Said. London: Pluto, 100–29.

Le Billon, Philippe. 2012. *Wars of Plunder: Conflicts, Profits and the Politics of Resources*. New York: Columbia University Press.

Lebow, Richard Ned. 2010. *Why Nations Fight: Past and Future Motives for War*. New York: Cambridge University Press.

Legatum Institute. 2014. *Prosperity Index*. London.

Leigh, David, and Rob Evans. 2007. "BAE Accused of Secretly Paying £1bn to Saudi Prince." *Guardian*, June 7.

Leigh, Lamin, Yuan Xiao, and Nir Klein. 2009. "IMF Lends Angola $1.4 Billion to Support Reserves, Reforms." www.imf.org/external/pubs/ft/survey/so/2009/car112309b.htm (Accessed April 25, 2015).

Leite, Carlos A., and Jens Weidmann. 1999. "Does Mother Nature Corrupt? Natural Resources, Corruption, and Economic Growth." papers.ssrn.com/sol3/Papers.cfm?abstract_id=259928 (Accessed April 25, 2015).

Lenin, V. I. 1965. *Collected Works*. Vol. 27. Trans. Clemens Dutt. Ed. Robert Daglish. Moscow: Progress.

Leon-Portilla, Miguel. 1992. *The Broken Spears: The Aztec Account of the Conquest of Mexico*. Expanded and updated ed. Trans. Lysander Kemp. Boston: Beacon.

Lepora, Chiara, and Robert E. Goodin. 2013. *On Complicity and Compromise*. Oxford: Oxford University Press.

Lessig, Lawrence. 1995. "The Regulation of Social Meaning." *University of Chicago Law Review* 62(3):943–1045.

Leventhal, John M. 1998. "Epidemiology of Sexual Abuse of Children: Old Problems, New Directions." *Child Abuse & Neglect* 22(6):481–91.

Levin, Carl, and Tom Coburn. 2010. *Keeping Foreign Corruption Out of the United States: Four Case Histories*. Washington, DC: US Senate Permanent Subcommittee on Investigations.

Lichtblau, Eric, David Rohde, and James Risen. 2011. "Shady Dealings Helped Qaddafi Build Fortune and Regime." *New York Times*, March 24.

Lincoln, Abraham. 1953. *Collected Works*. Ed. Roy P. Basler. New Brunswick: Rutgers University Press.
Lincoln, Abraham. 2015. *Lincoln's Selected Writings*. Ed. David S. Reynolds. New York: Norton.
Lintner, Bertil. 2000. *Burma in Revolt: Opium and Insurgency Since 1948*. 2nd ed. Seattle: University of Washington Press.
Lipton, Eric. 2010. "U.S. Intensifies Air Screening for Fliers from 14 Nations." *New York Times*, January 3.
List, Christian, and Mathias Koenig-Archibugi. 2010. "Can There Be a Global Demos? An Agency-Based Approach." *Philosophy & Public Affairs* 38(1):76–110.
List, Christian, and Philip Pettit. 2011. *Group Agency: The Possibility, Design, and Status of Corporate Agents*. Oxford: Oxford University Press.
Listhaug, Ola. 2005. "Oil Wealth Dissatisfaction and Political Trust in Norway: A Resource Curse?" *Western European Politics* 28(4):834–51.
Locke, John. 1988. *Two Treatises of Government*. Ed. Peter Laslett. Cambridge: Cambridge University Press.
London Metal Exchange. 2012. "Copper: Production and Consumption." www.lme.com/en-gb/metals/non-ferrous/copper/production-and-consumption (Accessed November 17, 2014).
Lossan, Alexei. 2014. "Russia's Largest Oil Platform Goes into Operation in Far East." rbth.co.uk/business/2014/07/04/russias_largest_oil_platform_goes_into_operation_in_far_east_37953.html (Accessed January 19, 2015).
Luft, Gal, and Anne Korin. 2013. "The Myth of US Energy Dependence." www.foreignaffairs.com/articles/middle-east/2013-10-15/myth-us-energy-dependence (Accessed May 11, 2015).
Lugar, Richard G. 2006. "US Energy Security—A New Realism." Washington, DC: Brookings.
Lujala, Päivi. 2009. "Deadly Combat over Natural Resources Gems, Petroleum, Drugs, and the Severity of Armed Civil Conflict." *Journal of Conflict Resolution* 53(1):50–71.
Lujala, Päivi. 2010. "The Spoils of Nature: Armed Civil Conflict and Rebel Access to Natural Resources." *Journal of Peace Research* 47(1):15–28.
Maass, Peter. 2009. *Crude World: The Violent Twilight of Oil*. New York: Knopf.
Maathai, Wangari. 1999. "Developing Anti-Corruption Strategies in a Changing World: Global Challenges to Civil Society." 9iacc.org/papers/day1/plenary/dnld/d1pl_wmaathai.pdf (Accessed May 11, 2015).
MacFarquhar, Neil. 2011. "In Saudi Arabia, Royal Funds Buy Peace for Now." *New York Times*, June 8.
Machiavelli, Niccolo. 1998. *The Prince*. Trans. Peter Bondanella and Mark Musa. Oxford: Oxford University Press.
MacQueen, Norrie. 2007. *Colonialism*. Abingdon, UK: Routledge.
Maddison Project. 2013. *Database 2013 (Update)*. www.ggdc.net/maddison/maddison-project/data/mpd_2013-01.xlsx (Accessed January 31, 2015).
Magaloni, Beatriz. 2010. "The Game of Electoral Fraud and the Ousting of Authoritarian Rule." *American Journal of Political Science* 54(3):751–65.
Mahdavy, Hossein. 1970. "The Rentier State: The Case of Iran." In *Studies in the Economic History of the Middle East*, ed. M. A. Cook. Oxford: Oxford University Press, 428–67.
Malanczuk, Peter. 1997. *Akehurst's Modern Introduction to International Law*. 7th ed. New York: Routledge.

Malaquias, Assis. 2001. "Diamonds Are a Guerrilla's Best Friend: The Impact of Illicit Wealth on Insurgency Strategy." *Third World Quarterly* 22(3):311–25.

Manea, Elham M. 1998. "Yemen, the Tribe and the State." www.yemenwater.org/wp-content/uploads/2013/03/Manea-Elham-M.-1995.pdf (Accessed April 25, 2015).

Manning, Sanchez. 2013. "Britain's Colonial Shame: Slave-Owners Given Huge Payouts After Abolition." *Independent*, February 24.

Manson, Katrina. 2013. "Somalia: Oil Thrown on the Fire." *Financial Times*, May 13.

Manzo, Kate, and Pat McGowan. 1992. "Afrikaner Fears and the Politics of Despair: Understanding Change in South Africa." *International Studies Quarterly* 36(1):1–24.

Maritime Connector. 2014. "Oil Tanker—Mont (Knock Nevis, Jahre Viking, Happy Giant, Seawise Giant)." maritime-connector.com/worlds-largest-ships/ (Accessed December 10, 2014).

Marques de Morais, Rafael. 2012. "Growing Wealth, Shrinking Democracy." *New York Times*, August 29.

Marshall, Monty G., and Benjamin R. Cole. 2009. *Global Report 2009: Conflict, Governance, and State Fragility*. Vienna, VA: Center for Systemic Peace.

Martell, Peter. 2009. "Dancing Bashir Scoffs at Darfur Warrant." news.bbc.co.uk/1/hi/world/africa/7926813.stm (Accessed January 29, 2015).

Martin, S. I. 2011. "How African Slaves Created a Prosperous New Britain." *The Voice*, August 23.

Martin, Steve. 1999. *Britain and the Slave Trade*. London: Channel 4.

Marx, Karl. 1959. *Economic and Philosophic Manuscripts of 1844*. Trans. Martin Milligan. Moscow: Progress.

Marx, Karl. 1977. *Capital*. Vol. 1. Trans. Ben Fowkes. New York: Vintage.

Marx, Karl. 1992. *Early Writings*. Trans. Rodney Livingstone. New York: Penguin.

Marx, Karl. 2000. "On the Jewish Question." In *Selected Writings*, ed. David McLellan. Oxford: Oxford University Press, 146–70.

Marx, Karl. 2008. *The Poverty of Philosophy*. Trans. Harry Quelch. New York: Cosimo.

Masetti, Oliver. 2014. *Nigeria: The No. 1 African Economy*. Frankfurt: Deutsche Bank.

Mazzetti, Mark, and Emily B. Hager. 2011. "Secret Desert Force Set Up by Blackwater's Founder." *New York Times*, May 14.

McCullough, Erskine. 1990. "Rubies Are Swelling the War Coffers of Cambodia's Feared Khmer Rouge Rebels." *Los Angeles Times*, November 18.

McDougall, Dan. 2009. "The Return of the Bloody Diamonds: Miners at Gunpoint in Zimbabwe." *Daily Mail*, September 19.

McElroy, Damien. 2014. "Iraq Oil Bonanza Reaps $1 Million a Day for Islamic State." *The Telegraph*, 11 July.

McHarg, Aileen, et al., eds. 2010. *Property and the Law in Energy and Natural Resources*. Oxford: Oxford University Press.

McKendrick, Ewan. 2013. *Contract Law*. 10th ed. Oxford: Oxford University Press.

Mehlum, Halvor, Karl Moene, and Ragnar Torvik. 2006. "Institutions and the Resource Curse." *The Economic Journal* 116(508):1–20.

Mehlum, Halvor, Karl Moene, and Ragnar Torvik. 2012. "Mineral Rents and Social Development in Norway." In *Mineral Rents and the Financing of Social Policy: Opportunities and Challenges*, ed. Katja Hujo. Basingstoke: Palgrave Macmillan, 155–84.

Melander, Erik, Magnus Oberg, and Jonathan Hall. 2009. "Are 'New Wars' More Atrocious? Battle Severity, Civilians Killed and Forced Migration Before and After the End of the Cold War." *European Journal of International Relations* 15(3):505–36.

Meyer, Michael. 1998. "Suharto Family Values." *Newsweek*, January 26.

Miklian, Jason. 2013. "Rough Cut." *Foreign Policy*, January 2.

Milanovic, Branko. 2011. "Inequality and its Discontents: Why So Many Feel Left Behind." www.foreignaffairs.com/articles/global-commons/2011-08-12/inequality-and-its-discontents (Accessed May 11, 2015).

Mill, John Stuart. 1909. *Principles of Political Economy, with Some of their Applications to Social Philosophy*. 7th ed. Ed. William J. Ashley. London: Longmans, Green.

Mill, John Stuart. 1989. *On Liberty and Other Writings*. Ed. Stefan Collini. Cambridge: Cambridge University Press.

Mill, John Stuart. 2001. *Utilitarianism*. 2nd ed. Ed. George Sher. Indianapolis: Hackett.

Miller, David. 1995. *On Nationality*. Oxford: Oxford University Press.

Miller, David. 2007. *National Responsibility and Global Justice*: New York: Oxford University Press.

Miller, Michael K. 2013. "Democratic Pieces: Autocratic Elections and Democratic Development since 1815." dx.doi.org/10.1017/S0007123413000446 (Accessed May 19, 2015).

Miller, Zeke J. 2014. "Obama: US Working to 'Isolate Russia.'" *Time*, March 3.

Millis, Walter. 1931. *The Martial Spirit*. New York: Houghton Mifflin.

Montagu, Caroline. 2010. "Civil Society and the Voluntary Sector in Saudi Arabia." *Middle East Journal* 64(1):67–83.

Montesquieu. 1989. *The Spirit of the Laws*. Eds. Anne M Cohler, Basia Carolyn Miller, and Harold Samuel Stone. Cambridge: Cambridge University Press.

Moore, Malcolm. 2011. "Sudan's al-Bashir Given Red Carpet Treatment by China." *Telegraph*, June 29.

Moran, Theodore H. 2011. *Foreign Direct Investment and Development*. Washington, DC: Peterson Institute.

Moravcsik, Andrew. 2000. "The Origins of Human Rights Regimes: Democratic Delegation in Postwar Europe." *International Organization* 54(2):217–52.

Morgan, Peter. 2005. "An Overview of the Legal Regime for Mineral Development in the United Kingdom." In *International and Comparative Mineral Law and Policy*, eds. Elizabeth Bastida, Thomas Wälde, and Janeth Warden-Fernández. The Hague: Kluwer, 1081–94.

Morris, Ian. 2014. *War! What Is It Good For? Conflict and the Progress of Civilization from Primates to Robots*. New York: Farrar, Straus and Giroux.

Morris, Ian. 2015. *Foragers, Farmers, and Fossil Fuels: How Human Values Evolve*. Ed. Stephen Macedo. Princeton: Princeton University Press.

Morrison, Kevin M. 2009. "Oil, Nontax Revenue, and the Redistributional Foundations of Regime Stability." *International Organization* 63(1):107–38.

Morrison, Kevin M. 2012. "What Can We Learn About the 'Resource Curse' from Foreign Aid?" *World Bank Research Observer* 27(1):52–73.

Moss, Todd. 2011. "Oil to Cash: Fighting the Resource Curse Through Cash Transfers." Working Paper 237. Washington, DC: Center for Global Development.

Moss, Todd, Caroline Lambert, and Stephanie Majerowicz. 2015. *Oil to Cash: Fighting the Resource Curse Through Cash Transfers*. Washington, DC: Center for Global Development.

Motavalli, Jim. 2012. "Natural Gas Signals a 'Manufacturing Renaissance.'" *New York Times*, April 10.

Moyn, Samuel. 2010. *The Last Utopia: Human Rights in History*. Cambridge: Harvard University Press.

Mueller, John. 2009. "War Has Almost Ceased to Exist: An Assessment." *Political Science Quarterly* 124(2):297–321.

Mueller, John, and Mark G. Stewart. 2014. *Responsible Counterterrorism Policy*. Washington, DC: Cato.

Munday, Roderick. 2010. *Agency: Law and Principles*. Oxford: Oxford University Press.

Murphy, Caryle. 2013. *A Kingdom's Future: Saudi Arabia Through the Eyes of Its Twentysomethings*. Washington, DC: Wilson Center.

Myers, Nathaniel. 2010. "Out of the Earth Nation-Building in South Sudan." *Virginia Quarterly Review* 86(1):190–99.

Naím, Moises. 2006. *Illicit: How Smugglers, Traffickers, and Copycats Are Hijacking the Global Economy*. New York: Anchor.

Naím, Moises. 2009. "The Devil's Excrement: Can Oil-Rich Countries Avoid the Resource Curse?" *Foreign Policy*, August 22.

National Intelligence Council. 2012. *Global Trends 2030: Alternative Worlds*. Washington, DC.

Natsios, Andrew S. 2012. *Sudan, South Sudan and Darfur: What Everyone Needs to Know*. New York: Oxford University Press.

Natural Resource Governance Institute. 2015. *Natural Resource Charter*. www.resourcegovernance.org/issues/natural-resource-charter (Accessed January 21, 2015).

Natural Resources Canada. 2015. "Mining Regulations." www.nrcan.gc.ca/mining-materials/policy/legislation-regulations/8726 (Accessed February 1, 2015).

Naylor, Tony. 2007. "In Jello Biafra We Trust." *The Guardian*, November 3.

Nee, Victor, and Sonja Opper. 2012. *Capitalism from Below: Markets and Institutional Change in China*. Cambridge: Harvard University Press.

Neumeister, Larry. 2010. "NY Judge: Kazakh Bribe Defendant is Cold War Hero." www.boston.com/news/nation/articles/2010/11/19/ny_judge_kazakh_bribe_defendant_is_cold_war_hero/ (Accessed April 25, 2015).

New Revised Standard Version Catholic Bible. 2008. New York: Harper Collins.

New York Times. 2004. "Late Nigerian Dictator Looted Nearly $500 Million, Swiss Say." August 19.

Newell, Terry. 1982. *Statesmanship, Character and Leadership in America*. New York: Palgrave Macmillan.

Ng'Wanakilala, Fumbuka, and George Obuslutsa. 2013. "China's Xi Tells Africa He Seeks Relationship of Equals." www.reuters.com/article/2013/03/25/us-china-africa-idUSBRE92O0D220130325 (Accessed April 25, 2015).

Nicholas, Barry. 1962. *Introduction to Roman Law*. Oxford: Oxford University Press.

Nickel, James. 1997. "Group Agency and Group Rights." In *Nomos XXXIX: Ethnicity and Group Rights*, eds. Ian Shapiro and Will Kymlicka. New York: New York University Press, 235–56.

Nickel, James. 2007. *Making Sense of Human Rights*. Malden, MA: Blackwell.

Nietzsche, Friedrich. 1998. *Beyond Good and Evil: Prelude to a Philosophy of the Future*. Trans. Marion Faber. Oxford: Oxford University Press.

Nietzsche, Friedrich. 2006. *On the Genealogy of Morality*. Trans. Carol Diethe. Ed. Keith Ansell-Pearson. Cambridge: Cambridge University Press.

Nigeria National Bureau of Statistics. 2014. *Foreign Trade Statistics, First Quarter 2014*. Abuja.

Nili, Shmuel. 2011a. "Conceptualizing the Curse: Two Views on Our Responsibility for the Resource Curse." *Ethics & Global Politics* 4:103–24.

Nili, Shmuel. 2011b. "Democratic Disengagement: Towards Rousseauian Global Reform." *International Theory* 3:355–89.

Nili, Shmuel. 2013. "Rawlzickian Global Politics." *Journal of Political Philosophy* 21:473–95.

NOIA. 2013. "History of Offshore." www.noia.org/history-of-offshore/ (Accessed January 19, 2015).

Nolan, Leigh. 2011. *Policy Briefing: Managing Reform? Saudi Arabia and the King's Dilemma*. Doha: Brookings.

Nordhaus, William D. 2011. "Energy: Friend or Enemy?" *New York Review of Books*, October 27.

Norges Bank Investment Management. 2015. *The Fund's Market Value*. www.nbim.no/en/ (Accessed January 19, 2015).

Norman, Helmi. 2013. "Saudi Arabia to Impose Restrictions on Online Content Production, Including on YouTube." opennet.net/blog/2013/12/saudi-arabia-impose-restrictions-online-content-production-including-youtube (Accessed February 4, 2015).

North, Douglass C., John Joseph Wallis, and Barry R. Weingast. 2009. *Violence and Social Orders: A Conceptual Framework for Interpreting Recorded Human History*. New York: Cambridge University Press.

Norwegian Ministry for Petroleum and Energy. 2011. *An Industry for the Future—Norway's Petroleum Activities*. Oslo.

Nossiter, Adam. 2009. "Underneath Palatial Skin, Corruption Rules Gabon." *New York Times*, September 14.

Nossiter, Adam. 2011. "U.S. Engages with an Iron Leader in Equatorial Guinea." *New York Times*, May 30.

Nossiter, Adam. 2012. "Under Pressure, Nigerian Leader Relents on Gas Price." *New York Times*, January 16.

Nowak, Manfred. 2010. *Report of the Special Rapporteur on Torture and Other Cruel, Inhuman or Degrading Treatment or Punishment*. New York: UN Human Rights Council.

Nozick, Robert. 1974. *Anarchy, State and Utopia*. New York: Basic.

Nussbaum, Arthur. 1962. *A Concise History of the Law of Nations*. New York: MacMillan.

Nussbaum, Martha. 2000. *Women and Human Development: The Capabilites Approach*. Cambridge: Cambridge University Press.

Nye, Joseph S. 2011. *The Future of Power*. New York: Perseus.

O'Murchu, Cynthia. 2014. "Asset Tracing; Following the Money." *Financial Times*, August 13.

Obama, Barack. 2004. *Dreams from My Father: A Story of Race and Inheritance*. New York: Random House.

OECD. 2011a. *Society at a Glance 2011*. Paris.

OECD. 2011b. *Update on Tax Legislation on the Tax Treatment of Bribes to Foreign Public Officials*. Paris.

OECD. 2012. *Economic Surveys: Norway*. Paris.

OECD. 2014a. *Better Life Index: Education*. www.oecdbetterlifeindex.org/topics/education/ (Accessed January 21, 2015).

OECD. 2014b. *StatExtracts*. data.oecd.org/ (Accessed November 19, 2014).

OECD. 2014c. "Summary Overview of the Arrangement." www.oecd.org/trade/xcred/summaryoverviewofthearrangement.htm (Accessed February 12, 2015).

Oilandgasinfo.ca. 2014. "Products Made from Oil and Natural Gas." www.oilandgasinfo.ca/oil-gas-you/products/ (Accessed January 21, 2015).

Okoh, George. 2011. "Nigeria Spend $4.2bn on Food Imports." *This Day*, August 22.

Okonjo-Iweala, Ngozi. 2011. "Foreword." In *The Puppet Masters: How the Corrupt Use Legal Structures to Hide Stolen Assets and What to Do About It*, eds. Emile Van der Does de Willebois, Emily M. Halter, Robert A. Harrison, Ji Won Park, and J. C. Sharman. Washington, DC: World Bank, ix–x.

Okonjo-Iweala, Ngozi. 2012. *Reforming the Unreformable: Lessons from Nigeria*. Cambridge: Massachussetts Institute of Technology.

O'Neill, Onora. 2002. *A Question of Trust: The BBC Reith Lectures*. Cambridge: Cambridge University Press.

OPEC. 2013a. *Annual Statistical Bulletin*. Vienna.

OPEC. 2013b. "World Proven Crude Oil Reserves by Country." www.opec.org/library/Annual%20Statistical%20Bulletin/interactive/current/FileZ/XL/T31.HTM (Accessed November 20, 2014).

OPEC. 2014. *Annual Statistical Bulletin*. Vienna.

Outram, Quentin. 2001. "The Socio-Economic Relations of Warfare and the Military Mortality Crises of the Thirty Years' War." *Medical History* 45(2):151–84.

Oxford English Dictionary. 2014. www.oed.com/ (Accessed February 1, 2015).

Paes, Wolf-Christian. 2009. "From Failure to Success: The Impact of Sanctions on Angola's Civil War." In *Putting Teeth in the Tiger: Improving the Effectiveness of Arms Embargoes*, eds. M. Brzoska and George A. Lopez. Bingley: Emerald, 137–62.

Paine, Thomas. 2000. *Political Writings*. Ed. Bruce Kuklick. Cambridge: Cambridge University Press.

Park, Jihang. 1990. "Trailblazers in a Traditional World: Korea's First Women College Graduates, 1910–45." *Social Science History* 14(4):533–58.

Partnership Africa Canada. 2009. *Zimbabwe, Diamonds and the Wrong Side of History*. Ottowa.

PBS. 2009. "Corruption Case Exposes Scope of Bribery in Nigeria." www.pbs.org/newshour/bb/africa-jan-june09-nigeria_04-24/ (Accessed April 25, 2015).

PBS. 2014. "Jimmy Carter: Proposed Energy Policy." www.pbs.org/wgbh/americanexperience/features/primary-resources/carter-energy/ (Accessed February 7, 2015).

Peel, Michael. 2009. *A Swamp Full of Dollars: Pipelines and Paramilitaries at Nigeria's Oil Frontier*. London: I. B. Tauris.

Pepys, Samuel. 2000. *Diary*. Vol. 6. Ed. Henry B. Wheatley. Berkeley: University of California.

Perlo-Freeman, Sam, Elisabeth Sköns, Carina Solmirano, and Helén Wilandh. 2012. *Trends in World Military Expenditure, 2012*. books.sipri.org/files/FS/SIPRIFS1304.pdf (Accessed May 11, 2015).

Persily, Larry. 2011. "Norway's Different Approach to Oil and Gas Development." www.arcticgas.gov/norway%E2%80%99s-different-approach-to-oil-and-gas-development (Accessed January 21, 2015).

Petraeus, David H., Robert B. Zoellick, and Shannon K. O'Neil. 2014. *North America: Time for a New Focus*. Washington, DC: Council on Foreign Relations.

Pettit, Philip. 1996. "Freedom as Antipower." *Ethics* 106(3):576–604.

Pettit, Philip. 1997. *Republicanism: A Theory of Freedom and Government*. Oxford: Oxford University Press.

Pettit, Philip. 2007. "Responsibility Incorporated." *Ethics* 117(2):171–201.

Pettit, Philip. 2014. *Just Freedom: A Moral Compass for a Complex World*. New York: Norton.

Pew Research Center. 2011. "Muslim-Western Tensions Persists." www.pewglobal.org/2011/07/21/muslim-western-tensions-persist/ (Accessed February 7, 2015).

Philips, Matthew. 2014. "U.S. Oil Imports from Africa Are Down 90 Percent." *Bloomberg Businessweek*, May 22.

Pilling, David. 2011a. "How Oil Affects the Price of Peas in China." *Financial Times*, January 12.

Pilling, David. 2011b. "Why the Mad Migration of Parts for your iPhone Matters." *Financial Times*, October 26.

Pinker, Steven. 2011. *The Better Angels of Our Nature*: London: Penguin.

Pinker, Steven, and Andrew Mack. 2014. "The World Is Not Falling Apart." www.slate.com/articles/news_and_politics/foreigners/2014/12/the_world_is_not_falling_apart_the_trend_lines_reveal_an_increasingly_peaceful.html (Accessed January 31, 2015).

Pitt, William. 1806. *The Speeches in the House of Commons*. Vol. 1. London: Longmans.

Plato. 1991. *The Republic*. Trans. Allan Bloom. New York: Basic.

Pliny the Elder. 1991. *Natural History*. London: Penguin.

Plumer, Brad. 2012. "Why the Saudis Want $100-a-Barrel Oil." *Washington Post*, January 17.

Pogge, Thomas. 1994. "An Egalitarian Law of Peoples." *Philosophy & Public Affairs* 23(3): 195–224.

Pogge, Thomas. 2008. *World Poverty and Human Rights*. 2nd ed. Cambridge: Polity.

Pogge, Thomas. 2010a. *Politics as Usual: What Lies Behind the Pro-Poor Rhetoric*. Cambridge: Polity.

Pogge, Thomas. 2010b. "Responses to the Critics." In *Thomas Pogge and his Critics*, ed. Alison M. Jaggar. Cambridge: Polity, 175–250.

Pogge, Thomas. 2011. "Allowing the Poor to Share the Earth." *Journal of Moral Philosophy* 8:335–52.

Poggioli, Sylvia. 2010. "Radical Islam Uses Balkan Poor to Wield Influence." www.npr.org/templates/story/story.php?storyId=130801242 (Accessed January 27, 2015).

Pole Institute. 2010. *Guerillas in the Mist*. Goma.

Polgreen, Lydia. 2008. "Congo's Riches, Looted by Renegade Troops." *New York Times*, November 15.

President of Azerbaijan. 2012. "Ilham Aliyev Attended the Opening of a New Settlement for 423 IDP Families in Shaki." en.president.az/articles/5947 (Accessed February 1, 2015).

Prichard, Wilson, Paola Salardi, and Paul Segal. 2014. "Taxation, Non-Tax Revenue and Democracy: New Evidence Using New Cross-Country Data." papers.ssrn.com/sol3/papers.cfm?abstract_id=2496872 (Accessed April 25, 2015).

Proctor, Ian. 2013. "Read: Full Text of Newlson Mandela's 1990 Wembley Stadium Concert Speech." *Get West London*, December 6.

Publish What You Pay. 2014. "Transparency on the Move: Payment Disclosure by the World's Largest Oil, Gas & Mining Companies." pwypusa.org/sites/default/files/Company%20Coverage%20Fact%20Sheet_Final.pdf (Accessed February 14, 2015).

Publish What You Pay. 2015. "Our Activities." www.publishwhatyoupay.org/activities (Accessed February 14, 2015).

Purdy, Jedediah. 2010. *The Meaning of Property: Freedom, Community and the Legal Imagination*. New Haven: Yale University Press.

Purdy, Jedediah, and Kimberly Fielding. 2007. "Sovereigns, Trustees, Guardians: Private Law Concepts and the Limits of Legitimate State Power." *Law and Contemporary Problems* 70(3):165–211.

QNB. 2014. *Qatar Economic Insight*. Doha.

Racine, Jean 2010. *The Fratricides*. Vol. 1 of *Complete Plays*. Trans. Geoffrey Alan Argent. Philadelphia: Penn State University Press.

Rademayer, Julian. 2004. "Equatorial Guinea: Festering Ground for Coups." *Sunday Times*, April 25.

Radon, Jenik. 2005. "The ABCs of Petroleum Contracts: License-Concession Agreements, Joint Ventures, and Production-Sharing Agreements." In *Covering Oil: A Reporter's Guide to Energy and Development*, eds. Svetlana Tsalik and Anya Schiffrin. New York: Open Society Institute, 61–99.

Raic, David. 2002. *Statehood and the Law of Self-Determination*. The Hague: Kluwer.

Railton, Peter. 1984. "Alienation, Consequentialism, and the Demands of Morality." *Philosophy & Public Affairs* 13(2):134–71.

Rajaratnam, Julie Knoll, et al. 2010. "Neonatal, Postneonatal, Childhood, and Under-5 Mortality for 187 Countries, 1970–2010: A Systematic Analysis of Progress Towards Millennium Development Goal 4." *Lancet* 375(9730):1988–2008.

Randall, Tom 2012. "Highest & Cheapest Gas Prices by Country." www.bloomberg.com/slideshow/2014-12-02/highest-and-cheapest-gasoline-prices-by-country-petrol-ranking-oil-subsidies.htmls (Accessed May 11, 2015).

Randhawa, Kiran. 2014. "Stephen Hawking: We Will Have Cleaner and Cheaper Power in 10 Years." *London Evening Standard*, October 20.

Raskin, Jamin B. 2001. "A Right to Vote." *American Prospect* 12(15):10–12.

Rasmussen, Tobias N., and Agustin Roitman. 2011. "Oil Shocks in a Global Perspective: Are They Really that Bad?" Working Paper 11/194. Washington, DC: International Monetary Fund.

Rathborne, John Paul, and Eduardo Garcia. 2013. "Mexico Opens Up its Energy Sector." *Financial Times*, August 12.

Ravallion, Martin. 2013. "How Long Will It Take to Lift One Billion People Out of Poverty?" *The World Bank Research Observer* 28(2):139–58.

Rawls, John. 1971. *A Theory of Justice*. Cambridge: Harvard University Press.

Rawls, John. 1999. *The Law of Peoples; with the Idea of Public Reason Revisited*. Cambridge: Harvard University Press.

Rawls, John. 2005. *Political Liberalism*. Expanded ed. New York: Columbia University Press.

Raz, Joseph. 1986. *The Morality of Freedom*: New York: Oxford University Press.

Raz, Joseph, and Avishai Margalit. 1990. "National Self-Determination." *Journal of Philosophy* 87(9):439–61.

Reddy, Sanjay, and Christian Barry. 2008. *International Trade & Labor Standards: A Proposal For Linkage*. New York: Columbia University Press.

Reed, Jason. 2006. "Photo Op Frames a Shot at Iran." www.washingtonpost.com/wp-srv/photo/postphotos/orb/asection/2006-04-17/10.htm (Accessed February 7, 2015).

Renner, Michael. 2002. "Breaking the Link Between Resources and Repression." In *State of the World*, ed. Linda Starke. Washington, DC: Worldwatch, 149–73.

Reno, William. 2003. "Sierra Leone: Warfare in a Post-State Society." In *State Failure and State Weakness in a Time of Terror*, ed. Robert Rotberg. Washington, DC: Brookings, 71–100.

Reporters Without Borders. 2014. *World Press Freedom Index*. Paris.

Revenue Watch Institute. 2013. *Resource Governance Index*. New York.

Ridge, Michael. 2014. "Moral Non-Naturalism." In *Stanford Encyclopedia of Philosophy*, ed. Edward N. Zalta. plato.stanford.edu/entries/moral-non-naturalism/ (Accessed April 25, 2015).

Risse, Mathias. 2012. *On Global Justice*. Princeton: Princeton University Press.

Risse, Thomas, Stephen C. Ropp, and Kathryn Sikkink, eds. 1999. *The Power of Human Rights: International Norms and Domestic Change*: Cambridge: Cambridge University Press.

Risse, Thomas, Stephen C. Ropp, and Kathryn Sikkink, eds. 2013. *The Persistent Power of Human Rights: From Commitment to Compliance*: Cambridge: Cambridge University Press.

Roberts, Adam. 2006. *The Wonga Coup: Simon Mann's Plot to Seize Oil Billions in Africa.* London: Profile.

Robertson-Snape, Fiona. 1999. "Corruption, Collusion and Nepotism in Indonesia." *Third World Quarterly* 20(3):589–602.

Robinson, James A. 2013. "Botswana as a Role Model for Country Success." In *Achieving Development Success: Strategies and Lessons from the Developing World,* ed. Augustin K. Fosu. Oxford: Oxford University Press, 187–203.

Robinson, James A., and Thierry Verdier. 2013. "The Political Economy of Clientelism." *Scandinavian Journal of Economics* 115(2):260–91.

Robinson, James A., Ragnar Torvik, and Thierry Verdier. 2006. "Political Foundations of the Resource Curse." *Journal of Development Economics* 79(2):447–68.

Rodrigues, Jason. 2013. "Lincoln's Great Debt to Manchester." *Guardian*, February 4.

Rogers, Simon. 2010. "Immigration to Europe: How Many Foreign Citizens Live in Each Country?" *Guardian*, September 7.

Rogin, Josh. 2014. "America's Allies Are Funding ISIS." www.thedailybeast.com/articles/2014/06/14/america-s-allies-are-funding-isis.html (Accessed April 25, 2015).

Roosevelt, Eleanor. 1999. *Courage in a Dangerous World: The Political Writings of Eleanor Roosevelt.* New York: Columbia University Press.

Roosevelt, Theodore. 1910. "Nobel Lecture: International Peace." www.nobelprize.org/nobel_prizes/peace/laureates/1906/roosevelt-lecture.html (Accessed February 1, 2015).

Roosevelt, Theodore. 1911. "The Peace of Righteousness." *Outlook*, September 9.

Root, Hilton. 2008. *Alliance Curse: How America Lost the Third World.* Washington, DC: Brookings.

Root, Hilton, and Emil Bolongaita. 2008. *Enhancing Government Effectiveness in Yemen: A Country Analysis.* Washington, DC: USAID.

Rosato, Sebastian. 2003. "The Flawed Logic of Democratic Peace Theory." *American Political Science Review* 97(4):585–602.

Ross, Brian, and Anna Schecter. 2011. "'Grand Theft Nation': Ali Bongo Goes to the White House." abcnews.go.com/Blotter/obama-invites-ali-bongo-white-house/story?id=13791159 (Accessed February 6, 2015).

Ross, Michael. 2004. "Does Taxation Lead to Representation?" *British Journal of Political Science* 34(2):229–49.

Ross, Michael. 2007. "Mineral Wealth, Conflict and Equitable Development." In *Institutional Pathways to Equity: Addressing Inequality Traps*, eds. Michael Walton, Anthony J. Bebbington, Anis A. Dani, and Arjan de Haan. Washington, DC: World Bank, 193–215.

Ross, Michael. 2008. "Blood Barrels: Why Oil Wealth Fuels Conflict." *Foreign Affairs* May/June.

Ross, Michael. 2012. *The Oil Curse: How Petroleum Wealth Shapes the Development of Nations.* Princeton: Princeton University Press.

Ross, Michael. 2014. "What Have We Learned About the Resource Curse?" ssrn.com/abstract=2342668 (Accessed April 25, 2015).

Ross, Michael, and Eric Voeten. 2013. "Oil and Unbalanced Globalization." papers.ssrn.com/sol3/papers.cfm?abstract_id=1900226 (Accessed May 11, 2015).

Rothney, John. 1969. *The Brittany Affair and the Crisis of the Ancien Régime*. Oxford: Oxford University Press.

Rouleau, Eric. 2002. "Trouble in the Kingdom." *Foreign Affairs*, July/August.

Rousseau, Jean-Jacques. 1826. *Oeuvres Complètes*. Vol. 6. Paris: Dalibon.

Rousseau, Jean-Jacques. 1968. *The Social Contract*. Trans. Maurice Cranston. New York: Penguin.

Rousseau, Jean-Jacques. 1997. *The Social Contract and Other Later Political Writings*. Ed. Victor Gourevitch. Cambridge: Cambridge University Press.

RT.com 2014a. "Putin Acknowledges Russian Military Servicemen Were in Crimea." rt.com/news/crimea-defense-russian-soldiers-108/ (Accessed January 31, 2015).

RT.com. 2014b. "Putin Breaks Ground on Russia-China Gas Pipeline, World's Biggest." rt.com/business/184176-russia-china-gas-siberian-power/ (Accessed May 11, 2015).

Rubinstein, Alvin Z. 1981. "The Soviet Union and Iran Under Khomeini." *International Affairs* 57(4):599–617.

Ruggie, John. 2006. *Report of the High Commissioner for Human Rights on the Outcome of the First Annual Meeting with Senior Executives from a Particular Sector of Transnational Corporations and Other Business Enterprises*. New York: UN Economic and Social Council.

Ruggie, John. 2012. *Keynote Remarks at Association of International Petroleum Negotiators*. business-humanrights.org/sites/default/files/media/documents/ruggie/ruggie-remarks-association-intl-petroleum-negotiators-20-apr-2012.pdf (Accessed May 11, 2015).

Ruggie, John. 2013. *Just Business: Multinational Corporations and Human Rights*. New York: Norton.

Rungswasdisab, Puangthong. 2010. "Thailand's Response to the Cambodian Genocide." www.yale.edu/cgp/thailand_response.html (Accessed January 29, 2015).

Ruseckas, Laurent. 2009. "Iraqi Oil: Good News, Actually." www.thefastertimes.com/internationalenergy/2009/07/21/iraqs-oil-auction-got-bad-press-but-was-actually-a-good-sign/ (Accessed February 14, 2015).

Rusling, James. 1903. "Interview with President William McKinley." *Christian Advocate*, January 22:17.

Ryan, Yasmine. 2011. "Tunisian Revolution Yet to Solve Inequality." www.aljazeera.com/indepth/features/2011/03/2011331172249350413.html (Accessed February 6, 2015).

Sachs, Jeffrey D., and Andrew M. Warner. 1995. "Natural Resource Abundance and Economic Growth." Working Paper 5398. Washington, DC: National Bureau of Economic Research.

Sachs, Jeffrey D., and Andrew M. Warner. 2001. "The Curse of Natural Resources." *European Economic Review* 45(4):827–38.

Sakwa, Richard. 2014. *Putin Redux: Power and Contradiction in Conteporary Russia*. New York: Routledge.

Sala-i-Martin, Xavier, and Arvind Subramanian. 2003. "Addressing the Natural Resource Curse: An Illustration from Nigeria." www.imf.org/external/pubs/ft/wp/2003/wp03139.pdf (Accessed April 25, 2015).

Salehyan, Idean, and Kristian Skrede Gleditsch. 2006. "Refugees and the Spread of Civil War." *International Organization* 60(2):335–66.

Sandbu, Martin. 2006. "Natural Wealth Accounts: A Proposal for Alleviating the Natural Resource Curse." *World Development* 34:1153–70.

Sandbu, Martin. 2009. "The Iraqi Who Saved Norway from Oil." *Financial Times*, August 29.

Sandholtz, Wayne. 2007. *Prohibiting Plunder: How Norms Change*. New York: Oxford University Press.

Sanford, Jr., William F. 1982. *The Marshall Plan: Origins and Implementation*. Washington, DC: US Department of State.

Sanger, David E., and Eric Schmitt. 2011. "US-Saudi Tensions Intensify with Mideast Turmoil." *New York Times*, March 14.

Sarchet, Penny. 2015. "Gerbils and Silk Road to Blame for Plague." www.newscientist.com/article/dn27014-gerbils-and-silk-road-to-blame-for-plague.html#.VPLizfmDkyp (Accessed March 1, 2015).

Sartre, Jean-Paul. 2004. *Critique of Dialectical Reason: Theory of Practical Ensembles*. Vol. 1. Trans. Alan Sheridan-Smith. Ed. Jonathan Ree. London: Verso.

Saudi Arabia Central Department of Statistics & Information. 2013. *Latest Statistical Releases*. www.cdsi.gov.sa/english/ (Accessed January 27, 2015).

Schaffnit-Chatterjee, Claire. 2013. *Sub-Saharan Africa*. Frankfurt: Deutsche Bank.

Scheffler, Samuel. 2013. *Death and the Afterlife*. Ed. Niko Kolodny. Oxford: Oxford University Press.

Schrijver, Nico. 1997. *Sovereignty over Natural Resources: Balancing Rights and Duties*. Cambridge: Cambridge University Press.

Schulze, Kirsten E. 2007. "The Conflict in Aceh: Struggle over Oil?" In *Oil Wars*, eds. Mary Kaldor, Terry Lynn Karl, and Yahia Said. London: Pluto, 183–224.

Schumpeter, Joseph A. 1991. *The Economics and Sociology of Capitalism*. Ed. Richard Swedberg. Princeton: Princeton University Press.

Science Insider. 2010. "How Many Have Died Due to Congo's Fighting? Scientists Battle over How to Estimate War-Related Deaths." news.sciencemag.org/2010/01/how-many-have-died-due-congos-fighting-scientists-battle-over-how-estimate-war-related (Accessed January 24, 2015).

Searle, John R. 1995. *The Construction of Social Reality*. New York: Free.

Seawright, Jason, and David Collier. 2014. "Rival Strategies of Validation: Tools for Evaluating Measures of Democracy." *Comparative Political Studies* 57(1):111–38.

Segal, Paul. 2011. "Resource Rents, Redistribution, and Halving Global Poverty: The Resource Dividend." *World Development* 39(4):475–89.

Sen, Amartya Kumar. 1999a. "Democracy as a Universal Value." *Journal of Democracy* 10(3):3–17.

Sen, Amartya Kumar. 1999b. *Development as Freedom*. New York: Knopf.

Sfakianakis, John, Daliah Merzaban, and Turki A. Al Hugail. 2011. *Saudia Arabia Economics: Employment Quandry*. Riyadh: Banque Saudi Fransi.

Shabrawi, Adnan. 2009. "Girl Gets a Year in Jail, 100 Lashes for Adultery." *Saudi Gazette*, February 8.

Shah, Sonia. 2004. *Crude: The Story of Oil*. New York: Seven Stories.

Sharansky, Natan, and Ron Dermer. 2004. *The Case for Democracy: The Power of Freedom to Overcome Tyranny & Terror*: New York: PublicAffairs.

Shaxson, Nicholas. 2007. *Poisoned Wells: The Dirty Politics of African Oil*. Basingstoke: Palgrave Macmillan.

Sick, Gary. 1985. *All Fall Down: America's Tragic Encounter with Iran*. London: Taurus.

Sidgwick, Henry. 1893. "My Station and Its Duties." *International Journal of Ethics* 4(1):1–17.

Sikkink, Kathryn. 2011. *The Justice Cascade*. New York: Norton.

Silverstein, Ken. 2003. "Oil Boom Enriches African Ruler." *Los Angeles Times*, January 20.

Silverstein, Ken. 2011. "Teodorin's World." *Foreign Policy*, February 22.
Silverstein, Ken. 2014. *The Secret World of Oil*. London: Verso.
Simmons, A. John. 1979. *Moral Principles and Political Obligations*. Princeton: Princeton University Press.
Simmons, Beth A. 1998. "Compliance with International Agreements." *Annual Review of Political Science* 1:75–93.
Simmons, Beth A. 2009. *Mobilizing for Human Rights: International Law in Domestic Politics*. New York: Cambridge University Press.
Simons, Marlise. 2011. "Prosecutor Confirms Accusations Against Sudan Leader." *New York Times*, January 1.
Simons, Penelope, and Audrey Macklin. 2014. *The Governance Gap: Extractive Industries, Human Rights, and the Home State Advantage*. Abingdon: Routledge.
Singer, Peter. 1981. *The Expanding Circle: Ethics and Sociobiology*. New York: Farrar, Straus and Giroux.
Sinnott-Armstrong, Walter. 2014. "Consequentialism." In *Stanford Encyclopedia of Philosophy*, ed. Edward N. Zalta. plato.stanford.edu/archives/spr2014/entries/consequentialism/ (Accessed April 25, 2015)
Skinner, Quentin. 2010. "Sovereignty: A Genealogy." In *Sovereignty in Fragments: The Past, Present and Future of a Contested Concept*, eds. Hent Kalmo and Quentin Skinner. Cambridge: Cambridge University Press, 26–46.
Slackman, Michael. 2011. "Bullets Stall Youthful Push for Arab Spring." *New York Times*, March 17.
Slater, Dan. 2012. "Strong-State Democratization in Malaysia and Singapore." *Journal of Democracy* 23(2):19–33.
Slaughter, Anne-Marie, and Thomas Hale. 2010. "Transgovernmental Networks and Multi-Level Governance." In *The Handbook on Multi-Level Governance*, eds. Henrik Enderlein, Sonja Walti, and Michael Zurn. Cheltenham, UK: Edward Elgar, 358–69.
Sloan, Stephen, and Sean K. Anderson. 2009. *Historical Dictionary of Terrorism*. New York: Rowman & Littlefield.
Smil, Vaclav. 2008. *Oil: A Beginner's Guide*. Oxford: Oneworld Publications.
Smil, Vaclav. 2010. *Energy Transitions: History, Requirements, Prospects*. Santa Barbara: Praeger.
Smillie, Ian. 2010. *Blood on the Stone: Greed, Corruption and War in the Global Diamond Trade*. London: Anthem.
Smillie, Ian. 2014. *Diamonds*. Cambridge: Polity.
Smith, Adam. 1904. *An Inquiry into the Nature and Causes of the Wealth of Nations*. 5th ed. London: Methuen.
Smith, Adam. 2002. *The Theory of Moral Sentiments*. Ed. Knud Haakonssen. Cambridge: Cambridge University Press.
Smith, Benjamin B. 2007. *Hard Times in the Lands of Plenty: Oil Politics in Iran and Indonesia*. New York: Cornell University Press.
Smith, Graeme. 2011. "China Offered Gadhafi Huge Stockpiles of Arms: Libyan Memos." *Globe and Mail*, September 2.
Smith, Martin. 1999. *Burma: Insurgency and the Politics of Ethnicity*. 2nd ed. New York: St. Martin's.
Smith, Vernon L. 2003. "The Iraqi People's Fund." *Wall Street Journal*, December 22.

Solana, Javier. 1998. "Securing Peace in Europe." nato.int/docu/speech/1998/s981112a .htm (Accessed January 30, 2015).

Sollund, Ragnhild. 2010. "Regarding Au Pairs in the Norwegian Welfare State." *European Journal of Women's Studies* 17(2):143–60.

Sprankling, John G. 2014. *The International Law of Property*. Oxford: Oxford University Press.

Sputnik. 2014. "Ukraine Chief of Staff Admits No Russian Troops in Donetsk." sputniknews .com/europe/20150129/1017514425.html (Accessed January 31, 2015).

Stanford Graduate School of Business. 2012. "Harnessing Mobile Tech and Students to Promote Development in Kenya." www.gsb.stanford.edu/stanford-gsb-experience/news-history/harnessing-mobile-tech-students-promote-development-kenya (Accessed January 16, 2015).

Statistics Canada. 2013. "Crude Oil and Equivalent—Imports—By Country of Origin." www.statcan.gc.ca/pub/57-601-x/2012001/t049-eng.htm (Accessed February 12, 2015).

Statistics Norway. 2012. "Attitude Towards Immigrants and Immigration Policy 2002–2012." www.ssb.no/a/english/kortnavn/innvhold_en/tab-2012-12-18-01-en.html (Accessed November 19, 2014).

Stead, W. T., ed. 1902. *The Last Will and Testament of Cecil John Rhodes*. London: William Clowes and Sons.

Stearns, Jason. 2011. *Dancing in the Glory of Monsters: The Collapse of the Congo and the Great War of Africa*. New York: PublicAffairs.

Stephen, Chris. 2014. "Libya: Western Countries Urge Citizens to Leave as Civil War Intensifies." *Guardian*, July 27.

Stern, Robert. 2006. "Hegel's *Doppelsatz*: A Neutral Reading." *Journal of the History of Philosophy* 44(2):235–66.

Stern, Roger J. 2010. "United States Cost of Military Force Projection in the Persian Gulf, 1976–2007." *Energy Policy* 38(6):2816–25.

Stiglitz, Joseph E. 2012. "From Resource Curse to Blessing." www.project-syndicate.org/commentary/from-resource-curse-to-blessing-by-joseph-e--stiglitz (Accessed January 21, 2015).

Stilz, Anna. 2015. "The Value of Self-Determination." www.philosophy.umd.edu/sites/philosophy.umd.edu/files/colloquium-papers/Stilz_Maryland.pdf (Accessed May 11, 2015).

Stodghill, Ron. 2006. "Oil, Cash and Corruption." *New York Times*, November 5.

Stoner, Kathryn. 2012. "Whither Russia? Autocracy is Here for Now, But is It Here to Stay?" *Perspectives on Politics* 10(4):969–77.

Stuart, Lucy. 2011. "Letter from London." *Al Arabiya*, May 27.

Sullivan, Kevin. 2013. "Saudi Arabia's Riches Conceal a Growing Problem of Poverty." *Guardian*, January 1.

Sunstein, Cass R. 1996. "Social Norms and Social Roles." *Columbia Law Review* 96(4): 903–68.

Sussman, David. 2005. "What's Wrong with Torture?" *Philosophy & Public Affairs* 33(1):1–33.

Tangermann, Stefan. 2002. *The Future of Preferential Trade Arrangements for Developing Countries and the Current Round of WTO Negotiations on Agriculture*. Rome: UN World Food Progamme.

Tarbell, Ida M. 1911. *The Tariff in Our Time*. New York: Macmillan.

Taylor, Jerome. 2011. "Iran Executes Three Men for Sodomy." *Independent*, September 7.

Telegraph. 2003. "Tony Blair's Statement." March 17.

Tessler, Mark, Amaney Jamal, and Michael Robbins. 2012. "New Findings on Arabs and Democracy." *Journal of Democracy* 23(4):89–103.

The National. 2013. "Arabs Not Yet Ready for Democracy." April 17.

Theobald, R. 1990. *Corruption, Development and Underdevelopment*: Basingstoke: Macmillan.

Thoreau, Henry David. 1983. *Walden and Civil Disobedience*. New York: Penguin.

Tilly, Charles. 1990. *Coercion, Capital and European States: AD 990–1992*. Malden, MA: Blackwell.

Time. 1972. "Black September's Ruthless Few." September 18, 1972.

Times (South Africa). 2009. "Bongo Looted Gabon with Impunity." June 10.

Tran, Mark. 2011. "Britain Must Get Tougher on Facilitators of Corruption, Says Report." *Guardian*, December 9.

Transparency International. 2013. *Corruption Perception Index*. Berlin.

Transparency International. 2014. *Corruption Perception Index*. Berlin.

Tuomela, Raimo. 1989. "Actions by Collectives." *Philosophical Perspectives* 3:471–96.

Turnell, Sean. 2011. "Fundamentals of Myanmar's Macroeconomy: A Political Economy Perspective." *Asian Economic Policy Review* 6(1):136–53.

Turner, Thomas, and Crawford Young. 1985. *The Rise and Decline of the Zairian State*. Madison: University of Wisconsin Press.

Twigg, Graham. 1993. "Plague in London: Spatial and Temporal Aspects of Mortality." In *Epidemic Disease in London*, ed. J. A. I. Champion. London: Institute of Historical Research, 1–17.

UK Foreign and Commonwealth Office. 2003. *Human Rights: Annual Report*. London.

UK Government. 2010. *UK Foreign Bribery Strategy*. London.

UN Development Programme. 2007/2008. *Human Development Report*. New York.

UN Development Programme. 2008–09. *Human Development Report Nigeria*. Abuja.

UN Development Programme. 2009. *Arab Human Development Report*. New York.

UN Development Programme. 2014. *Human Development Report*. New York.

UN Environment Programme. 2009. *From Conflict to Peacebuilding: The Role of Natural Resources and the Environment*. Nairobi.

UN Human Rights Council. 2008. *Report of the Working Group on Arbitrary Detention: Mission to Equatorial Guinea (8–13 July 2007)*. New York.

UN Secretary-General for Sudan. 2009. *Darfur Humanitarian Profile No. 34*. New York.

UN Treaty Collection. 2013. *Status of Ratification of Human Rights Instruments as of February 13*. www.ohchr.org/Documents/HRBodies/HRChart.xls (Accessed February 3, 2015).

UNESCO. 1948. *Human Rights: Comments and Interpretations*. unesdoc.unesco.org/images/0015/001550/155042eb.pdf (Accessed May 11, 2015).

UNESCO. 2013. "International Literacy Data 2013." www.uis.unesco.org/literacy/Pages/data-release-map-2013.aspx (Accessed February 1, 2015).

UNHCR. 2014. "An Introduction to Statelessness." www.unhcr.org/pages/49c3646c155.html (Accessed February 1, 2015).

UNICEF. 1999. "League Table: The Child Risk Measure." www.unicef.org/pon99/diceleag.htm. (Accessed November 24, 2014).

United Nations. 2012a. *The Millennium Development Goals Report*. New York.

United Nations. 2012b. "World Population Prospects: The 2012 Revision." esa.un.org/wpp/Documentation/pdf/WPP2012_Press_Release.pdf (Accessed May 11, 2015).

Urbina, Ian. 2009. "Taint of Corruption Is No Barrier to U.S. Visa." *New York Times*, November 16.

US Census Bureau. 2012a. *The Foreign-Born Population in the United States: 2010*. Washington, DC.

US Census Bureau. 2012b. *Gross Domestic Product in Current and Chained (2005) Dollars by Industry: 2000 to 2010*. Washington, DC.

US Census Bureau. 2013. *Table 2. Annual Estimates of the Population of Combined Statistical Areas: April 1, 2010 to July 1, 2012*. Washington, DC.

US Department of Commerce. 2011. *Compilation of Foreign Motor Vehicle Import Requirements*. Washington, DC.

US Department of Justice. 2007. *G8 Experience in the Implementation of Extraterritorial Jurisdiction for Sex Crimes against Children*. Washington, DC.

US Department of Justice. 2009. "Kellogg Brown & Root LLC Pleads Guilty to Foreign Bribery Charges and Agrees to Pay $402 Million Criminal Fine." www.justice.gov/opa/pr/kellogg-brown-root-llc-pleads-guilty-foreign-bribery-charges-and-agrees-pay-402-million (Accessed January 29, 2015).

US Department of Justice. 2011. "Assistant Attorney General Lanny A. Breuer of the Criminal Division Speaks at the Franz-Hermann Brüner Memorial Lecture." www.justice.gov/criminal/pr/speeches/2011/crm-speech-110525.html (Accessed February 7, 2015).

US Department of State. 1998. *Equatorial Guinea Country Report on Human Rights Practices*. Washington, DC.

US Department of State. 2006. "Remarks With Equatorial Guinean President Teodoro Obiang Nguema Mbasogo Before Their Meeting." 2001-2009.state.gov/secretary/rm/2006/64434.htm (Accessed February 7, 2015).

US Department of State. 2009. "U.S. President Barack Obama and First Lady Michelle Obama with World Leaders at the Metropolitan Museum in New York." www.flickr.com/photos/statephotos/3949359659 (Accessed February 7, 2015).

US Department of State. 2011a. "Country Reports on Human Rights Practices 2010: Nigeria." www.state.gov/j/drl/rls/hrrpt/2010/af/154363.htm (Accessed May 11, 2015).

US Department of State. 2011b. "Country Reports on Human Rights Practices 2011: Saudi Arabia." www.state.gov/j/drl/rls/hrrpt/humanrightsreport/index.htm?dlid=186447 (Accessed May 11, 2015).

US Department of State. 2011c. "Question Taken at the June 20, 2011, Daily Press Briefing." www.state.gov/r/pa/prs/dpb/2011/06/166559.htm (Accessed May 11, 2015).

US Department of State. 2011d. "Secretary Clinton at International Conference for South Sudan." iipdigital.usembassy.gov/st/english/texttrans/2011/12/20111214135248su0.8743664.html#axzz3KvH5EfW8 (Accessed February 7, 2015).

US Department of State. 2012a. "Country Reports on Terrorism 2011." www.state.gov/j/ct/rls/crt/2011/index.htm (Accessed May 11, 2015).

US Department of State. 2012b. "Country Reports on Human Rights Practices 2012: Equatorial Guinea." www.state.gov/j/drl/rls/hrrpt/humanrightsreport/index.htm?year=2012&dlid=204115 (Accessed May 11, 2015).

US Department of State. 2013. "Investment Climate Statement—Qatar." www.state.gov/e/eb/rls/othr/ics/2013/204718.htm (Accessed January 24, 2015).

US Department of State. 2014a. "534. Despatch from the Embassy in Thailand October 20, 1959." history.state.gov/historicaldocuments/frus1958-60v15/d534 (Accessed February 6, 2015).

US Department of State. 2014b. "Alerts and Warnings." travel.state.gov/content/passports/english/alertswarnings.html (Accessed November 26, 2014).

US Department of State. 2014c. "Country Reports on Human Rights Practices for 2013: Equatorial Guinea." www.state.gov/j/drl/rls/hrrpt/humanrightsreport/index.htm?year=2013&dlid=220108#wrapper (Accessed February 7, 2015).

US Department of State. 2014d. "U.S. Relations with Equatorial Guinea." www.state.gov/r/pa/ei/bgn/7221.htm (Accessed February 7, 2015).

US Department of State. 2014e. "U.S. Relations with Sudan." www.state.gov/r/pa/ei/bgn/5424.htm (Accessed January 29, 2015).

US Department of State. 2015a. "Independent States in the World." www.state.gov/s/inr/rls/4250.htm (Accessed May 4, 2015).

US Department of State. 2015b. "Country Reports on Terrorism." www.state.gov/j/ct/rls/crt/ (Accessed January 26, 2015).

US Energy Information Administration. 2013. "U.S. Household Expenditures for Gasoline Account for Nearly 4% of Pretax Income." www.eia.gov/todayinenergy/detail.cfm?id=9831 (Accessed November 18, 2014).

US Energy Information Administration. 2014a. "Frequently Asked Questions." www.eia.gov/tools/faqs/faq.cfm?id=32&t=6 (Accessed December 10, 2014).

US Energy Information Administration. 2014b. International Energy Statistics. www.eia.gov/cfapps/ipdbproject/IEDIndex3.cfm (Accessed February 12, 2015).

US Energy Information Administration. 2014c. Norway. www.eia.gov/countries/cab.cfm?fips=no (Accessed January 21, 2015).

US Energy Information Administration. 2014d. Petroleum & Other Liquids. www.eia.gov/dnav/pet/pet_move_neti_a_ep00_IMN_mbblpd_a.htm (Accessed February 6, 2015).

US Energy Information Administration. 2014e. "Qatar." www.eia.gov/countries/cab.cfm?fips=QA (Accessed November 21, 2014).

US Government Printing Office. 2014. *Fiscal Year 2014: Historical Tables—Budget of the US Government*. Washington, DC.

US Millennium Challenge Corporation. 2014. "Guide to the Indicators and the Selection Process, FY 2015." www.mcc.gov/pages/docs/doc/fact-sheet-the-fiscal-year-2015-selection-process (Accessed Februay 12, 2015).

US Navy. 2014. "Aircraft Carriers—CVN." www.navy.mil/navydata/fact_display.asp?cid=-4200&tid=200&ct=4 (Accessed December 10, 2014).

US Senate Committee on Banking, Housing, and Urban Affairs. 1977. *Foreign Corrupt Practices and Domestic and Foreign Investment Improved Disclosure Acts of 1977*. Washington, DC: US Government Printing Office.

US Senate Committee on Foreign Relations. 2008. *The Petroleum and Poverty Paradox: Assessing US and International Community Efforts to Fight the Resource Curse*. Washington, DC: US Government Printing Office.

US Senate Committee on Foreign Relations. 2013. "Testimony of John Prendergast." www.foreign.senate.gov/download/2013/04/16/testimony (Accessed April 25, 2015).

US Trade Representative. 2014. "The People's Republic of China." www.ustr.gov/countries-regions/china-mongolia-taiwan/peoples-republic-china (Accessed February 12, 2015).

USAID. 2011. *United States Official Development Assistance (ODA)*. eads.usaid.gov/usoda/docs/dcr/us/us_oda_2011.xls (Accessed May 11, 2015).

USAID. 2012. "First Paved Highway in South Sudan Constructed by USAID, Officially Opened." www.usaid.gov/news-information/press-releases/first-paved-highway-south-sudan-constructed-usaid-officially-opened (Accessed April 25, 2015).

Usher, Sebastian. 2013. "Saudi Preacher Jailed over Daughter's Death." *BBC News*, 7 October.

Van de Walle, Nicolas. 2007. "Meet the New Boss, Same as the Old Boss? The Evolution of Political Clientelism in Africa." In *Patrons, Clients and Policies: Patterns of Democratic Accountability and Political Competition*, eds. H. Kitschelt and S. I. Wilkinson. Cambridge: Cambridge University Press, 50–67.

Van Parijs, Philippe. 2000. "A Basic Income for All." *Boston Review*, October/November.

Vatikiotis, Michael R. J. 1993. *Indonesian Politics Under Suharto: The Rise and Fall of the New Order*. London: Routledge.

Vazquez, John A. 1993. *The War Puzzle*. Cambridge: Cambridge University Press.

Velleman, J. David. 1999. "Love as a Moral Emotion." *Ethics* 109(2):338–74.

Vicente, Pedro C. 2010. "Does Oil Corrupt? Evidence from a Natural Experiment in West Africa." *Journal of Development Economics* 92(1):28–38.

Victaulic. 2009. *Sevan Driller*. Easton, PA.

Victor, David G. 2007. "What Resource Wars?" *National Interest* 92(Nov–Dec):48–55.

Voltaire. 2006. *Candide*. Trans. Roger Pearson. Oxford: Oxford University Press.

Wallis, William. 2014. "Nigeria Bank Governor Alleges Oil Subsidy Racket." *Financial Times*, February 12.

Walsh, Nick Paton. 2003. "US Begins Secret Talks to Secure Iraq's Oilfields." *Guardian*, January 23.

Waltz, Kenneth N. 1959. *Man, The State and War*. New York: Columbia University Press.

Walvin, James. 2001. *Black Ivory: Slavery in the British Empire*. 2nd ed. Oxford: Blackwell.

Walzer, Michael. 1980. "The Moral Standing of States: A Response to Four Critics." *Philosophy & Public Affairs* 9(3):209–29.

Walzer, Michael. 2003. "Is There an American Empire?" *Dissent*, Fall.

Wan, William, and William Booth. 2011. "United States Recognizes Libyan Rebels as Legitimate Government." *Washington Post*, July 15.

Wang, Yi. 2013. "Sustainable Development--The Road to Achieve Chinese Dream and Human Progress." www.fmprc.gov.cn/mfa_eng/wjb_663304/wjbz_663308/2461_663310/t1081238.shtml (Accessed May 11, 2015).

Wang, Yudong, Congfeng Wu, and Li Yang. 2013. "Oil Price Shocks and Stock Market Activities: Evidence from Oil-Importing and Oil-Exporting Countries." *Journal of Comparative Economics* 41(4):1220–39.

Wantchekon, Leonard. 2002. "Why Do Resource Dependent Countries Have Authoritarian Governments?" *Journal of African Finance and Economic Development* 5(2):57–77.

Washington Post. 2006. "President Bush's State of the Union Address." January 31.

Weinert, Matthew S. 2007. *Democratic Sovereignty: Authority, Legitimacy and State in a Globalizing Age*. Abingdon, UK: Taylor & Francis.

Weinstein, Jeremy M. 2007. *Inside Rebellion: The Politics of Insurgent Violence*. Cambridge: Cambridge University Press.

Weiser, Benjamin, and William K. Rashbaum. 2010. "Liberia Aids U.S. in Drug Fight." *New York Times*, June 1.

Welch, Claude Emerson. 1980. *Anatomy of a Rebellion*. New York: State University of New York.

Wellman, Christopher. 2005. *A Theory of Secession: The Case for Political Self-Determination*. Cambridge: Cambridge University Press.

Wenar, Leif. 1998. "Original Acquisition of Private Property." *Mind* 107(428):799–820.

Wenar, Leif. 2010. "Realistic Reform of International Trade in Resources." In *Thomas Pogge and his Critics*, ed. Alison M. Jaggar. Cambridge: Polity, 123–150.

Wenar, Leif. 2016. "Popular Resource Sovereignty." In *Institutional Cosmopolitanism*, eds. Thomas Pogge and Luis Cabrera. New York: Oxford University Press, in press.

Wenar, Leif, and Branko Milanovic. 2009. "Are Liberal Peoples Peaceful?" *Journal of Political Philosophy* 17(4):462–86.

Wendt, Alexander. 1999. *Social Theory of International Politics*. Cambridge: Cambridge University Press.

White House. 2014. "Remarks by President Obama in Address to the United Nations General Assembly, September 24." www.whitehouse.gov/the-press-office/2014/09/24/remarks-president-obama-address-united-nations-general-assembly (Accessed January 27, 2015).

Wiegrefe, Klaus. 2013. "75 Years Later: How the World Shrugged Off Kristallnacht." *Spiegel International*, November 5.

Wiener, Margaret J. 1995. *Visible and Invisible Realms: Power, Magic and Colonial Conquest in Bali*. Chicago: University of Chicago Press.

Wiens, David. 2014. "Natural Resources and Institutional Development." *Journal of Theoretical Politics* 26(2):197–221.

Wiens, David, Paul Poast, and William Roberts Clark. 2014. "The Political Resource Curse: An Empirical Re-Evaluation." *Political Research Quarterly* 67(4):783–94.

WikiLeaks. 2009. "Nigeria: Trawler Owners' Association Questions Nigerian Navy Capabilities." www.wikileaks.org/plusd/cables/09LAGOS192_a.html (Accessed January 25, 2015).

Will, George. 2001. "Don't Place Bets on the IRA." townhall.com/columnists/georgewill/2001/10/29/dont_place_bets_on_the_ira (Accessed January 27, 2015).

Williams, Gabriel I. H. 2002. *Liberia: The Heart of Darkness*. Victoria, BC: Trafford.

Williams, Rowan. 2011. "Archbishop's Sermon to the Anglicans in Zimbabwe." rowanwilliams.archbishopofcanterbury.org/articles.php/2204/archbishops-sermon-to-the-anglicans-in-zimbabwe (Accessed January 24, 2015).

Williams, Walter L. 1980. "United States Indian Policy and the Debate over Philippine Annexation: Implications for the Origins of American Imperialism." *Journal of American History* 66(4):810–31.

Wilson, Woodrow. 1925. *The Public Papers of Woodrow Wilson: War and Peace*. Vol. 1. New York: Harper & Brothers.

Wilson, Woodrow. 1981. *The Papers of Woodrow Wilson*. Vol. 36. Ed. Arthur S. Link. Princeton: Princeton University Press.

Wines, Michael. 2004. "Where Coup Plots Are Routine, One That is Not." *New York Times*, March 20.

Wingo, Ajume H. 2004. "Fellowship Associations as a Foundations for Liberal Democracy in Africa." In *A Companion to African Philosophy*, ed. Kwasi Wiredu. Oxford: Wiley-Blackwell, 450–59.

Wintrobe, Ronald. 2007. "Dictatorship: Analytical Approaches." In *The Oxford Handbook of Comparative Politics*, eds. Carles Boix and Susan C. Stokes. New York: Oxford University Press, 363–94.

Wisor, Scott. 2014a. "Gender Injustice and the Resource Curse: Feminist Assessment and Reform." In *Gender and Global Justice*, ed. Alison M. Jaggar. Cambridge: Polity, 168–90.

Wisor, Scott. 2014b. "Why Climate Change Divestment Will Not Work." www.ethicsandinternationalaffairs.org/2014/why-climate-change-divestment-will-not-work/ (Accessed February 12, 2015).

Withnall, Adam. 2014. "Saudi Cleric 'Issues Religious Edict Banning All-You-Can-Eat Buffets.'" *Independent*, March 18.

Wittgenstein, Ludwig. 2003. *Philosophische Untersuchungen*. Frankfurt: Suhrkamp.

Woods, Damon L. 2006. *The Philippines: A Global Studies Handbook*. Santa Barbara: ABC-CLIO.

World Bank. 2004. *Mainstreaming Anti-Corruption Activities in World Bank Assistance: A Review of Progress Since 1997*. Washington, DC.

World Bank. 2013a. "Equatorial Guinea Overview." www.worldbank.org/en/country/equatorialguinea/overview (Accessed November 26, 2014).

World Bank. 2013b. *International Debt Statistics*. Washington, DC.

World Bank. 2014a. "Adjusted Net Savings." data.worldbank.org/indicator/NY.ADJ.SVNG.GN.ZS/ (Accessed February 6, 2015).

World Bank. 2014b. "Gross National Income per Capita 2013, Atlas Method and PPP." databank.worldbank.org/data/download/GNIPC.pdf (Accessed January 24, 2015).

World Bank. 2014c. "GDP per Capita (PPP)" data.worldbank.org/indicator/NY.GNP.PCAP.PP.CD (Accessed December 27, 2014).

World Bank. 2014d. "Life Expectancy at Birth, Total (Years)." data.worldbank.org/indicator/SP.DYN.LE00.IN/countries (Accessed November 18, 2014).

World Bank. 2014e. "Population, Total." databank.worldbank.org/data/views/reports/tableview.aspx?isshared=true (Accessed May 4, 2015).

World Bank. 2014f. "Poverty Overview." www.worldbank.org/en/topic/poverty/overview (Accessed November 18, 2014).

World Bank. 2014g. "Unemployment, Total (% of Total Labor Force)." data.worldbank.org/indicator/SL.UEM.TOTL.ZS (Accessed November 19 2014).

World Bank. 2015a. *A Measured Approach to Ending Poverty and Boosting Shared Prosperity*. Washington, DC.

World Bank. 2015b. "Data." data.worldbank.org/ (Accessed May 11, 2015).

World Bank. n.d. "Corruption and Economic Development." www1.worldbank.org/publicsector/anticorrupt/corruptn/cor02.htm (Accessed November 20, 2014).

World Bulletin. 2008. "Libyan Officials Oppose Gaddafi Oil Money Plan." www.worldbulletin.net/index.php?aType=haber&ArticleID=31318 (Accessed February 1, 2015).

World Economic Forum. 2014a. *Global Gender Gap Report*. Geneva.

World Economic Forum. 2014b. *Out of the Shadows: Why Illicit Trade and Organized Crime Matter to Us All*. Davos-Klosters.

World Food Programme. 2005. "Bleak Future for Angola's Children." www.wfp.org/news/news-release/bleak-future-angolas-children (Accessed April 25, 2015).

World Rainforest Movement. 2002. "Liberia: Unique Forests Threatened by Logging." wrm.org.uy/oldsite/bulletin/64/Liberia.html (Accessed April 25, 2015).

World Steel Association. 2014. *World Steel in Figures 2014*. Brussels.

World Trade Organization. 2005. *Trade Policy Review: Egypt*. Washington, DC.

World Trade Organization. 2010. *World Trade Report 2010: Trade in Natural Resources*. Geneva.

Worth, Robert F. 2014. "Leftward Shift by Conservative Cleric Leaves Saudis Perplexed." *New York Times*, April 4.

Wortham, Christopher. 1996. "Shakespeare, James I and the Matter of Britain." *English* 45(182):97–122.

Wrage, Alexandra. 2010. "The Big Destructiveness of the Tiny Bribe." www.forbes.com/2010/03/01/bribery-graft-law-leadership-managing-ethisphere.html (Accessed January 29, 2015).

Wright, Gavin, and Jesse Czelusta. 2002. "Exorcizing the Resource Curse: Minerals as a Knowledge Industry, Past and Present." time.dufe.edu.cn/wencong/stanford/swp02008.pdf.

Wrong, Michela. 2000. *In the Footsteps of Mr. Kurtz: Living on the Brink of Disaster in Mobutu's Congo*. London: Fourth Estate.

Xenophon. 2009. *Hiero*. Trans. H. G. Dakyns. n.p.: Hard.

Yergin, Daniel. 2008. *The Prize: The Epic Quest for Oil, Money & Power*. New York: Free.

Yergin, Daniel. 2011. *The Quest: Energy, Security, and the Remaking of the Modern World*. New York: Penguin.

York, Geoffrey. 2012. "Inside the Clash for Congo's Mineral Wealth." *Globe and Mail*, November 30.

Ypi, Lea. 2011. *Global Justice and Avant-Garde Political Agency*. Oxford: Oxford University Press.

Zacher, Mark W. 2001. "The Territorial Integrity Norm: International Boundaries and the Use of Force." *International Organization* 55(2):215–50.

Zoepf, Katherin. 2007. "Saudi King Pardons Rape Victim Sentenced To Be Lashed, Saudi Paper Reports." *New York Times*, December 18.

Zoli, Corri, Sahar Azar, and Shani Ross. 2011. *Pattern of Conduct: Libyan Regime Support for and Involvement in Acts of Terrorism*. Syracuse, NY: Institute for National Security and Counterterrorism.

Index